Taking the Result as the Path

The Library of Tibetan Classics is a special series being developed by The Institute of Tibetan Classics aimed at making key classical Tibetan texts part of the global literary and intellectual heritage. Eventually comprising thirty-two large volumes, the collection will contain over two hundred distinct texts by more than a hundred of the best-known Tibetan authors. These texts have been selected in consultation with the preeminent lineage holders of all the schools and other senior Tibetan scholars to represent the Tibetan literary tradition as a whole. The works included in the series span more than a millennium and cover the vast expanse of classical Tibetan knowledge—from the core teachings of the specific schools to such diverse fields as ethics, philosophy, psychology, Buddhist teachings and meditative practices, civic and social responsibilities, linguistics, medicine, astronomy and astrology, folklore, and historiography.

Taking the Result as the Path

The tradition known as the Path with the Result or *Lamdré (lam 'bras)* is the most important tantric system of theory and meditation practice in the Sakya school of Tibetan Buddhism. This volume contains an unprecedented compilation of eleven vital works from different periods in the history of the Path with the Result in India and Tibet. The *Vajra Lines* of the great Indian adept Virūpa (ca. seventh–eighth centuries) is the basic text of the tradition and is said to represent the essence of all the Buddhist tantras in general and the *Hevajra Tantra* in particular. Sachen Künga Nyingpo's (1092–1158) *Explication of the Treatise for Nyak* is a fundamental commentary on Virūpa's succinct work and is among the earliest texts written in Tibet to explain Virūpa's mystical words. The collection of six writings by Jamyang Khyentsé Wangchuk (1524–68) includes a definitive history of the tradition and detailed explanations of its meditation practices as taught by his great master, Tsarchen Losel Gyatso (1502–66). A supplement to Khyentsé's history, written in the nineteenth century by Künga Palden and completed by Jamyang Loter Wangpo (1847–1914) in the early twentieth century, tells the stories of later masters in the lineage. An instruction manual composed by the Fifth Dalai Lama (1617–82) completes the unfinished work of Khyentsé Wangchuk. The volume concludes with a summation of all the teachings. Mangthö Ludrup Gyatso (1523–96), another of Tsarchen's principal Dharma heirs, composed this brief and eloquent text.

Most of these writings traditionally have been considered to be of a secret nature. The present translation has been made with the personal approval and encouragement of His Holiness Sakya Trizin, head of the Sakya tradition, and Chogyé Trichen Rinpoché, head of the Tsarpa branch of the Sakya tradition.

THE LIBRARY OF TIBETAN CLASSICS • VOLUME 4

Thupten Jinpa, General Editor

Taking the Result as the Path

Core Teachings of the Sakya Lamdré Tradition

Translated and edited by Cyrus Stearns

Foreword by H.H. Sakya Trizin

Wisdom Publications • Boston

in association with the Institute of Tibetan Classics

Wisdom Publications
199 Elm Street
Somerville MA 02144 USA
www.wisdompubs.org

First Edition
11 10 09 08 07 06
6 5 4 3 2 1

Library of Congress Cataloging-in-Publication Data

Taking the result as the path : core teachings of the Sakya lamdré tradition / translated and edited by Cyrus Stearns.
p. cm.
Includes bibliographical references and index.
ISBN 0-86171-443-1 (hardcover : alk. paper)
1. Lam-'bras (Sa-skya-pa) 2. Sa-skya-pa (Sect)—Doctrines. I. Stearns, Cyrus, 1949–
BQ7672.4.T35 2006
294.3'420425—dc22
2006027197

Cover & interior design by Gopa &Ted2, Inc.
Set in Diacritical Garamond 10.5/13.5
Plate on page 12: Detail from a thangka of four Lamdré lineage holders; Tibet, fifteenth century. (Tibet Collection: Barbara and Walter Frey, Zurich, F753)

Wisdom Publications' books are printed on acid-free paper and meet the guidelines for the permanence and durability set by the Council of Library Resources.

Printed in Canada

This book was produced with environmental mindfulness. We have elected to print this title on 50% PCW recycled paper. As a result, we have saved the following resources: 51 trees, 36 million BTUs of energy, 4.506 lbs. of greenhouse gases, 18,704 gallons of water, and 2,402 lbs. of solid waste. For more information, please visit our web site, www.wisdompubs.org

Message from the Dalai Lama

THE LAST TWO MILLENNIA witnessed a tremendous proliferation of cultural and literary development in Tibet, the "Land of Snows." Moreover, due to the inestimable contributions made by Tibet's early spiritual kings, numerous Tibetan translators, and many great Indian paṇḍitas over a period of so many centuries, the teachings of the Buddha and the scholastic tradition of ancient India's Nālandā monastic university became firmly rooted in Tibet. As evidenced from the historical writings, this flowering of Buddhist tradition in the country brought about the fulfillment of the deep spiritual aspirations of countless sentient beings. In particular, it contributed to the inner peace and tranquillity of the peoples of Tibet, Outer Mongolia—a country historically suffused with Tibetan Buddhism and its culture—the Tuva and Kalmuk regions in present-day Russia, the outer regions of mainland China, and the entire trans-Himalayan areas on the southern side, including Bhutan, Sikkim, Ladakh, Kinnaur, and Spiti. Today this tradition of Buddhism has the potential to make significant contributions to the welfare of the entire human family. I have no doubt that, when combined with the methods and insights of modern science, the Tibetan Buddhist cultural heritage and knowledge will help foster a more enlightened and compassionate human society, a humanity that is at peace with itself, with fellow sentient beings, and with the natural world at large.

It is for this reason I am delighted that the Institute of Tibetan Classics in Montreal, Canada, is compiling a thirty-two–volume series containing the works of many great Tibetan teachers, philosophers, scholars, and practitioners representing all major Tibetan schools and traditions. These important writings will be critically edited and annotated and will then be published in modern book format in a reference collection called *The Library of Tibetan Classics,* with their translations into other major languages to be followed later. While expressing my heartfelt commendation for this noble project, I pray and hope that *The Library of Tibetan Classics* will not only make these important Tibetan treatises accessible to scholars of Tibetan studies, but will create a new opportunity for younger Tibetans to study and take interest in their own rich and profound culture. Through translations into other languages, it is my sincere hope that millions of fellow citizens of the wider human family will also be able to share in the joy of engaging with Tibet's classical literary heritage, textual riches that have been such a great source of joy and inspiration to me personally for so long.

The Dalai Lama
The Buddhist monk Tenzin Gyatso

Special Acknowledgments

The Institute of Tibetan Classics expresses its deep gratitude to Claus Hebben for generously providing the entire funding for this translation project.

We also acknowledge the Hershey Family Foundation for its generous support of the Institute of Tibetan Classics' projects of compiling, editing, translating, and disseminating key classical Tibetan texts through the creation of *The Library of Tibetan Classics.*

Contents

Appendixes

Foreword

His Holiness Sakya Trizin
Head of the Sakya Order of Tibetan Buddhism

THE PITH INSTRUCTIONS of the precious and profound Lamdré teachings were received by the great mahāsiddha Virūpa directly from Vajra Nairātmyā herself. Ever since then, they have passed down from master to disciple in an unbroken stream of transmission for well over a thousand years. These teachings were transmitted to Tibet by the great translator Drokmi Shākya Yeshé.

The term *lamdré* means "path and result." This term indicates that this sacred system of teachings encapsulates the core Sakya philosophy and practices resulting in the realization of the indivisibility of samsara and nirvana. This indivisibility means that the very samsaric appearances that we experience now themselves transform into the pure appearance of primordial wisdom. There is no impure form separate from what the realized noble ones experience. There is no pure form separate from what we experience. The same base is experienced and seen by different beings, therefore it is called the indivisibility of samsara and nirvana. This is the pinnacle of all the sutra and tantra teachings of Lord Buddha.

If a practitioner of Buddhadharma receives the Lamdré teaching with pure motivation from a qualified master, with both master and disciple meeting all the prerequisites, then the Lamdré is a complete path for obtaining full enlightenment in one lifetime.

A very important aspect of these secret pith instructions is that, from their beginning until now, they have been held in the greatest respect and have only been available to those whose mental continuum has been ripened through the relevant preliminary practices and initiations. Without such a base, esoteric teachings such as these cannot actually be comprehended. It is vitally important, both for the ripening of disciples and for the maintenance of the authenticity of the teachings, that this respect and guardianship of these teachings continues in their transportation into the West.

His Holiness the Dalai Lama has greatly emphasized and commended the work of those translating works from the vast and profound Buddhadharma. This is very important work, and I congratulate Cyrus Stearns and the Institute of Tibetan Classics for their motivation and dedicated effort in translating this most treasured teaching.

May the availability of this translation support the turning of the wheel of Dharma for eons to come, spreading the glorious light of the precious teachings, so that all illusory appearances become the pure appearance of full enlightenment, liberating all sentient beings from all forms of suffering.

Sakya Trizin
December 2005

Note to the Reader

Most of the texts translated in this book are of an esoteric nature. Traditionally, they have been studied and practiced in Tibet only by people who have received the teachings of the Path with the Result. Four of the texts—the two historical works, the text that shows how to explain and practice the Dharma teachings, and the explanation of the Three Appearances—are appropriate for anyone to read and study without preparation. The minimum traditional requirement for studying the remaining works is the complete Hevajra initiation. Optimally, the student will have received the entire teachings of the Path with the Result from a qualified teacher. The authors of the texts translated here intended them only for practitioners of the Path with the Result, and the tantric practices described in these works should never be attempted by anyone who has not been taught how to perform them correctly. For, according to tradition, good results cannot come from study and practice of Vajrayana teachings unless the student has first received the initiations and careful guidance that can only be received from a living master. These texts have been translated for *The Library of Tibetan Classics* only with the permission of H.H. Sakya Trizin, head of the Sakya tradition, and the encouragement of my teacher Chogyé Trichen Rinpoché, senior master of the Path with the Result and head of the Tsarpa lineage of the Sakya tradition.

General Editor's Preface

The publication of this volume brings a very special collection of Tibet's deeply spiritual literature into the world's literary heritage. This volume, *Taking the Result as the Path: Core Teachings of the Sakya Lamdré Tradition,* is volume 4 in *The Library of Tibetan Classics,* and contains some of the most important religious texts of the Tibetan Buddhist tradition translated for the first time ever in any secondary language. Selected under the guidance of His Holiness Sakya Trizin, the head of the Sakya school of Tibetan Buddhism, the texts in this volume constitute a comprehensive anthology of *Lamdré* (Path with the Result) teachings, the heart meditative tradition of the Sakya school. It is with deep respect and honor that the Institute of Tibetan Classics offers the translation of these precious texts to those who seek the path to spiritual awakening and to the world at large.

Two primary objectives have driven the creation and development of *The Library of Tibetan Classics.* The first aim is to help revitalize the appreciation and the study of the Tibetan classical heritage within Tibetan-speaking communities worldwide. The younger generation in particular struggle with the tension between traditional Tibetan culture and the realities of modern consumerism. To this end, efforts have been made to develop a comprehensive yet manageable body of texts, one that features the works of Tibet's best-known authors and covers the gamut of classical Tibetan knowledge. The second objective of *The Library of Tibetan Classics* is to help make these texts part of global literary and intellectual heritage. In this regard, we have tried to make the English translation reader-friendly and, as much as possible, keep the body of the text free of scholarly apparatus, which can intimidate general readers. For specialists who wish to compare the translation with the Tibetan original, page references of the critical edition of the Tibetan text are provided in brackets.

The texts in this thirty-two-volume series span more than a millennium—from the development of the Tibetan script in the seventh century to the first part of the twentieth century, when Tibetan society and culture first encountered industrial modernity. The volumes are thematically organized and cover many of the categories of classical Tibetan knowledge—from the teachings specific to each Tibetan school to the classical works on philosophy, psychology, and phenomenology. The first category includes teachings of the Kadam, Nyingma, Sakya, Kagyü, Geluk, and Jonang schools, of miscellaneous Buddhist lineages, and of the Bön school. Texts in these volumes have been largely selected by senior lineage holders of the individual schools. Texts in the other categories have been selected primarily on recognition of the historical reality of the individual disciplines. For example, in the field of epistemology, works from the Sakya and Geluk schools have been selected, while the volume on buddha-nature features the writings of Butön Rinchen Drup and various Kagyü masters. Where fields are of more common interest, such as the three codes or the bodhisattva ideal, efforts have been made to represent the perspectives of all four major schools. *The Library of Tibetan Classics* can function as a comprehensive library of the Tibetan literary heritage for libraries, educational and cultural institutions, and interested individuals.

It has been a real privilege for me to be part of this landmark translation project. I wish first of all to express my deep personal gratitude to His Holiness the Dalai Lama for always being such a profound source of inspiration. I would also like to offer my sincere thanks to His Holiness Sakya Trizin for his counsel on the selection of the texts featured in this volume, for his kind approval to have these precious texts of the glorious Sakya tradition translated as part of *The Library of Tibetan Classics,* and for providing a special foreword to the volume. I thank Cyrus Stearns for doing a masterful job in translating these precious texts into English, and to the following individuals and organizations, I owe my sincere thanks: to David Kittelstrom at Wisdom for being such an incisive editor; to Gene Smith at the Tibetan Buddhist Resource Center for providing assistance with obtaining crucial Tibetan texts needed for the editing of the Tibetan texts; to the Central Institute of Higher Tibetan Studies in Sarnath for providing full access to its library to the Tibetan editors working on the critical editions of these texts; and to my wife Sophie Boyer-Langri for taking on the numerous administrative chores that are part of a collaborative project such as this. Finally, I would like to express my heartfelt thanks to Claus Hebben who most generously provided the entire funding for this translation project. Without his support, no amount of dedication on the part of the Institute or the depth of talent and skill on the part of the translator would have resulted in such a successful conclusion of the project. I would also like to thank the Hershey Family Foundation for its longstanding support of the Institute of Tibetan Classics, without which the task of creating *The Library of Tibetan Classics* simply would not have gotten off the ground. It is my sincere hope that the translations offered in this volume will be of benefit to many people. Through the efforts of all those who have been involved in this noble venture, may all beings enjoy peace and happiness.

Thupten Jinpa
Montreal, 2006

Translator's Introduction

The tradition known as the Path with the Result or *Lamdré (lam 'bras)* is one of the great tantric systems of Buddhism in Tibet. For nearly a thousand years this vehicle for enlightenment has been the central focus of meditation practice in the Sakya school of Tibetan Buddhism. According to Jetsün Drakpa Gyaltsen (1147–1214), one of the greatest masters of the Path with the Result, the name of the tradition emphasizes that the focus of practice is "taking the result as the path."[1] The result—the essence or innate true nature of a living being—is actually present at all times. Were this otherwise, the practices of the spiritual path would be futile. This essence is not transformed by the practices of the path because it is beyond conceptual elaboration. The qualities of a buddha, or enlightened being, are obtained instead through removing obscurations and transforming one's body, speech, and mind. This process includes concentrated focusing on the essence itself. The result that is already present at the beginning is thereby taken as, or made into, the spiritual path by means of tantric techniques. This basic theme of tantric Buddhism will be explained in detail in the works translated in this volume.

The texts of the Path with the Result in this book are divided into two parts. Part I opens with the fundamental treatise of the system, formulated by the great Indian adept Virūpa (ca. seventh–eighth centuries). This quintessential mystical document is said to embody the vital meaning of the entire Buddhist doctrine in general and of the *Hevajra Tantra* in particular. This treatise is usually referred to as the *Vajra Lines* and consists of the instructions Virūpa originally gave orally to his disciple Kāṇha. The *Vajra Lines* consist almost entirely of mnemonic phrases that list topics in a cryptic, unelaborated form. These lines are called *vajra* or *adamantine* because they are extremely difficult to penetrate without instructions from a master of the tradition. However, when they are understood, they are like a magic gem that fulfills all spiritual wishes. For at least eight generations, the *Vajra*

Lines were passed down in a unique oral transmission, spoken to only one person in each generation. The great translator *(lo tsā wa)* Drokmi Lotsāwa Shākya Yeshé (993–1077?) orally translated the *Vajra Lines* into Tibetan, but they were never written down until Sachen Künga Nyingpo (1092–1158) did so, probably in the year 1141. Until Sachen's time, teaching the Path with the Result meant transmitting the *Vajra Lines* as an experiential oral teaching, sometimes over a period of many years.

After receiving permission from his teacher Shangtön Chöbar (1053–1135), Sachen wrote the first texts to explain the esoteric meaning of the Path with the Result. The most important of Sachen's works are eleven commentaries on the *Vajra Lines* of Virūpa. These commentaries represent explanations given for the benefit of individual disciples (eight men and three women). The last of the eleven, also translated in part I, is known as the *Explication of the Treatise for Nyak.* Since then, this short work that Sachen wrote for his disciple Nyak Wangchuk Gyaltsen has been the primary text used when teaching the *Vajra Lines* in the Sakya tradition. It is considered the most profound of Sachen's complete commentaries, even though the others are more detailed.[2] Because the tradition was still largely oral at that time, many points are explained briefly or not at all in Sachen's text. However, topics directly connected to meditation practice are usually made clear in the other works translated in this book. Sachen's son Drakpa Gyaltsen added crucial and extensive annotations to his father's final commentary, which have not been translated here. In summary, the *Vajra Lines* and the *Explication of the Treatise for Nyak* present the theoretical and practical basis for the Path with the Result and are intended for dedicated yogins and yoginīs.

Part II contains a series of the most important texts of the lineage within the Path with the Result that is known as the *Lobshé* or Explication for Disciples, a term used to distinguish it from the *Tsokshé* or Explication for the Assembly. Such a distinction within the tradition was not drawn until the time of the Sakya throne-holder Dakchen Lodrö Gyaltsen (1444–95). The Explication for Disciples claims that its teachings represent the uncommon esoteric transmission that was passed down from Sachen's time forward only to his descendents, the Khön family of Sakya. Eventually, Dakchen Lodrö Gyaltsen bestowed the teachings on his Dharma heir, Künpang Doringpa (1449–1524), who was not a member of the Sakya family. However, the specific details that characterize the Explication for Disciples were not written down until the time of Tsarchen Losel Gyatso (1502–66), Doringpa's main disciple. Tsarchen's special teachings were primarily recorded by his two most important students, Jamyang Khyentsé Wangchuk (1524–68) and Mangthö Ludrup Gyatso (1523–96). Both Khyentsé Wangchuk and Mangthö Ludrup wrote extensively according to the Explication for Disciples, but Khyentsé's works have usually been favored when teaching and practicing the Path with the Result in this tradition.[3]

The texts of the Explication for Disciples were kept strictly secret and passed down only as handwritten manuscripts for more than three hundred years. Not until the beginning of the twentieth century were the works of Khyentsé and Ludrup, along with many other texts of the Path with the Result, finally cut onto woodblocks for publication by the famous Dergé printing house. This was due to the efforts of the master Jamyang Loter Wangpo (1847–1914). In 1904 and 1905, Loter Wangpo twice taught the Explication for Disciples in full. During that period he noted that complete sets of the texts were very scarce and that the tradition was in danger of dying out in the near future. He resolved to have the rare manuscripts of the tradition gathered from different locations and cut onto woodblocks for publication.

Loter Wangpo carried out publication despite opposition by some people who felt that the Path with the Result in general, and the teachings of the Explication for Disciples in particular, should remain secret. By way of explanation, he pointed out that the Path with the Result had been an oral tradition until the later part of Sachen's life, when he set the first texts down in writing. Much later, in the sixteenth century, Tsarchen, Khyentsé, and Ludrup had realized that future generations would not be able to uphold the special Explication for Disciples as an oral transmission and had decided to write down these teachings. To those who objected that it was wrong to have the profound teachings that were the heart blood of the ḍākas and ḍākinīs cut onto printing blocks, Loter Wangpo replied, "No matter what you say, I have the authority to do so!" As a result of his determined action, the books became more widely available, and the tradition spread and has remained vital until the present day.[4]

All of Jamyang Khyentsé Wangchuk's writings on the Path with the Result are translated in part II of this book. According to his autobiography, Khyentsé wrote these works in 1559, after receiving the transmission of the Explication for Disciples from Tsarchen near Shalu monastery.[5] These texts are summarizing notes compiled by Khyentsé to record Tsarchen's teachings. The first of Khyentsé's works is a history of the Path with the

Result. He tells the story of the Indian masters beginning with Virūpa, and then continues with a more detailed account of the early Tibetan teachers of the lineage. In composing this work, Khyentsé clearly used all the earlier historical writings of the Sakya masters Jetsün Drakpa Gyaltsen, Martön Chökyi Gyalpo (ca. 1198–ca. 1259), and others. However, he took much of the story of Virūpa and the lives of the early Tibetan masters directly from the fourteenth-century chronicles of Chagen Wangchuk Gyaltsen, which were clearly the main written source.[6] Chagen's work contained special information from the Shama transmission of the Path with the Result, and because Khyentsé combined this material with the accounts of the masters of the Sakya transmission, his work became a unique historical treasure for the later tradition. The contents of Khyentsé's text indicate that his teacher Tsarchen used all available earlier histories of the Path with the Result when teaching. For many readers of this book, it may be most beneficial to first read this history and the following supplement (which contain biographies of all the earlier authors) before turning to the other texts concerned with the specific theories and practices of the tradition.

The second text translated in part II is a supplement to Khyentsé's history. This work was mostly written by the master Künga Palden in the late nineteenth century. It was then brought up to date by Loter Wangpo at the beginning of the twentieth century, perhaps when he was preparing the Dergé edition of the entire collection. The work is a series of brief sketches of the lives of the primary masters of the tradition after the time of Müchen Könchok Gyaltsen (1388–1469). With the exception of the information about the Fifth Dalai Lama, who made significant literary contributions to the tradition but did not transmit the teachings, the content of these short biographies has been gleaned from the full-length biographies contained in the Dergé collection. The latter part of this supplement follows the transmission line through the abbots of Ngor monastery, with which Loter Wangpo was affiliated. Although not described in the text, a transmission of the Explication for Disciples through the masters of Nālendra monastery has also survived to the present day.

Following Künga Palden and Loter Wangpo's supplement, which was inserted into the original set of Khyentsé Wangchuk's works when the Dergé edition was prepared, there is a text by Khyentsé describing how to explain and practice the Path with the Result. This work clarifies the meaning of the name *Path with the Result* and describes a few of the distinguishing markers of the system, such as the four authentic qualities and the four oral transmissions. The contents of two early collections of instructions from the tradition, the *Yellow Volume* and the *Little Red Volume,* are also briefly discussed.

The Mahayana basis of the Path with the Result is fully presented in the explanation of the Three Appearances, which contains all the preliminary topics of meditation necessary for beginning the Vajrayana path. Here Khyentsé provides detailed instructions on a number of crucial subjects, beginning with taking refuge and awakening the enlightenment mind. The main section of the text begins with an explanation of the first of the three appearances: impure appearance, or how the world appears to living beings who are immersed in impure states of mind because of their afflictions. Here the practitioner reflects upon the faults of samsara, the difficulty of gaining a human birth with all the freedoms and endowments necessary to practice Dharma, and the causes and results of actions. Next comes reflection upon the second of the appearances: experiential appearance, or how various experiences appear to a yogin or yoginī who has cultivated meditative concentration. This topic is explained by means of reflection upon love, compassion, and the relative and absolute enlightenment mind. Finally, the pure appearance of a sugata or buddha is discussed. This is briefly explained in relation to the inconceivable secret and the omnipresence of enlightened body, speech, and mind. A short addendum of notes by the Fifth Dalai Lama, Ngawang Losang Gyatso (1617–82), has been added at the end of Khyentsé's work. These notes explain how the teacher should integrate the various reading transmissions and explanations of supplementary texts into the schedule when teaching the Three Appearances.

The next text in this volume is Khyentsé Wangchuk's summarizing notes on the Three Continua. The main practices of the Path with the Result begin with this work. The text is principally concerned with the meditative cultivation of an experiential realization of the indivisibility of samsara and nirvana. First is a brief presentation, by means of the three aspects of coemergence, to demonstrate that all phenomena arise from mistaken notions about the intrinsic nature of the mind, which is described from the three perspectives of lucidity, emptiness, and their essential unity. Next is an extensive explication by means of three key points of practice: establishing that appearances are the mind, establishing that the mind is illusory, and establishing that the illusory mind has no self-nature. Finally an extremely extensive explication is given by means of the three continua: the causal continuum of the universal ground, the method continuum of the body, and the resultant continuum of mahāmudrā.

The final two texts by Jamyang Khyentsé Wangchuk and a supplementary work by the Fifth Dalai Lama further elaborate the second of the three continua, the method continuum of the body. These summarizing notes explain the practices of the path in connection with the four initiations. They are sometimes very brief and may seem fragmentary because they are meant to be accompanied by the oral explanations of a living master. The two texts by Khyentsé Wangchuk explain the practice of the outer and the inner creation stage of the deity Hevajra. The creation stage of the deity is the practice of the path of the vase initiation, which is the first of the four initiations. In addition to the inner and outer creation stage meditations, Khyentsé also explains the view, the culmination of attainment, the practice of transference, and the intermediate-state practices in connection with the vase initiation. However, the work ends abruptly at this point without explaining the dream yoga, which is the sixth and final section of practice in regard to each initiation.

Jamyang Khyentsé Wangchuk passed away in 1568 at the age of forty-three, apparently leaving his series of compositions unfinished. For the next eighty years, when the Explication for Disciples was taught using Khyentsé's incomplete works, the final sections of the teaching were taught on the basis of the earlier writings of Lama Dampa Sönam Gyaltsen (1312–75) and the works of Tsarchen's other great Dharma heir, Mangthö Ludrup Gyatso. Finally, after receiving the complete transmission of the Explication for Disciples from the master Sönam Chokden (1603–59) in 1649, the Fifth Dalai Lama wrote a supplement to complete Khyentsé's work.[7] The Fifth Dalai Lama's summarizing notes on Sönam Chokden's explanations begin with the dream yoga of the vase initiation and go on to explain all the remaining topics of meditation in connection with the three higher initiations. Even more than Khyentsé's writings, this text by the Fifth Dalai Lama is clearly pieced together from notes made when he received the teachings, and many topics are very briefly treated and must be elaborated upon orally when the transmission is given.

As a fitting conclusion, the final text is Mangthö Ludrup Gyatso's brief, eloquent, and profound synopsis of the key points of practice according to Tsarchen's transmission of the Explication for Disciples. Ludrup composed this work in 1581, at least six years before writing his own complete series of detailed manuals of guidance.

The Path with the Result is a vast and complex system of theory and practice, said to contain everything necessary for the attainment of complete enlightenment in one lifetime. For anyone wishing to practice and understand this tradition, the works translated here will reward careful and sustained study and reflection. The tantric practices should only be attempted under the guidance of a qualified master of this system. The words of Sakya Paṇḍita Künga Gyaltsen (1182–1251), one of the foremost masters of the Path with the Result, remain particularly relevant today as the tradition spreads into cultures outside Tibet:

> Nowadays many are interested in mantra,
> but very few study secret mantra.
> If it is difficult for the intelligent to understand
> the intention of the tantras even if they are energetic,
> how could foolish people who have not studied
> understand the intention of the tantras?[8]

For most of us, it will only be possible to gain a thorough understanding of the intention of the Vajrayana scriptures and the systems of meditation and theory that evolved from them when much more of the tantric literature of India and Tibet has been translated into European languages. Translation is one of the forms of transmission and transmutation during the spread of a tradition from one culture to another. The spiritual and literary treasury of Tibet is incredibly rich. This book is a first step in the long-term process of translating the basic texts of one specific tradition, the Path with the Result.

Acknowledgments

This translation project could never have been undertaken without with the blessing, permission, and encouragement of His Holiness Sakya Trizin, the head of the Sakya tradition. When I first discussed the work with His Holiness in person in August 2000, I was pleasantly surprised to find that he fully supported the idea of translating a number of works that I had always previously been told were to be kept strictly secret. We continued to communicate by telephone and e-mail, and His Holiness approved the specific list of texts to be included in this volume. At the suggestion of His Holiness, I asked Geshé Thupten Jinpa, who had kindly invited me to make these translations for the Institute of Tibetan Classics, to also ask His Holiness the Dalai Lama to approve the list of texts. His Holiness the Dalai Lama gave his consent and also made the specific suggestion that something written by Mangthö Ludrup Gyatso be included in the volume. I then selected the short work by Mangthö Ludrup that is the final text among the translations.

The completion of this work is due to the great kindness and blessing of my teacher, Chogyé Trichen Rinpoché. It is my good fortune to have twice received the Path with the Result according to the Explication for Disciples from Chogyé Rinpoché, who has also answered my innumerable questions about these teachings over the years. In spring 2003, Rinpoché also discussed topics in the texts, answered a number of questions, and gave his approval to the translation project. I am grateful to Khenpo Appey Rinpoché, who patiently and clearly answered many questions about the meaning of the *Vajra Lines* in particular and the Path with the Result in general.

In spring 2003, Guru Rinchen Chödar and Jamyang Sangpo, both senior students of Chogyé Rinpoché and Khenpo Appey, kindly gave much of their time to help with the translations, especially the many colloquial expressions in the works of Jamyang Khyentsé Wangchuk. I also benefited from several fruitful conversations with David Jackson, who graciously agreed to read through much of the manuscript and made very helpful suggestions. Near the end of the project, John Deweese generously helped convey last-minute e-mail messages sent to Chogyé Trichen Rinpoché in Kathmandu, and Guru Rinchen Chödar once again spent time going through a list of my questions. For identifying many of the references from the classical Indian works contained in the Kangyur and Tengyur collections, I thank the editors of the new critical edition of the Tibetan text published by the Institute of Tibetan Classics. I am grateful to David Kittelstrom at Wisdom Publications for his skillful editorial guidance throughout this project. My thanks also go to Linda Sobottka for her insightful copyediting work on the book. Finally, I must thank Geshé Thupten Jinpa for his extraordinary dedication to the multi-volume project of *The Library of Tibetan Classics.*

It is a great honor to have been allowed to translate these texts. Whatever is of value in this work is due to the kindness of my teachers, while all mistakes are due to my own lack of understanding.

Technical Note

THE NAME OF THE TIBETAN TEXT is *Dpal sa skya pa'i lam 'bras kyi chos skor gces btus.* The full names of the individual works in this collection are listed by author in the bibliography of texts consulted by the translator. Bracketed numbers embedded in the translation refer to page numbers of the new critical and annotated Tibetan edition published in modern book format by the Institute of Tibetan Classics in New Delhi (2004, ISBN 81-89165-02-x) as volume 4 of the series entitled *Bod kyi gtsug lag gces btus.* This critical edition of the Tibetan text contains a large number of mistakes, some copied from the earlier Dehra Dun edition of the various works and some newly introduced. The original Dergé edition was not consulted. Thus my translations here basically follow the readings in the original Dergé edition and the 1983 Dehra Dun reprint. It is not practical to cite every mistake in the critical edition, so only some of the most significant have been mentioned in the endnotes to the translation. Also, classical Tibetan authors often wrote from memory when repeating quotes from authoritative sources. As a result it is not unusual to find that a quote in these texts sometimes differs from the lines located in the original source.

All Tibetan names in the main body of text are rendered phonetically in accordance with a style sheet developed by the Institute of Tibetan Classics and Wisdom Publications especially for the *Library of Tibetan Classics* series. There is a correspondence table at the back of the book where transliterated spellings can be found. Both phonetic and transliterated spellings are also provided in the endnotes and the index. Sanskrit diacriticals are used throughout, except for naturalized Sanskrit terms such as sutra, mandala, samsara, and nirvana.

Pronunciation of Tibetan phonetics:
ph and *th* are aspirated *p* and *t,* as in *pet* and *tip.*
ö is similar to the *eu* in French *seul.*

ü is similar to the *ü* in the German *füllen.*
ai is similar to the *e* in *bet.*
é is similar to the *e* in *prey.*

Pronunciation of Sanskrit:
Palatal *ś* and retroflex *ṣ* are similar to the English unvoiced *sh.*
c is an unaspirated *ch* similar to the *ch* in *chill.*
The vowel *ṛ* is similar to the American *r* in *pretty.*
ñ is somewhat similar to a nasalized *ny* in *canyon.*
ṅ is similar to the *ng* in *sing* or *hanger.*

Section and chapter headings have been inserted into the translation of Sachen's *Explication of the Treatise for Nyak* to clarify the structure of the work. It was traditionally assumed that any reader of this text would have memorized the *Vajra Lines* that it explains. Thus, the lines from Virūpa's root text are not always provided in Sachen's work when explaining their meaning. I have inserted all the missing lines into the English translation, since it seems quite unlikely that prospective readers will have the root text memorized. Jetsün Drakpa Gyaltsen's extensive annotations in the *Explication of the Treatise for Nyak* have not been translated. The occasional annotations in the other Tibetan texts have been translated in the endnotes.

The information in the table of contents of this book is necessarily abbreviated. The interested reader should consult the topical outline for the works by Sachen Künga Nyingpo, Jamyang Khyentsé Wangchuk, Künga Palden and Loter Wangpo, and the Fifth Dalai Lama. Only the texts by Jamyang Khyentsé Wangchuk and the Fifth Dalai Lama have numbered outlines in the original Tibetan. The outline is provided as an appendix in which all topics can be easily located according to their page numbers in the book. A glossary of selected technical terms has also been included. The reader is encouraged to become somewhat familiar with these terms before reading the translations.

In the bibliography and endnotes the various references from classical Indian works in the Kangyur and Tengyur are identified according to the numbers in the Tohoku catalogue of the Dergé edition of these collections: *A Complete Catalogue of the Tibetan Buddhist Canons (Bkaḥ-ḥgyur and Bstan-ḥgyur),* edited by Hakuju Ui, Munetada Suzuki, Yensho Kanakura, and Tokan Tada. Sendai: Tohoku Imperial University, 1934. When available, the numbers in the Peking edition of the Kangyur and Tengyur are also provided in the bibliography.

PART I

Vajra Lines
Virūpa

Explication of the Treatise for Nyak
Sachen Künga Nyingpo

Virūpa

1. Vajra Lines of the Path with the Result

Virūpa (ca. seventh–eighth centuries)

After bowing at the lotus beneath the feet of the excellent master, I will write a brief explanation of the Path with the Result.[9]

For a sentient being with afflictions, impure appearance occurs.

For a yogin with meditative concentration, experiential appearance occurs.

For a sugata with the ornamental wheel of inexhaustible enlightened body, speech, and mind, pure appearance occurs.

Since samsara and nirvana are complete in the causal continuum of the universal ground, it is the root continuum.

For the method continuum of the body and so forth, there is the causal initiation with four triads, the seats and so forth, and so forth.

Presentation by means of the four fives of the creation stage as the path and so forth.

Protecting the sacred commitments of meditative equipoise and so forth.

Propitiation of the vajra ḍākas and ḍākinīs and so forth.

With the five sensory objects and so forth, one should please and so forth.

Through meditation on the four initiations in four sessions of the path, and in dependence on the body, the obscurations to great bliss cease and enlightenment is clear, so it is the explanatory continuum.

Mahāmudrā, the resultant continuum, is omniscience by means of the four resultant initiations.

After establishing the result by means of the four authentic qualities, the poison of meditation is extracted by the triad free from flaws of contradiction and so forth.

Resorting to food, behavior, the vital wind, the drop, and the mudrā consort. The bliss of the five clear essences, the five sense organs, and resorting to the nectar without parting from the experience.

Total release in the four samsara channels and the cakras, and the others, and by opening the channel knots at each of the first and last spiritual levels, and through ten triads in between.

Extracting the poison of the view by meditating on a thought that purifies the mind, which is the path of eliminating entry.

Resorting to the nectar without the five types of consciousness rejecting the five objects.

Because pure phenomena arise as empty from the beginning, totally release them.

The oral transmission of secret mantra and four others are unbroken.

On the basis of an exceptional body, the dependently arisen connections set the limits of an entity.

Contingent, dependently arisen connections.

The path of great enlightenment.

The authentic quality of the description of the dependently arisen connections between all phenomena.

The universal ground consciousness, the pure great enlightenment.

The path is totally completed through five dependently arisen connections. [4]

A yogin who is over-inclined toward method is protected from obstacles on the path by firm faith, the protection cakra, mantra recitation, mantra knots, phenomena as the appearances of the nature of mind, the contingent, dependently arisen connections, and, since they are like reflected images, by not parting from the truth of the ocean of reality.

For wisdom, there are the outer māras, and a change will come in regard to the two paths and the eight views and culminations of attainment.

The inner change the ten of the paths and so forth, and come if the signs are not known. Protection is through knowing.

Protection from contamination, obscuration, and loss of the seminal drop.

From the path of accumulation, the four results separate from the body, speech, and mind of an ordinary person are achieved.

By means of the three modes of gathering the essential constituents, random events occur.

One is blessed by the vital winds and mind.

If one then progresses on the path according to the thirty-seven factors conducive to the objective of enlightenment, there are four bases for the miraculous by which meditation is not lost, which are the vital action winds, and due to the masculine, feminine, and neuter vital winds and the blazing fire of the primordial awareness of direct transcendence, at the first gathering of the essential constituents the channels are opened by the harsh winter wind.

The mind rests, dreams of horses occur, and pains of the channels and vital winds.

The knot of various channels and so forth. By arresting [five of] the ten, the ground, or root, vital winds, and so forth, which have seven specifics, the branch vital winds gradually cease within.[10]

Many drops bloom, blending together with the support.

Dependent on that, the mind rests within.

The five types of consciousness gather within.

The five aggregates are subdued.

The advance and retreat of primordial awareness.

The three triads of visual appearances, dreams, and experiences by which meditation is not lost, like those that are preceded by thought, appear as the entire three worlds.

If earth dissolves into water, there is mirage.

If water dissolves into fire, there is smoke.

If fire dissolves into wind, there are fireflies.

If wind dissolves into consciousness, there are blazing lamps.

If consciousness dissolves into clear light, it is like the cloudless sky.

If earth, water, fire, and wind gather together with the vital winds and mind, the three worlds appear as though on fire everywhere.

The vital wind of water, and the hairs and body are cold.

With the vital wind of wind, there is gathering and diffusion, one flies, and birds appear.

The vital winds of the four elements circulate together, and various goddesses offer dances.

Due to the vital winds of the four elements, there is a variety, and smells and tastes.

Together with space, the hairs and body are blissful.

The five nectars, the enlightened bodies of the tathāgatas, and so forth.

Frankincense and the sun. Camphor and the moon.

Tiny drops in the tiny channels. And stars.

In the channel strictures and so forth. [5] Tree trunks and so forth.

The five such as passion and hatred.

The channels of terror, grief, and ghosts.

In the channels of tears. Yawns and tears.

If the vital winds and mind gather together in the syllables of the six realms that first formed at the navel, there are the dances of the six realms, the mantras, being guided there, dreams, and similar experiences, which appear as the entire three worlds.

From *oṃ,* the meditative concentrations of meditation and so forth.

If perfectly dissolved in the *āḥ,* the space of the mother, the three worlds are space.

If dissolved in the mansion of the great mother Prajñāpāramitā and so forth, the dharmakāya reality body is experienced and there is freedom from subject and object.

From *hūṃ* there is lucidity, buoyancy, and naturally arisen primordial awareness. A very immaculate sky.

At the middle gathering of the essential constituents, the channels are opened by a vital wind of reduced harshness.

Pain of the drops, and stable visual appearances.

In brief, in the *rakṣa* and so forth, rākṣasa demons and so forth.

The sound of the one with a bell.

As with the pristine divine eye, one thinks that everything below the *peak* of existence appears in the experiences of meditative concentration.

The unexplainable is illustrated, and is secret on the five and the ten.

For the outer dependently arisen connections by which meditation is not lost, there are the three triads of the reversal of the vital winds and so forth, and since the inner five ḍākinīs and five enlightened bodies of the tathāgatas enact the dependently arisen connections for great enlightenment, it is understood that the attainments come from oneself, and that understanding clears away thoughts of hope and effort.

By understanding the māras and wrong turns as one's own path and dependently arisen connections, faults are upheld as qualities, and the warmths arisen either in sequence or not in sequence are allowed natural expression.

Since the devaputra māras come on the path of one who is over-inclined toward wisdom, protection is by means of the four tests.

As for the four applications of mindfulness by which meditation is not lost, when objects cease, oneself is the chosen deity, the necessity of the signs is reflected upon, and, because meditative concentration is in equilibrium, at the final gathering of the essential constituents the channels are opened by a vital wind without harshness.

Since the drops gather within the six sensory bases, the six subsequent mindfulnesses are perfectly understood.

Some nirmāṇakāya emanated bodies are seen.

As for the four perfect renunciations by which meditation is not lost, the awareness that occurs following the three initiations from the nirmāṇakāya emanated body is reflected upon, and the channel of a two-decade lotus lady who is pleasant and so forth is sought.

Because the *essence a* is at the tip of the central channel and the mind is entered by the refined slowly-circulating vital wind and so forth, body, speech, and mind assume the vajra position.

Since the vital winds are suppressed by the drops, the sound of a drum and so forth is not heard [6] because the māra of contentment and so forth has been vanquished.

The path of the inner buddhas.

Gone to the *peak* of existence.

The *forbearance* of emptiness, difficult to bear in relation to birthless phenomena.

The mind lapses into a nonconceptual state in the central channel. When the mind moves, there is *forbearance.*

Since the phenomena of samsara have been transcended and the phenomena of the path of nirvana are utterly complete, it is *sublime among phenomena.*

In that way, there are the flawed and flawless experiences, and after the vital winds and mind have gathered together up into the *external-shape a,* what occur on the paths are the essence, the nature, and the characteristic.

On the transcendent path, by means of the path of the outer and inner dependently arisen connections, the naturally spontaneous nirmāṇakāya emanated body is achieved.

Through the path of the creation stage, the vase initiation that purifies the body is perfected.

The signs of reality are seeing the seven branches of enlightenment, which are the four precious channel mansions and the three principals of the body mandala. The advance and retreat of thoughts.

The ability to shake a hundred vast domains of the nirmāṇakāya emanated body, listen, make a hundred gifts, spread forth a hundred lights, pass down a hundred explanations, and be absorbed in a hundred different meditative concentrations.

If the channels of the six realms, and in particular the support of human beings, are seen, there is joy and anxiety, and shame and disgust.

The indivisibility of samsara and nirvana, which was presented before by the master at the time of the cause, is realized at about that point.

Compassion is born. Tears fall.

The various minds of others are known. One is amused on seeing the various sensory objects.

Various miracles occur instantaneously because the inner vast domain is seen.

The outer are not seen without seeing the inner.

At about that point, the liṅga becomes firm.

As the seminal drop rests at the tip of the vajra, the place of coemergence, likewise the body is crazed with bliss, and one swoons.

Oneself and others are not recognized.

The inner sign is the cessation of the vital wind by one finger-width.

The outer sign is the drops stable in half the genital area.

The first spiritual level of the path of seeing.

Again the four fourfold initiations from the nirmāṇakāya emanated body.

From the second spiritual level of the path of meditation, there is the ability to shake, and so forth, a thousand vast domains of the nirmāṇakāya emanated body, and so forth.

The qualities and so forth increase.

Advance and retreat, and so forth, cease.

The inner sign is the cessation of the vital wind by six finger-widths.

The outer sign is the drops stable in the genital area, navel, and heart.

Some sambhogakāya enjoyment bodies are seen. [7]

The sixth spiritual level of the path of meditation.

Again the four fourfold initiations from the sambhogakāya enjoyment body.

Through the path of the stages of self-blessing, the naturally spontaneous sambhogakāya enjoyment body is achieved.

The secret initiation that purifies the voice is perfected.

The signs of reality are the five powers, gaining control of the vital winds of the five clear essences, the five abilities, and being unimpeded in the gazes.

The seeds of the six realms are seen in the bhaga mandala. Control is gained over the six seeds. One teaches Dharma in the languages of sentient beings, and is unimpeded in regard to the general and individual characteristics of phenomena.

After seeing at the navel the eight bases of the syllables, and the vowels such as *a* and the consonant-syllables such as *ka,* one is unimpeded in the twelve branches of scripture, such as the Dharma of the sutras.

The five nectars and the ability to enjoy the six tastes.

Those that become the melody of Brahmā are clarified by six, such as "The *a* [is the most sublime of all] phonemes."[11]

Above the seventh spiritual level, the mudrā seals of the four cakras. The ability to shake, and so forth, a hundred million vast domains of the sambhogakāya enjoyment body, and so forth.

The inner sign is the cessation of the vital wind by ten finger-widths.

The outer sign is the drops stable in the throat and the point between the eyebrows.

The tenth spiritual level of the path of meditation.

Again the four fourfold initiations from the dharmakāya reality body.

Through the path of the mandalacakra method, which purifies the mind, the naturally spontaneous dharmakāya reality body is achieved.

The initiation of primordial awareness dependent on an embodiment of wisdom is perfected.

The signs of reality, the five forces, are due to the five vital winds of the enlightenment mind and the clear quintessence of the clear essences that they have moved.[12]

After the mandala of the root enlightenment mind has been seen, the signs are displayed.

After the initiations of the three bodies of enlightenment, the five types of primordial awareness, and so forth have been received, if the five nectars are seen gathering in any channels, the buddhas are seen acting for the benefit of others.

If the drops are seen gathering in the emanation cakra and that of great bliss, the buddhas are seen residing in profundity in the realm of Akaniṣṭha.

If the five nectars and the five vital winds are seen gathering in the emanation cakra at the navel, the five spiritual families of the sambhogakāya enjoyment body are seen residing in the mother's bhaga and proclaiming the secret to fortunate bodhisattvas.

If the clear quintessence of the clear essences of the mudrā consort is seen, there is unimpeded paranormal ability.

If the clear essences are drawn into the channel syllables, there is unimpeded magical ability.

If they are transferred precisely there again, previous locations are recalled.

The inner sign is the cessation of the vital wind by twelve finger-widths.

The outer sign is the drops stable in the entire crown of the head.

The twelfth spiritual level of the path of meditation. [8]

Again the four fourfold initiations.

Through the ultimate path, the ultimate are purified by the ultimate dependently arisen connection.

Through the path of the vajra waves, there is the sublime attainment of mahāmudrā, the child of the female embodiment of pure awareness.

The path that totally purifies existence.

The naturally spontaneous svābhāvikakāya essence body is achieved.

The fourth, the initiation of body, speech, and mind, is perfected.

The signs of reality.

As for the noble path of eight branches, two results are achieved at the point of the purification of the eight types of consciousness.

This great earth is joyful, elated, and delighted. It shakes in six ways.

Sounds resound in Māra's places.

The three worlds are seen in the place of the mudrā consort.

Ḍākas and ḍākinīs gather from afar.

The eight qualities of the power and wealth of harima and so forth arise.

The inner sign is the entry of the vital winds of life and exertion into the central channel.

The outer sign is the drops stable in half the cranial dome.

The twelfth and a half spiritual level.

The fourth, the initiation of mind, is perfected.

The sign of reality is the attainment of a single result. The city of the young, the basic space of phenomena, is pierced by the piercer, the enlightenment mind.

As the result, there is the ability to shake, and so forth, ten trillion vast domains of the sambhogakāya enjoyment body,[13] and so forth.

At the point of gaining the thirteenth spiritual level, a female on the thirteenth spiritual level, and so forth, is mentally summoned.[14]

The master is the combined quintessence of the sugatas of the three times.

From the chosen deity and the master indivisible in the bhaga, the attainments are received, and due to the dependently arisen connection, there is the path that totally purifies existence.

The naturally spontaneous, utterly pure svābhāvikakāya essence body is achieved. The result is perfected.

The sign of reality, the result, is the ability to shake, and so forth, absolutely all the vast domains of the sambhogakāya enjoyment body,[15] and so forth.

The inner sign is the cessation of the vital winds of life and exertion in the central channel.

The outer sign is the drops stable in the entire cranial dome.

Since the flawed and flawless meditation experiences have been distinguished by means of the outer dependently arisen connection and the inner dependently arisen connection of the dissolution of the four pulsations, it is the thirteenth spiritual level.

Omniscience. On the thirteenth spiritual level of a vajra holder, the dependently arisen connections appear as aligned. At the point of buddhahood, there is buddhahood with one's circle, in a single group. [9]

The Vajrayana of secret mantra is the causal, path, and resultant initiations. Although conceptually comprehended, the realization is nonconceptual. The appearance of primordial awareness is like that.

The profound path of the master.

Sacred commitment.

A cessation through comprehension of the body.

The oral instructions, together with the esoteric instructions, of the Path with the Result are complete.

samāptam iti

2. Explication of the Treatise for Nyak

Sachen Künga Nyingpo (1092–1158)

I PROSTRATE with the crown of my head at the feet of the excellent master.

Let me explain the meaning of the words.

> **After bowing at the lotus beneath the feet of the excellent master,...**

The four "excellent masters" are: the excellent master who completely eliminates outer doubts; the master who presents the inner naturally arisen primordial awareness; the master who presents the secret coemergent primordial awareness; and the master who presents the utterly pure real nature of all phenomena in ultimate reality. If one touches the lotus beneath that vajra master's feet, all qualities will be produced in oneself. Therefore, motivated by an exceptional clear faith, one bows with body, speech, and mind.

> **...I will write a brief explanation of the Path with the Result.**

The path is the two mundane and transcendent paths, the two paths of the stiff and the spinning wheel, the two paths consisting of the warmths and consisting of the signs,[16] and the two paths consisting of the advance and retreat of primordial awareness and the advance and retreat of thoughts. By way of these synonyms, there are eight.

The result is of three types: the great degree of benefit for oneself, which is the five bodies of enlightenment[17] that come from aligning the dependently arisen connections and completely perfecting the assemblies; the great degree of benefit for others, which includes many qualities such as enabling the blind to gain sight; and the great degree of benefit for both oneself and others, which is buddhahood together with one's circle, in a single group.

Therefore this is known as the oral instructions of the path with the result; the oral instructions of the result with the path; the oral instructions of understanding many points by understanding one; [12] the oral instructions of removing impediments to meditation by recognizing meditative concentration; the oral instructions of removing impediments of the māras by recognizing obstacles; the oral instructions of upholding faults as qualities; the oral instructions of accepting obstacles as attainments; and the oral instructions that are like a gold-transforming elixir.

This is a "brief explanation" because, in accordance with the permission received from the nirmāṇakāya emanated body,[18] Virūpa presented a vast meaning in few words. In short, the meaning is: "I will write the real nature of the Tripiṭaka in vajra lines that are like a precious wish-fulfilling jewel."

The Path of Samsara and Nirvana in Common

Now the meaning of the treatise is explained by way of the seven sections of the path of samsara and nirvana in common.

The Three Appearances

The path presented as the three appearances includes impure appearance, experiential appearance, and pure appearance. Three topics apply to each of these appearances: what the support is, what the cause is, and what the appearance is.

> **For a sentient being with afflictions, impure appearance occurs.**

The support is a sentient being. Of the six types of sentient beings in general, this applies in particular to the mindstream of a single human being. The cause is referred to as the "appearance of affliction." Due to the power of the habitual propensities of karma and afflictions, the appearance is an impure appearance. This includes both confusing appearance and karmic appearance.

> **For a yogin with meditative concentration, experiential appearance occurs.**

The support is a yogin, of which there are three types: a person with a perfect body, a person with a pristine mindstream, and a person in whose mindstream experience has arisen. The cause is mentioned as "meditative concentration," but this is an implicit reference to the blessing by the vital winds and mind, which are the ten father and mother ḍākas and ḍākinīs within the mansions of the channel syllables. [13]

Concerning "experiential appearance," the following arise in the mindstream: the three paths such as that of eliminating entry—which are the path of eliminating entry, the path of severing attachment, and the path of great enlightenment; the three experiences—which are the physical experiences, mental experiences, and dream experiences; the three dependently arisen connections—which are the dependently arisen connections of the reversal of the vital winds, the visual appearances, and dreams; the three warmths—which are the warmth preceded by thought, the warmth of the gathering of the nine essential constituents, and the warmth of the blazing and gathering of the drops; and the three meditative concentrations—which are the meditative concentration of the characteristic as a variety, the meditative concentration of the nature as emptiness, and the meditative concentration of the essence as their unity. In that way, all fifteen experiences may arise, either in sequence or not in sequence, and should be recognized as meditative concentration and taken as the path.

For a sugata with the ornamental wheel of inexhaustible enlightened body, speech, and mind, pure appearance occurs.

The support is a sugata, of which there are four types: the sugata of outer shape, because one has gone to bliss through the path of the two assemblies; the sugata of inner mantra, because one has gone to bliss through the path of the central channel; the sugata of secret initiation, because one has gone to bliss in the space of the mother; and the sugata of ultimate reality, because one has gone to bliss through the path of the three gates to liberation.

The sugata's inexhaustible enlightened body consists of the inconceivable secret of enlightened body and the omnipresence of enlightened body. Similarly, inexhaustible enlightened speech consists of the inconceivable secret of enlightened speech and the omnipresence of enlightened speech. Inexhaustible enlightened mind consists of the inconceivable secret of enlightened mind and the omnipresence of enlightened mind.

Those [qualities] are *ornamental* because they beautify both oneself and others. They are a *wheel* because they are a wheel of enlightened activity. By means of both benefits being done and benefits that will be done, a sugata performs unceasing activities for the benefit of sentient beings until samsara has been emptied. [14]

That presents the support.

The dissolution of the four pulsations is the implicitly presented cause, which is explained later in the text and is not presented here.

The appearance is "pure appearance." In brief, one realizes that there are no separate appearances of samsara and nirvana beyond one's own utterly pure primordial awareness. At about that point, samsara and nirvana have a single taste, path and result have a single taste, being a buddha and being a sentient being are a single mindstream, and what is to be rejected and the antidote have a single taste. This is the meaning of "at about that point, what is to be accepted and rejected are nondual and what is to be abandoned and attained are nondual."

The Three Continua

Now the path is presented as the three continua, which are the causal continuum of the universal ground, the method continuum of the body, and the resultant continuum of mahāmudrā. These are also the root continuum of the universal ground, the method continuum of the body, and the resultant continuum of vajra body, speech, and mind.

Let me explain the meaning of the words.

> **Since samsara and nirvana are complete in the causal continuum of the universal ground, it is the root continuum.**

[The mind] is known as the "universal ground" because it acts as the ground of both samsara and nirvana, depending on whether or not the methods are applied. It is *causal* because of its potent ability to arise as the result. It is a *continuum* because of the continuity of reflexive awareness that extends from when one is a sentient being until one becomes a vajra holder, with the nature of mind, pure awareness, an unbroken stream. Samsara and nirvana are complete in the sense that all the phenomena of samsara are complete in the form of the characteristics; all the path of nirvana is complete in the form of the qualities; and all the phenomena of the result are complete in the form of the potency. [15] That same [universal ground] is also referred to as the "root continuum," because the mind, the universal ground, is to be realized through the alignment of the dependently arisen connections in the body.[19]

Now the method continuum of the body is explained by dividing the subject into five sections: the causal initiation, which is the first topic of the method continuum; the twenty topics of the path and so forth; the presentation of the group of sacred commitments; the presentation of the propitiation of the five ḍākas and ḍākinīs if [the sacred commitments] are damaged; and the presentation of the path initiation, which is the main topic of the method continuum.

> **For the method continuum of the body and so forth, there is the causal initiation with four triads, the seats and so forth, and so forth.**

First, this is called the "method continuum of the body" because the alignment of the dependently arisen connections in the body is the method that brings about the realization of the mind, the universal ground, which exists in the manner of a seed or cause. The "and so forth" includes the meaning "the body is also the explanatory continuum" (which is treated later in the text), because that mind that is the root of samsara and nirvana can be realized and mastered by means of aligning the dependently arisen connections in the body.

The four triads are the four sets of these three topics: from which mandala, which initiation is obtained, and which stains does that purify.

"Seats and so forth" applies to all four mandalas. The three seats are the seat of the buddhas and bodhisattvas, the seat of the female embodiments of pure awareness and the goddesses, and the seat of the wrathful males and wrathful females.[20] The seat of the buddhas is in the center, and the seat of the bodhisattvas is in the inner primary and intermediate directions. From among the female embodiments of pure awareness, the seat of the visualized female embodiment of pure awareness is in the center and the seat of the actual female embodiment of pure awareness is to the left. In the sense of being identical [with the bodhisattvas] and so forth, the seats of the goddesses are also in the inner primary and intermediate directions. The seats of the wrathful males and wrathful females are in the outer primary and intermediate directions. These are the exact arrangement for the mandala of colored particles, but for the remaining three mandalas, one should meditate that the three seats are complete and know them exactly. That is the first, the presentation of the mandala. [16]

The second topic is which initiation is obtained. This concerns obtaining the eleven aspects of the vase initiation, one of the three types of secret initiation, the two initiations of primordial awareness dependent on an embodiment of wisdom, and any one of the five types of the fourth initiation, such as with the support.[21]

The third topic concerns which stains are purified. The stains of body, speech, mind, and the entire triad of body, speech, and mind are purified. The ordinary is vanquished, one may meditate on the path and so forth, and one is thereby privileged to obtain the result of the four bodies of enlightenment.

These initiations are the *superior* if obtained in dependence on an actual female embodiment of pure awareness. They are the *medium* if obtained in dependence on a visualized female embodiment of pure awareness. They are the *inferior* if obtained by just the words.

This is called the "causal initiation" because it is first obtained from the master and is like cleaning a vessel or clearing a field.

These topics have explained the meaning of the words "the causal initiation, with four triads, the seats and so forth, and so forth."

Presentation by means of the four fives of the creation stage as the path and so forth.

This is the presentation of the twenty topics of the path and so forth in connection with the initiations. Each initiation consists of five topics: what the path is, what the view is, what the culmination of attainment is, what the practice when passing away is, and what the result is.

The five topics of the vase initiation are as follows: the path is the shape of the creation stage; the view is the three essences; the culmination of attainment is the indivisibility of samsara and nirvana; the practice when passing away is the upward transference; and the result is the naturally spontaneous nirmāṇakāya emanated body.

The shape of the path should be learned directly from a master. The three essences of the view are the essence of the apparent aspect, the essence of the empty aspect, and the essence of their unity. For each of these there is also the phenomenon that is the reverse of the appearances of ignorance, and the true nature that is free from artificial mind. These also have a single essence, [17] but different facets.

When the culmination of attainment as the indivisibility of samsara and nirvana is reached, during the six spiritual levels of the transcendent path one is able to fit the three-thousandfold world systems into a mustard seed without problem of size. One is unimpeded by such things as walls and mountains. One is able to cause a river to back up, hold heavenly bodies such as the sun and moon hostage, make many from one, make one from many, and so forth.

If the culmination of attainment is not reached, the upward transference is practiced when passing away. This upward transference consists of three types of practice: the transformation of appearances when passing away, the transference with a globe of light when passing away, and the transference with sounds when passing away. The stages of practice for these should be learned directly from a master.

The result of the naturally spontaneous nirmāṇakāya emanated body is not discussed here, because it will be explained in the section on the result.

These are the five topics of the vase initiation.

The five topics of the secret initiation are: the path of the stages of self-blessing; the view of the four types of naturally arisen primordial awareness; the culmination of attainment as clearly distinct and utterly complete; the clear light when passing away; and the result of the naturally spontaneous sambhogakāya enjoyment body.

In general, the Omniscient One taught an inconceivable variety of practices concerning the first of these five topics, the path of the stages of self-blessing. Their key points are included in a set of nine hundred. The key points of these instructions are condensed into seventy-five. If the esoteric instructions for their practice are summarized, they can be included in the following nine. The five practices not dependent on cakras are the feeding of the lamp flame, Brahmā's lightning, the channel yoga, the wheel of the fire drill, and the yoga of the drops. The three dependent on cakras are the practice dependent on one cakra, the practice dependent on two cakras, and the practice dependent on four cakras. The others [of the ninth practice] are quick because they are dependent on the key points of esoteric instruction. Thus [the practices of the path of the stages of self-blessing] are condensed into nine.

For the first practice [the feeding of the lamp flame], sit in the key physical position with the knees raised and so forth. Four finger-widths below the navel, clearly imagine a dark red, upside-down syllable *kṣa*. At the navel, clearly imagine a light-red *aṃ*. Then imagine that the vital winds meet at the lower tips of the channels, the fire in the lower abdomen ignites, and the syllable *kṣa* greatly blazes. When it strikes the *aṃ*, a fine stream of nectar flows from the *aṃ*, feeding the flame of the *kṣa*. Visualize the blazing and dripping in that way, and also unite the vital winds to a suitable degree. Train in the path, [18] sustain the view, and allow the natural expression of the warmths. Practice without a definite number of sessions or amount [of repetitions] in a session. Examine one's inclination.[22] Evaluate one's health.

For the second [Brahmā's lightning]:

> The arrow of fire on the bow of wind
> strikes the *haṃ* target of the enlightenment mind.
> Primordial awareness will quickly arise.
> There is no repeated application.

Allow the natural expression of all experiences. There is no fixed number of sessions, length of a session, and so forth.

For the third [the channel yoga], observe the appropriate key points, such as the body with crossed legs. In coordination with the exhalation of the vital wind, clearly imagine the rasanā to the right, with the nature of the sun and fire, and red in color. In coordination with the inhalation of the vital wind, clearly imagine the lalanā to the left, with the nature of the moon and water, and white in color. In coordination with the pause of the vital wind within, clearly imagine the central channel endowed with four qualities. Keep in mind that it is thin like the stem of a lotus, straight like the trunk of a plantain tree, bright like a sesame-oil lamp, and red like a fig-tree flower. By training over and over in this way, allow the natural expression of all the experiences of the warmths. Observe no certain amount in a session, and so forth.

For the fourth [the wheel of the fire drill], sit in the key physical position with the knees raised. Clearly imagine the central channel, red in color and with a suitable thickness, in the middle of the body from the navel up to the crown of the head. Clearly imagine both the right and left channels, white in color and with a suitable thickness. The two channels rub the central channel, or seem to act like a friction belt, rubbing the central channel. Intensely unite both the upper and lower vital winds. For this practice also, drive oneself with the stimuli of food and behavior, train on the path without fixed lengths and numbers of sessions, sustain the view, and allow the natural expression of whatever experiences arise.

For the fifth [the yoga of the drops], while appropriately observing the key physical points, and in coordination with the vital winds, there are four practices: the union of the sun and moon at the heart, the lone hero at the navel, the drop of bliss at the genitals, and the seed of white hair between the eyebrows. The practice should be requested directly from a master.

Those topics present the five types of practice that do not depend on cakras. [19]

Of the practices that are dependent on cakras, the first is dependent on one cakra. Sit in the key physical position with the knees raised and also completely perform the other branches of meditation. Clearly imagine the wind at the anus, the fire in the lower abdomen, the sixty-four branches of the outer circle at the navel cakra without an arrangement of syllables, the primary set of eight syllables in a clockwise circle as the eight branches of the inner circle, a very tiny *aṃ* in the center, and all the syllables red in color. Then the two lower vital winds meet at the lower tips of the channels and the vital winds ignite the fire in the lower abdomen. That strikes the *aṃ* of the navel, and fire that is red in color and hot in essence blazes from the *aṃ* for about four finger-widths or so. Focusing the visualization on that, gradually perform the union of the vital winds.

Practice without a definite number [of repetitions] in a session or definite length for a session. Also examine one's inclination and so forth, as before. Train in the path, sustain the view, and allow the natural expression of all experiences of the warmths.

For the practice dependent on two cakras, in addition to the previous navel cakra, imagine the eight channel branches of the heart cakra without an arrangement of syllables, in the center of which is a pale blue upside-down *hūṃ*. Then imagine that both the *aṃ* and the *hūṃ* are connected by a very tiny central channel. Then again [as in the practice dependent on one cakra], when the vital winds meet at the lower ends of the channels, a very tiny fire blazes from the *aṃ* up to the *hūṃ*. A tiny stream of the enlightenment mind drips from the *hūṃ* down to the *aṃ*. Focus the mind on the white and red form of the blazing and dripping. Gradually unite the vital winds. The amount in a session and so forth should be understood as before.

The visual appearances representing the warmths that occur here are ten: the five signs and the five signs of the signs. The first signs, in the context of the right channel, are like smoke, mirage, fireflies, burning lamp flames, and a cloudless sky. Those involving the left channel are like darkness, rainbows, lightning, moonbeams, and sunbeams. These may also arise as various visual appearances and dream experiences. Allow the natural expression of all experiences.

For the third practice, which is dependent on four cakras, the observance of the key physical points and so forth is the same as described previously. Then clearly imagine again the two cakras that perform the actions. [20] Then envision the sixty-four branches of the outer circle of the navel cakra as two sets of the sixteen vowels such as *a* in a counterclockwise semicircle and the consonant-syllables such as *ka,* minus *ha* and *kṣa,* in a clockwise semicircle. The eight branches of the inner circle are the same as described previously. All the syllables are red in color and upright.

Then envision the eight branches at the heart as the four of *bhrūṃ* and so forth in the four cardinal directions, the four of *māṃ* and so forth in the four intermediate directions,[23] and the *hūṃ* in the center as before. All the syllables are black in color and upside-down.

Envision the sixteen branches at the throat as the sixteen vowels such as *a* in a counterclockwise circle, and an *oṃ* in the middle. All the syllables are red in color and upright.

Envision the thirty-two branches at the top of the head as the sixteen vowels such as *a* in a counterclockwise semicircle, the sixteen consonant-syllables from *ka* through the dental *ta* in a clockwise semicircle, and a *haṃ* in the middle. All the syllables are white in color and upside-down.

Then the two vital winds of the fire channel and the sleep channel[24] meet at the tips of the three channels, igniting the fire in the lower abdomen. When it strikes the *aṃ* at the navel, that naturally warm vital wind goes through the rasanā on the right and incinerates the essential constituents of the syllables of the heart cakra. It travels through the rasanā again and incinerates the essential constituents of the syllables of the throat cakra. It goes through the rasanā once again, and when it touches the *haṃ* at the crown of the head, the *haṃ* melts into light and flows down through the lalanā. It restores and expands the syllables of the throat as before. It goes through the lalanā again, and restores and expands the syllables of the heart cakra. When it moves through the lalanā again and strikes the *aṃ* at the navel, the *aṃ* greatly blazes and the end of the central channel slightly opens. Like a streak of lightning, the fire goes through the central channel, completely destroying both the *hūṃ* of the heart and the *oṃ* of the throat, and just by its touch, a tiny stream of nectar flows from the *haṃ* down though the central channel. As the fire of that *aṃ* is gradually forced down from the throat to a spot about four finger-widths above the navel, visualize the blazing and dripping wherever one is inclined, and perform the union of the vital winds for a suitable period. Allow the natural expression of all experiences. The rest is the same as described previously.

For the practices that are dependent on the key points of esoteric instruction, sit in the key physical position with the knees raised. Perform the other branches of meditation as before. Then visualize one's body as a hollow cavity and imagine that the inside of the body is filled with pale red fire. Perform twenty-four counted and uncounted yogas of the vital wind.[25] Determine the length of the session by means of the vital wind yogas. [21] Drive oneself with the stimuli of food and behavior. Allow the natural expression of all experiences. Definitely perform four sessions [daily]. Move to the next visualization after three days for a superior, five for an average, and nine for an inferior yogin.

Then imagine a dark red *raṃ* on the soles of both feet. Fire blazes from them, goes through the channels of the ankles, enters through the large channels of the thighs, and gathers in the genital area. Focus on the sharp, quick, intense, and harsh fire. Everything else is like the previous practice.

The battle of the drops is like the previous practice. The cakra visualization is like the previous practice. The blazing of fire more than that is like the previous practice. The blazing of fire much more than that is like the previous practice. The blazing of everything on fire is like the previous practice. During all of these, allow the natural expression of the experiences.

The view of the four types of naturally arisen primordial awareness consists of the meditative concentration of naturally arisen affliction, the meditative concentration of naturally arisen thought, the meditative concentration of naturally arisen blankness, and the meditative concentration of lucidity, buoyancy, and naturally arisen great primordial awareness.

The culmination of attainment, which is clearly distinct and completely perfect, is as follows. During the four spiritual levels, qualities arise in one's mindstream, such as understanding the languages of the six realms, teaching Dharma in their languages, gaining control of the vowels such as *a* and the consonant-syllables such as *ka,* the sublime attainment of speech, awakening from conventional designations, gaining control of the four types of individual and perfect pure awareness,[26] and one's voice transforming into the melody of Brahmā.[27]

If the culmination of attainment is not reached, clear light is the practice when passing away. The vital wind of the moment of death acts as a catalyst; all the vital winds enter into the central channel; and a sublime meditative concentration that is lucid, yet empty, arises. By blending this concentration with the previous meditative concentration of naturally arisen primordial awareness, the culmination of attainment will be reached or one will become an upholder of pure awareness and so forth without an intermediate state.

The result of the naturally spontaneous sambhogakāya enjoyment body is not discussed here because it will be explained in the section on the result. [22]

Those are the five topics of the secret initiation.

The five topics of the initiation of primordial awareness dependent on an embodiment of wisdom are: the path of the mandalacakra method as the path; the view of the four joys of coemergent primordial awareness; the culmination of attainment as the blissful emptiness of lesser extent; the practice when passing away, which is the approach of Vajrasattva at the moment of death; and the result of the naturally spontaneous dharmakāya reality body.

The first of these topics, which is the path, consists of both extensive and condensed practices. The five topics of the extensive path are: equal body and speech, equal desire, equal blessing, the purity of the female embodiment of awareness, and retention by means of the key points of esoteric instruction.

The first topic of the extensive path is equal body and speech. Equal body refers to both oneself and the mudrā consort equally meditating on the deity by means of the four branches,[28] or instantaneously. Equal speech means equal recitation of the root mantra and so forth. The scripture also says:

> The mind of divine form
> and the mind of sacred
> commitment are identical.[29]

Equal desire means that one desires to actualize the coemergent primordial awareness and reach perfect enlightenment in dependence on the female embodiment of pure awareness and that the female embodiment of pure awareness also desires the same in dependence on oneself. Thus there is equal desire to attain perfect enlightenment.

Equal blessing is the mutual blessing of space and secret.[30] The father imagines that the space of the mother vanishes and from emptiness is blessed as an *āḥ* that becomes an eight-petal red lotus marked on the pistil with an *āḥ*. The mother imagines that the secret organ of the father vanishes and from emptiness is blessed as a *hūṃ* that becomes a five-pronged blue vajra marked in the center with a *hūṃ*. At its opening is a dark-red upright *phaṭ,* the jewel is blessed with *oṃ,* and from a *svā* appears a jeweled roof.

The purity of the female embodiment of awareness is the purity attained through birth and the purity that comes from training. The first consists of five types: the deer lady, the conch-bearing lady, the ox lady, the design-bearing lady, and the variegated lady. The characteristics of these should be carefully learned directly from a master. [23] The purity that comes from training consists of three types: total purity of the mindstream through learning, reflection, and study; purity through initiation; and purity through the meditative concentration of yoga.

The purity of the female embodiment of awareness comes first. Then comes equal body and speech, which is the blessing as the nirmāṇakāya emanated body. Then comes equal blessing, which is the blessing as the sambhogakāya enjoyment body. Then comes equal desire, which is the blessing as the dharmakāya reality body.

The fifth topic, retention by means of the key points of esoteric instruction, also consists of five points. Initial descent should be performed; then retention; then reversal; then distribution; and finally, preservation without loss.

For the first point, place the consort (who is a completely pure female embodiment of awareness) at a suitable distance and gaze at her form. This fully ignites the fire of passion, causing the seminal drop to descend. Meditate on the bliss. Protect with the extreme stare and practice the secret control.[31] In the same way, listen to her voice, savor her scent, and experience her taste. In the same way, go as far as touching various key points of her body, thereby igniting the fire of passion and causing the seminal drop to descend. Meditate on the bliss. Protect with the extreme stare and practice the secret control. During all of this, allow the natural expression of whatever experiences arise. In this way, the three phases known as "descent and expansion," "expansion and retention," and "retention and gradual reversal of the seminal drop" occur in linkage. This first moment is the primordial awareness of joy.

Then join together *bola* and *kakkola.*[32] Again the fire of passion causes the seminal drop to descend. Meditate on the bliss. Protect with the extreme stare and the changes of the gaze. Practice the secret control. This second moment is the primordial awareness of sublime joy.

Since the seminal drop descends and the force of bliss is great during these two, they are known as the "warmth of the blazing drops."

Then, when rubbing, a nonconceptual bliss arises. As before, the seminal drop descends. Meditate on that blissful and nonconceptual state. Protect with the extreme stare and practice the secret control. The second is crucial. This third moment is [24] the joy free from joy, and it is also known as the "warmth of the wavering of the seminal drop."

If it is difficult to retain the seminal drop at that point, preserve the seminal drop here by stopping the upper vital wind or by means of the six actions[33] and so forth. If it is easily preserved, preserve it at the fourth moment.

If various events occur at about this point, such as repeated anal contractions, a feeling of being weighed down and disturbed, feces, urine, and so forth sometimes not coming forth and sometimes not stopping, the roots of the hair tingling, and perspiration and tears arising, then the seminal drop has been retained.

At that point, seek the channel of a completely pure consort, preceded by the three blessings. The union of both vajra and lotus, the union of the two channels, the union of the two drops, and the union of the two vital winds will cause bliss and emptiness to fuse together and a meditative concentration free from a recognition of bliss to arise. Sustain that meditative concentration here. Protect with the extreme stare and so forth. Practice the secret control. The second of these is crucial.

Practice protection by means of the six actions: drying up the ocean around Mount Meru; bringing the four continents under control; putting the retainer of taste in its own place; raising up the sublime sense organs; inhaling with a vocally intense, long, and forceful *hūṃ;* and firing the arrow and bow of the *hūṃ* and *phaṭ* of meditative concentration and reversing the seminal drops. Then, the drops should be spread throughout the entire body by means of tying on the belt of the vital wind, hurling the lasso, rotating the body like the wheel of a plow, and using the behavior of a child.[34]

The fourth moment is coemergent joy, which is also called the "warmth of the drops stabilizing." The six types of protection from loss are not explained here because they will be discussed later in the context of protection against loss of the seminal drop.[35]

The condensed path:

> Maintaining the physical posture
> that increases physical vitality,

with the sun in the right hand
and the moon in the left,
cross them and cover the two knees.
Continuously train with nine long *hū*
and short *hu* forward,
three to the right and three to the left, [25]
by means of three exhalations
and three inhalations.
On the third day, the genitals
will retract into the cavity.

That was the preparation. This is the main practice:

After performing the blessings and so forth,
slightly constrict the anus.
Intensely suck both the forefingers
and the second fingers.
Stare upward with both eyes.
This will retain the seminal drop.

Or else, strongly exclaim *ha* and *hal*.
Also perform the other physical yogic exercises.
This will also retain the seminal drop.

This is the conclusion:

With the *hi* of an elephant,
the *ngur* of a tigress,
the retching of a carnivore,
and sniffing like a fox,
gradually draw it up to the navel,
heart, throat, and crown of the head.
Spread it through the body with
the mudrā movements of the liberated lion.

Four types of unskillfulness may occur during this practice. If the yogin is not skillful in the descent, the seminal drop is quickly lost. If not skillful in retention, the duration of bliss is short. If not skillful in reversal, the drops will combine with water. If not skillful in spreading, illness will arise.

The four skills should be applied as the antidote for these types of unskillfulness. Skill in descent is the movement of a turtle. Skill in retention is the three actions of body and one of voice. Skill in reversal is the four animal actions. Skill in spreading is the mudrā movements of the liberated lion. The others, such as tying on the belt of the vital wind, are the same as in the extensive path.

That is an approximate presentation of the path.

The view of the four joys of coemergent primordial awareness consists of the four joys according to sequence, the four joys according to location, the four joys according to what is to be rejected, and the four joys according to their own essence.

The first, the four joys according to sequence, was presented in the section of training on the path, so it is not discussed separately.

The second, the four joys according to location, consists of both the joy according to outer location [26] and the joy according to inner location. For the first [or outer location], if bliss arises in some locations of the body, it is joy. If it arises in most of the body, it is sublime joy. If it arises and pervades the entire body, it is joy free from joy. If all apparent things arise as bliss, it is coemergent joy. For the second [or inner location], from the top of the head down to the throat is joy. From the throat down to the heart is sublime joy. From the heart down to the navel is joy free from joy. From the navel down to the genital area is coemergent joy.

The third topic is the four joys according to what is to be rejected. The general cessation of thoughts of subject and object is joy. The general cessation of thoughts of self is sublime joy. The cessation of thoughts about the mudrā consort is joy free from joy. The cessation of the thought of joy free from joy is coemergent joy. These apply to the body.

The fourth is the four joys according to their own essence. A lesser experience of bliss is joy. A great blazing of bliss is sublime joy. Nonconceptual bliss is joy free from joy. Nondual bliss and emptiness is coemergent joy.

These [four joys] should also be applied to scriptural explanations.

The culmination of attainment as a blissful emptiness of lesser extent is realization of the various phenomena of nirvana and so forth as blissful yet empty. This occurs on the eleventh and twelfth spiritual levels.

If the culmination of attainment has not been reached, the practice when passing away is the approach of Vajrasattva at the moment of death. With the vital wind of death acting as the catalyst, the channel knots open and the essential constituent drops, which are the support of the mind, gather together. When these enter slightly into the central channel, a sublime blissful emptiness arises at the moment of death. *Vajra* is emptiness. *Sattva* is bliss. By blending this sublime blissful emptiness with the previous view of blissful emptiness, one will reach the culmination of attainment and so forth without an intermediate state.

The result of the dharmakāya reality body is not discussed here because it will be explained in the section on the result.

Those are the five topics of the initiation of primordial awareness dependent on an embodiment of wisdom. [27]

The fourth initiation consists of five topics: the path as the three vajra waves, the view of the four ascending joys as the utterly pure real nature of all phenomena, the culmination of attainment as a blissful emptiness of greater extent, the transference from mahāmudrā as the practice when passing away, and the result of the naturally spontaneous svābhāvikakāya essence body.

For the first topic, preceded by the physical trainings and so forth, fully perform the branches of meditation. Preceded by prāṇāyāma and so forth, meditate on the waves of the body, which are the movements of the lower vital wind, then the waves of speech, and then the waves of the mind in meditative concentration.

Training in the path dependent on an actual lotus lady or a visualized mudrā consort of primordial awareness consists of three topics: the purification of the mindstream of the male embodiment of method, then the purification of the female embodiment of wisdom, and then the individual purification of the mindstreams of both.

Perform the three practices of equal body and speech and so forth as during the path of the third initiation. Then the embodiments of method and wisdom instantly enter into union and the clear essences of the essential constituents of both father and mother arrive at the sublime pistil. These then change into the form of light rays, which go through the right channel of the rasanā and arrive at the navel. The navel cakra becomes pale like the dawn, bright like the sunrise, and expanded like an inflated lung.

Again the light rays go through the rasanā to the right and arrive at the heart. Keep the three qualities in mind. Again they go through the rasanā and arrive at the throat. Keep the three qualities in mind.

Again they go through the rasanā and radiate from the right ear in the form of light rays. Mandalas of the special deity radiate from openings in the light rays. These bestow the four initiations on the mindstreams of sentient beings, making sentient beings into the special deity. The two blend and change into the essence of nectar, which enters through one's aperture of Brahmā. Keep the three qualities in mind at the top of the head. The nectar goes to the throat and has the brilliance of a thousand suns. At the heart it changes into the form of five-colored light. Imagine that it emerges from the navel cakra through the path of the purified channel and rests in the space of the mother as before.

This paralyzes the waves of object (to the right) and is known as the "signless gate to liberation," which is the first result. [28]

Do the same with the left channel, which paralyzes the waves of subject. This is the *wishless gate to liberation,* which is the second result.

Also do the same with the central channel, which paralyzes the waves of both subject and object. This is the *emptiness gate to liberation,* which is the third result.

This presents the purification of the mindstream of the embodiment of method.

Do the same with the mindstream of the embodiment of wisdom. After the light rays have circulated through both the right and left channels, they arrive just at the openings of both the right and left ears but do not radiate out. When they go through the central channel, it makes no difference whether they radiate and return through the aperture of Brahmā or not. Understand that the paralyzing of the waves, and also the three gates to liberation, apply as before.

To individually purify the mindstreams of the embodiments of method and wisdom, the clear essences of the essential constituents then go through the central channel of the father again in the form of light rays and dissolve into the sublime cranial dome. Those of the mother also dissolve in that way. Keep in mind that both are also the spontaneous five bodies of enlightenment.

It is uncertain what experiences may occur, but allow the natural expression of whatever arises.

The view is the four ascending joys as the utterly pure real nature of all phenomena. It is taught:

> Being in conformity with the cause
> vanquishes white hair.
> The ripened grants strength.
> The personally created causes increase.
> The immaculate brings immortality.[36]

The first [result] is that one will become beautiful and attractive to all living beings. The second is that some paranormal abilities will arise. The third is that one will be able to enjoy all the tastes of the mundane realm. The fourth is that one will be able to display some magical ability.

Also, at the stage of the first [result], the meditative concentration of blissful emptiness is small. At the second, it is medium. At the third, it is great. At the fourth, it is greater than great.

The culmination of attainment as a blissful emptiness of greater extent occurs on the half spiritual level of the thirteenth spiritual level. One realizes the nature of samsara and nirvana in the state of a single blissful emptiness, without acceptance or rejection, and without abandonment or attainment. [29]

If one has not reached the culmination of attainment, the practice when passing away is the transference through the path of mahāmudrā. This consists of three topics: training, familiarity, and putting it into action.

Training is to train the vital wind. On the first day of any lunar month, maintain four definite sessions of seventeen repetitions of the vital wind of prāṇāyāma. In the same way, increase the repetitions one every day, train for twenty-one days, and on the last day practice thirty-seven repetitions of the vital wind of prāṇāyāma. Again, reduce it by one on the first day. In the same way, reduce it by one every day, so that the original amount will again be reached in twenty-one days. By training the vital wind in this way for forty-two days, the circulation will become clear and the form will become certain.

Familiarity consists of two topics: familiarity in relation to sounds and familiarity in relation to syllables. For the first, maintaining the key points of the body and so forth, draw it[37] up to the throat with twenty-one *"hi ka"* and rest with twenty-one *"ka hi."* In that way, train with four definite sessions per day for seven days.

Familiarity in relation to syllables consists of two topics: familiarity with the outer syllables and familiarity with the inner syllables. The outer are discussed in the section on the main practice. The inner are the same as the extensive *caṇḍālī* in dependence on the four cakras, except that in both the right and left channels there is an alternate arrangement of the sixteen upright red vowels such as *a,* one at a time, and the upside-down white consonant-syllables such as *ka,* two at a time, which block both the right and left channels. Furthermore, clearly imagine these from bottom to top at the time of exhalation. Clearly imagine them from top to bottom at the time of inhalation.[38] Become familiar with this practice by means of four definite sessions per day for seven days.

Putting it into action consists of four topics: application to the pleasant destinies, application to another living being, application to another realm and mode of birth, and application to mahāmudrā. Learn the stages of practice for these topics directly from a master.

The result of the svābhāvikakāya essence body is not discussed here because it is explained in the section on the result.

Those are the five topics of the fourth initiation.

In this way, the twenty topics such as the path have been presented in the context of a person of inferior faculties. [30]

Protecting the sacred commitments of meditative equipoise and so forth.

This is the medium path [for a person of medium faculties]. Each initiation has a sacred commitment of meditative equipoise, a sacred commitment of subsequent conduct, a sacred commitment of food, a sacred commitment of protection, and a sacred commitment of no separation.

The sacred commitment of meditative equipoise for the vase initiation is the creation stage. The sacred commitment of subsequent conduct is the three essences. The sacred commitment of food concerns the pills of the five nectars and the five meats. The sacred commitment of protection concerns the twenty-two root and branch sacred commitments. The sacred commitment of no separation concerns the vajra and bell.

The sacred commitment of meditative equipoise for the secret initiation is the channels and the vital winds. The sacred commitment of subsequent conduct is naturally arisen primordial awareness. The sacred commitment of food is empty lucidity. The sacred commitment of protection concerns everything that conflicts with the naturally arisen and the vital winds. The sacred commitment of no separation concerns the suitable peaceful or intense vital winds.

The sacred commitment of meditative equipoise for the initiation of primordial awareness dependent on an embodiment of wisdom is the mandalacakra. The sacred commitment of subsequent conduct is coemergence. The sacred commitment of food is bliss. The sacred commitment of protection concerns the six losses of the seminal drop. The sacred commitment of no separation concerns the actual or the visualized mudrā consort of primordial awareness.

The sacred commitment of meditative equipoise for the fourth initiation is the three waves. The sacred commitment of subsequent conduct is the utterly pure real nature. The sacred commitment of food is the blissful emptiness of great bliss. Of the two obscurations, the sacred commitment of protection concerns the obscuration of knowledge. The sacred commitment of no separation concerns the actual lotus lady or the visualized mudrā consort of primordial awareness.

Protection [of the sacred commitments] from damage consists of four topics: all of them perfectly arising in one's mindstream protects them from damage, subsequent mindfulness of their number protects them from damage, the arising of an experience protects them from damage, and exceptional devotion to an excellent master protects them from damage.

Damage is of two types: the damage of sacred commitments that draws one into the sufferings of existence, and the damage of sacred commitments that will long delay progress on the path. The first concerns the fourteen root infractions and so forth that the yogin first pledged and that are the sacred commitment of protection for the vase initiation. The second is called "damage of sacred commitment" because one's progress on the path will be long delayed and the attainments will be long delayed if the remaining sacred commitments are damaged. [31]

The method of propitiation is mentioned:

> **Propitiation of the vajra ḍākas and ḍākinīs and so forth.**

The vajra ḍākas and ḍākinīs are the masters. The ḍākas and ḍākinīs of primordial awareness are the sambhogakāya enjoyment body. The mātaraḥ ḍākinīs are the nirmāṇakāya emanated bodies. The carnivorous ḍākas and ḍākinīs are the Lords of the Charnel Grounds and so forth. The ḍākas and ḍākinīs of sacred commitment are the vajra relatives.

If sacred commitments are damaged, the five ḍākas and ḍākinīs must be propitiated. If all the sacred commitments have been damaged, the vajra ḍākas and ḍākinīs must be propitiated. A line from the treatise applies to this:

> **With the five sensory objects and so forth, one should please and so forth.**

The five outer sensory enjoyments concern things such as substances and possessions. The five inner sensory enjoyments concern the offering of an exceptional female embodiment of pure awareness, adorned with ornaments.

If the sacred commitment of meditative equipoise has been damaged, the ḍākas and ḍākinīs of primordial awareness must be pleased. One must sustain the view to the full extent.

If the sacred commitment of subsequent conduct has been damaged, the mātaraḥ ḍākinīs must be pleased. One must sustain meditation to the full extent.

If the remaining three sacred commitments have been damaged, the carnivorous ḍākas and ḍākinīs and the ḍākas and ḍākinīs of sacred commitment must be pleased. This is done by means of sacrificial cakes of flesh and blood and the enjoyment of a ritual feast.

Those topics present the propitiation if the twenty branch sacred commitments of the medium path have been damaged.

Now, to present the main topic of the method continuum, which is the four initiations of the path in connection with shape, it is said:

> **Through meditation on the four initiations in four sessions of the path,...**

The three extensive, medium, and condensed ways to take the initiations should be learned directly from a master.

> **...and in dependence on the body, the obscurations to great bliss cease and enlightenment is clear, so it is the explanatory continuum.**

"In dependence on the body" means that the initiation at the time of the cause is obtained by means of the body; the initiation at the time of the path is also received by means of the body; the five dependently arisen connections are aligned by means of the body; the spiritual levels and paths are also traversed by means of the body; and what is to be abandoned is abandoned by means of the body.

Concerning the obscurations to great bliss: in general, the eight flawed experiences are the obscuration of knowledge. But even the flawless experiences—the three of the unity of appearance and emptiness in relation to objects, the unity of lucidity and emptiness in relation to consciousness, and the unity of bliss and emptiness in relation to the body—cease in a single taste due to sublime blissful emptiness.

Enlightenment is "clear" because the result of the four bodies of enlightenment or the five bodies of enlightenment is clearly achieved precisely through the alignment of the dependently arisen connections in the body.

[The method continuum] is also called the "explanatory continuum" [32] because the root to be realized, which is the mind, is realized and mastered through the alignment of the dependently arisen connections in the body, which is the agent of realization, and thus the explanatory continuum.[39]

Up to this point the body as the method continuum has been presented.

Now for the resultant continuum of mahāmudrā:

> **Mahāmudrā, the resultant continuum, is omniscience by means of the four resultant initiations.**

Because this is an attainment dependent on a mudrā consort, it is also called the *attainment of the mudrā* or the *child of the female embodiment of pure awareness.* It is *mahā* (great) or sublime because there is nothing else above this.

The ultimate path, which is the immediate cause for the attainment [of the resultant continuum of mahāmudrā], is also mentioned: "by means of the four resultant initiations." The vase initiation [dissolves] the pulsations of the channels, the secret initiation [dissolves] the pulsations of the syllables, the initiation of primordial awareness dependent on an embodiment of wisdom [dissolves] the pulsations of the nectars, and the fourth initiation [dissolves] the pulsations of the vital wind.

The result achieved by that is called *omniscience,* which means omniscience of enlightened body, omniscience of enlightened speech, omniscience of enlightened mind, and omniscience of enlightened body, speech, and mind. It is the attainment of the four bodies of enlightenment and the five bodies of enlightenment.

Up to this point the path presented as the three continua has been presented.

The Four Authentic Qualities

Now, for the yogin to quickly progress on the path by means of producing exceptional confidence, the path is presented as the four authentic qualities. It is said:

> **After establishing the result by means of the four authentic qualities,...**

These are the authentic quality of scripture, which is the perfect word of the sugata; the authentic quality of the esoteric instructions experienced by one's master, who is a vajra master; the authentic quality of the subsequent mindfulness of one's experience as a yogin; and the authentic quality of the description of the dependently arisen connections that set the limits of an entity.

"After establishing the result by means of the four authentic qualities" is just an indication. It should be understood to mean: "After establishing the result by means of the four authentic qualities, after establishing each of the five topics such as the path, and after establishing the cause and all of samsara."

The Six Oral Instructions

Now, to quickly develop meditative concentration, and so forth, the path is presented as the six oral instructions. [33] This topic in the treatise begins, "The poison of meditation is extracted by the triad free from flaws of contradiction and so forth." The six oral instructions are the three of extracting the poison of meditation, resorting to nectar, and total release, and the three of extracting the poison of the view, resorting to nectar, and total release. The three of meditation are mentioned first in the treatise, but because the three of the view come first in the process of direct realization, they will be treated out of sequence. It is said:

> **Extracting the poison of the view by meditating on a thought that purifies the mind, which is the path of eliminating entry.**

In general, the view consists of two topics: classifying mere understanding to be the view and classifying the meditative concentration of experience to be the view. The first includes the view that eliminates doubts through learning and reflection, the view maintained in regard to an individual scriptural tradition, the view that is taken as the object of enthusiasm or understanding, the view that is equal to that of the Vehicle of the Perfections, and the view that is not apart from the truth of the ocean of reality. Even if such views have been understood, one will still be unable to alleviate the poison of the flow of thoughts. This will not become a taintless path and one will not see the truth, just as food with a hundred flavors is not beneficial if it contains poison.

The extraction of that poison is taught with words such as "path of eliminating entry." First fully perform the branches of meditation. Meditate on one of the vital wind yogas such as prāṇāyāma, with the vital winds and mind in conjunction. If the mind rests on precisely that, it is the path of eliminating entry. Synonyms for this are "a thought that purifies the mind," and "correct thought." If even that is absent, it is called the "path of severing attachment." If the mind rests on something else, such as smoke, it is held to be the "path of great enlightenment."

Since these experiences also arise either in sequence or not in sequence, recognize them as meditative concentration and allow their natural expression. [34]

If that does not expel the poison of the view, it is because the consciousness desires an object, like a thirsty person pursuing water, and so one should resort to the nectar of objects. It is said:

> **Resorting to the nectar without the five types of consciousness rejecting the five objects.**

By means of resorting to looking at various wonderful spectacles with the eyes, up to and including the experiencing of sensations, the consciousness will be satisfied by an object and will rest upon that object. "The warmth preceded by thought" is a name for the mind previously not at rest. For the mind at rest, "resorting to the nectar of various objects" becomes one of the eight enhancements.[40]

One might ask, "If objects were to become nectar, would all sentient beings also become endowed with meditative concentration by resorting to objects?"

They would not. It is said:

> **Because pure phenomena arise as empty from the beginning, totally release them.**

This is the meaning: objects are birthless emptiness from the beginning and are by nature the three gates to liberation, so they are not the causes of bondage or of liberation. Totally release them in birthless emptiness. Bondage and liberation depend solely on skill in method. If the key point of allowing the natural expression of experiences is understood, they will become the warmth preceded by thought; but if it is not understood, they will become the "series of thoughts," or the "thief of thoughts, who is the māra of meditation," which is ordinary thoughts. Therefore, know that [liberation] depends on skill in method and the total release of the objects in birthless emptiness.

That is the presentation of the three oral instructions concerning the view.

Now there are the three oral instructions concerning meditation. It is said:

> **...the poison of meditation is extracted by the triad free from flaws of contradiction and so forth.**

Even when the poison of the view has been expelled as just described, if the poison of meditation (the eight flawed experiences that are the obscuration of knowledge) arises, that poison should be expelled by the triad free from flaws. This is the meaning: concerning [the view of] the three essences, the essences of both the apparent aspect and the empty aspect are flawed because they include exaggeration and denigration. For [the view of the four types of] naturally arisen [primordial awareness], the three [meditative concentrations] of affliction, thought, and blankness are flawed, because they include dullness and agitation, because they will not become antidotes for what is to be rejected, [35] and because they are difficult to distinguish from the ordinary afflictions and so forth. For [the views of] coemergence and utter purity, the first three joys are flawed because they include craving.

Those eight poisons are extracted by the three flawless experiences: for the [view of the three] essences, unity free from flaw of contradiction; for great naturally arisen primordial awareness, lucidity and emptiness free from flaw of contradiction; and for coemergence and utter purity, coemergent joy and bliss and emptiness free from flaw of contradiction. By recognizing even the eight flawed experiences as meditative concentration, and by the key point of allowing their natural expression, the three flawless ones will arise and that poison will be expelled. If the three flawless experiences do not arise, the methods for making them arise should be learned directly from a master.

When the flawless have not arisen in that way or even the flawed themselves have not arisen, one should resort to the nectar. This consists of seven topics, which can be condensed into three groups. These seven comprise the five nectars that produce the meditative concentration that has not arisen, the enhancement of what has arisen, and the removal of flaws.

> **Resorting to food, behavior, the vital wind, the drop, and the mudrā consort.**

The first is food. What should be avoided: salt, anything extremely salty, mountain garlic, salty-sour beer, and rancid meat are disturbing foods that should be avoided. What should be resorted to: the "application of a stream of nectar," some garlic, soaking myrobalan plums in milk and continually chewing them, the esoteric instruction of boiling water and butter, the three fruits and honey, and feces and honey.[41] These act as curative techniques for establishing the enlightenment mind, which is transformed into sublime nectar.

For behavior, what should be avoided are fire, the sun, and exertion that causes perspiration. What should be resorted to is solely the nectar of mildness and relaxation.

Use any of the seven esoteric instructions of the vital wind.[42]

For the drop, any of the four yogas of the drop will bring sublime meditation.[43]

Resorting to the mudrā consort is like the path of the third initiation.

Those methods will produce meditative concentration that has not arisen. [36]

The bliss of the five clear essences,...

The "bliss of the five clear essences" acts as the enhancement. Wherever bliss has arisen, if one wants it to pervade the entire body or even wants all appearances to be pervaded with bliss, one should become accustomed to blocking the path of exertion, exhaling through the path of life,[44] and gazing slightly upward with the eyes.

...the five sense organs, and resorting to the nectar without parting from the experience.

"The five sense organs, and resorting to the nectar without parting from the experience" indicates the removal of flaws. Slightly focus the awareness wherever bliss has arisen in the body. Then, by means of either the calm or the intense vocal inhalation,[45] propel it to the opening of the sense organ. That will cause bliss and meditative concentration to arise in the body and will also remove flaws.

If meditative concentration has arisen by resorting to the nectar in that way, the pains of the channels and the vital wind may again occur, and so total release is presented.

Total release consists of three topics: total release in the location of the channels themselves, total release through strengthening the force of the vital wind, and total release through allowing the natural expression of the warmths of mental experience. The last two are mentioned below.[46]

Total release in the channels includes both total release in the samsara channels and total release in the nirvana channel.

First is total release in the samsara channels. In general, the six types of channels are like a wound-up ball of string, like an extended rope, like a coiled snake, like an open umbrella, like a spreading tree, and like tangled hair. Totally release [the pains] at this or that place.

Total release in the four samsara channels...

The four samsara channels are the rasanā and lalanā. These both exist above the navel in dependence on both the right and left [sides] of the body, but below the navel they split into four—two [that fork] to the right and left and two [that fork] to the front and rear—and are thus held to be four.

To the right is the channel that discharges and holds frankincense. To the left is the channel that discharges and holds camphor.[47] To the front is the channel that discharges and holds musk. To the rear is the channel that discharges and holds feces. These are known as *samsara channels* because they produce the body that is generated by karma, as well as the mind of subject and object.

...and the cakras,...

The two cakras in which the enlightenment mind [37] is immobile and the four cakras in which it is mobile add up to six. Another twelve cakras of the twelve major joints adds up to eighteen. Again, if pains of the channels arise, totally release them [as necessary] in this or that place.

...and the others,...

The others are the other thirty-two channels and other tiny channels. If pains occur, totally release them in those places.

Now, for total release in the nirvana channel: if the vital winds and mind are clear in the central channel, of the thirty-two narrow channel knots, a knot each is totally released at *delight,* which is the first spiritual level, and at *great primordial awareness,* which is the twelfth spiritual level. At each of the ten spiritual levels in between, three knots are totally released, which are the preparation or beginning, the main section or enjoyment, and the conclusion or total completion and dissolution. Therefore, it is said:

> **...and by opening the channel knots at each of the first and last spiritual levels, and through ten triads in between.**

In this way, the path has been presented as the six oral instructions.

The Four Oral Transmissions

Now the path is presented as the four oral transmissions. It is said:

> **The oral transmission of secret mantra and four others are unbroken.**

These [others] are the unceasing stream of initiation, the undeclined transmission of blessings, the undisrupted sequence of the oral instructions, and the ability to satisfy the mind with devotion.

The first consists of three topics: the unceasing stream of initiation at the time of the cause, the unceasing stream of initiation at the time of the path, and the unceasing stream of initiation at the time of the result. In brief, this is a treatise in which the path is totally completed by means of initiation.

The second [oral transmission] has the nature of the four culminations of secret mantra, which are: the culmination of practice, the culmination of experience, the culmination of blessings, and the culmination of attainment.

For the third, when the māras and obstacles such as rākṣasa demons that may appear or the many unpleasant things such as fear and despair that may arise [38] are precisely understood as the path, this is known as the "oral instructions in which impediments to meditation are removed through recognizing them as meditative concentration, the oral instructions in which impediments of the māras are removed by recognition of the obstacles, the oral instructions of knowing to uphold faults as qualities, and the oral instructions of knowing to accept obstacles as attainments."

The fourth [oral transmission] is the arising of an exceptional confidence that, as taught by the master, all obstacles and attainments, and all hopes and fears, arise from aligning the dependently arisen connections of the channels and vital winds in one's own body. Then the perception of the master as a buddha ensues.

The Five Dependently Arisen Connections

Now the path is presented as the five dependently arisen connections.

> **On the basis of an exceptional body, the dependently arisen connections set the limits of an entity.**
>
> **Contingent, dependently arisen connections.**
>
> **The path of great enlightenment.**
>
> **The authentic quality of the description of the dependently arisen connections between all phenomena.**
>
> **The universal ground consciousness, the pure great enlightenment.**
>
> **The path is totally completed through five dependently arisen connections.**

This is presented by means of seven topics: what the ground that aligns the dependently arisen connections is; what the limits of the dependently arisen connections are; what the dependently arisen connections themselves are; which it is of the four paths; which it is of the four authentic qualities; the meaning indicated and actualized by those dependently arisen connections; and how many dependently arisen connections totally complete the path. These topics apply in sequence to the phrases of the *Vajra Lines.*

Protection from Obstacles on the Path

Now protection from obstacles on the path for a yogin who is over-inclined toward method or wisdom [is presented]. For the yogin who is over-inclined toward method, there are eight protections from four obstacles; for the yogin who is over-inclined toward wisdom, there are eight protections from four obstacles; and fourteen protections apply in common to both yogins. On the mundane path and below, protection is by means of these thirty protections.

The first topic is presented by "over-inclined toward method" and so forth.

> **A yogin who is over-inclined toward method is protected from obstacles on the path...**

Over-inclination toward method includes both over-inclination due to devotion and engagement and over-inclination due to experience. For those persons, there are four obstacles, which occur at four different points: the obstacles of mundane phenomena when engaging the path, the obstacles of the outer māras when the path has been entered, [39] the obstacles of the increased force of the māras when the mind is slightly stable, and the obstacles of not recognizing meditative concentration when the mind is stable.

> **...by firm faith,...**

The first of these obstacles includes two topics: the obstacles of ties with loving relatives and so forth and the obstacles of the master and friends. Protection from the first is by firm faith preceded by minor material gifts. Protection from the second is by firm faith preceded by material gifts and a loving attitude.

> **...the protection cakra, mantra recitation, mantra knots,...**

Three things will definitely protect one from the obstacles of the outer māras: the protection cakra of the vajra fence and so forth, or the recitation of mantras such as *sumbhani,* or mantra knots and so forth from a capable master and from friends, depending on other circumstances.

Those are the four methods for protection from the obstacles of method.

Concerning the obstacles of the increased force of the māras, the protection cakra should be exchanged.

> **...phenomena as the appearances of the nature of mind, the contingent, dependently arisen connections, and, since they are like reflected images, by not parting from the truth of the ocean of reality.**

Three points provide protection: recognition that all three—oneself as the one being obstructed, the obstructing māras, and the obstacle—are the mind, recognition that the mind is illusory, and recognition that it has no self-nature.

These are the three protections from the obstacles of method by means of wisdom.

When the mind is stable, many unpleasant things may occur due to the gathering of the vital winds and mind together in locations such as the syllable *kṣa,* such as being attacked by rākṣasa demons and carnivorous ḍākas and ḍākinīs. At that time, recognition of these [experiences] as meditative concentration removes impediments to meditation, recognition of the obstacles removes the impediments of the māras, and knowing to uphold them as qualities and knowing to accept them as attainments pacifies the obstacles. In brief, protection is through understanding the contingent dependently arisen connections.

In this way, it is taught that the eight protections can also be condensed into three. The eight condensed into three are: the four protections from the obstacles of method by means of method, the three protections from the obstacles of method by means of wisdom, and the single protection from the obstacles of method by means of the dependently arisen connections.

For wisdom,...

The "path of wisdom" and so forth applies to two types of people: those who are over-inclined toward wisdom due to devotion and engagement [40] and those who are over-inclined toward wisdom due to experiences. Four obstacles apply to them both: the obstacles that produce experiences and suffering, the obstacles that display forms, the obstacles that express sounds, and the obstacles that change the views and culminations of attainment. Four protections apply to these in sequence; these are the four tests.

Furthermore, this connects with a statement that applies from a later part of the text, where it says:

> **Since the devaputra māras come on the path of wisdom, protection is by means of the four tests.**[48]

The four tests are: the test by means of experiences, the test by means of meditative concentration, the test by means of mantra, and the test by means of the view and culmination of attainment.

Let me explain some of the meaning of the words. It is said:

> **...there are the outer māras,...**

The "outer māras" are false guides who have been evil from the beginning and who only cause obstacles.

> **...and a change will come in regard to the two paths and the eight views and culminations of attainment.**

However, the change of the eight views and culminations of attainment in regard to the two paths is the fourth obstacle, and the other three obstacles should be understood by implication.

> **The inner change the ten of the paths and so forth, and come if the signs are not known. Protection is through knowing.**

Now the "inner māras" are mentioned. Again (as with the previous obstacles) there are four from which to be protected. One is protected from these by means of the signs of the four initiations. The inner māras are beneficial or harmful, and may affect both elimination and acceptance.[49] They are known as "inner māras" and also as "impediments."

The ten of the paths and so forth are the same as described previously. As for protection through knowing the signs, the physical signs are:

> Press the gathered five with the tip,
> make an *e* for a Veda
> with thumb and third finger,
> use the mudrā gesture of the sublime
> enlightenment mind,
> and symbolize space with the forefinger.

The branch signs are:

> Show the five fingers individually,
> clench the vajra fist,
> show the three-pronged vajra raised,
> and symbolize space with the forefinger.

The vocal signs, which are the four sets of *ka la śa a, ya ra la wa, e vaṃ ma ya,* and *oṃ āḥ hūṃ oṃ,* should be understood to be for the four initiations. These will definitely protect one from obstacles.

Those topics present the sixteen protections, eight each for those who are over-inclined toward method and wisdom. [41]

Now are the fourteen protections for both yogins in common. It is said:

> **Protection from contamination, obscuration, and loss of the seminal drop.**

These are the protections from the six contaminations, the six losses of the seminal drop, and the two obscurations.

The six contaminations are: contamination of sacred commitment, contamination of evil spirits, contamination of bad companions, contamination of food, contamination of place, and contamination of a corpse. The first is *great* contamination, the middle four are *medium,* and the last is *small.*

The three degrees of contamination can be understood in dream experiences by means of examining what becomes unclean. If the body is soiled, it is great, if the clothing is soiled it is medium, and if the residence is soiled it is small.

The six contaminations can also be individually understood in dream experiences. Great contamination robs the life force, the medium produces physical and mental suffering and robs meditative concentration, and the small also robs meditative concentration.

The removal of contamination: the great contamination is removed by means of initiation, the medium is removed by means of a ritual feast, and the small is removed by means of bathing.

Removal by means of bathing applies to three types: the great, medium, and small contaminations of evil spirits. For the great contamination, correctly perform the ritual of the vase. Pour in the ashes from a fierce fire ritual, black aconite, powdered human bones, and white mustard, and fill it with fragrant water. If one bathes at the three periods while reciting many of the heart mantras of the special deity, the contamination will be removed. Using the ashes of an extensive fire ritual will remove the medium contamination, and using those of a peaceful fire ritual will remove the small contamination.

For the elimination of a local epidemic and so forth, use the ashes of a powerful fire ritual and correctly perform the ritual. As for the general removal of all contaminations: they are removed by initiation; they are removed by means of a ritual feast at a special time; and they are also removed by means of bathing. They are also removed by means of clay molds, half of which should be left in an isolated place and half of which should be scattered in a large river. Otherwise, they are also removed by saving the lives of creatures, vocal atonement, and so forth.

Because these mainly cause obstacles during the first gathering of the essential constituents, the removal of contamination is extremely valuable. [42]

The six losses of the seminal drop are: loss due to the arousal of bliss and the filling of the channels; loss in a dream due to an evil spirit and habitual propensity; loss due to the confluence of an illness and water; loss due to the arousal of passion caused by the catalyst of the female embodiment of pure awareness; loss by natural depletion due to disagreeable food; and loss due to the confluence with perspiration caused by activities.

Protection from the first [loss due to the arousal of bliss and the filling of the channels] is by means of the six actions, the calm and the intense vocal inhalations, and especially the powerful *hūṃ* and so forth.[50]

For the second [loss in a dream due to an evil spirit and habitual propensity], mix together well the four ingredients of black tree-gum resin, human brains, ashes from burned white mustard seeds, and menstrual blood. In the evening time, smear it on the genitals and the waist.

Or else make twenty-one knots in a black thread and recite many heart mantras of the special deity. Then tie it around the waist.

The dirt of a woman's clothing will protect one from loss due to habitual propensity. Otherwise, the physical position, practices common to the action tantras, and so forth will also provide protection.

For the third [loss due to the confluence of an illness and water], in general, one should resort to nutritious food. Take a little powder of the three hot herbs[51] on an empty stomach. Wrap the genitals and waist with a warm garment, such as the skin of a carnivorous beast. Stand up and apply five or seven moxa at the points where the elbows reach. That will definitely alleviate it.

Protection from the fourth loss [loss due to the arousal of passion] is by means of the special protections of the six actions and the extreme stare. The other protections from this should be learned in detail directly from a master.

Concerning the last two losses, the methods are no different from what was presented in the context of resorting to the nectar of food and activities.

These [six losses] mainly cause obstacles during the middle gathering of the essential constituents, so the protections are extremely valuable.

The two obscurations are the obscuration of the afflictions and the obscuration of knowledge. The first is the continual flow of thoughts. One is protected from this obscuration by means of the three paths of eliminating entry and so forth. The obscuration of knowledge occurs when meditative concentration is present, but [the concentration] is the eight flawed experiences. One is protected from these by the key point of allowing their natural expression and by the three flawless experiences. If the flawless have not arisen, the methods for producing them should be learned directly from a master.

These points have basically presented the fourteen common protections, [43] and thus the thirty general protections have been presented.

In that way, the path of samsara and nirvana in common has been presented by means of dividing the treatise into seven sections.

The Mundane Path

Now the mundane path of the stiff wheel is presented. The treatise is taught in seven sections, but the general classification of the path consists of the three modes of guidance on the path and the two modes of progression.

A General Classification

The first of these topics includes guidance on the path by the vital wind, guidance on the path by the essential constituent nectars, and guidance on the path by the channel syllables.

First is guidance on the path by the vital wind. On the mundane path and below, one is guided on the path by the vital wind that brings harm during the first gathering of the essential constituents; one is guided on the path by the vital wind that is neither beneficial nor harmful during the middle gathering; and one is guided on the path by the vital wind that is beneficial during the final gathering. That completes the mundane path.

On the transcendent path, one is then guided on the path by the taintless vital wind. Then one is guided on the path by the vital winds of the five powers. Then one is guided on the path by the vital winds of the five forces. Then one is guided on the path by the total dissolution of the vital winds of life and exertion. Then the pulsations of the vital winds dissolve and they become only the vital wind of primordial awareness.

Second is guidance on the path by the essential constituent nectars. During the first gathering of the essential constituents, one is guided on the path by the essential constituents that have not been separated into clear essences and impurities. During the middle gathering, one is guided on the path by those that are somewhat clear. During the final gathering, one is guided on the path by those that are mostly clear. That completes the mundane path.

On the transcendent path, one is then guided on the path by the clear essences of the essential constituents. Then one is guided by the quintessence of the nectars. Then one is guided by the great clear essences of the essential constituents. Then one is guided by the great clear quintessence of the clear essences. Then the pulsations of the nectars dissolve, and they become the sublime clear essence.

Third is guidance on the path by the channel syllables. Again, during the first gathering of the essential constituents, one is guided on the path by the syllables that arise as indefinite confusing appearances. During the second gathering, one is guided on the path by those that arise as certain visual appearances. During the third gathering, one is guided on the path by those that arise as extremely certain lucid appearances. That completes the mundane path and below.

On the transcendent path, one is then guided on the path by the somewhat pure force of the syllables. [44] Then one is guided on the path by the mostly pure force of the syllables. Then one is guided on the path by the pure force of the syllables. Then one is guided on the path by the greatly purified pure force of the syllables. Then the pulsations of the syllables dissolve, and they change into the indestructible syllables.

Now, the two modes of progression on the path are: progression according to the five spiritual paths in the context of conformity to the scriptures, and progression on the path according to the thirty-seven factors conducive to enlightenment.

The first topic consists of the four paths of accumulation, such as the *outer-shape path of accumulation,* and—of the paths of application—the three of *warmth,* such as: *preceded by thought;* both an outer and an inner *peak;* one *forbearance* of emptiness that is difficult to bear in relation to birthless phenomena; and both a *sublime among phenomena* in which the phenomena of samsara have been transcended and a *sublime among phenomena* in which the phenomena of the path of nirvana have been perfected. In that way, the mundane path and below are completed by means of the two paths of accumulation and application.

The first set of three signs indicate the path of seeing. The eleven sets of three signs indicate the path of meditation. The dissolution of the four pulsations indicates the ultimate path.

The second topic is progression on the path according to the thirty-seven factors conducive to enlightenment. First, the four bases for the miraculous act as the antidotes when appearances rise up as the enemy. Then the four applications of mindfulness act as the antidotes when emptiness rises up as the enemy. Then the four perfect renunciations act as the antidotes when one swoons with bliss. These twelve complete the mundane path and below.

On the transcendent path, one then progresses by means of the seven branches of enlightenment up through the sixth spiritual level, the five powers on four spiritual levels, the five forces on two spiritual levels, and, on the first half of the thirteenth spiritual level, by means of the eight supported types of consciousness, which are the eight branches of the noble path. In that way the transcendent path is completed by twenty-five factors conducive to enlightenment.

The Brief Presentation of the Causes for the Arising of Meditative Concentration

Now let me explain the meaning of the words in sequence.

> **From the path of accumulation,...**

The "path of accumulation" consists of four paths of accumulation. The outer-shape path of accumulation begins with inviting the indivisible deity and master into the sky in front of one [45] and making the five offerings. Thus it is a path of accumulation.

The inner-mantra path of accumulation begins when the vital winds and mind accumulate in the location of the navel. Thus it is a path of accumulation.

The secret-initiation path of accumulation begins when the vital winds and mind accumulate in the space of the mother. Thus it is a path of accumulation.

The ultimate-reality path of accumulation begins when the vital winds and mind accumulate at the sublime pistil of the two-decade lotus lady who is pleasant and so forth. Thus it is a path of accumulation.

In brief, these are held to be the "path of accumulation" because the causes for the arising of meditative concentration are accumulated.

When that path joins with the warmth of the path of application, there are three levels of warmth. Due to the particulars of the three lesser, medium, and great levels of warmth, the three gatherings of the essential constituents follow in sequence.

> **...the four results separate from the body, speech, and mind of an ordinary person are achieved.**

In general, four results arise at the time of the cause, four results arise at the first culmination of attainment, and four results arise at each individual culmination of attainment.

The first of these are: the *separated* result, because one has separated from the body, speech, and mind of an ordinary person; the *ripened* result, because what is present in the universal ground has ripened in oneself; the *coemergent* result conforming to the cause, because it is experienced according to what was done; and the *personally created* or *immaculate* result, because it arises from the effort of the person and because the unfavorable factors that are to be abandoned, have been abandoned.

Concerning the first, after the experiences of warmth have gradually become stable, the bodies of oneself and others appear as the deity, speech arises as mantra, and the stream of nonconceptual meditative concentration is unbroken in the mind. This is the first result.

Also, at about that point one understands the various languages of the animals and so forth, knows how to speak a variety of them, and thinks that one is unimpeded by any apparent phenomenon. This is the second result.

Also, at about that point the stream of bliss is unbroken in the body and even painful circumstances cause bliss to arise. This is the third result.

Also, at about that point the incidental afflictions recede, the mind with thoughts of the eight worldly concerns[52] also gradually ceases, and one has little attachment to anything. This is the fourth result. [46]

Concerning the four results that arise at the first culmination of attainment: first one gazes upon the faces of buddhas who are nirmāṇakāya emanated bodies. One is also clearly the special deity, the creation stage is stable, and one has separated from an ordinary body. By means of speech, one explains the Dharma to a hundred disciples and so forth and has separated from the speech of an ordinary person. A meditative concentration in which there is no distinction between meditative equipoise and postmeditation arises in the mind, and one has separated from the mind of an ordinary person. This is the first result.

Also, at about that point one is unimpeded by walls and mountains, able to fit the three-thousandfold world systems into a mustard seed without problem of size, make many things from one or one from many, and so forth. This is the second result.

Also, at about that point the vital winds and mind are drawn into the central channel, the queen wraps [her legs] around one's waist, and the stream of taintless bliss is unbroken. This is the third result.

Also, at about that point various concepts such as the visual appearances subside. The unfavorable factors that are to be abandoned have little force. The antidote, primordial awareness, has great force, and an advance and retreat of thoughts occurs. This is the fourth result.

Concerning the four results of the individual culminations of attainment, the term *result* is given to the four culminations of attainment themselves.

Of these, the first four primarily arise during *warmth,* and should be recognized in that way.

Now, to present in a condensed form the causes of meditative concentration, the essence of meditative concentration itself, and all the benefits, it is said:

> **By means of the three modes of gathering the essential constituents, random events occur.**

The three modes of gathering the essential constituents are: the natural gathering of the essential constituents for one with residual karma, the gathering of the essential constituents through blessings for one with devotion, and the gathering of the essential constituents through exertion for one with diligence.

These are the seven random events applied to the first type of person [with residual karma]: because the residual karma is randomly awakened, the vital winds randomly reverse; that randomly ignites the flames of fierce fire; that randomly opens the channels; that randomly gathers the essential constituents; that causes the random arising of tainted paranormal ability; and that causes the random arising of taintless paranormal ability.

Similarly, seven random events apply to devotion and seven random events also apply to diligence, making twenty-one.

If one is thus endowed with all twenty-one, one will reach the culmination of attainment in this lifetime. [47] If endowed with fourteen, one will reach it in the intermediate state. If endowed with seven, one will reach the culmination of attainment within sixteen lifetimes.

The first of these [random events] are each the eventual cause of meditative concentration, the middle five are the essence of the meditative concentration itself, and the last are the benefit or result.

Now the three modes of the mind at rest are presented. It is said:

> **One is blessed by the vital winds and mind.**

The mind is at rest due to the reversal of the vital wind, the mind is at rest because one is blessed by the vital winds and mind, and the mind is at rest because the [essential constituents] have blended together with the support.

The first of these is like damming up water or reining in a horse. The second is like being knocked out by poison and so forth. The third is like pouring water into water or butter into butter.

Both the first and the last are explained below, but the blessing of oneself by the vital winds and mind has been presented here.

Now, for the presentation in the context of conformity to scripture, it is said:

> **If one then progresses on the path according to the thirty-seven factors conducive to the objective of enlightenment,...**

"Enlightenment" is the renunciations and primordial awareness of the thirteenth spiritual level. "Conducive to the objective" refers to the causes. "Thirty-seven" is the number of dependently arisen connections concerning the vital winds and so forth.

Of these thirty-seven factors, the first topic concerns rapid entry or progress on the path. It is said:

> **...there are four bases for the miraculous by which meditation is not lost,...**

Meditation is not lost because all the dependently arisen connections are aligned in oneself and everything is meditative concentration.

Regarding the four bases for the miraculous, the vital wind of earth produces an exceptional meditative concentration, so the vital wind of earth has become a base for the miraculous. The same also applies to the other three vital winds.

> **...which are the vital action winds,...**

The "vital action winds" are vital action winds because they perform ten actions on the mundane path and below.

In general, this section includes the four infusions of the vital action winds, the ten divisions, the seven key points of practice, and the seventy key points of esoteric instruction.

Concerning the first topic:

> **...and due to the masculine, feminine, and neuter vital winds and the blazing fire of the primordial awareness of direct transcendence,...**

The infusion of the masculine vital wind causes bouncing, the feminine vital wind causes shaking, the neuter vital wind causes stability, and the infusion of the blazing fire of the primordial awareness of direct transcendence causes leaping, running about, and many other actions.

It is said:

> **...at the first gathering of the essential constituents...**

The ten fathers and mothers—the vital winds and mind—gather in the mansions that are the four gathering places and so forth, in the manner of the ḍākas and ḍākinīs of sacred commitment and primordial awareness. [48]

> **...the channels are opened by the harsh winter wind.**

At about that point, pains of the channels and vital winds occur because they have not been refined before. For example, this is like the intense cold sensation of the winter wind.

> **The mind rests, dreams of horses occur, and pains of the channels and vital winds.**

The resting of the mind is the mental experience. Dreaming of horses is the dream experience. The arising of the pains of the channels and vital winds is the physical experience.

The actual presentation consists of ten divisions: the five ground, or root, vital winds and the five branch vital winds.

Regarding this, the seven key points of practice concern the four vital winds of a person: exhalation, inhalation, the pause, and the combination of them, which are known as "one breath."

The last of these will be explained first. Completely perform the branches of meditation. First begin with the vital wind of exertion. Then begin with the vital wind of life.[53] Then gradually strengthen them. Allow the natural expression of all experiences. Examine one's inclination. Evaluate one's health.

Then, for stabilizing and enhancing, the oral instruction of expelling the breath is the branch of exhalation. This consists of three topics: exhalation through the path of life while blocking the path of exertion,[54] strong exhalation through both, and exhalation with sound through the mouth.

Also, for stabilizing and enhancing, the oral instruction of drawing in the breath is the branch of inhalation. This consists of two topics: inhalation through the mouth without sound, and inhalation through the path of life while blocking the path of exertion.

Also for stabilizing, enhancing, and so forth, or primarily for the breath that has been drawn in, the oral instruction of the pause of the breath is the union of the vital winds. Concerning this, completely perform the branches of meditation. First draw up the lower vital wind. Then draw in the upper vital wind. Then draw up the lower vital wind. It is imperative to not be mistaken about these three key points. Focus the attention on the *a* of the navel, and so forth. It is said:

> Exceptional exertion is without interruption.
> Excellent exertion is for sixty-four.
> Medium is explained as thirty-two.
> Inferior exertion is indefinite. [49]

Since all the experiences may arise either in sequence or not in sequence, allow the natural expression of all warmths.

It is said:

> **By arresting [five of] the ten,[55] the ground, or root, vital winds, and so forth, which have seven specifics,...**

This section consists of the seventy key points of esoteric instruction. Each of the vital winds includes seven topics: its name, its resting place, the action it performs, the pain of arresting it, the meditative concentration, the fault of paralysis, and the method for treatment.

The name is "life-sustaining." Its resting place is the life channel. Its action is keeping the body and mind inseparable and causing the clinging to "I" and "me." If it is arrested, palpitations of the heart, aches and pains in the upper torso, and sighing occur. The meditative concentration is the arising of empty lucidity for a long period. If it is paralyzed, morbid depression[56] and so forth occur. The three methods of treatment are total release, blessing, and meditation on bliss.

The name is "resting with fire." Its resting place is in the navel. Its action is the digestion of food and the separation of the clear essences and the impurities. If it is arrested, the pain is swelling of the stomach, and stomach rumbles and so forth are released. The meditative concentration is the arising of blissful emptiness for a short period. If it is paralyzed, dropsy and so forth occur. The method of treatment is the same as described previously. Those are the seven.

The name is "downward-clearing." Its resting place is the genital area. Its action is the discharging and holding of frankincense and camphor, and the discharging and holding of feces and musk.[57] If it is arrested, the pain is aches and pains between where feces and urine pass. The meditative concentration is the arising of blissful emptiness for a long period. If it is paralyzed, diarrhea, an inability to move the lower torso, and binding of the feces, urine, and so forth occur. The method of treatment is as before. Those are the seven.

The name is "upward-circulating." Its resting place is in the throat. Its action is causing speech and laughter, and the swallowing and vomiting up of food. If it is arrested, the pain is swelling and illness of the throat. The meditative concentration is the arising of a lucid awareness for a long period. If it is paralyzed, boils of the larynx and so forth occur. The method of treatment is the same as described previously. Those are the seven.

The name is "pervasive." Its resting place is in the top of the head and the twelve great joints. Its action is to enable leaping, running, lifting, placing, and so forth. If it is arrested, the pain is headaches and aches in all the groups of joints. The meditative concentration is the arising of the entire body as a blissful yet lucid form. [50] If it is paralyzed, the limbs become shriveled, bent, and so forth. The method of treatment is the same as described previously. Those are the seven.

Those present the thirty-five topics of the five ground, or root, vital winds.

Now the branch vital winds are described.

The name is "circulation." Its resting place is in both eyes. Its action is to cause awareness of the three types of form: superior, medium, and inferior. If it is arrested, the pain is aches and pains in the eyes and the eye sockets. The meditative concentration is invulnerability to those objects, which later serve as an aid to the primordial awareness of realization. If it is paralyzed, blindness and so forth occur. The method of treatment is the same as described previously. Those are the seven.

The name is "total circulation." Its resting place is in both ears. Its action is to cause awareness of the three types of sound: superior, medium, and inferior. If it is arrested, the pain is aches and pains in the ear canals, and some difficulty hearing. The meditative concentration is invulnerability to those objects, which later serve as an aid to the primordial awareness of realization. If it is paralyzed, deafness and so forth occur. Sometimes dripping of pus and blood occurs. The method of treatment is the same as described previously. Those are the seven.

The name is "extreme circulation." Its resting place is in the bulb of the nose. Its action is to cause awareness of the three scents: superior, medium, and inferior. If it is arrested, the pain is aches in the nose and the nasal bones. The meditative concentration is invulnerability to those objects, which later serve as an aid to the primordial awareness of realization. If it is paralyzed, the nose flattens and scents are not perceived. The method of treatment is the same as described previously. Those are the seven.

The name is "obvious circulation." Its resting place is in the tongue and uvula. Its action is to cause awareness of the three tastes: superior, medium, and inferior. If it is arrested, the pain is swelling and aches in the tongue and uvula. The meditative concentration is invulnerability to those objects, which later serve as an aid to the primordial awareness of realization. If it is paralyzed, muteness and so forth occur. The method of treatment is the same as described previously. Those are the seven.

The name is "perfect circulation." Its resting place is in the channels, skin, and all the masses of body hair. Its action is to cause awareness of the three sensations: superior, medium, and inferior. If it is arrested, the pain is heat, pressure, and so forth in all the body and hairs. The meditative concentration is invulnerability to those objects, which later serve as an aid to the primordial awareness of realization. If it is paralyzed, the skin cracks, becomes itchy, and so forth. The method of treatment is the same as described previously. Those are the seven.

The first method of treatment is total release. This consists of three topics: total release in the location of the channels themselves, total release through strengthening the vital wind, [51] and total release through allowing the natural expression of the warmths of mental experience.

Blessing consists of six topics: blessing by the excellent master, blessing by the special deity, blessing by the outer and inner ḍākas and ḍākinīs, blessing by the words of the profound sutras and tantras of the Mahayana, blessing by various appearances, and blessing by profound dependently arisen connections.

Meditation on bliss consists of two topics: meditation on bliss in dependence on the waves of enjoyment above and meditation on bliss in dependence on the secret union below.

Now the meaning of the words will be discussed.

> **The knot of various channels and so forth.**

The knot of various channels is the navel mansion. The other mansions of the four gathering places are included in the words "and so forth." The seven specifics are the seven of the name and so forth as presented previously.

It is said:

> **...the branch vital winds gradually cease within.**

By virtue of arresting the five ground, or root, vital winds, the five branch vital winds such as *circulation* also gradually cease within. Know that three points are presented by implication: "the blazing of the flames of fierce fire, its opening of the channels, and its gathering of the essential constituents."

Many drops bloom,...

Many drops bloom from the clear essences of the essential constituents, like the butter of churned yogurt.

...blending together with the support.

"Blending together with the support" occurs when both the drops that originally exist in the precious channel mansions and those that have appeared due to the force of meditation blend together like the ḍākas and ḍākinīs of sacred commitment and the ḍākas and ḍākinīs of primordial awareness, and one is blessed.

Dependent on that, the mind rests within.
The five types of consciousness gather within.

Therefore, the mind rests within: the conceptual mind is arrested. The five types of consciousness gather within and the eyes and so forth do not pursue objects.

These points present both the cause for the arising of meditative concentration and the essence of the meditative concentration itself.

The five aggregates are subdued.

This is the benefit. First the incidental afflictions somewhat recede. Attachment to everything becomes smaller and so forth, and the four malleable qualities gradually appear.[58]

The advance and retreat of primordial awareness.

This is how meditative concentration arises. [52] For a beginner, at times such as the first gathering of the essential constituents, even though a nonconceptual meditative concentration may arise, it is unstable. Thoughts are in control; so, even when primordial awareness arises, it [soon] retreats and is of little benefit, like the sun in the midst of clouds.

Now the ways meditative concentration arises are presented in a condensed form by means of the specifics of the three warmths.

> **The three triads of visual appearances, dreams, and experiences by which meditation is not lost,...**

"By which meditation is not lost" is the same as described previously. The visual appearances are smoke and so forth. The dreams are the dreaming of horses and so forth. The experiences are physical experiences such as the pains of the channels and the vital wind and so forth.

> **...like those that are preceded by thought,...**

The specifics of the three warmths include nine topics: the three visual appearances and so forth that are preceded by thought, and similarly the three of the gathering of the nine essential constituents and the three of the blazing and gathering of the drops.

> **...appear as the entire three worlds.**

Other appearances are not evident, because one rests on precisely those [three warmths] as meditative concentration.

Now the three modes of guidance on the path are mentioned.

For the extensive presentation of meditative concentration by means of guidance on the path by the vital wind, it is said, "If earth dissolves into water, there is mirage," and so forth.

> **If earth dissolves into water, there is mirage.**
> **If water dissolves into fire, there is smoke.**
> **If fire dissolves into wind, there are fireflies.**
> **If wind dissolves into consciousness, there are blazing lamps.**
> **If consciousness dissolves into clear light, it is like the cloudless sky.**

Furthermore, this includes the experiences of arresting the five vital winds in their own locations, the experiences of the increased force, the experiences of the vital winds and the four elements arrested in equilibrium, and the experiences of the sixteen arrested in equilibrium. Of these, "If earth dissolves into water, there is mirage," means that if the vital wind of earth is arrested at its own location, the navel, mirages will arise as all three experiences.[59] The others should be understood in the same way.

If the vital winds are arrested in the sublime location, which is the central channel, the mirages and so forth will be extremely lucid and extremely stable.

Just how to follow the treatise should also be learned directly from a master. [53]

Now the experiences of the increased force of the vital winds of the five elements are mentioned.

> **If earth, water, fire, and wind gather together with the vital winds and mind, the three worlds appear as though on fire everywhere.**

"Earth, water, fire, and wind" are originally present as the ḍākas and ḍākinīs of sacred commitment. "Gather together with the vital winds and mind" indicates blessing by the ḍākas and ḍākinīs of primordial awareness.

In particular, if one is blessed by the vital wind of fire, it is said that "the three worlds appear as though on fire everywhere." This is the visual appearance. As dream experiences, a great city burning with fire and so forth occur. And as physical experiences, all the hairs and the body are hot and tense. These two experiences should be understood by implication.

> **The vital wind of water, and the hairs and body are cold.**

If one's mindstream is blessed by the increased force of the vital wind of water, the physical experience is cold. As dream experiences, one also dreams of sailing a boat on the ocean and so forth. And as visual appearances, one also sees the four oceans and so forth. These two should be understood by implication.

A line from later in the text applies here:

> **Together with space, the hairs and body are blissful.**

If one is blessed by the increased force of the vital wind of space, as physical experiences all the hairs and body are content and blissful and one cannot be harmed by conditions of suffering. The mental experience is a great proportion of emptiness. As dream experiences, one dreams of being unimpeded by any apparent phenomenon. These two [experiences] should be understood by implication.

> **With the vital wind of wind there is gathering and diffusion, one flies, and birds appear.**

If one is blessed by the increased force of the vital wind of wind, "gathering and diffusion" occurs. These are the mental experiences. Without resting for even a single moment, the mind engages in a continuous gathering and diffusion of the stream of thoughts, and even sleep is broken. If sleep does occur, as dream experiences, one dreams of flying and of many flocks of birds. As the physical experience, one runs as fast as a horse. The last two [experiences] are presented by implication.

The experiences of the vital wind of earth are presented by implication. If one is blessed by the increased force of the vital wind of earth, as physical experiences, all the hairs of the body feel heavy and one cannot move. As mental experiences one sees the gold substratum of the universe and so forth, and appearances manifest as yellow. As dream experiences, one dreams of being unable to move on a great plain and so forth. All three[60] of these are presented by implication.

To simplify the *Vajra Lines,* those lines applied the experiences of the vital wind of fire to the visual appearances [54] and the other two [experiences] were presented by implication. The vital wind of water and the vital wind of space were applied to the physical experiences and the other two were presented by implication. The vital wind of wind was applied to the mental experiences and the dream experiences and both the physical experiences and the visual appearances were presented by implication. All three experiences of the vital wind of earth were presented by implication. In that way, these should be understood as fifteen experiences.

Now the experiences of the vital winds of the four elements in equilibrium are mentioned. It is said:

> **The vital winds of the four elements circulate together, and various goddesses offer dances.**

If the four sets of the 225 vital winds of the four elements are arrested as a single set of nine hundred, as visual appearances and dream experiences, various singing goddesses offer songs and dances. Since the physical experiences are insignificant here, they are not mentioned.

Concerning the sixteen elements in equilibrium, it is said:

> **Due to the vital winds of the four elements, there is a variety,...**

Arresting in equilibrium the vital winds of two cycles creates an inner dependently arisen connection and one thinks that various things are experienced externally.

> **...and smells and tastes.**

One thinks that various smells and various tastes of the world are experienced. Only physical experiences occur here, and no visual appearances or dream experiences.

These are experiences of the characteristic appearing as a variety. Since the other experiences of the nature as emptiness and the essence as unity arise either in sequence or not in sequence, allow the natural expression of all warmths.

On the transcendent path, one is guided on the path by the vital wind. Since the remaining paths of the vital wind have already been presented in the classification of the path in general and will be explained during the [presentation of the] transcendent path itself, they are not discussed here.

Now guidance on the path by the essential constituent nectars is mentioned.

> **The five nectars, the enlightened bodies of the tathāgatas, and so forth.**

If one is blessed by the five nectars in equilibrium, as all three experiences, a variety of the five tathāgatas, their spiritual families, colors, and so forth will appear.

Frankincense[61] and the sun.

In particular, if one's mindstream is blessed by the essential red constituent obtained from one's mother, as visual appearances and dream experiences, one sees the suns of the three-thousandfold world systems and so forth. As the physical experiences, the body is surrounded by red light. [55]

Camphor and the moon.

If the force of the moon—the enlightenment mind obtained from one's father—increases, one sees the moons of the three-thousandfold world systems and so forth as the visual appearances and dream experiences. As the physical experiences, one is surrounded by white light.

Tiny drops in the tiny channels. And stars.

If the tiny drops increase in the 72,000 tiny channels that branch off from the major channels, as visual appearances and dream experiences, one sees the stars of the three-thousandfold world systems and so forth. As physical experiences, many planets, stars, and so forth radiate from the pores of the body.

Those are experiences of the characteristic appearing as a variety. The other two experiences are presented by implication. The remaining guidance on the path by the nectars will be understood on the transcendent path itself.

Now guidance on the path by the channel syllables is mentioned.

The treatise is divided into the sections of guidance on the path by the ordinary syllables, guidance on the path by the fourteen syllables, and guidance on the path by the inconceivable syllables.

In the channel strictures and so forth.

If the vital winds and mind gather together in the great channel strictures, in all three experiences, mountain cliffs appear.

Tree trunks and so forth.

If the vital winds and mind gather in the small channel strictures, in all three experiences, tree trunks appear.

The five such as passion and hatred.

If the vital winds and mind gather together in the syllables of the five afflictions, such as the *hūṃ* of the heart cakra, the five afflictions naturally arise in one's mindstream and appear to arise in the mindstreams of others. One sees the forms of the five afflictions destroyed. One sees the poison of passion destroyed, the fire of hatred extinguished, the darkness of ignorance removed, the mountain of pride demolished, and the chains of jealousy released.

The channels of terror, grief, and ghosts.

"The channels of terror" are inside both kidneys. If the vital winds and mind gather there, as mental experiences and dream experiences, fear and terror arise. And as physical experiences, terrified behavior occurs.

The channels of grief are mainly in the two big toes of the feet. They are also commonly in the two thumbs of the hands. If the vital winds and mind gather together in them, grief naturally arises in all three experiences.

The channels of ghosts are mainly in the two ring fingers of the hands. They are also commonly in the fourth toes of both feet. If the vital winds and mind gather there, in all three experiences, it will seem as though one is afflicted by ghosts. [56]

In the channels of tears. Yawns and tears.

The channels of yawns and tears are outside both kidneys below, and in two coils at the corners of the eyes above. If the vital winds and mind gather together there, an unbroken stream of only yawns and tears occurs as the physical experiences alone.

Those lines present guidance on the path by the ordinary syllables. These are experiences of the characteristic appearing as a variety. Since the two other experiences also arise either in sequence or not in sequence, allow the natural expression of all warmths.

Now guidance on the path by the fourteen syllables is mentioned. It is said:

> **If the vital winds and mind gather together in the syllables of the six realms that first formed at the navel, there are the dances of the six realms, the mantras, being guided there, dreams, and similar experiences, which appear as the entire three worlds.**

If the vital winds and mind gather together in the white syllable *a,* the seed of the gods, one has the experiences of a god, feels happier than before, and thinks that one is a god. The dances are the changes in physical behavior, such as wearing a garland of flowers. The mantras are to speak the languages of the gods, such as Sanskrit. Furthermore, the experiences arise in the mind, the dances occur for the body, and the mantras arise as speech. Three visual appearances arise: one sees the places of the gods, such as a fine victory mansion; one sees the sons, daughters, and so forth of the gods themselves, adorned with all ornaments; and one also sees oneself and others guided there. The dream experiences are these occurring in various ways in dreams. These are the seven.

If the vital winds and mind gather together in the blue syllable *nri,* the seed of human beings, human experiences of more extreme delight and attachment to worldly concerns than before arise. The dances are the behavior and costumes of various countries. The mantras are to speak the languages and tell the various tales of each country, and in particular those of Magadha in India and so forth. The three are the same as described previously.[62] The three visual appearances arise: one sees the four continents, which are the places of human beings, and sees in particular Magadha and so forth; one sees human beings themselves, with many contrasting bodies, such as with great noses; and one sees oneself and others also guided there. [57] The dream experiences are these occurring in various ways in dreams. These are the seven.

If the vital winds and mind gather together in the yellow syllable *su,* the seed of the anti-gods, anti-god experiences of more fury, anger, and so forth than before arise. The dances are the physical attitudes of carrying clubs, carrying weapons, and so forth. The mantras are to utter many exclamations, such as "Hit!" and "Kill!" The three of the arising of the experiences in the mind and so forth are the same as described previously. The three visual appearances arise: one sees the cavern in Mount Meru, which is the place of the anti-gods, and so forth; one sees many of the fighting anti-gods themselves; and one sees oneself and others also guided there. The dream experiences are these occurring in various ways in dreams. These are the seven.

If the vital winds and mind gather together in the red syllable *pre,* the seed of the hungry spirits *(preta),* the experiences of a hungry spirit occur, such as being hungry even though one has eaten and thirsty even though one has drunk, having an obstructed gullet, and so forth. The dances are the behavior changed by hunger and thirst. The mantras are to say *"pre,"* and tell tales of food and drink. The three of the arising of the experiences in the mind and so forth are the same as described previously. The three visual appearances arise: one sees the great city of Sergya, the place of the hungry spirits; one sees red and unattractive houses and so forth; one sees the many hungry and thirsty spirits themselves; and one sees oneself and others also guided there. The dream experiences are these occurring in various ways in dreams. These are the seven.

If the vital winds and mind gather together in the smoky syllable *du,* the seed of the animals, the experiences of an animal occur, such as being more foolish than before and having less thought of cleanliness than before. The dances are the many behaviors of animals, such as dogs and cattle. The mantras are to make many animal sounds. The three of the arising of the experiences in the mind and so forth are the same as described previously. Three visual appearances arise: one sees the many places of the animals, such as the great ocean; one sees the animals themselves, such as crocodiles and great fish; one sees oneself and others also guided there, and so forth. The dream experiences are these occurring in various ways in dreams. These are the seven.

If the vital winds and mind gather together in the black syllable *tri,* the seed of the hells, the experiences of the hells are experienced, which are many sufferings of heat and cold, and so forth. The dances are engaging in many actions of suffering, such as having the body chopped into thirds. [58] The mantras are to make exclamations of suffering, such as "Alas!" and "Woe!" The three of the arising of the experiences in the mind and so forth are the same as described previously. Three visual appearances arise: one sees the places of the hells, such as the houses of Glowing Iron and Total

Blazing. One sees the many beings of the hot and cold hells. One sees oneself and others also guided there. The dream experiences are these occurring in various ways in dreams. These are the seven.

These are also experiences of the characteristic appearing as a variety. Furthermore, since those experiences of the nature as emptiness and the essence as unity also arise either in sequence or not in sequence, allow the natural expression of all experiences.

If these forty-two purifications of the places[63] have been suitably perfected, outer and inner parasites will be eliminated, the confidence of not going into the three lower realms will be gained, and the name "Bodhisattva Who Cannot Fall Back" will be obtained.

For now, that is just a rough presentation of the experiences of the desire realm.

> **From *oṃ,* the meditative concentrations of meditation and so forth.**

If the vital winds and mind gather together in the syllable *oṃ of meditation,* the experiences of the four meditations in the form realm arise. These are a meditative concentration of the precise application of discursive and analytical wisdom, a joyful and blissful meditative concentration, a meditative concentration of mere joy separate from bliss, and a meditative concentration of utterly pure equanimity. Since these also arise either in sequence or not in sequence, allow the natural expression of all warmths.

> **If perfectly dissolved in the *āḥ,* the space of the mother, the three worlds are space.**

If the vital winds and mind gather together in the *wisdom āḥ,* the experiences of the four formless sense cognitions arise. These four—of all phenomena as mere space, as mere consciousness, as absolutely nothing, and as beyond existence and nonexistence—also arise either in sequence or not in sequence.

For now, that is the presentation of just some of the various experiences of the three realms.

Now the transcendent experiences are mentioned.

If dissolved in the mansion of the great mother Prajñā-pāramitā and so forth, [59] the dharmakāya reality body is experienced and there is freedom from subject and object.

If the vital winds and mind gather together in the *essence āḥ,* one thinks that the thoughts of subject and object that are to be abandoned have been abandoned, and one thinks that the great bliss of the dharmakāya reality body that is to be obtained has been obtained.

From *hūṃ* there is lucidity, buoyancy, and naturally arisen primordial awareness. A very immaculate sky.

If the vital winds and mind gather together in the *hūṃ of unity,* a meditative concentration of great naturally arisen primordial awareness occurs. Lucidity is for the mind and buoyancy is for the body. "A very immaculate sky" is the simile. Since these all also arise either in sequence or not in sequence, allow the natural expression of all warmths.

These complete the presentation of the various experiences of the first gathering of the essential constituents.

At the middle gathering of the essential constituents,...

This is when the assembly of vital winds and mind, which are the ten fathers and mothers,[64] have become somewhat clearer and assemble in the mansions, which are the four gathering places and so forth.

...the channels are opened by a vital wind of reduced harshness.

As the sensation of cold is reduced in the spring wind, similarly the pains of the channels and the vital winds are somewhat reduced.

Pain of the drops, and stable visual appearances.

Concerning the pain of the drops: at about that point, the drops greatly blaze and a blissful pain occurs. Protection from their loss is also crucial here.

Concerning the stable visual appearances: since the essential constituents have become somewhat clear and the vital wind is somewhat stable, the signs of smoke and so forth are infallibly seen.

An Extensive Presentation in a Condensed Form

Now an extensive presentation in a condensed form is given.

> **In brief, in the *rakṣa* and so forth, rākṣasa demons and so forth.**

"In brief, in the *rakṣa* and so forth," refers to the syllable *kṣa* below the navel, which is the location of the rākṣasa demons, and also the location of all the carnivores, and the bhūta, yama, and yakṣa spirits, and so forth.

If the vital winds and mind have gathered together there as visual appearances and dream experiences, many things will happen, such as being struck, threatened, and so forth, by many ugly beings such as rākṣasa demons. The path free from fear should also be understood by means of this.

Therefore, a line from later in the treatise is applied here, which says:

> **As with the pristine divine eye, one thinks that everything below the *peak* of existence [60] appears in the experiences of meditative concentration.**

The visual appearances are stable, so a tainted visual paranormal ability arises.

> **The sound of the one with a bell.**

The sublime one with a bell[65] is the central channel, and if the vital winds and mind have gathered there, a sound like the buzzing of a bee occurs. The [channel] that is not sublime extends from the left ear down to the *wisdom āḥ*. If the vital winds and mind have gathered there, various near and distant sounds of the three worlds are heard "as with the pristine divine ear," which should be understood by implication.

> **The unexplainable is illustrated,...**

This phrase presents guidance on the path by the inconceivable syllables. When the vital winds have gradually cleared, the nectars become malleable. That releases the channel knots, and the channels become malleable. Precisely that causes the channel syllables to appear in various shapes, and the syllables become malleable. The force of these changes removes obstacles such as elemental disturbances in the body, and the malleability of enlightened body also occurs.

In brief, of the four malleable qualities, the force of the malleability of the syllables and the nectars causes whatever phenomena are in samsara and nirvana to arise as experiential appearances to the yogin. This is known as "the esoteric instruction of the akṣara syllables," "the esoteric instruction of infallible truth," or "the esoteric instruction of understanding many points by understanding one." What is unexplainable—even in ten million years—can be understood by a single phrase of the esoteric instructions of the syllables.

> **...and is secret on the five and the ten.**

The five are the perfection of the five spiritual paths known from the Vehicle of the Perfections. The ten are the bodhisattvas of the ten spiritual levels. Because the four malleable qualities and the esoteric instructions of the meaning of the syllables are unknown even to those bodhisattvas, they are secret; like the word for cattle, which is unknown on the island of Narikeri.[66]

These points have presented the causes for the arising of meditative concentration, the brief presentation of meditative concentration, and the extensive presentation of the path in a condensed form.

The Path Free from Hope and Fear

Now the path free from hope and fear is mentioned. This presentation consists of four topics: the presentation of the cause or reason for freedom from hope and fear; the presentation of the path free from hope; the presentation of the path free from fear; [61] and, for that very purpose, the presentation of allowing the natural expression of all warmths.

Let me discuss the meaning of the words.

> **For the outer dependently arisen connections by which meditation is not lost, there are the three triads of the reversal of the vital winds and so forth,...**

"By which meditation is not lost" is the same as described previously. The "outer dependently arisen connections" are called outer dependently arisen connections because they appear coarsely externally. Bouncing, shaking, and so forth are the dependently arisen connections of the reversal of the vital winds. The dependently arisen connections of the visual appearances (such as smoke) and the dream experiences (such as dreaming of horses) are included in the "and so forth." The phrase "three triads" indicates that, by the specific [threefold classification of each] of the three warmths, there are nine.

> **...and since the inner five ḍākinīs and five enlightened bodies of the tathāgatas enact the dependently arisen connections for great enlightenment,...**

Concerning the inner dependently arisen connections, which are the causes for those [warmths] to occur, the "inner five ḍākinīs" are the five vital winds and the five enlightened bodies of the tathāgatas are the five essential constituent nectars. Those ten inner father and mother ḍākas and ḍākinīs come and go in the spaces of the four precious mansions of the channels. Moreover, they blend together in the manner of the ḍākas and ḍākinīs of sacred commitment and the ḍākas and ḍākinīs of primordial awareness, thus blessing one's mindstream. This is the meaning of "enact the dependently arisen connections for great enlightenment," which is to enact the dependently arisen connections for the path of the thirteenth spiritual level.

Those points have presented the reason for freedom from hope and fear.

Now, for the purpose [of freedom from hope and fear], the path free from hope is presented, which begins with "the attainments" and so forth:

> **...it is understood that the attainments come from oneself, and that understanding clears away thoughts of hope and effort.**

The attainments are the four culminations of attainment, the five enlightened bodies, and so forth. These "come from oneself" because they are from the ten father and mother ḍākas and ḍākinīs. "Understanding" means this is first understood from the master and later by means of the authentic quality of the subsequent mindfulness of one's own experience. "Clears away thoughts of hope" means one is freed from the hope of receiving attainments from the outer conquerors, such as the nirmāṇakāya emanated bodies. [62] Concerning "effort," one is freed from the effort of outer offerings to the deities, sacrificial cakes, burnt offerings, and so forth.

Now the path free from fear is mentioned.

> **By understanding the māras and wrong turns as one's own path and dependently arisen connections, faults are upheld as qualities, and...**

Concerning "the māras and wrong turns," for a yogin who does not understand [the path], these are to be attacked by rākṣasa demons and carnivores, to be afraid and terrified, to be haunted by ghosts, and so forth. But for a yogin who understands the path, these are the path and the dependently arisen connections, like such things as a bridge, a precipitous pathway, or a boat on a river.

Therefore, these are known as "the oral instructions of removing hindrances to meditation by recognizing meditative concentration," "the oral instructions of removing hindrances of the māras by recognizing obstacles," "the oral instructions of knowing to uphold faults as qualities," and "the oral instructions of knowing to accept obstacles as attainments."

For just that purpose, the warmths are allowed natural expression, as in the statement about "arisen either in sequence or not in sequence."

> **...the warmths arisen either in sequence or not in sequence are allowed natural expression.**

Both the hopeful and the fearful come from the alignment of dependently arisen connections either in sequence or not in sequence, so the experiences also arise either in sequence or not in sequence. Thus, without accepting or rejecting either, a yogin allows the natural expression of all warmths.

The Four Tests

Now the path is presented as the four tests. It is said:

> **Since the devaputra māras come on the path of one who is over-inclined toward wisdom, protection is by means of the four tests.**

This will not be discussed here because it should be understood from before, in the context of the presentation of the thirty specific methods of protection for those over-inclined toward method and wisdom. In particular, it was treated out of order in the context of the protections by means of wisdom.

In brief, up to this point, in the context of guidance on the path by the vital wind, the four bases for the miraculous have been presented as the antidote for appearances rising up as the enemy.

The Four Applications of Mindfulness

Now the four applications of mindfulness are used as the antidote for emptiness rising up as the enemy. It is said:

> **As for the four applications of mindfulness by which meditation is not lost,...**

This is in the context of the mind being primary.

> **...when objects cease,...**

In general, of the nine types of emptiness, [63] five types of emptiness arise in the experience of a meditator: the emptiness in which visual objects cease because of the dissolution of the vital winds and mind in the *wisdom āḥ;* the emptiness that is free from subject and object—which are to be abandoned—because of the dissolution in the *essence āḥ;* the emptiness in which the six groups of consciousness cease because of the dissolution in the channel of the absorption of cessation; the emptiness empty of meditative concentration as a quality because the vital wind of wind has the force of a razor; and the emptiness in which one swoons from bliss because of the dissolution in the *external-shape a*.[67]

Of these [types of emptiness], the first is known to be flawed because it is empty of entities and conceptual marks, empty of calm abiding and penetrating insight as qualities of meditative concentration, empty of meditation in the meditation hut,[68] and empty of the various visual objects that are to be abandoned.

The antidote for this is the lesser conduct of the four applications of mindfulness.

> **...oneself is the chosen deity,...**

This is the application of subsequent mindfulness of the body. The subsequent mindfulness of the deity, which is the summoning and entering of the primordial awareness aspect, and the subsequent mindfulness of mantra, which is the heart mantra of the special deity, are implicitly presented.

> **...the necessity of the signs is reflected upon, and,...**

This is reflection upon the necessity of the six ornaments.[69] This is in the context of the meaning of the words. The true meaning is treated in the lines from the scripture beginning with the following:

> The cakra is worn for the purpose
> of homage to the master, Vajradhara.[70]

> **...because meditative concentration is in equilibrium,...**

Although an experience of emptiness alone had arisen before, because appearance and emptiness are united in this way, one is freed from the precipitous pathway of emptiness rising up as the enemy, and appearances arise as the sphere of the mandala of the special deity. All sound arises as mantra. One thinks that the stream of blissful primordial awareness is stable. And at about that point, one obtains the name "One for Whom the Creation Stage Is Somewhat Stable."

After thus becoming accustomed to the stream of this meditative concentration, on some occasions or constantly, one may think that precisely this is the great taintless bliss, or seeing the truth, or reaching the culmination of attainment. This is the māra of contentment. The "precipitous pathway of great dullness," in which one will not move elsewhere, comes from precisely this. This is due to the force of the vital winds and mind gathering in the *external-shape a.*

The Four Perfect Renunciations

The antidote for this [māra of contentment] is to use the greater conduct of the four perfect renunciations. The meaning is the authentic fourth initiation, which should be understood by means of four topics: the source from whom initiation is taken, the support from whom it is obtained, [64] the essence of the initiation itself, and the benefits that come from it.

Let me discuss the meaning of the words.

> **...at the final gathering of the essential constituents the channels are opened by a vital wind without harshness.**

"The final gathering of the essential constituents" is the point when the accumulated vital winds and mind that are mostly purified have gathered in the manner of the ten father and mother ḍākas and ḍākinīs of sacred commitment and primordial awareness.

The "vital wind without harshness" alleviates the pains of the channels and vital winds and is beneficial.

> **Since the drops gather within the six sensory bases,...**

The clear essences of the drops gather in the locations of the six sensory bases, such as the eyes.

> **...the six subsequent mindfulnesses are perfectly understood.**

Thus a tainted paranormal ability randomly arises, in which one sees forms at any distance with the eyes and so forth.

Some nirmāṇakāya emanated bodies are seen.

Due to the dependently arisen connections of the clear essences of the essential constituents, one sees between one and ten authentic nirmāṇakāya emanated bodies of various kinds.

As for the four perfect renunciations by which meditation is not lost,...

"By which meditation is not lost" is the same as discussed previously. The four perfect renunciations are: perfect renunciation because all thoughts are renounced when the channel of the two-decade lotus lady who is pleasant and so forth is discovered; similarly, because all thoughts are renounced when the refined slowly-circulating vital wind and so forth enter into the mind; because all thoughts are renounced when body, speech, and mind assume the vajra position; and because all thoughts are renounced when the drops suppress the vital wind. These points can be understood in detail as described following.

...from the nirmāṇakāya emanated body,...

This presents the source from whom the initiation is received.

...the awareness that occurs following the three initiations is reflected upon...

This is the fourth initiation with the support, and the experience of the four ascending joys that comes from a young prophesied lotus lady.

Now, to show that the essence of that initiation itself arises from four dependently arisen connections, the phrases such as "pleasant and so forth" are mentioned.

...and the channel of a two-decade lotus lady who is pleasant and so forth is sought.

A lotus lady is not unpleasant, but produces pleasure; she is not lacking characteristics, but is endowed with the characteristics; she is not disrespectful, but extremely respectful and passionate; and she does not lack blessings, but is blessed. A lotus lady is in the class of young lotus ladies who have the designs of eight-petal lotuses on their feet and hands, and so forth. A two-decade lady is two decades or twenty years old.

One seeks the channel by means of the yoga of preparing a saddle. One should also know that the channel is endowed with four qualities: fine like the stem of a lotus, sharp like the point of a spear, [65] [capable of] cutting, like the edge of a sword, and smooth like the surface of a mirror.

That presents the first perfect renunciation.

> **Because the *essence a* is at the tip of the central channel and the mind is entered by the refined slowly-circulating vital wind and so forth,...**

The *essence āḥ* is the support of the dharmakāya reality body. When it "arrives at the tip of the central channel," it enters the tip of the central channel in the form of drops, and the *[external-shape] āḥ* moves up from it.

The "slowly-circulating vital wind and so forth" refers to the five ground, or root, vital winds. "Refined" means "purified." "Mind" refers to the central channel, into which they enter. This presents the second perfect renunciation.

> **...body, speech, and mind assume the vajra position.**

"Body" is the rasanā to the right, "speech" is the lalanā to the left, and "mind" is the central channel. They "assume the vajra position" when they inseparably change into the shape of a letter *cha.*[71] This presents the third perfect renunciation.

> **Since the vital winds are suppressed by the drops,...**

The clear essences of the essential constituents arrive at the spot where the three channels join, thereby suppressing the vital winds of both the right and left channels. This causes the arising of a tainted bliss that is the most sublime experience below the stage of *sublime among phenomena.* This presents the fourth perfect renunciation.

> **...the sound of a drum and so forth is not heard because the māra of contentment and so forth has been vanquished.**

"The sound of a drum and so forth is not heard," because at about that point, although there is a tainted bliss in the mind, one takes it to be a taintless bliss. This causes one to swoon, and one cannot be awakened even by such things as a hundred great drums, a bass trumpet, or a pair of cymbals. Precisely this is also called "the māra of contentment." Generally, there are many types of contentment: contentment with the view, contentment with experience or meditative concentration, contentment with the oral instructions, and so forth. But here, "the māra of contentment and so forth has been vanquished" is mentioned because the māra of contentment, in previously clinging to a taintless bliss below the path of the applications of mindfulness, has been vanquished, and, by means of the four perfect renunciations, an exceptional meditative concentration has arisen that is close to the first spiritual level and comparable to a taintless bliss. Absolutely all the māras of contentment are vanquished by the path of seeing.

Because a meditative concentration consisting of the three warmths arises during the three gatherings of the essential constituents, of the four paths of application, those topics have presented the path of *warmth.*

Now the remaining three paths of application are established by means of the different qualities of warmth. [66] "The path of the inner buddhas" and so forth is mentioned.

> **The path of the inner buddhas.**
> **Gone to the *peak* of existence.**

"The inner buddhas" are the vital winds and mind, the ten fathers and mothers. "The *peak* of existence" is the tip of both right and left channels, and the *peak* beyond that is the tip of the central channel, into which the [vital winds and mind] have gone. Therefore, the second path of application has been presented by means of its different qualities.

> **The *forbearance* of emptiness, difficult to bear in relation to birthless phenomena.**

"Difficult to bear in relation to birthless phenomena" means that a meditative concentration of emptiness may have arisen before on the mundane path and below, but terror also arose. At this point, when the vital winds and mind have gathered in the central channel, a meditative concentration arises in which samsara and nirvana are realized to be emptiness, but one has fearless *forbearance.*

The inner dependently arisen connection for that is mentioned:

> **The mind lapses into a nonconceptual state in the central channel. When the mind moves, there is *forbearance.***

That is the third path of application.

> **Since the phenomena of samsara have been transcended and the phenomena of the path of nirvana are utterly complete, it is *sublime among phenomena.***

"The phenomena of samsara have been transcended" means that even though meditative concentration arose on both the paths of accumulation and application below [this level], one was not able to stop the intense sufferings and feelings of existence. *Sublime among phenomena* and *nirvana* transcend those [phenomena of samsara], and [*nirvana*] is the taintless first spiritual level. "The phenomena of the path are complete" means that absolutely all the dependently arisen connections of the four perfect renunciations are complete.

In this way, the fourth path of application has been presented by means of the two *sublime among phenomena.*

A Final Summary

Now a summary of the treatise that has presented the paths in that way is presented.

> **In that way, there are the flawed and flawless experiences, and after the vital winds and mind have gathered together up into the *external-shape a,...***

"In that way, there are the flawed experiences" refers to the eight, and the flawless are the three. "The vital winds and mind have gathered together up into the *external-shape a*" means that, after having transcended the channels, syllables, enlightenment mind, and vital winds of the mundane path and below, these [vital winds and mind] enter the central channel. That is the meaning of "the transcendent path begins."

Now, to condense into three the meditative concentrations arisen from the two previous paths[72] and the meditative concentrations that arise on the transcendent path, it is said:

> **...in that way what occur on the paths are the essence, the nature, and the characteristic.**[73]

Treated in reverse order, these are "the characteristic as a variety, the nature as emptiness, and the essence as their unity."

By means of these points, the treatise has been divided into seven sections, [67] and both the paths of accumulation and application and the twelve factors conducive to enlightenment have been divided into the three gatherings of the essential constituents, thereby presenting the oral instructions of the mundane path.

The Transcendent Path

A General Classification

Now the transcendent path is described. The general classification of the path is: according to the paths, the three of the path of seeing, the path of meditation, and the ultimate path; according to the factors conducive to enlightenment, twenty-five factors; and according to the spiritual levels, twelve and a half levels. The entire path is thereby complete.

However, if the spiritual levels are temporarily divided into groups, they can be condensed into four: six spiritual levels are the spiritual levels of the vase initiation, four are the spiritual levels of the secret initiation, two are the spiritual levels of the initiation of primordial awareness dependent on an embodiment of wisdom, and one half is the spiritual level of the fourth initiation.

Also, the creation stage is stabilized during the first, the self-blessing is stabilized during the second, the mandalacakra is stabilized during the third, and the vajra waves are stabilized during the fourth.

Also, one gains control of the vast domains of the nirmāṇakāya emanated body during the first, control of the vast domains of the sambhogakāya enjoyment body during the second, control of the vast domains of the dharmakāya reality body during the third, and control of the vast domains of the svābhāvikakāya essence body during the fourth.

Also, the body mandala is actualized during the first, the bhaga mandala during the second, the mandala of the root enlightenment mind during the third, and the mandala in which the quintessence of the sugatas of the three times are gathered is actualized during the fourth.

Also, the culmination of attainment that is the indivisibility of samsara and nirvana is reached during the first, the culmination of attainment that is clearly distinct and utterly complete is reached during the second, the culmination of attainment that is blissful emptiness of lesser extent is reached during the third, and the culmination of attainment that is blissful emptiness of greater extent is reached during the fourth.

Now the meaning of the *Vajra Lines* will be discussed in the context of each spiritual level. Four topics should be understood for each spiritual level: the presentation of the causes, the presentation of the signs, the presentation of the results, and the presentation of a final summary.

The Six Spiritual Levels of the Vase Initiation

The two causes in the context of the first spiritual level are the eventual causes and the immediate causes. The eventual causes include both the initiation and the path. The first includes both obtaining the vase initiation from the master at the time of the cause and meditating on the vase initiation oneself during four sessions and so forth. [68] The path is the shape[74] of the creation stage. The two immediate causes are the outer dependently arisen connection and the inner dependently arisen connection. The outer dependently arisen connection is receiving the four initiations from the nirmāṇakāya emanated body. The inner dependently arisen connection is seeing the body mandala.

The three signs are: the outer sign that arises in the drops, the inner sign that arises in the vital winds, and the signs of reality that arise in the mind.

Now the meaning of the words will be discussed.

> **On the transcendent path,...**

After both the paths of accumulation and application have been transcended, the path of seeing begins.

Now the immediate causes are presented.

> **...by means of the path of the outer and inner dependently arisen connections,...**

On the mundane path and below, progression on the path was by means of the three dependently arisen connections; but here, in the context of the immediate causes, the outer dependently arisen connection is receiving the four initiations from the nirmāṇakāya emanated body. The inner dependently arisen connection is seeing the body mandala, which is mentioned later.

> **...the naturally spontaneous nirmāṇakāya emanated body is achieved.**

This is the result. The meaning is: the cause, which has existed as the channels, actualizes on the thirteenth spiritual level as the result, the omnipresence of enlightened body, the nirmāṇakāya emanated body.

...the vase initiation that purifies the body is perfected.

This is the initiation as the eventual cause. The creation stage as the path should also be understood by implication.

Now there is the inner dependently arisen connection as the immediate cause.

The signs of reality are seeing the seven branches of enlightenment, which are the four precious channel mansions and the three principals of the body mandala.

Concerning "the seven branches of enlightenment," enlightenment is the primordial awareness of the first spiritual level and the branches are its immediate cause. One sees these seven: the channel knots of the four cakras in the shape of mansions, which exist as the four *e vaṃ ma ya*, and the three channels of the rasanā, the lalanā, and the central channel.

The advance and retreat of thoughts.

This is how what is to be abandoned is abandoned. In general, the twelve great and medium concepts are abandoned during the transcendent path. All of these are not the incompatible opposites that are to be abandoned—the causes that produce the sufferings of existence and intense feelings—but they are obscurations that will delay the actualizing of the spiritual level of a vajra holder and progression to higher and higher spiritual levels. In brief, it should be understood that what is to be abandoned has little force and the antidote has great force, so that although a thought may occur, it immediately dissolves into primordial awareness, like a wave in the ocean. [69]

Now the signs are presented. The treatise is divided into four sections: the presentation of the seven sets of a hundred qualities; specifically establishing this as the first spiritual level and the path of seeing; the presentation of other special qualities; and the presentation of which of the sixteen untainted joys these are.

The ability to shake a hundred vast domains of the nirmāṇakāya emanated body, make a hundred gifts, spread forth a hundred lights, pass down a hundred explanations, and be absorbed in a hundred different meditative concentrations.

"Shake a hundred vast domains of the nirmāṇakāya emanated body" means that one shakes a hundred vast domains, such as the realm of the fearless world of Jambudvīpa,[75] and gazes upon the faces of those buddhas and listens to Dharma from them. The "hundred gifts" are the display of a hundred different acts, such as giving away an eye or one's head. The "hundred lights" are a hundred acts such as radiating white light and seeing it return as red. The "hundred explanations" passed down is the teaching of the Dharma to a hundred different disciples who are inferior to oneself, in accordance with the inclinations of each. In regard to "a hundred different meditative concentrations," one is absorbed in a hundred different meditative concentrations, like those of "heroic motion" and "the majestic lion," which are mentioned in the *Sutras of the Perfection of Wisdom.* This line from later in the treatise also applies here:

Various miracles occur instantaneously because the inner vast domain is seen.

"Various miracles occur instantaneously" means that one displays a hundred miracles such as fire blazing from above and water erupting from below, and creating many from one or one from many. Seeing the inner vast domain is the inner dependently arisen connection for the seven sets of a hundred qualities such as these to occur and to appear externally. It is said:

The outer are not seen without seeing the inner.

These are the same seven branches of enlightenment that were mentioned previously.

Now this is established as the path of seeing and the first spiritual level:

If the channels of the six realms, and in particular the support of human beings, are seen,...

Seeing the blue syllable *nri* acts as the secret dependently arisen connection.

> **...there is joy and anxiety,...**

Infallible *joy* refers to the outer experiential appearance. Because the meaning of the untainted truth that was not seen before is seen, an exceptional joy arises. As for *anxiety*, because one sees all the sufferings previously experienced when one was still a worldly being (such as those of a sentient being in hell, and all the suffering of confused living beings), [70] fear may arise and one may think, "I am free from confusion and not experiencing those sufferings, but I may yet experience them." Thus anxiety arises.

> **...and shame and disgust.**

This means that shame and disgust may occur because one is despondent about one's previous behavior in samsara (when one was a confused sentient being), such as having taken one's mother [of a previous life] as a bride, and having taken the impure to be pure.

Now the exact way in which other special qualities of this first spiritual level occur is presented.

> **The indivisibility of samsara and nirvana, which was presented before by the master at the time of the cause, is realized at about that point.**

What was presented by the master in the context of the twenty topics of the path and so forth arises here at the first culmination of attainment. Many qualities arise in one's mindstream, such as being able to fit the three-thousandfold world systems into a mustard seed without problem of size, being able to turn back rivers, hold the sun and moon for ransom, and be unimpeded by walls and mountains.

> **Compassion is born. Tears fall.**

"Compassion is born" means that a nonreferential compassion is born for confused sentient beings. By virtue of that, tears fall.

The various minds of others are known.

The minds of passionate desire and so forth of those sentient beings with human bodies are seen with untainted paranormal ability.

One is amused on seeing the various sensory objects.

Without attachment, one sees and enjoys the sensory objects that are the previously unseen celestial mansion, Rūpavajrā, and so forth, which are untainted primordial awareness.

Now which of the sixteen untainted joys these are is presented. It is said:

At about that point, the liṅga[76] becomes firm.
As the seminal drop rests at the tip of the vajra, the place of coemergence, likewise the body is crazed with bliss, and one swoons.

"The liṅga becomes firm" means that the vital winds and mind gather together up into the *external-shape a,* the first knot of the central channel is opened, and the clear essences of the essential constituents become stable in half of the genital cakra. Thus, at about that point, the liṅga is never flaccid. "The tip of the vajra" is from the *external-shape a* until the first knot. Concerning the "place of coemergence," the seminal drop also becomes stable at the place of the sixteenth descending joy, and at the places of the first, second, and third ascending joys. [71] "The body is crazed with bliss, and one swoons" means that when the primordial awareness of the first spiritual level is obtained, the body is crazed with untainted bliss and the mind swoons with joyful bliss.

Oneself and others are not recognized.

Absolutely all the concepts that are to be abandoned on the path of seeing have been abandoned.

Those lines have presented the signs of reality that arise in the mind.

The inner sign is the cessation of the vital wind by one finger-width.

This is the amount that the vital wind ceases: one finger-width out, two finger-widths in and out.[77] As for the number, one set of 1,800 vital winds[78] dissolves into the central channel.

The outer sign is the drops stable in half the genital area.

The first knot of the central channel is opened and the clear essences of the essential constituents fill half the genital cakra and will not again return below.

The first spiritual level of the path of seeing.

"The first spiritual level" is a final summary. In conformity to scripture, this is the spiritual level of *delight.*

Now the presentation of the five remaining spiritual levels included in the vase initiation begins with the words "Again the four fourfold initiations."[79]

Again the four fourfold initiations from the nirmāṇakāya emanated body.

As presented previously, this also consists of the four topics such as the presentation of the causes. As before, it also should be understood that the presentation of the causes includes both the immediate causes and the eventual causes, that the eventual causes also include both the initiation and the path, and that the immediate causes include both the outer dependently arisen connection and the inner dependently arisen connection.

The real presentation of the result is the nirmāṇakāya emanated body.

Of the three signs, the first is in the context of the signs of reality that arise in the mind. It is said:

From the second spiritual level of the path of meditation, there is the ability to shake, and so forth, a thousand vast domains of the nirmāṇakāya emanated body, and so forth.[80]

It should be understood that the previous seven sets of a hundred qualities multiply into seven sets of a thousand, seven sets of ten thousand, seven sets of a hundred thousand, seven sets of a million, and seven sets of ten million.

The qualities and so forth increase.

Therefore, that is also the meaning of this line, which applies to the sixth spiritual level and below.

Advance and retreat, and so forth, cease.

This is also how what is to be abandoned is abandoned. Of the twelve great and medium concepts, the first six have ceased, and also of the twelve links of dependent arising, the six up through feelings have ceased in reverse order.

The inner sign is the cessation of the vital wind by six finger-widths.

The vital wind ceases for the amount of six finger-widths out, twelve finger-widths in and out. As for the number, six sets of 1,800 vital action winds cease.

The outer sign is the drops stable in the genital area, navel, and heart. [72]

With two spiritual levels at each of the three cakras, sixteen knots of the central channel are opened. The clear essences of the essential constituents become stable and will not again return below.

Some sambhogakāya enjoyment bodies are seen.

The faces of between one and ten [sambhogakāya enjoyment bodies] are seen, and they are seen blessing oneself.

The sixth spiritual level of the path of meditation.

This is a final summary. In conformity to scripture, the second spiritual level is taught to be *immaculate,* the third is *light-producing,* the fourth is *radiant light,* the fifth is *difficulties purified,* and the sixth is *actualization.*

In that way, the spiritual levels of the vase initiation have been presented by means of the six spiritual levels.

The Four Spiritual Levels of the Secret Initiation

Now the lines "the four fourfold initiations from the sambhogakāya enjoyment body" and so forth present the four spiritual levels included in the secret initiation. This should also be understood by means of four topics: the presentation of the causes, the presentation of the signs, the presentation of the result, and the presentation of a final summary.

The first topic, the causes, includes both the immediate causes and the eventual causes. And the eventual causes also include both the initiation and the path. Concerning this, as applied to the treatise, it is said to be the "secret initiation":

> **The secret initiation that purifies the voice is perfected.**

Of the paths, it applies to "through the path of self-blessing":

> **Through the path of the stages of self-blessing,...**

Of the initiations, it is said that "the secret initiation is perfected."

The immediate causes are also two in number. The outer dependently arisen connection is receiving the four initiations from the sambhogakāya enjoyment body in innumerable sessions:

> **Again the four fourfold initiations from the sambhogakāya enjoyment body.**

The inner dependently arisen connection applies to lines from later in the treatise:

The seeds of the six realms are seen in the bhaga mandala.
Control is gained over the six seeds.

The result is presented by this line:

The result[81] of the naturally spontaneous sambhogakāya enjoyment body is achieved.

The signs are presented by means of three topics. The signs of reality that arise in the mind are mentioned by the words "the five powers" and so forth:

The signs of reality are the five powers,...

When the vital wind of earth has become powerful in the central channel, one cannot be afflicted by harm from the element earth. The other three vital winds should be understood in the same way. When the vital wind of space has become powerful in the central channel, one is not frightened even by an abyss of a thousand leagues and so forth. The inner dependently arisen connection for these to occur is presented by the following line:

...gaining control of the vital winds of the five clear essences,... [73]

Also, at about that point, from the seventh spiritual level up through the tenth, the vital winds of earth and so forth have become somewhat forceful in the central channel. Various abilities will arise, such as the ability to emanate as earth.

...the five abilities,...

At about that point, the four abilities of being able to emanate as earth and so forth, and the fifth of being able to invisibly conceal oneself and others, will arise to a suitable degree.

...and being unimpeded in the gazes.

Since one has achieved the power to gather the vital winds and the mind at the openings of the eyes, at about that point, one also gains control of the four gazes, the eight gazes,[82] and so forth.

> **The seeds of the six realms are seen in the bhaga mandala. Control is gained over the six seeds. One teaches Dharma in the languages of sentient beings, and...**

Seeing the six such as the *a* seed of the gods is the secret dependently arisen connection. Externally, "One teaches Dharma in the languages of sentient beings." One teaches Dharma in each of the languages of the six types of sentient beings and in accordance with each of their inclinations.

> **...is unimpeded in regard to the general and individual characteristics of phenomena.**

One is unimpeded in regard to the general characteristics that are similar and common and the individual characteristics that are different and uncommon.

> **After seeing at the navel the eight bases of the syllables, and the vowels such as *a* and the consonant-syllables such as *ka*, one is unimpeded in the twelve branches of scripture, such as the Dharma of the sutras.**

The "eight bases of the syllables" are the eight *a ka ca ṭa ta pa ya śa* of the inner circle of the navel cakra. "Seeing the vowels such as *a* and the consonant-syllables such as *ka*" is seeing the fifty syllables of the outer circle. This is the secret dependently arisen connection. Externally, one is "unimpeded in the twelve branches of scripture, such as the Dharma of the sutras."[83] This point is known as "the time of becoming a great master of speech," "the time of total awakening from conventional designations," "the time when absolutely all the sublime attainment of speech has been realized," and "the time when control is gained of the four types of individual and perfect pure awareness."[84]

> **The five nectars and the ability to enjoy the six tastes.**

Since the clear essences of the essential constituents have risen and stabilized in the throat cakra, one enjoys the six tastes in the external mundane realm.

Those that become the melody of Brahmā...

"Become the melody of Brahmā" and so forth means that the *essence āḥ* also moves as far as the throat cakra, acting as the secret dependently arisen connection, and the branches of melodious enlightened speech, such as the sixty and the sixteen, occur externally. These are one's speech being pleasant to the ears of oneself and others, audible near and far, and so forth. Therefore, it is said, "become the melody of Brahmā."

...are clarified by six, such as "The *a* [is the most sublime of all] phonemes."

As for clarification by the six [verse feet] such as "The *a* [is the most sublime of all] phonemes," [74] the *Magical Net* says:

> The *a* is the most sublime of all phonemes.
> Of great benefit, it is the excellent syllable.
> Arising from within, yet birthless.
> It defies expression as a word.
> It is the sublime cause of all expression.
> It totally clarifies all words.[85]

Concerning the presentation of the inner dependently arisen connection for those events to occur, the meaning is that there are four internal cakras, with two spiritual levels at each of the cakras, and that those events occur by virtue of the clear essences of the essential constituents becoming actually stable and not moving from those cakras.

Another point that should be understood is that, on the sixth spiritual level and below, the nirmāṇakāya emanated body is clear with the six ornaments, but here the six ornaments are clear on the sambhogakāya enjoyment body as the essence of the six spiritual families.

Now the signs of reality are presented as other qualities that arise in the mind. It is said:

> **Above the seventh spiritual level, the mudrā seals of the four cakras. The ability to shake, and so forth, a hundred million vast domains of the sambhogakāya enjoyment body, and so forth.**

Before, on the sixth spiritual level and below, the sets of qualities such as the hundred vast domains of the nirmāṇakāya emanated body multiplied by seven. But here it should be understood that the seven sets of a hundred million vast domains of the sambhogakāya enjoyment body and so forth multiply by four.

> **The inner sign is the cessation of the vital wind by ten finger-widths.**

This means ten finger-widths out, twenty finger-widths in and out. As for the number, ten sets of 1,800 vital action winds cease in the central channel.

> **The outer sign is the drops stable in the throat and the point between the eyebrows.**

When twelve knots of the central channel have been released at the two cakras, the clear essences of the essential constituents become stable and will not move from there.

Those lines have presented the three signs.

> **The tenth spiritual level of the path of meditation.**

This is a final summary. In conformity to scripture, the name of the seventh is *far gone,* the eighth is *immobile,* the ninth is *fine intelligence,* and the tenth is *cloud of Dharma.*

The Two Spiritual Levels of the Initiation of Primordial Awareness Dependent on an Embodiment of Wisdom

Now the two spiritual levels of the initiation of primordial awareness dependent on an embodiment of wisdom are presented. This also consists of the four topics of the presentation of the causes and so forth. The causes also include both the eventual causes and the immediate causes. The eventual causes include both the initiation and the path.

The initiation applies to "the initiation of primordial awareness dependent on an embodiment of wisdom":

> **The initiation of primordial awareness dependent on an embodiment of wisdom is perfected.**

The path applies to "the path of the mandalacakra method":

> **Through the path of the mandalacakra method, which purifies the mind,...**

The immediate causes also include both the outer and the inner dependently arisen connections. [75]

> **Again the four fourfold initiations from the dharmakāya reality body.**

The outer dependently arisen connection is mentioned with the words "again the four fourfold initiations," which refers to receiving the four initiations in innumerable sessions from the conquerors, the undifferentiated nirmāṇakāya emanated bodies and sambhogakāya enjoyment bodies.[86]

Concerning the inner dependently arisen connection, a line from later in the treatise also applies here, which says, "the mandala of the root enlightenment mind has been seen":

> **After the mandala of the root enlightenment mind has been seen, the signs are displayed.**

Those topics have partially presented the causes.

> **...the naturally spontaneous dharmakāya reality body is achieved.**

This is the result, which is not discussed here because it will be explained in the context of the result.

Now the three signs are presented. In the context of the signs of reality that arise in the mind, "the five forces" and so forth are mentioned.

> **The signs of reality, the five forces, are due to the five vital winds of the enlightenment mind and the clear quintessence of the clear essences that they have moved.**

When the five vital winds of the five clear essences and the enlightenment mind—the five nectars—have blended together internally in a single taste, they become forceful in the central channel and the five forces arise externally. Since the vital wind of earth has become forceful in the central channel, one is able to emanate as the element earth. It is the same for the other three vital winds. When the vital wind of space and its enlightenment mind have become forceful in the central channel, one is able to invisibly conceal oneself and others.

Now the qualities concerning the initiation of primordial awareness dependent on an embodiment of wisdom will be calculated in the context of both the immediate and eventual causes. It is said:

> **After the initiations of the three bodies of enlightenment, the five types of primordial awareness, and so forth have been received,...**

After blessing with the three perceptions a mudrā consort who is a totally pure support, the male embodiment of method and the female embodiment of wisdom enter into union. Thus the clear essences of the essential constituents of the body are melted by the fire of subsequent passion and, from locations in all the channels, gather into the *haṃ* of the crown of the head.

The enlightenment mind moves from the top of the head down to the throat. Since the experience of bliss is small at that point, it is the primordial awareness of joy. Half the afflictions that are to be abandoned have been alleviated, but half have not. The path of the arhats is completed.

The enlightenment mind moves to the heart. Since the experience of bliss expands, it is the primordial awareness of sublime joy. Three quarters of the afflictions that are to be abandoned have been alleviated, but one quarter has not. The path of the prayekabuddhas is completed.

Concerning those two, since bliss is enjoyed, the initiation of the sambhogakāya enjoyment body is obtained.

The enlightenment mind moves down to the navel. The bliss is enhanced by a nonconceptual state, and when these unite, it is the primordial awareness of joy free from joy. All the afflictions that are to be abandoned are alleviated, and so the path of the bodhisattvas is completed. Since a nonconceptual state in which all elaborations have been completely alleviated is realized, the initiation of the dharmakāya reality body is obtained. [76]

Those clear essences of the essential constituents move down to the genital area. Since bliss and emptiness are united, this is the primordial awareness of coemergent joy. The alleviation of all the afflictions that are to be abandoned has stabilized, and so the path of great enlightenment is completed. By virtue of the drops being unstable, the initiation of the nirmāṇakāya emanated body is obtained.

In that way, this is the initiation of the three bodies of enlightenment.

This can also be classified as the initiation of the five types of primordial awareness. Since the birthless essence of all phenomena is clear, it is the initiation of mirrorlike primordial awareness. Since samsara and nirvana are realized as equal, it is the initiation of the primordial awareness of equality. Since it is perfectly realized that the jasmine-white relative enlightenment mind cannot be lost,[87] it is the initiation of the primordial awareness of discrimination. Since reality is accomplished in oneself, it is the initiation of the all-accomplishing primordial awareness. By virtue of the truth of the nonconceptual state, it is the initiation of the primordial awareness of the basic space of phenomena.

This can also be classified as the initiation of the five mudrā consorts. Since the coemergent primordial awareness does not touch the thoughts, it is the initiation of the brahmin woman. Since the thoughts do not touch the coemergent primordial awareness, it is the initiation of the outcaste woman. Since one's own mindstream is transformed into great bliss, it is the initiation of the dancer woman. Since everything else is transformed into great bliss, it is the initiation of the dyer woman. Since it is fierce in killing the conceptual marks and thoughts, it is the initiation of the fierce woman.

This can also be classified as the initiation of the eleven herukas. These eleven are the six of the heruka of form and so forth, oneself as the heruka of sacred commitment, the other heruka of primordial awareness, the designated or symbolic heruka, the labeled heruka of name, and the heruka of absolute primordial awareness.

In that way, those [twenty-four] reside in one's body and bless it. By virtue of one's relishing of the bliss, one is the deity, and thus this is the initiation of the twenty-four aspects of the real nature of the deity.[88]

Whatever is done with the hands of a yogin endowed with such experience becomes a mudrā gesture, so this is the initiation of the real nature of the mudrā. Everything done with the feet becomes the mandala, so this is the initiation of the real nature of the mandala. Whatever is expressed with the voice becomes secret mantra, so this is the initiation of the real nature of mantra. Whatever is thought with the mind becomes meditation, so this is the initiation of the real nature of meditation. If one is endowed with experience and realization of the four aspects of the real nature, "the initiation of primordial awareness dependent on an embodiment of wisdom is obtained."[89] [77]

In brief, it should be understood that this initiation is treated at this point because it acts as the cause for the culmination of attainment on the eleventh and twelfth spiritual levels.

Now, since the signs of reality dawn in the mind because of the two outer and inner dependently arisen connections, the other infallible qualities of the dependently arisen connections of reality are presented.

> **...if the five nectars are seen gathering in any channels,...**

The inner dependently arisen connection is seeing the five nectars of the clear essences of the essential constituents gathering indivisible from the five vital winds in the four gathering places of the channel mansions and so forth.

> **...the buddhas are seen acting for the benefit of others.**

This is seeing the conquerors—the nirmāṇakāya emanated bodies and sambhogakāya enjoyment bodies—benefiting their individual disciples by means of enlightened body and speech, which is totally pure and absolute enlightened activity.

> **If the drops are seen gathering in the emanation cakra and that of great bliss,...**

The clear essences of the essential constituents gather temporarily in the emanation cakra of the navel and then also gather in the cakra of great bliss at the top of the head. If the clear essences stabilize, this infallibly occurs as an experiential appearance:

> **...the buddhas are seen residing in profundity in the realm of Akaniṣṭha.**

It should be understood that the conquerors, the sambhogakāya enjoyment bodies, do not stray from the unique blissful emptiness of the dharmakāya reality body free from elaboration, yet also act for the benefit of disciples while remaining in that state. It should also be understood that precisely this is "seeing the vast domains of the dharmakāya reality body."

> **If the five nectars and the five vital winds are seen gathering in the emanation cakra at the navel, the five spiritual families of the sambhogakāya enjoyment body are seen residing in the mother's bhaga and proclaiming the secret to fortunate bodhisattvas.**

Also, at about this point, seeing the five nectars and the five vital winds gathering in the emanation cakra at the navel acts as the inner dependently arisen connection. Then, externally, as appearances of a taintless meditative concentration, the fathers and mothers of the five spiritual families of the conquerors, the sambhogakāya enjoyment bodies, are seen in the unique location of the supporting mandala (the mansion that is a manifestation of primordial awareness inside the tetrahedron) proclaiming the meaning of the words of the sublime secret of the profound Vajrayana, the unique Dharma that is to be presented to the unique audience of fortunate bodhisattvas on the eleventh and twelfth spiritual levels.

> **If the clear quintessence of the clear essences of the mudrā consort is seen, there is unimpeded paranormal ability.**

In regard to "seeing the clear essences of the mudrā consort," when the great, clear essences of the essential constituents in the channel locations of the mother [78] are seen without impediment, externally, as experiential appearances, the five paranormal abilities are unimpeded.[90]

> **If the clear essences are drawn into the channel syllables, there is unimpeded magical ability.**

The shapes of one's own channel syllables also transform into various shapes. If the clear essences of the [mudrā consort's] vital winds and mind are drawn there,[91] externally, various magical abilities of transformation into various forms arise without impediment.

> **If they are transferred precisely there again, previous locations are recalled.**

"If they are transferred precisely there again" means that, if the clear essences are transferred and left in precisely those locations of the *a* syllable and so forth, which are the mansions from which they were first drawn, externally, many lifetimes of other sentient beings and also of oneself will be remembered.

These lines have presented the signs of reality that arise in the mind due to the four dependently arisen connections of the outer, the inner, the secret, and reality.

> **The inner sign is the cessation of the vital wind by twelve finger-widths.**

The vital wind ceases for twelve finger-widths out, twenty-four finger-widths in and out. As for the number, twelve sets of 1,800 vital action winds have ceased in the central channel and, of the twelve links of dependent arising, down through ignorance have ceased.

> **The outer sign is the drops stable in the entire crown of the head.**

After the four knots of the central channel at the cakra of the crown of the head are opened, the clear essences of the essential constituents become stable and will not descend from there.

> **The twelfth spiritual level of the path of meditation.**

By means of the concealed meaning, "the twelfth spiritual level" refers to the eleventh spiritual level of *primordial awareness without simile* and the twelfth of *great primordial awareness.*

The Half Spiritual Level of the Fourth Initiation

The half spiritual level of the fourth initiation also consists of four topics: the presentation of the causes, the presentation of the signs, the presentation of the result, and the presentation of a final summary. The presentation of the causes includes both the eventual causes and the immediate causes. The eventual causes are the initiation and the path.

> **The fourth, the initiation of body, speech, and mind, is perfected.**

The initiation is the fourth, as said beginning with the words "the fourth, the initiation of body, speech, and mind."

> **Through the path of the vajra waves,....**
> **The path that completely purifies existence.**[92]

The path is "the path of the vajra waves." "The path that completely purifies existence" also applies here.

> **Again the four fourfold initiations.**

Concerning the outer dependently arisen connection of the immediate causes: dependent on an utterly pure female embodiment of awareness who is on the twelfth spiritual level, one appears to receive the four initiations from the conquerors, the indivisible three bodies of enlightenment.

The inner dependently arisen connection is precisely the initiations that dissolve the four pulsations.

> **Through the ultimate path, the ultimate are purified by the ultimate dependently arisen connection.**

In conformity to scripture, of the five paths, precisely that immediate cause is referred to with the words "through the ultimate path." It should be understood that, of the five dependently arisen connections, that is also the ultimate dependently arisen connection, and of what are to be abandoned, it purifies the ultimate obscurations of knowledge. [79]

Of the meaning of the words, it was said, "The path that completely purifies existence." "Existence" means the three channels, the triad of exhalation, inhalation, and resting of the vital wind, the three poisonous afflictions, the triad of body, speech, and mind, and the three worlds. The "path that completely purifies" these is the three waves.

> **As for the noble path of eight branches, two results are achieved at the point of the purification of the eight types of consciousness.**

"Noble" refers to the five types of primordial awareness. "Branches" refers to the eight types of consciousness, which are their causes. "Two results are achieved" means that, from the paralysis of the right waves of object, the signless liberation occurs, and from the paralysis of the left waves of subject, the wishless liberation occurs.

> **The signs of reality.**

Now the signs of reality that arise in the mind during the half spiritual level of the thirteenth spiritual level of the ultimate path are mentioned.

> **This great earth is joyful, elated, and delighted. It shakes in six ways.**

Concerning "This great earth is joyful, elated, and delighted," at the second moment when our Teacher, the perfectly complete Buddha, became enlightened, the earth goddesses of the three-thousandfold world systems were at the first moment joyful, at the second, elated, and at the third, delighted, like a child seeing its mother.[93] The earth shook in six ways with the sound of their laughter, which should be understood as "wavering, severe wavering," and so forth, as they occur in the Conqueror's *Sutras of the Perfection of Wisdom.*

Sounds resound in Māra's places.

Vanquishing the four māras is the miracle of breaking Māra's pride. The sounds of falling meteors, the great ocean in complete turmoil, and so forth occur, and sounds like cymbals that scramble the brains of the māras. This also applies to "the time without obstacles, at the time of subduing Māra in the evening."

The three worlds are seen in the place of the mudrā consort.

All the phenomena of samsara and nirvana abide in the bhaga[94] of the mother who is a mudrā consort on the thirteenth spiritual level and so forth. All these phenomena of samsara and nirvana are seen there in a single drop of the great, clear quintessence of the clear essences of the essential constituents, without restriction of size or space, so that what is looked at and the looking are no different in a single taste, a single state, and a single manner. This is one small omniscience.

The eight qualities of the power and wealth of harima[95] and so forth arise.

At about that point, all the vital winds of life and exertion in both channels enter into the central channel, and eight signs arise:

> Subtlety, buoyancy,
> disappearance in the subtle, [80]
> and the ability for enjoyment,
> great being, joyful delight,
> everything under control,
> and performing whatever one wishes
> are the eight qualities of power and wealth.[96]

Ḍākas and ḍākinīs gather from afar.

At about this point, the inner ḍākas and ḍākinīs gather from afar. One sees the great, clear quintessence of the clear essences of the essential constituents of all the channel locations gathering in the mansion of the central channel in the manner of the ten fathers and mothers. The outer ḍākas and ḍākinīs also gather from afar. One sees the ḍākas and ḍākinīs—who are the nirmāṇakāya emanated body, the sambhogakāya enjoyment body, and the dharmakāya reality body—indivisibly blessing every hair follicle of the meditator. It is taught:

> Just as a flock of geese gathers
> at the attractive site of lotuses,
> so also the ḍākinīs,
> even though they reside afar,
> will bless the site
> of the sacred commitments.[97]

Those lines also present what is known as "the time of direct enlightenment at dawn" and "the time of liberation."

The inner sign is the entry of the vital winds of life and exertion into the central channel.

The vital winds of life and exertion in the two channels enter from the *external-shape a* up to half of the cranial dome.

The outer sign is the drops stable in half the cranial dome.

The clear essences of the essential constituents become stable in half the cranial dome of the head. At about that point the shaft of the penis retreats into the pelvic cavity, and the Dharma conch, the curl of hair at the heart, and the tuft of hair between the eyebrows are also established.[98]

The twelfth and a half spiritual level.

This is a final summary. The first moment that is the cause of the thirteenth spiritual level—the ultimate path that is the dissolution of the four pulsations—is itself given that name.

Now, for an extensive presentation in the context of a single result, detailed phrases beginning with "the fourth, the initiation of mind," are given.

> **The fourth, the initiation of mind, is perfected.**

This is "the fourth" because it is the spiritual level included in the fourth initiation. Concerning "the initiation of mind," the right channel is body, the left is speech, and the central channel is mind. The meaning is that, of these, all the vital winds and mind of the two channels first enter into the central channel and then cease and dissolve. "Perfected" refers to the signs of reality, which are preceded by both the outer sign and the inner sign. The signs of reality arise in the mind, and although "sambhogakāya enjoyment body" is mentioned in lines later in the treatise, this should be understood to apply to "the ability to shake, and so forth, absolutely all the vast domains of the dharmakāya reality body, and so forth."[99]

> **The sign of reality is the attainment of a single result.**

"Result" [81] refers to the emptiness gate to liberation, the termination of absolutely all thoughts of subject and object. The real meaning of this is presented with the statement about "the piercer" and so forth:

> **The city of the young, the basic space of phenomena, is pierced by the piercer, the enlightenment mind.**

"The piercer" is the great, clear quintessence of the clear essences of the vital winds and mind. What is to be pierced is the central channel, the basic space of phenomena, the city of the new[100] buddha, the emptiness gate to liberation, the ultimate mansion. Although it is said, "pierced by the [piercer], the enlightenment mind," the great clear quintessence of the clear essences of the vital winds and mind pierce the central channel, its mouth is opened, and the four pulsations finally dissolve into the sublime cranial dome.

In the context of the signs of reality that arise in the mind due to this half spiritual level, it is said:

As the result, there is the ability to shake, and so forth, ten trillion vast domains of the sambhogakāya enjoyment body, and so forth.

Nevertheless, it should be understood that this applies to the twelfth spiritual level, and that the "absolutely all" mentioned later in the treatise applies to the half spiritual level here.[101]

Concerning the words "The inner sign is the entry of the vital winds of life and exertion into the central channel": at first they enter, and during the second moment they cease.

Now, for an extremely extensive explanation by means of the support for that [fourth initiation], the lines beginning with these words are given:

At the point of gaining the thirteenth spiritual level, a female on the thirteenth spiritual level, and so forth, is mentally summoned.

If one has progressed up to the thirteenth spiritual level in dependence on a lotus lady who was previously prophesied during the final gathering of the essential constituents, or if one has been on the rapid path of the messenger before, a [different] support is not necessary. Even if that is not the case, as included in the "and so forth," it should be understood that when one is on the first spiritual level, the female embodiment of pure awareness is also on the first spiritual level, and similarly, that when one is on the seventh spiritual level, the female embodiment of pure awareness is also on the seventh spiritual level, and similarly, that when one is on the tenth spiritual level, the female embodiment of pure awareness is also on the tenth spiritual level.

Concerning "mentally summoned": this is accomplished by mere recollection, without reference to external substances and so forth.

Now one receives the four initiations that dissolve the four pulsations on the ultimate path. The source from whom the initiations are received is mentioned beginning with these words:

The master is the combined quintessence of the sugatas of the three times.

"The three times" are the three cakras in sequence from above, or the three channels, or the triad of exhalation, inhalation, and resting of the vital wind, or the triad of the melting, bliss, and nonconcept of the drops, or, in brief, [82] the great, clear quintessence of the clear essences of the three mandalas,[102] which is about the size of the tip of a hair.

> **From the chosen deity and the master indivisible...**

Precisely that same drop and so forth have actually become undifferentiated from the master who is an ordinary person, the master who is the nirmāṇakāya emanated body, the master who is the sambhogakāya enjoyment body, the master who is the dharmakāya reality body, and the master who is the svābhāvikakāya essence body of the conquerors.

> **...in the bhaga,...**

This refers to the location where that excellent master resides, at the sublime pistils of the mothers who are on the thirteenth spiritual level and so forth.

> **...the attainments are received, and due to the dependently arisen connection, there is the path that totally purifies existence.**

"The attainments are received" because, in the second moment after the initiations that dissolve the four pulsations, one receives from that master the attainments that actualize the five bodies of enlightenment. "The path that totally purifies existence" also refers to the initiations that dissolve the four pulsations. The meaning of the words is the same as described previously.

Those lines have presented the immediate causes.

> **The naturally spontaneous, utterly pure svābhāvikakāya essence body is achieved. The result is perfected.**

This means that the four enlightened bodies of the transformed support, and also the enlightened body of the transformed supported mind, which are a single substance, are achieved. This is the result.

> **The result is the ability to shake, and so forth, absolutely all the vast domains of the sambhogakāya enjoyment body, and so forth.**

So it is said, but it should be understood that one has the ability to shake absolutely all the vast domains of the svābhāvikakāya essence body.[103]

> **The inner sign is the cessation of the vital winds of life and exertion in the central channel.**

Due to the cessation of the vital winds of life and exertion in the two channels, the four pulsations dissolve in the sublime cranial dome.

> **The outer sign is the drops stable in the entire cranial dome.**

This means that after the sublime cranial dome of the head has been established, absolutely all the support and what was supported have transformed.

For now, in conformity to scripture, those lines have presented absolutely all the paths of both the mundane and the transcendent paths by means of five topics according to the paths, thirty-seven according to the factors conducive to enlightenment, and twelve and a half according to the spiritual levels.

The Result

Now the result achieved by these paths is presented. It is said:

> **Since the flawed and flawless meditation experiences have been distinguished by means of the outer dependently arisen connection and the inner dependently arisen connection of the dissolution of the four pulsations, it is the thirteenth spiritual level.**
>
> **Omniscience. On the thirteenth spiritual level of a vajra holder the dependently arisen connections appear as aligned.**

At the point of buddhahood there is buddhahood with one's circle, in a single group.

This is the meaning: [83] the presentation of the perfection of the assemblies for oneself, which includes how the dependently arisen connections are aligned and the transformation of the five bodies of enlightenment; in particular, the presentation of the great degree of benefit for others, which is awakening the enlightenment mind in those for whom it has not awakened, and so forth; and the presentation of the great degree of benefit for both oneself and others, which is buddhahood together with one's circle, as a single group.

Concerning the first of these, [the perfection of the assemblies for oneself], when [the vase initiation] has gradually dissolved the pulsations of all the channels, they become the sublime central channel. From that arises "the omnipresent nirmāṇakāya emanated body," appearing in any form, beginning with the Blessed One, Great Vajradhara, blazing with the major and minor marks, or the sublime emanations such as Śākyamuni, and including the forms of any living being and anything in the environment, such as a heavenly tree, for the benefit of all disciples.

The secret initiation [dissolves] the pulsations of the syllables, and the pulsations of all the syllables gradually dissolve. The colors dissolve into white and the shapes dissolve into the indestructible syllables of unity, *aham iti;*[104] and when their force dissolves, these become as forceful as the *hūṃ* that overwhelms the four māras. From that [dissolution] arises "omnipresent enlightened speech, the sambhogakāya enjoyment body," in the language of any living being, beginning with Sanskrit; the sounds of all the elements; and even from the sky the sound of utterly pure enlightened speech, for the benefit of disciples.

The initiation of primordial awareness dependent on an embodiment of wisdom dissolves the pulsations of the nectars. After the nine essential constituents have gradually cleared, their pulsations dissolve into the sublime clear essences of the essential constituents, the nectars are transformed, and "omnipresent enlightened mind, the dharmakāya reality body," the primordial awareness that knows the precise nature and precise extent of everything, is actualized exactly according to the alignment of the dependently arisen connections.

The fourth initiation [dissolves] the pulsations of the vital winds. The vital action winds very gradually dissolve and transform into the vital wind of primordial awareness. The vital winds are transformed and "omnipresent enlightened body, speech, and mind, the svābhāvikakāya essence body," is actualized. When there is omnipresent enlightened body, there is also omnipresent enlightened speech and enlightened mind. The same applies to both [enlightened speech and enlightened mind]. Thus these [three] are beneficial for all disciples in the manner of a single substance.

Those points have presented the four enlightened bodies of the transformed support. [84]

The transformation of the supported mind is known as "the spontaneous enlightened body of the utterly pure svābhāvikakāya essence body." All four such bodies of enlightenment are a single, utterly pure primordial awareness actualizing in appearance as one or another particular aspect. In that way, the *Magical Net* says:

> A buddha endowed with the quintessence
> of the five bodies of enlightenment.[105]

Their essence as a single enlightened body is also mentioned in the same source:

> The single eye of primordial awareness
> is immaculate.[106]

The great degree of benefit for others is inconceivable qualities of greatness, such as: awakening the enlightenment mind in those for whom it has not awakened, advancing from spiritual stage to spiritual stage, direct enlightenment, and the blind obtaining sight. These are not discussed here.

The great degree of benefit for both is "buddhahood together with one's circle, in a single group." This is the simultaneous liberation of the pentad of oneself as the meditator, one female embodiment of awareness whose mindstream is utterly pure, one lineal master, one blessed ḍākinī, and one disciple who is an utterly pure recipient.

Because the meaning has been presented, one is able to understand the words by way of that presentation, and so the meaning of the words will not be analyzed.

That is the presentation of the result.

A Condensed Presentation of the Treatise

Now these lines of "secret mantra" and so forth provide a condensed presentation of the treatise.

> **The Vajrayana of secret mantra is the causal, path, and resultant initiations. Although conceptually comprehended, the realization is nonconceptual. The appearance of primordial awareness is like that.**

This is "secret" because it is not within the range of Brahmā, Viṣṇu, and Maheśvara, or even of all the transcendent arhats and pratyekabuddhas. It is "mantra" because it blesses one within. It is the "Vajrayana" because one's own four supporting mandalas of the body and so forth, and the four results of the enlightened-body vajra and so forth, are indivisibly made into the path. The "causal" initiation is first received from the master, the "path" initiation is one's own meditation on the four initiations in four sessions and so forth, which causes the "resultant" initiations that dissolve the four pulsations.

"Conceptually comprehended" is the path, "realization is nonconceptual" is the view, and "the appearance of primordial awareness" is the result. Also, "conceptually comprehended" is the mundane path, "realization is nonconceptual" is the transcendent path, and "the appearance of primordial awareness" is the result. Also, "conceptually comprehended" is the characteristic as a variety, "realization is nonconceptual" is the nature as emptiness, and "the appearance of primordial awareness" is the essence as their unity. [85]

Now the following lines are given so as to also condense the paths that have just been presented into the profound, the medium, and the inferior.

> **The profound path of the master.**

A person with superior faculties is perfected by means of the master. For one with superior faculties, by means of devotion and honoring the master—even if the master has not taught a single word and the disciple has not meditated for a single session, the dependently arisen connections will align themselves, the culmination of attainment will be reached, and so forth.

Sacred commitment.

This is the medium path. A person with medium faculties trains in the twenty sacred commitments by way of the three modes of training, and, if [the sacred commitments] are damaged, propitiates by means of the five modes of propitiation. A person with medium faculties will thus also complete the path, reach the culmination of attainment, and so forth.

A cessation through comprehension of the body.

This is the path of a person with inferior faculties, who is inferior because the experiences do not arise easily and it is difficult to align the dependently arisen connections and to have confidence. This is known as "a cessation through comprehension of the body" because the five dependently arisen connections are gradually aligned in the body, because the body acts as the antidote, and because what is to be abandoned is abandoned by the body.

Those points have presented the esoteric instructions of the Path with the Result without omissions or additions.

The Conclusion

Now, to show that those lines have completed the treatise, it is said:

The oral instructions, together with the esoteric instructions, of the Path with the Result are complete.

"Path" and "result" are as previously explained in the context of the promise to explain. The "oral instructions" are those of the mundane path and the "esoteric instructions" are those of the transcendent path. Also, the "oral instructions" are those of the path and the "esoteric instructions" are those that establish the result. In addition, the "oral instructions" are those subsequently presented by the master and the "esoteric instructions" are those that arise from the authentic quality of one's own subsequent mindfulness in experience. In that way, these are synonyms.

"Are complete" is the final phrase that shows this is not too much or too little, has no omissions and additions, and is not insufficient. That is the meaning in Sanskrit of "***samāptam iti.***"

Samāptam iti[107]

Part II

The Path with the Result According to the Explication for Disciples

3. Expansion of the Great Secret Doctrine

Summarizing Notes on the History of the Oral Instructions

From the Comprehensive Explanation of the Precious Teaching of the "Path with the Result"

The Infallible Version of Khau Drakzongpa
The Practice of the Old Monk Khyentsé[108]

Jamyang Khyentsé Wangchuk

I PROSTRATE AND TAKE REFUGE at all times at the feet of my holy spiritual father, great Vajradhara, Losel Gyatso Drakpa Gyaltsen Palsangpo[109] of matchless kindness, the essence of all the buddhas of the past, present, and future. I pray that you bless the mindstreams of all sentient beings such as me.

The comprehensive explanation of the precious teaching of the Path with the Result, the unique path traveled by all the sugatas of the three times, consists of three main parts:

I. The history of the oral instructions, which is for the purpose of confidence and establishing the validity of the source
II. How to explain and learn the Dharma
III. How to benefit others after the practice has been perfected[110]

I. The History of the Oral Instructions

This consists of two topics:

A. The origin of the oral instructions in the noble land of India
B. The spread of the oral instructions in the land of Tibet

A. *The origin of the oral instructions in the noble land of India*

This consists of two topics:

1. The appearance of our Teacher, the Buddha
2. The origin of the doctrine of the excellent Dharma

1. *The appearance of our Teacher, the Buddha*

In general, both illuminated eons and dark eons arise. Buddhas appear in the first, but not in the second. And in the first, eons of creation, eons of abiding, and eons of destruction arise. Of these three, buddhas appear only in the middle eons of abiding, but not in either the first or the last eons. During the middle ones, in the eons during which lifespans have increased up to eighty thousand years, human beings have long lives and a great proportion of happiness, so thoughts of dissatisfaction do not occur. Therefore, these people are not recipients for the teaching of the Dharma, and so buddhas do not appear. Nor do they appear during the time of the decrease of lifespans. Buddhas do appear anytime when human lifespans are between eighty thousand and one hundred years. For example, an illuminated eon sometimes appears amid the majority of dark eons, like the flash of a streak of lightning in the midst of pitch darkness on a summer night enveloped in heavy rainfall. [88] Thus my master taught.

Furthermore, at the beginning of this current eon, a thousand and two golden lotuses rose from within the ocean. Beholding such an omen of virtue, the gods proclaimed: "Wonderful! A good eon!" Therefore, by virtue of the opinions in individual sutras about this "eon in which a thousand lotuses were beheld," or this "good eon," many statements have been made about how one thousand buddhas will appear, one thousand buddhas and two bodhisattvas will appear, and so forth.

In any case, infinite eons ago our present Teacher, this King of the Śākyas, had accumulated the assemblies[111] for three countless eons and had already actualized perfect buddhahood. Nevertheless, to train disciples by means of the twelve deeds at a time when lifespans were one hundred years, he displayed how to actualize perfect buddhahood at the Vajrāsana in Magadha.[112]

To grace the disciples who were inclined toward the inferior teachings, the Buddha turned the Dharma wheel of the Śrāvakayāna; for the disciples who were inclined toward the vast, he turned the Dharma wheel of the causal Pāramitāyāna; and for the superior disciples who were inclined toward the profound, he turned the Dharma wheel of the four classes of tantra in the Vajrayana.[113] After establishing the superior and inferior disciples in the individual paths and results, in a grove of two sāl trees he finally displayed how to completely pass into nirvana.

2. *The origin of the doctrine of the excellent Dharma*

This consists of three topics:

a. The spread of the excellent Dharma in general
b. The origin of the Nine Cycles of the Path in particular
c. The specific origin of the Precious Teaching

a. *The spread of the excellent Dharma in general*

In that way, the Teacher entered into meditative equipoise in the basic space of phenomena due to the karma of the disciples, but the excellent Dharma he taught has remained for a long period here in this worldly realm and thus brought inconceivable benefit and happiness to sentient beings. Concerning the Dharma that has remained, it is taught:

> The excellent Dharma
> of the Teacher has two aspects,
> with the nature of scripture and realization.[114]

The Dharma thus consists of two aspects. Concerning the first, [89] the *Sutra Requested by a Son of the Gods* says:

> All Dharma is included within these two: the Buddha's words and the treatises.[115]

Thus the *Dharma* is the words eloquently spoken by the Buddha and the great treatises that comment on their intention.

How long will the Dharma survive? Several different opinions exist. One point of view is that it survives for ten five-hundred-year periods. During the three five-hundred-year periods of the result, many people actualize the result, such as the four results of the śrāvaka, which are the *foe destroyer*, the *stream winner*, the *once returner*, and the *never returner*. During the three five-hundred-year periods of practice, the three trainings are energetically practiced.[116] During the three five-hundred-year periods of scripture, the explanation and study of the vinaya, the sutras, and the abhidharma is foremost. During the single five-hundred-year period of adherence to just the signs, merely a reflection of the Buddhist doctrine exists. Thus my master taught.

In that way, the majority of great spiritual guides appeared in the noble land of India, including the perfect Buddha, and those who attained the four results of the śrāvakas, the great bodhisattvas of the Mahayana, the great adepts such as Saraha, Nāgārjuna, Virūpa, Tilopa, and Nāropa, the six ornaments, and the supreme pair.[117] Therefore, this is known as "how the Dharma first spread in the noble land."

According to the uncommon accounts of the followers of the Path with the Result itself, the story of the tradition in Tibet was related first. And where did that tradition come from? In the way that headwaters are traced to the white glaciers, "It was transmitted from 'this expert and realized master of the noble land.'" Thus the story of its Indian origins can be known from the writings of the venerable lord Drakpa Gyaltsen in the *Volume*. But the customary practice is [to explain the Indian origins first,] as in the composition by Ngorchen Dorjé Chang, which agrees with the general histories of the Dharma.[118] Thus my master taught.

b. *The origin of the Nine Cycles of the Path in particular*

In that way, as mentioned, the majority of those expert and realized masters who appeared in the noble land of India made only the unexcelled Vajrayana the heart of their practice. If absolutely all the systems of the Vajrayana path are summarized, they can be included within the "six crucial points."[119] And if all six of these are distilled for practice, they can be included within the Nine Great Cycles of the Path.

In the opinion of lord Lama and his predecessors, [90] the Nine Cycles of the Path were formulated by eight individuals.[120] However, the carefully analyzed account by lord Dorjé Chang, who held the opinion that they were formulated by nine individuals, is best.[121] Thus my master taught.

Each of these nine cycles is also explained by means of four topics: which teacher formulated it, which tantra it depends on, what treatise was composed dependent on that tantra, and what the yoga of guidance is for the practice of that treatise.

1) *The Path with the Result*

When seated in an assembly row [of the sangha], the master Vajrāsanapāda simultaneously beheld the faces of the eighty-four great adepts in a vision and composed a eulogy in which he says:

> He turned back the great river
> and held the sun ransom for beer.
> I prostrate to that master
> known as Virūpa.[122]

The object of this eulogy is the lord of yogins, Virūpa. In general, two bearers of the name Virūpa appeared in India: the one known as Eastern Virūpa and this venerable lord. The former was the formulator of the practices of Varāhī with the Severed Head and became the master of Sukhasiddhī and others.[123] The latter was the one famed as the venerable and powerful lord Virūpa. He composed the root treatise of the *Vajra Lines* based, in general, on all the unexcelled yoga tantras—in particular, on the *Tantra Trilogy* (the root and explanatory tantras of Hevajra), and, specifically, on the *Two-Part Root Tantra.*[124] The guidance for its practice is the instructions of the precious teaching of the Path with the Result.

2) *The Instructions Received in Front of a Stupa*

> While in the form of a monk,
> he reached attainment
> and was offered nectar
> by a forest goddess.
> I prostrate to that master
> known as Nāgārjunasāra.[125]

The teacher Nāgārjuna composed the treatise of *Commentary on the*

Enlightenment Mind, based on the chapter [treating the topic] of the enlightenment mind in the root tantra of the *Guhyasamāja Tantra* and in the *Direct Enlightenment of Vairocana.* The practice is known as "The Instructions Received in Front of a Stupa" because Āryadeva, the best of his disciples, reached a decisive conclusion about the nature of his mind in front of a stupa.[126]

3) *Realizing Coemergence*

Both Ḍombi Heruka and Śrīparam Ḍombipa appeared in India. The first is the object of this eulogy:

> Spreading his mat,
> he crossed the Ganges,
> and reached attainment
> riding on a tiger.
> I prostrate to that master
> known as Ḍombi Heruka.[127]

Ḍombi Heruka composed the treatise *Realizing Coemergence,* [91] based on the *Tantra Trilogy of Glorious Hevajra.* The practice is the guidance of "Threefold Coemergence."[128]

4) *The Complete Path by Means of the Mudrā Consort*

This master was the second of the three Indrabhūtis to appear in the land of Oḍḍiyāna.

> Of the royal line residing
> in the land of Oḍḍiyāna,
> both brother and sister
> reached attainment.
> I prostrate to that master
> known as Indrabhūti.[129]

Indrabhūti composed the treatise known as the *Stages of Qualities in the Initiation,* based on the *Drop of Primordial Awareness,* which is a tantra compatible with the *Hevajra.* The practice is the Complete Path by Means of the Mudrā Consort.[130]

5) *The Nine Profound Means*

Three holders of the name Padmavajra appeared in the land of Oḍḍiyāna. The senior was Anaṅgavajra, the middle was the great adept Saroruha, and the junior was Padmasambhava of Oḍḍiyāna. They are classified as senior and junior by virtue of having appeared earlier and later. Thus my master taught. This concerns the middle one, Saroruha:

> He reached attainment
> although he was of the candra caste,
> and lived with a lotus lady.
> I prostrate to that master
> known as Saroruhavajra.[131]

Saroruha composed the treatises *Saroruha's Method for Accomplishment* and *Like the Tip of a Lamp Flame,* based on the *Two-Part Root Tantra.* The practice is known as "The Nine Profound Means."[132]

6) *The Inconceivable*

> In the body of a farmer
> of the Tharu caste,
> he reached attainment with a mudrā consort.
> I prostrate to that master
> known as Kuddāla.[133]

Kuddāla composed the treatise of the *Complete Path by Means of the Five Aspects of the Inconceivable,* based on the *Sampuṭa Tantra.* The practice is the guidance on the *Inconceivable.*[134]

7) *The Complete Path of Fierce Fire*

Many holders of the name Kṛṣṇa or Kāṇha appeared in India, such as Kāṇha of Deliberate Behavior, Kṛṣṇacāryavajra, Kṛṣṇasamayavajra, and Kṛṣṇa Śāntibhadra.[135] Of them:

> Breaking the master's command
> and engaging in the conduct,

he became a perfect buddha
in the intermediate state of existence.
I prostrate to that master
known as Kṛṣṇacārin.[136]

Kṛṣṇacārin composed the treatise of the *Four Stages,* known as *Olapati* in the symbolic language of the ḍākinīs, based on the root and explanatory tantras of the *Cakrasaṃvara.* The practice is the guidance of "The Complete Path of Fierce Fire."[137]

8) *Straightening the Crooked*

He abandoned austerities
and engaged in the conduct,
used the gazes and reached attainment.
I prostrate to that master
known as Kṛṣṇavajra.[138]

The object of this eulogy, Kṛṣṇa Utsiṭa the Immortal, composed the treatise *A Verse on Drawing the Vital Winds into the Central Channel,* based on all the mother tantras. The practice is known as "Straightening the Crooked."[139]

9) *The Unwritten Mahāmudrā*

He was of the royal caste,
traveled on a sunbeam,
and used medicinal pills,
eye salve, and subterranean ability.[140]
I prostrate to that master
known as Vāgīśvara.[141] [92]

This expert and realized master composed the treatises known as *Illuminating the Fourth,* the *Seven Branches,* and *Precious Reality,* based on the *Glorious Hevajra Tantra* and a prophecy from venerable Tārā. The practice is known as "The Unwritten Mahāmudrā."[142] Thus my master taught.

c. *The specific origin of the Precious Teaching*

This consists of two topics:

1) The life of the Lord of Yogins, who is at the root of the lineage
2) An account of the Lord of Yogins' followers

1) *The life of the Lord of Yogins*

This consists of two topics:

a) When he lived
b) The story of his life at that time

a) *When he lived*

The *Mañjuśrī Root Tantra* says:

> Four hundred years after I,
> the Tathāgata,
> have passed away,
> a monk called Nāga will appear.

And so forth, until:

> He will live for
> six hundred years.[143]

Thus Nāgārjuna appeared four hundred years after our Teacher Śākyamuni passed into nirvana. He lived for six hundred human years in this world of Jambudvīpa.[144] His disciple in later life was Āryadeva. It is explained that the Lord of Yogins was Āryadeva's disciple.

Asaṅga appeared nine hundred years after the Teacher passed into nirvana. It is taught:

> He will live for one hundred
> and fifty years.[145]

Thus it is explained that Asaṅga lived for a century and a half. It is taught that the Lord of Yogins was a disciple of Asaṅga, and that the abbot

Śāntarakṣita was a disciple of the Lord of Yogins.[146] Therefore, in brief, the Lord of Yogins appeared about 1,020 years after the Teacher passed into nirvana.

b) *The story of the Lord of Yogins' life at that time*

At about that time, in a great city in east India known as Bekṣasa ("King of Medicine"), the Lord of Yogins was born as the son of King Sergyi Khorlochen, who was the son of King Mukhyüchen. When he was shown to a brahmin astrologer, it was prophesied that he would be one who clarified the doctrine by means of power. He was given the name Ngülgyi Khorlochen.

When the Lord of Yogins grew older, he took ordination from the abbot Vinayadeva and the teacher Jayakīrti at the temple of Somapūri in the east. Relying on that teacher, he studied to the point of expertise in all fields of knowledge. He constructed at that monastery [93] a small stone chapel filled with representations of the Three Jewels, and established a fine stream of offerings to purify the obscurations of his father and mother. He pleased the abbot, the teacher, and the sangha with excellent feasts and service. Then he brought his activities in that area to a close for the time being and traveled to the temple of glorious Nālandā, a place where the excellent Dharma had greatly spread.

The Lord of Yogins received complete ordination from the abbot, Dharmamitra, "Friend of Dharma." He trained in an incredible number of excellent Dharma teachings connected with the Mahayana and the Hinayana. Because that abbot was also highly pleased with the Lord of Yogins, he freely taught all the Dharma. In particular, as a secret Dharma for the teacher alone, Dharmamitra said, "In general, for rapid buddhahood the Vajrayana is necessary. Of the Vajrayana teachings, Cakrasaṃvara is especially profound and rapid."

Dharmamitra completely instructed him with ripening initiation and liberating guidance. In brief, he became famous as the great expert Śrī Dharmapāla, "Glorious Dharma Protector."

Then, after some time, when the abbot passed into nirvana, he said in a last testament, "This Śrī Dharmapāla is a great expert no different from me. I pass this monastic seat of mine to him. Treat him just as you have treated me!"

When the abbot's remains were offered for cremation, all the remains transformed into images of deities and relics. All the monks and patrons, such as the king, became filled with even more faith than before. By the abbot's command, the teacher Śrī Dharmapāla was installed as the abbot of Nālandā, and everyone honored him, bowing to him with the crowns of their heads.

During the day, the teacher Śrī Dharmapāla accomplished vast activities for the doctrine, such as explaining, debating, and composing Dharma of the Mahayana and Hinayana. During the night, he single-mindedly cultivated the meditative concentration of Cakrasaṃvara, as instructed by the teacher Dharmamitra. He lived in this way until he was about seventy years old.

Śrī Dharmapāla had hoped, "If I meditate with intense effort on a path such as this, will good signs of attainment arise?"

But not even a good dream had arisen, in addition to which, all his old illnesses had returned and he was inflicted with many new ones. Unbearable physical pain and mental suffering arose, and he was tormented by many evil beings, such as carnivorous spirits and rākṣasa demons. [94] Even in his dreams, many disagreeable appearances arose, such as: fire blazing from the lower part of a valley and water cascading from the upper part; lightning; rainfalls of hail, earth clods, and pieces of ice; and appearances of the master, the chosen deity, friends with the same sacred commitments, and so forth, upside down, with their faces slashed, their noses cut off, and their eyes plucked out, with blood flowing freely from the gaping wounds.

Śrī Dharmapāla fell into despair and thought, "I have done so much practice, but not even as much as a good dream has arisen. Only bad signs like this have arisen. If I interpret this, it is certain that I am one who has absolutely no link with the Vajrayana in this life. Therefore, I will now spend my time solely in study and explanation of the common Vehicle, without doing any secret mantra practice whatsoever."

On the evening of the twenty-second day of the fourth month in the spring, he threw his rosary into the latrine, and began to take it easy.

Regarding these events, this teacher Śrī Dharmapāla had reached the end of the path of accumulation and had also traveled most of the path of application. When the vital winds and mind had gathered into the *kṣa, ma,* and so forth below the navel, he had arrived at the point at which he was about to reach the path of seeing. The previous oral instructions of the abbot had been in a slightly unresolved form. Thus my master taught.

In any case, in a dream while he was sleeping at dawn, the venerable Vajra Nairātmyā appeared in the form of a blue ordinary woman, who was beautiful, enchanting, and adorned with many silks and jewels. She said, "Son of good family, it is not good that you did such a bad thing at the point of reaching attainment. In general, there is no greater or lesser compassion among all the buddhas. Specifically, I am the deity with whom you have accumulated karma. Therefore, I will bless you. But take the rosary out of the latrine! Wash it with perfumed water, and practice as before!"

When she disappeared, he awoke from the dream. With great joy he did as she had commanded, and on the evening of the twenty-third, the fifteen-goddess mandala of venerable Vajra Nairātmyā actually appeared and bestowed initiation in a great emanated mandala. The primordial awareness of the initiation, the nonconceptual primordial awareness of the path of seeing, was born in his mindstream. [95]

Furthermore, because he completely obtained the four initiations in a great emanated mandala, the stream of initiation did not cease.

Because he actualized the primordial awareness of the first spiritual level of the path of seeing during the initiation, the transmission of blessings did not decline.

Śrī Dharmapāla understood those disturbing experiences that had arisen before to be the pains of the channels, the pains of the vital winds, and the great mental changes that come because the knots of the channels have been opened during the first gathering of the essential constituents while being guided on the path by the warmths and the signs of the vital winds and the fierce fire. And he understood that the appearance of rākṣasa demons and carnivorous spirits had arisen because of the dependently arisen connections of the vital winds and mind gathering in the *ma, kṣa,* and so forth below the navel.

He understood that the fire blazing from the lower valley, the water cascading down from the upper valley, and so forth, had arisen as dream experiences because of the dependently arisen connections of the fierce fire blazing up from below and the enlightenment mind moving down from above while being guided on the path by the blissful yet empty drops during the middle gathering of the essential constituents. And he understood that those rains of hail, pieces of ice, and so forth, had occurred on the basis of the coming and going of the drops in the tiny channels.

While being guided on the path by flawless and genuine primordial awareness during the final gathering of the essential constituents, all the present passionate attachments are repulsed, which was indicated by the arising of the slashed faces of the master, the chosen deity, and so forth. Since Śrī Dharmapāla had not been graced before by the oral instructions of the excellent master, he had taken all those experiential appearances to be faults that should be rejected. But now, based on the oral instructions of Vajra Nairātmyā, he recognized them all to be meditative concentrations, and was naturally freed from all impediments and obstacles. Because those three gatherings of the essential constituents arose in his mind without disorder in sequence, the sequence of the oral instructions was undisrupted.

On the basis of those oral instructions, Śrī Dharmapāla reached the decisive conclusion that venerable Vajra Nairātmyā was the combined essence of all the buddhas. He thought, "Now all the buddhas of the three times could come, but there would be nothing more than this." Irreversible faith was born, and his mind was satisfied with devotion. Thus he became endowed with the four oral transmissions.[147]

Sustaining the stream of that primordial awareness, he advanced through the realization of one spiritual level each day, and after six days he had become a great bodhisattva residing on the sixth spiritual level.

Then, to present an offering of gratitude to the master and the chosen deity and to enhance his own realization, Śrī Dharmapāla gave orders to a trustworthy friend and secretly obtained the sacramental substances of meat, beer, and so forth. [96] When he performed a ritual feast, word of the carrying of meat and beer traveled from one monk to the next, and several who became aware of it said, "Let's investigate what is happening."

They looked through a crack in the abbot's door. At that time, when those with pure karma saw the teacher performing the meditative concentration of the venerable father Hevajra, he was residing in the midst of eight women, and when he was resting in the meditative concentration of the venerable mother Nairātmyā, he was in the midst of fourteen women.[148] Those monks with slightly impure karma saw him enjoying meat and beer in the midst of eight blazing lamps, fourteen lamps, and so forth.

Therefore everyone became doubtful, but since Śrī Dharmapāla was the great abbot of them all and as famous as the sun and the moon, no one dared to speak out. To avoid harm to the doctrine and to refute the lack of faith by others, the teacher accepted that he was bad when everyone said he was bad. To demonstrate his bad behavior, he offered in front of the Three Jewels all the articles required by a monk, such as the Dharma robes and alms bowl. Wearing a single cotton loincloth, he said, "I am the one called 'the naked bad one, Virūpa.'" He left abruptly[149] and robbed some merchants of a garland of flowers with which he decorated his body. In India the turnip is used for food by the lower castes, so he begged some from the turnip sellers, and robbed several more. Some of the turnips he stuck in his mouth and some he carried in his armpits. The entire sangha was shocked and began the rites of expulsion. Concerning this, if the gong is struck, a return is permitted later if a request is made. If the double-faced drum called a *paḍaha* is struck, there is no return in the future. Both of these were struck, and he was expelled. So he sang a song:

> Alas, good sangha,
> I've called myself bad.
> The drum was struck,
> the gong was struck,
> and I was expelled
> from the sangha.
>
> My mind that's like
> the immaculate moon
> is difficult for the sangha
> to comprehend.
>
> Blocking the leaking sense organs
> terrifies them.
>
> Virūpa will drink beer
> and hold the sun hostage.
>
> When the blue lily has risen
> it isn't covered with water.
>
> Therefore, Virūpa knows a lot.[150]

Then, on the road leading to Vārāṇasī, Virūpa arrived at the edge of the Ganges River. "You are very clean," he said, "I'm bad. If I touch you, you'll become polluted, so you should give me a pathway."

The Ganges backed up, and the teacher went on the pathway that was revealed. The sangha then realized that he had reached attainment. [97] They offered apologies and begged him to stay.

"Generally, in the world, when many good people have gathered, they have the right to eject a bad one," he replied. "But many of you bad people gathered and ejected me, a good person. This was not right. Nevertheless, it was for the sake of the doctrine. And hereafter, if a person appears who harms the doctrine, eliminate him!"

He forgave them, but did not agree to stay.

Virūpa lived in a forest in the Vārāṇasī area, some say for six years and some say for six months, so certainly for at least six months. In any case, he stayed only in meditative concentration, without taking any interest in food, clothing, and so forth. Therefore, his entire body was afflicted by the sun and the wind and he became very frightening in appearance.

He was seen there by the cowherds and others, and word passed from one to the next. These rumors were heard by Govindacaṇḍa, "The Fierce Cowherd," who was the king of Vārāṇasī and a practitioner of a non-Buddhist religion. He decreed, "If he is a non-Buddhist yogin, he must be invited here and honored since he is in difficulty. If he is a Buddhist yogin, there is danger that he may harm the people of Vārāṇasī, and so he should be eliminated. Find out which he is!"

The ministers came to the teacher, but as much as they examined him, they still could not tell. So they said, "He must be examined by the king himself. Bring him to the king!"

The teacher was invited from the midst of the forest. Along the road, the teacher put many small creatures such as insects and butterflies into his mouth.

"This one is bad!" people exclaimed.

Even when the creatures flew out of his mouth without having died, people said, "This one is bad!"

So Virūpa sang a song:

> I kill many creatures,
> and they say, "He's bad!"
>
> I revive many creatures,
> and they say, "He's bad!"
>
> I don't know how I should act![151]

Virūpa came to the king. But no matter what the king asked, he did not respond. The king became angry and said, "This one has no marks of Īśvara, so he is not a non-Buddhist yogin. He is a Buddhist yogin, so bind all his limbs with iron chains and throw him in the river!"

They did so, but the teacher arrived back in the presence of the king before those who had thrown him in the water arrived. When they had done this many times, the king said, "This one knows the art of controlling water, so stab him now with many weapons and kill him!" [98]

The executioners stabbed him with many weapons, but it was like hitting a boulder. So they put the teacher into a deep pit dug in the ground. And into that they dumped molten metal and many iron boulders. On top of that they heaped much earth, upon which they made many elephants stand. But the teacher arrived unimpeded in front of the king, before the men who had done that work arrived. Then the king became filled with faith and begged forgiveness. Virūpa established all the areas around Vārāṇasī in the Vajrayana.

On the road leading to southern India, Virūpa then arrived on the bank of the Ganges and said to the ferryman, "Take me across."

"In this world there is no custom of taking someone across without the ferry toll," the ferryman replied. "I want the ferry toll."

"I can give you this river itself as ferry toll," Virūpa said. "But would you prefer this river large, or would you prefer it small?"

"For the king's army, and for such purposes as watering the sugar cane, large is preferable," he replied. "But for such people as those who dwell in grass huts on the riverbanks, who are afraid of their homes being flooded, small is preferable."

Virūpa pointed his finger at the water, and the river backed up. The homes of those who dwelled in grass huts on the riverbanks were nearly submerged, and everyone was terrified. When they looked to see what had happened, the ferryman cried, "This yogin did it!"

Therefore, along with King Calabhadra and his retinue, some people offered jewels, some offered gold, some offered horses, some offered cattle, some offered grain, and so forth. They prayed to Virūpa, and by just snapping his fingers, the teacher made the water flow as before and removed the fears of those dwelling in the grass huts.

When Virūpa gave the ferryman the valuables that the people had offered, the past karma of the ferryman was awakened and he thought,

"Having met such an adept as this, I have no need for these valuables." He followed Virūpa as his servant, and the valuables, which had not been ruined or lost, were enjoyed by the individual owners. In that way, the Ganges was turned back for the second time. Virūpa also sang a song at that point.[152]

That ferryman was famed as Ḍombi Heruka, the disciple fit to be guided by the instantaneous path of the fortunate.

Then both the teacher and his disciple traveled to the region known as Ḍākinipāta in southern India. There they bought beer from the beer-seller woman called Kāmarūpasiddhi, "Attainment of Desirable Form." [99]

"What payment will you give?" she asked.

"When we're satisfied we'll give you a payment!" he replied.

She did not believe him, so he drew a line at the edge of the shade from the sun, and said, "When the shadow moves past this, we'll pay you."

They drank up all her beer. Then they slowly drank up all the beer in eighteen districts, but the shade from the sun did not even move a little. All the king's sundials and water clocks were also disrupted. All the people and cattle became totally exhausted from sleep deprivation and so forth. The king investigated what was happening and when he realized that it was a demonstration of the Lord of Yogins' ability, he asked Virūpa to release the sun.

"I have nothing to give in payment for the beer!" Virūpa replied.

The king gave the beer-seller women what payments were required for the beer. When Virūpa released the sun, it set in a red streak. About two days and half of one night had passed.

In that way, Virūpa turned back the Ganges twice and held the sun hostage, so his fame filled all directions.

Then, to grace Kāṇha, the disciple fit to be guided by the gradual path, and to tame Bhīmesara, they traveled to the land of Bhīmesara in southern India. There was a non-Buddhist king there called Nārapati, "Lord of Men," who kept five hundred longhaired sadhus as priests. There was an Īśvara phallic image erected by the past king Bhīmasena, to which many tens of thousands of goats and buffaloes were slaughtered and offered on each occasion of sacrifice.

They went there, and Virūpa offered many eulogies in the Sanskrit language according to the Vedas. The king was delighted and proclaimed, "It is difficult to find a great expert like this. He is fit to be the leader of the five hundred longhaired sadhus."

Thus the king appointed Virūpa his royal priest, and the teacher also resided as such. When the longhaired sadhus offered prostrations, flowers, and so forth to the Īśvara image, from the midst of his long hair the teacher extracted a volume said to be the *Two-Part Hevajra* or the *Perfection of Wisdom in Eight Thousand Lines,* and he made prostrations and offerings to that. The longhaired sadhus told the king, but the king did not believe it to be the truth and said, "How is it possible that a expert like him, one who has mastered the Vedas, does not make prostrations and offerings to Īśvara? You are just jealous." [100]

When the sadhus accused Virūpa again and again, even the king became doubtful. One time, when the sadhus were making prostrations and offerings together with the king, the teacher made prostrations and offerings as before to that volume of scripture. So the king asked, "Why don't you make prostrations to the Īśvara image?"

"It couldn't endure my prostrations," Virūpa replied.

The king insisted, "If there is no one greater than this god in the desire realm, how could he not endure a prostration? Make it!"

The teacher said to the image, "I am powerless against a sinful king. May you withstand it, O god!"

He put the palms of his hands together, said "Namo Buddhaya," and the phallic image split one-third [of the way down to the ground]. With "Dharmaya," it split two-thirds of the way, and with "Sanghaya," it split completely in half. Terrified, the king and his retinue touched Virūpa's feet and prayed for him to reassemble the image. Virūpa put a black stone image of Mahākaruṇika[153] on top of the head of the reassembled image and said, "If this is removed the image will be destroyed. As long as this remains, the image will not be destroyed." Then he left.

At that time, of the group of five hundred longhaired sadhus, one became disgusted with the wrong view and behavior of the non-Buddhists. Seeing the good qualities of the Lord of Yogins, his mind was captivated, and he followed him. This was Eastern Kāṇha, who is also taken as the basis for the definition of a person who "has not entered into the Buddhist doctrine, but wishes to enter." Thus my master taught.

Then the trio of master and disciples traveled for some distance south. A king named Dzeṃgi had made a copper image of Īśvara about 120 feet tall, known as Tambrapratima, in the form with three heads and six arms. They came to that place where offerings were made on each ceremonial occasion with the flesh and blood of many thousands of slaughtered creatures. Many non-Buddhist practitioners were gathered there making offerings. When the teacher and his disciples squeezed inside, they were told, "We'll give your share outside. You can't fit in here. So don't come!"

The teacher replied, "If we can't fit, it's you who ought to go," and with his foot kicked a stone at the image. Its consecration in the non-Buddhist tradition was thus damaged, and the image came tottering after the teacher for about seven steps. When it arrived outside the door, it fell face down. All the non-Buddhist practitioners there became terrified and touched Virūpa's feet. [101] When they begged him to put the image back, he made many threats, saying "I will put it back if you make offerings with the three white substances of rice and so forth, without sacrificing life. If not, I will lead it away!"

They agreed to do so, and he put it back.

As they traveled along the road in this way, it was proclaimed, "Virūpa is destroying all the non-Buddhist images!" and everyone was frightened. When he saw that to correct their mistakes the people had placed a Buddhist image upon the head of each non-Buddhist image, he was pleased to think that just his name alone was doing what needed to be done for the doctrine.

A statue of venerable Tārā had been placed upon the head of one non-Buddhist image. When the teacher circumambulated it, the face of Tārā swiveled around to see wherever the teacher went, and so it became known as "Tārā with the Turning Face." When the teacher offered a flower to firmly establish the Tārā, it became inseparable from the head of the image. The non-Buddhist practitioners had planned to remove it as soon as the teacher went outside, but they were unable to take it away. Thus my master taught.

Then they traveled further south. Many non-Buddhist yoginīs were living at a spot where a naturally arisen stone image of the goddess Caṇḍikā (known as Sahajadevī) stood. Everyone who came in that direction was led into the temple, and a naturally arisen trident stabbed them in the throat and they died. The flesh and blood of those who died was used for a ritual feast.

When Virūpa arrived to subdue them, those yoginīs were pleased and said, "Come inside."

He told his two servants, "You must hold your breath and stay here without speaking to them."

When the teacher went inside, the yoginīs said, "Call your two friends."

"Call them yourself," he replied.

They called, but received no answer. When they used their forefingers to touch the disciples' navels, excrement oozed out, so they said, "They're rotten," and left them.

When the teacher went into that temple, the trident began to vibrate and jingle. Virūpa reduced it to dust with a slap of his palm. The stone image rose, but when he slapped the palm of his hand on the crown of its head, the head sunk down between the breasts. The yoginīs vomited blood and fainted.

"You Buddhists have great compassion," they cried, "Don't act like this."

"It is precisely because of great compassion that I do just this," Virūpa replied. [102]

He placed a stupa on the top of the head of that image. All those yoginīs were brought into the Buddhist doctrine and became Buddhist yoginīs.

Then Virūpa blessed the ferryman who had followed after him before, when he had turned back the Ganges, so that the ferryman became a great spiritual hero on the sixth spiritual level, equal in realization to Virūpa himself. He sent him to subdue the malevolent non-Buddhist king Dehara, who lived at the Kaṃkana palace in the city of Natsok Draden in the land of Rāḍha in east India.[154] Using poisonous snakes for the bit and headstall, the breast collar and crupper, and so forth, on a man-eating jungle tiger, and holding such things as a large poisonous snake in his hand, this great adept Ḍombi Heruka subdued that king and established the entire land of Raḍa in the Vajrayana. Thus my master taught.

Both the teacher, the Lord of Yogins, and his disciple, Kāṇha, traveled to the ravine of Devīkoṭa in southeast India. They performed prostrations and circulambulations at the Khasarpaṇa image[155] that had been invited from Potala by the lay practitioner Chakyi Jinpachen, who was also known as the teacher Ajitaguptamitra. When Virūpa explained how he had performed actions for the doctrine, from first taking ordination up to the subduing of Sahajadevī, Mahākaruṇika said, "Son of good family, with your ability you could certainly reduce even Mount Meru to dust. However, since the different karma of sentient beings is inconceivable, you must awaken great compassion without making the non-Buddhist practitioners so frightened."

Virūpa replied, "In the west many thousands of creatures are slaughtered and offered on each occasion to the one known as Somanātha.[156] I will subdue him and then act according to the order of Mahākaruṇika."

Mahākaruṇika commanded, "In that case, you must also subdue him through skillful means, not subdue him with deliberate behavior!"[157]

When the master and servant departed from there with the intention to subdue Somanātha, he perceived it with his tainted clairvoyance. To welcome them, he emanated as two pure brahmins with deer skins wrapped around their lower bodies and with the purifying substances of kusha grass and so forth. They met coming along the road. Although Somanātha knew the answer, he asked, "Where are you yogins going?"

The teacher also recognized him, [103] and replied, "I am going to destroy Somanātha."

"If you Buddhists have great compassion, with what are you going to destroy him?"

"I use just that to destroy."

"He has gone to Videha in the east and isn't here."

"I will go even there and destroy him," Virūpa replied. "He could go to the four continents and the world of Brahmā, and I would still go there and destroy him."

Terrified, Somanātha revealed his true form that very instant and pleaded, "I am he. Please don't destroy me!"

"In that case," Virūpa replied, "build an establishment for the sangha and construct a Buddhist temple there. Draw my figure above its door. When making offerings, do not sacrifice living creatures. Make offerings with such things as rice and pastries, first to the representations of the Three Jewels and afterwards to me. With the leftovers, offerings may be made to you. If this is done, you will be allowed to stay. If it is not done in that way, I will smash you into dust."

Somanātha accepted this, and begged the teacher to stay as the priest for as long as the sun and moon remain. The teacher also accepted.

Somanātha gave prophecy in a dream to the king of Tiśala in western India, who was called Candradeva, telling him to accomplish in three months everything explained before, and that if he did not do so, his country and retinue would be destroyed. The king also became frightened and accomplished what he had been told. "What is that lord of yogins, Virūpa, whom even the god Maheśvara must fear, like?" he wondered. The king and his retinue happily welcomed and honored Virūpa with incredible welcoming arrangements.

When one travels about a quarter of a day's journey from Somanātha, one arrives in a region called Gujarat, which is captivating and extremely pleasant, with marvelous trees, flowing streams, meadows, and so forth. Virūpa went there, where a temple was constructed, a sangha of about a hundred was also honored, and animals such as goats and buffalos, whose lives had been spared, could wander comfortably without anyone being able to harm them.

Virūpa then bestowed the *Vajra Lines* on his disciple Kāṇha, who was not equal to him in realization, and blessed him to be equal in realization. He sent him away for three purposes: to subdue a malevolent non-Buddhist king in east India, [104] to grace the teacher Ḍāmarupa, and, from the land of Oḍḍiyāna in the west, to invite the *Five Cycles of Scripture*[158] that serve as supports for the *Vajra Lines.*

In accordance with the command of Avalokiteśvara, the teacher himself discontinued for a while his performance of deliberate behavior in Jambudvīpa. It is said that he dissolved into a stone image, which is also said to be the teacher himself. In any case, the image has a form in which the right hand makes the gesture of holding the sun hostage. The palm of the left hand, which is in the gesture of granting the sublime attainment, holds the stone whose touch transforms anything into gold; this stone is about the size of a medium myrobalan plum.

This image has wonderful qualities. Even very small children, if they offer with devotion to it, are able to offer garlands of flowers on the top of its head. But if one makes offerings with bad intent, no matter how tall one is, one cannot reach the top of its head. In front of the image is a stone skull-cup that never overflows or drips, even if many hundreds of thousands of vats of beer are poured into it. Both a mute, who is an emanation of Vajrapāṇi, and an emanation of Vajravarāhī who sometimes appears as a leper woman and sometimes appears as a mute woman, are continuously present in front of the image.

On one occasion, it is said that a destitute monk (or, according to another account, a destitute brahmin) prayed to him, and Virūpa gave him the stone whose touch transforms anything into gold. The monk made much gold, but when a king heard and began to take it, the monk said, "It is not mine. It belongs to the Lord of Yogins. So I will offer it into his hand. Then take it."

When the monk offered the gold-transforming stone into the image's hand, the hand closed up because he did not want to give it to that greedy king. When the king became angry and was about to break the hand, that vandal vomited blood and died right there. From that time on, no more than a crack has appeared in the hand, into which a fine iron wire can pass. The gold accumulated from inserting an iron wire into that crack is used as the basis for the offerings that are made.

The non-Buddhists say this image is called Puṇyahara, "Merit Robber," because it is one who robs the merit of Maheśvara, and if offerings are not made to the image, many nonvirtues will appear in the world. Therefore, they are especially diligent in making offerings. The Buddhists make offerings to it as glorious Balanātha, "Lord of Power."

In brief, among all the images existing in Jambudvīpa, [105] it is known that the Khasarpaṇa residing at Devīkoṭa in the southeast is best for continuous offerings, the Mahābodhi is best for special offerings, and none are better than Somanātha for both continuous and special offerings.[159]

In this way, the venerable Lord of Yogins spread the doctrine in Jambudvīpa through deliberate behavior and then actualized the citadel of a vajra holder on the thirteenth spiritual level. Even in the present period, he acts as the priest for Kumāra Kārttikeya and actually resides at Somanātha.[160]

It is known that Virūpa came three times to engage in deliberate behavior on this continent. The second time was when he was famed as the yogin called Sarupa or Siropa, who appeared in the land of India when a mad elephant called Nyima Charwa was destroying all the forests, towns, and cities. He mounted the mad elephant and vanished without a trace, like a rainbow.

The third time was to reassemble that destroyed image of Bhīmesara. It is said that he has already come, and it is also said that he has yet to come. Thus my master taught.

In brief, no matter how many powerful, expert and realized masters have appeared in the noble land of India, no one else has performed deeds in this way for the doctrine by means of deliberate behavior. Therefore, the upholder of the doctrine through deliberate behavior was the great adept, the Lord of Yogins, the upholder of the doctrine through debate was the glorious Dharmakīrti, and the upholder of the doctrine through power was the Dharma king Aśoka.[161] They are as famous as the sun and the moon.

This is how that king upheld the doctrine. One called "The Blue Robed Paṇḍita" had a huge following for the perverted teachings that he had devised. When no one was able to subdue him, the Dharma king Aśoka agreed to be his patron and summoned him with all his retinue and servants. They were put into a large shellac building, surrounded by many soldiers, and burned in a fire. Even the name of their evil tenets was annihilated. Thus my master taught.[162]

In brief, it is prophesied in the *Mañjuśrī Root Tantra,* beginning with these words:

> With the syllable *dha,*
> and diligent in vows.[163]

This is usually considered to be a prophecy about glorious Dharmakīrti, [106] but according to the opinion of Drokmi Lotsāwa and his followers, it is explained to be a prophecy of the Lord of Yogins. "With the syllable 'dha,' and diligent in vows," refers to *Dharma,* the first part of the name Dharmapāla. The same source also says, "Famous in the south." No specific accounts of Dharmakīrti subduing non-Buddhists in the south have appeared, but this venerable lord Virūpa mostly subdued non-Buddhists through the performance of deliberate behavior in the south. The same source also says:

> While diligent in vows,
> he will also master mantra.

To master mantra is to achieve the sublime attainment of mahāmudrā, but no accounts of Dharmakīrti specifically mastering mantra have appeared. Therefore, it is established as a prophecy of this venerable lord Virūpa. Thus my master taught.

2) *An account of the Lord of Yogins' followers*

Eastern Kāṇha, who was mentioned previously, is also called Kāṇha of Deliberate Behavior, because this teacher also perfected the performance of deliberate behavior. The area where he was born was called Karṇa, so he was also known as Karṇapa. He actualized the realization of the sixth spiritual level. He first practiced meditation on Mount Ujjayanta. Then, in accordance with the command of the Lord of Yogins, from the land of Oḍḍiyāna in the west he brought the *Five Cycles of Scripture,* which were fragments of the *Hevajra Root Tantra* in 500,000 lines and which serve as supports for the *Vajra Lines.* These do not seem to have been translated in Tibet. Thus my master taught.

Similarly, there was a king in eastern India who was going to fall into the lower realms because of attachment to his retinue of queens. Kāṇha saw that he was a potential disciple and went into the palace of the queens. When the king heard about it he was furious and ordered Kāṇha to be quickly killed. When the killers went inside, the teacher went straight outside without impediment. While they went outside, he came straight inside. When all the palace, inside and out, was filled with soldiers, from the single teacher there appeared a hundred, from the hundred, a thousand, and so forth, to an infinite number. The king and retinue became filled with faith and were established in the Vajrayana.

Similarly, Kāṇha also subdued a king of Magadha, who became known as Dhamapa or Ḍāmarupa. As prophesied by the Lord of Yogins, Kāṇha instructed him by means of the four oral transmissions. The secret name of this Kāṇha of Deliberate Behavior is known to have been Padmavajra. [107] Thus my master taught.

When the great adept Dhamapa engaged in deliberate behavior, he held a ḍāmaru skull-drum in his hand, and engaged in the behavior, rattling and shaking the ḍāmaru in all the twenty-four sacred lands and thirty-two sacred sites. Therefore, he was known as Ḍāmarupa. To subdue a malevolent non-Buddhist king, he led a man-eating jungle tiger in front of the king. When Ḍāmarupa suddenly grabbed the king by the topknot and put him on one shoulder and the tiger on the other shoulder and raced about, all the retinue were frightened and pleaded with him. He said, "If you abandon the non-Buddhist tenets, I'll put him down! If you don't, I'll feed him to the tiger!"

The king and his retinue were terrified, abandoned the tenets practiced by the non-Buddhists, and were established in the Vajrayana.

As prophesied by Eastern Kāṇha, Ḍāmarupa also subdued a king of Magadha known as Sengé Nampar Tsenpa, and instructed him by way of the four oral transmissions. The secret name of Ḍāmarupa is known to have been Buddhavajra. Thus my master taught.

Ḍāmarupa's disciple Avadhūtīpa was that great king of Magadha known as Sengé Nampar Tsenpa. After he had obtained the instructions from the great adept Ḍāmarupa, he cast aside the kingdom like dust. Because he lived and played in the midst of groups of children in the alleyways of the city, engaging in the "conduct of the renunciation of duality,"[164] he was famed as Avadhūtīpa. His secret name is known to have been Asamavajra.

The one graced by Avadhūtīpa was lord Gayadhara.[165] The land of his birth was Bengal, in eastern India, when the king was Candarupakṣi. His caste was that of a royal scribe, known as *kayāstha.* His name was Gayadhara. Gaya means "go," and since clouds go above and nāgas go below, his name means either "cloud holder" or "nāga holder." This was the opinion of our ancestors such as Drokmi.

Gayadhara was extremely skilled in all fields of knowledge. While he was acting as the king's scribe, Avadhūtīpa sent him a letter (as had been prophesied by Ḍāmarupa) which said, "You are fit to be my disciple. Come to me."

Gayadhara gladly went and was instructed by way of the four oral transmissions. [108]

In that way, from the Lord of Yogins to lord Gayadhara, each predecessor prophesied each successor, and the instructions were passed down in a single, unique transmission. Therefore, the Precious Teaching was known in India, but it was barely known; and it remained extremely secret, unheard of by most expert and realized masters.

Although this Lord of Yogins is accepted as authentic by all expert and realized masters, and is cited as a source in such works as the *Compendium of Deeds*[166] and the commentary on Vīraprabhāsvara's collection of the songs of the eighty-four adepts,[167] even these authors appear not to have been among those who received the esoteric instructions. Thus my master taught.

B. *The spread of the oral instructions in the land of Tibet*

This section contains three topics: the spread of the excellent Dharma in general, an account of the Nine Cycles of the Path in particular, and the specific history of the Precious Teaching.

1. *The spread of the excellent Dharma in general*

At first there was not even a single human being here in Tibet. The land was occupied by birds and wild creatures such as eagles and lions in Ngari, by animals such as deer, wild ass, and antelope in Central Tibet and Tsang, and by monkeys, tigers, leopards, bears, elephants, and so forth in Kham. It was owned by numerous demonic spirits and others such as the twelve masang siblings, who were neither human beings nor demons. Without any acceptance of virtues or rejection of sins, they harmed one another, and ate their own relatives' flesh and drank their own relatives' blood. Doing only nonvirtue, as soon as they died they went to the lower realms, like turning a leather bag of sand upside down.

With his compassion, the Lord of Sages, Śākyamuni, smiled and gazed intently at Avalokiteśvara, urging him to subdue them. In the same way, he also urged Tārā to act as his companion. And so they directed their attention to Tibet.

Then, at one point, in the first month of autumn in a bird year, all monkeys had the same dream. They dreamed that it was said, "In the horse month all the rākṣasa demons in the land of rākṣasa demons became intoxicated with blood and fell asleep. In the hawk month they will wake up, and all the rākṣasa demons will arrive in Tibet and eat all the monkeys."

When the monkeys told each another, they all said in agreement, "I also dreamed that."

All the monkeys became frightened, and when they told the monkey king Hanumantha, he said, "In general, there is no certainty in dreams. [109] However, if all sentient beings of the same species dream in that way at the same time, it might be true. We must strive for a way to prevent it. Moreover, if we aren't able to do it now when they have fallen sleep, we won't be able to later."

They planned to set the tail of the monkey king Hanumantha on fire, and he would burn down the house of the rākṣasa demons, after which all the other monkeys would pile up like a throne to bring Hanumantha down from the top of the castle, extinguish the fire on his tail, and so forth. But monkeys are the epitome of instability, and when Hanumantha actually set the house of the rākṣasa demons on fire, they all scattered without a trace. With no one to bring Hanumantha down, extinguish the fire, and so forth, Hanumantha had to jump, and he broke his arms and legs. He was unable to put out the fire on his tail, and while he lay there in great misery, noble Avalokiteśvara arrived and asked, "Hanumantha, what is wrong with you?"

When Hanumantha told the story, he was taught that all samsara has the nature of suffering. He was given the five basic precepts of a lay practitioner[168] and sent away with the command, "Go to Tibet and meditate!"

Hanumantha meditated and lived in the cliffs at Samyé Chimphu. One day a rākṣasa rock-demoness appeared there and said, "We should live together."

Hanumantha refused, saying, "I am a lay practitioner of Mahākaruṇika. It would not be right for me to act like that."

"If you and I are not together," she replied, "I will have relations with a rākṣasa demon, and five hundred young rākṣasa demons will be born. Together with them I will harm many sentient beings and go to hell. And if that doesn't happen, I will commit suicide."

The monkey felt compassion. "In that case," he said, "I will ask the Noble One. You be patient!"

In a single leap he arrived at Potala.[169] When he told the Noble One the reason, Avalokiteśvara prophesied, "Wonderful. Do that! Dependent on your children, grandchildren, and descendants, the excellent Dharma will spread."

Hanumantha returned to Tibet again in one leap. From union with the rākṣasa rock-demoness, five offspring were born whose forms were like the father but without tails. They were taken and left in a forest called Maja Tsokchen. They grew up, and from their joining with the female monkeys there, about five hundred children were born in one year's time. [110] They had little to eat and were very miserable, so they went to Potala and told Avalokiteśvara. He gave them the five grains such as barley and said, "I give you these. In the future, the descendants of your children will enjoy the five precious substances." And he scattered gold and so forth in the land of Tibet.

When those grains were planted at Sothang in the center of Yarlung, they grew perfectly. The male and female monkeys enjoyed them and gradually multiplied. By the dependently arisen connection of all their spirit forms being in the forms of yaks, horses, deer, and sheep, most human beings also came to have facial shapes similar to their spirit forms. And so, by classification of their spirit forms, first the four great human clans appeared, which were the pair Dong and Tong and the pair Sé and Mu. The Asha branched off from the Sé, and the Dru branched off from the Mu, making six great human clans. All Tibet became filled with the many that descended from them.

Moreover, since the father was of the monkey race, all Tibetan males have many unstable traits, such as not being content to just look with their eyes at any property and so forth, but needing to get it into their hands. Since the mother was of the rākṣasa rock-demoness race, all the females are very hateful and have evil tempers.

In brief, the human beings of Tibet descend from that couple, the monkey emanation of Mahākaruṇika and the rākṣasa rock-demoness emanation of Tārā. In particular, it is explained in the *Commentary on the Eulogy to the Exceptionally Noble*[170] that King Rupiṇi fled to Tibet and the human beings of Tibet descended from him. Although descent from him did occur, descent also occurred in a similar way from China, Mongolia, and so forth. Nevertheless, Tibetans mainly descended from the monkey and the rākṣasa rock-demoness. Thus my master taught.

Although human beings appeared in Tibet in that way, for a long time there were no kings and so forth. At some point while they were living as they liked in isolated groups, a son was born to King Pāṇḍava in India. He was endowed with the major marks, such as eyes that closed from the bottom like those of a bird, and fingers that were connected with webs. He was shown to a seer, who said that he would either vanquish all enemies or seize his father's kingdom.

This was too extreme, so the boy was given to subjects of the king who were mountain people, without acknowledging his identity. When they raised him, [111] he had many meritorious traits. He did not eat the leftovers of what they ate, the forest provided him cool shadows, protection from the wind, and so forth, the birds, monkeys, and other creatures offered him fruit and so forth, and light coiled about wherever he stayed.

When he grew up, he asked, "Whose son am I?" When he learned the story he became depressed. He wandered, passing from one forest, mountain, and so on, to the next, and arrived on the slope of Yarlha Shampo. Then he went to the peak of Sheldrak. At that time, many shepherds tending the cattle that were moved daily to graze on the grass saw a great light clearly descend on that mountain. The next day, many people, led by twelve knowledgeable Tibetans such as Thoklha Bönpo, came to that mountain to make offerings to the gods.

"Your offerings to the gods are good," the shepherds explained. "Last night a god took the form of light and descended at the edge of the pool where juniper is offered and cleansing done."

When the people who were making the offerings to the gods went there, at the edge of the pool they saw a young boy with the nature of light, who was endowed with the marks.

"Where have you come from?" they asked, and he pointed a finger at the sky.

"He has certainly descended from the sky. Let's invite him to be our leader!" the people exclaimed. They joined together all their pickaxes, shovels, and so forth, and made a throne. Because they carried him on the napes of their necks, the first king of Tibet was known as Nyatri Tsenpo, "Lord Enthoned on the Nape of the Neck."

Then, in the twenty-fifth generation, a manifestation of noble Samantabhadra called Lha Thothori Nyanshal appeared. At that time, as though riding the morning sunbeams, a jeweled chest descended onto the roof of the king's palace. Within it were the *Cintāmāṇidhāraṇī* of Uṣṇīsavimala, the *Seal of the Mudrā* written with four gold *oṃ* in a casket, the *One Hundred Rites of Renunciation and Fulfillment,* a crystal stupa, and so forth.[171]

Some say that a king called Mangpö Jé, who was in the heriditary line of the Dharma king Aśoka in India, had attached that chest to the tip of a victory banner and made offerings to it. On one occasion a great wind suddenly arose and the chest came to Tibet as though carried by the wind.

Some also say that the abbot Bodhisattva and the paṇḍita Lijin both came to Tibet, but since there was no written language and so forth, they were unable to spread the doctrine. [112] Bodhisattva Śāntarakṣita was known by the name Buddhirakṣita and Lijin was known as Lithesé. The two of them placed that chest in the hands of the king, prophesied, "In the future, your heriditary line will come to understand the meaning of this," and returned to India.

In any case, although the king and his retinue did not understand what it was, it was given the name "Awesome Secret" since incredible happiness and joy had arisen in Tibet just from its arrival. They made offerings to it with sacred libations and blue turquoise. Therefore, it is known that "the beginning of the excellent Dharma" was during the time of this king.

Then, after five generations, King Songtsen Gampo, who was an emanation of noble Avalokiteśvara, appeared. The Nepalese Queen, the Chinese Queen, and so forth invited many images such as the lords Akṣobhyavajra and Śākyamuni. The pair of Thönmi Saṃbhota and the paṇḍita Lijin translated the *One Hundred Rites of Renunciation and Fulfillment* and so forth. The king constructed the Rasa Trulnang Temple as a residence for those images, as well as many temples to subdue the borders, subdue beyond the borders, and so forth, thereby widely introducing the custom of the ten virtues.[172] However, because there were no ordained persons and so forth, who are the root of the doctine, this is known as merely the "introduction of the custom of the excellent Dharma." Thus my master taught.

Then, after five generations, King Trisong Deutsen, who was an emanation of Mañjuśrī, appeared. He invited many such as the Indian paṇḍita Bodhisattva and the teacher Padmasambhava, and constructed the Immutable and Spontaneous Temple of Samyé. Many were ordained, such as the "seven men on trial," and trained to be translators.[173] The 108 great translators, the 1,008 lesser ones, and so forth translated an inconceivable number of the excellent Mahayana and Hinayana teachings. Many centers for meditation practice and for explication and study were established. In brief, because the absolutely complete doctrine appeared, it is known that this king "spread and expanded the excellent Dharma." Thus my master taught.

After him, King Senalek, also known as Jingyön, built the temple of Karchung and performed vast actions for the doctrine.

Similarly, the sovereign Tri Ralpachen, about whom it had been prophesied, "A patron called Ralpachen will appear in a city called Dojok," controlled two-thirds of Jambudvīpa. [113] He constructed the temple of Ushang Do and invited many Indian paṇḍitas such as Jinamitra. Many translators, such as the trio of Ka, Chok, and Shang, translated much Dharma that had not been translated before.[174] They also applied a new standardized terminology to those texts that had been translated before but which had many different terms from individual regions, thereby making them easier to understand. This king performed incredible actions such as these for the doctine. The period up to this point is known as the "early spread of the doctrine." Thus my master taught.

After that king passed away, the one called Langdarma or Darma Udum served as king.[175] For several years he ruled the kingdom according to Dharma, but then an evil spirit possessed his heart. Most of the representations of the Three Jewels were taken to India. The image of lord Śākyamuni was hidden in the sand dunes. Some of the ordained were disrobed, some were killed, some were used as stools to mount horses, and so forth. Some were given shaman tambourines and sent to hunt wild beasts.

At that time, Lhalung Palgyi Dorjé, an emanation of the bodhisattva Vajrapāṇi, was meditating and living in the cliffs of Yerpa. When he saw monks hunting wild beasts, he asked why. They replied, "A wicked king has extinguished the doctrine, and we are powerless not to act in this way."

In accordance with a prophecy from the goddess Remati, he rubbed his white horse, cloak, spear, and so forth, with charcoal and made them black. He went to Samyé[176] and met a servant girl fetching water. He sent a message for an audience with the king and was told, "He has now gone to the grove of Lawa, so you may have an audience there."

King Langdarma had become tired of playing chess in the grove of Lawa and was reading the writing on the obelisk. Acting as though he were offering a prostration on meeting, it is said that Palgyi Dorjé stabbed the king with a spear or shot him with an iron arrow. In any case, he assassinated the king, who said, "This is either three years too early or three years too late," and died. Palgyi Dorjé made his horse, cloak, and spear white, then fled, saying, "I am the god called Namthel Karpo."

It was late in the day, so Palgyi Dorjé's pursuers did not catch him. He slept that night at Ogyal Thang, and arrived at Yerpa the next day. [Sitting inside a cave] he turned a vulture-skin cloak inside out and wore it. [114] When he bound the feet of a pigeon and forced it to fly about, the wings of the circling pigeon brought down all the soot and dust [in the cave], on the surface of which he released many beetles he was keeping in his fists. With pigeon feathers covering the ground, which was crisscrossed with beetle tracks, his pursuers all believed [he was dead] and left. But one pursuer placed a hand to Palgyi Dorjé's heart, realized that the heart was beating, and said, "This is the assassin of the king, the ghoul called Lhalung Palgyi Dorjé, but there is no point in adding my personal salt to the food in general,"[177] and left.

Unable to stay there, Palgyi Dorjé traveled toward Kham. In this way, that bodhisattva assassinated the wicked king, but the doctrine had severely declined and he was unable to restore it.

During that time, the three called Tsang, Yo, and Mar[178] had been living at Chuwori, but they were also unable to stay there. They loaded the Dharma texts of the monastic discipline and so forth on the back of a white female donkey and fled. First they traveled to the land of Mongolia, but were unable to spread the Buddhist doctrine because the language was different there. They stayed in Kham at either the rock cave of Dentik Shel or the rock cave of Anyen Shel.

At that time, a bodhisattva of the Bönpo spiritual family awakened to his past spiritual family, wished to enter the doctrine, and asked the three of them. They showed him the *One Hundred Parables on Deeds*[179] and so forth and said, "Look and see whether or not you are capable of being like this."

He had great faith in it. Lhalung Palgyi Dorjé was asked to fill the quota[180] when that man was ordained, and replied, "Since I assassinated the wicked king, I cannot fill the monk quota, but I will search for someone to fill it."

Two Chinese monks who were found filled the quota, and the man was fully ordained. He was given the name Gewa Rapsal, "Brilliant Virtue." Later, since his realization was very high, he was known as Gongpa Rapsal, "Brilliant Realization." Thus my master taught.

During that time, five or ten or so men of Central Tibet and Tsang traveled to Kham and took vows. They eventually returned to Central Tibet and Tsang and founded individual establishments of the sangha and so forth. However, because the doctrine had greatly declined, the teaching institutes were very bad. Nothing happened except just saying that such and such a commentary in black ink was probably used to explain such and such a root text in red ink. Practice was performed only with the most extreme hardship and difficulty. Although Chom Ral[181] distinguishes this as the "intermediate spread of the doctrine," [115] our tradition accepts it as "retrieving the embers of the doctrine from eastern Tibet" during the later spread of the doctrine.

Concerning how the embers of the doctrine were retrieved from western Tibet: when the king Langdarma died, no one but a young son survived him, and so for some time there was no king and so forth. Then the kingdom was divided between Yumten and Ösung. Tashi Tsekpa Pal and Kyidé Nyima Gön, the sons of Ösung, went to western Tibet. The first stayed at Lhatsé and so forth. The second traveled to Gugé and so forth and had two sons, Songé and Khoré. When ordained, Songé was called by the name Lha Lama Yeshé Ö. This Dharma king had been prophesied:

In the kingdom of glacial mountains,
in a family line called the royal line,
one called Yeshé Ö will appear.[182]

Yeshé Ö generously gave gold to seven intelligent boys, their seven servants, the servants of the seven servants, and so forth, and sent them to India to study Dharma. Most met with obstacles, and none benefited Tibet except for the great translator Rinchen Sangpo[183] and the lesser translator Lekpai Sherap. The great translator became a consummate expert, invited the three paṇḍitas with the word *kara* in their names, and so forth, and they translated countless Dharma texts of the sutras and the Vajrayana.

In a similar way, Lama Jangchup Ö invited Jowo Lhachik.[184] Jowo Lhachik introduced rituals where there were no rituals for the living, virtuous practices where there were no virtuous practices for the dead, dedication where there was no dedication of virtue, and so forth.

Similarly, Shangshung Gyalwai Sherap received the vows from the paṇḍita Dharmapāla and learned the practice and explanations. These were sequentially transmitted and became known as the "tradition of western Tibet."[185] And so forth.

In brief, the doctrine was completely translated by many translators and paṇḍitas. They established it through explanation and study, and spread the doctrine. Thus my master taught.

2. *An account of the Nine Cycles of the Path in particular*

These Nine Cycles of the Path are like the culled essence of all the Vajrayana practices that appeared in such a way in Tibet. Who brought them here to Tibet? Although Patsap Lotsāwa,[186] and later Gö Lotsāwa[187] and so forth, brought a few, only the venerable lord Drokmi completely possessed all nine. Moreover, this venerable lord Drokmi Lotsāwa [116] received the Precious Teaching of the Path with the Result, the Complete Path of Fierce Fire, Straightening the Crooked, and the Path of Padmavajra[188] from lord Gayadhara. He received the *Inconceivable*, the Instructions Received in Front of a Stupa, and *Realizing Coemergence* from the great adept Vīravajra. He received the Path of Indrabhūti from Prajñāgupta, the paṇḍita from Oḍḍiyāna,[189] and the Unwritten from the paṇḍita Amoghavajra.[190] In brief, because Drokmi pleased four powerful, expert and realized masters, and completely received the Nine Cycles of the Path, this venerable lord had the greatest Vajrayana oral instructions.

3. *The specific history of the Precious Teaching*

This consists of three topics:

a. The initial introduction of the tradition by lord Gayadhara
b. The spread of the tradition by lord Drokmi and his disciples in the interim
c. The final spread and expansion of the tradition by the venerable lords of Sakya, father and sons

a. The initial introduction of the tradition by lord Gayadhara

The great adept Avadhūtīpa had prophesied to lord Gayadhara, "Give these instructions to a monk vajra holder living on the banks of the Lohita River who received a prophecy from, and was graced by, noble Avalokiteśvara, and who has become the master of a king."

Realizing that the worthy disciple was in Tibet, Gayadhara traveled to Tibet to search for him. At that time he first met Purang Lotsāwa, who was called Shönu Sherap.[191] When Gayadhara gave several instructions, that translator became filled with faith and begged him for much Dharma. Gayadhara replied, "I have something of great importance to do in Central Tibet and Tsang, so I will go there for a while. I will come here again and give you the Dharma teachings you wish."

They agreed that Gayadhara would return in three months, the translator would offer fifty ounces of gold, and Gayadhara would give him the complete Dharma. Then Gayadhara left to slowly search for Drokmi.

During that time Drokmi was being honored by the three divine and venerable brothers of Lhatsé.[192] One night while staying in retreat at the Lhatsé cliffs, in this cave now said to be the cave of lord Gayadhara, Drokmi had an extremely significant dream such as he had never experienced before.

In the dream, lord Drokmi was staying in a three-story house. A terrifying black man about the size of the side of a mountain, who said he had come from the south, [117] arrived flying through the sky. He vomited a conch-shell-white lion from his mouth. It vomited a gold vajra from its mouth. From the center of the gold vajra came a gold vase filled with water. When this dissolved into Drokmi's body, an inconceivable primordial awareness of great bliss was born in his mindstream. Then three globes of light separated from his body and filled the three-story house with light. Again, everything melted into light and dissolved into Drokmi's own body. His body also melted into light and dissolved into his two feet. His two feet also vanished like a rainbow in the sky, and in that state he awoke from the dream.

This is called the "sealed dream of Drokmi," which was unwritten. Passed down in an oral transmission, it was not explained to anyone except when the Precious Teaching was taught. Thus my master taught.

When a mendicant's horn trumpet sounded at the closed door just after the dream had occurred, lord Drokmi sent someone to see what it was, because he was fond of Indian yogins. He was told, "There is an Indian mendicant wearing a red robe, who said, 'I have come from India to give you something, so I must have an audience. You must give me wealth.'"

Drokmi sent a reply in Sanskrit, "Since I am in strict retreat, we cannot meet. I have no wealth to give. Eat food!"

When excellent food and drink was given to him, the mendicant was very displeased and became angry. He would not even glance with his eyes at the food and drink. After they met, Drokmi asked the reason.

"You deeply offended me," Gayadhara replied. "You said many bad words."

Drokmi exclaimed, "I said, 'I have no wealth to give. Eat food!'"

"You didn't say that. This is what you said," Gayadhara replied. He put his right foot at his navel, extended his left leg, squeezed his waist with both hands, and said, "You said, 'Take your black hand,' and so forth."

When they scratched it on the ground and grammatically translated it, it turned out to be "Take your black hand, cover your ass, and get out!"

Drokmi fell into despair and wept, "I stayed that long in India. I met about eight paṇḍitas, and now I still don't know the proper grammar for even this!"

"You don't need to cry about it," the paṇḍita said. "The limits of grammar are like the ocean and no one knows them. You don't need all the minute subtleties. Even I don't know them. Just to know this much is exceptional. [118] In comparison to other translators, you are a great expert."

When they engaged in a Dharma discussion, and Drokmi realized that Gayadhara possessed the Vajrayana in general, specifically the mother tantras, among them Hevajra, and in particular the oral instructions of the Lord of Yogins, he was delighted. He remembered the previous prophecy by Khasarpaṇa, and touched Gayadhara's feet.[193]

First they examined the connection between teacher and disciple by means of the *Fifty Verses on the Master*,[194] and each was very pleased. As the first Dharma connection, Drokmi received the guruyoga of Amoghasiddhi.

He requested several further Dharma teachings and offered about ten ounces of gold. Then he begged Gayadhara for the Precious Teaching.

Gayadhara replied, "I made an agreement to go to the place of a translator in Purang, so I will go there for a while. I will use the gold, such as that given by him, for ritual feasts to accumulate the assemblies at the sacred places of India, and for making offerings and so forth to the masters. And I also need to get some Indian texts, so I will briefly return to India. I will come back in about three years at the latest, and at that time completely bestow the instructions. I will need about one hundred ounces of gold as a gift for the explanation of the tantras and four hundred ounces as a gift for the oral instructions. So you must accomplish that!"

Teacher and disciple made an oral agreement.

At that point Purang Lotsāwa arrived with five escorts and five horses. They invited Gayadhara and he left. During that time, lord Gayadhara had a red robe, due to which he was known as the honorable Red Mendicant or as the Red Cloaked Master, but he is not the same as the one in the lineage of Maksorma and so forth.[195] Thus my master taught.

Gayadhara stayed for a while at the place of Purang Lotsāwa and then traveled to India.

Then lord Drokmi was invited by a childless rich nomad couple at a place called Namthang Karpo in Padro. While Drokmi was staying in retreat at the Mangsang cliffs, Gayadhara was traveling again to Tibet on the road through Dromo, about five months after he had returned to India. A letter arrived that said, "The paṇḍita is coming, so come welcome him!"

To reassure the paṇḍita, the great master Drokmi sent a messenger to tell him that he would arrive to welcome him in two months, and happily rushed back to Lhatsé. [119] He requested support from the three divine and venerable brothers and others, and with many arrangements for welcome, and many articles fitting for a paṇḍita, such as a parasol, a throne, and a palanquin, and fine things for honoring him, the teacher and about thirty disciples departed.

Lord Drokmi and his disciples invited Gayadhara back through southern Latö in western Tsang, and because the translator and the paṇḍita were very famous, many came to honor them. Then, due to the large quantity of gold [that had been offered], they invited Gayadhara to northern Latö in western Tsang and traveled to Lhatsé by way of Gephu Pass.

How they slowly traveled to Mugulung and how Gayadhara taught the oral instructions and so forth is explained in detail later in this text.

Again Gayadhara returned to India to accumulate the assemblies and so forth using the gold offered by the great master.

At some point Gayadhara came again at the invitation of Gö Lotsāwa. Gö had been a disciple of the great master Drokmi, but later, when the teacher and disciple no longer got along very well, he tried to harm the great master. Gö even made many accusations about lord Gayadhara, saying these sort of things: "What kind of paṇḍita is this? He is a wandering mendicant who wants wealth and barely knows how to read Sanskrit."

Gö Lotsāwa decided to outdo them, and asked which paṇḍita was the most expert. The great paṇḍita Maitrīpa was very famous, so he went to invite him.[196] Gö poured gold into a complete human skull and made many designs on it with red ochre and indigo. As he traveled along, it was said to be a Tibetan ghost, and he had no problem on the outbound road. When he arrived at Dromo there was a paṇḍita being carried in a palanquin. Gö investigated who he was, and he replied, "I am Maitrīpa." Gö was extremely pleased and invited him.

By the blessing of Sé Mönlam Sherap[197] being willing to sacrifice his life for the sake of the master and so forth, they also traveled the inbound road without impediment.

When the old disciples from before recognized the paṇḍita and said, "Gayadhara has arrived!" Gö cried, "The lord has lied to me!"

"Are you not seeking Dharma?" lord Gayadhara replied. "I am more expert in Dharma than Maitrīpa."

Gö had been pleased with the instructions and had finished requesting several Dharma teachings; so he invited Gayadhara, because it would have been difficult to reject him. Gayadhara gave many teachings, primarily the instructions of the Ārya tradition of Guhyasamāja, the commentaries on the tantra, and so forth, which they translated.[198] [120]

On one occasion the translator and the paṇḍita were both invited by Sur Shākjung.[199] While they were staying at Shong, Drokmi came to meet Gayadhara, and the paṇḍita was extremely pleased. When he made Drokmi translate the Dharma teachings he was giving, Gö couldn't stand it and said, "The two of us must just take turns and translate."

The paṇḍita replied, "I was hoping to benefit you. Between the two of you there is a great difference in skill. If you translate, Drokmi will identify many errors. Therefore, bad things will be said about you. If you are not afraid of that, you alone may translate."

Therefore, it would appear that Gö had slightly less ability in translating. Thus my master taught.

When Gayadhara and Gö went and stayed at Tsongdü Gurmo, lord Drokmi again came to visit and said, "The lord has broken his promise."[200]

Lord Gayadhara replied, "With that, your own sacred commitments will be damaged. Gö is satisfied with the scriptures and has not even inquired about the oral instructions."

Gayadhara gave the Hevajra initiation to lord Drokmi alone and in secret. When Gö heard in the morning and expressed his disappointment, lord Gayadhara replied, "Just the water from my vase is preferable to the complete four initiations of another," and gave him water from the vase. Gayadhara scolded Gö, saying, "At first you were a disciple of Drokmi, and so it is not right to compete with him now. Not only that, didn't you complain a lot about me, too, saying, 'He just barely knows how to read Sanskrit,' and so forth?"

"That was not disrespect for you," Gö said, "I spoke hoping to harm Drokmi. Nevertheless." And he offered much gold and confessed. It was extremely upsetting. Thus my master taught.

During that trip lord Gayadhara was known by the name Prince Tringyi Shukchen.[201] It has been said that he is the object of a eulogy in the *Eulogy to the Eighty-Four Great Adepts:*

> He was from the royal caste,
> skilled in the fields of knowledge,
> and eliminated doubts
> by asking a deity in the sky.
> I prostrate to that master
> known as Tringyi Shukchen.[202]

Gö made many offerings of gold and so forth. Gayadhara traveled to India once more.

At some point lord Gayadhara was invited again by Gyijo Lotsāwa Dawai Özer.[203] On this occasion, Gayadhara probably thought it was now acceptable to teach because the great master Drokmi had already passed away. He also completely gave the Path with the Result to Gyijo. While there appear to be miscellaneous texts concerning the prediction of practice and so forth that were transmitted from Gyijo, there does not appear to be a transmission these days. Thus my master taught. [121]

During that time, Gayadhara was invited by Nyö Jungpo, Yönten Drak[204] by name, who requested much Dharma. While staying at his place, the signs of dying appeared to the paṇḍita. Hearing that both Sé and Rok[205] were in Kharak Thöphu, he said, "I have two spiritual grandsons in Thöphu. Take me there!"

"No one is there except two disciples of Drokmi," Nyö replied. "Since we are your own disciples, lord, you should stay right here."

"That won't help. Take me!" he said, and they brought him there.

When they arrived there, Gayadhara said to both Sé and Rok, "All my sons, be diligent in meditation! Going back and forth between India and Tibet, I have not had much time to meditate, but when a mantra practitioner dies, he dies like this."

When Gayadhara ejected his consciousness from the crown of his head, a white light about the size of a large pot emerged, inside of which was a very clear figure of Hevajra with eight faces and sixteen arms that was about eighteen inches in size. With sounds, lights, and a rain of flowers, it went to the west, seen by all the people at Barthang.

In brief, as special qualities, this expert and realized master Gayadhara had achieved stability in the creation stage, possessed the magical ability of emanating such things as single and multiple forms, was able to take materials from within a burnt offering while the flames were blazing, was able to leave his vajra and bell in space, and so forth.

Gayadhara had about five translators as disciples, beginning with Purang Lotsāwa and ending with Nyö Lotsāwa. While it appears that he made about four trips to Tibet, in the present account these are treated as three, with the initial journey to Purang and the invitation by the great master Drokmi counted as one. In brief, this expert and realized master was extremely kind to Tibet. Thus my master taught.

b. *The spread of the tradition by lord Drokmi and his disciples in the interim*

This consists of two topics:

1) The great master Drokmi's exceptional qualities
2) How followers came to him

1) *The great master Drokmi's exceptional qualities*

The three sons of King Tashi Tsekpa Pal were Pal Dé, Ö Dé, and Kyi Dé, who were known as the "Three Dé of Mé" or the "Three Divine and Venerable Brothers of Lhatsé." When they were pondering, "We need a royal priest. Who would be suitable?" they heard that the spiritual father Lotön Dorjé Wangchuk and the spiritual son Chetsün Sherap Sengé were maintaining the doctrine during that time at Shalu Gyengong.[206] [122] They offered a letter saying that they needed a royal priest to be sent, and Lotön and Chetsün replied, "That is excellent, because it will be a cause for the increase of our doctrine."

They gladly sent the trio of Gya Shākya Shönu, Sé Yeshé Tsöndrü, and Nyang Dorjé Gyaltsen, with five fully ordained monks, five novices, and two lay practitioners as their attendants. They stayed in the temple of Drompa Gyang, accomplished many ordinations, and established a great institute of the sangha.

During that time, the great master Drokmi was born in the area called Mangkhar Chudé.[207] He was known as Drokmi, "Man of Drok," because he was born into the family line called Drok, in the Jeu clan. His ordination name was Shākya Yeshé, derived from the names of the abbot and the teacher.

While Drokmi was engaged in listening and reflection, the patrons and priests all decided, "We now have nothing but just the explanation and study of the monastic code. We cannot do without the complete doctrine here. So it would be best to send several knowledgeable and capable monks to India to study the Dharma."

The trio of abbot and teachers assembled the entire sangha. The three offered food and drink from their own hands and conferred incredible gifts and honors. They spoke of their previous discussion and then asked, "Who is capable of going on such a trip?"

The trio of Drokmi Shākya Yeshé, Leng Shākya Tsöndrü, and Tak Yeshé Shönu accepted, but no one else. The abbot, teachers, and patrons were all pleased and gave many praises, honors, and compliments. The advice they gave the three was: "Study the monastic code because it is the root of the doctrine, the Vehicle of the Perfections because it is the heart, and the Vajrayana because it is the quintessence. Then return!" The patrons also agreed to provide whatever awards and services were fitting when the three returned after learning those subjects.

At that time, Gya Shākya Shönu was apparently somewhat impetuous and gave preferential treatment to Leng. He furtively gave him ten ounces of gold, a hundred musk pods, and a donkey-load of salt, and quickly sent him off in secret. He gave strict instructions: "Now I am doing retreat and no one is to come within its boundaries." [123]

The trio were supposed to use Dharma supplies and so forth in common and travel together. But because the abbot had already sent Leng ahead, Tak and Drokmi were left without a patron. At that point, with great determination Sé Yeshé Tsöndrü gathered all the patrons, such as the three divine and venerable brothers, and told the story. When he asked for donations, they all gave many praises, honors, and compliments, many individually agreed to offer this much or that much, and for two months the offerings were made. During that period the great master Drokmi made a retreat and studied the vernacular with an itinerant Indian mendicant who was posing as a paṇḍita. He learned enough so that it was unnecessary to employ a translator for their immediate activities.

Then Drokmi and Tak combined the incredible offerings of wealth they had received and took more than one hundred ounces of gold, about a thousand musk pods, and other things such as tails. They each had an attendant, and with the itinerant mendicant making five, they set off on the road. Because the auspicious land of Mangyul is the route traveled without impediment by all translators, they went there. The water was pleasant, and they stayed for about two months.

Then, since Leng was also there, they eventually traveled together with him to Nepal. They met the eldest of the four Nepalese Phamthingpa brothers, who was known as the Newar Jaḥ Hūṃ or as Śāntabhadra.[208] They listened to grammar, epistemology, and so forth, as well as many Dharma teachings of secret mantra. The great master Drokmi was able to understand Dharma in the Sanskrit language quite well.

They asked the master Śāntabhadra, "We are thinking of going to India. Which paṇḍita is most expert?"

He replied, "In that case, because it will bring the auspicious connections into alignment to begin with, make offerings at the Mahābodhi of the Vajrāsana. Then, of the 'experts at the six gates' of the temple of Vikramaśīla, the paṇḍita guarding the east gate is Śāntipa, who is also my master. He is also a second Omniscient One in the kāliyuga, so you should rely on him."

Śāntabharda even sent his younger brother, the Newar Adepa as their guide, and they traveled to the Vajrāsana. They made prostrations, offerings, and prayers, and the omens were also quite excellent.

Then Drokmi traveled to Vikramaśīla. Concerning the "experts at the six gates": [124] at the eastern gate was Śāntipa, whom he primarily questioned about grammar and epistemology. At the southern gate was the expert and realized master Vāgīśvarakīrti, who had been directly graced by venerable Tārā. At the western gate was Prajñākara, whom Drokmi primarily questioned about the non-Buddhist philosphical tenets. At the northern gate was the venerable lord Nāropa, whom he primarily questioned about the Vajrayana. The two central pillars were Ratnavajra and Jñānaśrī, who were called "the pillars," but they were not more expert than the others.[209]

Among them, Śāntipa was known as a second Omniscient One. This is the reason: he was an expert born to the west in Oḍḍiyāna, and while he was living there his chosen deity had prophesied, "You must go to Magadha without asking anyone. Vast benefit will come to the Buddhist doctrine."

In accordance with the prophecy, Śāntipa loaded many volumes on two elephants. When he left with a small retinue, an elder of the sangha in that land dreamed that he was told, "The entire Buddhist doctrine has gone to Magadha."

The sangha was immediately gathered, and when they searched in all directions they found the teacher Śāntipa leaving with his disciples. They understood that the dream had been a sign of this. No matter how much they tried to delay him they were unable to do so, and he traveled to Vikramaśīla and did what was to be done for the doctrine. Thus my master taught.

Drokmi primarily relied on that great expert and studied all fields of knowledge. He also received a Dharma connection from each of the others and stayed for eight years.

Then Drokmi decided to return to Tibet, and he went to visit the Khasarpaṇa residing in the Devīkoṭa ravine to the south because it was a very famous shrine.[210] If one kneeled and joined the palms of the hands on the top of the head, a position called "stuck to the earth," and made prayers for seven days without any consideration of food, drink, and so forth, Khasarpaṇa would actually grant a prophecy about the desired goal. The great master Drokmi did so, and Khasarpaṇa prophesied, "You will be graced on the road by an adept who holds the lineage of the Lord of Yogins.

In the land of Tibet a master possessing the complete instructions of the Lord of Yogins will come to deliver the oral instructions to your door. Practice them and eliminate any further inclination to search for other masters and oral instructions." [125]

Then, traveling through the middle of a dense jungle called Kuwa Grove in southern India, Drokmi heard the sound of a monk's staff.[211] Thinking, "A village is here," he looked. He saw a very handsome monk in the three Dharma robes and carrying an alms bowl and a monk's staff touching the trunk of a tree with the staff. A woman's arm adorned with gold bracelets extended from the tree as far as the shoulder and was offering nectar into his alms bowl.

Drokmi was totally amazed and an uncontrived faith arose in his mind. He decided that this was the adept prophesied by Avalokiteśvara and made prostrations and circumambulations. He placed the monk's feet on top of his head and asked to be graced. He was accepted and given a gift of nectar that had the taste of a hundred flavors. A meditative concentration was also born in his mindstream. And he saw signs of attainment when the monk decided to leave, such as the leaves of the tree drawing together and offering dew drops to cool his face.

"To instruct you, I need to give an initiation," the handsome monk said.

"I received initiation from the Newar Jaḥ Hūṃ and from Śāntipa," Drokmi replied.

"For my Dharma you need my initiation," the monk said, and in a village at the edge of Kuwa Grove he bestowed a Hevajra initiation for three nights. He also gave Drokmi the tantra and various instructions.

When Drokmi begged him for much Dharma, the monk replied, "My provisions are provided by the great, medium, and lesser nonhuman beings, so I have no use for wealth. But the auspicious connections are crucial in the Vajrayana. Therefore, if you need oral instructions, rush to your country and bring back wealth!"

"Master, where will you be staying?" Drokmi asked.

"I had thought to go to the glorious mountains of Śrīparvata,"[212] he replied. "But a king called Canaka has been begging me for three years, so I will stay in his palace for seven years.[213] You should also come meet me there."

That great adept was Prajñendraruci, "Beautiful with Powerful Wisdom," a disciple of the teacher Durjayacandra. He is the one known by the secret name Vīravajra. Thus my master taught.

When Drokmi and his companions were then about to return to Tibet, Tak Lotsāwa said, "I'll stay and perform circumambulations at the Vajrāsana. I'm not going to Tibet." But he finally went when the two of them insisted. [126]

The three traveled to Drompa Lhatsé. The abbot, teachers, sangha, and patrons arranged incredible honors, such as a welcoming reception. The great master Drokmi had become a consummate expert and Leng had become an average one. But Tak Lotsāwa knew nothing except how to recite the *Heart Sutra* in the Indian language. When asked, "Why does Drokmi know this much, while you don't know anything except that?" it is said that he replied, "He went off elsewhere carrying a skull-cup. I became devoted to the Mahābodhi of the Vajrāsana[214] and stayed doing circumambulations."

However, by virtue of his pure moral discipline and the blessings of the Mahābodhi that had entered him, Tak Lotsāwa established a great center of the Sangha known as Takdé.

Leng said, "Here in Tibet, where the people are as stupid as cattle, no distinction is made between experts and fools, so I'm going back to India."

He traveled again to India. He did became an expert, but it seems that his activities were not very great. Thus my master taught.

The great master Drokmi had become incomparable, so that even the abbot and the teachers received the Vajrayana through his kindness. The three divine and venerable brothers also took him as their master. The daughter of King Pal Dé called Lhachik Dzeden Öchak was offered as a support for Drokmi's realization of coemergent primordial awareness. And her brother Lhatsün Kali was offered as his attendant. Drokmi stayed for a while at the Lhatsé cliffs, practicing, working for the benefit of others, and so forth.

Then Drokmi announced, "I am going to travel again and request instructions from the great adept Vīravajra. You should offer gold and so forth. I will give you the instructions I obtain there."

Pleased and happy, everyone offered much gold. Father Drokmi and mother Lhachik took it and traveled together to India. They met the master staying in the palace of King Canaka. Drokmi offered wonderful things such as gold and musk, and also Lhachik. Lhachik acted as the initiation support for Drokmi's request of the Hevajra initiation, and the extensive initiation was given. Similarly, Vīravajra also bestowed initiations in thirteen mandalas of unexcelled yoga tantra, together with the oral instructions. Drokmi received all the profound instructions transmitted and passed down from Ḍombi Heruka. Furthermore, he received the ripening initiations, the liberating guidance, the explanations, the entrustments of pure awareness, and about fifty ritual permissions, practices, and so forth, for about eighty great tantras, with the *Tantra Trilogy* foremost, and one hundred and sixty small tantras such as the *Rali*.[215] [127] He also received many esoteric instructions. They stayed for four years.

Then, when Drokmi and Lhachik decided to return to Tibet, the master Vīravajra said, "A long time has passed. For three months the two of you should do some enjoyable activities and, to lift your spirits, you should go see the sights." During their travels they saw three great sights.

The First Sight

Once they saw a large crowd that had gathered but had suddenly become terrified and was scattering. When they asked the reason, everyone told them in despair, "King Canaka has taken control of many kingdoms and is very famous. So the infinite armies of fifteen kings such as the western king Bhojantahara have arrived at a place five days' journey away. It is the consequence of this king's great deceit, cunning, and guile. Now it is certain that we will die and this city will be vacated!"

When Drokmi and Lhachik told the master about the armies of the fifteen kings, he said, "This King Canaka is devoted and faithful to the Three Jewels, so he has great merit. Nothing bad will happen."

However, everyone else (except for some few who were endowed with clairvoyance) was certain they would be annihilated and said so unanimously, so that even the king became dejected.

When Canaka entered into battle, a battle station for the king to stay in was made on the back of a gigantic elephant. Many representations of the Three Jewels were placed in the center of it. An elaborate array of offerings was arranged in front of these and ten monks and ten brahmins presented the offerings. The king sat in front of them on a throne. To the right and left his retinue were stationed, such as the royal turban-bearers and nose-wipers. A great strongman was positioned on top of the elephant's head holding a huge bronze mace made from twenty loads of Magadha bronze.[216] Many of the retinue were stationed on the elephant's neck, such as ten strongmen to cast out iron hooks and ten directors above them.

Around the central elephant stood twenty-five battle elephants and around them, fifty ordinary elephants, each mounted by fifty soldiers. [128] Outside of this horde of elephants were the chariots, outside of them was the cavalry, and outside of them was the surrounding infantry. With an infinite horde of these four kinds of troops, the king entered into battle.

Then, because it was the custom for the two kings to fight first and for the others not to battle until that fight had been decided, Canaka and the fierce opposing king fought for about half the day, but there was no obvious victory on either side. When King Canaka's elephant was exhausted and about to collapse, Canaka called out the name of the great adept Vīravajra three times in a loud voice. After that, he said to the strongman, "The time has come for you to summon your strength. If you can win this battle, I will give you my daughter by the senior queen and all the territory that is newly acquired."

The strongman smashed the great bronze mace into the center of the forehead of the opposing king's elephant and killed it. The forces of the fifteen kings were defeated at that very moment. Canaka and his retinue were victorious in battle, and all the minor kingdoms were made into subjects. However, Canaka had become weary of samsara, and as soon as the forces were dispersed he passed the kingdom to his eldest son. With a retinue of about one hundred and fifty, including Canaka himself, five queens, seven ministers, and individual attendants for each member of the retinue, Canaka boarded a ship carrying provisions that would last for fifty years, and left saying he was going to an island in the ocean to meditate on the oral instructions given by Vīravajra.

The Second Sight

Drokmi and Lhachik saw a young girl eight years of age, who said she was a ḍākinī of primordial awareness and who cast off shame and made herself naked. She did and said whatever she thought, dancing in space and stamping the earth in dance.

The Third Sight

Drokmi and Lhachik saw a mad elephant charge from the depths of the jungle and lay waste to all the trees. It picked up creatures with the end of its trunk and killed them by throwing them into the distance. When it was about to destroy many villages, it picked up the eight-year-old girl with the end of its trunk, circled a village, and placed her on top of a stupa. The girl's blessings cured even that elephant of madness, and it returned to the depths of the jungle. The girl vanished like a rainbow in the sky. [129]

As a Dharma teaching upon departure, Drokmi also heard the Path with the Result without the root text.

Drokmi and Lhachik returned to Tibet, and Drokmi founded the center of Mugulung. While he was mostly staying at the cliffs of Lhatsé, he first met lord Gayadhara as explained previously. Later he invited Gayadhara to Lhatsé by way of Gerphu. When Drokmi asked him to begin the Teaching, Gayadhara replied, "A special place is required for that."

When they searched they heard the sound "mumu" from a stream and Gayadhara said, "Let's investigate the sound of this, and I will teach the Dharma where it dissolves into the earth."

They investigated and discovered the stream of Mangkhar. They traveled along it as far as Mugulung, where it dissolved. "*Mukta* in Sanskrit means 'liberation,'" Gayadhara said, and they stayed there.

Gayadhara had agreed to stay in Tibet for five years and completely bestow the Precious Teaching. Drokmi was to offer five hundred ounces of gold. But while Drokmi was listening to the oral instructions, Gayadhara said, "Three years have passed, and I'm leaving now."

When Drokmi mentioned the earlier promise, Gayadhara replied, "If the Dharma teachings were not completed, I would stay. Why should I stay when the Dharma has been completed? You may reduce your gold and make the offering."

"If I reduce the amount of gold, it would damage the auspicious connections," Drokmi thought. "So I will offer exactly what I said before."

He did not have quite enough, but since Surpoché[217] was very famous in lower Tsang at that point, very prosperous, and also an old former disciple, Drokmi sent him a message: "I will give you Dharma. Bring wealth!"

Surpoché had been invited by Surchung to Sampa Wadong in Shang and was staying in retreat practicing Yangdak[218] when the message arrived. For several days no one delivered the message. Then, during a break, he received the message. Others said, "It is an obstacle to the practice. You should stay."

But Surpoché replied, "The reason I was practicing was to strive for attainment. The root of attainment is the Dharma. In general, lord Drokmi has great instructions. In particular, a paṇḍita called Gayadhara arrived before, and it is said that Drokmi has been listening to many Dharma teachings, so I am certain that he definitely has profound instructions. This is not an obstacle. It is an attainment!" Surpoché happily left Surchungpa[219] as the leader for the remaining practices.

Surpoché had subdued the nāga of Sampa Wadong, and the nāga had said, "Take out gold until some that resembles creatures appears!"

Some said it was taken from that same place and some said it was taken from the ocean. [130] The nāga offered much gold and Surpoché himself took many offerings, including a hundred ounces of gold, and traveled to Mugulung. The great master Drokmi was also pleased, and when he gave several instructions such as *Saroruha's Method for Accomplishment* and the *Inconceivable,* Surpoché said, "This old guy's Mental Series has been enriched by the oral instructions of the great master."[220]

When briars grew in the autumn, Surpoché carried briarwood on his cloak for Drokmi. People exclaimed, "The briars will ruin your cloak. Please don't do that!"

While performing the work, Surpoché replied, "If Surpoché is not ruined, the cloak will not be ruined," and showed his devotion in many ways.

The great master Drokmi poured all five hundred ounces of gold into a basin in front of the paṇḍita and at the same time made incredible offerings of about a thousand musk pods, about two hundred bright six-foot-long white tails and a hundred black tails, and others such as cloth and silk. Because there was much too much gold, Gayadhara was afraid it was an illusion and did not believe it. He took the gold and went to where most of the people were in Mangkhar Drilchen.

"What is this?" he asked, and showed it to them.

"This is gold," they all agreed. "And of the different kinds of gold, the most excellent kind is like this."

Gayadhara was delighted and said to Drokmi, "What do you need now?"

"If you still have some remaining instructions for this Precious Teaching," he replied, "please bestow them."

"I don't have anything left now," Gayadhara said. "You are not the type who needs this, but it is my custom."

Gayadhara hung a scroll painting of Pañjaranātha[221] on his back, put his rosary around his neck, held a sacrificial cake on the top of his head, and swore an oath that he had no remaining instructions. Then he asked, "Now what do you need?"

Drokmi said over and over, "I don't need anything," but Gayadhara would not listen.

Some accounts say that the great master Drokmi thought, "Will the lord not accept just this?" and said, "In that case, I need you to not give these instructions to anyone except me." Gayadhara was very pleased, thinking that the great master valued the Dharma because he understood the profound key points of the instructions, and gave his approval.

But some accounts say that when Drokmi spoke in that way, the paṇḍita replied, "I don't completely understand your request. What you said about not giving it to others and so forth slightly disrupts the auspicious connections. No benefit will come from your heriditary lineage, but your Dharma lineage will flourish." [131] So it also appears that Gayadhara spoke as Nāropa did to Marpa.[222] Thus my master taught.

Similarly, when the Path with the Result had been completed, lord Gayadhara also gave some prophecies and interpreted the meaning of the extremely significant dream that had come to the great master Drokmi. The interpretation was as follows: The three-story house symbolized the three realms of samsara. The black man who came from the south was the Lord of Yogins. The conch-shell-white lion vomited from his mouth was conch-shell white because it symbolized the white-robed lord Gayadhara, who was an emanation of the compassion of the Lord of Yogins. It was a lion because it symbolized that he was a lion of speech that no one could withstand. The gold vajra vomited from its mouth symbolized the Precious Teaching, the heart of the Vajrayana doctrine. The gold vase filled with water that came from it symbolized the unbroken four oral transmissions of the unceasing stream of initiation and so forth. Its dissolving into the top of Drokmi's head meant that such instructions would be passed down to lord Drokmi himself. That three lights came from his body and filled the three-story house meant that his three types of disciples who fully received the scriptures, fully received the instructions, and reached attainment, together with their disciples, would remove the darkness of the three realms. That everything melted into light and dissolved into the great master meant that their minds and the mind of the great master would blend together. That the great master himself dissolved into his two feet and that they also vanished in the sky meant that he would have two sons but that they would pass away and the heriditary lineage would disappear.

Paṇḍita Gayadhara happily returned to India. The great master Drokmi was totally satisfied with the instructions. In accordance with the prophecy by Khasarpaṇa, he eliminated the inclination to search for other masters and instructions.

On one occasion while Drokmi was living in Mugulung alternately practicing and benefiting others, the master Vīravajra arrived flying through the sky.

"Why have you come?" Drokmi asked.

"I have come to see the kingdom of glacial peaks and to resolve some of your doubts, my son," Vīravajra replied, and stayed for about a month. He composed a method for accomplishment, the *Blazing Jewel*.[223] One morning he said, "In the western land of Oḍḍiyāna the ḍākinīs are holding a ritual feast using the flesh of one who has been a brahmin for seven lifetimes. I will go there." [132]

When Drokmi offered him much gold, Vīravajra said, "I have no need for that." He quickly flew into the sky riding a sunbeam and departed.

On another occasion a paṇḍita arrived flying through the sky. "Who are you?" Drokmi asked.

"I am called the sovereign Maitrīpa," he replied. "I have come from the glorious mountains of Śrīparvata to give you some instructions. Keep it a secret and don't tell anyone."

Maitrīpa gave many profound instructions such as the initiation of Vajrayoginī. They did everything in secret during that time, but the secret slipped out and, passed from one person to the next, it became widely known that lord Maitrīpa had come to Mugulung. When many people came wanting to meet him, lord Maitrīpa flew into the sky and quickly traveled to Śrīparvata.

In this way, many expert and realized masters delivered oral instructions to Drokmi's door. He ripened and liberated many fortunate disciples. Lhachik Dzeden Öchak bore two sons named Indra and Dorjé.

After Drokmi had completed with that body everything beneficial to disciples, he passed into nirvana in a way consistent with Gayadhara's prophecy: "On the basis of a slight dependently arisen connection, you will not attain buddhahood in this life without abandoning the body."

It is accepted that Drokmi lived to the age of eighty-two or, according to some, ninety-five years. In any case, at the point of passing away he made a last testament that said, "I will enter again into this body and actualize the citadel of mahāmudrā, so you must not even touch this corpse of mine for seven days! If you act in this way, I will accomplish the great goal. However, you'll make a mistake, won't you?"

Accordingly, the consort and sons did as Drokmi had ordered, but there was a paternal relative of Drokmi, a malevolent man called Drilchen Tangawa who had turned his back on the doctrine of actions and their results. With his eye on the inheritance of the great master, he came there and made inquiries in the guise of affectionate concern. When they explained about the last testament, he said, "That is impossible. Where is there even a story about a dead person returning again? When left for that many days the corpse will rot and bring disgrace to the master himself. Burn it now!"

But they would not listen. So he said, "In that case, since there are this many of us who are paternal relatives, astrological advice would be indispensable." [133]

He influenced the astrologer with secret bribes. So the astrologer said, "If the corpse is not burned by the morning of the fourth day it will be very bad for the paternal relatives, the consort, and the sons."

Some disciples also said, "With the great master no longer living, nothing is more valuable than the consort and sons," and moved the body without permission. Its warmth had not faded, but the astrologer gave many vague explanations, saying, "It happens like this with some types of corpses." It was brought to where the Black Mausoleum of Drokmi is now, and cremated.

The worst gossip claimed that that paternal relative also burned the two sons in a fire of the bundles of offerings, but that does not seem to be true.

In any case, when they had finished doing these bad things and seven days had passed, the nonconceptual primordial awareness of the great master Drokmi's mind took the form of a white light about the size of a large pot and, with sounds, lights, and a rain of flowers, arrived in search of the body. When it was not found, it went briefly to the spot where the body had been and departed into the open sky.

Though Drokmi did not accomplish the sublime attainment of mahāmudrā in dependance on that very body, in the intermediate state he actualized the citadel of a vajra holder of the thirteenth spiritual level. Thus my master taught.

The paternal relative then forced even the consort and sons to obey him. The disciples became extremely upset with each other about whose fault everything was. Due to the breaking of the sacred commitments in that way, the consort Dzeden Öchak also passed away.

Drokmi's son [Dorjé] fell into a morbid depression and died. The noble son Indra did not want to stay in the area and traveled in the direction of eastern Tibet. At Chökhor Shongma he met Nyan Lotsāwa.[224] They engaged in a discussion of Dharma and the noble son Indra barely won, but he made many unnecessary harsh comments. Nyan Lotsāwa became angry and put a fatal curse on him.

Then Indra traveled on. When he arrived in the vicinity of Rongmu, many came to make offerings, saying, "He is the son of Drokmi." The bundles were piled up in a circle and, fearing that thieves would take them, Indra slept in the middle. He fastened the straps of the loads around his waist and went to sleep after placing a butter lamp beside him. The flames spread, the bundles were consumed in the fire, and he died.

As was clear in Drokmi's dream, it did not turn out very well for his sons, the hereditary lineage, and so forth, [134] but his disciples, their disciples, and the upholders of the lineage have spread and expanded the precious doctrine up to the present day. Thus my master taught.

2) *How followers came to the great master Drokmi*

Since this venerable lord Drokmi had great instructions and great fame, he was relied upon and bowed to by most of his contemporaries, both the influential and the weak. But he valued the Dharma highly and was extremely strict about bestowing the oral instructions, saying, "I don't explain Dharma to four ears," and did not teach the profound Dharma instructions from his one cushion to more than one other. He said, "No Dharma for more than six ears," and did not teach most secret-mantra Dharma from his cushion to more than three. Because of such restrictions, other than having Dharma connections with him, it would appear that no one received his complete Dharma.

Drokmi's three main types of disciples were:

a) Disciples who fully received the scriptures
b) Disciples who fully received the oral instructions
c) Disciples who reached attainment

a) *Disciples who fully received the scriptures*

Five disciples fully received the scriptures. Gyijang Ukarwa of Lhatsé, Draktsé Sonak of Shang, Ré Könchok Gyalpo of Trangok, and Khön Könchok Gyalpo of Sakya were the four known as "the four who fully received the scriptures earlier." Master Ngaripa was known as "the one who fully received the scriptures later."

(1) *Gyijang Ukarwa*

According to the account of the followers of the Path with the Result, Gyijang Ukarwa is said to have offered a milk cow and a plot of land that could be plowed by a bull in one day; and he appears to have been a native of present-day Drompa Lhatsé. However, he was actually born near where the great local spirit known as Shakra Lhatsé lived in Kham. Gyijang Ukarwa studied the *Tantra Trilogy* under the great master Drokmi. In particular, he was expert in the *Sampuṭa.* He also received many instructions from Indian masters such as the Red Mendicant and Nakpo Rozin. He was one who drew his strength from the protector.[225]

Gyijang Ukarwa agreed to offer sixty ounces of gold to Drokmi as a Dharma gift and traveled to Kham. At Tsongkha Tsongön in the eastern Tibetan region of Domé he gained the position of master to the king of Tsongkha. Many offerings came to him, but when he started to leave to offer a hundred ounces of gold and countless similar things to the great master Drokmi, the king would not release him. Gyijang Ukarwa sent a person with the offerings and said, [135] "As proof that this was received, please give me a blessed object that I know about."

Some of the offerings were lost and no more than about sixty ounces of gold were delivered into Drokmi's hands, but the accompanying letter was delivered without obstacle. The great master was delighted and, in return, sent Gyijang Ukarwa the gift of a painted image of Hevajra that had been the meditation object of Gayadhara. Thus my master taught.

(2) *Draktsé Sonak of Shang*

Draktsé Sonak was the eldest son of a rich merchant called Tsongpön Pal in a place called Draktsé in Shang. Draktsé Sonak had a fine physique, a sharp mind, and great knowledge. The merchant made many trips for business in the region of western Tibet and had Dharma connections with the great master Drokmi. One time the merchant came to the great master and said, "I have a son of fine physique and sharp mind who I had thought might receive Dharma from the great master. However, we have a local chieftain who gave his daughter to him to cherish, and he is with her. If it were possible to part him from her and bring him here, could it happen?"

"Wonderful!" Drokmi replied. "But he doesn't have to separate from the woman. She may also be admitted into the Dharma. Bring both of them, husband and wife!"

When the merchant told the couple, they were delighted and traveled to Mugulung carrying countless things to offer. They held an incredible Dharma banquet and so forth. They also presented countless offerings to the master and the consort. Drokmi bestowed the complete explanation of the *Tantra Trilogy* and also various instructions such as the *Inconceivable*.

They again returned to their home, and Sonak accomplished some benefit for others such as his own relatives, producing about ten disciples who fully received the tantras. He mostly concentrated on meditation. Thus my master taught.

(3) *Ré Könchok Gyalpo of Trangok*

At a place called Trangok in Phulchung, Ré Könchok Gyalpo was the eldest of six, the five sons and one daughter of a very rich man of the Ré clan. [136] He had a good disposition and was skilled in serving his parents and so forth. He became a disciple of one of Surpoché's disciples and also knew several Nyingma practice activities and so forth. He was the type of person who also performed some ritual feasts.

He once gave food and drink to some mendicants who arrived at Trangok and then asked them, "You who are called yogins travel everywhere and so you have much information. Who is regarded as a good master in Central Tibet and Tsang now?"

They replied, "By virtue of the spread of the doctrine now, there are many everywhere who think, 'I am an expert. I am good.' But everyone agrees that Drokmi Lotsāwa is the one beyond all comparison. Since he is near you, do you know a lot about him?"

A great joy arose in Ré's mind at just hearing the name of the great master. He carefully investigated the story. When he asked his parents about going to Drokmi, they said, "This son of ours has good character and respects his parents. When he rattles the drum during the practice activities, all of us in the area feel pleasant and contented. He would seem to have a good propensity for Dharma, so this is right."

He loaded much wealth on five good horses, took five servants armed with bows and arrows, mounted a fine horse himself, put on a fine turquoise ear ornament, and traveled to Mugulung. When he first met Drokmi's consort, she said, "You seem like the dear child of a rich man, who has run away for the Dharma. What has happened?"

Ré told his story, and she exclaimed, "Wonderful! Excellent! I will be your helper."

Ré met the master and presented vast offerings, such as the ear ornament and the five fine horses with the loads. He provided a superb banquet for the tantras, a banquet for the reading transmissions, complete sets of robes, and so forth. His retinue returned to Trangok.

Ré stayed in Mugulung and heard the explanation of the *Tantra Trilogy* and also several esoteric instructions such as the *Inconceivable.* He returned again to his home and, while he did also benefit others a little, he mostly just practiced meditation. It appears that this man and Khön Könchok Gyalpo were called "the two Könchok Gyalpos" and were especially close to Drokmi. Thus my master taught. [137]

(4) *Khön Könchok Gyalpo of Sakya*

When Khön Könchok Gyalpo and his elder brother were staying at Jakshong in Yalung, the elder brother said, "Because the Nyingma practitioners have proclaimed the secrets by publicly performing the sacred dance of the twenty-eight Wangchukma and so forth, the blessings have declined.[226] You should now enter the door of the new secret-mantra tradition and practice that."

Könchok Gyalpo decided to travel to lord Drokmi's place. He put a load of mixed barley flour and butter on a donkey and added three dressed sheep carcasses on top of that. He gave one dressed carcass and some bags of butter to a servant called Ajo Gyalé and started off through Draphu Pass. Just as he reached the entrance to the pass, a monk horseman wearing the hat of a paṇḍita arrived at the pass with a retinue of four. A great feeling of joy was born in Könchok Gyalpo's heart at the mere sight of the monk horseman.

"Who are you?" he asked.

"I am a junior translator in the retinue of Drokmi Lotsāwa," the man replied. "I am the one called Balti Lotsāwa and also Khyin Lotsāwa." He also asked, "Where did you come from?" and so forth.

"I came from a place called Jakshong in Yalung," Könchok Gyalpo replied. "I am going to lord Drokmi."

Balti said, "In that case, you will not reach Mugulung tonight, and there are no other villages, so stay in my monastery. We also need to talk some."

He led them to his monastery at Balphuk and said to him there, "This wealth of yours will not even get you an audience with lord Drokmi, let alone get you Dharma. Specifically, he is now in retreat, so it is probably futile to go. Stay here for a while. I will offer the Dharma you want. Then I will also go to request initiation when the retreat is over. If you go with me at that time, you can see whether it is possible to obtain an audience and Dharma teachings."

"Generally speaking, I am grateful to you," Könchok Gyalpo replied. "But I must also ask the Three Jewels for a sign as to whether or not you and I have a karma connection and so forth. I must think about it some, so I will offer my reply tommorrow."

"Do that!" Balti Lotsāwa said and escorted him to the guest quarters. [138]

Lord Könchok Gyalpo arranged a fine ritual feast and offering of sacrificial cakes there and extensively carried out all the practice activities. When he prayed to the masters, the Three Jewels, and the protectors and guardians of the Dharma, he had many obscure dreams during the night. At dawn he had good dreams, a meditative concentration arose in his mindstream, and so forth.

The next day Balti Lotsāwa asked, "What signs occurred?"

"Good ones occurred," Könchok Gyalpo replied. "But that's not enough. I have an elder brother who is also my master and my chosen deity. It is not right for me to decide without asking him."

"Wonderful! A practitioner of secret mantra must primarily keep the sacred commitments," Balti said, and was pleased.

Könchok Gyalpo gave a letter to Ajo Gyalé and sent him to get his brother's opinion. The venerable elder brother gave his consent in a sealed message to Khyin Lotsāwa: "My younger brother and you have a karma connection. You will also benefit him, so I am entrusting and giving him to you. Care for him kindly. There are some signs of obstacles for you, so be energetic in the methods to repel them!"

Könchok Gyalpo stayed in Balphuk and concentrated on the *Hevajra Root Tantra.* When the great master Drokmi had finished his retreat, Könchok Gyalpo traveled as a companion with Khyin Lotsāwa and his disciples, who were going to request initiation. When he met the great master and asked for his blessing, Drokmi held his hair for a long time and said,

"Young student, the feel of your hair is completely unlike the feel of others'. This family line of yours is a family of people who will bring vast good to the Buddhist doctrine."

"He also needs to be given initiation," Khyin Lotsāwa said.

"Has he received initiation?" Drokmi asked.

According to the custom of the great master, the tradition was to give three initiations called "the initiation to first open the door of the Dharma," "the initiation to mend the sacred commitments in between," and "the initiation to finally clarify realization."

Khyin Lotsāwa said, "I performed the initiation to open the door of the Dharma."

"Fine," replied Drokmi.

Könchok Gyalpo was also allowed to remain there as an attendant while the great master and his disciples performed the creation and offerings, and he received from Drokmi the initiation of Hevajra during three nights.

Again he returned with the teacher Khyin Lotsāwa and his disciples to Balphuk. [139] When eighteen months had passed in the teaching and study of the tantras, Khyin Lotsāwa suddenly passed away amid sounds, lights, and a rain of flowers.

Könchok Gyalpo took all the possessions of Khyin Lotsāwa on seventeen horses with upper and lower loads, and offered them to the great master. When he supplicated him with requests for the Dharma, Drokmi replied, "Have you come to your grandfather when your father has died? You are not mistaken to come. If you want Dharma, bring wealth!"

Könchok Gyalpo traveled to Jakshong. He divided the wealth with his brother. By selling all the fields that he obtained as his share, he got thirteen horses with loads. When he took them and offered them in Mugulung, Drokmi said, "I'm not going to provide for these horses. You take them and bring back some other wealth."

Könchok Gyalpo offered a rosary of jewels and said, "Please use this to pay for grass."

"Can't argue with that," Drokmi replied and accepted. He gave Könchok Gyalpo the complete explanation of the tantras and also several instructions such as the *Inconceivable*.

Then Könchok Gyalpo requested the Precious Teaching of the Path with the Result.

"I made a vow not to explain the scriptures to those who fully received the instructions and not to explain the oral instructions to those who fully received the scriptures," Drokmi replied and did not give them.

In this way, of Drokmi's five or four spiritual sons, this venerable lord Könchok Gyalpo alone was of the greatest benefit to others. Thus my master taught.

(5) *Master Ngaripa, the one disciple who fully received the scriptures later*

Master Ngaripa's father was a Purang monk called master Dorjé Phurpa. When he stayed at a place called Yopso in Jang to perform the rituals for a man who had died, master Ngaripa was born from the union of Dorjé Phurpa with the deceased man's wife.

When master Ngaripa was a child, his father said, "Since you are the son of a monk, you need good qualities. And for that you must know how to read, so read this," and gave him the volume of the *Compendium of Lessons*[227] and left to recite the Dharma. When he came back, the boy was playing among the children.

His father scolded him, "Are you like other children? Not studying how to read, and acting like this!"

"I have nothing to read," Ngaripa replied.

"Where did the volume of the *Compendium of Lessons* go?"

"I memorized it, down to the small notes."

His father led him inside and tested him. He had memorized it without confusion down to the minor annotations. His father was astounded, but Ngaripa added, "Not only that. I had forgotten this from yesterday, [140] but now I've refreshed my memory," and repeated many Dharma teachings from memory, such as those concerning conduct.[228] In brief, an understanding of all fields of knowledge sprang up naturally in Ngaripa, without any need for study.

A man called Old Paṇḍita lived in that area, and he said, "Ratnakīrti, you also practiced the Mahayana Dharma in the last life. And in this life, too, your practice is amazing. But due to my sacred commitments to the master, I will not explain your family line, name, and so forth," and did not give further indications.

This perfect great expert who led many disciples, even from the age of eight, traveled to Mugulung. He offered vast wealth and possessions.

Drokmi was also pleased with his discernment, knowledge, and so forth, and completely gave him the explanation of the scriptures.

At a banquet for the tantras, master Ngaripa provided superb offerings to the master and about two hundred of Drokmi's retinue and disciples. He offered a hundred dressed carcasses and a hundred ounces of butter to the master, fifty dressed carcasses and fifty ounces of butter to the consort, twenty-five of each to each of the two sons, one dressed carcass and one ounce of butter to each of the monks, and so forth.

Again, as a private party, Ngaripa invited the master Drokmi and his consort with the inner circle to his residence and held a fine banquet, again making vast offerings. At that time, the summarizing notes he had made concerning the difficult points in the tantra as taught by the great master were in a book holder. The great master saw them and took them, saying, "For you to understand like this is like Vajragarbha[229] appearing in the world. I need this."

When Ngaripa asked for it later, Drokmi said, "It's lost among the master's own books and not available," and did not wish to return it.

When Ngaripa begged Drokmi for oral instructions he was told, "If you need Dharma, bring wealth!"

Ngaripa traveled to Kongpo and had many disciples. When he received twenty-six horses at one time he used one as his mount and offered to Drokmi the other twenty-five superb horses together with their loads.

Ngaripa had a dream in which there were many bright white doors said to be the treasury of the great master. He dreamed that he was given the key to one.

"Lord," he said. "You control many treasuries of the Teaching, but you do not give them to your subject."

"If I do not give them to you, who would I give them to?" Drokmi replied and gave several instructions such as the *Inconceivable*. [141]

In brief, of all the disciples who fully received the scriptures, the best was this master Ngaripa. Thus my master taught.

b) Disciples who fully received the oral instructions

Three disciples fully received the oral instructions: the inferior recipient Lhatsün Kali, the middling recipient Drom Depa Tönchung, and the superior recipient Sé Kharchungwa. Although they were similar in having fully received the path, they are classified as superior, middling, and inferior according to the amount of benefit they brought to others.

(1) *Lhatsün Kali*

Lhatsün Kali was the son of the sovereign Pal Dé, and, since he was also the brother of Machik Dzeden Öchak, the complete oral instructions were given to him in consideration of familial attachment. But he passed away at a young age and did not benefit others, so he is referred to as "a recipient by virtue of family ties." Thus my master taught.

(2) *Drom Depa Tönchung*

A man called Drom Tsandawarti in the eastern Tibetan region of Domé slowly traveled westward to a place called Chekha in Phenyul and settled there. In this family line the one called Trogyal Yeshé had three sons and daughters. The eldest son was called Drom Depa Shākya Gyal, the middle one Depa Tönchung, and the daughter Namkha Dorjé.[230] This Depa Tönchung was an expert in the Nyingma transmission of mantra, Mamo Bötong[231] in general, and, within that, the *Realization of the Goddess's Life-force.*

At that time, the ḍākinīs gave Drom a prophecy. He traveled on the trail through Lakpa Pass and extracted an esoteric instruction called the *Four-Finger-Width Dart of the Goddess* from a treasure trove in the middle floor of Samyé. When he practiced according to its contents, after twenty-one days he actually beheld the face of the goddess with light rays like the shining moon.

"If you have something to say, say it!" she demanded. "I am swift."

He spoke all at once the names of three enemies who sickened his heart, and said, "These must be eliminated."

The next evening the heads of those three were dropped on the surface of the mandala at the same time, and Drom was told to set the time of death at seven days for those three with seven in each of their retinues or, it is also said, for seven enemies with three in each of their retinues. [142] He sent a message to the enemies and set the time, "If you have something to eat, eat it! If you have something to wear, wear it! And so forth, for you will die in this many days."

Twenty-five people vomited blood and died within seven days. The fame of Drom's sorcery became equal to the extent of the sky. Supplicants, those requesting support, and so forth made countless offerings of wealth. Although he became very rich, he also became despondent about having killed so many people at the same time. He taught the sorcery to his younger brother named Özer Dorjé and performed many basic acts of virtue as a means of confessing his sins. He took the older of his two wives as an attendant and placed the younger, to whom his sons and daughters had been born, in the care of his elder brother Depa Shākya Gyal.

With a retinue of about thirty, Drom took much wealth and traveled toward Mugulung. Even along the road many came to make offerings to him, and he arrived comfortably with many possessions. He made a large offering to the great master Drokmi and arranged a superb banquet for the guidance. When he asked for the oral instructions, Drokmi gave them.

Furthermore, Drom requested each Dharma session by offering as gifts a tenth of an ounce of gold, several brocade foot cushions, several silk cloths when those ran out, and a Dharma sacrificial cake that could barely be carried by two men. When most of the oral instructions had been completed and just four Dharma sessions were left, his gold ran out.

Drom explained the reason, and asked, "Is it acceptable to offer something instead of gold?"

Drokmi replied, "If your gold has run out, my Dharma has also run out," and did not want to give even those four Dharma sessions.

Drom offered many valuables in exchange for the gold he had already offered to Drokmi's consort and bought it back. When he said, "I have obtained the gold now," Drokmi carefully gave the rest of the oral instructions.

On one occasion, Drom's wife had a dream that many women came flying through space from the west and said, "This husband of yours is traveling to Oḍḍiyāna soon. Wouldn't it be best to join us now and go?" She dreamed that they led her by the hand and she flew away.

She told it to Drom and asked, "Wouldn't it be good to have some methods to dispel this omen of impending death?"

Drom asked the great master Drokmi, and the great master said, "Oh! I had also thought I should mention it, but forgot until now. If you want to dispel it, [143] you should bathe your wife, adorn her with much jewelry, and offer her as my consort for seven days. If you utterly abandon your possessions, it will be averted, but since you people from Central Tibet are tight with your wealth, how will you do that?"

The wife of the great master Drokmi was aghast and said, "This man has presented offerings and service in this way for so many years, and yet you say, 'You people from Central Tibet are tight with your wealth.' Nobody speaks like this!"

"I hoped to benefit him. It makes no difference to me," Drokmi replied.

When Drom went to their residence, his wife was seated in meditation posture and glistening with perspiration. When he gave the advice about bathing and so forth, she said nothing. When he looked again, she had already passed away into Khecara.[232]

When Drom offered all his wife's jewelry and so forth to the great master, held a banquet for all the Drilchen people of Mangkhar, and made measureless donations and so forth, it was known that "Drom has opened up an inexhaustible treasury."

In this way Drom stayed for eight years. He pleased Drokmi with unbelievable constant and special services. He also completely received the oral instructions.

When he decided to travel home with his disciples and asked for a loan of three horses for his own mount, to carry books, and so forth, the great master replied, "You are trying to sweet-talk me. There is no custom of a master making offerings to a disciple. You can stay here and not go to your own home."

Drom's retinue became angry and made many slanderous comments. Even he became somewhat despondent and said, "Up to now Mugulung was Vajrāsana and the great master was Śākyamuni. But I may not be able to come back. After taking so much wealth from my home and staying here for a long time, I would be ashamed to finally return home on foot, so I will first go in search of some horses."

When Drom traveled in the direction of Dingri, he was said to be a spiritual son of the great master Drokmi and became very famous. Many came to request Dharma and make offerings, and he received about twenty horses.

When Drom gave several disciples the blessing for the *Inconceivable*,[233] blood gushed from his nose and he was stricken with chills. At daybreak a great clairvoyance arose in him. He passed into nirvana after leaving a last testament containing statements such as these: "That master of mine is

Vajradhara himself. He was testing my worthiness. [144] But I did not understand that, and so there has been a slight backlash. Nevertheless, I will be graced in the intermediate state. Offer into his hands whatever possessions I have and these bones. If you request oral instructions, he will give the oral instructions without the necessity of such hardship as mine."

When Drom's body was cremated, sounds, lights, a rain of flowers, and so forth appeared. His disciples took the bones, seventeen horses with upper and lower loads, and so forth and traveled up the lower valley of Mugulung blowing conches. The great master Drokmi heard them while he was sitting and performing the regular offering of sacrificial cakes. He cried, "I think my heart is being torn out. Look!"

When they looked, it was those disciples. They told Drokmi the story and offered him the wealth. He took the bones into his lap, said, "Has the son come back to the father?" and wept.

"Several masters told me, 'Examine the worthiness of disciples!'" he explained, "But some faults have occurred from excessively harsh examination. If any among you want oral instructions, I will give them."

Although not many requested oral instructions, they did request a Hevajra initiation. The three among them who requested some clarification of the instructions were the two called Mara Serpo and Rokpo from Phenyul, and Phakpa Chönang.[234]

In brief, Drom completely obtained the instructions by means of wealth and possessions. Although the *Incisive Vajra* says no spread of his lineage occurred, that is slightly incorrect.[235] The lineage through this master lasted for about six or seven generations and then ceased, so he is classified as the middling recipient. Thus my master taught.

(3) *Sé Kharchungwa*

Sé Kharchungwa's birthplace was Chidrum in Dokmé.[236] His clan was the Sé, within which were both the Kya subclan and the Ché subclan. All of the people born into the Ché subclan were eloquent and had sharp intellects, pleasant voices, good physiques, and fine faces. He was born into a family line of that type.

Sé had many yaks. Once in autumn his yak herder was occupied with other work, so he went himself to tend the yaks in the mountains. He saw that most of the sky was extremely clear just above Mugulung, with a white cloud about the size of a field that could be planted with one load of grain, surrounded at the edges by many rainbows and with the fine tips of the rainbows shimmering in all directions. [145] He immediately thought, "I am sure that beneath that cloud there is a master who teaches a Dharma that brings certain buddhahood."

Equal joy and sadness arose in his mind, and he felt he could not bear it. When he had gone a short way from there, he came to some young men digging sod and asked them, "You all, what is beneath that white cloud over there?"

"In general," they replied, "the area over there is called Kochak Plateau. More specifically, the area right there is called Mangkhar Mugulung. A master called Drokmi Lotsāwa who knows how to make people into buddhas lives there."

Hearing that, tears gushed from Sé's eyes, the hairs on his body stood on end, and for a while his mind slipped into an inexpressible swoon. When he recovered and remembered the master, he felt he could not bear it. The young men were also acting like they could not bear it physically or mentally, saying, "Should we not go to that master?" joining hands, singing songs, and stamping out dances.

Sé then drove his yaks down early and went to the place of his maternal uncle, Tönchung Daryé, who loved him very much. He said to his uncle, "I have something to tell you that I haven't mentioned before, and also questions about some important topics of discussion, so let's go to an isolated place tonight."

"We don't have much to discuss and so forth, do we?" his uncle replied. "But in any case, we can do that."

Sé brought a load of wood, a lot of beer, and a good torso of meat. The two of them stayed in an empty house. They started a fire and consumed the beer and the torso of meat. Sé told the story of what had happened and said, "I absolutely must go to that master."

His uncle said, "I am also aware of the talk, but I am not free to go. And you are not able to go."

At the end of much discussion about who could and who could not go, the uncle said, "So the two of us will go together. Recently my mother bought six-tenths of an ounce of gold from a nomad, wrapped it in wool, and hid it in a crevice in the wall. I'll steal it and bring it, and borrow some from you." Their discussion of the matter was settled.

As the two of them were traveling, they met a mixed group of about twenty mantra practitioners and monks, who were Drokmi's emanations.

When the two told their story, the travelers replied, "If you are going to Mugulung, we have many aquaintances and can protect you from the dangers of the road."

They joined together and traveled to Mugulung. [146] They had great merit and arrived when the great master was to give a Hevajra initiation. As soon as they met, a physically and mentally unbearable faith was born in Sé. The inside of his body was piercing hot, like the heat of a blazing fire. A violent shudder wracked his body, and he let out a cry from within.

"Young nomad, what is wrong with you?" the great master Drokmi asked.

"Something is in my mind that I don't know how to express," Sé replied.

The great master was pleased and said, "Young man with the sharp nose and even teeth, it seems that my blessing has entered you. This family line of yours is a line that will bring vast good to the Buddhist doctrine."

In the morning the emanated mantra practitioners and monks had vanished. Drokmi gave the Hevajra initiation to the two of them for three nights. For several days he then taught the explanation of the root downfalls, the six-branch Hevajra method for accomplishment, and the yoga of the sacrificial-cake offering. Sé understood them well. When that was finished, the great master stayed in retreat. Although there were no audiences or Dharma teachings, Sé and his uncle carefully served the consort as attendants. They also performed the autumn and spring chores with care and diligence.

Once, during a ritual feast, Drokmi said, "Sing a song!"

When no one else knew how, the consort said, "That young Jang man from a while ago knows how. Should I call him?" Drokmi gave permission and was delighted when Sé sang a song.

Moreover, since lord Sé had a handsome face and body, pleasant speech, and was very skilled in songs and so forth, the consort was fond of him. She gave him good food and so forth, but he knew it came from the religious gifts. When he told stories, sang songs, and so forth during weeding and other times, it attracted flocks of patrons. And so he also made a living in that way.

During the harvest that autumn, Sé and his uncle tended with care and diligence to harvesting the crops that had been planted for the master. The great master saw them and asked, "Who are those two over there?"

"Those two are the two young men from Jang who came last year," the consort replied.

"Are they still staying here?" Drokmi asked.

"They have stayed," she said. "They want to request Dharma. As soon as you met him last year you were very complimentary. Aren't you going to teach even one session of Dharma now?"

"I'll give the Dharma," he replied.

The consort told the two of them, [147] "Stay at the private entrance to the master's residence, and when the master comes, make your request!"

When they spoke, Drokmi called them before him and said, "What are you doing, staying here until now?"

"We request the Dharma," they replied.

"I'll do just that," he said.

They used two ounces of gold as a gift for the initiation and one for a ritual feast. They obtained the second initiation to mend the sacred commitments.[237] Sé is the only person to have obtained an initiation from the great master with just three ounces of gold. Thus my master taught.

"Now don't stay here," Drokmi said. "Get out! And don't come back again!"

When Sé insisted that he had to be allowed to return, Drokmi asked, "What are you doing?"

"I am asking the lord for the Precious Teaching," he replied.

"If you need Dharma, bring wealth! Don't come without wealth!"

Sé returned home. When his wealth was calculated, he obtained about thirty male and female yaks as his share. In the autumn, at a time when people were busy, he said, "You others do some other work. In combination with doing some recitations of mantra, I will tend to the yaks."

He took them grazing for grass several times, going into the mountains and returning after about three or four days, thereby fooling people. After that he drove the yaks and went to the Lhatsé ferry.

"Take us across," he said.

"For every six male and female yaks, I want one," the ferryman demanded.

If he were to do that, Sé thought, there would be no offering for the master. He prostrated in the direction of Mugulung, made prayers, and offered a sacrificial cake to the Dharma protectors. After all the male and female yaks rushed into the river led by a female yak with a white patch on the forehead, Sé quickly crossed the river holding the tail of the black yak at the rear and arrived on the other side. The ferrymen were extremely upset with each other about whose fault this was.

As Sé drove the beasts along, he met the master Drokmi and his consort out on an excursion in the lower valley of Mugulung. When he offered the male and female yaks, Drokmi commented, "Your offering is not large. But it is useful for decorating the upper portion of the valley. Do these female yaks have calves?" He showed his pleasure in many ways, giving each beast a name, and stroking them with his hands.

In that way, lord Sé Kharchungwa stayed for eight years and completely received the Precious Teaching with the associated instructions. The Later Cycles of the Path were completed in four years. There had been one year before that, so he stayed with Drokmi for a total of thirteen years. [148] There was nothing great about the things Sé offered, but because he pleased the master with his conduct, he completely obtained the Precious Teaching together with the Cyles of the Path.

The great master Drokmi once said, "All my oral instructions have been lost through techniques of thievery to this smooth-talking Sé."

Sé wept and asked, "Am I not your disciple?"

"I was joking," Drokmi replied. "If I didn't give them to you, to whom would I give them?"

After all the oral instructions had been completed, Sé wanted to receive the scriptures and made a request.

"I made a promise to one of my masters," Drokmi replied. "If you are interested in the scriptures, go to Khön Könchok Gyalpo."[238]

At Sé's departure, the master said to him, "You have completely obtained the oral instructions because you have a fine disposition and have acted skillfully in showing respect for superiors and friendliness toward your peers. In particular, you received them because of your eloquent voice. This voice has been very kind to you, so use your voice. Sing a song right now!"

Sé sang a song eulogizing the body, speech, mind, qualities, and activities of the master. Drokmi was delighted and demonstrated his love by stroking Sé's head many times, twisting his ears, pouring beer from his mouth into Sé's mouth, and so forth.

Then Sé said, "I am going to Sakya, but I also need to be given a sealed letter of introduction to deliver there. If Könchok Gyalpo tells me he needs the Precious Teaching, am I allowed to explain it?"

"I do not want you to completely explain it," Drokmi replied. "It is acceptable to explain just the inner structure and outline of the esoteric instructions."

Sé traveled to Sakya carrying a sealed letter in which the great master Drokmi said to Khön Könchok Gyalpo, "You are the best of all my disciples who fully received the scriptures. Sé is the best of all the disciples who fully received the oral instructions. I am the best of all of both your masters. Spread the best doctrine, given by the best to the best!"

When Sé met Khön Könchok Gyalpo and delivered the sealed letter, Könchok Gyalpo seized Sé's hand, began to stamp his feet in dance, and cried, "The master makes compliments like this! Now no one on the surface of this earth is happier than the two of us!"

Könchok Gyalpo raised many banners at his residence [149] and also held a fine ritual feast of celebration. "I will completely offer you all the instructions," he said. "An exchange of goods is not necessary. We are both of one family."

But Sé replied, "I can't do that. I will provide the goods," and went home.

Because of his fame as "the one spiritual son of lord Drokmi," the people from his home received Sé with a welcome of horsemen, masked dancers, and so forth. For all the people of his home, he held a great ceremony for awakening the enlightenment mind, and about fifty ounces of gold were offered. To a gathered group of the best among them, Sé twice gave the two-night initiation of Cakrasaṃvara and received many offerings.

In brief, Sé took what amounted to about two hundred ounces of gold, went to Sakya, and made a vast offering. He stayed for six years and mastered the study of all three tantras.[239] He even served as Khön Könchok Gyalpo's personal attendant, which delighted him.

Then Sé said, "I asked the master if I could offer you this Precious Teaching, and he told me it was permitted to explain just the inner structure of the esoteric instructions. If that is agreeable to you, master, I will offer it."

Könchok Gyalpo replied, "I was unable to request it. If I obtained even just that much, it would be a great auspicious connection, so I certainly request that."

The two of them taught each other, back and forth.

Then Sé went home. To enhance his realization, he lived for six years in all the dangerous places as far as Jang and Ra. He meditated single-mindedly on the Precious Teaching and inconceivable experience and realization was born.

Because Sé had perfected the energy of the root mantra, he subdued the nāga demoness of Kharchung, bound her to a vow, moved her residence, and established a monastery there. Those who had been stricken by leprosy that was the fault of the nāga demoness were benefited by just rubbing his saliva or urine on the sores.

Sé perfected the path of the third initiation, and even though he had a wife, they had no children because he had made the seminal fluid workable. He gained powers of clairvoyance and magical abilities such as multiplying many bodies from one.

In brief, because this Path with the Result—which was transmitted from the great master Drokmi and has remained unbroken until the present day—was transmitted through Sé, he was the best among the disciples who completely received the oral instructions. Thus my master taught. [150]

c) *Disciples who reached attainment*

Among Drokmi's disciples, three men and four women reached attainment.

(1) *The three men who reached attainment*

Three men reached attainment:

(a) Gyergom Sewo
(b) Shengom Rokpo
(c) The Glutton of Central Tibet

(a) *Gyergom Sewo*

Gyergom Sewo was the only son of a rich man, born into the Jeu family line in Gyerda, the lower valley of Gyerphu. He gained faith in the great master Drokmi and went to request Dharma. Gyergom rode a fine horse and wore fine armor worth a thousand ounces of gold called "fine and worth a thousand," a helmet worth seven ounces of gold, a leather shield worth three ounces of gold, and other elaborate armaments required by a warrior, such as a knife, lance, and arrows. He traveled with a retinue of one young man in armor riding a fine horse, and about five others.

The great master Drokmi was staying at Takpoché when they met, and he prophesied, "Son, with this impressive outfit of yours, you will be victorious in battle with the afflictions."

Gyergom offered all the horses and armor, as well as much other wealth, and requested instruction. Drokmi bestowed initiation and gave the oral instructions.

Meditating right there for thirteen years, Gyergom obtained infinite magical abilities and clairvoyance and then left, saying he was going to the glorious mountains of Śrīparvata in the south.

(b) *Shengom Rokpo*

Shengom Rokpo's home was in Tanak, his clan was the Shen, his name was Shentön Yungdrung Drup, and he was the son of a Bönpo master. After his father passed away, he collected offerings from Rutok in Jang. The great wealth that came to him was used in memory of his father.

Shengom did not believe in the religious teachings of the Bönpo tradition. His mind was captivated by the reputation of the great master Drokmi, and he traveled to Mugulung carrying many offerings. He requested the oral instructions and reached attainment by meditating for thirteen years in places such as Semodo and Namtso Chukmo to the north.

Then Shengom said, "Many Bönpo holders of pure awareness live at the glacial peak of Kailash, so I will go to turn them from a bad path and establish them on a perfect path."

He mounted a sunbeam and quickly went to Kailash. There he turned all the Bönpo holders of pure awareness away from a wrong path and led them to Khecara. He lives even now on Mount Kailash without having abandoned his body. Thus my master taught.

(c) *The Glutton of Central Tibet*

This man was known in Phenyül as the Slaughterer Tashi Sengé. [151] Even though he was not actually a butcher, he acted as the leader of many hundreds of depraved men, and was a powerful thug who engaged only in robbery and plunder. Once he had intercourse with his own twenty-year-old sister and she became pregnant. At that point, he became disgusted with all of his actions and gave his sister to the Slaughterer Jaur Drak. He took some valuables, such as a priceless turquoise he had robbed from his fine bride, and fled.

Tashi Sengé arrived at a small monastery near Chushül. On the side of a slippery blue slate mountain across from it, two deer were standing together. By firing a single arrow he was able to kill them both at the same time. He butchered one carcass and carried it back. The dedicated meditators of that small monastery had gone to benefit disciples, and in their absence he tore down the walled-up door to a hut and had a look. He found a sack of barley flour and three vats of beer. He mixed the barley flour into the beer and drank it, finishing off most of the beer and barley flour. He took out his sword and put it in front of him, used his knife, lance, and arrows as a pillow, and went to sleep.

Those meditators returned. Seeing Tashi Sengé's demeanor they were frightened and amazed and cried, "Are you a rākṣasa demon? You cannot be human. Get away from here now! The patrons are coming behind us and will definitely kill you!"

They made many comments hoping to frighten him, but Tashi Sengé replied, "I have done a bad thing, but otherwise I am not someone who is afraid of your patrons."

The meditators said, "You seem to be one who does all kinds of crude and violent acts. That behavior of yours will take you nowhere but hell. Instead of that, wouldn't it be better for you to go to the man called lord Drokmi in the place called Mangkhar Mugulung, who knows how to make people into buddhas?"

As soon as Tashi Sengé heard the great master Drokmi's name, he fainted. When he recovered he said, "I am grateful to you. Just hearing that master's name made me happy. In return for that favor and in place of the barley flour and beer I consumed, you must take this deer carcass and also the deer carcass on the slope of slate over there."

Tashi Sengé took his knife, lance, arrows, and so forth and left. At the entrance to the Silma Pass he met [152] many returning traders from Latö in western Tsang and traveled in their company. At the Kharak Pass many robbers appeared. When the traders were terrified, Tashi Sengé said to the robbers, "I came to escort these traders. Let them go as they please, without robbing them."

When they did not listen to what he said, he told them, "In that case, to see whether or not you will be able to stand up to me, three of you young men grab your shields and stand in the distance with about six feet between each of you."

He shot a single arrow that pierced straight through the three men and their shields and penetrated about one handspan into a boulder. The rest of the robbers all fled to who knows where. The traders exclaimed, "You are like an emanated body!" and gave him fine rewards and offerings.

They eventually arrived at Mugulung. Tashi Sengé made many offerings to Drokmi, including the turquoise, property, and other wealth. Drokmi gave him various oral instructions and said to his own consort, "At all three mealtimes, give him two measures of barley flour, a side of meat, and a full measure of beer."[240]

Once, when someone offered a ritual feast to the great master Drokmi, Tashi Sengé's share was a sacrificial cake made from one load of barley flour,[241] a half side of meat, and a jug of beer, all of which Drokmi gave to him. When he consumed it then and there in the assembly row, the great master remarked, "The previous amount wasn't enough, so we'd better give him three times more than that."

On another occasion, when the great master Drokmi was invited to a Dharma council in the lower valley of Mangkhar, he took Tashi Sengé as his attendant and said, "You should also go for amusement today. Bring your ornaments such as your knife, lance, and arrows!"

Tashi Sengé competed in sports with the young men gathered there. When he shot one of his thick arrows, five long arrow shots of the others just reached it, and after he jumped once from the jumping platform, the others barely reached him with five jumps. Similarly, he ate by himself at one time a great mountain of kneaded barley flour together with a barrel of beer that would certainly have sufficed for about a hundred young men.

Tashi Sengé also participated in a contest of strength in which he held the ends of twenty-five good ropes while twenty-five young men seized each rope. With one jerk he snatched the ropes from the hands of the young men, spun the ropes around in the sky, [153] and sang a song:

> I am the great strongman famous in Mangkhar.
> I am the great pillar supporting the great master.
> I am the dear child of Dzeden Öchak.[242]
> I am the doctrine protector of meditators.

When Tashi Sengé did such things, everyone was amazed and said, "The great master has enslaved a strongman."

He became famous in those circles. When he turned those abilities to practices such as the yogic exercises, many channel knots were unraveled, producing a great enhancement of his meditative concentration.

As soon as Tashi Sengé arrived back at Mugulung, he achieved many magical abilities and clairvoyance, and flew to the glorious mountains of Śrīparvata. He remains there even now without having discarded the body. Thus my master taught.

(2) *The four women who reached attainment*

Four women reached attainment:

(a) Tömo Dorjetso
(b) Remo Köné
(c) Shapmo Chamchik
(d) Chemo Namkha Yeshé

These women are also used as examples for the four modes of gathering the essential constituents.[243]

(a) *Tömo Dorjetso*

Tömo Dorjetso was born in the area of Mangkhar called Tötso. She went to be the wife of a Mangkhar man called Dradül Jepa. They were very rich and six sons were born to them. But some other people of that area plotted against them, murdered the father and his six sons at the same time, and took all their wealth. That acted as a catalyst, her grief caused a gathering of the essential constituents, and she went insane. When the great master Drokmi heard the talk about her madness, he said, "She is a vessel for my Dharma."

Several relatives carried her on a stretcher and she arrived in front of Drokmi. When he bestowed initiation and taught her the oral instuctions, she reached attainment and traveled to the western land of Oḍḍiyāna. This is referred to as "the natural gathering of the essential constituents for a person with residual karma." Thus my master taught.

(b) *Remo Köné*

Remo Köné was called Remo because she was born in Mangkhar at the place now called Re. Her name was Mönmo Gökyi, but she was called by the nickname Köné, "Rare One," because that family had none except the one daughter. She married a nomad, but went insane when this sole beloved husband died. Unaware of what was going on around her, she would scream the name of her husband about three times and then fall unconscious. When she awoke, she would scream his name again. She made a loud sound of weeping day and night. When the great master Drokmi traveled back and forth in that area, he heard the loud sound of weeping and asked what it was. When told the story, he said, "She is a vessel for my oral instructions." [154]

Köné's brother brought much wealth and came to Drokmi leading the crazy woman. When the great master gave her teachings, she did not say anything. Even when her brother put his mouth to her ear and shouted, she only wept in that way, staring with eyes from which no tears would flow and wailing loudly. When cold water was thrown in her face, she slightly regained consciousness. She gathered her garments and said, "What has happened to me? I'm a bit sick."

The great master replied, "I am focusing meditation on you. Keep weeping!"

Köné wept three loud sobs and fell unconscious. When she recovered from that she said, "My mouth is dry. Bring beer."

She was given a full jug of beer laced with dried meat, which she drank in gulps. Drokmi put her to sleep that night between her mother-in-law and sister-in-law, and said, "If she says, 'Bring food and drink,' give her whatever she wants. Do not discuss such things as death," and left her.

Köné slept that night. When she woke up the next morning she pressed herself everywhere exclaiming, "Did I tumble from a mountain peak? It seems like my entire body was beaten. Was my head smashed?"

The great master was invited and said, "You did not tumble down. I am focusing meditation on you. You must weep without distraction!"

She became somewhat more conscious and her mind calmed down. Drokmi said, "Now initiation can be bestowed."

He bestowed a Hevajra initiation. When he gave her guidance on the *Inconceivable,* Köné felt certainty in these words:

> The nondual primordial awareness
> realized by means of the visual
> consciousness is so amazing.[244]

She remained at that hermitage immersed in a single meditative concentration until a morning seven days later. Then she gradually reached attainment.

While she was living in Köné Cave, a cave to the east in the upper valley of Mangkhar, lord Sé Kharchungwa came to Mangkhar on the way back from going to make wooden covers for a volume of many sutras. He sent his retinue on the main road and said, "I'm going to meet a Dharma sister."

Sé went to her and spent the night there. They made many comparisons of their experiences. She cooked and served food by a large river there. "Yesterday there was a big fuss below here," she said. "What was all that?"

"Those were the escorts who brought the offerings made to me by the Shama sister and brother,"[245] Sé replied. [155]

"Well!" Köné exclaimed. "Even you have been carried away by Māra!"

Sé is said to have remarked that from the time of his birth he had never been more embarassed than that.

Then Köné was invited by Nakgyal[246] to be the priestess of the yakṣinī demonesses and lived there for a while. Then she traveled to Oḍḍiyāna.

However, the story is told that when lord Sakya Paṇḍita[247] traveled to Mongolia, Köné was asked for advice, and they met. Even today it appears that at various places in Nakgyal the sound of her hand cymbals is heard, fresh sacrificial cakes are found, and so forth. So it appears that she still comes around sometimes.

Because Köné was liberated by the arising of certainty in the words of the master, she is used as the example of the gathering of the essential constituents through blessings for one with devotion. Thus my master taught.

(c) *Shapmo Chamchik*

Shapmo Chamchik was from the Jetsé family line in Shap. She and six brothers were born to wealthy parents, and so she was known by the title Chamchik, "Single Sister." She possessed all the complete characteristics of a lotus lady mudrā consort.

The great master sent a sealed message to her: "Being of the lotus lady mudrā consort type, it is a waste for you to stay among ordinary people. Come here! I will give you oral instructions."

Chamchik was overjoyed and came with much wealth. When Drokmi performed the initiation of Hevajra, she was introduced to coemergent bliss during the third initiation and an excellent meditative concentration was born.

"Since the primordial awareness of great bliss has been born in my mindstream, I am in a state of bliss," she cried. "Brothers, be at ease!"

The great master relied upon her for five years as a support for the birth of coemergent primordial awareness. Chamchik was liberated by the path of the third initiation and finally traveled to Oḍḍiyāna. This is called "the gathering of the essential constituents due to great bliss for one with residual karma." Thus my master taught.

(d) Chemo Namkha Yeshé

Namkha Yeshé was called Chemo, "Sister," because she was the sister of Drom Depa Tönchung.[248] She had the complete characteristics of a lotus lady consort. From her childhood she spoke only of the great master Drokmi, everywhere she went.

Drom Shākya Gyal once had a dream in which many women appeared and said, "Will you escort this sister of yours to the great master's place? Or should we lead her now?"

Therefore, Drom Depa Shākya Gyal said, "From the time she was little, without any information about the great master, she talked only about him. [156] She has a karma connection. It is right to send her."

Chemo was escorted with much wealth and about eight servants. At that time, the great master was staying at the Mangsang cliffs of Dringtsam. Chemo arrived there without impediment and offered much wealth. The great master also fully gave her the esoteric instructions of the creation stage of Varāhī Khecarī, the completion stage of the central channel, the practices for controlling the yakṣinī demonesses, and so forth.[249]

In order to practice, Chemo made a hut of leaves on the main road of Shun Drakrum and begged food on the road. She practiced and reached attainment.

In particular, because she had gained control of the yakṣinī demonesses, Chemo said, "If you act like me, it will happen like this," and when she waved an empty leather bag in the air it would be filled with a quantity of food and when she held out an empty bowl in the air it would be filled with beer. She gave some in this way to all travelers.

Some also say that Chemo did not achieve other than the ordinary attainments.

The first three women all went to Khecara without discarding their bodies. Chemo is used as the example of the gathering of the essential constituents through exertion for one with diligence. Thus my master taught.

3) *The disciples of Sé Kharchungwa*

Similarly, how did followers come to those best disciples of the great master? Although those who fully received the scriptures and those who reached attainment had many disciples and grand-disciples, that subject will be left alone for the time being.

The subject to be discussed now is how disciples came to lord Kharchungwa, the best of the disciples who fully received the oral instructions. Because he had great blessings and profound oral instructions, there were about two hundred of his disciples who certainly began the path and in whom realization arose, and about thirty-seven who fully received the explanation of the tantras. But the main ones were known to be the two Shangtön brothers who were the superior recipients of the Precious Teaching, the Shama sister and brother who were the middling recipients, and Segom Jangyé who was the inferior recipient.

a) *The two Shangtön brothers*

The Shangtön brothers[250] were born into the Jeu family line at Ding, in the region known as Latö in western Tsang. Both brothers mainly depended on income from their handiwork of calligraphy, grinding gold into powder, the finishing[251] of scriptures, and so forth. They also had some fields and houses. [157] Because they were of such virtuous character and skilled in the techniques of their craft, they had many customers for their work.

Lord Kharchungwa called on them for the gold grinding, finishing, and so forth of the covers he was making with gold for a volume of many sutras and the *Sutra of the Perfection of Wisdom in One Hundred Thousand Lines*. The brothers and one student went. Because they were of fine character, had handsome faces and bodies, had little desire for food, and were able to perform exquisite work, lord Sé was delighted. During break periods and free moments he did not call for other artisans, but called these brothers to him and engaged in many enjoyable discussions.

"Brothers," he said, "I am pleased by these good qualities you have. Come here at every break period. We will have discussions."

He also said to the other artisans, "Foremen, if you do work like the two Shangtön brothers, we patrons will become filled with faith. This will also be good for you."

When the brothers themselves also became filled with deep faith and modestly honored him, lord Sé said, "We are the patrons now and you are the objects of offerings, so you do not need to act like this. In the future, if the auspicious connections for performing honors come into alignment, you should do so without any hesitation."

The brothers discussed this and decided to beg the master for the Precious Teaching.

The volume of many sutras and the *Sutra of the Perfection of Wisdom in One Hundred Thousand Lines* were finished. Lord Sé gave fine gifts and a good banquet was held for the artisans. After they had dispersed, the two brothers offered a fine banquet to the master and his inner circle. They offered everything they had received as gifts and said, "Lord, you possess what is called the Precious Teaching. You must give this to us."

Lord Sé replied, "Because this is the income from your own handiwork, to be used for your food, I will not take it. If you want oral instructions, bring wealth from home."

The brothers returned to their home. They did much selling of the wealth from the gifts, their own fields, and so forth. They got about fifty ounces of gold, which they took and traveled to Kharchung. They requested the oral instructions. The elder brother Shangtön Chöbar said, "I will mostly meditate. You mostly study," and they did so. Through their devotion, their daily behavior, and so forth, they pleased the master and also completely received the oral instructions.

Master Sé also praised them, saying, "This Dharma of mine is understood by the two Shangtön brothers. [158] Of the two, it is understood by Shangtön Sijibar."

In that way, the elder brother gained greater understanding and so forth on the basis of the *Vajra Lines* through actual meditation than the younger brother did through closely adhering to the oral discussions and studying.

In brief, because the transmission is unbroken and has spread widely up to the present day, and because the brothers obtained the oral instructions without anything left out, they are known as the "superior recipients of the Precious Teaching." Thus my master taught.

b) *The Shama sister and brother*

The Shama sister and brother were from the area of Phadruk in southern Latö in western Tsang. Their father was Shama Dorjé Gyaltsen, who was known by the nickname Jiwa Hapsha, and their mother was called Gyalmo Men. Six children were born to this couple. The eldest was Shama Sengé Gyaltsen, second was Shama Gyaltsen, third was the sister Machik Gyalmo, fourth was lord Khumbuwa, also called master Dzongpa, fifth was Gyalchungpa, and sixth was Lopön Tsünchung.

Machik Gyalmo and lord Khumbuwa were the best. In general, Machik was endowed with the characteristics of a lotus lady. In particular, she also had amazing marks on her skin—a red lotus with three petals above the navel, the image of three rows of jewel necklaces from the throat to the navel, a victory banner with a sun and moon crest at her forehead, vermilion spirals of joy at both shoulders, the image of a blue lily with a sword in the center marked by a letter *tāṃ* under her tongue, and so forth.

When Machik reached the age of fourteen she went to be the wife of a man in Phadruk. She did not want to stay there, and was able to divorce by pretending to be insane.

Regarding Machik: during the early spread of the doctrine, King Songtsen Gampo was an emanation of Avalokiteśvara, the Chinese queen Ongjo was an emanation of Tārā, and Thönmi Saṃbhoṭa was an emanation of Mañjughoṣa. At this later time, the king was born as the Kaśmīri hermit Jayānanda. The Chinese queen was born as Machik Shama and Thönmi was born as Ma Lotsāwa Chöbar. At that time, such masters as the Kaśmīri hermit, Tsami, and Abhaya gave similar prophecies to Ma Lotsāwa: "In Tibet lives an emanation of Tārā who is of the lotus lady mudrā consort type. Use her as a support for realizing coemergent primordial awareness. If you practice Saṃvara, you will quickly reach attainment."[252]

Accordingly, Ma Lotsāwa returned to Tibet. He inquired about the consort, and she was Machik Shama. [159] He took her, and she went happily. When Ma Lotsāwa utilized Machik as the initiation support when receiving initiation from the chosen deity, she actually saw them—father and mother—as the chosen deity, and a vision of herself changing into the eight offering goddesses and making offerings and so forth also arose.

After some time, Ma Lotsāwa then took ordination and traveled to Central Tibet and Tsang, where he was poisoned. He died at Shap. His death acted as a catalyst, and a violent gathering of the essential constituents occurred within Machik. Seven great signs of obstacles occurred, such as a daily discharge of enlightenment mind about the size of a white mustard seed, and ravens not eating her sacrificial cakes.[253]

When Machik inquired about which master had the greatest oral instructions for dealing with these obstacles, she heard that Dampa Gyagar at Dingri was very famous and traveled there.[254] When she told him the reason she had come, Dampa said, "It is a consequence of not having offered gifts when requesting initiation from the master, sitting on his seat without the master's permission, acting as another's consort without asking the master, and so forth. Make offerings to the master if he is still living, or if not, to his stupa or to someone dear to him, such as his son."

Machik replied, "I did not offer initiation gifts because the master and I had combined our wealth and made no distinction between 'mine and yours.' I had no wealth kept aside."

"Your brother secretly took a horse as payment for you," Dampa said.[255] "I need many things to fix this. Bring a side of meat, a skull-cup full of beer, the egg of a black hen, and so forth."

When Machik offered those things, Dampa used the meat and beer for a ritual feast for about eighty people. The egg was inserted into Machik's vagina and left for a day. When it was removed, the inside of the egg was filled with black blood, from the midst of which an iron scorpion actually emerged.

It is said that at Dampa's command Machik fixed an ornamental finial upon master Ma Lotsāwa's outer reliquary, and also that she made offerings to his son. These cured the gathering of the essential constituents, and she was healthy for one year.

Again the essential constituents gathered as before, and when Machik spoke to Dampa, he told her to consult some sutras and tantras, and to travel around part of the country. She observed a retreat and consulted many sutras and tantras, but to no benefit. While she was traveling around the country, at the edge of a river in the lower valley of Khulung in Rong, she heard some of Nubpa's[256] young monks and students [160] singing a song:

> Ah! The secret of all the buddhas.
> Perfect buddhahood is birthless.
> From a birthless state everything is born.[257]

Hearing this, she gained certainty. A great change occurred in her mind, and it was beneficial.

After a year Machik again became ill as before and told Dampa. He gave her a drum and said to strike it. When she struck it, it made a great sound. When she requested a remedy for the impediments, he made a sign telling her to go away. She was not allowed to stay. She decided that his oral instructions were ineffective.

Meanwhile, lord Sé Kharchungwa had traveled to Phadruk to make the wooden covers for a volume of sutras and for the *Sutra of the Perfection of Wisdom in One Hundred Thousand Lines.* While he was staying at the place of Kechakpa Khyungpo Hūṃkara of Dingri, Sé became very famous as the excellent spiritual son of the great master Drokmi.

Khyungpo Kechakpa sent a message to Machik Shama saying, "Aren't you going to ask this lord Kharchungwa about a remedy for your impediments?"

Sister and brother loaded much butter and barley flour on a horse and came there. They offered the master the buttered flour, as well as the horse. When Machik told her story, lord Kharchungwa was sitting with his legs extended. Tapping his staff on a decoration on his boot, he commented, "Didn't it happen like this to you first? Then didn't it happen like this?"

When he spoke in such detail, and it matched just what had happened to her before, she knocked her head on the ground and prostrated. She felt great devotion and exclaimed, "Lord, are you the one called Buddha?"

When she requested a remedy for her impediments, lord Kharchungwa performed a Hevajra initiation. He gave her some remedies for the impediments and said, "If you want it in more detail, bring wealth to Kharchung."

"I have a brother," she said. "If I brought him, could he be included?"

"He may come," he replied.

Both sister and brother presented offerings of threefold purity three times.[258] They also pleased the master by enduring many hardships. He wished to give the complete oral instructions, but at one point they became satisfied with the oral instructions they already had, and prepared to leave.

Lord Kharchungwa told the Shangtön brothers, "These Shamas are fine people, and also fit vessels for the Dharma, so I intend to give them the complete oral instructions. But they are preparing to go. According to the custom of this lineage, there is no custom of giving without a request. You brothers should discuss this with them!" [161]

The Shangtön brothers told the Shama sister and brother, "Lord Kharchungwa's oral instructions seem to be still not quite complete. Since he is also very pleased with you, you should still stay, supplicate him, and hear the rest of the oral instructions. By your kindness we would also benefit."

The Shamas replied, "Honored brothers, what is this you're saying? We have stayed this long. And we made offerings of threefold purity three times. We traveled around as far as Jang and Ra. With nothing but a single coarse red cloth each to protect us from the intense cold, we will have to travel and sleep at the bellies of yaks.[259] The master also kept us close to his heart, and he completely gave the oral instructions. Even if he says he still has some, the lord could be lying." Then they left.

Therefore, in the accounts of this transmission through Shang, it is said, "Their oral instructions were slightly incomplete." However, some that we do not have were given to them. Nevertheless, they divided the practice by means of the four states as in *Saroruha's Method for Accomplishment*[260] and used the view in common with the Vehicle of the Perfections as the view of the time of the cause, without using the indivisiblity of samsara and nirvana, which are signs of slightly incomplete oral instructions. Thus my master taught.

In any case, because Machik made practice the essential thing, she possessed the paranormal ability of knowing something if she thought about it, and was able to emanate one body or many. She once said to a female attendant, "Let's go pick garlic. You go first."

Machik did not come. Wherever the attendant went, a pigeon came along. When she returned carrying garlic, Machik was sitting on her mat with a handful of garlic.

"Who offered the garlic?" the attendant asked.

"I picked it myself," she replied. "I was beside you on the rocky cliff when you almost fell."

Once, when Machik emanated as a pigeon and went to listen to the *Perfection of Wisdom* taught by Tsalung Dongtön, some young students flicked pebbles at her.

"The Dharma was profound," she said, "but some bad children, some nasty children, pelted me with pebbles and wouldn't let me listen."

When offerings were being made at the Vajrāsana, Machik magically traveled there and, in the dress of a Tibetan woman seated in the vajra position, performed circumambulations in the sky. The great Tsami[261] recognized her and spoke about her. The Indians became supremely faithful and four mendicants came to Tibet to request Dharma.

"In general," Machik said, "because I am a person from the borderland, [162] and in particular, because I am a woman, I am not qualified to be a master," and did not give them the Dharma. She gave them four ounces of gold and sent them away.

Similarly, Machik gained control of many magical abilities. Because she had enslaved the four gateway goddesses of Saṃvara, by just saying, "Hawkface, draw water! Owlface, start a fire!" water would appear in an empty pot and blazing fire on an empty hearth.

In brief, although Machik did become a powerful woman of attainments, lord Gönpawa commented, "This little Shama woman would have reached the culmination of attainment in this life, but her excessive fondness for songs of experience became a slight obstacle on the path."[262]

In any case, the transmission from both Machik and her brother Shama Chökyi Gyalpo, who was known as lord Khumbuwa, included about eight transmissions with the designations "male transmission" and "female transmission." But today nothing seems to be left of them except miscellaneous reading transmissions of texts. In any case, they are known as "the middling recipients." Thus my master taught.

c) *Segom Jangyé*

When a rich man of Phadruk called Segom Jangyé took much wealth and went to Mugulung, he could not meet the great master Drokmi. Segom said, "Even if he does not give oral instructions, if I just meet him I will offer the famous, fine horse that I have."

The consort and others said to Drokmi, "Before, you always told disciples to bring wealth if they needed Dharma. Now much wealth is offered, but you do not give the Dharma. Even if you just grant an audience, he will offer much wealth such as a fine horse, so you should just meet him."

Drokmi replied, "Before, when I said, 'Bring wealth,' I said it to emphasize the greatness of the Dharma and to examine the worthiness of the disciple. Now the Dharma teachings have been given to the individual owners. I have absolutely no need for wealth." He did not even grant an audience.

Segom took much wealth and traveled to Kharchung. When he requested the oral instructions, Sé Kharchungwa bestowed the complete oral instructions. Because Segom did not sustain the practice, develop wisdom, and so forth, or because he did not benefit others, he is known as the inferior recipient. Thus my master taught. [163]

c. *The final spread and expansion of the tradition by the venerable lords of Sakya, father and sons*

This section consists of three topics:

1) The life of the great venerable lord of Sakya, who opened up the tradition
2) How he received the Precious Teaching
3) How followers came to him

1) *The life of the venerable lord of Sakya, who opened up the tradition*

As explained previously, Khön Könchok Gyalpo had many good qualities. The younger of his two wives was called Machik Shangmo because she was the daughter of Shangshung Guruwa, or Machik Khargolungma because she lived in Khargolung. Sachen[263] was born to her.

Sachen was an emanation of the one known as Bodhisattva Dhanaśrī, or as Dha Bodhisattva, the elder brother or nephew of the great majestic lord Atiśa. Although some now claim that this venerable lord Sachen was an emanation of Avalokiteśvara, but not an emanation of Mañjughoṣa, and do not even count him among the seven Mañjughoṣas of the lineage, the tradition of this transmission considers him, to the contrary, to be an emanation of Mañjughoṣa and to be the chief of the seven Mañjughoṣas of the lineage.

The majestic lord Atiśa prophesied that from the auspicious connection of having seen seven *dhīḥ* syllables on the surface of the white earth of Sakya, seven emanations of Mañjughoṣa would appear at this place in the future. Accordingly, the great venerable lord Drakpa Gyaltsen actually says, "Mañjuśrī, assuming human form."[264] Therefore, this tradition considers the seven to be the trio of the father Sachen and his two sons, the uncle (the Dharma lord Sakya Paṇḍita), the nephew (Chögyal Phakpa), and the brothers Jamyang Dönyö Gyaltsen, whom some saw as

Mañjughoṣa mounted on a lion, and lord Lama Dampa,[265] whom Geshé Sherap Dorjé saw as Mañjughoṣa radiating light.

Being thus an emanation of Mañjughoṣa would not mean that Sachen was not Avalokiteśvara. When a man from Kham said, "You are known to be Avalokiteśvara, so if you do not show me proof, I will commit suicide," Sachen showed an eye in the palm of his right hand, held in the gesture of granting the sublime attainment, to symbolize Avalokiteśvara's one thousand arms and one thousand eyes. As indicated by such stories, he is also known by the name Venerable Lord of Great Kindness. Thus my master taught.

This excellent master, Sachen, obtained the Hevajra initiation and also various scriptures and instructions from his father. [164] When his father passed away, astrological calculations were performed. The predictions indicated that if appointment to the monastic seat, laying the foundation of the outer reliquary, and completion of the funeral rites were performed in a single day, all that followed would be excellent.

The monks and patrons wanted to appoint lord Sachen himself to the monastic seat, but his mother insisted, "That is not correct, because he must study while young. His father also said, 'This Dharma of a translator contains little deception,' and valued it greatly, so it is better like this."[266]

They invited lord Bari Lotsāwa,[267] who lived at the Yukharmo of Sakya. His appointment to the monastic seat, laying the foundation of the Khön Reliquary, and completion of the funeral services were all accomplished in a single day.

Lord Bari Lotsāwa said, "As a nobleman's son, you must understand the Dharma. And for that you need wisdom, so you should first practice this." He gave the ritual permission of Mañjughoṣa Arapacana. Here in the famous Mañjughoṣa Grotto of Sakya, Sachen practiced Mañjughoṣa with Bari accompanying him in the practice. When some signs of obstacles arose, Bari gave him the water protection of the wrathful blue Acala[268] and so forth.

By practicing, Sachen became free from obstacles. After six months, he directly beheld the face of the venerable lord Mañjughoṣa, in color like refined gold, with both hands making the gesture of the Dharma wheel, and seated on a jewel throne with both legs extended in the "good position." To the right and the left of Mañjughoṣa stood bodhisattvas, each the color of refined gold. Mañjughoṣa spoke to Sachen the *Instructions on Parting from the Four Attachments*,[269] the condensed essence of the Mahayana path. From then on, Sachen understood all Dharma teachings without impediment.

At that time, the Sakya elders had a discussion and decided, "Lord Sachen should engage in study. Moreover, because the abhidharma is important as a basis for the explication of Dharma, it is correct to study it first. Drangti Darma Nyingpo is an expert, so it would be best to go to him."

When Sachen came to Drangti at Ngurmik in Rong, all the monks had already gathered. Unable to obtain a house, he hung a blanket in an alley and stayed there. A monk called Yardrok Khoplewa became ill with a type of black smallpox[270] and had no nurse or other helper. [165] Unable to bear that, Sachen served and carefully helped him, but caught the disease himself and became ill.

At that time, in Sakya there was a man called Apho Phaktön who some said had lucid visions because of his spiritual practice and some said just saw ghosts. He was sitting in the sun after breakfast. Above the Drachung of Sakya, a man quickly raced toward him mounted on a black horse, wearing a long embroidered robe and a ceremonial wide-brimmed hat, whipping his horse.[271] He reined in the horse at Sakya and said, "Künga Nyingpo is ill and approaching death! What are you Sakya people thinking about?"

When Apho Phaktön told the story to Sachen's mother, she said, "What Apho says definitely comes true. This is no good."

Then a messenger also arrived with the news that had been passed from one person to the next. The mother thought, "If the lord dies, there will be no reason to return to Sakya now or later." Except for the Dharma estate of Sakya, she converted what there was into gold, took it, and left.

When mother and son met, the son shed tears because he was young and desperately ill in a distant place. His mother encouraged him, saying, "It would be fine if you died in the midst of this oceanlike assembly of monks."

In any case, Sachen recovered from the disease and expertly learned the abhidharma from Drangti and the assistant teacher called Jangchepa Khyung.

Then he decided to study epistemology, and stayed in the upper Nyang valley receiving the *Precision of Epistemology*[272] from Khyung Rinchen Drak and the assistant teacher Medikpa. At that point the Sakya elders invited him to Sakya, saying, "You can receive epistemology later. Bari has reached an advanced age, so you should come here first and request the oral instructions."

From lord Bariwa, Sachen fully received the cycles of Cakrasaṃvara, Hevajra, and Yamāri, and all Bari's instructions, such as the *One Hundred Methods for Accomplishment*.[273] Bari passed the leadership of the monastic seat to the venerable lord Sachen himself. Bariwa traveled to a place known as the Lingbar Cave of Jang, and there passed into nirvana.

Again the elders told Sachen, "Now, since our ancestral Dharma is the scriptures and oral instructions transmitted through lord Drokmi, you must manage to receive them perfectly."

When Sachen investigated where they could be received, [166] and realized that Khön Dralhabar[274] was a paternal relative and also expert in the scriptures, he traveled to him at Gyichu in Jang.

There Sachen had a dream after receiving the preliminary section of the Hevajra initiation. He dreamed that three bridges made with bridge supports of balls of kneaded dough spanned a great red and murky water, said to be the ocean of existence. Many people pleaded, "Please take me across to the other shore! Please take me across!"

Sachen took three people across all three bridges. He took seven people across two bridges. He took many people across one bridge. Then he rested in the sun on the slope of a mountain said to be Malaya.[275]

When he told master Gyichuwa in the morning, the master joked, "With your strength, how could you take more than three people across?"

Master Gyichuwa held Sachen in very high regard, and also freely gave him the teachings. Sachen received and mastered the Dharma cycle of Hevajra transmitted from lord Drokmi to Ngaripa Salwai Nyingpo, Hevajra transmitted through lord Gö Lotsāwa in the tradition of the great adept Kṛṣṇa, Cakrasaṃvara transmitted through Phamthingpa, which Gyichuwa had received from Mal Lotsāwa, and so forth.[276]

At one point, Sachen heard talk about lord Sé Kharchungwa coming to sit at the head of the rows of a Dharma council in Dokuk. Many of Gyichuwa's young students were preparing to go to the spectacle. In general, the great master Sachen did not enjoy spectacles and so forth, but because of the great reputation of lord Kharchungwa, he wanted to meet him in person, and traveled together with them.

Seated at the head of the rows, lord Kharchungwa made many extravagant statements and questioned each of Gyichuwa's young students. When he arrived at the great master Sachen, he asked, "Noble son, who are you?"

"I am from over at Dromphuk," Sachen replied.

"One of my masters lived there," Sé said. "Now he has passed away. I wanted to visit, but haven't. It was said that one called Bariwa was there, but I didn't want to go. What is it like there now?"

"I am his unworthy son."

"Noble son, do not tell lies! My master had no son!" Sé exclaimed.

The great master Sachen was unable to say anything. But when the young students told his story, lord Kharchungwa sat for a moment with his eyes squeezed shut and said, "If I observe my spiritual practice and the signs of my vital winds, that is correct. [167] The saying, 'The living and the dead do not meet,' is untrue. The meeting time has come."

Sé placed the great master Sachen on his lap, held him to his heart and face, and shed tears. They stayed with their cushions together for three days. Sé gave Sachen a brilliant exposition of the inner structure and outline of the oral instructions of the Precious Teaching. "There is Dharma inside this decrepit old man," he said. "So come quickly. If you think 'I can come slowly,' by that time I will have died."

Sachen and his companions returned to Gyichu. The great master planned to go to Kharchung immediately. When he had finished gathering his things into a bundle, his monk friend Tönpa Dorjé Ö said, "In general, whatever a practitioner of secret mantra does is done after asking the master. In particular, among us—among this many monks—there is no one for whom our master Gyichuwa has higher regard than you. It is not correct to go without asking permission."

"I have no suitable gift. I cannot ask," Sachen replied. So Dorjé Ö gave him a full silk scarf. Realizing that what Dorjé Ö had said was true, Sachen asked Gyichuwa.

"Why are you going?" Gyichuwa said.

"To request the Precious Teaching."

"He is called Smooth-Talking Sé. He has collected and explains some remnants of my master Ngaripa's[277] Dharma teachings. He does not have any oral instructions. Do not go," Gyichuwa replied, and did not give permission.

In gratitude for having completed the scriptures under the guidance of Gyichuwa, Sachen invited him to Sakya. He held a great Dharma council and fulfilled his wishes.

Then Sachen decided that he should go to Kharchung. Just when he had finished getting the necessary goods ready—mainly about three hundred loads of barley—Gyichuwa became ill, and a person came to summon Sachen. When he arrived there, Gyichuwa had already passed away, leaving a last testament saying, "Take monastic ordination and maintain this Khön establishment!"

Sachen completely performed Gyichuwa's funeral rites and so forth. When he had returned to Sakya and prepared the monk's robes, master Nam Khaupa[278] heard about it and summoned him.

"What is the meaning of preparing the yellow robes?" he asked.

Having heard the story, Nam Khaupa ordered, "Masters are equal, but instead of the dead face of the dead master, look at the living face of the living master—me, and do not take ordination!"

Because Sachen obeyed him, the venerable brothers[279] and so forth would later be born, and so this master Nam Khaupa was very kind to the Sakyapa. Thus my master taught. [168]

Although Sachen did not take monastic ordination, he did maintain Gyichuwa's monastic seat.

Because Gyichuwa had been Mal Lotsāwa's disciple, Sachen took his teacher's many Cakrasaṃvara texts and went to Mal Lotsāwa in Gungthang. As it appeared to his disciples, master Mal did not appreciate the great master Sachen's understanding and commented, "Some spend their lives with the Dharma. Some understand it in just an instant."

When the teacher and several disciples were deciphering a mantra of Bhairava, but were completely at a loss, the great master Sachen came from where he was sitting some distance away and suggested, "It would work if you said it like this."

Master Mal exclaimed, "Those I thought did know, do not know. Those I thought did not know, do know," and abruptly left.

The great master Sachen was embarassed and sat depressed some distance away. When their texts were swept away by the wind when nobody was holding on to them, and carried to where the great master was sitting, he collected them and offered them into master Mal's hands.

"It is a good omen!" Mal Lotsāwa exclaimed, and made similar remarks, but was not especially pleased, and gave Sachen some miscellaneous esoteric instructions such as the *Eight Branches.*[280]

When Sachen was returning home, master Mal said, "Some types of people will say, 'I am performing the bestowal of an initiation,' draw with barley flour a lotus with eight petals upon a ruined shield in a corral, and wrap wool around the neck of a pitcher. Do not act like that. Do not let my Dharma be wasted!"

"How could I treat the master's Dharma like that?" Sachen replied, and left for home.

On the road back, Sachen traveled among the Sangyü nomads, and because he was very famous as the "noble son of Sakya," seventeen ounces of gold came into his hands by the time he reached Sakya. He gave it all to a mantra practitioner and sent him to offer it to Mal Lotsāwa.

Mal Lotsāwa had gone to lead an assembly, and when a message was delivered, he said, "It is probably a hungry person with no food. If there is some meat and beer, take it to him at the door."

Told that there was an offering, Mal himself went to the messenger and said, "What offering do you have?"

"Some gold."

"How many tenths of an ounce?"

"I have seventeen ounces," the messenger said.

Master Mal added a full ounce from his own pouch and said, "It is the noble son of Sakya's offering. You have eighteen ounces of gold. Offer them in the center of the assembly!"

Sachen received a message saying, "You are extremely trustworthy, but I did not fully understand that. Now this old man has Dharma, so come quickly." [169]

Sachen went immediately. Mal Lotsāwa completely passed to him the Cakrasaṃvara uncommon explication for disciples, transmitted from the great adept Nāropa; the esoteric instructions of Yamāri; the yoga tantras; and Pañjaranātha transmitted through Lochen, and so forth. He also gave Sachen sacred objects, and completely passed on his doctrine.[281] Thus my master taught.

2) *How the venerable lord of Sakya received the Precious Teaching*

At the end of Gyichuwa's Dharma council, the great master Sachen had intended to go immediately to Sé Kharchungwa, but Sé had passed away at about the same time as Gyichuwa, so he was unable to receive the Precious Teaching.

When Sachen now investigated who was the best person from whom to receive the Precious Teaching of the Path with the Result, he was told that the two Shangtön brothers were the best of Sé's disciples. Of the two of them, the younger brother Sijibarwa was expert, but he had passed away. Now the elder brother, Chöbar, remained. Sachen decided to go, and spoke to master Nam Khaupa.

"What are you doing?" Nam Khaupa asked.

"I am requesting the Precious Teaching," Sachen replied.

"The so-called dedicated meditators are great liars. He does not have any oral instructions at all. If you want buddhahood, I will teach you a method for accomplishment, and you can meditate."

"I am certain myself," Sachen insisted, and was permitted to go.

Sachen gave a coat of armor to a man called Apo Gyalpo. When the two of them arrived as master and servant, lord Gönpawa was sitting in an archery field in Ding, with dank matted hair, naked, and wearing a goatskin cloak over his lower robe. He was spinning thread and engaging in much random talk.

The great master Sachen stayed to the side in a gully there and asked a girl, "Where does the one called Shang Gönpawa Chöbar live here?"

"I do not know a Shang Gönpawa," she said. "If you need Uncle Chöbar, he's the one over there," and showed him.

"Ask him to please come here," he said.

When Shangtön arrived, Sachen spread out a white robe he had, and said, "Please sit here."

But Shangtön did not wish to sit. When Sachen offered prostrations, Shangtön said, "Aren't you mistaken? You seem like a student from far away. And of such students, you seem to be a follower of the new translations."[282] [170]

"I am not mistaken," he replied, and offered the armor as a gift.

"Oh, now what mistake are you making?" Shangtön exclaimed. "With nothing but the food I seek each morning and seek each night, what could I have to loan that would require armor for collateral?" and became alarmed.

"I was not requesting a loan. I am requesting the Precious Teaching."

"What are you talking about?" Shangtön asked. "As for the Precious Teaching, I have never even heard of it except for right now, let alone know it. As for the minor Dharma teachings I explain, I explain some of the *Great Perfection of Tsamunti* and the *Cycle of the Brahmin.*[283] Since you followers of the new translations have great suspicions about those, aren't you suspicious? You should go!"

Wondering whether Shangtön might possibly still give it if he continued to insist, Sachen said, "Since it is late this evening, I would not arrive anywhere, so I ask for a place to stay."

"I have no house or anything fit for a guest," Shangtön replied. "So there is no place for you to stay. You can go or stay, do what you like!"

Sachen left, not wishing to reply.

"And take the armor!" Shangtön called out.

"I don't want to take now what I have already offered," Sachen replied.

Since neither Sachen nor Shangtön took it, the armor was left in that dry gully.

The great master Sachen thought, "From his present behavior, it might be true that Shangtön does not have the Precious Teaching. Since Nakrong Lotsāwa is now in Chakthang, I will go there and investigate closely."

Sachen left for Chakthang, and had arrived at the point where there was a branch in the road, when Tönpa Dorjé Ö (also later called Shang Kyabpa), who was the father of José Öchok, said to lord Gönpawa, "What did the one who was just now asking to meet you want?"

"He said he needed the Precious Teaching," Shangtön replied.

"Well, what did you say?"

"I said I didn't know it."

"When we were staying in Kharchung, some of Gyichuwa's young students came. That man may be the one to whom Sé Kharchungwa said, 'You are my master's son,' took him on his lap, and shed tears. If so, wouldn't it damage your sacred commitments?"

"Ah!" Shangtön exclaimed. "In that case, it would. I didn't know. Now, you run and see whether it is him or not. If not, let him go. If it is, bring him back."

Tönpa Dorjé Ö ran off and caught up with Sachen after the fork in the road. When they discussed the story, and Tönpa Dorjé Ö found that Sachen was indeed the one, he was invited back. [171]

"I do not want people to be aware of our meeting," Shangtön said. "Let's meet in private."

Sachen was led to a ravine in upper Ding, where Shangtön asked, "Who informed you that I had the Precious Teaching?"

"I heard from lord Kharchungwa," he replied.

"In that case, why didn't you request it from lord Kharchungwa himself?"

"When lord Gyichuwa did not give permission, I could not receive it."

"As the saying goes, 'Some māras appear as abbots and teachers,'" Shangtön commented.

"It was not that," Sachen said. "Lord Kharchungwa also passed away at the same time as master Gyichuwa. So if I had gone at that time, Gyichuwa's Dharma would have been left incomplete. And I would also not have received the oral instructions of lord Kharchungwa. He knew that."

"I was joking," Shangtön replied. "How could he have been mistaken?"

In brief, lord Gyichuwa knew that this great master was to be trained by Shang Gönpawa. Thus my master taught.

Then master Shangtön said, "I have completely received the oral instructions, but because there are no texts and I have never taught anyone, I need to think about them some. It is also not right to explain them immediately upon request. You must make at least three requests."

"I made requests yesterday and now, which is two," Sachen answered. "If I make it three by requesting tommorrow as I leave, will that be enough?"

"You did receive the inner structure of the Precious Teaching from lord Kharchungwa, so I should at least listen to your request," Shangtön said. "In any case, many great paṇḍitas and junior paṇḍitas have now been invited here for a memorial Dharma council for Setön Dorjung. It would be unattractive for an old yogin to also teach Dharma at this place where they are explaining Dharma. This fall I must also collect some gifts for explaining Dharma to some laywomen. Come next year in the spring."

Sachen did as he was told. He came bringing an offering of about thirteen ounces of gold and, for Öchok's father in return for his kindness, a heavy cloak. But the father had passed away, so he gave it to Öchok himself.

In brief, this great master completely received the Precious Teaching beginning when he was twenty-eight years old. It was completed in eight years: four years for the Precious Teaching and four years for the Later Cycles of the Path. [172]

Furthermore, lord Gönpawa mostly maintained a deliberate behavior of secrecy, acting as if he did not even meditate, let alone teach the Dharma, except for just a few Dharma sessions with some laywomen. He put on the appearance of passing his time in the activities of an ordinary person—helping in the work of the local people and, between those jobs, collecting all the human and dog excrement on the pathways and heaping it on his own field, and so forth.

When he collected excrement in the springtime, no matter how many villagers said, "Uncle Chöbar, come collect our excrement," he accepted each request.

His wife argued with him, "Are you going to do them all at once, or are you picking a fight?"

The master displayed a physical form at each of their places and satisfied their wishes.

Similarly, during the tilling of the fields, the harvesting of crops, and so forth, he manifested simultaneous physical forms, but each person simply assumed it was him, and no one appears to have known that he was manifesting physical forms. Thus my master taught.

Of those types of miracles, after the oral instructions were completed, Shangtön led lord Sachen to the roof at the time of giving the prediction of practice. "In this Vajrayana, meditation alone is the crucial point," he said. "We were two brothers. My younger brother made a great study of the explication of the treatise, and I meditated. Of the two of us, I gained the greater understanding on the basis of the treatise. And I also did not meditate that much. But for you to believe, I will show you a spectacle."

Shangtön put on his goatskin cloak and went outside. He went under a large shabby basket that was there, and put the goatskin cloak on top of the basket. After a while, many wild creatures made from many precious substances, with various shapes, fur, and colors Sachen had never seen before, emerged from under the basket and covered all the ground of Ding. Later, they dissolved one into another, and went back under the basket.

Again countless birds made from various precious substances, with different colors and shapes, emerged from under the basket and filled all the ground of Ding. They dissolved as before.

Then, in front of the basket in midair, Shangtön displayed the figures of the lords of the three spiritual families,[284] with the nature of light, in the midst of rainbows and lights. That also dissolved as before.

Then lord Shangtön Gönpawa displayed figures of himself, indivisible form and emptiness, filling the entire valley of Ding. [173] Then lord Gönpawa himself went and sat on top of each basket. When an infinite light of various colors radiated from his body, the entire valley was transformed into the nature of light. Finally, when they had all dissolved one into another, he emerged from under the basket, shook the goatskin cloak and put it on, and came inside.

Shangtön made the prediction, "If you make practice the essential thing, you will realize mahāmudrā without discarding the body. If you mostly teach, you will have three disciples who achieve the sublime attainment, seven who attain *forbearance,* and about eighty endowed with realization. Do not write these oral instructions down in texts for eighteen years. Do not mention that you have them, even if only by name. Then, whatever you do—teach or set them down in writing—you will be the owner of the doctrine."

This lord Sachen received fragments, but not the complete Precious Teaching, from Kyura Akyap, Shama Könchok, and Drangyul Olkawa. The first two later became lord Sachen's disciples. Thus my master taught.

Sachen reviewed the *Vajra Lines* once every day and the extensive path once every month without break. He had been poisoned before by a monk he had been with in Gungthang who hated him, and then cured by a medicine called *somo tsitsi* that had been offered to him. But the residue of the poison arose again while he was staying at Drongchung monastery in Yeru, and he slipped into a coma for about twenty days. He later recovered from the illness, but it had caused him to forget all the Dharma.

"For the other instructions, I can depend on companions, books, and so forth," Sachen thought. "But for the Precious Teaching, the master is not living. There are no books and companions. Even if I went to India, it would be difficult to learn these instructions."

Sachen went into retreat in the Mañjughoṣa Cave of the eastern palace that is called the Old Residence. When he made prayers, Shang Gönpawa appeared in a dream and spoke the oral instructions. He made intense prayers, and lord Gönpawa actually came and completely taught the oral instructions.[285] Sachen also regained the forgotten ones. [174]

When Sachen made strong prayers again, he beheld the faces of five figures—the main one and a retinue. The body of the venerable Lord of Yogins, Virūpa, was deep red in color, with the majestic light of ten million suns. With both hands making the gesture of the Dharma wheel, he covered Sakya from Baldrok to Möndrok[286] with his legs crossed in the vajra position, and used the slope of white earth as a backdrop. To the right was the great adept Kāṇha, with his left hand resting in the meditation gesture and his right blowing a horn trumpet. To the left was Gayadhara, wearing the bulky white cotton robes of a paṇḍita, with his legs crossed, and holding a vajra and bell crossed at his heart. To the rear, Koṭalipa held a parasol. In front, Vīṇāpa held a skull-cup with both hands and served nectar.[287] The three adepts were each dark blue in color, with braided topknots, and wore short trousers of white cotton.

Then Virūpa appeared, sometimes with the retinue and sometimes alone, and for one month Sachen received the profound-path guruyoga, the common and uncommon Virūpa protections, Vidāraṇā in the tradition of Virūpa, and seventy-two tantras.[288] In that way, with the direct transmission that he actually heard from the Lord of Yogins, two transmissions came together in Sachen.

The eighteen years of the restriction commanded by Shang Gönpawa expired, and the bodhisattva Aseng, who was the son of Kyura Akyap, supplicated Sachen: "You have the Precious Teaching, but you have never even mentioned it to us. Now you must teach."

Because the expiration of the eighteen years and the supplication by Aseng occurred at the same time, Sachen decided that the auspicious connections had been aligned by master Shang, and taught it once to Aseng alone. At his supplication, Sachen also composed the *Summary: An Explication of the Treatise*.[289] This was the first of all the explications of the scripture in the tradition of this lineage. Thus my master taught.

Similarly, Sachen gradually taught the Path with the Result to three, five, twenty-five, and—although he did not teach as in these public explications nowadays—even to somewhat more than twenty-five. At first he held three ritual feasts every time. Later he held two: one at the initial commencement and one at the point of mending the sacred commitments.

After thus ripening and liberating infinite disciples, [175] Sachen demonstrated how to pass into bliss at the monastery of Kyawo Khadang in Jang. At that time, four of his physical forms traveled simultaneously to four pure lands. One traveled to Sukhāvatī and one to Potala, because these are the places where Avalokiteśvara's sambhogakāya enjoyment body and nirmāṇakāya emanated body reside. One traveled to the mundane realm of Serdokchen, to purify that land for a main spiritual son.[290] One went to Oḍḍiyāna, symbolizing that he was the lord of the entire Vajrayana, since all the Vajrayana tantras reside there. Thus my master taught.

When Sachen's physical remains were offered for cremation, most disciples saw him as Cakrasaṃvara and several saw him as Hevajra. When the ashes of his body were sprinkled on the lake in the springtime, the surface of the lake was covered with a red film that took the form of the supporting mandala and supported deities of Cakrasaṃvara. In the ancient texts it says that this was used as a model and painted on the ceiling of the mausoleum. Now it is explained that the painting was created from the images in the smoke from the cremation of the body. Thus my master taught.

In what way did the great master of Sakya compose texts on this Precious Teaching? If all that he composed himself and that disciples wrote as accounts of his words and so forth are combined, there appear to be about twenty explications of the treatise. But the main ones are those known as the Eleven Commentaries. Many different identifications of these have appeared, but in the opinion of Dakchen Rinpoché,[291] they were for [1] Aseng, [2] Shu, [3] Lok, [4] the Wife, [5] the Sons, [6] Da, [7] Sang, [8] Ga, [9] Mang, [10] Ah U, and [11] Nyak. The *Eulogy to Lord Sachen* composed by Shuché[292] says:

> You instructed in writing
> eight male and three female disciples
> who completely received the oral instructions.

The ancient text with annotations applying to this, which has come from the hands of Yarlungpa,[293] will thus be taken as authoritative:

[1] The first commentary, as mentioned previously, was the *Summary* composed at the request of the bodhisattva Aseng.[294] There were both larger and smaller versions of the *Summary*.

[2] The *Explication for Shuché* was requested by Shuché Ngödrup.

[3] The *Explication for Lokya* was requested by Lokya Chödrak of Gyerbu.

[4] The *Explication for the Wife* was composed for the benefit of Machik Tsetsa, the senior of the great master's two wives, and the mother of the eldest son Künga Bar. Cakrasaṃvara was used for the creation stage. [176] It was slightly different from the one now held to be the *Explication for the Benefit of the Wife*. Thus my master taught.

[5] The *Explication for the Benefit of the Sons* consists of the miscellaneous accounts of the many difficult points of the *Vajra Lines* recorded for the benefit of Sachen's physical sons, the venerable brothers, and edited by his spiritual son, Nyen Phuljungwa Tsuktor Gyalpo, also known as Sönam Dorjé.

[6] The *Explication for Dagyal* was composed for the bodhisattva Dawa Gyaltsen.

[7] The *Explication for Sangri* was composed for the benefit of the spiritual friend Sangri Phukpa.

[8] The *Explication for Gatheng* was composed for the benefit of a man from Kham called Gatheng after Sachen realized that the account of his words recorded in Gatheng's summarizing notes was slightly corrupt.

[9] The *Explication for Mangkhar* was composed for the benefit of Lady Mangchung.

[10] The *Explication for Lady Ah U* was composed for the benefit of the woman called Lady Ah U Ma, who had howled "Ah U! Ah U!" after the purification of birth as a dog had arisen.[295]

[11] The *Explication for Nyak* was composed for the benefit of the spiritual friend Nyak Shirawa Wangchuk Gyaltsen.

These are the eleven. Of them, the *Explication for Aseng* is a Dharma text composed by Sachen. Most of the others were written down exactly according to Sachen's words, and are authentic because they were offered for him to see and he corrected them. Thus my master taught.

In this lineage, the reading transmissions of the *Explication for Aseng*, the *Explication for the Benefit of the Sons*, and the *Explication for Nyak* are the only such transmissions that still remain. Thus my master taught.

3) *How followers came to the venerable lord of Sakya*

Most learned and realized masters during that time became Sachen's disciples, as mentioned in the prophecies of lord Gyichuwa and lord Gönpawa. Yet it has been said that his main disciples were three who achieved the sublime attainment, seven who attained *forbearance*, and about eighty who were endowed with realization. No individual identifications are made for the latter.

a) *Three who achieved the sublime attainment*

(1) *The Ceylonese mendicant*

On the island of Ceylon near India, an abbot who was a sthavira arhat prophesied to another monk that there was now in Tibet an emanation of Virūpa called Sakyapa. He would obtain the sublime attainment from him.

Accordingly, two mendicants came from Ceylon, but one turned back in Nepal. One came before the great master Sachen while he was staying in Gungthang. He offered many different medicines and a fine brocade canopy called a *gagula*. When initiation was bestowed and the oral instructions were taught, he obtained the sublime attainment after six months, and traveled to the glorious mountains of Śrīparvata without discarding the body. [177]

(2) *Gompa Kyibar*

The one called Gompa Kyibar was born in Mangkhar Trangok. When he practiced the great and small vocal inhalations of the path of the fourth initiation[296] at Samling, a voice like a brass trumpet was heard at Taktsé Pass, loud enough to make the nomads' dogs bark. Relying on the path of the fourth initiation, he attained mahāmudrā without discarding the body.

(3) *Bodhisattva Tak*

Bodhisattva Tak was born at Takdé Sengé Lung in Latö in western Tsang. He had an extremely fine disposition. He also requested instructions from the great master Sachen. In general, he requested the Path with the Result, and in particular, the guidance of the profound path.[297] When he meditated, although he discarded the body for a while, he later entered into the same supporting body and passed into Khecara without discarding the body.

These were the three taken across all three bridges in Sachen's earlier dream. Thus my master taught.

b) *Seven who attained forbearance*

These seven were the precious venerable lord Drakpa Gyaltsen, Shuché Ngödrup, Nakgom Sönam Gyaltsen, the Tsarkha yogin, Gatön Dorjé Drak, Gompa Ötrak, and Lady Mangchungma.

(1) *The precious venerable lord Drakpa Gyaltsen*

Drakpa Gyaltsen was in essence Mañjughoṣa, but as perceived by his disciples, he said in the *Dream Biography:*

I will not be liberated on the path taken by Bodhisattva Tak. I will go on the path taken by Shuché Ngödrup.[298]

Therefore, he took the way of attaining *forbearance* on the path of application. Thus my master taught.

(2) *Shuché Ngödrup*

Shuché Ngödrup was the nephew of Shutön Rokpo, a teacher of the Vehicle of the Perfections in Latö in western Tsang. He wanted to go to the great master Sachen, and asked over and over, but his uncle did not give permission. One time he insisted, and was scolded, "I hope this continuing detailed explanation for these young monks will benefit you. Why would you go?"

Shuché stared at his face for a long time and replied, "In our Vehicle of the Perfections it says that some māras come in the form of abbots and teachers. Is that you?"

His uncle was embarassed and did not say anything, and Shuché was allowed to leave. He went to the great master Sachen and received instructions. When he told the previous story, it is said that Sachen remarked, "To speak in that way after you had heard the Vehicle of the Perfections and so forth from him was a little too extreme."

After Shuché had completely received the instructions, he said, "I cannot survive here in Tibet. I am going to India," and left.

Once when the great master Sachen was sitting on the slope of white earth at Sakya, [178] a great vulture flew up from the south. As soon as it arrived in front of the great master, it changed into a monk and offered prostrations. The monk stayed with Sachen for a while. Again he changed into a vulture and flew away. When everyone saw this and asked about it, Sachen said, "It was Shuché Ngödrup, who said he came to ask whether I was happy. He came from India."

Not long after the great master Sachen had passed away, the venerable brothers were holding a ritual feast in the Gorum Temple and remarked,[299] "It would be nice if Apo Shuché were here tonight."

After a moment there was a knock at the door. When they looked, it was Shuché. He offered as gifts a fresh garland of mayapple and some stalks of rice.

"When did you come?" they asked.

"I came when you said it would be nice if I were here."

The venerable lord Drakpa Gyaltsen said, "Few people are here tonight, and those have pure sacred commitments, so perform a miracle."

"Please do not say that," Shuché replied, and became nervous.

When Drakpa Gyaltsen insisted, Shuché went into a small hole beside the chapel of the protectors. A little later, one Shuché came out. He prostrated, and sat in the row. Seven like him lined up, and finally he himself appeared. Finally one dissolved into another, and Shuché flew off to India.

Shuché was the type to be living even now. As illustrated by this episode, he gained control of miracles and clairvoyance. Thus my master taught.

(3) *Nakgompa Sögyal*

Nakgompa Sögyal's birthplace was Tanak. His parents and other relatives died when he was young. He wandered around and found work in Tsal Gungthang as the servant of a mantra practitioner who was meditating on the form of the deity Yamāri that was known as Langtso Marpo. Sögyal learned by watching him meditate. When Sögyal chanted where the cattle grazed, at one point the animals became Yamāri and their voices reverberated as *hrīḥ kṣṭi*.[300] When he told the mantra practitioner, he said Sögyal had residual karma and performed a blending ritual.[301]

Sögyal eventually met the great master Sachen, who taught him the instructions. When he meditated, he attained *forbearance* on the path of application.

(4) *The Tsarkha yogin*

After the great master Sachen had peacefully passed away, the spiritual friend Nyak[302] traveled among the Sangyü nomads. An old nomad there, who had the sign of the drops stabilized below his throat, [179] said, "The master was extremely kind to me, but I am not able to make a great offering right now."

He presented many offerings of a hundred items of gold, of salt, of blocks of tea, of butter, and so forth, together with the pack animals to carry them.

"Are you not mistaken?" Nyak said. "The great master never traveled here after leaving Gungthang."

"How am I mistaken?" he replied. "The great master arrived in Tsarkha on this month and year, and stayed for three years. When he gave guidance to about thirty dedicated meditators, these signs of the path also appeared within me through his kindness."

Similarly, all the old disciples compared their experiences. Sachen had displayed six physical forms simultaneously: being Mal Lotsāwa's disciple in Gungthang, giving the instructions in Tsarkha, explaining the Dharma of the Precious Teaching in Sakya, benefiting living beings among the Sangyü nomads, turning the Dharma wheel at Gonga in Shap, and opening the mandala of Namkha Drimé and performing the consecration of the temple of Drönla Cham in Dringtsam. But it appears that no one understood until later. Thus my master taught.

(5) *Gatön Dorjé Drak*

Gatön Dorjé Drak was of the Ga family line of Kham. He was a disciple of both Sachen and the venerable lord Drakpa Gyaltsen. He made many earlier and later offerings. In particular, he delivered a great offering while the venerable lord was staying at Nyilung monastery in Jang. In response, the venerable lord gave the oral instruction called the *Epistle to Gatön,* one of the most crucial texts of the Path with the Result.[303] Thus my master taught.

(6) *Gompa Ötrak*

When Gompa Ötrak meditated, the purification of birth in the hells occurred.[304] There was a large tree in one of the fields of Sakya. When Gompa Ötrak arrived at its top, hot water was bubbling and boiling at its root. When he thought, "I hope I don't fall down," he tumbled down, and all his flesh was stripped bare to the white bones.

As soon as he thought, "I wish this water were cold," it instantly froze. His body was stuck there and he could not pull himself out. With effort, he pulled out half his body, but half remained stuck, and the appearance arose of his lungs and heart hanging out. Thus my master taught.

(7) *Lady Mangchungma*

Lady Mangchungma's birthplace was Gara. When she meditated at Samling, many purifications of birth as an animal occurred.[305] In particular, the experience of a hybrid yak arose. While it was hobbling on a main road, many yaks came racing along. It tried to flee, but could not get away. The catalyst of being crushed by the yaks woke her from the experience. [180] It is said that the experience was so vivid that when she looked there were many yaks going by. Afterward, appearances arose as bliss. The feeling of yak-hair cloth and so forth, and of stones, thorns, and so forth, all arose as great bliss. She was one who stayed wherever it was uncomfortable and meditated. Thus my master taught.

Thus, although Sachen had many disciples, his main disciples were his descendants and Dharma sons, the two venerable brothers.

The precious teacher Sönam Tsemo

The precious teacher Sönam Tsemo was not listed with the previously discussed disciples because he and lord Sachen were actually not two, or because they were equal in realization. Thus he was not discussed separately.

Moreover, this venerable lord Sönam Tsemo had previously taken birth in India as eleven paṇḍitas, such as Durjayacandra.[306] When he was born in Tibet, the ḍākas and ḍākinīs attached a notice above the gate of the Vajrāsana. When it was proclaimed in all directions by the paṇḍita Devaśrī of Kauśambī, he was discovered. He was an unimpeded expert in all fields of knowledge.

When Sönam Tsemo was teaching the Path with the Result in the Old Tower of Sakya, he established nineteen disciples in the state of pure appearance, simultaneously displaying three different visual appearances, including appearing as Mañjughoṣa for the venerable lord Drakpa Gyaltsen. When he gave the causal initiation to the great venerable lord, he actually displayed the supporting mandala and supported deities of glorious Hevajra. Since the bestowal of the initiation was thus received as it had been by Virūpa from Nairātmyā, a direct transmission can also be traced from this event.

Furthermore, Sönam Tsemo gained mastery of many magical abilities, including being able to go to and return from such sacred places as Potala[307] in about half a day and to engage in deliberate behavior together with the assemblies of spiritual heroes and yoginīs residing in those places. It has been said:

> I bow to and rejoice in you
> who are on *near proximity*.[308]

With these words, it was accepted that he resided on the second spiritual level, *immaculate,* called *near proximity*. Thus my master taught.

Although Sönam Tsemo is known to have passed into Khecara without discarding a body, it has been said:

> From within the physical remains of the precious teacher, a sound like great bees emerged.[309]

If these words are evaluated, it seems as though Sönam Tsemo probably did leave physical remains. In any case, he completed two of four intended introductory treatises, such as the *Entrance Gate for Children,* the *Entrance Gate to the Dharma,* and the *Entrance Gate to Expertise.* He also composed commentaries on the *Two-Part Root Tantra* and the *Sampuṭa;* the *Method for Accomplishment,* the *Stream of Initiation,* and so forth for the Hevajra tradition of esoteric instructions; [181] and several texts of oral instruction, such as *Application to Precisely This Scripture.*[310]

Further details about the venerable lord Drakpa Gyaltsen

In that way, of the two brothers, the great venerable lord Drakpa Gyaltsen was the kindest and most important for this Precious Teaching. This exceptional and extremely direct transmission of the instructions that did not come to other disciples of lord Sachen, such as the precious teacher Sönam Tsemo, came through Drakpa Gyaltsen. He also edited the single volume that had not existed before, and so forth.

Drakpa Gyaltsen's extensive biography is told in other texts, but the following miraculous stories are not mentioned in them.

When the Old Tower of Sakya was built, many scattered red boulders were at the spot where an evil black nāga called Khün lived. One could hardly even walk in that area.

The venerable lord Drakpa Gyaltsen told that nāga, "I am building a temple here, so you must move."

The nāga was miserable and replied, "There will not be time to move even my gold, not to mention my other wealth."

It was not necessary to drive him far away. Drakpa Gyaltsen stopped him with a vow not to harm general and specific living beings. When Mön Vajra Rāja led the way with water from the vase, and the great venerable lord held a vajra and bell and exorcised the nāga from behind, not only did he move, but even the boulders where he lived scurried away like driven sheep. Those are the red boulders now behind the eastern palace. Malevolent ghouls were not able to even slightly transgress Drakpa Gyaltsen's commands.

Similarly, when the great paṇḍita of Kaśmīr[311] arrived in Sakya, the junior paṇḍitas agreed beforehand, "He might be a great vajra holder, but we are paṇḍitas famous in all parts of India, from east to west, so you should not return his prostrations."

Following behind the great paṇḍita was a spirit who had been a man who had had a stable creation stage of Vajrabhairava, but since he had not combined it with compassionate emptiness, and in conjunction with bad conditions, had been born as an evil spirit called Stack of Nine Goiters. When Drakpa Gyaltsen saw him coming and placed his vajra and bell in space, exorcising the impediment, the spirit could not retreat to India nor could he remain in Tibet, and he quickly fled to a distant ocean shore of China.

When the venerable lord Drakpa Gyaltsen made prostrations to the great paṇḍita, the great paṇḍita himself returned the prostrations. [182] Afterward, when the junior paṇḍitas asked why, he is said to have replied, "He is great Vajradhara in the mandala of Guhyasamāja. Should I not offer prostrations to him?"

Once the great paṇḍita told lord Sakya Paṇḍita, "Let us go see what your uncle is doing."

"I will go in advance," Sakya Paṇḍita replied.

"Do not do that. Let us go together," he said.

When they arrived, the venerable lord Drakpa Gyaltsen had finished the creation stage of Guhyasamāja and was intending to make the offerings of the front creation. He was sitting and holding the vajra and bell in his hands. When the great paṇḍita suddenly arrived, Drakpa Gyaltsen left his vajra and bell in midair above the surface of the table, as though anxious at the thought that no welcome had been prepared.

The great paṇḍita thought that he had done so deliberately and said, "Nothing amazing about that."

The venerable lord replied, "I was not hoping to amaze you," and placed them again on the table.

When the great paṇḍita stayed with his cushion next to that of the great venerable lord and examined him, he found no faults whatsoever in his actions of body, speech, and mind. When Drakpa Gyaltsen used leather cords for the string of a rosary, the great paṇḍita is said to have commented, "You are great Vajradhara. It is correct to braid nine threads for the string of a rosary as explained in the tantras."

On another occasion the great paṇḍita, together with his disciples, announced that a solar eclipse would occur. The venerable lord said that it would not happen. In that situation, the great paṇḍita traveled to Shang with his disciples. On the day the sun was to be eclipsed, the teacher and all his disciples said that an eclipse was coming and that the venerable lord did not know. They looked for it, but the great venerable lord had halted the circulation of the sun, Rāhu[312] was unable to affect the sun, and no eclipse occurred.

The great paṇḍita was forced to say, "An old layman practitioner up in western Tsang is bursting with pride."

In this way, Drakpa Gyaltsen was able to overwhelm with his brilliance even the consummate great paṇḍitas.

Drakpa Gyaltsen once stayed at Nyilung monastery in Jang, where there were two parallel caves. The venerable lord stayed in one and a kitchen was set up in the other, with a hole made between them. At one point, many hundreds of horsemen arrived on the plain in front of the caves, and they all went inside the cave where the venerable lord was staying. [183] While an attendant watched carefully through the hole, many men in Mongol costume seated themselves in rows. In the midst of them, a white youth with a turquoise topknot acted as interpreter, translating and speaking their requests in Tibetan and translating and explaining the venerable lord's statements in Mongolian. Indeed, this was the Mongolian deity Namthel Karpo, respectfully giving the many reasons for the venerable lord to visit Mongolia.

"I am old now," the venerable lord replied. "I have no great karma connection with you Mongols, so it would not be beneficial. In the future, invite my nephew Künga Gyaltsen![313] Great benefit will come to you." The interpreter was the deity Nyen Thanglha.[314]

"Don't we have some beer?" the venerable lord asked. There was about half a skull-cup, which was offered to him. When the venerable lord blessed it with the three syllables and sprinkled it about, there was drink enough for all to get drunk and tipsy. As the night passed they sang songs in Mongolian, danced about, and displayed many signs of joy. They dispersed at sunrise.

In that way, the great venerable lord bound the Mongolian deity Namthel Karpo to a vow, and the benefit earned was that lord Sakya Paṇḍita was later invited by the Mongol Prince Ködan. Thus, bringing the three regions of Tibet under control was also due to the kindness of the great venerable lord Drakpa Gyaltsen.[315]

In particular, forty-four years after lord Sachen had passed into bliss, the venerable lord Drakpa Gyaltsen himself reached the age of fifty-six. While he was staying in the Tsangkha monastery of Nyemo, the great venerable lord Sakyapa appeared again and again in his dreams. He remembered that it was known that when lord Sachen had met the Lord of Yogins before, he had also first appeared again and again in dreams.

"I do not know what this is," he thought. He observed a strict retreat and made prayers, and after a while the venerable lord Sachen actually appeared. Sachen gave him a smooth white square stone with *hūṃ* and *aṃ* in the center of a lotus with eight petals, the syllables *ya ra la wa* in the four directions, and the four intermediate petals empty.

"Son, the meaning of all the Dharma I taught you before is included here," Sachen said, and spoke the verses, "First, take the true nature of phenomena as the base," and so forth.

Concerning this, "First, take the true nature of phenomena as the base" [184] is the view of the time of the cause. "Second, seize the vital winds" is the yoga of the vital winds. "Fully generate the heat of the fierce fire" is the yoga of the drops. "Draw the stream of the enlightenment mind into the central channel" is the yoga of the consort. "Bring the elements of earth and so forth under control" is the vajra waves. "Actualize the five types of primordial awareness and attain the immortal state" is the result. Sachen spoke this exceptional instruction called the *Clarification of the Meaning Through Symbols,* in which the entire path of the Precious Teaching is presented by means of symbols.[316]

In brief, the great venerable lord Drakpa Gyaltsen had instructions that came through both the sequential transmission by way of three lineages and through the direct transmission. The three lineages converged in him because he received the entire path from four masters: the father, lord Sachen; the son, Sönam Tsemo; Nyen Phuljungwa Tsuktor Gyalpo;[317] and Gyagom Tsultrim Drak.

Concerning the lineage of the direct transmission, these verses written at the end of an explication of the treatise were composed by the precious teacher Sönam Tsemo, although they are now claimed to be the words of the venerable lord Drakpa Gyaltsen:

> The moon of primordial awareness
> appeared to immaculate eyes.

The good qualities
of the Tripiṭaka were clarified.
Beautiful like a jewel within the ocean,
this is realized by the clear-minded,
but not by others.[318]

The moon of primordial awareness (great Buddha Vajradhara,[319] first in the lineage, as indicated by the symbol of a single moon) instructed the eyes, the Lord of Yogins (second in the lineage). Lord Sachen (third in the lineage, as indicated by the three baskets of the Tripiṭaka) clarified the scriptures and instructions. The ocean is the precious teacher Sönam Tsemo, fourth in the lineage. A direct transmission such as this cannot be realized except by the intelligent.

Similarly, Ram Dingmawa Jungné Dorjé asked the precious venerable lord Drakpa Gyaltsen what the lineage of the seventy-two tantras was. The verses of his reply are now written at the end of the *Summary:*

The unexcelled—the directions multiplied
by the mountains plus the eyes—
were clarified by the Vedas
and assigned by the hands to the fire.
The ocean clarified by its light
flowed into the elements.
If the intelligent understand the meaning of this,
they should speak![320]

The meaning: the unexcelled yoga tantras [185] are the directions—which are ten—that become seventy when multiplied by the seven mountains.[321] Enhanced with two eyes, these become seventy-two, which are clarified by the esoteric instructions of the methods of explanation, symbolized by the [four] Vedas. This way of grouping and explaining the tantras by means of the four authentic qualities and all the esoteric instructions by means of the four oral transmissions was taught by the hands (Virūpa, the second in the lineage) to the fire (Sachen, the third in the lineage). The ocean of all his tantras and oral instructions (possessed by the precious teacher Sönam Tsemo, the fourth in the lineage) flowed into the precious venerable lord Drakpa Gyaltsen, the fifth in the lineage, as indicated by the symbol of the

[five] elements. By the rhetorical question, "Do the intelligent understand such a meaning?" Drakpa Gyaltsen indicated that he understood.

In brief, most of the esoteric instructions of the Precious Teaching in those transmissions existed only as oral transmissions. Except for the highly cherished miscellaneous texts kept in a leather box, there was no arrangement of the teachings into a single volume. This venerable lord Drakpa Gyaltsen composed many texts, such as the *Root Text and Commentary on the Indivisibility of Samsara and Nirvana* and the *Four Fundamental Treatises of Guidance.*[322] He collected all of these texts, with a catalogue, into a single volume, and was therefore extremely kind to these instructions. Thus my master taught. At that time, as both the wooden cover of the volume and the cloth were yellow, it became known as the *Yellow Volume.*

In this way, Drakpa Gyaltsen illuminated the precious doctrine, and has already actualized perfect buddhahood in the northern buddha field of Serdokchen. Thus my master taught.

Sakya Paṇḍita and his main disciples

Drakpa Gyaltsen had many disciples, but his Dharma son, his nephew and the crown jewel of all his disciples was the great venerable lord Sakya Paṇḍita. The biography of this master should be taught in more detail as it appears in the separate texts. Sakya Paṇḍita composed many texts on the oral instructions, such as the *Text on the Five Dependently Arisen Connections* and the *Seal of the Four Mandalas.*[323] By now, a long time has passed since he attained perfect buddhahood. This can be known from Phakpa Rinpoché's comment in *Replies to the Kadam Master Dokorwa's Questions:*

> Several years have passed since the buddhahood of our master, the Dharma lord.[324]

Thus my master taught.

The assembly of Sakya Paṇḍita's disciples included many monastic students, such as those with the last name of Pal and those with the last name of Gyaltsen. [186] Of these disciples, the stream of the vow of individual liberation transmitted through Khangtön Özer Gyaltsen is presently maintained unbroken in the region of Lophu.

Sakya Paṇḍita's many main disciples included the pair of Lhopa and Mar, who upheld the lineage of explication, the pair of the adept Yönten Pal and Tsokgom, who upheld the transmission of the oral instructions, and Gyalwa Yangönpa,[325] who upheld the transmission of practice.

Mar Chökyi Gyalpo recorded the *Incisive Vajra Biographies, Mar's Explication of the Treatise,* and so forth, exactly according to the words of lord Sakya Paṇḍita. Mar gave them to Gangtön Sherap Bum. Karpo Drakpa Rinchen Sengé received them from him, and the transmission is unbroken to the present day.[326]

Lhopa Rinchen Pal endured many hardships for these esoteric instructions, such as traveling to China to request the texts of guidance from lord Sakya Paṇḍita. While he also composed miscellaneous texts, a transmission for them does not appear to have survived.

The adept Yönten Pal[327] served as the personal attendant of lord Sakya Paṇḍita for six years. He obtained most of the Dharma that lord possessed, such as the oral instructions of the entire Path with the Result.

Tsokgom Rinpoché[328] studied under the great learned and realized lord Sakya Paṇḍita for thirteen years, receiving all the Dharma he possessed, and the entire path of the Path with the Result in particular. At Gyerphu Dzilung, also called Samten Ling, he mainly engaged in meditation.

Chögyal Phakpa and his main disciples

The chief of all Sakya Paṇḍita's disciples was the king of Dharma, Phakpa Rinpoché, who was his Dharma son and paternal nephew. Furthermore, Phakpa's father, Sangtsa Sönam Gyaltsen,[329] had focused his practice on the deity Gaṇapati, who knew that the master Setön Ripa of Langri Thang in Ngari had the ability to take control of the threefold universe. When Gaṇapati supplicated him, Setön Ripa purposely took rebirth as Phakpa Rinpoché, whose extensive biography should be taught according to the separate texts.

Many disciples came to Phakpa, but his official activities were very great and he never stayed in one place for very long; thus, few disciples completely received the tantras and oral instructions from him. Gendenpa Tashi Pal completely received the explication of the *Tantra Trilogy* in little stages like the progress of a hybrid yak-cow.[330]

Master Shang Könchok Palwa[331] also completely received guidance on the Teaching in little stages like the progress of a hybrid yak-cow. [187]

Furthermore, Gelong Künlo and he both followed Phakpa Rinpoché to China for the sole purpose of requesting the oral instructions. They met Phakpa Rinpoché at a place called Tsodo Nesar in Dokham as he was returning to Tibet. When they told their story, Phakpa Rinpoché said, "While many people of the three districts of Central Tibet, Tsang, and Kham are coming to me nowadays, most do so for the sake of this life alone; none are seeking Dharma. You two seeking Dharma from a great distance is amazing."

Over a period of three years they completely received the path. Shang Könchok Palwa became master Phakpa's chief spiritual son. Gelong Künlo, other than furthering his own meditation, did not uphold the lineage. Thus my master taught.

The great adept Drakphukpa and later transmissions

The great adept Drakphukpa[332] received the Path with the Result from Shang Könchok Palwa. Furthermore, the trio of Tsokgom, the adept Yönten Pal, and the nephew Phakpa Rinpoché was extremely significant for the Precious Teaching. This master Drakphukpa received the transmission of the instructions from all three. Furthermore, Shang Könchok Palwa had received the entire path of the Precious Teaching from Ra Nyipa Gyalwa Rinchen, also known as Rinchen Gyaltsen, a disciple who had received the entire path from the adept Yönten Pal. Shang Könchok Palwa had received it again from Phakpa Rinpoché, considering him to be the owner of this Dharma. From master Shang, Drakphukpa received the two transmissions from the nephew Phakpa Rinpoché and the adept Yönten Pal. Because lord Drakphukpa also completely received the path from the great adept Nyenchenpa,[333] the disciple of Tsokgom Rinpoché, he combined the quintessence of all three transmissions.

Because this lord Drakphukpa had become the authority on Sakyapa Dharma, even lord Lama Dampa,[334] who had first received the Teaching from Guru Palden Sengé of Phoma Takri, received it again from Drakphukpa. Even to the present day, all major and minor points of practice are judged according to whether they existed or not in Drakphukpa's time. Thus my master taught.

The disciples of the great adept Drakphukpa who completely received the path were lord Lama Dampa, Ritröpa Lodrö Tenpa,[335] and Drakphukpa Könchok Gyaltsen. [188]

Drakphukpa's disciple, the master of the Path with the Result called Lodrö Karpo of Lingtsang in Kham, also received the Teaching. While Lodrö Karpo was doing much teaching and study in Kham, Gyönjo Yeshé Pal of Kham requested the Teaching. He later came to Drakphukpa in Central Tibet and Tsang, but just after he received the instructions on the Three Appearances, Drakphukpa passed away. The remaining guidance was completed by Ritröpa. Then Lodrö Karpo traveled to Phakrika and practiced and studied intensively for many years. When he traveled to Sakya, he was known as the Path with the Result master Yeshé Pal,[336] and did much teaching and study. His disciple was Chölingpa Losang Karmo of Kham, later known as the Path with the Result master Losang Karmo.[337] Those masters and disciples also engaged in much explication and practice.

In the lineages that flowed from them, a stream of the reading transmission of Sachen's eleven commentaries has been upheld. But they have texts said to have been composed for the benefit of the great venerable lord Drakpa Gyaltsen and so forth that are somewhat different from the eleven nowadays. Therefore, those reading transmissions are insufficient. Thus my master taught.

Lord Palden Tsultrim[338] received the Teaching from both lord Lama Dampa and Ritröpa. The trio of the great adept Buddhashrī,[339] Sharchen Yeshé Gyaltsen,[340] and the Menyag teacher Rinchen Dorjé received it from Palden Tsultrim. The latter passed away at an early age in Kham, and was not beneficial to others.

When lord Palden Tsultrim gave the prediction of practice to Sharchen, he restricted him by command for eighteen years. This was just as Gönpawa had done to Sachen, but with lord Gönpawa it turned out exactly. In this case things did not turn out exactly. Before the expiration of the commanded restriction, Sharchen passed away; and he had not been able to give the complete Teaching, other than just the Hevajra initiation in the tradition of the esoteric instructions, and minor instructions of the profound path, the Virūpa protection, and so forth.

Therefore, when Ngorchen Dorjé Chang wished to receive the Precious Teaching, he went to Lotsāwa Kyabchok, a very famous disciple of lord Lama Dampa. But when Ngorchen had received the Teaching up through the Three Appearances, he was unsatisfied because it was not quite the unadulterated Sakya tradition. In accordance with a prophecy in a dream, he traveled on, and when he investigated, he heard that the great adept Buddhashrī was the best. When Ngorchen came to him, the house, the man guiding him with incense, the physical shape of the master himself, and so forth were just as they had been in the dream, so he was pleased. He completely obtained the oral instructions. Lord Sempa Chenpo[341] received them from him. [189] The great Dakchen Dorjé Chang[342] received them from Lord Sempa Chenpo. Thus my master taught.

Following the trio of Tsokgom, the adept Yönten Pal, and the nephew Phakpa Rinpoché, the trio of La, Nyen, and Shang[343] were extremely significant.

Laruwa was born into the family of chieftains called Laru Serkhangpa. Studying under Sharpa Dorjé Özer, he learned the *Tantra Trilogy* together with the esoteric instructions. While he was feeling great, thinking, "I am an expert," he met the adept Yönten Pal, and everything before became just words. He requested the entire path of the Path with the Result.

Laruwa Sönam Sengé's disciple was Dönri Drakchen, and Drakchen's disciple was the omniscient Gangtröpa.[344] Paṇchen Mati received the complete path from Gangtröpa, but said that the meditative concentration of individual withdrawal in the six-branch yoga that he had received from the omniscient Jonangpa kept the stream of initiation from ceasing.[345] Although Thekchen Chöjé completely received the Teaching from Mati Paṇchen, he saw that it would not be the real transmission of the meaning because Mati did not perform the Time of the Path without break.[346] Later he received it in Sakya from the master called Butön Wangchuk Dar or Wangchuk Gyalpo, a disciple of Drakphukpa Könchok Gyaltsen, and so received both the transmission of the word and the transmission of the meaning. The venerable father[347] received it from Thekchen Rinpoché.

Also, Lachen Künga Gyaltsen completely received the Teaching from lord Lama Dampa, and Dakchen Jamyang Chenpo received it from him.[348]

Similarly, the realized expert Nya Ön received the teaching from Lama Dampa. The great adept Künlo of Tsechen received the entire path from Nya Ön, but because Nya Ön was also in Mati's tradition, he received it again from Yakdepa Namkha Sönam.[349] Yakdepa received it from Drakphukpa Köngyal, who was also known as Latö Köngyal. This master also composed a text of liner notes to the Hevajra initiation that is very highly regarded. Thus my master taught.

From the great adept Künlo the Teaching was received by Jamyang Könchok Sangpo.[350] The great Dakchen Dorjé Chang received it from Könchok Sangpo. The transmissions of both the word and the meaning were also in this lineage.

In brief, the venerable lord Künpang Chenpo[351] received all the esoteric instructions of the three combined transmissions as explained previously. He received the Explication for the Assembly four times from the great Dakchen Dorjé Chang, [190] together with a yearlong Explication for Disciples, and the four oral transmissions remained unbroken.

My spiritual father and master[352] himself received the Explication for the Assembly twice from Künpang Chenpo, and he received the Explication for Disciples three times. He eliminated all doubts about the words and the meaning, and was instructed by means of the four oral transmissions. Thus my master taught.

In that way, of those systems of transmission, the instructions of this transmission from lord Dorjé Chang[353] are mainly upheld for the following reasons. Those practitioners of the Path with the Result [in the other lineages] who appeared during the interim period were all endowed with experience and realization because the transmission through the masters had not declined and because they concentrated on practice. However, they did not totally eliminate doubts concerning all the tantras and esoteric instructions by means of study and reflection. Due to this, explanation by means of the four authentic qualities was claimed, but the sequence stated in the tantras, the sequence in which the four authentic qualities first arise, the sequence of practice, the sequence of experience, and the sequence in which these become authentic qualities did not definitely occur for them. On the basis of that, the traditions of explanation became varied, and even in regard to the *Vajra Lines,* it became somewhat difficult to teach, because the statements from the explications of the treatise, the analysis as applied to the authentic quality of the treatise, and the analysis as applied to the authentic quality of experience during guidance were not individually differentiated.

In particular, for most guidance in tantric teachings now given in Tibet, due to ordinary considerations of convenience, the master bestows an initiation first. Then he begins the appropriate guidance. This sequence was also imposed on these teachings, even though it does not fulfill the intentions of the tantra and the treatise of the *Vajra Lines.* Why not? Because the *Root Tantra* says:

> The vows of renewal and
> purification should be given first,
> and after that the ten topics of training.
> Present to them the Vaibhāṣya,
> and likewise the Sautrāntika.
> Then the Yogācāra,
> and after that present the Madhyamaka.
> When all the stages of mantra
> have been understood,...[354]

After saying the stages of the view and the stages of the conduct should be studied, the tantra says, "...after that, begin Hevajra."[355] Concerning how to begin Hevajra, it is taught to begin through both ripening initiation and liberating guidance. But here in the other traditions [of the Path with the Result], initiation is bestowed first. Then the common path is presented. Then the uncommon path is presented. This is somewhat incorrect.[356] It is also taught:

> Afterward, perfectly present reality.[357]

Thus the other traditions are extremely incorrect in view of the statement that immediately after the bestowal of initiation, the "view of the time of the cause" should be presented to prevent the misconception of an individual self and so forth concerning the primordial awareness of the initiation. [191]

The other traditions are also somewhat incompatible with the statement in the *Vajra Lines* about the causal continuum of the universal ground, which is made in the context of the ground of purification only after the Three Appearances have been first presented:

> For the method continuum of the body and so forth, there is the causal initiation with four triads, the seats and so forth, and so forth.[358]

They are also incompatible with the statement in the *Summary:*

> The ground of the path is formed
> by the Three Appearances,

> and absolutely all the practice
> is understood through the Three Continua.[359]

They are also incompatible with the *Reply to Dratön's Request,*[360] and so forth.

In brief, it is very important in this tradition to never be in conflict with the writings of the early venerable lords of Sakya.

Ngorchen Künga Sangpo

The great Ngorchen Dorjé Chang[361] was prophesied in the *Sutra of the White Lotus of the Excellent Doctrine:*

> At that time the monk
> Künga Sangpo will appear.[362]

And also in the *Noble Sutra on Upholding Basic Virtue,* beginning with the words:

> At that time the monk
> Künga Sangpo will appear.[363]

Even the denigration by Dharma lord Khedrup, who said, "This is not a sutra," was prophesied with the statement:

> Another angry, fierce, and extremely
> harsh monk will dispute it.[364]

Ngorchen's buddhahood was prophesied with such statements as:

> He will also be known as
> Ngönpar Shepa Thop.

And:

> In the field of Abhirati,
> Beautiful to Gaze Upon.[365]

Thus it was prophesied that he would become the tathāgata Ngönshé

Thopai Gyalpo in the buddhafield Abhirati, Beautiful to Gaze Upon. He was an indisputable founder of the tradition.

Specifically, Ngorchen appeared to take deliberate rebirth for the sake of the precious doctrine of the venerable lords of Sakya. Through study and reflection, he eliminated doubts about all the sutras and tantras in general and all the writings of the early masters of Sakya in particular, and unmistakably established them.

Müchen Könchok Gyaltsen

Ngorchen's main spiritual son was lord Müchen.[366] When Khyenrap Rinpoché[367] was receiving the *Saṃvara Root Tantra,* until the tantra was completed he actually saw Müchen as Cakrasaṃvara, with four faces and twelve arms.

Also, when Müchen traveled from Ngor to Mü, lord Sangyé Palsang went to welcome him, and as he was traveling up the precipitous path he actually saw the supporting mandala and supported deities of Saṃvara in the tradition of Kṛṣṇa vividly approaching. [192] In a state of high excitement, he composed a eulogy to Śrī Heruka.

As illustrated by these examples, Müchen was known to be an emanation of Cakrasaṃvara. The transmission received through him is the main one. Because the other two transmissions also possess many profound key points of esoteric instruction, many practices of the profound key points are not totally dependant on what the followers of Ngor themselves practice.

In brief, there does not appear to have been a classification separating the Explication for the Assembly from the Explication for Disciples; the classification in that way was taught in a unique transmission by lord Ngorchen Dorjé Chang to Müchen Sempa Chenpo. Sempa Chenpo also separated the teachings and gave them to Dakchen Dorjé Chang alone. The disciples who were constantly present, such as lord Sangyé Palsang, realized that whenever lord Sempa Chenpo became red in the face, snapped his fingers, and exclaimed, "I should not go beyond that," he was talking about the Explication for Disciples. They received fragments of the teachings by listening closely to his oral comments.

In brief, because lord Sangyé Palsang and so forth completely received Dakchen Dorjé Chang's Explication for Disciples, they had the Explication for Disciples. Those who said, "We did not completely obtain it," were the middling. Those who said, "We did not obtain it, so we do not have it," were the inferior. Thus my master taught.

All the traditions up to this point are the unadulterated Sakya tradition alone. Thus my master taught.

The combined transmissions

Some traditions of the Path with the Result are also called "combined transmissions." If one is uncertain about how those appeared, one may become doubtful about the many stray texts or when hearing some exaggerated rumors. Therefore, these transmissions should also be understood.

Phakmodrupa

The first of all combined transmissions was that of Deshek Phakmodrupa.[368] He first studied under lord Sachen for twelve years. When he practiced below the Mañjughoṣa Cave, it is known that a spring emerged because of his practice. He recorded an explication of the treatise called the *Library Explication* or the *Treasury of Explication,* written exactly according to Sachen's words.

Phakmodrupa later met Dakpo Lhajé[369] of the Kagyü, and after accepting the Kagyüpa tenets, he taught the Path with the Result combined with the six doctrines of Nāropa, the mahāmudrā, and so forth. His disciples, such as Thatsawa Sengé Gyaltsen and Prajñākīrti, [193] also wrote explanatory commentaries combining the mahāmudrā and so forth with the *Library Explication.* That is the reason for this statement:

> To discard the six doctrines and,
> while meditating on the oral instructions
> of others, such as the Path with the Result
> and the mahāmudrā,
> trace them to Nāropa's lineage,
> conflicts with one's own tradition,
> not to mention that of others.[370]

Thus my master taught.

Chegompa

After Phakmodrupa, Chegompa requested the Path with the Result from Gyaltsa Talphukpa, a disciple of Sachen.[371] There was a Chegom from Central Tibet and one from Tsang. This was the one from Tsang, who became a disciple of Lady Machik Rima. He also wrote an explication of the treatise combined with the mahāmudrā and so forth.

Kodrakpa

The great adept Kodrakpa completely obtained the path of the Path with the Result in the Shama tradition and received the six-branch yoga from the great paṇḍita Vibhūticandra.[372] He combined those two, and when he practiced at a place in Rasa for twenty-four years, he met the Lord of Yogins.[373] He directly beheld the channel locations of the vajra body and wrote many compositions as they arose in his mind, such as the *Ocean of Visualized* Ha *Syllables for the Removal of Impediments* and texts that combined the six-branch yoga and the Path with the Result.

Chagen

After Kodrakpa, the one known as the White Adept or Chagen completely received the path of the Precious Teaching of the Shama tradition and the Sakya tradition from Lady Machik Nyitri.[374] When he practiced single-mindedly for eighteen years, he reached attainment. He beheld the face of the Lord of Yogins, who was red in color, and received permission to write a complete set of texts for the Path with the Result combining the Sakya tradition and the Shama tradition. Some of these are extremely authoritative, and are known as the *Sealed Path with the Result.*

Chagen taught Künpang Drakgyal. Künpang Drakgyal taught Tai Situ Jangyal, who kept saying, "I will teach."[375] But he was distracted by other business and it never happened. Today no transmission remains.

Although these are different transmissions, all were transmitted through a lineage, and hence they had valid sources. Thus my master taught.

Jonang Künpang Chenpo

Jonang Künpang Chenpo[376] received the Sakya tradition from Jamyang Tsangnak Phukpa Sherap Özer and the Shama tradition from Jangpa Charpa Rinchen Özer. After receiving permission from Sé Kharchungwa[377] in a dream, Künpang Chenpo made revisions to the *Vajra Lines* using the two versions for which he had the transmission. He rearranged much of the text from beginning to end and composed an explication of the treatise according to this version, which he combined with many esoteric instructions of the Drom tradition for which he did not have the transmission. [194]

Latö Wangyal

Künpang Chenpo's disciple Latöpa Wangyal combined those three lineages with the six-branch yoga, making four. Considering all paths complete within the meditative concentration of individual withdrawal, he made classifications of *three necessary points, three unnecessary points,* and so forth. This was similar to the Chinese *hoshang,* who denigrated all means.[378]

Therefore, of the combined transmissions, these last two are corrupt. Thus my master taught.

Similarly, Jangchup Pal of Kham (also known as Khamchen Genlhepa because he lived at Genmodrok in Sakya) possessed eighteen slightly different transmissions, which were designated "the eighteen systems of the Path with the Result." Dzimpa Gyaltsen Pal requested these from him. The omniscient Gangtröpa requested them from Dzimpa. Because Mati Paṇchen received them from Gangtröpa, the transmission of the Shama tradition is also actually unbroken.[379] Thus my master taught.

Also, Lochen Jangtsé[380] requested the Teaching from lord Lama Dampa. Tsipriwa Kashipa Namkha Özer requested it from Lochen Jangtsé, and even created a small volume in which he made numerous additions and deletions to the texts of the *Volume.*

All of these traditions are included among the combined lineages. Thus my master taught.

Even the slightest ray of his speech
causes every lotus
of knowledge to blossom.

A glance from the corner
of his loving eyes
liberates us from the terrible,
great ocean of samsara.

Just hearing the drumbeat of his
auspicious name fills the heart
with a result delightful to all.

These words of the master,
whose kindness is endless,
clarify the fundamental nature
of absolutely all phenomena.

Aha! The master possessing
the transmission has amazing stories.

Stories this pleasing to the heart
delight everyone with their glory.

Glory unequalled, when heard,
causes great bliss to flow.

Flow and long remain—
this is the master's kindness.

Without even knowing the heritage
of their own fathers,
those who proudly think,
"I am so exceptional,"
are experts mumbling nonsense,
seated on lofty thrones in the midst of fools.

To study at the feet of the wild father,
the excellent master,
great Vajradhara assuming human form,
and relish the glory of the nectar
of the Sublime Vehicle,
is certainly the result of infinite
accumulated merit.

Thus I have written what I have retained in mind of the essential explanation of the history of the oral instructions.

Mastu sarva jagataṃ

4. Blazing of a Hundred Brilliant Blessings

A Supplement to the Expansion of the Great Secret Doctrine, *Summarizing Notes on the History of the Oral Instructions*

From the Comprehensive Explanation of the Precious Teaching of the "Path with the Result"

Künga Palden (nineteenth century) and Loter Wangpo (1847–1914)

Your compassion, a natural clear light
like the center of space,
causes clouds of great love to form,
and a gentle rain of elegant explication
falls to delight all experts.
May your hoisting of the victory banner
of the doctrine protect me![381]

To establish the authenticity
of the masters of the uncommon teaching
of the Explication for Disciples,
the story of the lineage
as well as a supplement
are given here as a service.

UP THROUGH NGORCHEN DORJÉ CHANG, both the Explications for the Assembly and for Disciples actually existed, but they were not given individual names. According to the custom of lord Sempa Chenpo, Dakchen Dorjé Chang separated and individually bestowed the common and uncommon esoteric instructions. From then on, these were known as the Path with the Result for the Assembly and the Path with the Result for

Disciples. The transmission of both of these is what has remained without decline until the present, and still remains.

Dakchen Lodrö Gyaltsen

The great Dakchen Dorjé Chang, the source of the doctrine of the Explication for Disciples, who separated the Explications for the Assembly and for Disciples into two, was born in a wood-mouse year (1444). This lord Lodrö Gyaltsen was the great Sakyapa Künga Nyingpo himself, purposely taking birth once again to spread the doctrine of the oral transmissions such as the Precious Teaching of the Path with the Result. [196] That this was the case is shown by the following examples. Without impediment, lord Lodrö Gyaltsen recognized Sachen's handwriting without anyone else offering the information. This lord said that a text on the application of actions, of which no one knew the location, was in the rhinoceros-hide amulet on the image of the protector,[382] and had been concealed as a treasure by Sachen. When others asked how he knew this, he replied, "There is a very great reason, but that's enough. Don't tell anyone." In numerous ways, the lord himself accepted that he was Sachen's emanation.

From childhood he possessed an unimpeded wisdom. From the time he was two or three years old until he was six, he received from his father, Jamyang Chenpo,[383] absolutely all the instructions of the oral transmissions, such as the inner family transmission of the Path with the Result and the Dharma cycles of Mahākāla. And he mastered these precisely according to the meaning of the words. Thereafter, until the age of thirteen, he studied at the lotus beneath the feet of Jamyang Könchok Sangpo[384] and received many teachings of sutra and tantra; in particular, he received the Precious Teaching once.

In accordance with a prophecy of Dakchen Künga Wangchuk,[385] Lodrö Gyaltsen then secretly traveled to Mü. Together with all the assembly, he received from Müchen Könchok Gyaltsen the Three Appearances and a rough explanation of the mantra path. The lord alone received the uncommon, profound key points, without omission.

In accordance with Müchen's system of practice, Dakchen Lodrö Gyaltsen observed the individual distinction of the Explication for the Assembly from the Explication for Disciples, and bestowed the Path with the Result many times at numerous monastic establishments in the three regions of

Central Tibet, Tsang, and Kham, such as the great monastic seat of Sakya, and Nālendra[386] in Phenyul. In total, he gave it more than twenty times.

Dakchen Lodrö Gyaltsen also composed many indispensable texts required for the explanation of the Teaching, such as guidance concerning the indivisibility of samsara and nirvana, a ritual for bestowing the path initiation, an explication of the sacred commitments, and a manual for creating nectar pills.[387]

Lodrö Gyaltsen directly beheld the profound body mandala within and possessed unimpeded paranormal ability and signs of attainment. After spreading the Buddhist doctrine by means of explanation, disputation, and composition, he displayed the manner of gathering his rūpakāya form bodies into the basic space of phenomena on the fourth day of the ninth month in a wood-rabbit year (1495), when he was fifty-two years old. [197]

The venerable lord Doringpa

Lord Dakchen Lodrö Gyaltsen had countless disciples, but his main disciple was the venerable lord Doringpa.[388] This master was born in an earth-snake year (1449) as the son of Governor Doringpa. He ruled until the age of thirty-seven and also received various Dharma cycles of secret mantra from the spiritual father, Ngorchen Dorjé Chang, and the spiritual son, Müchen. Then he requested ordination from Drathangpa Sherap Dawa.

Once, when Doringpa was practicing in a hermitage, food became a bit scarce, and he offered a sacrificial cake to Kurukullā.[389] That night he received a prophecy: "Toward the end of your life great wealth will come. Tomorrow a person will come to deliver food." It came to pass exactly like that.

Then, in his dreams, many magical displays appeared of numerous emanations of the protector inviting him to Sakya, but the lord paid no attention. Then the same thing happened to a close attendant, who was frightened by the magical displays and said, "Now it is surely best that you go. If you don't go, I won't be able to stay as your attendant."

Since Doringpa was urged so strongly, he traveled to Sakya. From the king of Dharma, Dakchen Lodrö Gyaltsen, he first received (for four months) the Path with the Result in the tradition of the Explication for the Assembly. After that—as experiential guidance—he received guidance according to the Explication for Disciples, together with the associated instructions, for eighteen months and totally eliminated his doubts regarding the meaning of the words. After that, like an empty vase being filled by a full vase, he also received and mastered the Explication for the Assembly three times, as well as absolutely all the instructions of the oral transmissions such as the Thirteen Golden Dharmas and the large and small protectors.[390]

By virtue of having performed the basic recitation retreat of the *aṣṭā*[391] three times, Doringpa also liberated many people from the disability of muteness on many occasions merely by bestowing his spittle. Not only that, when he performed the removal of impediments for numerous people who had become insane due to a gathering of the essential constituents, and for whom nothing else was beneficial, they were immediately cured. Simply by deliberately focusing his visualization on the malevolent, he liberated them into the basic space of phenomena. His amazing deeds such as these transcend the limits of the imagination.

From the time Doringpa first received the Path with the Result until he passed away, he performed the unbroken practice of the Time of the Path in four sessions daily. He also bestowed the Path with the Result many times. When he was close to passing away, he bestowed absolutely all the remaining oral instructions upon Tsarchen Dorjé Chang, in the manner of passing on the doctrine. [198] And he said, "You faithful ones will not be parted from me. Lord Drokmi's advice says, 'Even though a master may dwell in the hell of Supreme Torture, if one feels that he is a buddha and offers prayers, the blessings of a buddha will enter one's mindstream. An indivisible dependently arisen connection abides in the true nature of them both.' This will definitely come to pass."

Finally, on the fifteenth day of the tenth Mongol month of a wood-monkey year (1524), when he had reached the age of seventy-six, Doringpa passed into Khecara by means of the profound practice at the point of passing away.

Both Gorumpa and Tsarchen, the lords of the Explication for Disciples, were his spiritual sons.

The venerable lord Gorumpa

The first, the great venerable lord Gorumpa,[392] was born in a fire-bird year (1477), in the hereditary line of the great Metön of Tsangrong, who was the spiritual son of Marpa of Lhodrak.[393] At the age of seventeen Gorumpa received the complete path of the Path with the Result from Dakchen Dorjé Chang. At the descent of primordial awareness during the initiation, the illustrative, symbolic primordial awareness arose in his mindstream. Then he received the Path with the Result in the tradition of the Explication for Disciples once from the great lord Doringpa, the Explication for the Assembly twice from Jegyurwa Sönam Sengé, and the Explication for the Assembly once each from Salo Künga Sönam and Shalupa Könchok Tsultrim.[394] He definitely mastered absolutely all the meaning of the words.

Gorumpa took the Path with the Result as the core of his meditation, with about 2.5 million recitations of the *aṣṭā* and so forth. He said that when he clearly imagined the body mandala, the catalyst of the entry of the primordial awareness aspects always caused a great bliss to arise. He possessed inconceivable qualities of experience and realization, such as emanating two bodies and reading texts in the dark.

At the age of sixty-eight, on the twenty-ninth day of the sixth month in a wood-dragon year (1544),[395] Gorumpa passed into great Khecara.

Tsarchen Dorjé Chang

The second, the great Tsarchen Dorjé Chang, who was an emanation of the venerable lord, the powerful master Virūpa, was the spiritual son of lord Doringpa and the sole backbone of the doctrine of oral transmission. This lord Tsarchen was born in a water-dog year (1502), in the Dong clan. He received ordination from the omniscient Gendün Gyatso.[396]

Once when Tsarchen was staying and studying at Tashi Lhunpo,[397] the monks proclaimed, "Dharma lord Tsarpa does not study!" [199]

So one day he went to the Dharma arena, debated everyone present there, and defeated them. Then the lord said, "I'm Losel Gyatso, who just lies around sleeping, but I know this much. Now bring it on!"

Everyone in the Dharma arena lacked the confidence to debate, and became filled with faith.

One day while Tsarchen was staying there a woman said over the opening of the well, "You are summoned into the presence of the venerable lord, the great Doringpa. This is his gift."

She offered into his hands a book, and then vanished. When he opened the book, it was the Dharma cycle of Khecarī.[398]

He went to the venerable lord Doringpa and offered him the book, telling him the previous story.

"The other day this Khecarī went to invite you," Doringpa replied.

"And this book is her Dharma cycle. Now, for the time being, you should put it in the book stacks."

Tsarchen went to the library as he had been told. Among the many volumes in the stacks, there was a gaping hole where a book had been removed. When he put the book there, it fit exactly. He was amazed and filled with an uncommon faith.

From then on Tsarchen studied at the lotus beneath the feet of the venerable lord Doringpa. As experiential guidance, he received the Precious Teaching in the tradition of the Explication for Disciples three times and in the tradition of the Explication for the Assembly twice. He mastered absolutely all the meaning of the words. He also received many esoteric instructions other than those, such as the Golden Dharmas and the large and small protectors. In brief, he received absolutely all the profound Dharma possessed by that lord, thoroughly investigated those teachings down to their minor practices, and became the lord of all the oral transmissions.

For the explanation of the Precious Teaching in the tradition of the Explication for Disciples, Tsarchen composed such works as the indispensable *Sunbeams Explication* and the *Rosary of Jewels,* which is a supplement to the *Stream of Initiation.*[399]

The venerable lord Doringpa, on the verge of passing away, bestowed absolutely all the remaining teachings. He sometimes gave some of the profound oral instructions in a small teahouse he had. Sometimes he said he was going somewhere like a meadow, or to circumambulate a stupa, and said, "Come as my attendant." He would stay at a place where there were no other people and give the instructions as a unique transmission to lord Tsarchen alone. Doringpa also gave him sacramental substances of Phakpa Rinpoché, Dakchen Rinpoché's nectar pills and the manual for creating them, and oral directions needed for creating the nectar pills. [200] He also gave him the lord's own bell, and saying "Dharma lord, ring this and bestow initiations!" installed him as the lord of the doctrine.

Lord Tsarchen also received many profound Dharma teachings from lord Gorumpa, such as the Path with the Result.

In his continual meditations, he recited every day without break a thousand each of the *aṣṭa,* the *oṃ gsum ma,* the *yamarāja,* and the *śāsana.*[400] When he was young, he saw the ground in all directions entirely filled with figures of the buddhas and was unable to place his feet on the ground. Furthermore, he repeatedly beheld the faces of many calm and wrathful chosen deities, such as powerful Khecarī, the Great Master of Oḍḍiyāna, Hevajra, and glorious Vajrabhairava. He had the inconceivable ability to command an ocean of oathbound protectors, such as Pañjaranātha and Caturmukha, as if they were slaves.

Tsarchen gave the Path with the Result many times in numerous monastic establishments of Central Tibet and Tsang, making the doctrine of the Path with the Result in the tradition of the Explication for Disciples as brilliant as the sun.

At the age of sixty-five, on the fifteenth day of the seventh month of a fire-tiger year (1566), he passed away to become the assembly leader of the spiritual heroes and ḍākinīs of Khecara.

Although lord Tsarchen had countless expert and realized disciples, on this occasion the stories of just six of his great expert and realized students who were totally peerless on the face of the earth will be explained in sequence.

Jamyang Khyentsé Wangchuk

The first, Jamyang Khyentsé Wangchuk, was born in a wood-monkey year (1524), into the hereditary line of Asha. From his childhood he lived with the great lord Gorumpa and received many profound Dharma teachings; he received the Precious Teaching twice. Then he traveled to Tanak Thupten to study dialectics. During that time he received a condensed Path with the Result from Dakchen Ngakgi Wangpo of Tsedong.[401]

Khyentsé Wangchuk later invited the Dharma king Tsarchen to Palpuk[402] and received as experiential guidance a very extensive teaching of the Path with the Result. Furthermore, he received and mastered absolutely all the instructions of the oral transmissions, such as the Golden Dharmas, Pañjaranātha, and Caturmukha.

When Khyentsé Wangchuk was performing the basic recitation retreat and had reached the point of about three hundred thousand repetitions of the *aṣṭa,* he dozed off a little while reciting as the sun rose in the east. In the sky before him, he beheld glorious Hevajra with eight faces and sixteen arms, together with the mother. Hevajra's body was like the color of azure turquoise, [201] clear, lucid, and pristine, with the nature of light. For some time Khyentsé rested free from grasping.

He also made these summarizing notes known as the *Expansion of the Doctrine,* the guidance manual for the Explication for Disciples, in which the immaculate words of Tsarchen Rinpoché are recorded in writing. Thus the great kindness of this lord Khyentsé Wangchuk toward all future teachers and meditators of the Path with the Result in the tradition of the Explication for Disciples is obvious.

Khyentsé Wangchuk served as the abbot of many large and small monasteries, such as Shalu. He kindly bestowed the Precious Teaching repeatedly to many worthy disciples. Moreover, he received most of the oral instructions of the new and the old traditions and spread them through teaching and listening. He beheld the faces of numerous special deities. All the ḍākinīs and Dharma protectors listened to him like slaves, and he had inconceivable pure visions. That he had wisdom equal to Mañjuśrī's was established in everyone's opinion.

At the age of forty-five, on the twenty-first day of the fifth month in an earth-dragon year (1568),[403] lord Khyentsé Wangchuk passed away into Khecara.

Mangthö Ludrup Gyatso

The omniscient Ludrup Gyatso, who was "like the cream of Tsarchen's disciples," was born in a water-sheep year (1523), into a family of the gold mine supervisors of Nyak. He brought to perfection the study of all sutra and mantra. He received the Path with the Result once from the venerable lord Künga Drolchok,[404] and from Tsarchen Dorjé Chang, the Path with the Result in the tradition of the Explication for the Assembly once and that of the Explication for Disciples once.

The experiences that are like smoke and like mirage continually arose.[405] When Ludrup Gyatso made summarizing notes on Tsarchen Rinpoché's words of guidance for the Explication for Disciples[406] and offered them to him to read, Tsarchen was extremely pleased and exclaimed, "You have understood my Explication for Disciples exactly. You are like the cream of my disciples."

Ludrup Gyatso also made Hevajra his continual meditation. Once his arm was afflicted by the harm of a nāga. While he was reciting the Hevajra mantra with deliberate visualization, in a dream a black snake almost emerged from his mouth, but when he pulled on it with his hands it broke in the middle. Again he recited the mantra with the visualization, and when he slightly dozed off, in a dream the snake emerged, except for just the tail. [202] When he awoke from that, on the basis of reciting the mantra with visualization, he had a dream in which all the rest emerged. When he awoke from the dream the affliction was cured. There are countless amazing stories such as this about him.

He bestowed the Teaching of the Explication for Disciples, with the complete associated instructions, upon many worthy disciples such as Paṇchen Ngawang Chödrak.[407]

By bestowing the explanatory teachings of the *Tantra Trilogy of Hevajra* as a careful explication, this lord Mangthö Ludrup Gyatso was extremely kind to the Hevajra cycle, the ancestral Dharma of Sakya. In general, he performed vast deeds for the doctrine by means of explanation, disputation, and composition in regard to the oceanlike scriptural traditions of sutra and mantra. In his seventies, he passed away into Khecara.[408]

The venerable lord Bökharwa

The great venerable lord Bökharwa,[409] who reached perfection of experience and realization, was born in a fire-pig year (1527), into the hereditary line of the Dharma kings of Tibet. He was amazing from an early age, with the syllable *a* gleaming clearly on his tongue, and so forth. When he got a bit older, he received ordination from Bumrampa Sherap Gyaltsen and perfected his studies at Kyetsal in Dreyul.

Bökharwa went as a visiting scholar to the great Ngamring Dharma institute in Jang. At first, he felt intimidated by the huge assembly. Then the intention arose in his mind: "I must accumulate the assemblies by means of this opportunity to teach in the midst of such a sangha as this." When he visualized the sangha members on the crown of his head[410] and gave teachings, even the meanings that had not revealed themselves before became vividly evident.

After Bökharwa returned to Kyetsal and was attending the assembly as he had before, on one occasion Tsarchen Rinpoché, wearing a red hat and saffron robes, gazed upon the assembly through a skylight. Lord Bökharwa had never met Tsarchen before, but just the sight of his face filled him with inexpressible faith. As soon as the assembly was adjourned, they met, and when Bökharwa received the ritual permission of the protector Dong Nyenchen[411] as an initial Dharma connection, the auspicious connections for accomplishment of the fierce actions were aligned.

Then slanderers told malicious rumors to the head of state,[412] and many of Bökharwa's paternal relatives were murdered, he was robbed of all his valuable possessions, and other disasters occurred. [203] This served as a catalyst, and Bökharwa went to Tsarchen Rinpoché. He requested an extremely detailed Path with the Result in the tradition of the Explication for Disciples, and inconceivable instructions of the oral transmissions. Their minds blended together as one. By means of the application of the enlightened actions of Vajra Mahākāla, he eliminated the slanderous enemies of the doctrine.

All the dignitaries of Central Tibet and Tsang honored Bökharwa as the lord of spiritual families. Constantly turning the Dharma wheel of the Precious Teaching and so forth, he accomplished incredible benefit for the doctrine and living beings.

At the age of sixty-one, in a fire-pig year (1587), Bökharwa passed away into Khecara, together with sounds, lights, and a rain of flowers.

Ngakchang Sönam Chöphel

The powerful master of Dru, Ngakchang Sönam Chöphel, who was an emanation of the glorious Buffalo-faced Mighty Enemy of Time,[413] was born in a fire-pig year [1527]. He received ordination from Jamyang Sönam Paljor and reached the perfection of learning and reflection.

In the presence of the Dharma king Tsarchen, Sönam Chöphel was ripened by the Path with the Result in the tradition of the Explication for Disciples, which he requested in detail. He immediately performed the basic recitation retreat, and when about three months had passed, the great Doringpa repeatedly appeared in his dreams and prophesied that he would be a lord of the oral transmissions.

On that occasion Tsarchen Dorjé Chang said, "This king spirit of Nenying is repeatedly going to your meditation hut, so is some form of obstacle not coming? That spirit offered to Doring Rinpoché a pledge not to harm the upholders of our lineage. I will also perform whatever visualizations and so forth would be best. Be diligent in offering some sacrificial cakes intended for that spirit and in performing spiritual practice. Especially, make intense prayers during this profound path of the guruyoga. This is the sole remover of impediments and deliverer of enhancements."

Then Sönam Chöphel completed the recitations. Later, in the presence of the omniscient Khyentsé Wangchuk, he received most of the Dharma cycles of the oral transmissions possessed by that lord, such as the Path with the Result in the tradition of the Explication for the Assembly twice, and that of the Explication for Disciples once. He achieved consummate skill in all of the practices, down to the most minor aspects. Because he immediately asked questions to resolve his doubts and so forth, he became expert.

As prophesied by lord Doringpa, while Sönam Chöphel was explaining the teaching in the tradition of the Explication for Disciples at Namgyal Tsé in Dar, he also beheld the faces of lord Doringpa and Tsarchen, the spiritual father and son. When he thought to ask about a minor doubt that he had, they spoke:

> Hey! The fine path is "fine,"
> and that's it. [204]
> So a statement is unnecessary.
> Not the slightest result
> exists elsewhere.
> As intelligent as you are,
> what else do you need?

Then they disappeared.

In this way, since he established the spread and explanation of the oral transmissions of the Precious Teaching and so forth, lord Sönam Chöphel was also extremely kind to the doctrine of the oral transmissions. He passed away into Khecara on the twelfth day of the twelfth month in a water-rabbit year (1603),[414] when he had reached the age of seventy-seven.

Khenchen Shönu Lodrö

The great abbot Shönu Lodrö, who was "like the pillar of the doctrine," was born in a fire-pig year (1527). He perfected learning and reflection in regard to the oceanlike techniques of profound and vast Dharma. In particular, he received from Tsarchen Dorjé Chang himself the Precious Teaching in the tradition of the Explication for Disciples, as well as all the instructions of the oral transmissions of the Golden Dharmas, such as Nāro Khecarī, and of the Dharma protector cycles. He concentrated solely on these for meditation.

Later, Shönu Lodrö founded Tashi Chödé monastery in an earth-rabbit year (1579), thereby establishing a pillar of the Khaupa doctrine.[415] By turning the Dharma wheel of suitable and appropriate teachings for definitely worthy vajra disciples, and so forth, he achieved incredible benefits for the doctrine and living beings.

When Shönu Lodrö was seventy-three, on the twenty-fifth day of the twelfth month of an earth-pig year [1599], he passed away into Khecara, together with marvelous signs.

Dingmawa Lapsum Gyaltsen

Dingmawa,[416] the backbone of the doctrine of the oral transmissions, was born in a fire-dog year (1526). While he was studying sutra rituals under the expert and realized Lodrö Chöphak, during the section on merit in general he beheld many forms in the sky, sometimes divine palaces, sometimes such things as hanging internal organs and entrails. These experiences, which are explained as signs of the sublime path in such traditions as the Great Perfection and the Kālacakra, arose again and again.

From the Dharma king Tsarchen, Dingmawa then received the Precious Teaching in the tradition of the Explication for Disciples, together with the associated instructions and, furthermore, many Dharma cycles of the oral transmissions, such as the Thirteen Golden Dharmas and the large and small protectors. At a gathering for the Dharma teachings during that period, when the arrival of lord Dingmawa was slightly delayed, [205] Tsarchen Rinpoché commented, "This honorable master will benefit the doctrine, so we must wait." This was a prophecy that he would later become a great backbone of the doctrine.

At the feet of the omniscient Khyentsé Wangchuk, Dingmawa received the oceanlike instructions of the new and the old traditions. Foremost among these, he received the Precious Teaching in the tradition of the Explication for the Assembly once and that of the Explication for Disciples twice.

While he was performing the basic recitation retreat of Hevajra at Palpuk, as a lucid appearance of blended dream and clear light, two young women each offered him skull-cups filled with nectar during one session. When he drank them, an inexpressible primordial awareness of great bliss was born in his mind. He told Jamyang Khyentsé Wangchuk about it, who said it was a sign of obtaining the seven branches of union.[417]

When Dingmawa bestowed the Precious Teaching upon many worthy and fortunate disciples (such as Yapjé Künga Lodrö and Wangchuk Rapten), during the causal initiation, the spiritual father Tsarchen, and the spiritual son Khyentsé Wangchuk performed the ritual of granting the initiation while sitting in front of him in the sky until the initiation was finished. Dingmawa exclaimed, "I have taught you exactly according to the spiritual father and son's words of initiation. What joy!" He had inconceivable pure visions such as that.

At the age of fifty-two, on the third day of the tenth month in a fire-ox year (1577), lord Dingmawa reached the sublime citadel, together with rainbow lights and a rain of flowers. Both this master and the great Ngakchang of Dru[418] were disciples of both Tsarchen and Khyentsé.

Paṇchen Ngawang Chödrak

Paṇchen Ngawang Chödrak, the spiritual son of both the great Ngakchang Sönam Chöphel and Ludrup Gyatso, was born in a water-monkey year (1572). He received ordination from Jenga Könchok Gyatso, who said, "I will give you the name of my master." He bestowed the name Ngawang Chödrak, and looked after him very carefully.

When Ngawang Chödrak had completed his studies of the sutra tradition, he received from the omniscient Ludrup Gyatso the guidance of the Precious Teaching in the tradition of the Explication for Disciples, together with the associated instructions, and a ripening and extensive explanation of the *Tantra Trilogy of Glorious Hevajra*. Then he also composed many profound and extensive texts, such as summarizing notes on the guidance of the Path with the Result, together with the associated instructions, a complete set of summarizing notes for the explication of the *Tantra Trilogy*, and a commentary on the *Two-Part Hevajra*.[419] [206]

While receiving the Path with the Result, in a dream Ngawang Chödrak joined and traveled along the headwaters of a huge river and arrived in Lhasa together with the river. When he looked in at many monks reciting scriptures in the temple where the Jowo resided, they were reading only golden volumes in which just the *aṣṭā*[420] was written. Ngawang Chödrak said that this was a sign that he would go up to the monastic seat of Sakya and offer the Dharma cycles of the Explication for Disciples.[421]

Later, from the great abbot Wangchuk Palsang, he completely received the path of the Teaching in the tradition of the Explication for the Assembly.

Engaging in incredible explanation and study of sutra and mantra, with the Precious Teaching foremost, Ngawang Chödrak was extremely kind to the Buddhist doctrine in general and to this doctrine in particular.

At the age of seventy, on the eighth day of the fourth month of an iron-snake year [1641], lord Ngawang Chödrak passed away into Khecara, together with marvelous signs.

Wangchuk Rapten

Dorjé Chang Wangchuk Rapten was born in an earth-sheep year (1559). On the seventh day, Tsarchen Rinpoché was asked for a name, and named him Namkha Döndrup Wangpo. That night, in the clear light of Tsarchen's meditation, a prophecy occurred three times: "This child is the rebirth of Tsultrim Gyaltsen."

At the age of thirty-one, Wangchuk Rapten received full ordination from the great abbot Ngawang Rapten. Before and after this, he received many Dharma cycles of the oral transmissions from the spiritual father Tsarchen, the spiritual son Khyentsé Wangchuk, Ngakchang Sönam Chöphel, and lord Lapsumpa.[422] In particular, he was ripened by the profound Explication for Disciples that he received from Lapsumpa in an extensive way.

While performing the great recitation retreat of the *aṣṭā* at Chölung in Nup, Wangchuk Rapten actually beheld the faces of the nine deities of glorious Hevajra, with the supporting mandala and supported deities, about one story tall. And one evening he also had a vision of each of the Three Venerable Lords in White,[423] seated with smiling faces on top of something like a wooden wall frame.

On the evening Wangchuk Rapten arrived at Palpuk, an experience arose in the manner of a dream in which the Dharma king Tsarchen bestowed the initiations, blessings, and guidance of the Precious Teaching.

In many Dharma institutes of Central Tibet and Tsang, Wangchuk Rapten showered down an inconceivable rain of profound Dharma teachings, foremost of which was the Precious Teaching, and countless worthy disciples were produced. [207]

Just before Wangchuk Rapten passed into a pure land, the intention arose in his mind to concentrate only on the practice of Padmasambhava of Oḍḍiyāna, because he was now advanced in years and it was difficult to cope with the complete practices of the great mandalas. That night, in a dream, Hevajra clearly appeared, with the great teacher Padmasambhava seated in his heart. Wangchuk Rapten realized that it would not work if he consolidated his practice, and so he performed the Time of the Path in two sessions daily without interruption until he passed away.

At the age of seventy-eight, on the second day of the tenth Mongol month of a fire-mouse year (1636), lord Wangchuk Rapten passed away into Khecara, together with sounds, lights, and a rain of flowers.

Khyapdak Kangyurwa

The great Khyapdak Kangyurwa[424] was born in a water-rabbit year (1603). From an early age he studied at the lotus beneath the feet of lord Wangchuk Rapten. Like an empty vase being filled by a full vase, he received absolutely all the instructions of the Sakyapa oral transmissions, most importantly the Teaching in the tradition of the Explication for Disciples, and, furthermore, countless Dharma teachings of ripening initiation and liberating guidance in the new and old mantra traditions.

Kangyurwa sought out and received from pristine sources the reading transmissions of all the words of the Conqueror that had been translated in this glacial realm, and spread the reading transmissions. The fact that the transmission of the Kangyur has survived until the present day is certainly due to the kindness of this lord Kangyurwa alone.

Kangyurwa was extremely diligent in meditation, completing the recitation retreats according to the number of mantras and length of time for 108 chosen deities taught in the four classes of tantra. He also sponsored the copying of new sets of the precious Kangyur and of the collected works of Tsarchen, the spiritual father, Khyentsé Wangchuk, the spiritual son, and Wangchuk Rapten.

As pure appearance, Kangyurwa had visions of a very large and clear Virūpa and of the great lord Sakyapa, who wore a blue robe sparkling with light and had a bright red countenance. He also beheld the nine deities of Hevajra residing in the heart of Padmasambhava, the Great Teacher of Oḍḍiyāna. Such marvelous episodes of his spiritual life transcend comprehension. In particular, because he had perfected the enlightenment mind, he performed countless deeds to benefit others.

At the age of fifty-seven, on the fourteenth day of the ninth month in an earth-pig year (1659), Kangyurwa passed away into Khecara by using the meditation for the point of passing away.

Lord Kangyurwa had many spiritual sons, but Shalu Khenchen and the all-seeing Fifth Dalai Lama were both very kind to the upholders of the Khaupa tradition.

Shalu Khenchen

The first of Lord Kangyurwa's spiritual sons, Shalu Khenchen, was born in a water-tiger year (1602) as the son of Governor Menkhangpa.[425] From an early age he was extremely diligent in study. He received many general and specific profound Dharma teachings, [208] but in particular, in a wood-sheep year (1655) he received from Tsultrim Tashi of Nyima Ling all the initiations, blessings, explications of the treatise, reading transmissions, and esoteric instructions of the Path with the Result in the Gongkar tradition.[426]

After that, from the great Khyapdak Kangyurwa, Shalu Khenchen received for three months and eighteen days the experiential guidance of the Teaching in the tradition of the Explication for Disciples and mastered the profound key points without omission. As recompense for the Dharma, he offered impressive places such as a delightful residence he had at Riphuk. Then he traveled to Shalu and performed vast deeds for the doctrine.

In the earth-pig year (1659) Shalu Khenchen performed the great recitation retreat of Hevajra. While he was counting repetitions of the *devapicu*,[427] Dorjé Chang Wangchuk Rapten appeared in a dream, seized with his hand the mantra rosary that was circling from Shalu Khenchen's mouth, and said, "If you don't need this, give it up." Again, one evening, much blood flowed from his left hand, but a man said, "The rest of the blood still remains." These seemed to be omens that he would have to leave the retreat unfinished. But when he told the venerable lord Kangyurwa the situation, he did not say anything except that he would offer more details later. And that turned out to be the case.

Then, because the venerable lord Kangyurwa had passed away to a pure land, a letter from the all-seeing great Fifth Dalai Lama arrived, and Shalu Khenchen had to leave the retreat unfinished and go to perform the cremation. However, he later completed an extremely extensive great recitation retreat at Gongkar. Then he made the doctrine of the Explication for Disciples as brilliant as the sun by means of teaching and spreading vastly the Path with the Result in the tradition of the Explication for Disciples many times, as well as the Dharma cycles of the oral transmissions.

At the age of eighty, in an iron-mouse year (1681),[428] Shalu Khenchen displayed the manner of dissolving the array of his rūpakāya form bodies back into space.

The Fifth Dalai Lama

The great Fifth Dalai Lama[429] was born into the Sahor clan in a fire-snake year (1617). He was very sympathetic in general to philosophical tenets, without distinction, and in particular to the doctrine of the Tsar tradition. Moreover, from the great venerable lord Kangyurwa he received an extremely detailed teaching of the Path with the Result in the tradition of the Explication for Disciples, together with the complete Cycles of the Path, and made it his primary meditation.

The Dalai Lama also made summarizing notes as a supplement to the guidance manual for the Explication for Disciples.[430] Among the biographies of the lineage masters of the Path with the Result, in addition to what biographies there were of the early masters of the Tsar tradition, [209] he kindly composed four new biographies of Tsarchen, Kangyurwa, Wangrap, and Shalupa. In total, he prepared the woodblocks for printing fourteen biographies, as well as many Dharma cycles of Hevajra, such as the *Sunbeams* and the *Supplement to the Stream of Initiation.*[431]

From Kangyurwa, Shalu Khenchen, and Surchen,[432] the Dalai Lama received—like an empty vase being filled by a full vase—all the instructions of the glorious Sakyapa oral transmissions, such as the Thirteen Golden Dharmas and the large and small protectors, as well as all the profound Dharma teachings, such as the collected works of Tsarchen Dorjé Chang. And he acted as a mainstay for the tenets of the Khaupa tradition.

As a result of the Dalai Lama's accomplishment of the trilogy of red deities, who bring the three realms under control, he brought all the dignitaries, headed by the eastern emperor, and the population under control.[433] At a time when the minor chieftains in Central Tibet and Tsang were trying to reduce each other to servants and constantly held the evil intention to be victorious themselves and defeat the others, the Dalai Lama arose as the religious and political lord of the glacial land of Tibet in order to protect it from the continuous eruption of conflicts, disputes, and other evil actions. He ruled and subdued the entire vast kingdom as smoothly as if he were unfolding a bolt of silk and naturally gathered all the wealth of the four directions.

At the age of sixty-six, on the twenty-fifth day of the second month in a water-dog year (1682), the great Fifth Dalai Lama demonstrated the manner of temporarily dissolving his mind back into the basic space of phenomena.

Khyenrap Jampa

Dorjé Chang Khyenrap Jampa Ngawang Lhundrup was born into the Ché clan of clear light in a water-bird year (1633). From an early age he lived with his paternal uncle, Dorjé Chang Tenzin Sangpo,[434] and brought the study of sutra and mantra to perfection. He also completed the recitation retreats of calm and wrathful special deities, such as the basic recitation retreat of Hevajra.

In general, Khyenrap Jampa received many profound and vast Dharma teachings. In particular, he received many times the Path with the Result known as the *Blue Volume*,[435] in which all three lineages passing through the uncle and nephew of Tongra had been gathered into one. These three lineages were the two transmissions of the Path with the Result received by the omniscient Rongtön from Thekchen Chöjé and Dorjé Gönpo of Latö in western Tsang, as well as the transmission of the lineage from Ngorchen the spiritual father and Müchen, his spiritual son, to Dorjé Chang Khyenrap Chöjé.[436]

During the second [transmission of the Path with the Result], while receiving the teachings of the Three Appearances, when the sufferings, length of life, and so forth in the cold hells were taught, Khyenrap Jampa dreamed that he traveled to the places of the cold hells and witnessed numerous sentient beings tortured with suffering. [210] Such exceptional experiences of purifying the places arose.[437] During the causal initiation, he actually beheld his root master Tenzin Sangpo as Hevajra, the father with the mother. From then on, he thought, "This master is really a perfect buddha," and a deep faith arose in which his master never appeared as his uncle or as an ordinary person, even for a single instant.

Once Khyenrap Jampa was struck by a serious illness as a result of poisoning. In an extremely lucid vision, he beheld Sachen in the midst of rainbow light and a Hevajra palace of rainbow light, with the supporting mandala and supported deities, numerous divine boys and girls making offerings with such things as victory banners and pennants, surrounded by the charnel-ground stupas, skeletons, rainbow clouds, field protectors, and so forth. He was cured of the illness. He had numerous pure visions such as this.

When he received from lord Ön Rinpoché[438] the Path with the Result in the tradition of the Explication for the Assembly, on the day that the master gave the main section of the causal initiation, Khyenrab Jampa actually beheld an emanated mandala in space above the mandala of colored sand. He was filled with boundless devotion and thought, "This master is really Hevajra."

Khyenrap Jampa received from Khyapdak Shalupa[439] an extremely extensive teaching of the Path with the Result in the tradition of the Explication for Disciples. As soon as it was finished, Shalupa presented the volume of the Explication for Disciples to lord Khyenrap Jampa and said, "You are the lord of this Dharma, so you must spread its explication and practice!"

To worthy disciples, such as Morchen Dorjé Chang, lord Khyenrap Jampa also gave careful explications of the guidance of the Path with the Result in the tradition of the Explication for Disciples in very great detail, together with the guidance of the Path with the Result in the *Blue Volume* transmitted from Rongtön.[440] One evening, while he was bestowing the initiations, blessings, and reading transmissions, without combining even the minor aspects of the practices of each transmission, he beheld, as in a dream, the face of the great venerable lord Drakpa Gyaltsen, who was holding a vajra and bell, and those of Shuché and Sangtsa in the retinue.[441] Khyenrap Jampa was delighted, and signs of blessings also arose.

Before and after this, lord Khyenrap Jampa gave the Path with the Result for the Assembly and for Disciples a total of about twenty-five times, the *Vajra Rosary* seventeen, the twelve mandalas for purification[442] about three hundred times, about six hundred causal initiations, and about five hundred path initiations. Furthermore, he taught and spread numerous types of initiations, blessings, and ritual permissions countless times, so that the existence today of the unbroken transmission of these common and uncommon profound Dharma teachings of the Sakyapa should be realized to be due to the kindness of this lord Khyenrap Jampa alone. [211] In that way, he performed incalculable benefit for the doctrine and living beings.

At the age of seventy-one, just at the break of dawn on the second of the double thirtieth days of the fifth month in a water-sheep year (1703), Khyenrap Jampa passed away into Khecara.

Morchen Dorjé Chang

The great Morchen Dorjé Chang, the sovereign of an ocean of oral transmissions, was born in a wood-horse year (1654). At the age of five, when Jamgön Ameshap[443] visited Central Tibet, they met at Rawa Mé. When

Morchen offered his topknot, taking initial ordination, he was given the name Künga Lhundrup. He requested such teachings as a longevity initiation, the ritual permission of the ten wrathful deities, the guidance of the six transmissions of the *Perfection of Wisdom,* the upper actions of Vajrakīla, and the *One Hundred Methods for Accomplishment.*[444]

Then Morchen eventually traveled to Mor and perfected the ritual practices. He brought the study of dialectics to perfection at Rawa Mé. He went to Sakya as a visiting scholar, and when he was unimpeded in explication, discussions, and so forth, the Dakchen and his son[445] perfectly looked after him.

At the age of twenty-five, Morchen accepted full ordination from Rikzin Pema Trinlé. Several years after that, three of his younger brothers passed away from a disease causing violent headaches. When the lord was also seized by that disease and nearly passed away, a faithful person offered him a bit of nectar, and he became more comfortable. That evening, he dreamed that he was swallowed by the great Rikzin Pema Trinlé, stayed for a while in his stomach, and passed out through his urethra. When he woke from the dream, the entire disease had vanished, like a snake shedding its skin. He wondered, "Am I still dreaming? Previously I could only be lifted onto a palanquin and carried."

He suddenly stood up, took about five or six steps, and found that he could walk without impediment. He was overjoyed, and thinking, "If I can get up now, this very daybreak, I'll be so happy!" he did not sleep any more. As soon as daybreak came, he got up and walked, and without difficulty was even able to descend the nine-step stairs in his residence. His father, mother, and all the retinue expressed their joy and amazement, and were extremely relieved.

When the great Rikzin Pema Trinlé had given the Precious Teaching before, Morchen had been ill and unable to request it. Now he realized that there was no greater source for the Path with the Result than Dorjé Chang Khyenrap Jampa at Nālendra in Phenyul. [212] First he approached him to offer the request. Then he returned and received as experiential guidance the Path with the Result in the traditions of both the Explication for Disciples and the Explication for the Assembly. He stayed for more than one year.

Later on he lived with Khyenrap Jampa for thirteen years, sharing the same sleeping quarters; and he acted as master of offerings when Khyenrap Jampa gave Dharma teachings, and as tutor of his nephew Ngawang Khyentsé for seven years. In brief, all the Dharma teachings he received, he received like an empty vase being filled by a full vase, including the Path with the Result for the Assembly and for Disciples twelve times in total, and the *Vajra Rosary* eight times.

Morchen later served as the abbot of many major and minor monasteries, such as Mor monastery, Rawa Mé, and Tashi Chödé. He constantly spread the teachings, with the Path with the Result in the tradition of the Explication for Disciples foremost. He established until the end of existence the unbroken transmission of the Conqueror's doctrine in general and the doctrine of the great secret Explication for Disciples in particular.

At the age of seventy-five, on the twelfth day of the eleventh month of an earth-monkey year (1728), Morchen passed away directly into great Khecara.

Khyapdak Nesarwa

Khyapdak Nesarwa,[446] the great Vajradhara of the kāliyuga, was born into the Asha royal family in a wood-monkey year (1704). During his childhood, when he had severe stomach pains, a medium possessed by Dorjé Lekpa[447] was consulted. The medium operated with a knife and removed and ate the diseased tissue. He placed his hands on the outside of the child's robe, and before long the cut was also healed and the illness was cleared away.

Nesarwa was then invited to Tashi Chödé, where he carried out the studies of sutra and mantra. From Morchen Dorjé Chang, he received the transmision of the three white deities, the outer, inner, and secret Rock Fortress, the *Vajra Rosary,* and twice the Path with the Result in the tradition of the Explication for Disciples. Furthermore, he fully received the profound dharmas of the Tsar tradition, such as Nāro Khecarī, the cycle of the Golden Dharmas, and the large and small protectors.[448]

Nesarwa completely performed the recitation retreats according to the number of mantras and length of time for many deities of the new and old mantra traditions, such as the basic recitation retreat of Hevajra. By virtue of his continual refinement of the creation and completion practices, even when he was conversing with another person, he was able to clearly visualize the supporting mandala and supported deities of Hevajra inside the pupils of that person's eyes.

Lord Nesarwa gave the Precious Teaching seven times. When he was offering the secret guidance of Caturmukha to Yapjé Dorjé Chang[449] at

Sakya, [213] Hevajra and the brahmin form of Caturmukha arose as visual appearances. Many stories exist of his beholding the faces of numerous such special deities in visions.

All Tibetan dignitaries without exception honored his feet on the crowns of their heads, and he caused the unbroken, fine transmission of the profound and vast Dharma to expand like a summer lake in Central Tibet, Tsang, and Kham.

At the age of fifty-seven, on the sixteenth day of the sixth month of an iron-dragon year (1760), Nesarwa displayed the manner of gathering in the array of his rūpakāya form bodies.

Künga Lodrö of Sakya

Lord Nesarwa had countless spiritual sons. Of them, Yapjé Dorjé Chang Künga Lodrö of glorious Sakya, the excellent expert and realized master of this system of the transmission of the Explication for Disciples, was born in an earth-bird year (1729) into the Khön family line endowed with three sublime names.[450] From an early age he received many Dharma teachings, such as the Path with the Result, from his father, Yapjé Sönam Rinchen. The marvelous episodes of Künga Lodrö's life transcend comprehension, such as beholding in visions the faces of noble Nāgārjuna and the five early patriarchs of Sakya, being able to sit in midair with the weight of his body supported only by a stick of incense, and repeatedly beholding the eight deities of Pañjaranātha, as well as the protector of Nyen.[451]

Then Künga Lodrö accepted Nesar Dorjé Chang as his spiritual lord. He received from him, and mastered absolutely, all the instructions of the oral transmissions of the Sakya ancestral Dharma teachings, such as: being ripened by the key points of the Teaching in the tradition of the Explication for Disciples, all the initiations, ritual permissions, and reading transmissions of the volumes for the cycle of the Golden Dharmas; and all the initiations, ritual permissions, guidance, and reading transmissions of the volumes for Pañjaranātha and Caturmukha. Because he performed the basic recitation retreat of Hevajra three times, he repeatedly beheld the supporting mandala and supported deities, actually and in visions.

Künga Lodrö gave the Teaching in the tradition of the Explication for the Assembly many times, and, in particular, gave an extremely detailed and extensive guidance of the Teaching in the tradition of the Explication for Disciples in an iron-ox year (1781). On that occasion, during the blessing of Nairātmyā, the inner offering boiled up and overflowed, and when he poured it into the hands of disciples, it felt so hot it seemed unbearable. He beheld in visions the face of Ngorchen Dorjé Chang, who gave him a prophecy concerning his four future disciples, his hereditary line, and so forth.

On the thirtieth day of the lunar month, when Künga Lodrö was to give the outer and inner Virūpa protection, all the resident and visiting astrologers were certain that a solar eclipse would occur. They even pasted up an announcement on the door. The lord commented, "While it is certain that there is to be a solar eclipse today, this old man is to arise as the Lord of Yogins. [214] So you should all watch a show in relation to the solar eclipse, as well as the astrologer's announcement!" By his blessing Rāhu was unable to approach the sun.[452] He displayed inconceivable signs of attainment such as that.

For the excellent upholders of the doctrine, he bestowed whatever was needed such as initiations, ritual permissions, and reading transmissions, and performed vast activities to expand the doctrine to the end of existence.

At the age of fifty-five, on the second day of the last of the double fifth months in a water-rabbit year (1783), Künga Lodrö gathered his rūpakāya form bodies back into the basic space of phenomena.

Jampa Namkha Chimé

The great abbot Jampa Namkha Chimé was the supreme disciple graced by lord Künga Lodrö. He was born[453] into a line in which excellent individuals who reached attainment had appeared from the time of Drangti Gyalnyen Kharphuk, one of the nine royal physicians of the Dharma king Songtsen Gampo in former times. He had inconceivable good qualities, such as the recollection of previous lives.

After traveling to the Thartsé palace at glorious Ewaṃ,[454] Jampa Namkha Chimé mastered the outer and inner fields of knowledge, as well as numerous treatises of sutra and mantra, such as the seven treatises necessary for all and the four small tantric texts.[455] From the great Khangsar abbot Ngawang Chökyong Sangpo,[456] he received the Path with the Result in the tradition of the Explication for the Assembly.

Jampa Namkha Chimé received the vows of complete ordination from Jinpa Tashi, the abbot of glorious Sakya. From Jamgön Ngawang Künga Lodrö[457] he received all the instructions of the oral transmissions endowed with the four authentic qualities, chief of which were both the Path with the Result for the Assembly and for Disciples, and he established these in his mind through listening, reflection, and meditation. From more than fifty excellent teachers, such as the Phenkhang uncle and nephew, and Kyoda Lama, he received instructions profound and vast like the ocean, and he practiced according to each tradition, without combining even the minor practices.

He beheld in visions the faces of the special deities, such as the great master Padmakāra,[458] and openly displayed the signs of dwelling on the level of attainment, such as plunging his ritual dagger into stone. He was enthroned on the abbatial throne of lord Dorjé Chang,[459] and ripened and liberated worthy beings for many years.

Jampa Namkha Chimé went to be the royal priest of the great Dharma king of Dergé. In all the large and small Dharma institutes that follow the Ngor Ewaṃ tradition in that region, it is by his kindness that the legacy of the authentic preservation of the doctrine of explication and practice (such as the spread of the initiations, the reading transmissions, and the explications of the esoteric instructions, as well as the ritual practices and the yogas of the two stages) has survived to the present. [215]

Throughout his life, Jampa Namkha Chimé bestowed numerous instructions of the profound and vast Dharma, for instance the Teaching in the tradition of the Explication for the Assembly numerous times, and those of the Explication for Disciples twice, thereby producing many individuals who upheld the doctrine. When he saw that the extent of his disciples in this realm had been reached for the time being, he quietly granted a last testament to such people as his nephew, the yogin Jampal Sangpo, and Sawang Lachen.[460]

At the age of fifty-six, Jampa Namkha Chimé displayed the manner of gathering in the array of his bodies of enlightenment, together with numerous amazing signs.[461] The Dharma king, master, and disciples, became even more filled with faith and devoted than before, and they completed his funeral ceremonies.

Jampa Künga Tenzin

Dorjé Chang Jampa Künga Tenzin, the nephew and spiritual son of lord Jampa Namkha Chimé, and our guardian lord and sole sovereign, was born in the fire-monkey year (1776) of the thirteenth cycle, into the family of the Drangti experts. As a youth he was endowed with numerous good qualities and transcended the behavior of a child.

Jampa Künga Tenzin came to the Thartsé palace of Ngor Ewaṃ Chöden. Beginning with the Dharma rituals that were regularly performed, he mastered without difficulty the great scriptural traditions of sutra and mantra, such as the seven treatises necessary for all.[462] From Dorjé Chang Namkha Chimé, he received the kindness of the three vows, and became the lord of the entire doctrine of the Sage. Because he had not been tainted by the accumulation of faults for many lifetimes, it was obvious to all that wherever he stayed was pervaded in every direction by the sweet fragrance of moral discipline.

He understood without error the meaning of the words of the oceanlike instructions and minor practices of the oral transmissions of the venerable lords of Sakya that he received from twenty-five masters.

Because he had completed the recitation retreat of glorious Hevajra twice, as well as those of such deities as the large and small protectors, the chosen deities granted him attainments, and many signs arose in his mindstream that the Dharma guardians were carrying out his enlightened activities. The Lord of Sages, Śākyamuni, accompanied by the sixteen sthaviras, Teacher Padmasambhava, who was a second Buddha, and so forth, displayed their smiling faces. [216]

During nine years as abbot on the Dharma throne of lord Dorjé Chang, Jampa Künga Tenzin expanded the doctrine of that second Conqueror even more than before, through explanation, disputation, and composition, as well as through enlightened actions of knowledge, love, and ability. He was twice invited by the great Dharma king of Dergé, and he carried out enlightened activities with which any connection was meaningful. He bestowed the vows of complete monastic ordination upon the great Dharma king.[463]

Throughout his life, Jampa Künga Tenzin ceaselessly turned the Dharma wheel of the Path with the Result in the tradition of the Explication for the Assembly ten times, the Explication for Disciples four times, the *Vajra Rosary* twice, and so forth. He bestowed every kindness of ripening initiation and liberating guidance on the spiritual sons who upheld the secret of his teaching and were like a golden rosary of the crown jewels of scholars and superb practitioners. These included the Sakya Dakchen, Yarlung Choktrul (both uncle and nephew), the omniscient Khyentsé Wangpo, Jamgön Ngawang Lekdrup, Khuna Sherap Gyaltsen (a great paṇḍita who knew the five fields of knowledge), Sawang Lachen, the powerful expert Künga Palden, and so forth.[464] He reigned like a second Buddha on the crowns of the heads of the upholders of the doctrines of the glorious Sakya, Ngorpa, and Tsarpa traditions.

He brought vast benefit to living beings, such as improving the laws of both secular and religious systems in the principalities of Dergé.

It is clear that the great elevation of the prestige of the Thartsé palace after lord Dorjé Chang Jampa Künga Tenzin's return to Ngor Ewaṃ Chöden came from his merit. From the time of his return until he reached the age of eighty-seven, except for offering Dharma teachings a few times at Sakya and making several trips to hot springs, he lived at Ewaṃ itself, passing his time only in teaching and practicing.

Then Jampa Künga Tenzin saw that the merit of living beings in this land had expired, and seeing the potential disciples in another realm, from the first Mongol month in a water-dog year (1862), at the age of eighty-seven he displayed the manner of his health progressively deteriorating. On one occasion, he said that the absence of parasites in or on the body is explained as a sign of reaching the *peak* of the path of application, and that after reaching the *forbearance* of the path of application one would not go into the lower realms. In regard to this, he repeatedly asked, "How are the signs of reaching those paths of application explained?"

When a few pages of a commentary on the *Ornament of the Sutras* were offered by our Vajradhara [Jampa Künga Tenpai Gyaltsen] for him to consider, [217] he acted very intent, reading them closely and so forth. Thus it is certain that he accepted that he had reached one of those paths of application.

On the fifteenth day of the third month of that year, Jampa Künga Tenzin explained that since that day was the fifteenth day, it was necessary for him to consume a multiplied relic of the Buddha. So one was offered and he consumed it while making prayers. That night he sat with legs crossed and held his body up straight. Just as the sun rose on the seventeenth day, the lord pointed his index finger at the sky, indicating to those around him, "I will not stay here."

When our excellent guide [Jampa Künga Tenpai Gyaltsen] said three times, "Now that you are peacefully passing away, please do not relax your meditation," he merely nodded his head and gathered his array of the rūpakāya form bodies back into space. At that point, numerous amazing signs were apparent, such as rainbows of various colors appearing in the sky.

For three days, the radiance of his body was even finer than usual, his skin was white, and the skin of his face became youthful, with hardly any wrinkles. When three days had passed, that ephemeral radiance of his face faded, and his head bent slightly forward. When just a short stream of red enlightenment mind descended from his right nostril, again he rose from clear light in the enlightened body of unity. Various different offerings were presented by countless spiritual heroes and yoginīs equal in number to the grains of sand found in the river Ganges, and Jampa Künga Tenzin passed away into the sublime city, accompanied by auspicious rituals performed by infinite hosts of buddhas and bodhisattvas. Without doubt, he actualized a vajra holder's enlightened body of primordial awareness.

At the cremation, when the fire of primordial awareness blazed by itself from his body, and the smoke of the body joined with the rainbows of various colors spiraling from the sky and faded away, everyone's hearts were deeply moved with waves of faith, devotion, and wonder.

In accordance with the established customs of the great palaces of Ngor, the subsequent funeral services were completed in a lavish and extensive way by our sublime guide, certainly the true Vajradhara, the honorable Jampa Künga Tenpai Gyaltsen. [218]

Jampa Künga Tenpai Gyaltsen

Our root preceptor, certainly the true Vajradhara, Jampa Künga Tenpai Gyaltsen, was the nephew and spiritual son of lord Jampa Künga Tenzin. Together with marvelous omens, the flower of the major and minor marks blossomed anew in the family of the Drangti experts in the earth-ox year (1829) of the fourteenth cycle.

From his youth, his eyes would glisten with tears of great compassion at the sight of the flesh and blood of sentient beings that had been killed. He delighted in secluded places. The excellent propensities from bestowing initiations, explaining Dharma, and so forth, had not been lost. Since he was especially attracted to the ordained life, he came to glorious Ngor Ewaṃ Chöden at the age of four.

Beginning with the alphabet, Jampa Künga Tenpai Gyaltsen memorized in a short time and mastered without difficulty the collection of Ngor Ewaṃ recitations, the seven treatises necessary for all,[465] and so forth. He renounced the luxuries of samsara, which produced intense revulsion in him. In order to complete the good qualities of stability and learning, he received full ordination by means of the three stages in succession[466] from his uncle, the great abbot Jampa Künga Tenzin, who acted as abbot, with the yogin Jampal Sangpo as master of ceremonies, and so forth.

He kept all the necessities of a monk, and guarded like his own eyeballs all the subtle and coarse precepts about what was prescribed and what was prohibited, not transgressing them. He repeatedly took the vows of the three Mahayana systems for awakening the enlightenment mind. In the tradition of the Jowo Kadampa,[467] he received all the existing cycles of the treatises, oral instructions, and esoteric instructions of mind training in regard to the precious enlightenment mind, and made them the center of his meditation.

From masters such as his uncle, Khenchen Dorjé Chang, Jampa Künga Tenpai Gyaltsen received all the existing cycles of initiation, guidance, and esoteric instruction in connection with the four classes of tantra, which completely filled his mindstream. Thus he became a great vajra holder endowed with the three vows.[468]

From both Jamyang Khyentsé Wangpo, the great paṇḍita of the ten fields of knowledge, and Jampaiyang Ngawang Lekdrup, who were as famous as the sun and the moon, Jampa Künga Tenpai Gyaltsen received instructions on the outer fields of knowledge, such as grammar, epistemology, poetics, metrics, synonymy, and medicine, together with the associated topics. The fame of his reputation as a "great paṇḍita of the ten fields of knowledge" rose to the peak of existence. [219]

Jampa Künga Tenpai Gyaltsen received the reading transmissions of the entire Kangyur, and those transmissions that remained for the Tengyur; the explanations of the tantras such as the *Kālacakra,* the *Two-Part Hevajra,* and the *Litany of the Names of Mañjuśrī;* the eighteen famous treatises[469] and so forth; and numerous types of oral instructions, treatises, and anthologies of the new and old Kadam traditions. Thus he became a unique receptacle of sutra and mantra teachings.

Not only did he receive them in that way, he continually examined and considered all the approaches to the profound and vast Dharma day and night without break. Not mixing them up, he saw how each philosophical system upheld its view and meditation, its practical conduct, its secret key points of esoteric instruction, its acceptance of the philosophical tenets, its classifications of the ground, path, and result, and so forth. Gaining fearless confidence in disputation concerning points of doubt, he became a superb teacher.

From his uncle, Khenchen Dorjé Chang, Jampa Künga Tenpai Gyaltsen received all the instructions with the four oral transmissions and authentic qualities, such as the Precious Teaching for the Assembly and for Disciples, and perfected reflection upon them. Moreover, he did not stop at merely receiving them, but mastered them even to their minor practices. Bringing them into experience by never emerging from the yoga of four daily sessions, except during times of explanation, disputation, and composition, he actualized the warmths and realizations of the two stages. He beheld the naked, genuine, true nature of phenomena, coemergent primordial awareness. All appearances of phenomena arose as the sphere of the deity. The vajra Dharma protectors served him like slaves.

Jampa Künga Tenpai Gyaltsen was continually engaged in spreading the teachings of the profound and vast Dharma. He bestowed the profound instructions, foremost of which were the Teaching in the tradition of the Explication for the Assembly eight times and the Explication for Disciples five times. Furthermore, he bestowed many common and uncommon stages of guidance, such as the *One Hundred Systems of Guidance,* the eight great systems of guidance in our own tradition, the Stages of the Path, and Mind Training. He bestowed countless initiations, such as: the seven mandalas of Ngor twice; the *Vajra Rosary* twice; the tantras for purification twice; and limitless kinds of separate teachings. He bestowed a great many types of ritual permissions, foremost of which was the *Ocean of Methods for Accomplishment* three times.[470] He taught the explanations of the major scholastic treatises, as well as the common guidances of grammar, poetics, and so forth. He also gave countless cycles of the supportive reading transmissions of collected works, anthologies, and so forth, foremost of which were the Tengyur and the collected works of the spiritual guides of Tibet. [220] About five volumes of his wondrous compositions exist. He established the great spiritual vehicles of all the precious tantra classes that survive in this glacial land.

Born from his speech, many disciples appeared who upheld the doctrine and gained expertise and attainments. Descending from them, a countless host of direct disciples and grand-disciples has appeared, completely filling this vast earth at the present day. All of them spread the precious doctrine in all directions and sought to place absolutely all creatures in the higher realms and in the lofty citadel of the definite excellence of enlightenment.

In particular, throughout his life about one hundred crown jewels of scholars and superior practitioners became Jampa Künga Tenpai Gyaltsen's spiritual sons, to whom he passed the doctrine of the Teaching in the tradition of the Explication for Disciples. Foremost among these were the great Khangsar abbot Jampaiyang Ngawang Sönam Gyaltsen; the great abbot and sun of speech Jamyang Sherap Gyatso; Palden Lodrö Gyaltsen, who was the precious abbot of Phenkhang and a great bodhisattva who will never regress; the great abbot Jamyang Rinchen Dorjé, who was his relative who honored him with the three tributes his entire life; the noble and sublime Thupten Jigmé Chökyi Wangchuk, who was a superb teacher and the Gyatrul Rinpoché of Chamdo; Rinchen Losang Khyenrap, who was the master of Risur who upheld the doctrine of the omniscient Butön Rinpoché; Künga Jamyang, who was the backbone of the doctrine of the oral transmissions and the Dharma lord of Ngari; and Jikmé Palden, a great paṇḍita who knew the five fields of knowledge. Even one as inferior in the two religious and secular traditions as myself was allowed to sit at the end of the row of fortunate beings who were his disciples.[471] Several of these disciples actualized the result of attainment through meditation, and the individuals upholding the doctrine made the doctrine of the Explication for Disciples as brilliant as the rising sun.

During that period, Jampa Künga Tenpai Gyaltsen's disciples (who filled all the areas of the three districts of Ngari in western Tibet, the four "horns" of Central Tibet and Tsang in the middle, and the six ridges of Do and Kham in eastern Tibet) filled the surrounding directions with the exclamation, "Ah! Our tasting such nectar from the mouth of one who is like a buddha actually appearing on the earth is similar to what the five fortunate beings in the retinue of the Blessed One tasted in the past. Fantastic!" [221]

In that way, by means of both explication and practice, Jampa Künga Tenpai Gyaltsen spread the precious doctrine in all directions his entire life. To urge toward the Dharma those disciples who were clinging to permanence, and because he saw that the time had come for training those in other realms, at the age of forty-two, in the early morning of the fourth day in the last of the two ninth months in an iron-horse year (1870), he sat in the posture of Guru Ratnasambhava, displayed to the ḍākinīs the uncommon signs of the four initiations, and gathered the array of his rūpakāya form bodies back into space. During that time, the orb of his face was more brilliant than before, his body was resplendent, and so forth, corresponding to the statements that a total transformation of one's previous condition occurs, and that the sense faculties of individuals who have gained the nectar of unexcelled primordial awareness become totally clear, the color of their faces becomes pure, the color of their skin becomes white, and so forth.

Suddenly, a constant shower of gentle rain fell, many marvelous rainbow clouds formed and, in particular, a cloud in the shape of a stupa appeared from the eastern direction.

On the morning of the eighth day, when he was closely examined, the white enlightenment mind had flowed from both nostrils. It had pervaded his entire body, which was an obvious sign that, from the clear light of death—the dharmakāya reality body—Jampa Künga Tenpai Gyaltsen had risen again in the sambhogakāya enjoyment body of unity and was ceaselessly turning the Dharma wheel of the Mahayana for bodhisattvas on the tenth spiritual level.

When the body was offered for cremation on a day in the tenth month, the fire of primordial awareness blazed by itself. Inconceivable mundane and transcendent omens and miracles were actually displayed then as well, such as rainbow clouds shaped like the offering substances and a fine aroma spreading in all directions.

In accordance with the established customs of the great palaces of Ngor, the subsequent funeral services were completed in a lavish and extensive way, with the participants (led by Jampa Künga Tenpai Gyaltsen's spiritual son Jamyang Rinchen Dorjé) attentively conducting them with faith and devotion in memory of his kindness. The funeral rites were carefully observed in all respects. [222]

> In that way, by the merit of recording
> the condensed biographies
> to establish the authenticity
> of the masters of the Teaching
> in the tradition of the Explication for Disciples,
> may I be liberated by the path of the master.

Beginning with the biography of Dakchen Dorjé Chang, through about half of the biography of Dorjé Chang Jampa Künga Tenzin, this supplement to the biographies of the lineal masters of the Explication for Disciples in the uncommon Ngor tradition of the Teaching was composed by the eastern Dharma lord Künga Palden,[472] a superb teacher of sutra and tantra. The remainder, the condensed biography of Jampa Künga Tenpai

Gyaltsen, certainly the true Vajradhara, the title, the expression of offering, and the colophon, are new additions by me, Loter Wangpo, done with the intention of offering service by reviving the reading transmission. May this merit become a cause for all living beings such as me to be graced in all lifetimes by that venerable lord Vajradhara.

Sarva maṅgalaṃ
Good fortune to all!

5. Summarizing Notes on How to Explain and Practice the Dharma

From the Comprehensive Explanation of the Precious Teaching of the "Path with the Result"

The Infallible Version of Khau Drakzongpa
The Practice of the Old Monk Khyentsé

Jamyang Khyentsé Wangchuk (1524–68)

I PROSTRATE AND TAKE REFUGE at all times at the lotus beneath the feet of the venerable lord Vajradhara of matchless kindness, the holy Dharma king Tsarchen, the essence of all the buddhas of the past, present, and future. Please grace me with your great love.

> Glorious in nature, with pristine intellect,
> your clear light fills all samsara and nirvana.
>
> Born from the ocean of the four ripening initiations,[473]
> your orb of the two famous stages is vast.
>
> Wreathed by rosaries of the light rays
> of the sacred commitments and vows,
> you are the friend who causes the lotus grove
> of attainments to bloom.
>
> I bow with the crown of my head
> at the feet of the master who,
> with the light of the four bodies of enlightenment,
> removes the darkness of disciples.

The overlord of the sphere of unity
is hero Hevajra embraced by mother Nairātmyā.

The powerful lord, the emperor of attainment,
is famous in the three worlds as honorable Virūpa.

The sublime sovereigns of the infallible doctrine
are the great masters of Sakya, together with the lineage.

May the toenails of Dharma lord Tsarpa,
the master embodying them all,
rest forever on the crown of my head.

Hearing a small portion of it removes
the darkness of impenetrable ignorance,
and undistracted attention to its meaning
increases the light of the vast Dharma.

If meditated upon correctly,
it definitely bestows the citadel endowed
with threefold greatness in this life.[474]

I bow with devotion to the speech of the master,
and compose this essential memory aid.

II. How to Explain and Learn the Dharma

This consists of three topics:

A. The identification of the Dharma to be explained
B. The oral instructions that explain it
C. The precise way these explain it

A. *The identification of the Dharma to be explained*

The Dharma teaching is the esoteric instructions of the Path with the Result. This also consists of two topics:

1. What is to be described—how the "path with the result" actually exists [224]
2. The description—how the "path with the result" is presented in the treatise

1. *What is to be described—how the "path with the result" actually exists*

The "path with the result" is actually presented. But the "path with the cause,"[475] the "cause with the path," the "cause with the result," the "result with the cause," and the "result with the path" are also presented by implication.

The "cause with the path": the functions of the path are present in the cause as potential activity.

The "cause with the result": the result is present in the cause as natural spontaneity. If a flawless seed meets with the circumstances, a seedling can potentially arise as the result. Similarly, the result can potentially arise if the oral instructions are met with as the circumstance.

The "path with the cause": at the time of the path, the stains of the cause can potentially be purified. If that were not the case, one would not know what path to meditate upon in relation to what ground of purification.

The "path with the result": at the time of the path, the result is potentially obtainable, because if that were not the case it would be useless to meditate on the path.

The "result with the cause": at the time of the result, the cause is present in a transformed state. A gold-transforming elixir transforms the base element of iron into gold, but the iron is not made totally nonexistent. In the same way, the cause has also transformed into the result, but it has not become totally nonexistent.

Similarly, because all the qualities of the path are present in increasingly complete form, it is said to be the "result with the path."

In brief, all of those are one's own mind alone, beyond conceptual elaboration, appearing in a particular form. But they are not established outside of the mind. Due to temporary influences, that very mind appears in individual forms, but its essence is not established as better or worse. It is like the following example. When a piece of copper is used for a dog dish, it is an inferior thing and an object of disgust, but when the very same copper is used for an ornament, whether an anklet or a bracelet, or something like the plate of a king, there is no feeling of disgust and, in addition, it becomes a beautiful and amazing thing. When that same copper has been made into something like a buddha image, and consecrated, it is used as an object for prostrations and offerings, on the basis of which it becomes an object for the accumulation of the assembly of merit. Although it appears in this way in temporarily sublime or inferior forms, the essence of the copper itself has not improved in the least. [225]

Therefore, to say, "The ground, the path, and the result are indivisible," is like saying, "The ground is the path," "The path is the result." Yet, when that very essence of buddhahood at the time of the ground—unrecognized and obscured by the incidental stains—is purified by the time of the path, parted from the stains, and then its very essence recognized, it is designated by the name *result.* That is also the meaning of this statement:

> Teaching the meaning of the indivisible
> triad of ground, path, and result,
> who other than Künga Gyaltsen Palsangpo,
> a member of the Khön family,
> a sublime son of the Śākya born into the vajra family,
> speaks in conformity with the meaning?[476]

Therefore, the *Root Tantra* says:

> Sentient beings are buddhas,
> but obscured by incidental stains.
> Once these are removed, they are buddhas.[477]

This teaches, "One is a buddha at the time of the ground, but not recognizing that to be so, one is unable to perform the actions of a buddha."

"Once these are removed" specifies the path that purifies the stains, and "they are buddhas" specifies buddhahood at the time of the result.

Briefly, in the context of not distinguishing the actual and the designated, the *Great Proclamation* of Gyaltsap Dampa says:

> If the ground is established,
> it is logically implied to be Hevajra,
> but when the actual and the designated
> are distinguished, that logical
> implication does not hold.[478]

2. *The description—how the "path with the result" is presented in the treatise*[479]

This consists of three topics:

- a. The path
- b. The result
- c. The meaning of the names of both together

a. *The path*

This consists of two topics:

- 1) The path to be traveled
- 2) The path that transports one

1) *The path to be traveled*

According to its essence, the path can be divided into both mundane and transcendent paths. As long as the truth of the first spiritual level on the path of seeing has not been seen, it is the mundane. After that, it is the transcendent.

Among the twelve paths of the stiff wheel and the spinning wheel (those consisting of the warmths and consisting of the signs, and so forth), that of the stiff wheel is the mundane path. For example, when the wheels of a cart are new and have not yet been broken in, sometimes they do not turn even when pulled with much effort and sometimes they turn easily. Similarly, on the mundane path, because the four supporting mandalas have not been refined, experiences arise either in sequence or not in sequence. So it is taught, "The warmths should be allowed natural expression." In this way, various experiences occur, with meditative concentration sometimes seeming to arise effortlessly and sometimes not arising even with effort. [226] The path of the spinning wheel is the transcendent path. When the wheels of the cart have been carefully broken in, they will easily turn wherever the cart is pulled. In a similar way, on the transcendent path, all the experiences consisting of the three signs arise in sequence.

Similarly, the path consisting of the warmths is the mundane and that consisting of the signs is the transcendent.

The path consisting of the views is the mundane and that consisting of the culminations of attainment is the transcendent.

The path of the advance and retreat of primordial awareness is the mundane. Primordial awareness shines a little, then it is obscured, and then it shines again, like the sun between clouds. The path of the advance and retreat of thoughts is the transcendent path. Mundane thoughts may arise, but they cease immediately.

The path on which the master does not progressively evolve is the mundane path. Except to one for whom samsara has almost stopped, he usually appears as an ordinary human master. The path on which the master does progressively evolve is the transcendent path. During the six spiritual levels of the vase initiation the master of the nirmāṇakāya emanated body appears. During the four spiritual levels of the secret initiation the master of the sambhogakāya enjoyment body appears. During the two spiritual levels of the initiation of primordial awareness dependent on an embodiment of wisdom, the master of the dharmakāya reality body appears.

According to the paths, those are condensed into five; according to the spiritual levels, into twelve and a half; and according to the factors of enlightenment, into thirty-seven. Thus my master taught.

2) *The path that transports one*

This consists of two topics:

- a) The three extensive, medium, and condensed paths
- b) The three for those of superior, medium, and inferior faculties

a) *The three extensive, medium, and condensed paths*

This consists of three sections:

(1) Eighteen topics for the extensive path
(2) Five topics for the medium path
(3) Three topics for the condensed path

(1) *The extensive path*

The treatise of the *Vajra Lines* includes three general parts. The first part, the path of samsara and nirvana in common, consists of seven topics: the path presented as the three appearances, the path presented as the three continua, the path presented as the four authentic qualities, the path presented as the six oral instructions, the path presented as the four oral transmissions, the path presented as the five dependently arisen connections, and the presentation of protection from obstacles for yogins who are over-inclined toward method and wisdom. The reason that these are referred to as the path of samsara and nirvana in common is that each of them presents the complete phenomena of the ground, the path, and the result.

The second part, the mundane path of the stiff wheel, consists of seven topics: the brief presentation of the cause for the arising of meditative concentration, an extensive presentation in a condensed form, the presentation of the path free from hope and fear, the presentation as the four tests, the presentation of the applications of mindfulness as the cause, the presentation of the four perfect renunciations as the result, [227] and the presentation of their final summary. The reason these are defined as the mundane path is that they produce the mundane meditative concentrations that have not arisen, enhance those that have arisen, and so forth.

The third part, the transcendent path of the spinning wheel, consists of four topics, which are the four culminations of attainment: the indivisibility of samsara and nirvana for the six spiritual levels of the vase initiation, the clearly distinct and completely perfect for the four spiritual levels of the secret initiation, the blissful emptiness of lesser extent for the two spiritual levels of the initiation of primordial awareness dependent on an embodiment of wisdom, and the blissful emptiness of greater extent for the one spiritual level of the fourth initiation. In most explications of the treatise of the *Vajra Lines,* this consists of the four topics of the causes, the signs, the results, and the boundaries. But in either of the two methods of classification, these are considered to be the transcendent path, because they produce the transcendent meditative concentrations and so forth.

In that way, the extensive path has eighteen topics.

(2) *The medium path*

This consists of five topics: the presentations of meditative concentration, its cause, its benefits, its obstacles, and its boundaries.

(3) *The condensed path*

This consists of three topics: the essence, the nature, and the characteristic.

b) *The path presented for those of superior, medium, and inferior faculties*

(1) *The superior*

A person who is liberated at the time of the initiation, like King Indrabhūti,[480] is said to have "utterly superior faculties," and it is unsuitable for him to be guided by any of these paths. A person with superior faculties is a person who obtains the authentic ripening initiation, based on which he reaches the decisive conclusion that the master from whom he obtained the initiation is endowed with the four bodies of enlightenment and the five types of primordial awareness; and, certain without the slightest doubt or hesitation, offers supplications as though unaware of day and night. It is taught that "He is liberated by the profound path, the path of the master." The sacred commitments are also naturally protected, and he will reach the culmination of attainment without having to depend on any of the paths of creation, completion, and so forth with even the slightest effort. Thus my master taught.

(2) *The medium*

Although a person may have great faith, devotion, and so forth toward the master, when he has not reached the decisive conclusion that the master is endowed with the four bodies of enlightenment and the five types of primordial awareness, he cannot be liberated by the path of the master alone even if he is energetic in offering supplications. Therefore, he has medium faculties. In addition to the previous practices, by protecting the twenty sacred commitments by means of the four modes of protection,[481] and valuing them as he values his life, he will quickly obtain the result. [228] This is "the medium, the path of the sacred commitments and the vows." Thus my master taught.

(3) *The inferior*

One who is not quite untouched by minor infractions of the sacred commitments and so forth has inferior faculties and, in addition to the previous practices, must correctly practice the yogas of creation and completion. This is "the inferior, a cessation through comprehension of the body, the path consisting of the five dependently arisen connections." Thus my master taught. The meaning of this will be explained in detail later in the text.

b. *The result*

The result is threefold greatness: the greatness of benefit for oneself, which is being endowed with the four bodies of enlightenment and the five types of primordial awareness; the greatness of benefit for others, which is enabling the blind to regain sight and so forth; and the greatness for both oneself and others, which is buddhahood together with one's circle in a single group.

c. *The meaning of the names of both together*

This is known as the oral instructions of the path with the result, the oral instructions of the result with the path, the oral instructions of understanding many points by understanding one, the oral instructions of upholding faults as qualities, the oral instructions of accepting obstacles as attainments, the oral instructions of removing impediments to meditation by recognizing meditative concentration, the oral instructions of removing impediments of the māras by recognizing obstacles, the oral instructions with which to understand the real nature of the Tripiṭaka, the oral instructions that are like a gold-transforming elixir, the oral instructions that are like a wish-fulfilling jewel, and the oral instructions of knowing to uphold faults as qualities and to accept obstacles as attainments. Thus it is endowed with eleven, ten, or eight exceptional features.

In brief, this teaching is known as the *Path with the Result* because the ground, the path, and the result, or all the phenomena of samsara and nirvana are presented completely and without error. Whatever other profound esoteric instructions of the creation and completion stages may exist, they may be called "profound esoteric instructions" or "profound guidance," but they do not even merit the mere name "path with the result." Thus my master taught.

B. *The oral instructions that explain the Dharma*

It is taught:

> Doubts are eliminated by means
> of the four authentic qualities
> and oral transmissions.[482]

Therefore, most doubts about the oral instructions are eliminated by means of the four authentic qualities and the four oral transmissions.

1. *The four authentic qualities*

The *Vajra Lines* say:

> After establishing the result by means of the four authentic qualities,[483]

The authentic quality of scripture applies to what is determined by inference, so the establishment of the result is actually stated, [229] but by implication the ground and the path are also both established. The great venerable lord Drakpa Gyaltsen said:

> All phenomena are established
> by means of the four authentic qualities.[484]

This section consists of three topics:

a. The essence of the authentic qualities
b. The definite number of the authentic qualities
c. The sequence of the authentic qualities

a. *The essence of the authentic qualities*

As known in conventional mundane usage and to dialecticians, an authentic quality is *infallible.* This means, "Whatever goal is desired, it is infallible or perfect in achieving it." Thus my master taught.

b. *The number of the authentic qualities*

The number is definitely four. Why? These are the four authentic qualities of the perfect words and so forth. Thus, the reasons for certainty regarding that number are that all the factors of a person's path to buddhahood are included in these four; no more than these are necessary, and if they were fewer everything would not be included.

One might ask, "In that case, does that not contradict the *Kālacakra,* which explains that there are three authentic qualities? It says:

In this Vajrayana three circumstances were taught by the Blessed One: the initial circumstance of the tantra, then the circumstance of the master, and then the circumstance of oneself."[485]

Because these are the intentions of each of the two individual tantras, one cannot be refuted by the other. However, there is also no contradiction here. In the context of obtaining a teaching from an authentic great adept in person, those three are sufficient, and it is not necessary to establish the authentic quality of the treatise because the opinion of that great adept himself is already unmistakably known. Since it is not necessary to question the treatise composed by him, three authentic qualities are sufficient for people like Eastern Kāṇha and Ḍombi Heruka.[486] Similarly, the mention of three in the *Kālacakra* was made in the context of obtaining a teaching directly from the Buddha or an authentic great adept. Here in the Path with the Result it is necessary to depend on a transmission from one master to another, at which time it is necessary to eliminate doubts by means of listening and reflection concerning the authentic quality of the treatise. So four have been identified. This is the meaning of the following statement:

> Understand that it has been transmitted from one to one.
> Receive it directly from a superior master.[487]

Thus my master taught.

c. *The sequence of the authentic qualities*

This consists of four topics:

1) The sequence stated in the tantra
2) The sequence in which they first occur

3) The sequence of practice
4) The sequence in which they become authentic qualities

1) *The sequence stated in the tantra*

One might ask, "Is there a definite sequence for these?"

There is. The *Sampuṭa* says:

> The authentic quality of the treatise,
> the teacher, following the scripture,
> and awareness of reality.[488]

These are the authentic quality of the treatise, the authentic quality of the master, and the authentic quality of scripture. [230] "Awareness of reality" is the authentic quality of experience, from the ultimate experience of the real primordial awareness that is illustrated, to the various experiences that may arise. These are mixed up and stated out of order in the tantra to prevent dialecticians from using the tantra as they please. Thus my master taught.

2) *The sequence in which they first occur*

"In that case," one might ask, "if that statement from the tantra is out of order, what exactly is the sequence that is not out of order?"

As headwaters originate in the white glaciers, the instructions must be based on an immaculate tantra spoken by the completely perfect Buddha, and so [1] the authentic quality of scripture, the perfect words, occurs. Concerning infallible commentary on the intention of those words, it is taught:

> Based on the oral instructions
> of adepts such as Nāgārjuna,
> who was prophesied,
> or such as Virūpa,
> who was blessed by the ḍākinī,...[489]

Because the treatises of commentary by authentic commentators appear in this way, [2] the authentic quality of the treatise occurs. Because an excellent master who teaches the treatise appears, [3] the authentic quality of the master occurs. Because he teaches the oral instructions, [4] the authentic quality of experience occurs. The authentic quality of experience is the arising of the fifteen experiences—the five sets of three—and so forth, because those oral instructions have been practiced.[490] Also giving the name "authentic quality of experience" to the oral instructions that produce [experience] is giving the name of the product to the producer. Thus my master taught.

3) *The sequence of practice*

"In that case," one might ask, "are they also in that order when practiced?"

They are not. First is the authentic quality of the master. When one practices according to just what that master explained, the experiences arise exactly in one's mindstream just as the master taught. This is the authentic quality of experience. At that time, the doubt may arise, "Is this a deception, something created in arrogance or out of convenience by the master himself?" That is not the case. The teacher, the Lord of Yogins, the great Virūpa, explained it in this way. When eliminating doubts by means of study and reflection on the *Vajra Lines,* one realizes, "It is in the treatise of the Lord of Yogins, just exactly as the master said," and confidence arises. This is the authentic quality of the treatise. And this is not something the Lord of Yogins created haphazardly or out of arrogance. [231] It is the extracted quintessence of the meaning to be expressed in all the sutras and tantras, the words of the Sugata in general, and specifically, of secret mantra teachings; among them, the unexcelled yoga tantras; among them, the mother tantras; among them, both the Cakrasaṃvara and the Hevajra cycles; among them, the *Tantra Trilogy of Hevajra;* and among them, the *Two-Part Root Tantra.* By applying quotations from the tantras to each phrase of the *Vajra Lines* and teaching it, a certainty that it is the heart of the tantras will arise. This is the authentic quality of scripture, the perfect words. Thus my master taught.

4) *The sequence in which they become authentic qualities*

Those are the authentic qualities, but if experience has not arisen in the individual, they will not become authentic qualities in one's own essence, and nothing but indecision and doubt will arise. Whenever experience does arise in one's mindstream and one thinks, "This master of mine is a buddha," a faith that others cannot steal will arise. This is the authentic quality of the master. Similarly, when one thinks about the treatise and the tantra, "These are infallible, without error, and extremely profound," and a faith that others cannot steal arises concerning the master, the deity, and the oral instructions, they have become authentic qualities. Thus my master taught.

2. *The four oral transmissions*

The treatise says:

> The oral transmission of secret mantra and four others are unbroken.[491]

This consists of three topics:

a. Their essence
b. Their definite number
c. Their sequence

a. *Their essence*

This consists of four topics:

1) The unceasing stream of initiation
2) The undeclined transmission of blessings
3) The undisrupted sequence of the oral instructions
4) The mind satisfied with devotion

1) *The unceasing stream of initiation*

This is the unceasing stream of initiation at the time of the cause, the time of the path, and the time of the result.

2) *The undeclined transmission of blessings*

Although this is also the individual blessings in connection with the Teaching, such as the blessing of the venerable Vajra Nairātmyā, it is primarily the four culminations of secret mantra: the culmination of practice, the culmination of experience, the culmination of blessings, and the culmination of attainment.

3) *The undisrupted sequence of the oral instructions*

Some in the Shama tradition maintained that the term *sar kha* meant, "the transference of the master's realization to the disciple, like making an imprint." The Path with the Result master Yeshé Pal[492] and so forth maintained that, as the edge *(kha sar)* of a sword cut others, the term *sar kha* meant that these oral instructions cut other thoughts and so forth. These are mere fabrications. In our tradition, *sarga* is understood as an archaic Tibetan term with a meaning like "sequence" or "section." Without an examination of the connection between master and disciple, the initiation is not bestowed. [232] Without the bestowal of the initiation, the oral instructions are not explained. When the oral instructions have not been explained, the treatise is not explained. When the treatise has not been explained, the prediction is not given. When the prediction has not been given, the seal is not applied. Thus these are taught without mistakes in the sequence.

4) *The mind satisfied with devotion*

When one practices in that way and the warmths and the signs are actualized just as they were explained, a faith that others cannot steal arises concerning the master and the oral instructions. This is the result of the oral transmission, which is given its name. Thus my master taught.

b. *Their definite number*

Because a person's entire path—from when the path is entered up to the citadel of unity—is included in those four, more are not necessary, and if any one is missing, it will not be an unmistakable path to buddhahood. So there are definitely four.

c. *Their sequence*

If the initiation is not obtained, blessings cannot be imparted. The oral instructions come from those endowed with the culmination of practice and so forth. From practicing [the oral instructions], devotion arises. This is their sequence. Thus my master taught.

C. *The Precise Way These Explain the Dharma*

The Dharma is explained by means of the four authentic qualities and the four oral transmissions.

1. *Explanation by means of the four authentic qualities*

This consists of three topics:

a. Explanation by application of the sixty articles of Dharma contained in the *Volume* to the four authentic qualities
b. Explanation by application of the *Little Red Volume* to the four authentic qualities
c. Specific explanation of the four fundamental treatises of guidance for the purpose of producing the authentic quality of experience

a. *Explanation by application of the sixty articles of Dharma contained in the* Volume *to the four authentic qualities*

This consists of two topics:

1) The identification of the sixty articles of Dharma
2) How to apply these to the four authentic qualities

1) *The identification of the sixty articles of Dharma*

In the opinion of lord Müsepa, the number sixty includes the catalogue.[493] However, since the catalogue is the "book shepherd"—the guide to the sixty articles of Dharma, or their shepherd—this is somewhat incorrect, like counting fifty-nine yaks and adding the yak shepherd as the sixtieth when sixty yaks are needed.

Some in the Ngor tradition reach the number sixty by adding other minor esoteric instructions, but this directly contradicts the great venerable lord Drakpa Gyaltsen's statement:

> Unable to write a catalogue for the other minor esoteric instructions, I will leave that alone.[494]

In our tradition, according to the opinion of Dakchen Dorjé Chang, the number sixty includes the *Vajra Lines.* [233] It is counted because most of the profound Dharma teachings of the Sakyapa are included here in the three catalogues to the *Volume,* the ancestral Dharma teachings, and the *Tantra Trilogy,* which were composed by the great venerable lord Drakpa Gyaltsen. If the *Vajra Lines* is not counted in any of these three, the fault will occur of the *Vajra Lines,* which is the main text, not being anywhere. Therefore it is reasonable to count it. Thus my master taught.

Furthermore, according to this very same lineage, until lord Sachen, not a single written text existed. The *Vajra Lines* were learned and transmitted orally. This is also the key point concerning the absence of an Indian language text and a translator's colophon for Drokmi's translation. Shang Gönpawa told lord Sachen, "Whether you write it down in texts, or whatever you do, you are the owner and have great power." Thus Sachen received both the commanded restriction and the permission.[495]

As soon as the eighteen-year commanded restriction had expired, Aseng, who was from Kham, begged Sachen to teach. Because this happened at the same time as the expiration of the commanded restriction, Sachen realized that his master had brought the auspicious connections into alignment, and he gave guidance to Aseng alone. Sachen also wrote down the *Vajra Lines* at that time and composed the *Summary for Aseng,* the first of all the commentaries.[496] Because the miscellaneous texts that Sachen gradually composed were of great value, they were kept in a leather box and were known as the *Leather Case Collection.* Later, the great venerable lord Drakpa Gyaltsen arranged them into a volume. To symbolize that this Dharma is difficult to understand, but that all needs and wishes are fulfilled if it is understood, he drew a vajra on the face of the front cover-board and a jewel on the back one. To indicate that the teachings are understood from the oral instructions of a master endowed with the transmission, he drew the figures of the transmission line of the Teaching on the inside of the cover-board. Since it had a yellow cloth on it, it was known as the *Yellow Volume.*

To prevent dialecticians from using them as they please, the texts are not arranged in a certain sequence. The *Vajra Lines* as the root text, the *Explication of the Treatise for Nyak,* the twenty-two small texts of clarification, and the *Explication for Aseng*—which is the condensed meaning of those—are the twenty-five in regard to the authentic quality of the treatise.[497]

As a continuation of that, seventeen Dharma teachings supplement the meaning, six of which are contained here [in the *Yellow Volume*]. As a continuation from "the causal continuum of the universal ground,"[498] there is the root text and the commentary on the indivisibility of samsara and nirvana.

As a continuation from "there is the causal initiation with four triads, the seats and so forth, and so forth," [234] there are the key points of esoteric instruction for bestowing the three supreme initiations dependent on the path of liberation,[499] and for condensing all the rituals of the four initiations. As a continuation from "presentation by means of the four fives of the creation stage as the path and so forth," there is the condensed outer creation stage. As a continuation from "protecting the sacred commitments of meditative equipoise and so forth," there is the creation of the nectar pills for the sacred commitment of continual food. As a continuation from "the oral transmission of secret mantra and four others are unbroken," there is the memory aid for the blessing of Vajra Nairātmyā.

The seven Dharma teachings for beginners in common are the great stream of initiation and the four-branch extensive method for accomplishment, composed by the precious teacher Sönam Tsemo; and the six-branch medium method for accomplishment, the method for accomplishment of the venerable mother Nairātmyā, the *Rejection of Confusion About the Root Downfalls,* the ritual feast of the sacred commitment of food at special times, and the replenishing, achievement of the accumulated deeds, and burnt offering of the recitation retreat, all composed by the venerable lord Drakpa Gyaltsen.[500]

The four fundamental treatises of guidance are the fundamental treatises of guidance precisely according to the treatise of the *Vajra Lines,* guidance by means of the six key points of oral instruction, guidance by means of the eleven key points, and guidance by means of the paths for those of superior, medium, and inferior faculties.

The five Dharma teachings for producing realization concern: utilizing and dispensing with the paths; utilizing and dispensing with the mudrā consort; the seven esoteric instructions beneficial to know; the blending of the paths, together with the four pulsations; and the twelve outer and inner deeds.

The four texts for the removal of impediments concern the seven precipitous paths on which meditation is discarded, the four key points not to be allowed natural expression, the removal of elemental physical disturbances by means of the vital winds and behavior, and the thirty-two yogic exercises.

For the authentic quality of scripture, the perfect words, there are the condensed application to precisely this scripture,[501] the detailed application, and the condensed application to all scriptures.

For the authentic quality of the master, there is the story of the masters in India and the story of the masters in Tibet.

Those are the sixty.

2) *How to apply these sixty articles of Dharma to the four authentic qualities*

These sixty articles of Dharma must be applied to the sequence of the four authentic qualities. Furthermore, they must be applied to the sequence of practice. First, in the context of the authentic quality of the master, there are the life stories of the masters in India and the life stories of the masters in Tibet.

For the authentic quality of experience, [235] there are thirty articles of Dharma. Concerning the four fundamental treatises of guidance, the five Dharma teachings for producing realization and the four texts for the removal of impediments are to be inserted within the first of the fundamental treatises. Then come the great stream of initiation, the bestowal of the three supreme initiations dependent on the path of liberation, the condensed version of all the rituals of the four initiations, the *Rejection of Confusion About the Root Downfalls,* the creation of nectar pills, the ritual feast, the root text and the commentary on the indivisibility of samsara and nirvana, the four-branch and the six-branch methods for realization, the condensed outer creation stage, the method for accomplishment of Nairātmyā, the burnt offering, the memory aid for the undeclined transmission of the blessing, the medium path without the root text, the condensed path that has a brief treatise of its own, and a guruyoga text.

For the authentic quality of the treatise, there are the twenty-five texts. For the authentic quality of the scripture, there are the three texts of the detailed application to precisely this scripture, the condensed application, and the condensed application to all scriptures. The detailed application to all scriptures has not been placed in writing because it would be too long.

In that way, those sixty articles of Dharma are applied to the sequence of the four authentic qualities and taught at the appropriate points. Thus my master taught.

b. *The application of the minor texts or the* Little Red Volume[502] *to the four authentic qualities*

This consists of two topics:

1) Their identification
2) Their application to the four authentic qualities

1) *Their identification*

These are the "minor texts" composed by individual masters, from the great lord of Sakya to Ngorchen Dorjé Chang; the miscellaneous texts that are not complete bodies of work like the *Black Volume.*[503] From the prayer to the lineage of the Path with the Result in the context of the authentic quality of the master, through the Dharma connections with the six gatekeepers (which are counted as one), there are sixty texts. The titles of the ten compositions by Ngorchen Dorjé Chang, such as *Opening the Secret Door,* which concerns the method for explaining the Path with the Result, are listed in the catalogue.

The seven texts composed by lord Müchen are the stream of initiation, the explanation of the need for the toothstick and so forth, the supplement to the earth ritual, the six-branch method for direct realization, the commentary on the sacrificial-cake ritual, and the two manuals of guidance for the Path with the Result. The works composed by Dakchen Rinpoché are the ritual for awakening the enlightenment mind, the explication of the root downfalls, the basic explication of the process of direct enlightenment, how to create the nectar pills, the summarizing notes on the indivisibility of samsara and nirvana, the guidance manual for the *Clarification of the Meaning through Symbols,* and the guidance manual for the *Path Concealed and Explained.* [236] The individual explications composed by those two lords are not included among the minor texts in the *Little Red Volume.*[504]

2) *Their application to the four authentic qualities*

This can be known elsewhere.[505]

c. *The specific explanation of the four fundamental treatises of guidance for the purpose of producing the authentic quality of experience*

One might ask, "What are the four fundamental treatises?"[506]

They are these four that are precisely according to the treatise of the *Vajra Lines* and so forth.

One might wonder, "For what reason is the first of these labeled 'precisely according to the treatise?'[507] Are the last three fundamental treatises not also precisely according to the intention of the treatise?"

All four fundamental treatises are equal in commenting precisely according to the intention of the *Vajra Lines,* but the other three fundamental treatises are not guidance precisely according to the sequence of the treatise. Because the first provides guidance precisely according to the sequence of the treatise, it is named in that way.

Moreover, this first fundamental treatise completely presents all the paths, from that of the most inferior person with lesser good fortune suited to the gradual approach, who has not entered the Buddhist doctrine but wishes to enter, to that of a yogin of unity. As for the meaning of "a person of lesser good fortune suited to the gradual approach," one is of "lesser good fortune" because one has not had the good fortune in this life to have actually entered the Vajrayana without interruption by other paths. Such a person is "suited to the gradual approach" because it is necessary to be trained gradually by means of the views in sequence and so forth.

This explanation includes two topics:

1) Those suited to the gradual approach in the context of the explanation of the tantra
2) Those suited to the gradual approach in the context of guidance by the esoteric instructions

1) *Those suited to the gradual approach in the context of the explanation of the tantra*

It is taught:

> The vows of renewal and
> purification should be given first,
> and after that the ten topics of training.
> Present to them the Vaibhāṣya,
> and likewise the Sautrāntika.
> Then the Yogācāra,
> and after that present the Madhyamaka.

And so forth, through:

> When all the stages of mantra
> have been understood,...[508]

Thus train in the conducts and views in sequence. The meaning of "the stages of mantra" is mentioned in the uncommon explanatory tantra in lines such as the following:

> Action tantras for the inferior.
> Not the action for yogins above them.
> The sublime yoga for sublime sentient beings.
> The unexcelled yoga for those above that.[509]

In that way, at the end of training in those four classes of tantra and the paths of the father tantras such as the *Guhyasamāja* and the mother tantras such as the *Cakrasaṃvara,* in order to emphasize the greatness of the quintessential *Hevajra,* it is said:

> After that, begin Hevajra.[510] [237]

Thus it is accepted that one enters into the ripening initiation and liberating guidance of glorious Hevajra, by which the sublime attainment is rapidly achieved. Those points should be learned in detail from the *Jeweled Tree for Direct Realization.*[511] Thus my master taught.

2) *Those suited to the gradual approach in the context of guidance by the esoteric instructions*

All of the practices, from "the vows of renewal and purification" up to "the stages of mantra have been understood," are completed by the guidance of the Three Appearances.

"In that case," one might ask, "what are the practices of the action tantras, the performance tantras, and so forth?"

Although these are not individually identified as "such and such a practice," according to the statement that the Path with the Result is "the extracted quintessence of the meaning of all the sutras and tantras, the words of the Sugata," it is the collected essence of the meaning of them all. In brief, this means that all the realizations from training in the views and conducts in sequence are complete here. Thus my master taught.

Therefore, as mentioned, this path is suitable for guiding all persons. However, since the mindstream of a person of good fortune who is suited to the instantaneous approach already contains all the realizations of those previous paths, they have been achieved, and one merely needs to practice. For example, a person whose mindstream contains all the realizations of a śrāvaka or all the realizations of the "lesser individual" can be guided beginning with love and compassion. Similarly, one with all the realizations of the Mahayana in his mindstream can be guided beginning with the bestowal of initiation. However, because it is difficult nowadays to clearly distinguish such categories, and in order to facilitate the guidance of other disciples of medium and dull faculties and so forth, guidance precisely according to the treatise of the *Vajra Lines* is used.

Furthermore, the reason that the actual presentation of the treatise is in the tradition of guidance for one suited to the gradual approach is that this treatise was formulated for Eastern Kāṇha. He was the most inferior of those suited to the gradual approach, because he had not entered into the Buddhist doctrine and had just come from the midst of the five hundred longhaired sadhus of Bhīmesara. He wished to enter the doctrine and followed after the Lord of Yogins. Therefore, Virūpa gave him the *Vajra Lines* as a list of the oral instructions, exactly according to how he had guided him.

The two middle fundamental treatises are the paths of guidance for persons of good fortune who are suited to the instantaneous approach. [238] Concerning this, because they can enter into the unexcelled Vajrayana without needing to enter other intervening paths in this life, they are of "good fortune." Because they do not need to train in other paths, they are "suited to the instantaneous approach." Here there are the two internal divisions of those with superior faculties and those with medium. Guidance by means of the six key points concerns what is present as the cause, what is obtained through initiation, familiarity with the path, experiencing the view, arising of the culminations of attainment as the signs, and actualization of the result. "What is present as the cause" concerns just the presentation of the ground for practice of the path. Beginning with the bestowal of initiation, it is necessary to meditate on the paths in sequence, which is the path of those with medium faculties. For guidance by means of the eleven key points,[512] obtaining the initiation serves as the ground. Just having the creation stage as the support, the paths of the third and fourth initiations are alternately practiced, which is the path of those with superior faculties. Thus my master taught.

Guidance by means of the paths for those of superior, medium, and inferior faculties is for the three Śrāvaka, Mahayana, and Vajrayana types.

Each of these three is also divided into the three categories of superior, medium, and inferior, and the path is taught by means of these twelve topics. This applies to both those suited to the gradual approach and those suited to the instantaneous approach. Thus my master taught.

Four texts are for the removal of impediments.[513] Concerning "the seven precipitous paths on which meditation is discarded," in the past the Lord of Yogins was forced to throw his rosary into the latrine and make the vow that he would not practice the meditations of secret mantra. Similarly, when various disturbing experiences arise while practicing the path and one can do nothing about them oneself and the master's methods are also ineffective, one may say, "It is better if I stop now." When such things happen, and it is necessary to stop while spiritual practice is still in progress, meditation is discarded. Seven such precipitous paths may occur.

In general, all experiences should be allowed natural expression, and if the natural expression of whatever impediments occur is allowed for at least seven days, no problems will arise. However, if severe upper respiratory seizures, severe lower respiratory pressure, and so forth, are permitted to continue even for a single day, they can take one's life, and so must be quickly removed. Therefore, four key points must not be allowed natural expression.

When the mental obstacles to meditative concentration become denser, an elemental disturbance in the body that visualization alone will not completely remove must be removed by by means of the vital winds and behavior.

Concerning the thirty-two yogic excercises, most maintain that the yogic exercises and the physical trainings are one, but this tradition accepts those two to be separate. [239] First is the twenty physical trainings and so forth, and second is the thirty-two yogic excercises. Thus my master taught.

2. *Explanation by means of the four oral transmissions*

These are the unceasing stream of initiation and the other three.

a. *The unceasing stream of initiation*

This consists of three topics:

1) The unceasing stream at the time of the cause
2) The unceasing stream at the time of the path
3) The unceasing stream at the time of the result

1) *The unceasing stream of initiation at the time of the cause*

Concerning the mandala in which the initiation is bestowed, Vajraghaṇṭā said:

> The essence of the two that are made
> is determined by the faculties of the disciple.[514]

For the benefit of those with inferior faculties, who will not be confident if an image of the deity in a form with faces and arms is not made in the mandala, one is drawn on cloth. Knowing that those with medium faculties will be confident when introduced after just a seed syllable or a hand implement or a droplet has been depicted, even though there is no form with faces and arms, one of colored particles is used. He also said:

> That is not the practice for experts,
> because they are liberated
> at the sight of the perfect truth.[515]

When the channels and essential constituents of the body are explained as the nature of the gods and goddesses, certainty arises in those with superior faculties, for whose benefit the body mandala is taught.

Although these three mandalas are mentioned, and during the time of that great adept Vajraghaṇṭā it was suitable to bestow the ripening initiation in the body mandala, nowadays even those with superior faculties are worse than those with inferior faculties during that time. Therefore, nowadays it is definitely necessary to obtain the initiation in either of the two outer mandalas before the bestowal of initiation in the body mandala. Thus his tradition of ripening initiation is somewhat inappropriate [today].

In particular, lord Sakya Paṇḍita said:

> Nowadays it is taught that for all superior,
> medium, and inferior persons
> initiation should be bestowed

in a mandala of colored particles;
other ripening initiations
are refuted in the tantra.[516]

Thus, for the tantras in general, and specifically here in the context of the tradition of the esoteric instructions of Hevajra, it is definitely necessary to bestow the ripening causal initiation in a mandala of colored particles. The *Root Tantra* says:

The mandala of colored particles
should be with the excellent colors,
or else the middling should be
with the powder of the five
precious substances,
or else with rice and so forth.[517]

In the actual presentation, only the mandala of colored particles is mentioned, and the one drawn on cloth, or the body mandala, does not appear at all. Although the eight gateways of the ritual corresponding to Hevajra's eight faces[518] are not complete in the one drawn on cloth, it has been said elsewhere that as a slight simplification, it is also acceptable to bestow the ripening initiation in a mandala drawn on cloth.

Furthermore, the meaning of *ground initiation* or *causal initiation* is that after a person who has never entered the Vajrayana before obtains that initiation, [240] it serves as the ground for meditation on the path, or that initiation acts as the cause and one meditates on the path.

In brief, from the time when an initiation in any mandala of an unexcelled tantra has been obtained, until the time of initiation that connects one to the result, initiation alone becomes that person's path, whether initiation was obtained in a mandala of colored particles or one drawn on cloth. Although it is said to be the *causal initiation,* this is just a label. Thus my master taught.

"The stream of initiation at the time of the cause" refers to the arising in the mindstream—from the descent of primordial awareness, up to the introduction of the fourth initiation—of the real primordial awareness that is illustrated, which is the superior; the illustrative symbolic primordial awareness, which is the medium; or the certainty or experience of the introduction to the grounds to be purified and the purifying agents, which is the inferior. If nothing such as that occurs, one has merely sat in the row of those receiving the initiation, but not obtained the initiation.

One might wonder, "When does that stream come to an end?"

If the primordial awareness of the bestowal of the initiation in the coarse mandala of colored particles by means of the coarse ritual has not been sustained for up to seven days, or at the least, if the certainty of the introduction to the grounds to be purified and the purifying agents has not arisen, even if the written words of the method for direct realization are unbroken, it is an unbroken mumbling, and the stream of initiation will cease. Thus one should produce and meditate on a lucid manifestation of each aspect. Thus my master taught.

2) *The unceasing stream of initiation at the time of the path*

In general, as mentioned, after having received an authentic ripening initiation, whether one takes initiation from another person or performs the self-entry in a mandala of colored particles or one drawn on cloth, and so forth, all of these are solely initiations at the time of the path. Here that general name is given to the specific. Its stream of initiation is the same as described previously.

As for when it ceases, because it is an extremely subtle primordial awareness unlike the coarse and the general, it will cease if even the slightest amount of time elapses past the time at which the initiation was obtained. Therefore, if the Time of the Path is performed in one session daily it is definitely necessary to complete it before the time at which the initiation was obtained. This is difficult, and because of the great risk of breaking [the stream of initiation], the key point is to perform the meditation in either four or two sessions daily.

Moreover, with the words "In four sessions of the path" and so forth, the *Vajra Lines* also explains that one is liberated by the Time of the Path alone.

One might ask, "Why does it also teach that during the first gathering of the essential constituents one is guided on the path by the vital wind, the fierce fire, and the warmths and the signs?" [241]

The adept Yönten Pal and Tsokgom,[519] the two direct disciples of the Dharma lord Sakya Paṇḍita, had different opinions about this. In the opinion of the adept Yönten Pal, one should target the key points of the vital wind and practice the yogic exercises during the four sessions of meditative equipoise. In his opinion, the Time of the Path should be practiced between sessions so as not to break the stream of initiation. If this becomes the path, it is a fast method for reaching attainment, but if the techniques for the removal of impediments, and so forth, are not successful, one can easily become a great lunatic. So there are great advantages but also great risks. In the opinion of Tsokgom Rinpoché, one should take the four initiations during the four sessions and meditate on the vital wind and the fierce fire between sessions. Since this has great advantages and little risk, this practice is followed. Thus my master taught.

3) *The unceasing stream of initiation at the time of the result*

From the first spiritual level onward, the initiations are received from the four bodies of enlightenment, such as the nirmāṇakāya emanated body. Thus my master taught.

b. *The undeclined transmission of blessings*

These are the four of the culmination of practice and so forth.

1) *The culmination of practice*

Doubts about the meaning to be meditated upon are eliminated through learning and reflection. Understanding well the oral transmission, the symbolic transmission, and the observed transmission, and carefully perfecting the master's infallible practice, even down to the way he arranges the offerings, is what is to be practiced. So this is the culmination of practice.

2) *The culmination of experience*

Although the practice is understood in that way, experiential realization will not arise if one does not practice. If it has not arisen, one will not become endowed with the four oral transmissions. To practice until various experiences have arisen in the mindstream, such as the fifteen experiences (the five sets of three),[520] is the culmination of experience.

3) *The culmination of blessings*

When one practices in that way, the ten father and mother ḍākas and ḍākinīs of the vital winds and mind gather in the four mansions, the gathering places. They cause a self-blessing of all the vital winds and mind, which gather into the central channel; and, in a naturally arisen way, a nondual primordial awareness arises from within. This is the culmination of blessings.

4) *The culmination of attainment*

The actualization of the culminations of attainment as the indivisibility of samsara and nirvana, and so forth, is the culmination of attainment. Thus my master taught.

c. *The undisrupted sequence of the oral instructions*

This consists of two topics:

1) What is to be described—the undisrupted sequence in the context of the oral instructions
2) The description—the undisrupted sequence in the context of experience [242]

1) *What is to be described—the undisrupted sequence in the context of the oral instructions*

This is teaching without error in the sequence, beginning with not bestowing the initiation without examining the connection between master and disciple, down to not applying the seal without having given the prediction.

2) *The description—the undisrupted sequence in the context of experience*

This is the arising of the experiential realizations in the mindstream without error in the sequence.

d. *The mind satisfied with devotion*

In that way, experiential realization arises in the mindstream, at which point a devotion to the master, the deity, and the oral instructions arises that cannot be stolen away by other circumstances. Thus my master taught.

If these are applied to the four authentic qualities, the mind satisfied with devotion is the authentic quality of experience. On the basis of that, the other three become authentic qualities.

III. How to Benefit Others after the Practice Has Been Perfected

In regard to the application of the seal of the ten secrets and the beneficial advice to a fortunate disciple, it is not really appropriate to explain the ten secrets here. For giving the prediction of practice, it is best if one has clairvoyance like lord Gönpawa.[521] Even if that is not the case, if one is able to request permission from the chosen deity, one can give the permission by saying, "For a period of such and such years, practice in a such and such a site. When such and such a disciple appears in such and such a place, teach!" If one is not endowed with either of those qualities, since it is said, "Request the oral instructions endowed with the four authentic qualities from a master endowed with the four oral transmissions,"[522] it is done by just saying, "Practice until the authentic quality of experience arises in your mindstream. When you become endowed with the four oral transmissions, teach a fortunate disciple!"

Furthermore, if one does not obtain the prediction of practice, even if one practices, experiential realization will not arise, or even if it does arise, it will not be stable, and outbreaks of impediments, and so forth will occur. If the prediction of teaching has not been obtained, even if one teaches, disciples will not gather, or even if they have gathered, experiential realization will not arise, and so forth, and it will be difficult for things to turn out properly. Therefore, obtain the prediction of practice and teaching. If one acts in that way, all the auspicious connections for accumulated excellence will naturally come into alignment. Thus my master taught.

These points are what I have retained in mind, and are just a little of the essence of the comprehensive explanation that was taught in detail. [243] With a devotion that is extremely difficult to achieve, I have written this as a memory aid concerning the teachings of my holy spiritual father and master, great Vajradhara.

> In accord with the inclinations
> of limitless disciples,
> you instantaneously opened a hundred
> doors of the measureless Dharma.

You freely gave a precious banquet
of countless elegant explications
to endless living beings of good fortune.

Ah! The powerful lord Dharmapāla
took new saffron robes,
and appearing as the glory of all
living beings in the north,
is famous here as the Dharma king Tsarchen.[523]

The total quintessence
of the renowned Vajrayana,
undiscovered by a thousand famous experts,
is owned by you alone,
whose famous reputation exceeds
the peak of existence and who are endowed
with meaningful pure fame.

Unique father with the sweet
glistening nectar of the oral transmission,
at the lotus of your feet with stamens
of compassion in bloom,
I, a devoted bee, am totally crazed
with the bliss of the fresh honey
of the Explication for Disciples.

Wrapped up in ten million
needless distractions,
I've mostly slept in the bed
of terminal ignorance.

Occupied by the turmoil
of many worthless activities,
I've been an idiot taking
trivial things to be Dharma.

But I've actually seen
the fine face of the unique father,

which is much greater than relying
on other methods for an eon.

With my motives and actions
of undivided devotion undamaged,
his compassionate protection is certain,
whatever I do.

Therefore, from today
until enlightenment is obtained,
may I uphold the treasury
of my venerable lord and master's teaching,
and spread the infinite benefit
and happiness of countless disciples,
together with the master's doctrine.

May this also spread and expand the profound doctrine of the Explication for Disciples in all directions!

Sarva maṅgalaṃ
Good fortune to all!

6. Summarizing Notes on the Path Presented as the Three Appearances

From the Expansion of the Great Secret Doctrine *Summarizing Notes of Guidance for the Precious Teaching of the "Path with the Result"*

The Infallible Version of Khau Drakzongpa

Jamyang Khyentsé Wangchuk (1524–68)

I PROSTRATE AND TAKE REFUGE at all times at the feet of the omniscient great abbot, the holy Losel Gyatso Drakpa Gyaltsen Palsangpo,[524] matchless in kindness, the essence of all the buddhas of the past, present, and future, and the refuge for all the world and the gods. Please grace me with your great love.

> With enlightened activities that are
> auspicious, all-pervasive, and pristine,
> you expand the benefit and happiness
> of fortunate beings and spread
> the great secret doctrine in a hundred directions.
> May the master, the source of all attainments,
> make virtue and goodness arise!

When bestowing the Precious Teaching according to the Explication for Disciples, my spiritual father and master, the holy and great lord of conquerors, Vajradhara, sat on a high and majestic throne in the midst of numerous beautiful arrangements. Above his head was a white parasol, to the right a victory banner, to the left a trident pennant, and in front were arranged the requisite offerings, beginning with the four waters, together with cymbals.[525] Saying that, for the gathered disciples, the Three Appearances are first explained in common with the Vehicle of the Perfections, he did not perform the Dharma sacrificial cake. He recited the *Heart Sutra* and the *Ocean of Good Qualities* three times [246] and the great homage and offering to the lineage of the Path with the Result once,[526] and then said:

"The citadel of perfect buddhahood must be reached for the benefit of all sentient beings. For that purpose, please listen to the profound instructions of the Precious Teaching of the Path with the Result with the intention to practice them, and clearly awaken your mind to sublime enlightenment.

"First it is necessary to 'present offerings and make supplications' in order to please the Dharma and the Dharma speaker with gifts and honors. For that purpose, visualize this: The present vajra master is not an ordinary person. He clearly appears in the form of the quintessence of the four enlightened bodies of unity, the overlord, the great Heruka with eight faces and sixteen arms, in union with mother Vajra Nairātmyā. On a jeweled throne supported by eight great lions, he stands on the seats of a lotus, a sun, and a stack of the four māras. He is surrounded by the masters of the lineage, a divine assembly of the complete three seats,[527] and countless spiritual heroes, ḍākinīs, and Dharma protectors and guardians.

"In front of him, as gifts for requesting the profound instructions of the Precious Teaching of the Path with the Result, imagine that you are presenting inconceivable offerings made from your body, possessions, and all the virtue that you accumulate in the three times. Please present the required offerings, beginning with the four waters."

Beginning with *oṃ guru buddha bodhisattva saprivāra,* present the requisite offerings from the four waters to *śabda,* accompanied with great music.[528] Emanating bodies of one's own equal in number to the particles of dust in a field, circumambulate the master three times.[529]

While the flowers are distributed and received, offer the seven-heap mandala. Recite once the prayer with the two quatrains beginning "Omniscient One, embodiment of primordial awareness."[530]

Again, circumambulate three times. Perform once the distributing and gathering of the flowers, the mandala, and the supplication.

Again, circumambulate three times. With a feeling of intense supplication, distribute and gather the flowers, and perform the supplication of the thirty-seven-heap mandala offering once, [247] from "One's own offering substances," to "May they be pleased by all the offerings that have been presented," and from *"oṃ guru"* to *"samaye hūṃ."*[531]

Once again, with a feeling of intense supplication, and with a handful of flowers, say three times, "Essence of all the buddhas of the three times, holy, glorious, and excellent master, please bestow your kindness and grace us, the disciples gathered here, with the stages of extremely profound guidance, the esoteric instructions of the Precious Teaching of the Path with the Result."

Think: "I have made the prayer and the prayer has been accepted. I have been born into the spiritual family of this Dharma," and feel incredible delight.

These offerings, supplications, and so forth are not just the master's desire for greatness or recognition. All the auspicious connections of the Vajrayana path come into alignment on the basis of having pleased the master. The teacher Nāgārjuna taught in the *Five Stages* beginning with the following words:

> With the wish for inexhaustible reality.[532]

"Reality" specifies what is to be realized. With that wish to achieve excellent benefit for oneself and others, equal to space and inexhaustible, one must offer gifts to the master. Concerning what should be offered:

> Everything, everything greatly pleasing.

The first "everything" is the outer offerings beginning with the four waters. The second "everything" is the articles for the inner offerings, the secret, and so forth. And those must not be the worst things; one must offer the things that are valuable to oneself, scarce, and pleasing.

> The most exceptional,
> pleasing, and excellent—
> offer those to the master.[533]

One must please him with the most exceptional and excellent, and with what is difficult to relinquish, from one's children and wife, to one's life. It is taught:

> If children and wife,
> and even one's life,
> which are difficult to give,
> should be relinquished,
> what need to mention
> ephemeral possessions?[534]

The reason for this is mentioned in the *Jewel Rosary*, a commentary on the *Five Stages:*

> For the diligent,
> it is what yields in this very life
> the buddhahood that is difficult
> to achieve in even a hundred million eons.[535]

The main cause for obtaining buddhahood is the two assemblies. [248] The assembly of primordial awareness arises from the accumulation of the assembly of merit, and the main method for accumulating merit is to please the master. The *Guhyasamāja* says:

> Just to massage with oil a single pore of the skin of the vajra master is exceptionally great merit, even more than honoring buddhas and bodhisattvas equal in number to the grains of sand in the Ganges river for eons equal in number to the grains of sand in the Ganges river.[536]

With the thought of serving him, to massage with oil a pore of the skin of an authentic vajra master is thus even more exceptional than to make offerings and to honor that number of buddhas and bodhisattvas for that length of time. There are inconceivable such ways to cultivate merit. Concerning what prevents [the cultivation of merit], the *Vajrapañjara* says:

> Whoever does not supplicate the master,
> will not be born into the spiritual family.[537]

If one does not supplicate the master, or if the master does not accept one's supplications, it is said that one "is not born into the spiritual family of this Dharma." Whatever meditation practice, study, and explanation is done, it will not turn out well, and the hardship will have been to no avail. But here the offerings and supplications have just now been made. Accepted by the master, one has been born into the spiritual family of this Dharma. Whatever study, reflection, and meditation practice is done, one will have received the initiation, and all the auspicious connections for accumulated excellence will easily come into alignment. Thus my master taught.

The clarification of conduct for listening to the Dharma

After the master and disciples have gathered, "the clarification of conduct for listening to the Dharma" should be presented as the initial topic for teaching and listening. It is taught:

> Sitting calmly in front,
> with a restrained manner
> of clothing and so forth,
> and kneeling with palms joined,
> make three requests
> with the desire to listen and so forth.[538]

In general, the physical conduct for listening to the Dharma is that one should sit directly in front of the master. Do not sit behind, to the side, and so forth. In particular, if one sits directly to the side there will be many obstacles, so this should be avoided. If there is no other option, and one must sit to the side and so forth, one should imagine that one is in front. The posture is mentioned as kneeling. But according to the statement "The *vajrāsana* is praised for Buddhists here in the Vajrayana," [249] the vajra position is best. If that is not possible, comfortably observe the heroic position, which is to hold the body straight, with a slight bow. Avoid all disrespectful actions, such as leaning back and forth, sleeping, covering the head, supporting the cheeks with the hands, and holding an umbrella or a weapon. Here in the Mantra Vehicle, the key points of the vajra body are targeted. Therefore, keenly observing the key physical points during all activities such as requesting the Dharma and practicing meditation brings the auspicious connections into alignment for the rapid birth of the primordial awareness of great bliss in the mindstream. Thus my master taught.

Concerning one's mental state, a sutra says:

> Listen carefully and thoroughly, and retain it in the mind.[539]

In this way, to listen carefully is to avoid the fault of a vessel turned face down. For example, if a vessel is turned face down and left in the summer at a place where rain constantly falls, no matter how much pours day and night without break for years or months, not even one drop will be able to enter into that vessel. Similarly, when listening to the Dharma, if one sits in the Dharma row in a drowsy state or allows the attention to stray elsewhere, no matter how much Dharma is explained it will just be a gurgling sound murmuring in the ears, without even a trace remaining in the mindstream or being comprehended. Even though the Dharma has been listened to in such a way for years or months, not only will no benefit whatsoever occur, but numerous problems will also arise while relying on the Dharma. Therefore, without letting the attention be distracted elsewhere while listening to the Dharma, one should engage in examination of the words and meaning of this Dharma, retain what one can in the mind, and avoid the fault of being like a vessel turned face down.

Similarly, the meaning of the statement "listen thoroughly" is to avoid the fault of a dirty vessel. For example, simply placing a vessel face up is not enough. If a bad substance that is inside it, whether poison or filth or even smoke or ashes, is not removed, whatever nurturing substance, from water to nectar, is poured within, it will cause loss of life, illness, or other bad consequences, and the nurturing substance will also be wasted. But if those impurities are removed, whatever nurturing substance, from water to nectar, is poured into the vessel, each will be able to faultlessly perform its function. Similarly, it is not enough just to retain the meaning of the words of the Dharma as intellectual knowledge. And concerning the motives for listening to the Dharma, [250] thoughts like, "I will listen to this Dharma and then humiliate someone whom I don't like" are motivated by hatred. Thoughts like, "I will sell such a Dharma in such a region, and gain wealth," is desire. Thoughts such as, "I will surpass those who are my rivals," are pride and envy. In brief, concerning any study, reflection, and meditation that is done motivated by thoughts of the three poisons, it is taught:

> Actions produced by desire, hatred,
> and ignorance are nonvirtuous.[540]

Although such actions may seem to be virtues at the moment, in the end they definitely create only the lower realms. Therefore, totally discard all evil motivations, adhere to the altruistic thought of wishing to obtain buddhahood for the benefit of all sentient beings, and avoid the fault of the dirty vessel. Thus my master taught.

Similarly, the meaning of "retain it in mind" is that the fault of a vessel with a broken bottom must be avoided. For example, no matter how much nutriment is poured into a vessel with a broken or cracked bottom, it runs out and none stays inside. Likewise, if the meaning of the words of the Dharma that is listened to is not comprehended and retained in the mind without forgetting, by the middle of the explanation the beginning will have been forgotten, and by the final explanation the middle will have been forgotten. When one rises from the Dharma gathering one will be completely ordinary and be unable to repeat the words one has heard, let alone explain their meaning. Therefore, it is very important to repeat the Dharma over and over with great attention and, until it has been experienced, to keep it clearly in mind without ever forgetting. Thus my master taught.

Similarly, the teacher Vasubandhu says in his *Correctness of the Explanation:*

> Pride, no faith, lack of enthusiasm,
> external distraction, absorption,
> and sadness are the stains of listening.[541]

Listening to the Dharma with pride is to think, "I am superior to the master in family, age, learning, and so forth. Nevertheless, I will listen just to obtain this Dharma." That type of listening is a very great fault. Cultivate the attitude that one is the patient and the master is the physician, and listen with very great respect.

"No faith" refers to having not even a trace of faith in the Dharma and the master. [251] Instead, only thoughts of their faults come to mind, and one thinks, "What does he have to say?" or, "What kind of Dharma does he have?" And one says, "These masters wander around anywhere and listen to anything nowadays. This Dharma is too much. It is too little. The master is not learned. He is not expert. Right here it was wrong, right there it was wrong." In the aphorisms of the Kadampa spiritual friends, "dragging a sheepskin robe" is mentioned. If one goes dragging a long sheepskin through the streets, not a single pure thing such as gold and silver will stick to it, but it will catch everything bad such as filth and debris. Similarly, if one does not see any of the good qualities of the master and the Dharma, but purposely grasps in this way at their tiniest faults, one will not receive even a trace of benefit from listening to the Dharma for an eon, in addition to which one will have accumulated inconceivably serious bad karma while relying on the Dharma. Therefore, develop faith by thinking, "Whatever appearances the master displays, my perception is impure. How could the master be bad?" And whether the Dharma is extensive or condensed, develop great faith by thinking, "The Sugata taught the Dharma in accordance with the inclinations of all potential disciples; how could he have taught with the intention that it was for me alone? Therefore, even though this particular teaching does not appeal to me, there are numerous other potential disciples to be trained by a particular teaching, and so the Buddha's teaching of the Dharma to everyone in accord with their inclinations is amazing." Thus my master taught.

"Lack of enthusiasm" refers to having no enthusiastic feeling when listening to the Dharma, but considering it to be like a supplementary teaching or an obligation. Taking the Dharma to be trivial, and immediate occupations to be the most important, without considering it a problem to miss the beginning and end of Dharma sessions, or even to drop an entire session, some people discard them without concern. Those types of actions are also incorrect. From the time the Dharma teaching begins until it is finished, just totally put aside everything else and think about nothing except that Dharma. Thus my master taught.

"External distraction" refers to allowing the six sense faculties to stray to their objects when one has arrived in the Dharma gathering. Sometimes one gazes up and examines the beams of the building. Sometimes one jokes around and laughs. Even if that is not the case, [252] one may lapse into a state of subconscious meandering, emerging only when one realizes that the Dharma teaching has finished. Those types of actions are incorrect. Therefore, apply body, speech, and mind as one, and listen.

"Absorption" refers to some people who do not continually emphasize spiritual practice, but who go into a state of good meditation when they arrive in the Dharma gathering, and rest in equipoise without directing their ears to the Dharma. And it refers to some who become absorbed within, like falling into a deep sleep, and do not direct their attention to the meaning of the words of the Dharma. Avoid such actions, open one's ears, and listen.

"And sadness, are the stains of listening" refers to sadness. "Sadness from not understanding" is the sadness of some beginners because they are unable to understand the exact meaning of the words, no matter how much they strive and try to listen. The thought may occur, "I just don't understand. I listen, but it seems futile. Should I give up?" What use would that be? Listening is necessary precisely because the teaching has not been understood. If understood, there would be no need to listen; it would be the same as working on what has already been finished. Therefore, by listening over and over, one's understanding will become better and better, and finally one will gain mastery of the entire meaning of the words. Purposely strive and listen.

"Sadness because the session is long" refers to some people who are unable to listen when the Dharma session is long, and for whom the thought occurs, "Now what should I do? I would like it to finish." What is wrong with a long Dharma session? In a past life, when the Lord of Sages, Śākyamuni, had been born as a king, the sound of the Dharma had not been proclaimed in that country, but the previous propensities of the king were awakened, and he became enthusiastic about the Dharma. For a single quatrain of the Dharma, he placed a thousand lamps on his body [as an offering] and listened to the Dharma. That we are able to effortlessly listen to the excellent Dharma without having to practice such austerities is due to the accumulation of merit for infinite eons.

Similarly, once when a monk was teaching the Dharma in a meadow, a frog that lived in a nearby pool emerged there and distinctly heard the sound of the Dharma in his ears. But a herdsman called Nanda planted his staff on the frog and the frog died. From the benefit of having died while hearing the sound of the Dharma, he was born as a god with control of others' emanations.[542]

A pigeon once died while sleeping in the attic of a home where a monk was continuously chanting the *Condensed Sutra on the Perfection of Wisdom,* and from the benefit of having heard the sutra he gained a human body. [253] He entered the gate of the Dharma and, without needing to study, knew the sutra up through what he had heard before while he was a pigeon.

If benefits such as these arose just from hearing the sound of the Dharma for animals who did not understand the meaning, then an entire human life would only be too short for hearing the Mahayana in general, or even more than that, the Vajrayana, or even more than that, a Dharma like the Precious Teaching. Therefore, think, "Hearing a Dharma like this is due to the accumulation of merit for numerous eons," and pay attention.

In that way, avoid the six faults and listen to the Dharma by means of the five attitudes. These are to develop the attitude that the master is the physician, the attitude that oneself is the patient, the attitude that the Dharma is the medicine, the attitude that the practice is the strenuous regimen, and the attitude that the companions are the nurses, and listen. Thus my master taught.

These points are explained on the basis of the *Gate for Entering the Dharma,* composed by the venerable lord Sönam Tsemo, which is the root text. Similarly, the divisions of the classes of tantras and so forth are made according to his *Classification of the Tantras in General*.[543] Make no mistakes about the basic philosophical tenets of our own tradition. In addition to that, it will be excellent and produce joy in experts if one knows how to teach by embellishing this explanation with elegant explications from the works of other experts that are not in conflict with our own system, and with an ocean of quotations from the immaculate sutras, tantras, and treatises. But if one has not identified the basic tenets, what point is there in a verbose, vague explanation based on many stray texts? Thus my master taught.

The Dharma to be explained and listened to

In that way, having understood the conduct for listening to the Dharma, here is the Dharma that is to be explained and listened to: it is the unique path traveled by all the buddhas of the three times, the extracted quintessence of the meaning of all the sutras and tantras that are the profound teachings of the buddhas, the oral instructions of the great Lord of Yogins, the great venerable lord Virūpa, the pathway to be traveled by experts, and the lamp illuminating absolutely all the sutras and tantras. Difficult for those without the merit to understand, it is the stairway for those entering the city of nirvana, [254] and presents the nature of emptiness sublimely endowed with all aspects. This is the Precious Teaching of the oral instructions of the Path with the Result, the oral instructions of the result with the path, the oral instructions of understanding many points by understanding one, the oral instructions of upholding faults as qualities, the oral instructions of accepting obstacles as attainments, the oral instructions of removing impediments to meditation by recognizing meditative concentration, the oral instructions of removing impediments of the māras by recognizing obstacles, and the oral instructions that are like a gold-transforming elixir. Thus the Dharma to be listened to and explained is this root text of the *Vajra Lines*, the small treatise that clarifies the real nature of the meaning of the Tripiṭaka and is like a wish-fulfilling jewel.

The teaching consists of three main topics: how the esoteric instructions that are the means of explanation are explained, the practice according to that explanation, and the application of the seal of the ten secrets for a practicing yogin and the beneficial advice to a fortunate disciple.

For the first, how the esoteric instructions are explained, it is taught:

> Doubts are eliminated by means
> of the four authentic qualities
> and oral transmissions.[544]

Therefore, most doubts about the oral instructions are eliminated by means of the four authentic qualities and the four oral transmissions. What are these four authentic qualities? The *Sampuṭa* says:

> The authentic quality of the treatise,
> the master, following the scripture,
> and awareness of reality.
> As for the actual secret meaning,
> understand that it has been transmitted
> from one to one.
> Receive it directly from a superior master.[545]

This explanation consists of four topics: the sequence in which the four authentic qualities first occur, the sequence stated in the tantra, the sequence of practice, and the sequence of experience or the sequence in which they become authentic qualities. The presentation of this according to the sequence of practice consists of the root of the path, which is how to rely upon a spiritual friend, or, for the authentic quality of the master, reflection upon the lives of the lineal masters, and offering supplications.

The second main topic, the practice according to that explanation, consists of the yoga of guidance to cause the authentic quality of experience to arise in the mindstream. This includes the four fundamental treatises of guidance for producing experience that has not arisen; the five Dharma teachings for producing realization that enhances what has arisen; and, for removing impediments, the four texts for removing impediments.[546] These are explained in a series. [255]

First is the four fundamental treatises of guidance. Of these, guidance precisely according to the treatise of the *Vajra Lines* is for the inferior person who has not entered into the Buddhist doctrine but has the wish to enter, like master Kāṇha, because he had not entered the doctrine and had just come from the midst of the five hundred longhaired sadhus of the Bhīmesara region. He wished to enter the doctrine and followed after the teacher Virūpa. Persons suited to the gradual approach are guided in a similar way. The path of guidance for those of good fortune, suited to the instantaneous approach, is by means of the six key points and the eleven key points. Guidance by means of superior, medium, and inferior faculties applies to both in common.[547] Thus my master taught.

The meaning of "guidance precisely according to the treatise" is accepted by some to be guidance precisely according to the meaning of the *Vajra Lines.* But why should the other three ways of guidance not also be the intention of the *Vajra Lines?* Therefore, in our tradition, this means "guidance precisely according to the actual presentation of the treatise." Concerning the way of guidance, it is taught:

> The ground of the path is formed
> by the Three Appearances,
> and absolutely all the practice
> is understood through the Three Continua.[548]

Accordingly, this includes both the preliminary way to proceed, by forming the ground of the path, and the practice of the actual path.

For the first, the preliminary way to proceed, lord Lama Dampa says in his *Clarification of the Hidden Meaning:*

> First bestow the initiation and provide guidance
> by means of the Three Appearances.[549]

This corresponds to most of the systems of guidance in Tibet, such as the *Five Stages.* And it certainly cannot be said that such an approach is unsuitable. Nevertheless, the first guidance manual in the tradition of this lineage is the *Guidance Manual for Jochak,* composed by the great venerable lord Drakpa Gyaltsen at the request of Mön Vajra Rāja, also known as Kartön Chakyi Dorjé. In the actual presentation of this work, it says:

> To a faithful disciple, one who listens to just what is explained
> by the master.[550]

Just this much is mentioned as the characteristic of a recipient to be taught the Three Appearances; there is no statement about obtaining initiation and so forth. And Drakpa Gyaltsen also makes a similar statement in the *Reply to Dratön's Request.*[551] That is not all. In the *Vajra Lines* itself, after the presentation of the Three Appearances with "For a sentient being" and so forth, the initiation is mentioned in the context of the Three Continua with the following words:

> For the method continuum of the body and so forth, there is
> the causal initiation with four triads, the seats and so forth,
> and so forth.[552]

The *Root Tantra* also says:

> When all the stages of mantra
> have been understood,
> after that, begin Hevajra.[553]

Therefore, this presentation will follow the *Guidance Manual for Jochak,* which was set down in writing by the great venerable lord Drakpa Gyaltsen exactly according to the statements of the venerable lord Sachen. [256] The points that are somewhat condensed there will be supplemented from lord Lama Dampa's guidance manual.[554] And the points there that do not agree with Drakpa Gyaltsen's work will be set aside.

In brief, the great Dakchen Dorjé Chang received from his venerable father a transmission of the teaching that he had received from Lachen Küngyalwa and Thekchen Chöjé. He also received a transmission of the teaching from Jamyang Könchok Sangpo, who had received it from the great adept Künga Lodrö, who had received it from the expert Nya Ön and Yakdepa Namkha Sönam. And he also received it from lord Sempa Chenpo.[555] Gathering together these three transmissions of the initiations and esoteric instructions, Dakchen Dorjé Chang also possessed many key points of esoteric instruction transmitted through them. In particular, he had numerous profound key points transmitted from the venerable lord, his father. But later he mainly used this exceptional system transmitted through Sempa Chenpo. Thus my master taught.

As mentioned previously, the characteristics of a disciple, a recipient to be taught the Three Appearances, were stated with the words "faithful" and so forth.[556] There are four kinds of faith: clear faith, keen faith, confident faith, and ultimate faith.

The first, clear faith, is when the mind is utterly delighted by just hearing the name of the master and the oral instructions. A state of mind arises in which there is enthusiasm for that alone. This is "like a lustful one in pursuit of a beauty," like a passionate man losing his mind at the sight of a beautiful woman.

The second is keen faith. Making numerous efforts to seek out such a master and oral instructions, one engages in any means to obtain them. Like a thirsty person seeking water, one engages in those means without shrinking from any hardship.

The third is confident faith. When one meets a master and obtains the instructions in that way, an exceptional certainty in all the profound key points of the particular teaching arises, like the meeting of a mother and child who are each confident in who they are.

The fourth is ultimate faith. A faith arisen due to influences like food and drink and so forth recedes if those are not given. A faith from having obtained just the common instructions, but not having experienced them, recedes on the basis of slight likes and dislikes and is called "unstable faith." [257] In contrast, a faith from having obtained the uncommon instructions and experienced them through practice is a faith that others cannot steal, "like an elephant entering a lake." When an elephant tormented by the heat of spring enters a lake, he goes in without worrying about anything else being there, such as logs and living trees. Similarly, with the stable certainty of having reached the decisive conclusion that the master who presented the path is actually a buddha, a faith will arise that cannot be stolen away by any other influence. Thus my master taught.

Even with such faith, if one does not listen to the master, the good qualities will not arise in the mindstream, so the instructions should be taught to one who practices exactly according to the statements of that master, without altering them.

By taking refuge and offering supplications, which is virtuous at the beginning of all practices, meditating on the individual key points, which is virtuous in the middle, and applying the seal of prayers, which is virtuous at the end, one should practice while passing the time in virtuous conduct sustained by mindful alertness. In lord Lama Dampa's guidance manual, the statements about the nine branches of meditation and so forth are merely placed in conjunction with the preliminaries.[557] These are not accepted to be meditations at the beginning of the key points of the Three Appearances, because the stages of the path would be reversed if the uncommon preliminaries were applied before the common preliminaries. Therefore, just the taking of refuge and the awakening of the enlightenment mind, which are virtuous at the beginning, must be done first.

Taking refuge

Concerning how to meditate on the sources of refuge, some maintain that they [should be visualized] filling all of space. Some in the Ngor tradition, on the basis of explanations corresponding to the opinion that the Three Appearances belong to the Vehicle of the Perfections, just say "The Buddha is the perfection of the renunciations and realizations, the Dharma consists of the path and cessation," and so forth, and that it is not possible to meditate on these as having forms. Some, with similar explanations, meditate on the Buddha in the form of the Lord of Sages, Śākyamuni, and so forth, and for taking refuge use the threefold formula and so forth.[558] But in our tradition, according to the oral transmission of the great Dakchen Dorjé Chang, it is done in the following way.

The area where one is staying is a ground of beryl created from the manifestation of primordial awareness. [258] Marked in a checkerboard design with gold from the Jambu River, it is soft if pressed, springs up if released, produces pleasure if touched, and is broad and level like the palm of the hand. In the center of this is a celestial tree created from the self-manifestation of primordial awareness, with superb branches, leaves, and fruits. At its tip is a lotus with four petals fully unfolded, in the center of which is a jeweled throne supported by lions, upon which are the seats of a lotus and sun. Upon this is the kind and excellent root master himself, in the form of great Buddha Vajradhara, whose body is the color of the clear autumn sky. He has one face, and two arms crossed at the heart with the right holding a five-pronged gold vajra and the left holding a pure silver bell with a handle made of a gold vajra. He sits with legs crossed in the vajra position. Adorned with silks and jewels, he is decorated with the major and minor marks, and has the brilliance of ten million suns. Extending from in front of him are the lineal masters seated in a clockwise circle, from the venerable lord Virūpa, the Lord of Yogins, to the great venerable lord Künpangpa,[559] appearing exactly according to their individual forms, like a string of pearls.

On the front petal is the divine assembly of the mandalas of the chosen deities, with the nine deities of Hevajra[560] foremost. On the right petal is the Lord of Sages, Śākyamuni, surrounded by all the buddhas of the ten directions. On the rear petal is the Dharma consisting of the path and cessation, in the form of volumes stacked up like a mountain, adorned with coverings of heavenly substances, dangling jewels, and so forth. On the left petal is the sangha of bodhisattvas, many with the costumes of ordination and of the sambhogakāya enjoyment body. Above and in all directions around them, imagine all the root and lineal masters, chosen deities, buddhas, bodhisattvas, spiritual heroes, yoginīs, ḍākinīs, and Dharma protectors and guardians, like an opened sesame pod or a gathered cluster of clouds.

On the ground in front of them, imagine oneself with one's father to the right and mother to the left. In front are the living beings of the six realms, led by one's worst enemy, as well as all the sentient beings of the intermediate state of existence, packed together like a crowd in a great marketplace. [259]

Think: "When observing the condition of myself and others—all sentient beings such as my father and mother—throughout samsara that cannot be measured or said to have begun at a particular point, until now there has been a profusion of suffering in which only varying degrees of suffering have been endured, but no intervals during which this suffering was experienced and this one not. If I do not meet an exceptional refuge even now, I will endure only suffering throughout samsara that cannot be measured or said to end at a particular point. I have no choice but to seek an exceptional refuge who will protect me from this.

"Moreover, I could go for protection to the mundane gods, the śrāvakas, the pratyekabuddhas, and so forth, but some endure nothing except suffering themselves because they are not free from samsara. Because some have not perfected the renunciations and realizations for their own benefit and are not expert in whatever training methods are necessary for the benefit of others, it would not be worthwhile to rely on them. Therefore, among all sources of refuge, the master and the Three Jewels are the ultimate and infallible. They have the wisdom with which to clearly understand the subtlest sufferings of sentient beings together with their causes, without mixing them up, seeing them as clearly as a myrobalan plum placed in the palm of the hand. Even if they understood, if they did not have love they could not perform benefits. Therefore, by virtue of their prayers to awaken the enlightenment mind during their training on the path, they are endowed with compassion toward all sentient beings, like the special love of a mother for a sick child. Even with love, if they did not have ability they would be unable to protect, like a mother with crippled hands whose child is swept away by the waters. But they have the ability, such as establishing many sentient beings in enlightenment just by focusing their attention or emanating a ray of light.

"Therefore, with the single-minded motive to request the refuge of liberation from samsara for myself and others—all sentient beings—not just by mouth and with words, but from the bottom of my heart and the marrow of my bones, I long for this as do all sentient beings long for it, and I respectfully bow and express it with my voice, as do all sentient beings express it."

Say: "I and all living beings, with my parents foremost, all sentient beings equal to the limits of space, [260] take refuge from this time until the heart of enlightenment[561] is reached.

> We take refuge in the glorious and excellent Masters.
> We take refuge in the perfect Buddhas, the Blessed Ones.
> We take refuge in the excellent Dharma.
> We take refuge in the noble Sangha."

Thus practice the fourfold taking of refuge a hundred times, a thousand times, and so forth, with body and mind united in one purpose, until the hairs of one's body flutter, tears gush from one's eyes, and one's body and mind cannot bear it. At the end, join the palms in the vajra gesture at the heart:

> I prostrate and take refuge
> in the master and the Three Jewels.
> I pray for you to bless my mindstream.

If done more extensively, recite the prayer of *Parting from the Four Attachments:*

> Please bless my mind to turn toward the Dharma.
> Please bless me to take the Dharma as the path.
> Please bless me that confusion about the path is removed.
> Please bless me that confusion arises as primordial awareness.[562]

If done more extensively than that, recite the following:

> Please bless me that love, compassion, and the uncontrived enlightenment thought arise in my mindstream without even a trace of irreligious thought occurring, and that I reach the citadel of omniscience and perfect buddhahood for the benefit of all sentient beings.

Thus recite between three and twenty-one times the suitable extensive or medium prayers. Light rays[563] emanate from the sources of refuge and, just by striking all sentient beings, purify their two obscurations together with the propensities, and complete the two assemblies. Reaching buddhahood with the mind as the nonconceptual dharmakāya reality body and the body as the taintless enlightened body of great bliss, sentient beings suddenly depart to the individual buddha lands, like a large flock of birds flying away. The sources of refuge gradually melt into light from the edges and dissolve into the excellent root master. He smoothly melts into blue light whose nature is great bliss, with the dazzling light of ten million suns. When that dissolves through the top of one's head, one should feel that the Three Jewels and one's own mind have been indivisibly blended together, and totally concentrate the pure awareness in that state. Then rest in wonder at the natural state, without focusing as much. If a thought arises, concentrate and clearly imagine the Three Jewels and one's own mind indivisibly blended together. Again, relax and so forth in alternation, for as long as possible. This is the absolute taking of refuge. Thus my master taught. [261]

When one wishes to rise from the session, think that if just expressing the name of the Three Jewels in that way has infinite benefit, the quantity of merit from taking refuge for the benefit of all sentient beings, meditating on the meaning of it, and so forth, cannot be calculated. With the thought that one is bringing together all such virtue of the three times and dedicating it for the benefit of all sentient beings, seal this with dedication prayers such as the following.

> By this merit may I obtain omniscience,
> defeat the faults that are the enemies,
> and liberate living beings from the ocean
> of existence turbulent with the waves
> of birth, old age, sickness, and death.

During all periods between sessions, pass the time in heartfelt devotion, thinking, "Master and Three Jewels, please be aware of me!"

Observe four sessions such as that. Or, in this context common to the three vehicles, it is also said:

> Three times during the day and night,
> one should recite the *Three Heaps*.[564]

Hence one may do this in three sessions. It is also excellent to practice it continually. Thus my master taught.

Awakening the enlightenment mind

Second, after taking refuge comes awakening the enlightenment mind. As mentioned, when the condition of sentient beings is examined, they appear to endure only the causes and results of unbearable suffering. None of these suffering sentient beings have not been one's father and mother. And they have been one's father and mother not just once, but countless times. Every time they have done so they have performed infinite benefit, and are all kind parents who have kindly and carefully cared for one. To illustrate this with an example, if the ears from each time one has been born as a sheep were gathered together, they would not fit in the three-thousandfold world systems. Similarly, for as many times as one has taken a physical body, during all of those times those sentient beings have been one's father and mother and one has been their child. But we have passed through many births and deaths, and because we do not recognize them, we now take some people to be enemies, and because we perform nothing but many inappropriate actions, we do not benefit them. Moreover, one can see that if one is separated from one's mother in this life when one is small and then meets her at some point after not having met for a long time, no mutual recognition and no perception of being mother and child arise. If there is no immediate recognition after having not met from just the beginning to the end of this life, [262] it goes without saying that there would be no recognition after passing through a rebirth.

Think with intense longing: "Wouldn't it be wonderful if these old mothers of mine were to reach the citadel of buddhahood?"[565]

Recite the following at least three times, while mindful of the meaning.

> I must reach the citadel of perfect buddhahood
> for the benefit of all sentient beings.
> For that purpose I will practice
> the oral instructions of the Precious Teaching
> of the Path with the Result.

The second topic, meditation on the individual key points, which is virtuous in the middle, contains three parts: impure appearance, experiential appearance, and pure appearance.

I. Impure Appearance

The *Vajra Lines* say:

> For a sentient being with afflictions, impure appearance occurs.[566]

"For a sentient being" indicates meditation on the faults of samsara; because the condition of a sentient being, when observed, is seen to have only the nature of suffering. "Afflictions" indicates the difficulty of gaining the freedoms and endowments, because sentient beings, through blind indulgence in the afflictions, mainly experience the three lower realms. Thus it is difficult for them to reach the higher realms. And in those higher realms, it is difficult for them to obtain a human body that is a superb support for the practice of Dharma. "Impure appearance" indicates meditation on the causes and results of actions. Therefore, the faults of samsara are presented first.

A. *The faults of samsara*

For liberation from samsara it is necessary to repudiate the attachments of samsara. To repudiate those it is necessary to understand the nature of samsara. Therefore the nature of samsara is presented. Thus my master taught.

If all the sufferings of samsara are summarized, they can be included within three topics:

1. The suffering of suffering
2. The suffering of change
3. The pervasive suffering of conditioned existence

1. *Reflection upon the suffering of suffering*

The great venerable lord Drakpa Gyaltsen said:

> First is the suffering of suffering,
> which is the suffering
> of the three lower realms.
> If one carefully thinks about that,
> one's flesh will crawl.
> If it actually happened,
> it would be unbearable.

Without creating the virtue to avoid it,
those who keep cultivating the crop
of the lower realms are pitiable,
wherever they are.[567]

And in the *Clear Reply to a Request* he said:

The suffering of suffering
is the locations of the three lower realms,
like abscesses on top of leprosy sores.
If one carefully thinks about that,
how could it be endured? [263]
Therefore, turn away from
nonvirtuous actions.[568]

In this way, the *suffering of suffering* is the suffering of the three lower realms of the hells and so forth. All of samsara has the nature of suffering, in addition to which these are extremely oppressive suffering. Therefore, they are referred to as "the suffering of suffering," because it is as if they have been doubled. For example, this is illustrated by the affliction of abscesses and sores on the surface of severe leprosy. The suffering of suffering consists of three topics:

a. The hells
b. The hungry spirits
c. The animals

a. *The hells*

One should first reflect upon the sufferings of these realms:

1) The cold hells
2) The hot hells
3) The peripheral and the minor hells

1) *The sufferings of the cold hells*

The sufferings of the cold hells are presented first. According to the custom of the practitioners of the Path with the Result itself, the presentation begins with the cold hells. This is because they are mentioned first in the *Guidance*

Manual for Jochak, and also because, if the greatest sufferings of the hot hells are explained first, some persons may possibly have severe upper respiratory seizures, vomit blood from the mouth, or react in other violent ways. Therefore, the intention is to mollify those people by explaining the hells in sequence, beginning from the smallest sufferings of the cold hells; or, since the peripheral and minor hells are in the four directions of each of the hot hells, to explain those in connection with them. Thus my master taught.

The first of these realms, the cold hells, consists of eight hells, each of which is explained by means of four topics: the place where one is born, the actions that cause birth there, the suffering produced by those actions, and the length of life with that suffering.

First is the place where one is born. In the context of the common vehicles, in which these hells are established entities, it is explained that twenty thousand leagues below Jambudvīpa, the hell known as "Supreme Torture" lies to the south. Then seven hot hells are stacked up in sequence. To the north of these are stacked the eight cold hells. Concerning their essence, it is taught:

> Who made the ground of glowing iron?
> Where did those fires come from?
> The Sage has taught that all
> such things are sinful mind.[569]

Thus these are the manifestations of each nonvirtuous mind, and the hell locations will be created here and there, wherever the sentient being is located. Thus my master taught.

Blistered

The first cold hell is known as "Blistered." All the ground below is a vast icy chasm, [264] surrounded on all sides by an unbroken range of glacial peaks. It is a murky, pitch dark land. A whirling blizzard of snow and intense wind howls down from everywhere above. No protective shelter exists that even a little bird could squeeze into. Nothing like clothing, not even a patched rag, is to be found, and no bright objects, not even starlight, are to be seen. It is extremely cold and gloomy in the dark.

In relation to the Three Jewels, the actions that cause birth in the first cold hell are eating the allocated offerings of the master and the Three Jewels; extinguishing offering lamps; stripping the garments from images of the deities and the brocade coverings from painted figures and so forth; stealing the wood of the sangha; stealing the clothing of sangha members; not giving warm tea, cooked vegetables, and so forth. And also throwing sentient beings in water, from the large (human beings, horses, bulls, and so forth) to the small (such as fleas and lice), burning their homes, and so forth. In brief, concerning all those actions that produce the sufferings of cold, it is said, "Similar in form produces similar in result." In brief, this is the case with all nonvirtuous actions produced by the intense three poisons.[570]

The manner of birth is that when one's individual life span, karma, and merit run out, one dies dully, like a lamp that has run out of oil and cannot be fixed, losing consciousness in a swoon without recognizing the clear light of death. From that state, the four elements appear in order, and one arises in the intermediate existence. Inconceivable sufferings are experienced for forty-nine days and so forth in the intermediate state, and during the second half of this period, the place where one will be born appears in the intermediate existence. The place where one will be born in the hells is utterly black in form, like a chunk of charcoal or a blanket of yak hair. And, as a result of grasping at the black olfactory light,[571] out of the midst of all the appearances, which are dark and gloomy, appear Yama, the coemergent ghosts, and so forth. With some leading one from in front and some threatening from behind, one is driven and plunges headfirst into the blackness, like falling helplessly into a great abyss. When arriving at the place where one will be born, one loses consciousness in a swoon, like dying. Immediately upon waking from that, by the power of karma one is born with a large body that has young flesh and very little tolerance to cold. The ground below is an expanse of ice, and since one cannot stand it, one thinks of fleeing and runs in all directions, but encounters only glacial mountains. [265] From everywhere above, a blizzard of snow and cold wind strikes with a howling sound. With no protector and no refuge, one is tormented with suffering and flees. Because one has stumbled and fallen in the intense cold, blisters from the size of one's head or the size of a fist, down to the size of a mustard seed, erupt white and bumpy over one's entire body without any spaces between them, and one has to experience unbearable suffering.

Concerning the length of life there, it is taught:

> By removing a single sesame seed
> once every one hundred years
> from a sesame bin, it will be exhausted.

> That is the life span of the Blistered.
> The life span of the others
> is twenty times that.[572]

A container filled with eighty loads of sesame calculated in the large measures[573] of the Magadha region in India is called a "sesame bin." When that sesame bin is exhausted by discarding a sesame seed every one hundred human years, according to the Hinayana, or every single human year, according to the teacher Asaṅga, the karma of the Blistered will be finished, and the life span exhausted. But it is also taught:

> I do not say where the life span of the Blistered will completely end.[574]

Think with utter sincerity: "I do not have the slightest confidence that I will not be reborn in this way and have to experience unbearable suffering, with no way to stand it, during a lifespan that cannot be measured or said to be of a particular duration. These actions that have been done every day motivated by the intense three poisons are actions that I am certain will bring rebirth, and since I have acted heedlessly, I will definitely be reborn. If I were reborn, it would be impossible to bear such suffering and there would be no escape, so I absolutely must act to not be reborn! I must practice the excellent Dharma. And of the Dharma, I will practice and definitely experience the oral instructions of the supremely profound Precious Teaching of the Path with the Result."

Similarly, the location, the body, and so forth for the following hells are the same as described previously, but because the karma of motivation and application twenty times greater than before has been accumulated, the suffering and the length of life are also twenty times greater and longer.

Burst Blisters

Because of the intense cold, all the blisters split open with snapping and popping noises. The oozing pus and blood become globs of ice. And from within the burst blisters emerge iron worms with sharp fangs that bore straight into all of one's bones. [266] This suffering must be endured for an endless life span in hell.

Crying "Alas!"

Because the suffering is too intense, one lets out ringing wails of misery, "Alas! Alas!" with absolutely nothing else to do.

Crying "Woe!"

Because of the intense cold, one resorts to just whimpering, "Woe!" without being able to even cry out.

Grinding Teeth

One is unable to make even those whimpering sounds; the teeth clench and the chin droops.

Split Open Like an Utpala Flower

Struck by the severe cold from the great wind, the globs of pus and blood are instantly peeled off. Bluish skin is fully revealed. With a snapping sound, this skin splits open into eight pieces, or sixteen, and so forth. Because the color is blue, like an utpala flower, this hell is called Split Open Like an Utpala Flower.

Split Open Like a Lotus Flower

By the force of the cold wind, that blue skin is instantly peeled off, fully revealing the tender flesh beneath, which is red like polished copper. That flesh also splits open into sixteen pieces, twenty-four, and so forth.

Greatly Split Open Like a Lotus Flower

Those pieces also rupture and split open into countless pieces. All the inner vital organs of the body also split open with crackling sounds. Even though the body has been turned inside out, one cannot die because one's karma has not been exhausted.

In brief, both the exhaustion of karma through experience and the exhaustion through purification are taught. "Exhaustion through experience" is like the sesame bin explained previously, where those life spans are multiplied twenty times, and there are no defined times for exhaustion and no limits that can be defined. "Exhaustion through purification" is like the experience of the Lord of Sages, Śākyamuni, when he was born as a chariot driver in hell. When intense love arose for his companions, his karma was exhausted and he transmigrated and was born in the heaven of the thirty-three gods. When an extraordinary altruistic motivation has arisen in oneself, or through the efficacy of a perfect ritual performed by those left behind or by someone like a master for the purification of one's sins, one may be liberated by an untimely death when one's karma has been exhausted even though the life span is not complete. Otherwise, unbearable suffering must be experienced for an endless life span in hell.

Think about this as before, with thoughts such as these: "No one can endure things like this. [267] It is impossible to endure putting just a foot or a fist in the middle of the winter ice now for even one day. How much pain comes if that is done? Therefore, I could never bear suffering like this in the midst of the ice in that gloomy, pitch dark land where the entire body is split open into pieces for not just one month, or even one year, but for an endless life span in hell. I absolutely must act so as not to be born there!"

To sum this up, seated on a comfortable seat in one's own place, let body, speech, and mind relax in a natural state. At the end of that, perform the taking of refuge and make supplications, which are virtuous at the beginning, or, if so inclined, one can also perform the awakening of the enlightenment mind. In either case, rest for as long as possible in the inexpressible state in which the sources of refuge and one's own mind are blended together.

When a thought suddenly arises, think: "Oh, no! This place where I have been born is called 'the three realms of samsara.' Among the confusing appearances and the sufferings, none whatsoever exist that I have not experienced. If all kinds of sufferings are summarized, they can be included within three. And of these, the 'suffering of suffering,' which is the suffering of the hells, must be experienced. The sufferings of the cold hells are like the least of these. And the sufferings of those are like this."

Thinking that, reflect upon them in order, from Blistered to Greatly Split Open Like a Lotus Flower. Reflect upon each of these until the thought that you have been born in such a place, and the thought that you have experienced such suffering, have clearly arisen in your mindstream.

When these thoughts have arisen, reflect upon this until you feel it in your flesh and it touches your marrow: "That would be impossible to bear. Unbearable as it is, not only do I have no confidence whatsoever that I will not be reborn there, but since I have done countless serious actions, and none whatsoever exist that I have not accumulated every day, these will certainly bring rebirth. Therefore, I am sure that I will definitely be reborn. If I am reborn, there will not be any way to bear or any method to withstand such suffering, so I absolutely must act to not be born there! Nothing else except the practice of the excellent Dharma alone will do. And from within the Dharma, I must gain definite experience in the oral instructions of the Precious Teaching of the Path with the Result, the extracted quintessence of the meaning of all the sutras and tantras, by which buddhahood is certain in one lifetime and in one body." [268]

When the mind has become weary, rest serenely in inexpressible pure awareness for as long as possible. When a stray thought floats up, think: "Oh, no! This place where I have been born is the three realms of samsara, an ocean of suffering."

Reflect upon the eight cold hells in various ways, such as in sequential order, in reverse order, and out of order. Meditate until a distinct renunciation and dissatisfaction arise. If dissatisfaction about the suffering occurs, a desire for liberation from it will naturally arise. Therefore, meditate with deep feeling, thinking, "I am practicing the path." When body and mind become wearied by this meditation, rest at ease in inexpressible pure awareness. This is meditation on the individual key points, which is virtuous in the middle.

When one wishes to rise from the session, think: "In that way, inconceivable merit will come from taking refuge in the master and the Three Jewels, producing such virtues as dissatisfaction with samsara and enthusiasm for liberation. By all such virtue in samsara and nirvana, may I and all sentient beings in common obtain buddhahood!" With that thought, apply the seal with dedications and prayers such as this:

> By this merit may I obtain omniscience,
> defeat the faults that are the enemies,
> and liberate living beings
> from the ocean of existence,
> turbulent with the waves of birth,
> old age, sickness, and death.

If one does not apply heartfelt mindfulness and yearning during all times between sessions by thinking: "Oh, no! I'm in the three realms of samsara. When will I be liberated from this?" and if all the time between sessions is given up to just anything, listening to the Dharma will have been worthless.[575] Therefore, it is very important to retain mindfulness and attention during all periods between sessions. Thus my master taught.

These practices are virtuous at the end and should be known to be so for all sessions. Thus my master taught.

If one knows how to explain these topics in detail from authentic sutras and from treatises such as the *Treasury of Abhidharma* and the *Main Practice of the Spiritual Levels,*[576] and if expert disciples are also present, it is excellent if the explanation is greatly expanded. If one does not have much to explain or, even if one does, if it will be too much explanation for the middling and lesser disciples, the essence will be lost. Therefore, a condensed explanation of the key points to be meditated on is more profitable. Thus my master taught.

2) *Reflection upon the sufferings of the hot hells*

These are the eight hot hells, each of which is presented with respect to its place, manner, suffering, and length of life.

Revival

The first hot hell is called "Revival." [269] Two traditions have arisen concerning its place. One maintains that all the ground below is a ground of glowing iron with blazing fire, surrounded on all sides by a network of red flaming iron mountains. The other tradition maintains that all the hot hells are in a square iron house.

The precise manner of birth is as follows. One who has accumulated the karma to be born in that place is led in the intermediate existence by threatening messengers of Yama; drops headfirst into the pitch dark; and when arriving at that place of birth, falls into an inexpressible swoon. Immediately upon arising from that clear light, the shape of the hell body and so forth are the same as described previously, but one is born with a large body that has young flesh and little tolerance, like newly healed flesh, and in particular with very little tolerance to heat.

Immediately upon birth, one is burned and frightened by the blazing fire of the glowing iron ground below everything and, with thoughts of fleeing in all directions and searching for protection or refuge, one runs away while still burning. But with no place to flee and no protection or refuge, one is surrounded by many horrible butchers, who are like one's worst enemy. With fierce roars of "Strike! Kill!" they shoot glowing iron arrows and giant arrows from a distance. When closer, they stab one with numerous weapons such as spears and lances, and those that come very near use swords, axes, and so forth, piercing straight through one's entire body. With intense hatred one also strikes back with everything at hand, which turns into glowing iron weapons blazing with fire. When the entire body has been burned and charred and one has lost consciousness in a swoon, from empty space a voice clearly proclaims, "Revive!" At the same moment a whispering cold wind blows. This acts as a catalyst, and one revives with a body recreated as before. Immediately upon reviving, the same thing happens as before, and day and night without rest one endures such suffering in that place of darkness, great pitch black darkness.

Concerning the length of life, a comparison to fifty human years is made. For the gods of the four races of the great kings[577] each day is equal to fifty human years, and they live for five hundred of their own years. Taking that lifespan as a single day, those in "Revival" live for five hundred of their own years. In brief, the suffering must be endured for an endless life span in hell.

Black Line

In the hot hell called "Black Line," the hell being flees in terror and is seized by the hell guardians, [270] who mark the length, the width, and so forth of the body with eight black lines, sixteen, thirty-two, and so forth. With glowing iron saws blazing with flames, they cut from the top of the head, but when they arrive at the navel all the upper wounds have healed without a trace. Again, they cut in the opposite way, but when the saws arrive at the upper body all the lower wounds have healed without a trace. However much the hell beings are cut open in this way without respite, chopped up with iron hatchets blazing with flames, pierced with chisels, and so forth, they do not have the good fortune to die until their karma has been exhausted.

Crushing

When one flees across the glowing iron ground, huge red mountains of glowing iron with the faces of whatever goats, sheep, yaks, and so forth one has killed are racing rapidly back and forth. Thinking, "Will I not be lost between those?" one flees and is crushed when two of them come together. The intestines, stomach, and all other organs spill out. The entire body is burned and charred and floats up as ashes. As soon as the two mountains pull apart, one's body is recreated as before. Again the suffering of being crushed occurs as before.

Similarly, one is wrapped up and left inside a closed iron blanket that blazes with fire, and the entire body is burned and charred. When it opens up, one's body is recreated as before. Again it closes.

The explanation that one is forced to take birth inside an iron basket blazing with fire, pounded with iron pestles blazing with fire, and so forth, appear to be the intended sense of individual sutras regarding the sufferings in this hell. Thus my master taught.

Screaming

When fleeing in terror from those sufferings of the glowing iron ground and so forth, one sees a white house. Thinking, "If I go over there it would be nice," one goes. But one enters a glowing iron house blazing with fire, the door seals itself, and one wails and screams, tormented with suffering.

Great Screaming

Entering inside doubled houses of glowing iron blazing with fire, the physical suffering is no different. But in the mind, because one is thinking, "It's possible to escape from the inner house, but I won't escape from the outer," the suffering is more severe. So this is known as "Great Screaming." Thus my master taught.

Hot

A glowing iron impaling stake, like a double-edged sword blazing with fire, is shoved through the anus and comes out at the top of the head, burning and charring all the inner vital organs of the body. [271] A mixture of flames and smoke flickers out from the mouth and nostrils. A mixture of scorched odors and smoke curls out at the top of the head. When the impaling stake is pulled out, the body is recreated as before. The withdrawal and insertion is done in that way without even an instant of respite.

Totally Hot

When an iron impaling stake with three points is stabbed through the anus and the two buttocks, and comes out at the top of the head and the two shoulders, one is burned as before.

Similarly, in the *Sutra of One Hundred Parables on Deeds,* Hot and Totally Hot are distinguished by being cooked in a single iron pot and being gradually cooked in a three-tiered pot.[578]

Supreme Torture

One is put inside an iron stove that is twenty thousand leagues in size. A great mass of roaring fire blazes from the ten directions and the center (which is the eleventh), and what is burned and the burning become indivisible. Except for the awful cries, there is barely even a sentient being, but the suffering is inconceivable.

In brief, this hell is named "Supreme Torture" because no suffering greater than this exists in the three worlds. Those who harm the body of a vajra master and those who perform any of the five inexpiable acts[579] are born there. Some traditions accept a direct descent without an intermediate state, in which one passes through a hole that has opened in the earth, without discarding the body, or in which one is born in this hell immediately after rising from the clear light of death, but the practitioners of the Path with the Result accept an intermediate state.

In any case, for the first six hot hells, the life spans are calculated in comparison to the six types of gods in the desire realm. Thus my master taught.

The seventh hot hell lasts for half an intermediate eon and the eighth for one intermediate eon. Thus my master taught. Concerning the length of these periods, the *Sutra of Maudgalyāyana's Rescue of His Mother from the Hell Realms*[580] tells of a square iron boulder four hundred leagues high and wide, upon which the sentient beings of the hells go back and forth, wearing down the boulder during half an intermediate eon. Two boulders such as that are worn down during one intermediate eon. Suffering must be experienced for that long. Therefore, as previously described, one must be diligent and so forth not to be born there. Thus my master taught.

3) *The peripheral and the minor hells*

This consists of two topics: reflection upon the sufferings of the peripheral hells and reflection upon the sufferings of the minor hells. [272]

a) *Reflection upon the sufferings of the peripheral hells*

It is said: "For all eight, sixteen more exist." Outside each of those eight hot hells, the four peripheral hells, such as the Pit, are located one after the other. These total sixteen, because the four must be experienced in each of the four directions. These four are taught:

> Blazing Coals, Swamp of Rotten Corpses,
> Path of Razors and so forth, and the River.[581]

(1) *Blazing Coals*

When the karma of having to experience the primary hot hells has been exhausted, and the hell being is driven by the hell guardians and flees in terror, the image of an open path to the east that was not there before appears. Similarly, one sees a barren ashen plain. Nothing except glowing iron blazing with fire was seen for all that time before, but now one sees a path and a barren ashen plain. Therefore, at the prospect of happiness, and because one is being driven from behind, one runs, only to arrive on top of a pit of blazing coals covered on the surface with pale ash. As one sinks, the flesh is stripped from the bones of all portions of the legs, and the white bones are clearly exposed. One faints, unable to bear the pain. The entire body is burned by those unbearable blazing coals. All the flesh is stripped and the white bones are fully exposed, but by the force of one's evil karma one is unable to die, and rises to the surface. The body is recreated as before, with no injury. When it sinks again into the pit it is burned. With the hell guardians pacing back and forth threateningly around the perimeter, one has nowhere to escape, and has to experience unbearable suffering for about one hundred human years.

(2) *Swamp of Rotten Corpses*

After finally escaping from that, one thinks, "A nice blue river is flowing over there." As one flees with the intense desire to go there, the hell guardians open a path and drive one from behind. The "Swamp of Rotten Corpses" is essentially made from the slime of the rotten corpses of hell beings that have died. It is extremely hot to touch, disgusting and filthy by nature, and causes fainting and death just at the smell of its stench. Furthermore, this outer iron fence is created from the collective merit of the beings of Jambudvīpa. If not shielded by this, sentient beings would certainly die immediately if they smelled the stench of the hell of rotten corpses. But, by the force of one's evil karma, a sentient being of hell sinks into that swamp, unable to die. [273] All one's sense orifices, including one's mouth and nostrils, are blocked with filth. Countless iron worms with sharp fangs in the midst of that swamp bore straight into all the bones of one's legs. Unable to bear the pain, one faints and falls face down. One's body burns and rots. One has to remain in such a state for about one hundred human years.

(3) *Path of Razors*

When the karma of having to experience such things has been exhausted, again the hell guardians make one flee along an unprotected path to the east. Going there one sees a vast green meadow. Thinking, "It's nice over there," one runs and arrives on a plain that is filled with sharp cutting razors, some as large as a wooden wall frame and some as small as a handspan or a thumbnail, without any gaps between them. As soon as a foot steps on that plain, it is totally chopped up. One faints, unable to bear the pain. As soon as one faints on top of the large razors, the entire body is totally sliced up into hundreds and thousands of pieces. Again, as soon as one revives, the body is recreated as before. Again it is sliced up. One has to remain like this for about one hundred human years. Thus my master taught.

When one escapes from that, one sees a thick, dark green, attractive forest. One runs there, but as soon as one tries to take a seat in the cool shade, an untimely, intense, howling wind rises. It shakes the trees, and all their branches and leaves turn into sharp weapons such as swords and axes and fall like rain. One's entire body is cut and sliced into countless hundreds and thousands of pieces, but one is unable to die and must remain in such a state for about one hundred human years.[582] Thus my master taught.

When the karma of having to experience such things has been exhausted, one escapes from there and flees. One sees a nice green mountain and goes there. But when one arrives at its base, inconceivable fierce and savage carnivorous beasts such as great multicolored dogs and vultures attack and eat one alive. While the entire body is being consumed, all the intestines and stomach are being torn out, and one is experiencing inconceivable suffering, [274] from the peak of that mountain the voice of a relative or a beloved friend clearly shouts one's name, crying, "Where are you? Come here!" As soon as one hears that, with simultaneous attachment for that person and fear of the carnivorous beasts, one quickly climbs up the mountain. On the mountainside sharp iron thorns about sixteen finger-widths long are growing without any gaps between them. They all point downward, and they perforate the entire body like a sieve. When one arrives at the mountain peak in agony, with streams of blood flowing, not only is no friend or relative around, not even a trace remains of one ever having been there. One becomes depressed and despondent, but cannot do anything about it.

Also, a bird known as "the mud-eating bird," with a wingspan of about sixteen leagues, as well as many similar savage birds, arrive in a dense cloud. When they have dug out one's brains, plucked out one's eyes, and picked the entire body into pieces and eaten it, the body is gradually recreated as before. An indescribable suffering is experienced.

Again one is called, this time from the base of the mountain. Racing down, tumbling and leaping with attachment and fear, one's entire body is perforated by the iron thorns, which all point uphill. On arrival at the base, not even a trace of that friend or relative remains. One is eaten by the multicolored dogs and carnivorous beasts.

Again, when one seems to be called from the mountain peak, one climbs up, and so forth. One must remain for about one hundred years in such a state of descending and climbing. This hell is called "the *śalamāli* trees." *Śala* means "weapon" and *māli* means "rosary," so this means "the weapon-rosary trees."

(4) *Impassable River*

When one escapes from that, one again sees something like a sandy plain. But when one runs there, it is the "Impassable Salt River," shaped like a blazing meadow sputtering with flames as when water is poured in the middle of a huge fire, hot and difficult to bear. As soon as one falls into this, all the flesh is burned away without a trace. White bones are all that remain, but one is unable to die, and threatening hell guardians guard the shores. One has absolutely nowhere to flee and nowhere to escape. When only pieces of bone remain, these are snared by the iron hooks of the hell guardians and pulled to the surface of the river. One's body is immediately recreated as before, with newly healed flesh of very little tolerance. [275] Again, one is burned. One has to remain in such a state for about one hundred human years.

Again, driven inward by the hell guardians, one roams in terror across the ground of glowing iron. Driven to the south, all the hells from Blazing Coals to Impassable River must be experienced as before. Likewise, they must also be experienced in the west and in the north. In that way, one is tortured for about six hundred human years: one hundred years each in Blazing Coals, Swamp of Rotten Corpses, Plain of Razors with its subcategories of Leaves of Swords and Śalamāli, and River of Hot Ash. Then one is born in a different hell, or else one transmigrates to another of the six realms. Thus my master taught.

b) *Reflection upon the sufferings of the minor hells*

In that way, the hells mentioned up to now exist for all hell beings, but these latter minor ones have miscellaneous forms, a variety of which exist even in the higher realms of the gods and humans. In comparison to those previous ones, these seem like no suffering, and so they are called *minor.* Thus my master taught.

What certainty could we have regarding the precise number? Nevertheless, Śāntideva, the son of the conquerors, condensed the meaning of about eighty sutras and mentioned the number of about eighteen minor hells in the *Compendium of Lessons.*[583] These eighteen are the three that come from the narrative of venerable Śrīmad, the twelve that come from the narrative of Saṅgharakṣita, and the three that come from the narrative of Nawajewa Nyishupa.

The first three are described as follows. When venerable Śrīmad was coming up the Vulture Peak and noble Maudgalyāyana was coming down from the peak, they met on the road. Maudgalyāyana looked at the sky and smiled. When Śrīmad asked, "Why did you smile?" Maudgalyāyana magically revealed the minor hells, which were beheld by Śrīmad: [1] In empty space some distance out from the Vulture Peak was a human shape with a body about the size of two houses, experiencing the suffering of blazing fire all over the outside and inside of his body. He had been a butcher who had slaughtered many cattle and been reborn in that condition. [2] In space a little closer than that was another human form, but with the flesh and skin of the body turned inside out; below the waist it was like a skeleton held together by a few ligaments. He had been a "supervising butcher" [276] who handed over the cattle to the butchers. [3] In space a little closer than that was a human form with a large body, but with testicles about the size of a mountain hanging down. With his body and his testicles held together by a rope of flesh about the size of a horsetail, he endured inconceivable suffering. The ripened result of having castrated livestock such as horses and donkeys was experienced in that way.

The twelve minor hells mentioned in the narrative of Saṅgharakṣita included four that were [1] like a cauldron, [2] like a pot, [3] like a broom, and [4] like a pestle. These were the ripened results of having done bad things to the cauldrons and so forth of the sangha, and having using them for one's own benefit and so forth. The next three, [5] like a pillar, [6] like a wall, and [7] like a rope, were the ripened results of having wiped filth on the pillars, walls, and so forth of a temple. [8] The ripened result of the actions of a sangha patron who, due to his stinginess, postponed what was to have been done today, was to be extremely miserable in a human shape that was about to break between the upper and lower parts. The ripened results of having given to one's relatives and so forth minor possessions and such things that had been dedicated to the sangha are known as the hells that are like [9] a tree trunk, [10] a branch, [11] a flower, and [12] a fruit.[584]

In brief, although appearing in forms like pillars and walls in various higher realms, these were in essence sentient beings who had to remain until their karma was exhausted, while experiencing inconceivable sufferings such as having to hold up what cannot be supported.

Three minor hells are mentioned in the narrative of Nawajewa Nyishupa. A courtesan once kept the layperson's vows during the day but indulged her carnal desires at night. The ripened result was that during the day she was worshiped by many divine boys and girls and had boundless happiness in a celestial palace of jewels, but at about sundown the celestial palace became a house of glowing iron blazing with fire and the divine boys and girls became iron wolves blazing with fire. While burning, she endured the inconceivable sufferings of being eaten, torn apart, and so forth. When sunrise came it was as before, and she became comfortable.

A butcher once took lives during the day and kept the layperson's vows during the night. By virtue of that he experienced sufferings the opposite of those just described.

Similarly, Nawajewa Nyishupa came to a sangha establishment that was on a seashore. When the noonday gong was struck and [277] many beings in the form of sangha members had gathered, he was given food before noon, told to go away and not watch the unpleasantness, and kicked out. But he carefully observed, and as soon as the meal was served the beings became angry with each other and quarreled, striking each other with the alms bowls and so forth, leaving everyone wounded. They experienced great suffering, with everyone fighting and arguing. After a while they dispersed. When Nawajewa Nyishupa asked about the reason for this, he was told that these members of the sangha had fallen to fighting as they partook of a meal. The ripened result of that was being reborn in a minor hell such as this and having to experience suffering like this every day until the karma was exhausted.

Similarly, the mother of the paṇḍita Smṛti[585] was born as a worm inside the fireplace of a rich man of Central Tibet who kept a fire going day and night. For many years the paṇḍita worked as that rich man's servant. Having not taken his wages on time, he calculated them once, and they amounted to a lot. He offered them all to the rich man and said, "I need this hearthstone for my wages."

But the man replied, "These so-called 'mendicants' are tricky. The hearthstone could be a gem."

Because the mother's karma was not exhausted, the man did not want to give up the stone. Smṛti took his wages and performed many methods for purifying his mother's sins. Finally he had to dig up the hearthstone and run away.

Similarly, nowadays there are worms that cannot be burned but are tormented by heat in the midst of such places as hot springs. If they were other animals, they would die in an instant, but because it is a minor hell they are unable to die.

In brief, one should reflect as before that these are the smallest sufferings of the hells, but since even they are unbearable, one must act to never be reborn there, and so on.

b. *Reflection upon the sufferings of the hungry spirits*

This consists of two topics:

1) The principal
2) The scattered

1) *The principal hungry spirits*

The hungry spirits are of three types:

a) Those with external obscurations
b) Those with internal obscurations
c) Those with obscurations of obscuration or obscurations of food

The location of these hungry spirits is five hundred leagues below Rājagṛha or the region of Vaiśālī.[586] Known as Sergya, the city of the hungry spirits, it is extremely revolting, and just a glimpse of it would cause a morbid depression. It is like a copper pot tarnished by the sun. The number of hungry spirits living there is inconceivable, but if the types are summarized, they can be included within thirty-six types. [278] And if those thirty-six are summarized, they can be reduced to these three types.

a) *Those with external obscurations*

Some hungry spirits with external obstructions are born from a womb. Some are magically born. As soon as they are born they have heads about as big as Mount Meru, mouths about the size of the eye of a needle, necks about the width of a longbow string, stomachs about the size of a mountain, and bellies about the size of a valley. Their arms and legs are thin like porcupine quills. Tortured at all times by hunger and thirst, when they are rushing about without any rest, searching for food and drink, they see a great mountain of rice or food somewhere. When more hungry spirits than can fit rush in that direction, the larger ones push down, knock over, and crush the smaller ones. With their bowstring throats unable to hold up their heads and their porcupine quill arms and legs unable to hold up their bodies, they fall down and are crushed. Their entire bodies are broken into pieces. After enduring so much suffering, when they continue on and arrive at the mountain, it has changed into a pile of something like earth or porcelain, without even a trace of food or anything edible having been there. Weeping, thrashing on the ground, beating their chests, and with similar actions, they experience inconceivable grief and suffering.

Similarly, when they see a great, gently flowing river, and go there, they see it become a dry open riverbed. And when they see a green tree with branches and fruits and go there, they see a depressing, dried-up tree trunk. Only such undesirable things happen. As it is taught:

> The body of a hungry spirit
> is like the withered top of a palm tree.[587]

b) *Those with internal obscurations*

The hungry spirits with internal obscurations search as those with external obscurations do, without finding food and drink. Even when they find a little, they only find things like feces, urine, and snot. Even then, they clench it in their hands without being able to eat it, and the poison of their hands dries it up. When it is eaten, that small thing will not at first pass through the mouth that is about the size of the eye of a needle, and tears it open. After it has entered the mouth, it disappears without a trace in the vast hollows of the cheeks. When it is swallowed, the gullet is too narrow and it cannot pass through. When it does arrive in the stomach, which is about the size of a valley and cannot be filled, their craving increases again and they become extremely hungry and thirsty. Weeping and wailing, they have to experience inconceivable suffering. Thus my master taught.

c) *Those with obscurations of obscuration*

For hungry spirits with obscurations of obscuration, as soon as the food or other good substance goes inside, it blazes with fire and burns up all their inner vital organs. [279] Fire and smoke flicker and blaze from their mouths and nostrils. They bang their entire bodies against the earth and weep.

Some types of hungry spirits have huge goiters, and it is as if the body were attached to the goiter. They are nourished only by the pus and blood of those ripened goiters.

Concerning all of these in common, it is taught:

> For the hungry spirits,
> even the moon is hot in summer

> and the sun is cold in winter.
> At just a glance,
> a tree becomes fruitless,
> and even a river dries up.[588]

In this way, during the warmer seasons such as the summer, even the moon is hot as fire, and during the colder seasons such as the winter, even the sun is cold as water. Therefore, they experience inconceivable sufferings of torment, terror, hunger and thirst, exhaustion, and so forth.

Concerning their life span, it is taught:

> They do not die in five thousand
> or even ten thousand.[589]

These hungry spirits live for five hundred of their own years, in which a human month makes one day. While human beings and so forth may die if seven days pass without food, because of their severe bad karma the hungry spirits are unable to die, although they have not heard even the names of food and drink for hundreds and thousands of years. Thus my master taught.

2) *The scattered hungry spirits*

The scattered hungry spirits are the eight tribes of gods, tsen spirits, king spirits, and so forth[590] that live in the various worlds of the gods and human beings. When seen by meritorious and capable human beings or others, the hungry spirits are frightened almost to death. With nowhere to escape and afflicted by hunger and thirst, they are never satisfied, even by drinking a rain of food, beer, or other substances constantly falling into their mouths. Thirsting for the lives and breath of sentient beings, such spirits inflict whatever harm they can upon them. In these circumstances, if a ritual such as the expulsion of impeding spirits is not performed, worn out by their terror they will engage only in evil actions such as taking whatever lives they can. Finally, they will be reborn in an inescapable hell and have to experience suffering.

Therefore, think about this as before, with thoughts such as these: "If we do not have food for just one day now, how much suffering occurs? If reborn in such a place, it would be impossible to endure such suffering, in which even the name of food and drink is not heard for many hundreds and thousands of years. I have no confidence that I will not be born in a place like this. All the nonvirtue that I have committed every day, such as stinginess and the hindering of generosity, which are actions certain to bring rebirth, have been done heedlessly, and so I will certainly be reborn. [280] Now I absolutely must act so as to not be reborn there!"

c. *Reflection upon the sufferings of animals*

This also consists of two topics, as described following.

1) *Animals living in the principal location*

These animals live mashed together in the great outer ocean, like the grains left over from barley beer. They are untold in number, from the large whales and so forth down to the small fish and tadpoles. They have what are known as "the sufferings of uncertain place and uncertain companions." When carried by the ocean waves and currents, the eastern go west, the western go east, the southern go north, and the northern go south, with no distinction between going here or there.

In the "darkness between continents," the grim, pitch dark regions not reached by the sun, animals large and small have only this for all their birthplaces, dwelling places, and death places. They are crammed and crushed together one on top of the other. Eating one another, they live in that pitch darkness where they cannot even see their own limbs. They experience inconceivable sufferings, such as the stench of the rotten putrid corpses of sentient beings that have died. They are commonly so stupid that it is like being crushed by a mountain. Without any acceptance of what is to be done and rejection of what is not to be done, they must experience such suffering living mashed together in the dark. Thus my master taught.

2) *The scattered animals*

The scattered animals are the ones in the realms of the gods and human beings. Those that are controlled by owners have the sufferings of being exploited and worked and, at the very least, having their fur sheared and their milk milked. Those that are not owned are stricken with terror all the time and, at the very least, must be watchful even as they eat a few blades of grass. They eat one another, with the big ones eating the little ones, many little ones gathering together and eating the big ones, boring into their bodies, and so forth. In brief, their nature is nothing but suffering.

Their lifespans are uncertain, from the longest of an eon, down to the shortest, which are years or months, or being born and dying each instant. Thus my master taught.

In brief, wherever one is born in those locations, one does nothing but suffer. When that suffering is recognized, an extraordinary aspiration for liberation will arise, because no one wants suffering. [281] Since absolutely no other method for liberation except the Dharma exists, an extraordinary desire to practice Dharma will arise. Therefore, this is known as "the guidance that turns the mind toward Dharma." Thus my master taught.

2. *Reflection upon the suffering of change*

The second section consists of two topics:

a. In general, reflection upon the impermanence of all composite things
b. In particular, reflection upon the changes of the gods, anti-gods, and human beings

a. *In general, reflection upon the impermanence of all composite things*

It is taught:

> The three worlds are impermanent,
> like autumn clouds.
> The births and deaths of living beings
> are similar to watching a dance.
> The lives of living beings
> are like lightning in space.
> So quickly they pass,
> like the stream of a waterfall.[591]

In this way, all composite things have impermanence and change as their nature. Even a universal ruler is born as a slave, Brahmā and Śakra are born as ordinary beings, and the gods of the sun and moon must be born in a dark house where they cannot see even their own noses. Similarly, at the destruction of the eon not even a trace will be left of all these solid and stable appearances of the four continents, Mount Meru, and so forth. Absolutely nothing permanent and stable exists.

b. *In particular, reflection upon the changes of the gods, anti-gods, and human beings*

Even if born as a god, an anti-god, or a human being as a result of having performed tainted virtues, one does nothing but suffer. Due to the merit of the gods of the desire realm, sensory objects appear effortlessly for them. Made proud by these and attached to them, they carelessly indulge themselves day and night without trying for even a moment to think of doing virtue. Even though the "great drum of the gods that presents the four summations" steadily proclaims from the sky the sound of the words, "All composite things are impermanent," and so forth,[592] because the gods are under the power of the sensory objects alone, it does not even slightly penetrate their minds. In such a state, when that karma is exhausted and they hear distinctly proclaimed from empty space the words, "In this many days from now you will die," inconceivable suffering arises. Similarly, it is taught:

> Body color becomes ugly,
> seats are disliked,
> flower garlands become old,
> clothing is soiled,
> and perspiration
> appears on their bodies. [282]
> These are the five omens
> heralding death and transmigration
> in the higher realms.[593]

In this way, five signs of dying occur. The previously extremely beautiful and attractive body changes, and now the body color becomes ugly. Until now one was relaxed anywhere, distracted there by the sensory objects, but now one cannot stay still in one place, and has no wish to sit on one's seat. Previously the flowers attached to one's body remained bright and glistening with dew, but now those attached in the morning become withered and old by the afternoon and those attached in the afternoon become withered and old by the evening. Perspiration appears on the body. Because of that, dark dirty stains now suddenly appear on the clothing where stains would not previously have occurred. These are the five signs of dying.

When the five signs of dying or the five approaching signs are seen (such as the luster of the body becoming dim, water clinging to the body when bathing, and so forth), even one's relatives, retinue, and others dear to one are unable to approach and, as though incapable of parting, just scatter flowers in one's direction from a distance. Gazing with tainted paranormal ability, one realizes that the virtues done before have been exhausted, and that one will be reborn in such realms as the hells as the ripened result of careless indulgence in the sensory objects due to the three poisons. Great mental suffering, which is 100,000 times greater than the physical sufferings of the Revival hell, must be experienced. Then, after death and transmigration, one must endure the sufferings of the hells and so forth. Thus my master taught.

The gods of the higher realms linger for long periods in their respective meditative concentrations. When waking from these, they are proud and think, "By cultivating meditative concentration for so long, I am now liberated from samsara." But gazing with paranormal ability, they see that they will be reborn in the hells and so forth, and a great wrong view arises, in which they think, "Oh, no! I have remained absorbed in meditative concentration for so long, but have not been liberated from samsara. Absolutely no 'liberation and freedom' exists in the world." In conjunction with this, they transmigrate from that place and must again experience the sufferings of the lower realms that cannot be measured or said to be of a particular magnitude. Thus my master taught. [283]

Those born as anti-gods are deeply angry and disturbed just by being born in that realm, and pass the time just fighting day and night without rest. In particular, due to their envy of such things as the wish-fulfilling tree and the daughters of the gods, in short, of all the wealth of the gods, they fight with the gods. Because the gods have great merit and the anti-gods have little merit, it is usually the anti-gods who are defeated, and their time passes in killing, destruction, and terror. In the realm of the anti-gods, when the female anti-gods look into the "lake in which everything appears," they see whatever killing and destruction is being done in the realm of the gods, like images appearing in a mirror. Weeping, beating their chests, and so forth, their time passes only in suffering. While in this state, the karma through which they were born there becomes exhausted, they transmigrate, and they are reborn in the Revival hell and so forth and must experience suffering.

Concerning those born as human beings, the great are tortured by mental suffering, the lesser are tortured by physical suffering, and all are tortured in common by the four great rivers of the sufferings of birth, old age, sickness, and death, without even an instant of rest. First conceived and then dwelling in the mother's womb, when the mother's stomach is filled with food, the suffering is like being squeezed between cliffs. When the mother is hungry, the suffering is like being dangled in a bucket. When she eats hot food or anything warm, the suffering is like being doused with fire. When she takes cold food and drink, the suffering is like being frozen in ice. When the mother does strenuous work, the suffering is like falling into an abyss. Similarly, one must dwell inside such a black, cramped, and stinking darkness.

At birth, the suffering is like being drawn through the eye of a sieve or having one's skin peeled off. Being born and falling on the surface of the cushion, the suffering is like falling into a pit of thorns. Being lifted by the mother onto her lap is like being a chick carried off by a hawk. And so forth. In brief, one does nothing but suffer. Thus my master taught.

Similarly, during old age all the strength of the body is lost. Taken as an object of disgust and ridicule by one's children, one's circle, and others close to one, one becomes depressed and dejected. One is tormented by illnesses, evil spirits, and so forth. [284] Finally, when the time of death arrives, it cannot be resisted by force, tricked by wealth, or turned back by rituals, and one dies darkly and dully attached to relatives, valuables, or similar things. And so forth. In brief, there is nothing but utter suffering.

Many people are reduced to one. The rich become beggars. The influential become weak. The opposite happens, and so on. In brief, the point here is this changing from moment to moment, without any possibility of permanence, that we actually see every year and every month. Thus my master taught.

3. *Reflection upon the pervasive suffering of conditioned existence*

This consists of three topics: no end to actions, no satisfaction with sensory objects, and no weariness of birth and death.

No end to actions

Wherever anyone is born in samsara, all the bewildering actions of various kinds done day and night without rest are never finished or ended, and one dies with things left to do. Once again, one must begin preparations for the next life. In brief, actions of body, speech, and mind have been done heedlessly until now. Not only are these all worthless efforts, but they mostly yield only the wrong results, so that one will have to wander through this samsara. Therefore, meditate with thoughts such as this: "I will utterly abandon these worthless activities and practice Dharma!"

No satisfaction with sensory objects

While we all have been wandering in different forms through samsara that cannot be measured or said to have begun at a particular point, no distinction has been made between using this and not using that for food and drink. When we were born as gods, we ate nectar. When we were born in the hells, we ate glowing iron. When we were born as bugs, we ate excrement. Even in just this lifetime, from birth until now, whatever superior, middling, and inferior food and drink we have eaten and drunk has never brought the slightest moment of complete satisfaction. This is the point.

No weariness of birth and death

While roaming through the six realms, like the turning of a potter's wheel, no distinction has been made between taking this body and not taking that one. For example, if the ears from each time we have been born as sheep were gathered they would not fit into the three-thousandfold world systems. Similarly, with no distinction between being born in one place and not being born in another, each of those times we have died and each time been helplessly born again by the force of karma and afflictions. Nevertheless, we have accumulated only causes for roaming through samsara, without becoming weary of those types of things or perceiving them as suffering. [285]

Now we must make energetic efforts to use every possible means for escaping from this samsara, like a bird in a burning forest, a swan in freezing water, or the child of a cannibal witch. Thus my master taught.

B. *The difficulty of gaining the freedoms and endowments*

In the *Vajra Lines* the word "afflictions" implicitly presents the difficulty of gaining the freedoms and endowments. Due to their blind indulgence in the afflictions, the sentient beings of samsara are helplessly born in the three lower realms. It is difficult to reach the higher realms in general and, specifically, to gain a human body with the freedoms and endowments. Thus one should understand the sufferings of samsara in relation to any of those forms and seek a means of liberation from that suffering. No method exists other than the excellent Dharma alone. Moreover, because the Dharma must also be practiced on the basis of a human body alone, the difficulty of gaining the freedoms and endowments is meditated on after reflection upon the sufferings of samsara. Thus my master taught.

This reflection consists of three topics:

1. Reflection upon the difficulty of gaining the freedoms and endowments
2. Reflection upon the great benefit of the freedoms and endowments that have been gained
3. Reflection that the beneficial freedoms and endowments will not last long

1. *Reflection upon the difficulty of gaining the freedoms and endowments*

This consists of four topics:

a. The difficulty of gaining these from the perspective of cause
b. The difficulty of gaining these from the perspective of essence
c. The difficulty of gaining these from the perspective of example
d. The difficulty of gaining these from the perspective of number or comparison

a. *The difficulty of gaining these from the perspective of cause*

In general, it is explained that the cause is virtue and, in particular, that a human body is obtained if moral discipline has been perfectly maintained. However, virtue is generally rare and, specifically, the pure preservation of moral discipline is rare. Because sentient beings in degenerate times blindly indulge in the afflictions, they will for the most part go into the lower realms, like turning a leather bag of sand upside down. Thus my master taught.

b. *The difficulty of gaining these from the perspective of essence*

Avoidance of the eight places where no opportunity exists to practice Dharma and possession of the ten endowments with which to practice Dharma are explained to be the eighteen aspects of the freedoms and endowments. What are these?

The eight are the four inopportune situations when one does not have a human body and the four inopportune situations when one has become a human being. First, it has been stated:

> The hell beings, the hungry spirits,
> the animals, the barbarians,
> the gods with long lives,
> having wrong views,
> the absence of a buddha,
> and being dumb,
> are the eight inopportune situations.[594]

Because those in the three lower realms are intensely tormented by suffering, they do not have the slightest leisure to practice Dharma. Even if they did, due to their bad karma they would not have the good fortune to hear even the sound of the Dharma. [286] Even though some kinds of animals do hear the sound, because of their stupidity, which is like being crushed by a mountain, they cannot understand what is and is not to be done. Because they do not understand anything, they do not have the merit. The gods with long lives are attached to sensory objects, and with the pride of thinking, "Nobody is greater than me," even when they hear the Dharma they do not have the good fortune to practice it. Thus my master taught. The "barbarians" are those born in countries where the Buddha's doctrine has not spread. Even if they have been born in a central country or elsewhere where the Dharma exists, some people, due to their bad karma, hold great wrong views in their minds, thinking that the Three Jewels, the causes and results of actions, and so forth, are not at all true. The "absence of a buddha" refers to having been born at a time when a buddha has not appeared in the world. In this context, "being dumb" does not refer to a fault in the speech faculty, but to being unintelligent because of a fault in the mental faculty. In brief, when the Dharma is not understood even though it is taught, and absolutely no discrimination is present, that is also an impediment to the practice of Dharma. Thus my master taught.

Of the ten endowments, the five endowments dependent on oneself are mentioned in the following lines:

> To be a human being,
> born in a central country,
> with complete sense faculties,
> without committing heinous acts,
> and with faith in the sources of refuge.[595]

If these endowments are absent, it is impossible to practice Dharma. In general, one must be born as a human being. Of them, one must be born in a country where the Dharma is present, such as a central country that is the hub of the Dharma, and not in a borderland country where no Dharma exists. Even if born there, if one is deaf, blind, dumb, and so forth, it will be an impediment to the practice of Dharma. So one must have no faults in the five sense faculties. "Without committing heinous acts" means not to commit any of the inexpiable or nearly inexpiable acts, and so forth. "Faith in the sources" is to have faith in the sources of refuge, the Three Jewels. This is to possess the five endowments dependent on oneself.

Even if one has those, if these endowments dependent on others are absent, it is impossible to practice Dharma. The endowments dependent on others are also suitably complete now. It is taught:

> The appearance of a buddha,
> his teaching of the Dharma,
> the survival of the doctrine,
> followers of it, and sincere
> love for the sake of others.[596]

In this way, a buddha has appeared in the world, he has taught the Dharma, the precious doctrine he taught has survived without disappearing, and followers of it remain, down to those upholding just the outer signs. Each of these is very important. Without any companions in the practice of Dharma, even if one's own karma is awakened and one wishes to practice Dharma, it is extremely difficult to begin. [287] Others, such as patrons, provide the favorable conditions for Dharma. These are the five.

Those endowments are suitably complete in these physical bodies that we all have obtained now. From numerous perspectives, it is extremely difficult for them to be complete in this way. Thus my master taught.

c. *The difficulty of gaining these from the perspective of example*

A hypothetical example is taught:

> A yoke tossing on a great ocean.[597]

Assuming that there were a golden yoke with a single hole in it, carried across the ocean by the wind, randomly drifting in all directions, and assuming that there were a blind turtle at the bottom of the ocean that emerged to the surface just once every one hundred years, it would be nearly impossible for the neck of the turtle to emerge through the hole in the yoke. In a similar way, luckily obtaining the freedoms and endowments is also barely possible.

Similarly, as taught in the *Sutra of a Bouquet of Flowers,* when many loads of white mustard seed are dumped onto a needle held with the point up, most will strike the ground.[598] It is barely possible that a white mustard seed will stick on the point of the needle. When beans are thrown at the side of a wall, the same thing happens. In this example, the number that strike the ground represent those born in the lower realms and the number that stick to the point of the needle represent those that obtain human bodies. Thus my master taught.

d. *The difficulty of gaining these from the perspective of number*

If one thinks, "Obtaining a human body is probably not that rare. Many human beings live in Tibet alone," then one has not examined this well. Who can count the number of valerian and mugwort plants on the mountain slopes of a single small valley? And the number of small sentient beings like tiny birds in each of those valleys is unimaginable, let alone countable. Similarly, how many large and small creatures live in the upper, lower, and middle parts of a house during a season such as the summer? However many human beings live inside that house, they can certainly be counted.

Who is able to count those creatures? Even considering something like one's own clothing, how many nits and lice live inside it? Similarly, it is explained that eighty-four thousand bacteria live inside the abdomen. And the outside of the body is swarming with different kinds of creatures such as nits and lice. Among all these, no human being exists except oneself alone. [288]

In brief, however one thinks about it, reflect upon it with thoughts such as this: "This physical body that I have obtained right now is extremely difficult to gain. Therefore, I absolutely must act to not leave empty-handed!"

2. *Reflection upon the great benefit of the freedoms and endowments that have been gained*

One might wonder, "In that case, if it is so difficult to gain, then the horn of a rabbit, the child of a barren woman, and so forth are also rare."

Those are just rare by reason of their nonexistence, which is referred to as "certainty in nonexistence," and have no essence whatsoever. But [being born in] this physical body is even more beneficial and exceptional than finding a wish-fulfilling jewel. If the jewel is found and supplications are offered, all unfavorable conditions are removed and whatever food, wealth, and so forth are wished for will appear. But this body is capable of accomplishing all actions such as these, and more. Its benefit is extremely great because all temporary and ultimate virtue and goodness—that nothing else such as a wish-fulfilling jewel can give—is accomplished on the basis of this body, from the levels of the gods and human beings in the future, and the enlightenment of the śrāvakas and the pratyekabuddhas, up to that of great unified Vajradhara. Thus my master taught.

3. *Reflection that the beneficial freedoms and endowments will not last long*

One may think, "Since I have now gained what is so difficult to gain, this itself is sufficient."

But this will also not last long. Here the practice should be done by means of four reflections: the certainty of death, death no matter what is done, the uncertain time of death, and that nothing will be beneficial at death except the Dharma. Thus my master taught.

In brief, the Kadampa and some others treat death and impermanence separately, but in the tradition of the Path with the Result these are included within the difficulty of gaining the freedoms and endowments. Thus my master taught.

C. *Reflection upon the causes and results of actions*

The *Vajra Lines* say, "impure appearance." The meaning of this is taught by means of two topics:

1. General confusing appearance
2. Specific karmic appearance

1. *General confusing appearance*

Even though they do not really exist, the various phenomena of self and others, samsara and nirvana, and the environment and its inhabitants arise due to the duality of subject and object. This is general confusing appearance.

2. *Specific karmic appearance*

That is further distinguished by the good and bad karma that each being has accumulated. For example, when the living beings of the six realms look at the same time at something like a bowl full of water, [289] different individual appearances arise, from the gods seeing nectar, to the beings of the hot hells seeing molten metal. Seeing such appearances is determined by the virtuous and sinful karma of those beings. Therefore, this stabilizes one's reflection upon the causes and results of actions, which consists of three topics:

a. Nonvirtuous actions
b. Virtuous actions
c. Neutral actions

a. *Nonvirtuous actions*

This also consists of three topics:

1) Reflection upon nonvirtuous actions
2) Reflection upon their results
3) Instructions to avoid nonvirtuous actions

1) *Reflection upon nonvirtuous actions*

It is taught:

> Actions produced by
> desire, hatred, and ignorance
> are the nonvirtues.[599]

Because of motivation, actions motivated by the three poisons—in whatever forms they appear—in essence yield nothing but wrong results. Of these, many are completely nonvirtuous in thought and application. If these are condensed by type, they can be grouped as the ten nonvirtues:

a) The three that are physical
b) The four that are vocal
c) The three that are mental

a) *The three that are physical*

Taking life means to deprive another being of life, or urge another to do so, by means of anything from poison, weapons, fire, water, and so forth, to magic and evil mantras, including rejoicing about it. *Taking what has not been given* means to make the valuable objects of others, those that one has no control of, one's own by means of robbing by force, or stealing by stealth, or even by means of flattery or hinting. *Sexual misconduct* means to have sexual intercourse with a woman other than the woman who belongs to oneself, whether she belongs or does not belong to another.

b) *The four that are vocal*

Lying means speech that deceives another. *Slander* means speaking divisive words, whether true or false, with the desire to divide others, whether they are mutually friendly or not. *Harsh words* means to speak, with intense force, words that strike at another's vulnerable points. *Idle speech* means all aimless, worthless talk, from study and reflection upon the bad treatises of the non-Buddhist outsiders and so forth, to conversations about business, war, prostitutes, and so forth.

c) *The three that are mental*

Covetousness means to think, "If I had that," "If it came to me," about something one sees, from another's land, castle, and so forth, down to a minor object. [290] *Malice* means to have no compassion for others who are suffering, and to do whatever one can to make them suffer. *Wrong view* means the continual wrong thoughts of maintaining that the Three Jewels, the causes and results of actions, and so forth, are not even true in the slightest degree.

2) *Reflection upon their results*

For each of those types of actions, three results occur:

a) The ripened result
b) The results corresponding to the causes
c) The dominant result

a) *The ripened result*

This is definite ripening only as a body in the lower realms. Moreover, due to the intensity or weakness of the thoughts, the many or few instances, and so forth, the greatest of those actions propel one into the hells, the middling propel one into the realm of the hungry spirits, and the lesser propel one into the realm of the animals. As explained, those sufferings must be experienced for hundreds, thousands, and millions of years. Concerning the last two middling and lesser actions, when escape from those locations of the lower realms becomes possible, even if one has been born in a suitable higher realm, one must still experience suffering until released from that karma.

b) *The results corresponding to the causes*

This consists of two topics: experiences corresponding to the causes and actions corresponding to the causes.

(1) *Experiences corresponding to the causes*

From having taken life, one will have a short life and many illnesses. From having taken what was not given, one will be poor and destitute. From sexual misconduct, one will have many enemies and one's wife will be troublesome. From having lied, wherever one is born one will be much maligned. From having slandered, one will have few friends and be parted from loved ones. From harsh words, one will hear only unpleasant talk. From idle speech, one's words will carry no force. From covetousness, everything considered as "one's hopes" will not be fulfilled. From malice, one will be afraid. From wrong view, one will have faith in and adhere to evil views.

(2) *Actions corresponding to the causes*

One will have the deep desire to perform particular actions again and again. By engaging in these actions, one will again be born in the lower realms. Thus my master taught.

c) *The dominant result*

The dominant result ripens as the environment where one will be born. It is taught:

> In a region of little glory,
> with many hailstorms,
> choked with dust, stinking,
> and with uneven terrain and alkaline soil,
> where the times are turbulent,
> the fruits are small, bitter, or nonexistent.[600]

In this way, each action produces three results. The reasons for this can be illustrated using the example of one, such as taking life. Because striking another with something such as a weapon produced pain and torment in body and mind, one will have many illnesses. Because of the actual taking of life, one will be tortured in the hells and so forth. [291] Because all of that victim's glory faded and he died miserable, one will be born in a place despised by oneself and everyone else, in a disgusting region with little glory. Thus my master taught.

3) *Instructions to avoid nonvirtuous actions*

Think: "If all these sufferings, from the sufferings of being born in the hells, to the slightest mental discomfort of a body in the higher realms, did not exist, they could be ignored. But all the sufferings that do exist are only results that have come from nonvirtue as their cause. Therefore, from this time forward, until I die, or until the sun rises tomorrow, or at least until I am finished with this session, I will not perform even the smallest and most minor nonvirtue, let alone the great!"

b. *Virtuous actions*

This consists of the three topics of reflection and so forth.

1) *Reflection upon virtuous actions*

It is taught:

> Actions produced with no desire,
> and without hatred and ignorance,
> are the virtues.[601]

Everything done without the three poisons as their causes are the virtues. If these are condensed by type, they can be grouped as the ten virtues. These are precisely the opposites of the previous ten nonvirtues.

2) *Reflection upon their results*

As with nonvirtuous actions, these results are threefold: the ripened result, results corresponding to the causes, and the dominant result. The ripened result is ripening as a suitable divine or human body in the higher realms. Actions corresponding to the causes are to delight in performing particular virtues due to the force of having been accustomed to them, and by engaging in these again and again one will later go from higher realm to higher realm until enlightenment is obtained. Experiences corresponding to the causes are the opposite of those [described in relation to the nonvirtuous actions], from having few illnesses and a long life, up to devotion to the perfect view. And the dominant result is that the country where one is born will be a region that is blazing with glory, delightful, and so forth.

3) *The instructions to cultivate virtuous actions*

Think: "In brief, everything that appears as happiness and pleasure in samsara and nirvana, from the obtaining of perfect buddhahood down to a being in the hot hells experiencing just the prospect of cold wind, come from virtue. Therefore, from this moment, until I die and so forth, I will cultivate and practice the virtues, down to the most minor!"

c. *Neutral actions*

This consists of three topics: reflection upon neutral actions; reflection upon their results; and training to transform neutral actions into virtues.

1) *Reflection upon neutral actions*

Neutral actions are everything such as eating, sleeping, traveling, and sitting, which are not mixed with any virtuous or nonvirtuous motives. [292]

2) *Reflection upon their results*

Neutral actions are not "worthless hardships," nonvirtues that produce suffering. They are also not virtues, so pleasant results will not arise. Nothing specific will come from them.

3) *Training to transform neutral actions into virtues*

Meditate by thinking: "From today forward I absolutely must transform all such neutral activities into virtues, without leaving them as worthless!"

Take refuge and make supplications at the beginning of the session, and energetically meditate in sequence on the individual key points during the main practice. At the conclusion, perform the dedication prayers and so forth as described previously.

During all times between sessions one must avoid even the smallest nonvirtues and cultivate the smallest virtues. For example, if a tiny spark of fire escapes into the midst of a great building filled with grass, like a barn, it will gradually spread and the entire building will be consumed by fire. Similarly, if one thinks, "I can bear a small sin like this," an increase in negativity will occur, and it will increase every day and become a serious nonvirtue until it is destroyed by a powerful antidote. But with intense mindfulness this can be avoided with little difficulty when it is small. Even if the antidote has not been applied, one should be energetic in confession with the four powers[602] and so forth. Thus my master taught.

Similarly, it is not right to give up small virtues, thinking, "Something like this is not really beneficial." It is like a vase filled by each accumulated drop of water, or Mount Meru created by each accumulated atom. Even the most minor virtues should be cultivated without disdain. It is explained that these are destroyed by wrong view, intense anger, and so forth, so be energetic in applying the seal of pure dedication and so forth before they are destroyed by something like that.

In brief, it is taught:

> The sages do not wash away sins with water
> and do not remove the sufferings
> of living beings with their hands.
> They do not transfer their realization to others,
> but liberate them by presenting the truth
> of the real nature of phenomena.[603]

It is taught that by presenting the truth of the real nature of phenomena the buddhas gradually remove suffering, but they do not wash it away with water, like dirt, or remove suffering with their hands, like pulling out a thorn.

Thus the causes and results of actions are the root of the presentation of the truth of the real nature of phenomena.

In brief, up through this point the paths of the lesser and middling individuals, or the practices of the śrāvakas and the pratyekabuddhas, are complete. Thus my master taught. [293]

II. Experiential Appearance

It is taught:

> For a yogin with meditative concentration, experiential appearance occurs.[604]

The meaning of this is discussed under two headings:

A. The meditations by a common yogin until the common experiences arise
B. The production of certainty about the experiences that will arise for an uncommon yogin

A. *The meditations by a common yogin until the common experiences arise*

A common yogin is a person who practices the path of the Vehicle of the Perfections. He meditates until the individual experiences of the common path of love, compassion, and the enlightenment mind arise. The uncontrived enlightenment mind arises on the basis of compassion. Moreover, it is taught:

> Love is the root of compassion.[605]

So compassion arises on the basis of love. Therefore, these three exist in the sense of causes and results or supports and what are supported. Thus my master taught.

1. *Cultivating love*

Concerning the essence of love, it is taught:

> The careful cultivation
> of benefit for living beings
> is great love.[606]

So love is the desire for sentient beings to be endowed with happiness. Thus my master taught.

Love is cultivated by means of four topics: cultivation for one's mother, cultivation for friends, cultivation for enemies, and cultivation for infinite sentient beings. Each of these should be practiced by condensing them into the three topics of cultivating love through recognizing one's mother, remembering her kindness, and wishing to repay her kindness.

The first of these is cultivation for one's mother. After completing the taking of refuge and supplications, clearly visualize one's actual mother in front of oneself, whether she is living or has died, with the exact size, shape, and color of her body, jewelry, dress, and so forth. If she died when one was small, or something like that, and one does not remember her form, clearly meditate that she is certainly present like an ordinary woman. Generate the deep feeling, "She is my mother."

Second is remembering her kindness. Think: "Oh, my! This mother of mine has been extremely kind to me. At first, when I was conceived in her womb and could be destroyed by even the slightest mishap, my mother ignored all her own pleasure and suffering and thought about what might be good for this body of mine. She turned to all favorable types of behavior and avoided all unfavorable types of behavior. My mother cherished me more than she cherished herself. When I was born, I was as feeble as a worm in a plowed furrow. If I had not been kept warm, or even if the palate butter[607] had been given late, I could have been parted from life in an instant. But because she pressed me to the warmth of her body, gave the palate butter, provided milk, and so forth, I did not die. [294] Therefore, she was extremely kind because she produced and gave me a body and life to begin with.

"Then, while I couldn't do anything, she gazed at me with loving eyes, called me by sweet names, fed me food and drink from her mouth, wiped away my filth with her hands, and thinking 'My baby!' thought of nothing but me. Wrapping me in clothing and so forth, she taught me about clean and dirty when I did not know about clean and dirty. Leading me by the hand, she taught me to walk when I did not know how to walk. By saying, 'Say "Papa!" Say "Mama!"' and so forth, she taught me to speak when I did not know how to speak. In brief, she carefully taught me everything to accept and reject, by saying, 'Mama's coming!', 'Oh, no!', 'You'll fall!', and so forth. If I knew how to say just 'Ah,' she was overjoyed and bragged about it to people. Similarly, my mother carefully gave me all the best food without eating it herself, and everything she would not give to others. Saying, 'I know about myself and about him. This child needs it,' she had no leisure during the day, did not sleep at night, and worked until her feet and hands were cracked open. She would care for me even to the point of deceit, denial, and theft. Therefore, she was extremely kind because she taught me discrimination during the middle period.

"Cared for in that way, my body grew, I reached maturity, I entered the gate of the doctrine, I met excellent masters, I have instructions like this Precious Teaching to practice, and so forth. Therefore, she was extremely kind because she put me in contact with the Dharma in the end."

To cultivate love in connection with longing, meditate with deep feeling over and over from the bottom of one's heart: "I would be glad if this mother of mine, who has been so kind in that way, were endowed with happiness and the causes of happiness and free from suffering and the causes of suffering. But just the opposite is true for her. Therefore, wouldn't it be wonderful if this mother of mine were to become endowed with happiness and all the virtues that are the causes of happiness?"

As a promise, think: "I will definitely cause this mother of mine to become endowed with all the virtues that are the causes of happiness."

Thinking that one is dedicating for her sake the virtues, bodies, possessions, and so forth that one accumulates during the three times, utterly give them up. As a prayer, think and say: "May this mother of mine become endowed with happiness and all the causes of happiness!" [295]

It is difficult to accomplish immediate benefit through one's longing and so forth, but if the masters and the Three Jewels are supplicated, whatever has been requested will infallibly be accomplished. Therefore, in the sky in front, clearly visualize the masters and the Three Jewels filling space. As a supplication, repeat the following one hundred times, one thousand, and so forth:

> Masters, Three Jewels, please be aware of her! Please bless this mother of mine to be endowed with happiness and all the causes of happiness!

Or use this supplication:

> Masters, Three Jewels, please be aware of this mother of mine!
> Let her be endowed with all the causes of happiness!

Similarly, imagine one's father, as though he were actually in front of one. Recognize him as one's father, thinking, "This is my father." In remembering his kindness, think that except for not having carried one in his body, he took care of one like one's mother. Cultivate love and so forth toward him as before.

In a similar way, imagine in front of one those toward whom attachment has arisen, from relatives and so forth to those that have merely looked upon one favorably. Reflect upon them with thoughts such as these: "These people benefited me, looked upon me with loving eyes, spoke nice words, and gave me valuable things. In similar ways, they have only cared for me with kindness. Not only just that, throughout beginningless samsara they have been my mothers. Moreover, they have done so numerous times. Every time they have been my mother they have only been kind, caring for me with kindness just like my present mother has cared for me."

Then call to mind all those toward whom hatred has arisen, as illustrated by one's worst enemy, and then infinite sentient beings, and do the practice as described before, by means of the four points in connection with a promise, a prayer, longing, and a supplication.

2. *Cultivating compassion*

It is taught:

> The total protection
> of those who are suffering
> is great compassion.[608]

Thus a sharply-focused desire to remove living beings from suffering is compassion. This consists of three topics:

a. Cultivating compassion for sentient beings
b. Compassion in regard to phenomena
c. Compassion in regard to the nonreferential

a. *Cultivating compassion for sentient beings*

This consists of the four topics of cultivating compassion for one's mother and so forth.

First is cultivating compassion for one's mother. Both the first step, which is recognition of one's mother, and the second, which is remembering her kindness, are the same as previously described. [296] For the third, cultivating compassion for her, do the practice in connection with longing, a promise, a prayer, and a supplication, with thoughts such as this: "This mother of mine lacks happiness and the causes of happiness, and is enduring suffering and the causes of suffering. Therefore, wouldn't it be wonderful if she were free from suffering and all the nonvirtues that are the causes of suffering?"

Most practitioners of the Path with the Result have not used more than the three of longing and so forth. This connection with a supplication is the custom of Dakchen Dorjé Chang.[609] In any case, it is acceptable to cultivate all four in sequence or to condense them into whichever one is most inspiring, such as a supplication, and meditate. Thus my master taught.

Second is cultivating compassion and so forth for one's father, which is done in the same way.

Third is cultivating compassion for enemies. Think: "This enemy is my mother, but because she has passed through births and deaths no recognition remains, and not recognizing that I was her child and that she was my mother, she has harmed me and so forth without self-control, like a crazy person. Similarly, she has performed many nonvirtues, which accumulate the causes of suffering, and due to that will have to endure only suffering without ever escaping from the three lower realms of the hells and so forth. How pitiful! If my mother of this life went crazy and attacked me with weapons and so forth, I would not hate her. Unable to bear the thought that my mother was crazy and in such a condition, I would find medicines, perform rituals, and so forth. Similarly, it is not reasonable to be angry with this person. After searching for a way that will definitely turn this mother of mine away from the causes and results of suffering, wouldn't it be wonderful if this mother were free from suffering and all the causes of suffering?"

The rest is the same.

The fourth topic is cultivating compassion for sentient beings. This is as described before, except that one should specially select and cultivate it for whoever has the most suffering, such as those in the hells. Thus my master taught.

b. *Compassion in regard to phenomena*

These sentient beings have to experience unbearable sufferings. This is solely due to ignorance—not recognizing one's very essence, which is the root of the twelve links of dependent arising. Therefore, repeat this any number of times: "Wouldn't it be wonderful if these old mothers, sentient beings equal to the limits of space, were free from ignorance, the cause from which suffering arises?" [297]

Repeat this any number of times: "May they be free from ignorance, the cause from which suffering arises!"

Repeat this any number of times: "Masters, precious Three Jewels, please be aware of them! Please bless these sentient beings to become free from ignorance, the cause of suffering."

c. *Compassion in regard to the nonreferential*

Think: "All phenomena do not transcend emptiness, which is beyond conceptual elaboration. But because this has not been realized, the mind is affected by dualistic thoughts and the untrue is taken to be true, the nonexistent is taken to be existent, and so forth. Due to this confusing appearance, sentient beings have to experience the infinite sufferings of the three lower realms. Wouldn't it be wonderful if they realized the view beyond conceptual elaboration? May they realize the view beyond conceptual elaboration! Masters, precious Three Jewels, please be aware of them! Please bless these sentient beings to realize the view beyond conceptual elaboration."

In that way, use longing, a prayer, and a supplication for refuge as described previously. Thus my master taught.

A number of different methods have been taught for meditation on the three topics of compassion in sequence, and for meditation by condensing them into one because the latter ones are categories within the former ones. But here it is practiced as described previously. The *Guidance Manual for Jochak* says:

> As the object, use sentient beings tormented by suffering, and cultivate compassion for sentient beings, while thinking, "May they be free from the causes of suffering!"
>
> Since ignorance is the cause of suffering, cultivate compassion with reference to phenomena, wishing "May they be free from ignorance!"
>
> All sentient beings are not perfectly established by nature, but with mental focusing on them as the point of reference, cultivate nonreferential compassion.[610]

This special section on compassion in the guidance manual for the Precious Teaching composed by Jamgön Khyentsé has been copied from the actual handwritten notes made by Dorjé Chang Wangrap.[611]

3. *Cultivating the enlightenment mind*

This consists of two topics:

a. The relative enlightenment mind
b. The absolute enlightenment mind

a. *Cultivating the relative enlightenment mind*

This consists of three topics:

1) Awakening the aspiration enlightenment mind
2) Awakening the application enlightenment mind
3) Training in the practice of the aspiration enlightenment mind and the application enlightenment mind

1) *Awakening the aspiration enlightenment mind*

Reflect upon this so that it strikes your flesh and penetrates the marrow of your bones: "In that way, even being energetic with promises, prayers, and so forth, I am not able to immediately remove living beings from suffering. [298] The great beings of the world who are superior to me, the noble śrāvakas and pratyekabuddhas who are superior to them, and also the bodhisattvas who are vastly superior to even them, have not perfected the good qualities of renunciation and realization, which is for their own benefit. They are not expert in the vast methods of gracing disciples, which is for the benefit of others. Therefore, they are not able to protect sentient beings from all suffering. Who possesses that ability? A buddha who has completely perfected all the good qualities of renunciation and realization possesses it. Therefore, wouldn't it be wonderful if I reached the citadel of perfect buddhahood in order to quickly liberate all sentient beings from this great ocean of suffering in samsara? I will definitely reach it!"

Recite aloud a hundred times, a thousand times, or more:

> For the benefit of all sentient beings, I will reach the citadel of omniscient and perfect buddhahood.

A practitioner of the Path with the Result who was known as Jatön Sengé Sangpo performed the awakening of the enlightenment mind one hundred thousand times in front of the lord in Kyirong,[612] and he did so using this method. Thus my master taught.

2) *Awakening the application enlightenment mind*

This also consists of two topics, as described following.

a) *Cultivating the equality of self and others*

Meditate again and again, thinking, "As I want to be happy, so do all sentient beings also just want to be happy. Therefore, may all sentient beings be endowed with happiness!"

And by thinking, "As I do not want to suffer, so do all sentient beings also not want to suffer. Therefore, may all sentient beings be parted from suffering!"

b) *Cultivating the exchange of self and others*

Think: "As I do not wish to suffer, so do all sentient beings also not wish to suffer. Therefore, may all of their sufferings, the causes as well as the results, ripen to me!"

Imagine that all of their sufferings are gathered together in a black heap, like hair shaved off by a knife. All of it, without as much as a speck left over, dissolves and is absorbed into the center of one's heart and fades into emptiness. All of one's own happiness and virtue radiates like sunshine from one's heart. As soon as it strikes all sentient beings they attain the superb glory of happiness and joy. [299] All sentient beings shine with light and go straight into great bliss. Do this again and again with that kind of longing.

For the purpose of supplication, practice by repeating this out loud a hundred times, a thousand times, or more:

> May the sufferings of all sentient beings ripen to me.
> By my virtue may they all achieve happiness![613]

3) *Training in the practice of the aspiration enlightenment mind and the application enlightenment mind*

This should be understood according to the way it is taught in such texts as the *Fine Path of the Bodhisattvas.*[614]

b. *Cultivating the absolute enlightenment mind*

This consists of two topics:

1) Calm abiding
2) Penetrating insight

1) *Calm abiding*

This is practiced by means of four key points:

a) A motionless support
b) An immobile body
c) Unblinking eyes
d) An undistracted mind

a) *The support*

A piece of wood, a small stone, and so forth have been recommended, and in the *Sutra of the King of Meditative Concentrations*[615] an image of the Buddha is recommended for mental focusing. But in the tradition of the Lord of Yogins, Virūpa, a blue flower is used for mental focusing. A blue flower of about four finger-widths should be drawn on something like silk or cotton, with a deep blue-black center and with the middle of the four petals blue but fading out toward the edges. At a spot measuring seven handspans in front, and level with the tip of one's nose, place such a flower on a stand of something like a straight reed that is completely immobile. The reason for this is that a flower is easily acceptable to the mind and blue does not irritate the eyes. Thus my master taught.

b) *The body*

Perfectly maintain the six-point or seven-point posture of Vairocana, with the hands in the gesture of meditative equipoise, the thumbs touching at the navel, and so forth.

c) *The eyes*

Gaze with half-closed eyes, not too open and not too shut, at a spot measuring seven handspans from the tip of the nose. This is the meaning of the saying, "Gaze about as far as a full wooden yoke." As a wooden yoke is seven handspans in length, here also the meaning is to gaze about that far; not further away than that and not closer in. Thus my master taught.

In that way, while maintaining the key physical points and the gaze, do not lean or wobble at all until the session is finished. In particular, since the channels of the thoughts are in the eyes, if they move the mind will never come to rest, so do not allow any blinking and rolling of the eyes. Rest gazing directly at the support in front, the blue flower. [300]

d) *The mind*

In that state, serenely rest the mind on the flower. Rest tranquilly, without scrutinizing its shape, color, and so forth. This practice has three aspects, referred to as "first concentrating," "relaxing in between," and "finally recognizing the natural state." First is "concentrating." With body and mind totally concentrated, rest the mind at ease upon the blue flower by drawing together as one the mind, the eyes, and the vital winds. Second is "relaxing in between." Deliberate grasping will lead to thoughts, so when the mind is stable upon the flower, just relax. Third is "finally recognizing the natural state." When resting in that way, if the mind and the flower serenely and freely blend together, it is known as "recognizing the natural state." Rest in just that state, without doing anything artificial.

If the mind drifts elsewhere, pull it back and practice as before, by means of concentrating, relaxing, and the natural state. If even more thoughts come from practicing in that way, they should be totally eliminated. As soon as a thought arises, totally eliminate it without letting the mind follow it. Rest again upon the blue flower. Or "look at the very nature of the thought." By deliberately looking at the essence of the thought itself, it will fade away without a trace. Relax in just that state. Use whichever of those two methods is preferable. Thus my master taught.

Whatever impediments of dullness and agitation occur while practicing like this, by clearing them away and meditating, the five experiences of movement, attainment, familiarity, stability, and perfection may arise in sequence or, since it is taught, "They may arise in sequence or out of sequence, so allow their natural expression," it is also possible that they may occur out of order. One should be well introduced to the nature of these, and be energetic in whatever methods bring the mind to rest.

In general, meditation is the most important point in the Vajrayana. In particular, this Precious Teaching is superior to others because of the four authentic qualities. If one has not meditated, the authentic quality of experience will not occur. If that has not arisen, where will the other three authentic qualities come from? Practitioners of the Path with the Result who possess the four authentic qualities are said to be rare, so one must meditate. If a good calm abiding has arisen here, it will be easy for the later paths to arise in sequence, so be energetic and meditate! Thus my master taught. [301]

2) *The cultivation of penetrating insight*

Lord Sakya Paṇḍita said:

> Pointing out the nature of the mind alone is the tradition of the non-Buddhists. To proceed on the Buddhist path it is necessary to point out the nature of appearances to be the mind.[616]

Accordingly, this consists of three topics:

a) Establishing that appearances are the mind
b) Establishing that the mind is illusory
c) Establishing that the illusory [mind] is inexpressible

a) *Establishing that appearances are the mind*

Thus, when the mind is lucidly at rest, think: "The appearances included here in apparent existence, samsara and nirvana—all of this that appears as myself, others, places, and bodies—is nothing except my own mind alone, which just appears as these by virtue of confusion. Not even the slightest external thing is established as true. All of this is the appearances of my own mind."

Reach a decisive conclusion and rest as before in just that state, without grasping at it.

b) *Establishing that the mind is illusory*

One may think: "Is the mind that arises in that way established as true in reality?"

Not even slightly. By the force of a sorcerer's enunciation of mind-altering mantras such as *jaḥ* and *hūṃ* upon mere trivial things such as a goat's horn or a monkey's tail, the people who have been drawn under his spell accept as true those appearances as various horses, cattle, and so forth, as if they were actually present. They experience desire and hatred, and many pleasures and pains, but when they are released from that spell and look around, just those trivial things remain, and not even a trace of horses, cattle, and so forth. Although the things did not actually exist, by virtue of the people's confusion, they experienced those pleasures and pains.

Similarly, the mind has been affected by various habitual propensities without beginning. When the many circumstances for awakening these propensities are encountered, they arise as various appearances—the places, bodies, possessions, enemies, friends, and so forth—although they do not exist and are not established as true from the moment of their arising. In brief, it is like an illusion and a dream. Reflect upon this, reach a decisive conclusion, and rest at ease in just that state, without grasping.

c) *Establishing that the illusory [mind] is inexpressible*

Thus, no one except a buddha is able to know why the various confusing appearances of mind arise in that way. It is taught:

> No one except an omniscient one
> is able to know the diverse aspects
> of the causes of the eye
> in a single peacock feather.[617] [302]

Thus, as one cannot say, "This is the reason," it is inexpressible. Rest in just that state, without grasping.

In brief, the Gendenpa[618] teach, "Calm abiding is like the ocean, and penetrating insight like a small fish," so that in the center of the abiding mind it is necessary to have a stark mindfulness that "this is not true." But in our tradition, when one has penetrating insight into the essence of the mind, if a calm abiding capable of resting upon that is absent, it will become merely intellectual knowledge and one will not remain in that state. Therefore, it is accepted that penetrating insight is like the lamp and calm abiding like the glass that protects the lamp flame from the wind. In brief, one must rest in just that recognition of the very essence of the mind, without any grasping. It is ineffective if grasping ensues. It is taught:

> If grasping ensues, it is not the view.[619]

With these topics, all the Mahayana practices up through those of the Madhyamaka have been presented without any omissions. Thus my master taught.

B. *The production of certainty about the experiences that will arise for an uncommon yogin*

In that way, the yogin of the common Vehicle knows that all of samsara has the nature of suffering and understands that the sentient beings wandering there are one's parents. While cultivating love, compassion, and so forth—the states of mind in which one wishes to liberate sentient beings from suffering—one might wonder, "When will we reach buddhahood?"

It is taught in one's own scriptures that the quickest will linger for three countless eons. When that is heard, this thought may occur: "Although that is marvelous if compared to wandering in samsara forever, nevertheless, if we linger for that long, it is impossible to calculate the various sufferings we will experience during each countless eon. Our parents will suffer too much for too long a period. For buddhahood, does a much quicker method than that exist, which was definitely taught by the Buddha in his great compassion?"

The thought to consult the vast sutras arises. When one looks, one finds that the Vehicle of the Perfections itself contains no statements about methods quicker than three countless eons. But in the sutra known as the *Definitive Commentary on the Intention* or as the *King Bestowing Oral Instructions,* one finds the statement beginning with these words:

> The causal Dharma for those
> inclined toward the cause,
> but...[620]

As soon as one sees this, one thinks, "Statements about a direct path do exist, statements about a method for quick buddhahood known as the Vajrayana, which definitely does not require three countless eons." [303] Confidence is thus gained on the basis of one's own scriptures.

When one asks the vajra master about this point according to the Vajrayana, one hears, "If what is known as the 'Vajrayana' is practiced, depending on the distinctions of good fortune and diligence, a superior person will be able to actualize the citadel of buddhahood in years or months, a mediocre one will do so in this lifetime or at the point of death, and an inferior one will do so in the intermediate state, or within seven lifetimes, or within sixteen lifetimes. That path consists of both ripening initiation and liberating guidance. When practicing it, numerous experiences arise, and one must persevere without rejecting or accepting them."

Hearing this, that common yogin thinks, "I absolutely must practice that path, the experiences will definitely arise in my mindstream, and I will also release them without aversion or attachment."

Similarly, he thinks, "Here I am also practicing the Precious Teaching. When the fifteen experiences—the five sets of three, such as the three dependently arisen connections—arise,[621] and similarly, whatever experiences of samsara and nirvana arise, I will allow them all natural expression, without attachment to the good ones and without viewing the disturbing ones as faults, and certainly be able to release them on the path."

The necessity or benefit of such thinking is that whatever gentle or disturbing experiences arise during the time of the main practice, one will be able to release them without aversion or attachment. Because the abbot Dharmamitra did not present this key point to the Lord of Yogins, it was necessary for the Lord of Yogins to display the manner of not recognizing the experiences. Thus my master taught.

III. Pure Appearance

It is taught:

> For a sugata with the ornamental wheel of inexhaustible enlightened body, speech, and mind, pure appearance occurs.[622]

One might ask, "At the point of reaching perfect buddhahood as the result of such practice, what kind of special qualities exist?"

A sugata who has gone to bliss—the result of the four bodies of enlightenment—through the blissful path of accumulating the two assemblies has inconceivable qualities of inexhaustible enlightened body, speech, and mind. Because this is beautiful and an object of aspiration, it is *ornamental.* Because it is unceasing, it is a *wheel.*

One possessing such qualities has the inconceivable secret of enlightened body and the omnipresence of enlightened body, and the same for enlightened speech and enlightened mind.

The inconceivable secret of enlightened body

The enlightened body of that buddha is just an appearance for each individual disciple, and cannot be calculated to be a particular size. [304] This is taught in the sutra about the bodhisattva Vegadhara calculating the size of the cranial dome of the Buddha's head.

The omnipresence of enlightened body

In brief, a buddha acts for the benefit of sentient beings by appearing in various forms, whatever is appropriate for a particular disciple, from the sublime nirmāṇakāya emanated bodies such as Hevajra and Cakrasaṃvara, to living beings such as a lion or a courtesan, and objects in the environment such as a boat or a bridge.

The inconceivable secret of enlightened speech

No one is able to calculate the extent of the enlightened speech of a buddha by saying, "It is this," as is taught in the sutra that describes how Maudgalyāyana searched for the limit of the enlightened speech of the Buddha.

The omnipresence of enlightened speech

A buddha is able to teach the Dharma in each individual language, from the language of the gods to that of intestinal worms.

The inconceivable secret of enlightened mind

When a buddha rests in equipoise in a worldly meditative concentration, he is seen to be like a worldly person, and so forth. The extent of enlightened mind is within the experiential range of buddhas alone; it cannot be reflected upon by anyone else.

The omnipresence of enlightened mind

Like a myrobalan plum placed in the palm of his hand, a buddha knows the causes and circumstances of all subtle and coarse entities of the environment and its inhabitants, to the roundness of a pea and the sharp point of a thorn, exactly as they are, without mixing them together.

A buddha possesses a collection of such qualities beyond the range of the imagination. So think again and again: "I will quickly reach the citadel of buddhahood endowed with such qualities." Thus my master taught.

How the Supportive Reading Transmissions and Explanations Are Given

During the teaching of the Three Appearances, the reading transmission of the life stories of the lineal masters and the comprehensive explanation of the history of the Dharma is given. As soon as the Three Appearances are completed, the awakening of the enlightenment mind is imparted.

After that, the reading transmission and the explanation of the root text and the commentary of *Twenty Verses on the Vows* are given.[623] Immediately afterward, disciples are accepted. After that, the disciples meditate on accumulation and purification, and the master performs the replenishing of the recitation and the preparation of the vase water.

Concerning the replenishing of the recitation, the Time of the Path is recited in four sessions. The vase is prepared at the end of the sessions. The vase, the Dharma conch, the dhāraṇī thread, and the inner substances are arranged in front of one. Immediately upon entering into the retreat, as soon as the first session of the recitation of the Time of the Path has been completed, the victory vase for the bestowal of the initiation is prepared, and so forth. The action vase is not necessary. [305] Holding the dhāraṇī thread and imagining nectar flowing from the enlightened body of the deity inside the vase, a number of recitations are performed and the offerings and eulogies are made. The deity does not dissolve. For all the sessions other than that one, just clearly visualize the deity inside the vase, without the necessity of the creation ritual, and perform the recitation. When the retreat is over, make the offerings and eulogies to the deity of the vase. After the offering water of the Dharma conch has been offered, the deity dissolves. That vase water is used for the vase water of the water initiation of Akṣobhya during the causal initiation.

After the causal initiation has been completed, the mantra path begins. As soon as the disciples have gathered, and at the end of an appropriate number of recitations of the one hundred-syllable mantra, recite the confession and vow beginning with the words, "I am ignorant and dull."

Then repeat three times:

> I take refuge until enlightenment
> in the Buddha, Dharma,
> and sublime Assembly.

By the merit of my acts
of generosity and so forth,
may I achieve enlightenment
for the benefit of living beings.[624]

This is followed by the four immeasurables,[625] the creation of the protection cakra of Uṣṇīṣa through the recitation of the warning threats of the *bhāyana* mantra, the supplication to the lineal masters and, following the seven-heap mandala, the inner, outer, and secret mandalas composed by Sakya Paṇḍita.[626] During this time, the master dedicates a sacrificial cake to the Dharma protectors.

Then the reading transmission of the *Volume* is given, as far as possible. Then the explanation of the *Fifty Verses on the Master*[627] is given, as far as possible if taught from memory, and just the reading transmission if not taught from memory. Then the explanation of the root downfalls is given, as far as possible. Then the key points of guidance on the indivisibility of samsara and nirvana are given in sequence.

When the mental focusing on the outer mandala has been finished, the path initiation is bestowed. After the explanation of the root downfalls has been completed, the explanation of the creation stage is given, and, together with that, the mental focusing on the body mandala. When the vase initiation has been completed, the initiation-blessing of Nairātmyā should be performed. Then the yogic excercises are taught, and the key points of the secret initiation are gradually imparted. When the explanation of the creation stage has been finished, the explanation of the inner mandala is given. During the initiation of primordial awareness dependent on an embodiment of wisdom, and during the fourth initiation, the blessing of the profound path and the guidance in the key points of how to meditate on it, the blessing of Nāro Khecarī, and the blessings of the outer and inner Virūpa protection, Guru Ratnasambhava, the threefold repetition, and so forth, are given as far as possible. The prediction of practice and the application of the seal of the ten secrets are given. After that, an elaborate ritual feast is held. The next day, an elaborate sacrificial-cake offering for Pañjaranātha and Caturmukha is arranged, and a lavish sacrificial-cake ritual is held as a form of thanksgiving.

These notes on how to give the reading transmission of the sacred commitments, as well as the explanations, have been written according to the oral teachings of the great venerable lord Kangyurwa.[628]

7. Profound Summarizing Notes on the Path Presented as the Three Continua

From the Expansion of the Great Secret Doctrine

Summarizing Notes of Guidance for the Precious Teaching of the "Path with the Result"

The Special Dharma of Khau Drakzongpa

The Practice of the Old Monk Khyentsé

Jamyang Khyentsé Wangchuk (1524–68)

I PRAY AT THE FEET of the essence of all the sugatas of the past, present, and future, the overlord of a hundred spiritual families, the guide in whom the three seats are complete, my spiritual father, holy Vajradhara, Losel Gyatso[629] of matchless kindness. I pray that you bless me to recognize the very essence of the fundamental nature.

The teaching of the path presented as the Three Continua consists of three explanations:

I. The ground—the fundamental nature of the phenomenon of samsara
II. The path—the precise way to meditate
III. The result—the spiritual level of ultimate buddhahood[630]

I. The Ground—the Fundamental Nature of the Phenomenon of Samsara

In the *Guidance Manual for Jochak,* the great venerable lord Drakpa Gyaltsen says that this topic is not presented here because it has been extensively presented in the Three Appearances.[631] As for the meaning, in general the *ground* refers to the person practicing the path. Moreover, by virtue of one's not having recognized the Hevajra of the time of the ground—the very essence of one's own mind free from conceptual elaborations—the mind arises as the confusing appearances of samsara, the various places, bodies, and experiences, even though they are actually nonexistent. The *places* are those of the various sentient beings, from the ground of glowing iron for hell beings, to the celestial palaces of jewels for the gods. The *bodies* appear in various forms, from those of the hell beings with very young skin and very little tolerance to heat and cold, those of the hungry spirits that are like a copper pot tarnished by the sun, those of the animals that have various colors and shapes, and those of the human beings that are male and female with various good and bad physiques, up to those of the gods that have numerous individual different shapes and colors. Dependent on that, the various *experiences* also arise, from the eating of pieces of glowing iron in the hot hells, up to the gods living on nectar, meditative concentration, and so forth. [308] And those are taken to be true.

In brief, actually and indirectly, all sentient beings of the six realms are fit to enter the Vajrayana and are fit to be recipients of the Vajrayana. Furthermore, during the Three Appearances, the explanation that it is necessary to practice the Dharma for liberation from samsara, and that a perfect human body is necessary as the support for that, is just a generalization. Here, dependent on the path of the uncommon Vajrayana, a flawless vajra body—born in Jambudvīpa, born from a womb, and endowed with the six constituents—is definitely necessary as the support for achieving the citadel of unity in one lifetime and with one body. This is because the beings of the three other continents[632] are *merit accumulators,* and the results of their actions done in this lifetime do not ripen during this lifetime, while the beings of Jambudvīpa are *karma accumulators,* and the results of their actions (karma) done in this lifetime are able to ripen during this lifetime itself. As for "endowed with the six constituents," the space, wind, fire, and so forth explained in the *Kālacakra* are complete in most sentient beings. But here it is necessary to be endowed with the father's white constituent having the clear quintessence of the clear essences with the resonance of the three seed syllables[633] and the potency to produce bone, brains, and fat, and to be endowed with the mother's red constituent having the clear quintessence of the clear essences with the resonance of the three seed syllables that produces flesh, blood, and skin. It is necessary to have a body endowed with these six, and with flawless sense organs such as the eyes and flawless limbs such as the arms. This is because in the Vajrayana the key points of the four supporting mandalas[634] are targeted. If the mandala of the channels in the body is damaged, the essential constituents, vital winds, and so forth within them will also not flow straight, which will cause an impediment to the arising of the flawless experiences of the path. That is also the crucial reason that practitioners of secret mantra do not do bloodletting, moxibustion, and so forth. Thus my master taught.

Similarly, Garbharipa says:

> Depending on cause, spiritual family,
> what are to be discarded, and conditions,
> four types of persons are explained.[635]

As for "spiritual family," it is taught:

> Akṣobhya is the deity
> of the yogin who is very black.[636]

And also:

> One with a nine-pronged vajra
> at the base of the ring finger
> belongs to Akṣobhya's
> sublime spiritual family. [309]
> Lord Amitābha's has a lotus,
> and Vairocana's a wheel,
> Ratnasambhava's has a jewel,
> and one of the Karma spiritual family
> has a sword.[637]

Thus, a person who is black or azure and has the shapes of one or many vajras, mainly at the base of the left ring finger, or at various other locations on the body, belongs to Akṣobhya's spiritual family. Similarly, one who is white and has the design of a wheel belongs to Vairocana's spiritual family, one who is yellow and has the design of a jewel belongs to Ratnasambhava's spiritual family, one who is red and has the design of a lotus belongs to Amitābha's spiritual family, and one who is green and has the design of a sword or crossed vajras belongs to Amoghasiddhi's spiritual family.

The five afflictions are "what are to be discarded." Followers of the Vehicle of the Perfections teach that these are to be discarded. However, absolutely nothing in their own nature binds or liberates. The difference is whether or not they are handled with skillful means. Here in the Vajrayana, the ground is not discarded. Therefore, the stronger the firewood of what are to be discarded, the greater the bonfire of the antidote. Similarly, according to the coarseness of the afflictions, the seal of a particular spiritual family is applied, thereby taking them as the path by means of the oral instructions of an excellent master, and the attainments of the particular spiritual family are quickly achieved. One should understand that a practitioner belongs to the spiritual family of Akṣobhya if hatred is predominant, to the spiritual family of Amoghasiddhi if jealousy is predominant, and so forth. Thus, if one practices according to the individual spiritual families, accomplishment will be easy and auspicious. When one belonging to the spiritual family of Vairocana makes glorious Hevajra the path, the manifestations of clear light will appear predominantly white, one will see the color of the enlightened body as white, and so forth. Accomplishment will occur in that way. Thus my master taught.

In regard to "depending on conditions," if a fertile rice or barley seed that is undamaged by frost and hail and has been kept in something like a box comes in contact with the conditions of water and fertilizer, it has the potency to produce a sprout. Similarly, the buddhahood of the time of the ground exists in such a way that, if it comes in contact with the conditions of the oral instructions, the buddhahood of the time of the result can arise.

II. The Path—The Precise Way to Meditate

This consists of three topics:

A. Preserving the sacred commitments as the ground
B. The stages of guiding the person
C. Producing an exceptional certainty, recognizing meditative concentration, and a classification of the boundaries of the path[638] [310]

A. *Preserving the sacred commitments as the ground*

This consists of two parts:

1. Topics concerning the initiation during which the previously unobtained sacred commitments and vows are obtained
2. Topics concerning the sacred commitments that have been obtained and are to be protected without damage

1. *Topics concerning the initiation during which the previously unobtained sacred commitments and vows are obtained*

When a seed comes in contact with the conditions of water and fertilizer, it produces a sprout. Similarly, when the unceasing stream of initiation is bestowed upon the four supporting mandalas of the time of the ground, the dependently arisen connections of the four bodies of enlightenment are brought into alignment. Just the arising of the sprout is not enough. If it is not cared for and nurtured, it will be wasted by drying out, being eaten by animals, and so forth. Similarly, just obtaining the vows during the initiation is not enough. If they are not carefully protected by means of attentive mindfulness, the root of all the attainments will vanish. So they must be protected.

2. *Topics concerning the sacred commitments that have been obtained and are to be protected without damage*

The twenty sacred commitments in connection with the four initiations are what are to be protected. This consists of two topics:

a. Damage to the sacred commitments that draws one into the sufferings of existence
b. Damage to the sacred commitments that will long delay progress on the path

a. *Damage to the sacred commitments that draws one into the sufferings of existence*

The sacred commitment of protection[639] in connection with the vase initiation includes the fourteen root infractions and the eight branch infractions, making twenty-two. Because any one of these creates the cause for birth in vajra hell and other bad places, they are said to "draw one into the sufferings of existence."

b. *Damage to the sacred commitments that will long delay progress on the path*

Damage to any of the remaining nineteen sacred commitments[640] produces negative consequences, such as postponing attainments that would otherwise have been achieved early in life to later in life, or postponing those that would otherwise have been achieved in this life to the intermediate state. It is taught that the commitments must be upheld precisely according to the explanations in the *Rejection of Confusion About the Root Infractions* and its clarification by the great Dakchen Dorjé Chang.[641] The critical reply composed by Paṇchen Shākchok against the criticisms of the *Rejection of Confusion* by the Gendenpa and Jamlingpa is most excellent.[642] Thus my master taught.

B. *The stages of guiding the person*

This consists of three explanations:

1. Meditation on the view of the indivisibility of samsara and nirvana in the causal continuum of the universal ground
2. Meditation on the path in connection with the four initiations concerning the method continuum of the body[643]
3. How the citadel of the four bodies of enlightenment and five types of primordial awareness is obtained[644] [311]

1. *Meditation on the view of the indivisibility of samsara and nirvana in the causal continuum of the universal ground*

The *Root Tantra* says:

> Afterward, perfectly explain precisely that.
> Not the slightest difference exists between
> the embodiment of pristine primordial
> awareness and the thoughts of samsara.[645]

The reason the view is presented immediately after the bestowal of the initiation is that during the initiation—at the point of the descent of the primordial awareness of enlightened body, speech, and mind, or at the point of the third initiation dependent on an actual mudrā consort or one that is an embodiment of primordial awareness—it is possible for the primordial awareness of great bliss to arise for those with acute sense faculties, good channels, and extensive essential constituents. The cultivation of calm abiding and penetrating insight in the context of the Three Appearances is a fine tradition, but it does not completely transcend intellectual knowledge. In the present practice, these qualities arise from within as experiential knowledge. So the previous [practice] is like pure water and this latter is like putting saffron in that water. Thus, when whatever appears arises as great bliss, it prevents wrong conceptions such as that of an individual self. This is necessary, because if all the paths that occur later have been pervaded by this [great bliss], they will also all become the primordial awareness of great bliss alone. Thus my master taught.

This consists of both wisdom—reaching a decisive conclusion by means of the view, and method—practice by means of meditation.

a. *Wisdom—reaching a decisive conclusion by means of the view*

This consists of three topics:

1) A brief presentation by means of the three aspects of coemergence
2) An extensive explication by means of the three key points of practice
3) An extremely extensive explication by means of the three continua

The first of these is the method for introduction, the second is the method for stabilizing that, and the third is the method for perfecting it. Therefore, they are not repetitious. Thus my master taught.

1) *A brief presentation by means of the three aspects of coemergence*

This consists of two topics:

a) The preliminaries
b) The main practice

a) *The preliminaries*

This consists of three topics:

(1) The yoga practice of the mandala to accumulate the assemblies
(2) The meditative recitation of the hundred syllables to purify sins
(3) The guruyoga for the infusion of blessings

(1) *The yoga practice of the mandala to accumulate the assemblies*

Arrange the offerings and so forth in front of the created mandala of five heaps. Prepare the offering mandala with the necessary substances. Seated on a comfortable cushion, take refuge and awaken the enlightenment mind in a suitable way. With the *svabhāva* mantra, clearly imagine that from a state empty of all the environment and its inhabitants a *bhrūṃ* emerges, which becomes a celestial mansion of great liberation as the residence, square, with four gates and archways, and all the complete characteristics. [312] In the center are the seats of a jeweled throne supported by lions, a lotus, a moon, a sun, and the four stacked-up māras. Upon them is the kind root master himself in the form of glorious Hevajra with eight faces and sixteen arms, in union with mother Vajra Nairātmyā. Extending from in front of him, in a clockwise circle, are the lineal masters of the Teaching, from the venerable Vajra Nairātmyā up to the great venerable lord Künpangpa,[646] seated in a clockwise circle like a string of pearls. On the front petal of the lotus are the chosen deities, with the nine deities of glorious Hevajra foremost. To the south are the nirmāṇakāya emanated bodies of the Buddha. To the west is the Dharma in the form of scripture, but in essence realization. To the north is the sangha of bodhisattvas.

Perform the outer offerings, the inner, the secret, and so forth, and offer praises with whatever eulogies one knows. When offering supplications, recite:

> Please complete the favorable conditions of the two assemblies in my mindstream, purify the unfavorable conditions of

> sins and obscurations, and cause the exceptional view of the indivisibility of samsara and nirvana to arise as the result.

In this way, be energetic in offering the mandala of seven heaps, of thirty-seven heaps,[647] the recitation of "One's own offering substances,"[648] and so forth, until the signs occur.

(2) *The meditative recitation of the hundred syllables to purify sins*

For the yoga practice of the hundred syllables, imagine as usual Vajrasattva upon a lotus and moon on the top of one's head. During the recitation, recite each mantra in conjunction with a vividly lucid visualization of nectar flowing like molten crystal from the syllable *hūṃ* on the lotus seat in his heart, passing through the shape of the body and so on, and finally coming down gradually through the top of one's head and so forth. All illnesses, evil spirits, sins, and obscurations exit in a black stream in the form of bloody pus, smoky liquid, and so forth. The vacant spaces are totally filled with pale nectar.

The body will actually feel buoyant and the pure awareness vividly clear, and further signs of the purification of sins will occur actually and in dreams and so forth. It is crucial for the mind to be lucid and single-pointed in visualization.

Also, examine the types of hot and cold illnesses one might have, male and female evil spirits, and so forth, and thus change the visualizations to cool and hot nectar, and so forth, and recite.

(3) *The guruyoga for infusing blessings into the mindstream*

The *Glorious Two-Part Hevajra* says:

> Inexpressible by another,
> coemergence is not found anywhere,
> and is to be known
> by resorting to the means
> of the time of the master,
> and from one's merit.[649] [313]

To reach the citadel of buddhahood in a single lifetime it is necessary to realize the nature of mind, coemergent primordial awareness. That cannot be presented by any scripture, reasoning, or logic. It is taught:

> Free from color, written words,
> qualities, and examples,
> it cannot be spoken of,
> and only vaguely indicated.[650]

And:

> I, Tilopa, have nothing to present.
> Show it to yourself and understand![651]

Not only can it not be described, but wherever it is sought in the environment and its inhabitants, outside or inside one's body, beginning with the flesh, blood, and internal organs, to external mountains and fences, the mind cannot be found because it is not even slightly established with a color, shape, and form.

"In that case," one might ask, "is there no means for realizing it?"

There is. It is taught:

> It is to be known
> by resorting to the means
> of the time of the master,
> and from one's merit.[652]

[The nature of the mind] will be realized on the basis of the means, which is devotion to the master, and the accumulation of the assembly of merit. It is taught:

> As long as the roots of merit
> have not been totally completed,
> that excellent emptiness will not be realized.[653]

The foremost method for the accumulation of merit is to supplicate the master. The *Glorious Guhyasamāja* says:

> Just to massage with oil a single pore of the skin of the vajra master is exceptionally great merit, even more than honoring

> buddhas and bodhisattvas equal in number to the grains of sand in the Ganges river for eons equal in number to the grains of sand in the Ganges river.[654]

The reason for this is that if all the sources for accumulating merit are collected together, they are included in the Three Jewels. And these are all complete in the master, whose body is the essence of the Sangha, whose speech is the essence of the excellent Dharma, and whose mind is the essence of the Buddha. Similarly, all the deities of the complete three seats are included in the master, whose five aggregates are the five conquerors; whose four elements, with extremely pure great bliss as a fifth, are the five mothers; whose internal sensory bases, such as the eyes, are the bodhisattvas; whose external sensory bases, such as form, are the six goddesses; and whose eight great joints and so forth are the ten wrathful beings. For the benefit of those with lesser good fortune, such as ourselves, he displays the form of the aggregates, the constituents, [314] and the sensory bases.

It is taught:

> Why did Vajrasattva himself
> take the form of a teacher?
> Intent upon the goal
> of training sentient beings,
> he displayed an ordinary form.[655]

Therefore, the *Guhyasamāja* says:

> Abandon all other offerings
> and begin perfect offerings
> to the master.
> By pleasing him,
> one will obtain the sublime
> primordial awareness
> of an omniscient one.[656]

Because it is sufficient to practice the best method and discard the inferior methods, if the offerings to the circle of the mandala and all offerings to the gods, spirits, and so forth are abandoned, and one is diligent in offerings to the master at all times and in all forms, the "primordial awareness of an omniscient one," the citadel of perfect buddhahood, will be reached. Nāgārjuna mentions the reason:

> If someone falls
> from the peak of Mount Meru,
> even though they think they will not fall,
> they will fall.
>
> If beneficial transmission is obtained
> by the kindness of the master,
> even though one thinks
> one will not be liberated,
> one will be liberated.[657]

"In that case," one might wonder, "is a long period needed to reach that attainment?"

No. The *Sañcārya,* an explanatory tantra of the *Cakrasaṃvara,* teaches:

> I bow to the lotus beneath the feet of
> the vajra master whose body is like a jewel,
> and by whose kindness great bliss
> arises in a single instant.[658]

By the kindness of the master, the coemergent primordial awareness of great bliss arises in an instant. For example, a wish-fulfilling jewel is the most exceptional thing in the world, but if it is only able to grant happiness and joy in this life, and cannot grant even the liberations of a śrāvaka and pratyekabuddha in the next life, it goes without saying that it cannot grant the citadel of a vajra holder on the thirteenth spiritual level. In contrast, the master is able to bestow such a citadel in this lifetime and at other times. So nothing in the world may be greater [than a wish-fulfilling jewel] as an example, but the master is even more exceptional than that. Similarly, the *Saṃvarodaya* says:

> The master is the Buddha,
> the master is the Dharma,
> and likewise the master is the Sangha.

> The master is the creator of everything.
> The master is glorious Heruka.[659]

The *Samputa* says:

> Learn these inner divisions
> directly from a master.
> Mantra and attainments
> cannot be accomplished
> from sentient beings who are
> less than masters.[660] [315]

The *Vajrapañjara* says:

> Displaying as a teacher,
> he is prostrated to by the buddhas.
> Know this one to be greater
> than our father and mother.[661]

"In that case," one might think, "is the master greater than even those chosen deities, buddhas, and so forth?"

The master and the buddhas are no different in terms of renunciation and realization, but the master is greater in terms of kindness. Although buddhas equal to the number of atoms in the universe reside upon a single dust mote, at this time when much bad karma has been accumulated, we do not have the good fortune to actually see their bodies. We do not actually hear their speech. Due to this situation, it is not possible for the primordial awareness of their minds to precisely enter us. Because the master displays a form corresponding to our good fortune, we actually see his body, hear and practice the Dharma he teaches, gradually cleanse the two obscurations, gradually complete the two assemblies, and are able to reach the citadel of buddhahood.

For example, even if the three conditions of a cloudless sky, hot sunlight, and dry tinder are present, if one does not have something like a fire crystal or a mirror to focus the light, no matter how hot the sun is, it will not be able to start a fire in the tinder. When the light is focused with something like a crystal, a fire will start in just an instant. Similarly, no matter how great the compassion of the buddhas, it is not possible for their primordial awareness to actually enter into sentient beings whose mindstreams have not been purified. By offering supplications to the master as the embodiment of all the buddhas, the blessings enter quickly. With this in mind, lord Sakya Paṇḍita says:

> Even though sunbeams are very hot,
> without a fire crystal a fire will not occur.
> Similarly, without a master, the blessings
> of the buddhas will not occur.[662]

Not only is it explained in that way in the scriptures of the Vajrayana, it is also taught in the Vehicle of the Perfections. The *Condensed Verses on the Perfection of Wisdom* say:

> The conquerors sublimely endowed
> with all good qualities have taught,
> "The buddhas and the Dharma
> depend on the spiritual friend."[663]

And also:

> Always rely on expert masters.
> If you ask why, it is because an expert's
> good qualities come from that.[664]

And also:

> As groups of the sick rely
> on a physician to be healed,
> so rely without distraction
> on a spiritual friend.[665]

And the *Sutra of the Salty River*[666] teaches:

> When the final five-hundred-year period occurs,
> I will take the form of the teacher. [316]
> Think that he is me, and awaken
> devotion to him at that time!

Similarly, this is often said in all the sutras and tantras, and also thus commented upon by all authentic commentators. In few words, but with extensive meaning, the Lord of Yogins says:

> The profound path of the master.[667]

Vajraghaṇṭā says:

> I will explain the stages of the blessing
> concealed in the *Cakrasaṃvara,*
> which arises in an instant
> by just the blessing of the master.[668]

Saraha says:

> When what the master
> has said enters the heart,
> it is like seeing a treasure
> resting in the palm of the hand.[669]

In brief, all the authentic realized experts who have appeared in India and Tibet have unanimously said this. In the Vajrayana tradition, the awakening of meditative concentration that has not arisen, the enhancement of what has arisen, the removal of impediments, and the stabilizing of meditative concentration all depend solely on the guruyoga. Even at the point when the citadel of ultimate and perfect buddhahood has been actualized, to not abandon the master is maintained as a sacred commitment of primordial awareness, and so forth. In brief, the master is taught to be foremost during all of the cause, the path, and the result. Thus my master taught.

How to offer supplications

Sit on a comfortable cushion in the meditation posture. Take refuge and awaken the enlightenment mind with a composed and certain mind. From a state purified into emptiness by the *svabhāva* mantra, visualize that the area where one stays becomes a square celestial mansion with four gates, ornaments, and archways, created from the manifestations of a pure, lucid, and nondual primordial awareness. In a form with all dimensions and characteristics totally complete, it is extremely tall and spacious, equal to the extent of the three-thousandfold world systems, with its jeweled pinnacle resplendent in the world of Brahmā.

Inside that, in the sky directly in front of the point between one's eyebrows, the kind root master himself, the essence of all the buddhas of the three times, is present in the form of glorious Hevajra, who is pleased with one. He has a body that is blue in color, with eight faces, sixteen arms, and four legs. He is joined together with mother Vajra Nairātmyā upon the seats of a jeweled throne supported by eight great lions, a variegated lotus, a moon, a sun, and the four stacked-up māras. [317] At his forehead, upon a full white moon mandala, is a white *oṃ,* the nature of the body vajra of all the buddhas of the three times. At his throat, in the center of a red lotus with eight petals, is a red *āḥ,* the essence of their speech vajra. At his heart, upon a sun, is a blue *hūṃ,* the essence of their mind vajra. Visualize these all like images appearing in a mirror, clear without and clear within, having the nature of light.

A mass of multicolored light and light rays radiates, floating out from the *hūṃ* at the master's heart. It fills all the buddha fields of the ten directions, such as the immense buddha fields above, Akaniṣṭha and so forth, and in a similar way, those of the eight directions and below. Stimulated by these light rays, the root and lineal masters of the three times residing in those locations (with those of the transmission of the Teaching foremost), along with the chosen deities, buddhas, bodhisattvas, spiritual heroes, ḍākinīs, Dharma protectors and guardians, and primordial-awareness aspects, all arrive from every direction as though they had been called, clustered together like a group of great clouds. They dissolve and are absorbed into all portions of the root master's body, from the crown of the head to the toenails, like snow falling on a hot stone, or water seeping into sand. Imagine that he is the combined essence of all the sources of refuge.

Offerings to him

The outer offering is to imagine that the five customary sensory offerings—created from the substance of one's body, possessions, and all basic virtue accumulated throughout the three times—emanate and are offered to fill the sky. The excellent master accepts them as his own, and his mindstream is pleased by the primordial awareness of great bliss.

The inner offering is to imagine the emanation of countless skull cups filled with the nectar of the five meats and five nectars that have the nature of the five types of primordial awareness and are created from the substance of one's body, possessions, and so forth. This is consumed by the vajra tube of the master's tongue, the skull cups filled with nectar dissolve into his body, and he is pleased by the primordial awareness of great bliss.

Similarly, the secret offering is to imagine that beautiful and enticing mudrā consorts, such as the conch-bearing lady, the lotus lady, and so forth, emanate and fill the sky. The master is pleased by their kisses, their embraces, joining with them, and so forth. [318]

Everything like that—what is to be offered, the act of offering, the offering substances, and so forth—is nothing but one's mind alone appearing in various forms, without anything established apart from the mind. To rest the mind for as long as it will remain in the inexpressible state of united lucidity and emptiness is the offering of reality.

The ground of purification is the respectful honors that have been lavishly offered to mundane rulers and so forth, and the requests made for a desired result if they are pleased. Similarly, imagine that due to the complete presentation of the four offerings, the mind of the excellent master is delighted by the primordial awareness of great bliss, and that he immediately bestows the coemergent primordial awareness of great bliss.

The eulogies

Praise him with whatever eulogies one knows that are stated in the immaculate tantras, such as these:

> I bow to the lotus beneath the feet of
> the vajra master whose body is like a jewel,
> and by whose kindness great bliss
> arises in a single instant.[670]

And:

> The master is the Buddha,
> the master is the Dharma,
> and likewise the master is the Sangha.
> The master is the creator of everything.
> The master is glorious Heruka.[671]

And:

> I prostrate to the masters,
> whose bodies embody all the buddhas,
> who are the very essence of the vajra holders,
> and who are the root of the Three Jewels.[672]

And:

> The body of the master
> is immutable body.
> The speech of the master
> is unceasing speech.
> The mind of the master
> is unconfused mind.
> I prostrate to the body, speech,
> and mind of the master.[673]

With intense devotional longing for the master's mind and one's own mind to blend together, and for the master to approach and dissolve into oneself, single-pointedly aim the attention, the eyes, and the vital winds directly at the master's heart or at the point between his eyebrows, and without allowing the mind to wander, recite this about a hundred times:

> I supplicate the precious master, the essence of all the buddhas of the three times. Please bless my mindstream.

Recite this an appropriate number of times:

> I supplicate the excellent master, the embodiment of all the root and lineal masters. Please bless my mindstream.
> I supplicate the excellent master, the embodiment of all the chosen deities. Please bless my mindstream.
> I supplicate the excellent master, the embodiment of all the buddhas. Please bless my mindstream.
> I supplicate the excellent master, the embodiment of all the excellent Dharma. Please bless my mindstream.
> I supplicate the excellent master, the embodiment of all the Sangha. Please bless my mindstream.

I supplicate the excellent master, the embodiment of all the ḍākas and ḍākinīs and Dharma protectors. Please bless my mindstream.

Offer these supplications an appropriate number of times:

I supplicate great unified Vajradhara. Please bless my mindstream.
I supplicate venerable Vajra Nairātmyā. Please bless my mindstream.
I supplicate the teacher, the Lord of Yogins, glorious Virūpa. Please bless my mindstream.
I supplicate the great adept Eastern Kāṇha. Please bless my mindstream.
I supplicate the great adept Ḍāmarupa. Please bless my mindstream.
I supplicate the great Avadhūtīpa, who renounced duality.[674] Please bless my mindstream.
I supplicate the excellent expert and realized master Gayadhara. Please bless my mindstream.
I supplicate Drokmi Lotsāwa Shākya Yeshé. Please bless my mindstream.
I supplicate the master Setön Künrik. Please bless my mindstream.
I supplicate the master Shangtön Chöbar. Please bless my mindstream.
I supplicate Künga Nyingpo, the venerable lord of Sakya, the glorious master of great kindness. Please bless my mindstream.
I supplicate the precious teacher Sönam Tsemo. Please bless my mindstream.
I supplicate the precious venerable lord Drakpa Gyaltsen. Please bless my mindstream. [319]
I supplicate the great Dharma lord Sakya Paṇḍita. Please bless my mindstream.
I supplicate the protector of living beings, the Dharma king Phakpa. Please bless my mindstream.
I supplicate Shang Könchok Palwa. Please bless my mindstream.
I supplicate the great adept, the great Drakphukpa. Please bless my mindstream.
I supplicate omniscient Sönam Gyaltsen. Please bless my mindstream.

I supplicate the Dharma lord Palden Tsultrim. Please bless my mindstream.[675]

I supplicate the great adept Buddhashrī. Please bless my mindstream.

I supplicate Dorjé Chang Künga Sangpo. Please bless my mindstream.

I supplicate Könchok Gyaltsen, in essence Cakrasaṃvara. Please bless my mindstream.

I supplicate the venerable lord Lodrö Gyaltsen Palsangpo, lord of all spiritual families. Please bless my mindstream.

I supplicate the venerable lord Dorjé Chang Künsang Chökyi Nyima Loden Sherap Künga Gyaltsen Palsangpo. Please bless my mindstream.[676]

I supplicate the root master of great kindness. Please bless my mindstream.

Precious master, bless my mind to turn toward the Dharma.
Bless me to take the Dharma as the path.
Bless me that confusion about the path is removed.
Bless me that confusion arises as primordial awareness.
Bless me that no traces of irreligious feelings arise.
Bless me to understand that whatever appears is the mind.
Bless me to realize that mental appearance is illusory.
Bless me to realize that the fundamental nature is inexpressible.

In brief, for the benefit of all sentient beings equal to space, bless me to reach in this very lifetime the citadel of the overlord, great Heruka, the quintessence of the four enlightened bodies of unity.

Bless me to reach it very quickly.
Bless me to reach it right now.
Bless me to reach it in this very spot.

Bless me that no unfavorable circumstances or impediments occur.

Please make all fortunate circumstances effortlessly and spontaneously present.

Again, relentlessly offer the supplication beginning, "I supplicate the precious master, the essence of all the buddhas of the three times,"[677] not just mouthing the words, but supplicating from the bottom of one's heart and the marrow of one's bones, until the hairs of one's body flutter, tears gush from one's eyes, one's attention is riveted on the master, and body and mind cannot bear it.

Similarly, it is also fitting to offer supplications by means of the *Ever Excellent*[678] supplication to the lineage of the Path with the Result, with insistent supplications to the root master, and by calling to the master from afar. These may be recited in a steady tone of voice, expressed in a great roar, or in other ways; in brief, by whatever means are most appealing. Without lingering in the various experiences, practice without distinguishing day from night. Through these actions, the coemergent nature of the mind will appear from within in a naturally arisen way through the blessing of the master. [320] Whether the following spiritual practices arise or do not arise depends on this, so practice single-mindedly! Thus my master taught.

The four initiations are also complete here. The indivisible blending together of the master's body and one's own body, and the entry of the blessing of his body, are the vase initiation. The blending together of his speech and one's own speech is the secret initiation. The blending together of his mind and one's own mind is the initiation of primordial awareness dependent on an embodiment of wisdom. The indivisible blending together of one's own three aspects and the master's body, speech, and mind is the fourth initiation.

Finally, seal the session by means of pristine dedication prayers such as these:

> In all lifetimes may I never be apart
> from the perfect master,
> enjoy the glory of the Dharma, and,
> after fully completing the qualities
> of the spiritual levels and paths,
> quickly reach the citadel of Vajradhara.[680]

And:

> By this virtue, just like young Sudhana,
> may I in all lifetimes please the excellent master
> who is like an ocean of good qualities.[681]

During all times between sessions, whatever apparent things[682] are seen, do not examine their forms. When looking at their essence, think, "It is naked emptiness. I have met the body vajra of my master as appearance and emptiness indivisible. Bless me!"

And think, "All sounds that are arising and will arise are the speech of the master."

Whatever thought arises in one's mind, look at its essence and think, "I have met the mind vajra of the master. Bless me!"

In brief, from a vivid state of birthless emptiness as the fundamental nature, and brilliant unceasing devotion as its radiance, energetically pass the time honoring the master with prostrations, circumambulations, and so forth. Thus my master taught.

b) *The main practice*

In the tradition of the Explication for the Assembly, guidance is not given in the three aspects of coemergence or the extensive explication of the Three Continua. When the teaching is done in that way, no decisive conclusion will be reached about the mind. So those practicing in that tradition may listen to the Path with the Result many times; but without anything to focus the attention upon during meditation, nothing happens except that they say, "When do we receive mahāmudrā?" and then go to the place of some foolish "realized one" who does not know anything, and sit with gaping mouths. [321]

The reason guidance is not provided is that, for those disciples fit to be included in the Explication for the Assembly, the profound key points are concealed and left vague. Nevertheless, some in the tradition of the Explication for the Assembly nowadays say that they eliminate doubts about the three aspects of coemergence and then meditate on the three key points of practice. They have even modified texts. This is in obvious contradiction to the great venerable lord Drakpa Gyaltsen's *Commentary on the Indivisibility of Samsara and Nirvana* and his *Guidance Manual for Jochak,* where the statement "Meditate until reaching a decisive conclusion about the mind" is written after each section, and also contradicts lord Sakya Paṇḍita's list in the *Catalogue of the Guiding Instructions* and the *Clarification of the Meaning Through Symbols,*[683] where these are counted in the sequence of practice.

In our tradition of the Explication for Disciples, a decisive conclusion is reached about the mind and an introduction made on the basis of these three root aspects of coemergence. The meaning of that introduction is stabilized and enhanced by means of the three key points of practice and brought to perfection by means of the extensive explication of the three continua. Therefore, the key points of guidance are provided for them all. Thus my master taught.

(1) *The three aspects of causal coemergence*

At the start of the practice, begin by taking refuge, awakening the enlightenment mind, and performing the guruyoga. After resting in inexpressible pure awareness, think: "I have received and am meditating on the Precious Teaching."

From within that teaching, the view of the indivisibility of samsara and nirvana must be cultivated in the mind. If this mind is not recognized, the guidance will never be effective even if the master and the oral instructions are most exceptional, as when a blacksmith is expert but cannot make anything without materials. If one does not discover one's mind by oneself, no one else is going to find it, so turn the attention inward and search for the mind. Think: does one have a mind or not? If not, one is no different from an inanimate object. But a flowing liveliness is present now. This is it. As it is, does it have the form of samsara or of nirvana? If it has the form of samsara, is it inanimate, cognitive, or a nonassociated conditioning factor? Similarly, what kind of shape and color does it have? In brief, where is it among the environment and its inhabitants—inside and outside of the body, from the top of one's head to the soles of the feet, from the flesh, bones, entrails, and vital organs, to the external mountains, fences, and buildings? Repeatedly search, over and over. [322]

When one has not discovered it, imagine the master in the sky in front as before. Offer intense supplications until one's body is exhausted. The master dissolves into oneself. Search again as before. Meditate until a decisive certainty arises and one thinks, "My mind is like this."

By searching in that way, nothing is to be discovered such as the mind being established as a form or shape, but this mere flow, mere awareness, mere dexterity of the mind will be recognized. That is called "lucidity, the characteristic of the mind," which is seeing one third of the qualities of the mind.

When looking at the essence of that lucidity, its distinct presence as emptiness, not being established as anything, is "emptiness, the nature of the mind."

Thus, the lucidity not discovered by searching is itself emptiness. The empty searcher itself is lucidity. These cannot be separated by saying, "This is lucidity and this is emptiness." This is called "unity, or the inexpressible, or the uncontrived, which is the essence of the mind."

The mind that is just that, united lucidity and emptiness beyond all theoretical knowledge and all possibility of expression, is called "the Hevajra of the time of the ground," "the indivisibility of samsara and nirvana," and "the buddhahood of the time of the ground."

How to practice [the three aspects of causal coemergence]

When looking at one's mind from a state in which the master's mind and one's own mind are indivisibly blended together, one should recognize the mere lucidity, the mere awareness, the mere flickering presence, the mere flow, the mere dexterity, and rest in that state for as long as one can remain without clinging. When a new thought suddenly arises, examine where the thought first came from, and in relation to just what object, at what time, and in what form it arose. Discovering nothing means that it is empty of a cause for arising. Examining where and in what way it endures in between [arising and cessation]—inside or outside of one's body, in the environment and its inhabitants, in samsara or nirvana—one finds that it does not endure anywhere and is not established as anything, and is therefore empty of an essence that endures in between. Because it cannot be seen to "cease or be exhausted at such and such point at the end," it is empty of the result of cessation at the end. Recognizing it to be emptiness free from the three—arising, duration, and cessation—serenely rest in unfabricated pure awareness.

In general, meditation is either resting meditation or analytical meditation. [323] Here it is analysis and meditation by means of discriminatory wisdom. If that has been done, but it has not worked exactly, offer supplications to the master as before. Thinking that the master's mind and one's own mind have indivisibly blended together, serenely rest in just that state without clinging. This is resting meditation. Practice those two alternately.

When meditating in that way, it is possible that a misconception may arise. One might think, "All the phenomena of samsara and nirvana are included in the mind. If the mind is united lucidity and emptiness in that way, what about all these chaotic external appearances?"

To remove that doubt, both the mode of existence of all phenomena in samsara and the mode of their appearance are considered.

Concerning the mode of existence, it is taught:

> From natural lucidity, emptiness,
> and their unity,...[684]

As explained previously, the united lucidity and emptiness of the mind is Hevajra, the buddhahood of the time of the ground, but it is not recognized to be so, and precisely that, by virtue of its coemergence in the context of the mode of appearance, arises as the various places, bodies, and experiences of samsara. The mode by which this arises is taught in the following lines:

> ...arise the afflictions, vital winds,
> syllables, channels, constituents,
> illnesses, evil spirits, and coarseness,
> all of which are threefold,
> making up the twenty-seven aspects
> of causal coemergence.[685]

In that way, the united lucidity and emptiness of the mind is the Hevajra of the time of the ground. But one does not recognize it to be so, and precisely that is called "coemergent lack of awareness," which is ignorance. Thus, not recognizing it as the inexpressible, one clings to it as an "I" or a self. When a self is established in that way, it is natural for an "other" to arise in reference to it. And so both desire and hatred arise, which are called "attachment to self and hatred toward others." These three root afflictions are called "the afflictions of affliction." Pride and greed are their qualities, jealousy their activity. Dividing from these are the six root afflictions, the twenty secondary afflictions, and so forth, the eighty-four thousand afflictions that are the incompatible opposites of the eighty-four thousand articles of Dharma. Dividing from these, the inexpressible avenues or pockets of the afflictions are established.

In that way, when the mental afflictions are established, the mobilizing vital winds also arise. When attachment to unity as true ensues, ignorance arises. The vital wind that mobilizes [ignorance] is the pause. [324] From confusion about lucidity, desire arises. The vital wind is inhalation. From confusion about emptiness, hatred arises. The vital wind is exhalation. Dividing from these are the five ground, or root, vital winds, the ten branch vital winds, and the 21,600 vital action winds. Finally, these divide until they are equal in number to all the thoughts.

Concerning the "syllables," the actual syllables are the tones of expression, but the channels in crooked shapes that are the supports for those are also referred to as syllables. For example, the sound of an instrument such as a lute or a trumpet comes from a person's fingering or breath, but because the lute or the trumpet is the support for that sound, one refers to "its sound." Furthermore, the short *a* in the form of a vertical line, which is the clear essence of the drops first obtained from the mother, is created as the first of all the syllables. *Oṃ* and *hūṃ* come from it. *A ka ca ṭa ta pa ya śa* come from those. Dividing from those are the vowels such as *a* and the consonant-syllables such as *ka*. And *puja, ou, a,* and so forth. These are created until they are finally countless.

Concerning the meaning of the "channels," when a sentient being of the intermediate state becomes attached to a womb at the point of conception, by the force of karma it sees the parents copulating, even though nonexistent. If it will be born male, it is conceived with hatred for the father and desire for the mother, and if it will be born female, with intense desire and hatred the opposite of that. It enters through the mouth or anus of the father, and together with his white constituent (the clear quintessence of the clear essences with the resonance of the three seed syllables), it exits through his vajra into the mother's lotus. When it blends together with the mother's red constituent (the clear quintessence of the clear essences with the resonance of the three seed syllables) and enters in between the white and red constituents, it dissolves into clear light. It does not recognize that [clear light] for what it is, and precisely that becomes a coemergent lack of awareness, forming the central channel about the size of a hair from a horse's tail split a hundred times. Then, when attachment to that lucidity as true ensues, the lalanā appears. Then, when attachment to emptiness as true ensues, the rasanā appears. Then, corresponding to the gradually increasing coarseness of the thoughts of subject and object, the four cakras appear, as well as the channels in which the enlightenment mind flows—the thirty-two channels, the seventy-two thousand tiny channels, and finally the mass of channels equal in number to the thirty-five million body hairs.

Concerning the "constituents," the *subtle* are the clear quintessence of the clear essences of the constituents, and both the white and red constituents, making three. Dividing from these are the five nectars, the thirty-two constituents that produce the teeth, nails, and so forth, [325] and finally those forming with the nature of light at all the hair follicles, as on the throat of a cuckoo or like the dew on the tip of a blade of grass.

Concerning "coarseness," after the body has been gradually created in that way in the womb for a period such as nine or ten months, when the time for birth arrives it is propelled by the vital action winds, is born, and this kind of coarse body called "the supporting container of the sense organs" appears as an object seen by everyone. The syllables and vital winds become coarser, and coarse speech arises as the various tones of the voice. Coarseness of mind refers to the countless thoughts that engage the confusing appearances of samsara. Thus my master taught.

Concerning "illnesses" and "evil spirits," when that kind of coarseness has been established in such a way, the illnesses and evil spirits that create disease in the body and suffering in the mind arise, even though nonexistent. Male evil spirits, female evil spirits, and nāga evil spirits make three. Hybrids of two of those and hybrids of three make five. Dividing from these, the fifteen great evil spirits that afflict children, the eighty thousand types of impeding spirits, the 360 types of evil spirits, and so forth arise. Illnesses of the blood and bile, the vital winds, and the phlegm make three. Combinations of two of those, and of three of those, make five. Dividing from these, countless types arise, such as the 404 types of illness.

In that way, as an umbrella held aloft in the sky casts a shadow on the ground, so also when the very essence of the triad of the lucidity, emptiness, and unity of the mind is not recognized, and attachment to lucidity as true ensues, exaggeration occurs. Taking emptiness to be nothingness, denigration occurs. Concerning unity, attachment [to lucidity and emptiness] as separate occurs. By virtue of this, while [lucidity and emptiness] are not even slightly established, these twenty-seven occur: one set of eight from confusion about lucidity, one set of eight from confusion about emptiness, and one set of eight from confusion about their unity (making twenty-four) together with the three of lucidity, emptiness, and their unity. Thus my master taught.

How to practice

After blending one's mind with the master, think: "All the phenomena included in apparent existence, samsara and nirvana, are not established outside of one's mind. In particular, this arising of the confusing appearances of samsara—the various places, bodies, and experiences—arises from confusion about the triad of the lucidity, emptiness, and unity of the mind."

Extend this as presented previously, reaching the decisive conclusion that each of these phenomena are lucidity, emptiness, and their unity, and rest in the inexpressible state. [326]

Also, if all the phenomena of samsara are summarized, they can be included in those twenty-seven. If these are also condensed, they can be included in the three poisons. Those also condense into lucidity, emptiness, and their unity. As for lucidity and emptiness, because emptiness is not discarded by lucidity and lucidity is not discarded by emptiness, they are united. The essence is inexpressible. Serenely rest precisely upon that, without clinging.

Again, offer supplications, rest evenly, and so forth, as before.

It is taught:

> If spontaneity is correctly realized in that way,
> the characteristics of cause and result
> in samsara and nirvana are understood,
> and after also correctly realizing all
> the outer and inner dependently arisen connections,
> absolutely all illnesses
> and evil spirits will be destroyed.[686]

Furthermore, saying that appearances are the mind is not significant just because it is a king's decree or in the scriptures.[687] Through such an introduction into how appearances are the mind, a realization that appearances are the mind will occur. On the basis of this realization, all the characteristics of cause and result, in which samsara is the ground of purification and nirvana the result of purification, are correctly recognized. By virtue of that recognition, a realization of all the outer and inner dependently arisen connections will occur. On the basis of that, all the sufferings and thoughts of samsara evaporate and, unoppressed by them, all appearances will definitely arise as the primordial awareness of great bliss. Therefore, this introduction to appearances as the mind is a great advantage.

If people are introduced to just the mind, things may seem fine while pursuing that practice alone, but when objects are encountered, many people are unable to cope with the circumstances. Nowadays, when those who have stayed in the mountains for many years and engaged in incomparable meditation arrive home, they behave with desire, hatred, and greed that is up to a hundred times greater than that of ordinary people. The descent of these people into a severely disturbed state is due to not having been introduced to appearances as the mind. Lord Sakya Paṇḍita teaches:

> Pointing out the nature of the mind alone is the tradition of the non-Buddhists.[688]

How could mahāmudrā and so forth be the actual tradition of the non-Buddhists?[689] Nevertheless, if compared to a teaching such as this, they are somewhat less profound. Thus my master taught.

When it has thus been realized [that appearances are the mind], and an illness of blood and bile occurs, since it is a confusing appearance arisen from attachment to lucidity as true, first clearly focus on the pain and so forth of that illness, and identify it as lucidity. Then investigate the source of those two [illnesses], and, when it is not discovered, rest in that state, thereby applying the seal of emptiness to lucidity. [327] When these are united, the illness will vanish without a trace.

Similarly, for an illness of the vital winds, first reach the decisive conclusion that the illness is emptiness. Then clearly focus on the form of that pain and rest in just that state, which is the seal of lucidity on emptiness.

An illness of phlegm is a confusing appearance arisen from clinging to unity as true. Therefore, first identify [the illness] as lucidity. Apply the seal of emptiness to that. Apply the seal of lucidity to [emptiness]. This is the conjunction of three seals or the application of the seal of unity to unity.

Similarly, by also practicing like that in regard to the three evil spirits, one will be naturally freed from all illnesses and evil spirits.

Mainly, as explained before, hope rests in the blessing of the master alone. If one is able to supplicate the master from the bottom of one's heart and the marrow of one's bones, without distinguishing day from night, realization will emerge from within in a naturally arisen way. It will not come from a quick approximation of the general meaning based on vague explanations found in random texts. While even that will unravel samsara, in order to reach the citadel of unity, realization must arise in the mindstream. As for how it arises, lord Sakya Paṇḍita says:

> My mahāmudrā is a primordial awareness
> that comes from initiation,

and a naturally arisen primordial awareness
that comes from the meditative concentration
of the two stages.[690]

In this way, for those of truly superior faculties, the nonconceptual primordial awareness of the path of seeing, up to that of the thirteenth spiritual level of a vajra holder, may arise during the initiation. But for those of medium or lesser faculties, the illustrative and symbolic primordial awareness may arise during the descent of primordial awareness, the third initiation, and so forth. To sustain its continuity, when the yogas of creation and completion are correctly practiced from a state in which the sacred commitments and the vows are maintained as the ground, the coemergent primordial awareness of the nature of the mind will nakedly emerge from within in a naturally arisen way. Because this is not analytically established through reasoning that it is free from single or multiple nature, or mentally created like a conceptual theory, it is called "naturally arisen primordial awareness."

In brief, reach a decisive conclusion and be certain that the master is the essence of all the buddhas of the three times. Offer supplications with intense force. Through becoming accustomed to precisely this—resting without clinging in a state where the master and one's mind are blended together—at some point, conceptual marks and thoughts will all calmly fade away. [328] This is *calm abiding.* At that point the present thoughts of subject and object will cease, and it will be impossible not to nakedly see the very essence of genuine mind. Thus a meditative concentration of united calm abiding and penetrating insight will arise in the mindstream.

Furthermore, of the three flawed and the two flawless types of calm abiding and penetrating insight mentioned by lord Sakya Paṇḍita in the *Reply to the Questions of Gomchen Truma,* this is the flawless, about which he said:

The two are calm abiding,
which is a complete calming
of conceptual marks and thoughts,
and penetrating insight,
which is a unity of bliss and emptiness.[691]

"A unity of bliss and emptiness" means that genuine mind free from all the sufferings of samsara is bliss; its essence is emptiness; and these are united. This is the point.

Therefore, although that calm abiding and penetrating insight in the context of the Three Appearances is obviously excellent, "appearances are the mind" and so forth are merely established through reasoning. Because they occur here in a naturally arisen way dependent on exceptional methods, this is very different. In summary, all the spiritual practices of the unexcelled Vajrayana must be for the arising of illustrative and symbolic primordial awareness. Thus my master taught.

(2) *The three aspects of path coemergence*

It is taught:

> Preceded by ripening initiation,
> the three aspects of the practiced path
> are creation, completion,
> and primordial awareness.[692]

Thus, when the very essence of lucidity, emptiness, and their unity is not recognized, the various places and bodies of samsara arise. Preceded by an authentic ripening initiation, the path for purifying precisely that is threefold: the creation stage that takes lucidity as the path; the completion stage that takes emptiness as the path; and, arisen from meditating on those two, the primordial awareness that takes their unity as the path. Each of these is threefold.

Because lucidity also has united lucidity and emptiness as its quintessence, vividly lucid meditation on the supporting mandala and supported deities as the creation stage (which is the method for targeting its key points) is taking lucidity as the path. From gathering the three realms—the environment and its inhabitants—into the protection cakra, to resting in a state where even the *nāda*[693] is not visualized, is taking emptiness as the path. Arising as the deity from that state, as a fish leaps from the water, is taking unity as the path.

Similarly, the completion stage also consists of three topics: complete body, complete speech, and complete mind. [329] Meditation on the three channels and five cakras, and union endowed with the three perceptions, is lucidity. Its nature is emptiness. The indivisibility of [emptiness and lucidity] is unity.

The primordial awareness arisen from those [two stages] consists of countless paths, such as the fifteen—the five sets of three.[694] If these are condensed, the yogin and the environment and its inhabitants lucid as the deity is the nature of lucidity as the characteristic. Clearly resting in emptiness, its nature not established as anything, like the space of the sky, is the meditative concentration of emptiness as the nature. Any of the manifestations of clear light, such as the five signs of smoke and so forth, and the five signs of the signs,[695] are the experience of unity as the essence.

In brief, the united lucidity and emptiness of the mind is the Hevajra of the time of the ground, but is not recognized to be so, which produces these confusing appearances of samsara. When these are purified by the united lucidity and emptiness of such a purifying path, the arising of an experience of united lucidity and emptiness is the Hevajra of the path. Reach a decisive conclusion and be certain that precisely that is the Hevajra of the time of the result, residing on the thirteenth spiritual level of a vajra holder. That this should be taken as the path is mentioned in the saying, "If engaged with attachment, the path is infallible due to the connection." Because a moon exists in the sky, a moon is reflected within the water. Similarly, the appearances of the time of the path arise by the blessing of the presence of the buddhahood of the time of the result, and so it is said that practitioners of secret mantra "take the result as the path."

In brief, by meditating in this way, the thoughts of samsara thin out more and more and experiential appearance becomes more and more lucid. Precisely that transforms into the primordial awareness of the time of the result and, when the incidental stains within the universal ground are purified into space and the very essence of united lucidity and emptiness is nakedly seen, that is the *result.* This is also the meaning of the indivisibility of the three: ground, path, and result.

Of the two traditions (of accepting that the ground of purification and what is to be purified are different, and accepting that those two are one ground distinguished by different facets), the tradition of the Sakyapa itself is the latter. Because it is the ground from which the stains are purified, it is the ground of purification. Because the incidental stains within it must be purified, it is also what is to be purified. Thus my master taught.

(3) *The three aspects of resultant coemergence*

It is taught:

> Lucidity is the nirmāṇakāya emanated body,
> emptiness is the dharmakāya reality body,
> and their unity is the sambhogakāya enjoyment body.[696] [330]

By thus taking it as the path, when the very essence of lucidity is recognized and transformed, the nirmāṇakāya emanated body arises. Moreover, the nirmāṇakāya emanated body comes from radiant unceasing lucidity. The dharmakāya reality body comes from emptiness as its essence. The sambhogakāya enjoyment body comes from the indivisibility of those two. Thus the nirmāṇakāya emanated body is also the quintessence of the three bodies of enlightenment. It is the same for the other two.

In brief, one's mind alone arises in various forms by virtue of encountering various good and bad conditions, but has no essence whatsoever that is established as good or bad, as demonstrated by the example of copper.[697] All these confusing appearances of samsara are not even slightly established as true in reality. They merely appear to a confused perception, but are not as they appear, like a yellow conch-shell seen by someone with an illness of the bile.

Therefore, when one understands that all the phenomena of samsara lack any self-nature, even though they may appear like samsara in their mode of appearance, they cannot perform the functions of samsara, as explained by the saying, "Ropes burnt by fire cannot bind."

Similarly, "a rope is mistaken for a snake." When a person terrified of snakes goes to some dark place in an area where snakes are known to exist, as soon as he sees a rope on the path he thinks it is a snake and flees in terror. At this point an informed person shows him, "This is not a snake, it is a rope." The object was never a snake, and just by that recognition, the terror of apprehending a snake is released into its natural state.

Similarly, through the force of being affected by beginningless habitual propensities, the mind has arisen as a variety of self and other, enemy and friend, and engaged in all the functions of attachment and hatred. When introduced by the excellent master, by just the recognition that the confusing appearances of samsara have never existed, all appearances arise as the primordial awareness of great bliss.

In brief, all the phenomena of the ground, path, and result are not established outside of one's mind. Identify that united lucidity and emptiness of the mind beyond all possibility of expression, and rest serenely in just that, without clinging.

As Mañjughoṣa taught Sachen:

> If clinging arises,
> it is not the view.[698]

And as the great venerable lord Drakpa Gyaltsen says beginning with the words:

> The unthinkable
> is not a topic for thought.[699]

The great key point of the view is to sustain it without clinging. Thus my master taught. [331]

2) *An extensive explication by means of the three key points of practice*

To stabilize and enhance the meaning of what one has been introduced to in that way, the extensive explication by means of the three key points of practice is given. It is taught:

> For the three key points of practice,
> which are the mind, the illusory,
> and no self-nature...[700]

Reaching a decisive certainty about spiritual practice that has arisen before will stabilize it. However, if [the spiritual practice] has not arisen before, or if it has arisen but only vaguely, by means of each example and its meaning here, it will clearly arise through explanation and meditation on how appearances are the mind. Therefore, it is enhanced. Thus my master taught.

This [explanation and meditation] consists of three topics:

a) Establishing that appearances are the mind
b) Establishing that mental appearance is illusory

c) Establishing that the illusory [mind] has no self-nature

Thus, these three in sequence target the key points of lucidity, emptiness, and their unity. Each of these also consists of three stages: the preparation, the main practice, and the conclusion.

a) *Establishing that appearances are the mind*

(1) *The preparation*

To make what is done meaningful and to establish the entire path as the path of great bliss, one begins by taking refuge and awakening the enlightenment mind. The secret mantra tradition is called "the path of the master," and so one practices the meditation of guruyoga that causes realization to arise from within by means of offering supplications to the master. To defeat ordinary attachment to appearances and for victory over the māras of the obstacles, one meditates on the creation stage.

(a) *Taking refuge and awakening the enlightenment mind*

Take refuge and awaken the enlightenment mind as much as possible as explained previously. The master dissolves into oneself.

(b) *Guruyoga*

Clearly imagine the root master as Hevajra with eight faces and sixteen arms, the father and mother on the seats of a lion throne, and so forth in the sky in front of one. Insistently offer supplications about seven or twenty-one times. The master dissolves into oneself. With minds blended together, stay for as long as one can remain.

(c) *Creation-stage meditation*

While remaining in this state, by pronouncing *hūṃ,* clearly imagine the protection cakra on the vajra ground, with the fence, the garlands, pavilion, canopy, and blazing fires of primordial awareness. By pronouncing *hūṃ,* instantly and clearly envision within it the celestial mansion complete with all the characteristics. By pronouncing *hūṃ,* clearly imagine in the center of it oneself as Hevajra with eight faces and sixteen arms, together with the mother, like an image appearing in a mirror. [332] At his three places, upon a moon, a lotus, and a sun, the three syllables *oṃ, āḥ,* and *hūṃ*—the essences of the body vajra, speech vajra, and mind vajra of all the buddhas of the three times—blaze with light, like images appearing in a mirror. Focus the mind on these and pronounce the three seed syllables three times. The protection cakra with the celestial mansion is the place. Meditation on oneself as the deity is oneself. Pronouncing the three seed syllables is the protection of the yogin. Thus my master taught.

(2) *The main practice*

This consists of two topics:

(a) The root examples
(b) The branch examples

(a) *The root examples*

It is taught:

> For the mind, there is being affected by sleep,
> substances, illnesses, and evil spirits,...[701]

The reason these are given the name *root* is that they are from the perspective of the confused mental faculty. Thus my master taught.

1' *Being affected by sleep*

This consists of three[702] topics:

a' Mindfulness of the example
b' Combining example with meaning
c' Resting evenly in that state

a' *Mindfulness of the example*

Clearly imagine something that one has dreamed, such as in last night's dream: meeting an attractive dear friend and relishing and enjoying sensory objects, the arising of a feeling of terror at enemies, ghosts, being bitten by carnivores, and so forth.

b' *Combining example with meaning*

Think: "I had a dream like that last night. While various feelings of attachment and hatred occurred, they only arose in that way because my mind was affected by sleep. Of course, when I awoke from sleep those objects toward which attachment and hatred had arisen had not come to this place; not even a trace of them existed. Similarly, because it is affected by beginningless habitual propensities, the mind arises as the various places, bodies, experiences, enemies, and friends in samsara, even though they do not exist. This arising of the various thoughts of attachment and hatred is not even slightly different than it was in the dream. They are equal in appearing to a confused perception, equal in not really existing, and equal in the performance of particular functions and the experience of pleasant and painful sensations, even though they do not exist."

c' *Resting evenly in that state*

When the essence of the mind of one who is confused is viewed in such a way, it is a perfectly inexpressible unity of lucidity and emptiness. Rest evenly upon that for as long as one can remain without clinging.

(3) *The conclusion*[703]

This consists of three topics:

(a) Dedicating the basic virtue
(b) Cultivating compassion for infinite sentient beings [333]
(c) Pervading all activities with resting evenly, and practicing without parting from that

(a) *Dedicating the basic virtue*

If one wishes to rise from that session, perform the appropriate dedication prayers, such as this:

> By this basic virtue done in this way, may I reach the citadel of complete buddhahood for the benefit of all sentient beings!

Or:

> By this merit may I obtain omniscience,
> defeat the faults that are the enemies,
> and liberate living beings from the ocean
> of existence turbulent with the waves
> of birth, old age, sickness, and death.

(b) *Cultivating compassion for infinite sentient beings*

Meditate with deep feeling over and over, while thinking: "These beings who engage solely in confusing appearances without realizing the fundamental nature of the mind are so pitiable! May these beings quickly realize the fundamental nature of the mind!"

(c) *Pervading all activities with resting evenly, and practicing without parting from that*

If hatred for an enemy arises, think: "I am confused. The enemy is not established as an external object. He is the united lucidity and emptiness of my own mind," and rest in the inexpressible. Similarly, reach the decisive conclusion that everything—attachment to friends, greed for valuables, traveling, walking, sleeping, sitting, food and drink, and so forth—are one's mind, and rest serenely in just that state.

2' *Being affected by substances*

This also consists of three topics.

a' *Mindfulness of the example*

When *datura,* spurge,[704] is eaten, appearances manifest as yellow. When *kashokanta,* scopolia,[705] is combined with beer and eaten, all appearances manifest as entirely turquoise. When *jinchen thulu*[706] is combined with those and eaten, all appearances manifest as a shield. If these are combined with *bocha gapa*[707] and eaten, all appearances manifest as armor. If that is combined with red incarvillea and eaten, all appearances manifest as entirely reddish.[708]

b' *Combining example with meaning*

Reach a decisive conclusion, thinking: "However those may appear, they are not established in reality. By virtue of the mind being affected by a particular substance, appearances arise in that way and a variety of attachment and hatred arises until the efficacy of that substance has faded. When the efficacy of that substance has faded, not even a trace of those appearances remains. Similarly, by virtue of one's mind also having been affected by various habitual propensities without beginning, and by its encountering various conditions, it appears as the various places, bodies, and experiences of samsara. The nature of one's mind appears as those things, but they are not even slightly established as objects external to it." [334]

c' *Resting evenly*

When certainty has arisen, rest the mind without clinging.

Similarly, the three topics of mindfulness of the example and so forth should be understood for all the following examples.

3' *Being affected by illnesses*

When an illness of the blood takes hold, all appearances manifest as red. When an illness of the bile takes hold, all appearances become yellow, and during some illnesses all appearances become dark. During some fevers, appearances occur of one's body manifesting as three or four, and so forth.

4' *Being affected by evil spirits*

For some people whose minds are affected by evil spirits, appearances arise of someone pursuing them, someone grasping them, and so forth. No matter what nearby people (who know the nonexistent to be nonexistent) say, they do not listen and they do many things because of their own confusion and fear, even leaping from cliffs or leaping into gorges.

In that way, although no pursuers and so forth exist, because the mind is confused, terror is experienced. In the same way, one should now understand all appearances to be similar to that.

(b) *The four branch examples*

These four are mentioned in the following lines:

> ...double vision, eye disease,
> swirling fire, and rapid spinning.[709]

These are defined as the four *branch* examples from the perspective of the confused sense consciousness.[710] Thus my master taught.

1' *Double vision*

In regard to "double vision," when one squeezes the eyes and looks at a single faraway object like a person or a stupa, it is seen to be two, three, and so forth, even though those multiples do not exist.

2' *Eye disease*

For people with some types of unclear vision, the sky and so forth, which are empty and in which nothing at all exists, are seen to be filled with dark spots or series of dark threads, like pieces of hair moved by the wind. This is called "the eye disease of falling strands of hair."

3' *Whirling fire*

When fire is lit on the tip of a thin stick and someone then rapidly whirls the stick, it appears as one solid ring of fire. But it only appears in that way by virtue of being rapidly whirled. That small fire does not itself become a circle at that time.

4' *Rapid spinning*

In regard to "rapid spinning," when one forcefully twirls around something like a pillar and then sits down, all the mountains, fences, and buildings spin, sky and earth seem to turn upside down, one wants to get up but falls down, and so forth. [335] Things appear in this way because one's mind is affected by the rapid spinning, but during those appearances the mountains, fences, and so forth do not actually spin at all.

Similarly, one should understand that dependent on one's mind being affected by various habitual propensities, it arises as the miscellaneous confusing appearances of samsara, all the places, bodies, and experiences, but that these are really not established at all externally. Rest without clinging in just that state.

In this way, dependent on confusion about lucidity, mind arises as various appearances. On the basis of those eight examples, all the confusing appearances that arise in such a way are established to be one's mind. Thus those examples are the extensive explication of lucidity. Thus my master taught.

b) *Establishing that mental appearance is illusory*

One might wonder, "If all appearances are thus one's mind, are they truly established as even mental appearance?"

They are not. They only appear in that way by virtue of a combination of causes and conditions. Because they are not really established as true from the moment of appearance, they are like an illusion.

The fact that this is the case is established by means of eight examples. The great venerable lord Drakpa Gyaltsen simply referred to these examples as the *first* and the *later* examples, but lord Lama Dampa called them *root* and *branch* examples.[711] These are not to be defined from the perspective of the confused mental consciousness and sense consciousness. In any case, the first set of these are the root examples.

(1) *The root examples*

These four are mentioned in the following lines:

> For the second point, there is illusion,
> mirage, the moon in water, and lightning,...[712]

(a) *Illusion*

Think: "By the force of a magician pronouncing the mind-confusing mantras *bhyoḥ, jaḥ, phaṭ,* and so forth over such trivial things as a worthless potsherd or the hair of a monkey's tail, a person is brought under his spell. Based on the efficacy of the combination of those substances, mantras, and spells, the various appearances of horses, cattle, homes, men, women, and so forth arise in that person's perception, even though they do not exist. For that person the thoughts of attachment and hatred concerning these illusory objects arise. The appearance of experiencing various pleasures and sufferings for a long time arises in the mind, but when the magician destroys the illusion, not even a tiny trace remains of horses, cattle, and so forth. [336] Only a short time passed, but because the mind was affected by the illusion, sufferings were experienced even though they did not exist.

"Similarly, when the mind, the universal ground affected by various habitual propensities accumulated from time without beginning, encounters various conditions, it arises as the various places, bodies, and experiences of samsara. But if the causes and conditions are in some minor respect not completely assembled, these will not arise. For example, by virtue of the combination of the karma of the previous lifetime and the conditions that awaken it, each one's own individual present appearances arise in this way. Again, when the conditions for this are exhausted and one dully dies, these appearances vanish without a trace. Again, because the causes and conditions for birth in the intermediate state have come together, the appearances of the intermediate state arise without impediment. Again, when the causes and conditions for that are exhausted, the appearances of the intermediate state vanish without a trace. By virtue of the coming together of the causes and conditions of the next lifetime, the appearances of the next life arise. Similarly, when the causes and conditions for whatever appearances of enemies and friends, places and bodies, and attachment and hatred come together, these arise. If any of the causes and conditions have not come together, these will not occur. Therefore, these are mere appearances, not really established as they appear, like an illusion."

When a decisive certainty has arisen, rest at ease without clinging.

(b) *Mirage*

As for "mirage," at midday during the hot season, when a person afflicted by thirst looks across the area of a vast plain, a quivering, sliding, shimmering appearance arises, like a body of water. Because wild beasts afflicted by thirst are brought to their deaths by chasing after this kind of appearance with the idea of drinking from it, it is also called "the seducer of wild beasts." When a person focuses on and moves toward something like that, it retreats further and further away, and disappears. Moreover, when any one of the causes and conditions presented before, such as the hot season, is lacking, this mirage does not occur; but if all the conditions come together, it does occur.

Similarly, these present appearances also arise from a combination of causes and conditions.

(c) *The moon in water*

When the three conditions of the moon present in the sky, space free from obscurations, and clear water come together, a reflection of the moon clearly appears within the water. Even when many hundreds of thousands of containers of water are present, a reflection of the moon appears within each of them. But when any one of the causes and conditions is not combined, the appearance of the moon in water does not occur. [337]

(d) *Lightning*

Meditate while thinking: "When waves moved by the wind in the ocean, eruptions of the fire of the horse's face,[713] and the summer rainy season come together, an appearance of lightning will flash in the sky. But if any one of those causes and conditions does not come together, it will not occur. Similarly, these present appearances arise from a combination of causes and conditions and are not really established, even as mere appearance."

(2) *The branch examples*

These are four in number, as mentioned in the following lines:

> ...Hari, a spirit town,
> clouds, and a rainbow.[714]

(a) *Hari*

The *Sampuṭa* says:

> The same as Haricandra's city,
> appearing like play in a dream.[715]

There was once a city called Harikela near the ocean in southern India. In the summertime, when rain fell during the night and the sun shone during the day, a reflection appeared in the sky in the shape of the city, down to the exact people and animals. The Indian commentaries on the *Sampuṭa* say that a reflection appeared of Haricandra (a past king of that country) and his retinue, going to Khecara without having discarded their bodies. In any case, that type of appearance arises from the combination of those dependently arisen connections: the rain falling in the night, the clear dawning of the sun in the morning, and the traveling of King Haricandra to Khecara.

(b) *A spirit town*

In regard to "a spirit town," when one looks across a great plain in India, the form can arise of a town, with numerous people and animals coming and going among the houses. Or, even in Tibet, at some places known to be encampments of masang spirits, bright white shapes of reed dwellings and so forth appear. When one approaches closer, wanting to look at these things, not even a trace of their having been at that place remains, for they will have moved behind one or somewhere farther away.

Moreover, this is not an example of the existent becoming nonexistent, but of recognizing the nonexistent to be nonexistent.

(c) *Clouds*

Dependent on the vapors of the ocean having gathered in the sky, white and black clouds appear in empty space with various colors and shapes, even though they do not exist as anything substantial.

(d) *A rainbow*

Concerning "iridescence" or "a rainbow," think: "When the conditions of a drizzling rain, the presence of some sunlight, and the summer season come together, [338] a clear rainbow appears with the five colors distinct, but when it is approached, it vanishes again. Similarly, all of these present appearances arise from a combination of the dependently arisen connections of causes and conditions, but are not really established as they appear, just like a rainbow."

When a decisive certainty has arisen, in just that state, while thinking, "Like a rainbow," rest serenely in the inexpressible, without clinging.

These examples confirm that, although appearances arise as a variety in that way, their essence is not at all established. Therefore, these are the extensive explication of emptiness. Thus my master taught.

c) *Establishing that the illusory [mind] has no self-nature*

This consists of two topics:

(1) Establishing that the illusory [mind] is dependently arisen
(2) Establishing that the illusory [mind] is inexpressible

The illusory [mind] is established as dependently arisen by means of examples primarily explained in the Vehicle of the Perfections. Because it is established as inexpressible by means of examples explained in the unexcelled Vajrayana, these are called the "uncommon examples."

(1) *Establishing that the illusory [mind] is dependently arisen*

This also consists of two topics:

(a) The root examples
(b) The branch examples

(a) *The root examples*

It is taught:

> For the third point, dependently arisen
> is the first of two topics,
> which includes recitation,
> lamps, a mirror, and a seal,...[716]

1' *Recitation*

This consists of three topics: reflecting on the example; combining example with meaning; and resting in that state.

a' *Reflecting on the example*

Concerning "recitation," when a teacher orally teaches something like a sutra to a disciple, dependent on that explanation by the master, the words as well as the meaning clearly appear in the disciple's mindstream and he understands. Furthermore, because they appear in the mindstream of the disciple dependent on the explanation by the teacher, they appear without cessation. But because the understanding of the master has not transferred to the mindstream of the disciple, no actual arising has occurred. Therefore, no duration occurs in between, and it is thus free from arising, cessation, and duration.

b' *Combining example with meaning*

Similarly, the confusing appearances of samsara at the time of the ground, which appear as these various places, bodies, and experiences, arise as merely an illusion due to various causes and conditions, even though nonexistent. They are not established even as just an illusion. Without dependence on the previous lifetime, the next will not arise, so no cessation occurs. Because the previous has not transferred to the next, no actual arising occurs. [339] Because no duration occurs in between, they are emptiness free from arising, cessation, and duration, and are referred to as "just dependently arisen."

Similarly, among all the phenomena consisting of dualistic appearances, such as the previous and following moment, east and west, and being on the point of going to sleep and having fallen asleep, not a single one occurs without dependence on another. Thus no cessation occurs. Because that previous one has not transferred to the next, no actual arising occurs. Because duration is not established in between, phenomena are free from arising, cessation, and duration. Although radiant, unceasing appearances arise in such a way as merely dependent and merely connected, one might ask, "Why are they like this, emptiness free from arising and cessation from the very moment of their appearance?"

Because the reason cannot be expressed as "this" or "that," one should reach the decisive conclusion that it is inexpressible.

c' *Resting in that state*

Thus, if certainty has arisen, remain for as long as one can in the inexpressible state without clinging to even that. When a thought suddenly arises again, reflect and practice as previously described: "All these phenomena included in apparent existence, samsara and nirvana, arise as various appearances, merely dependent and merely connected. From the very moment of their appearance, they are emptiness free from arising and cessation, not established as anything."

2' *Lamps*

When one burning lamp is touched to another cotton wick, the second wick will brightly burn. Furthermore, if that first burning lamp did not exist, the next would not occur. Although the next would not occur without depending on the first, the previous has not transferred to the next, because the first one continues burning.

3' *A mirror*

When one looks in a mirror that is completely clear of tarnish, one's face clearly appears inside it. Moreover, without dependence on the face, its reflection would not occur. Because its reflection appears dependent on the face, no cessation occurs. Even though it has appeared, because one's face has not transferred inside the mirror, no actual arising occurs.

4' *A seal*

When something like a stamp made from wood or horn is pressed into a material like clay, its exact form clearly appears in the clay. Without dependence on the stamp, the design would not be reproduced in the clay, but the design of the stamp has not transferred onto the surface of the clay.

(b) *The branch examples*

These four are mentioned in the following lines:

> ...a fire crystal, a seed,
> a sour taste, and an echo.[717] [340]

1' *A fire crystal*

When sunlight is focused by a fire crystal and touches dry tinder, combustion instantly occurs. Without dependence on the fire crystal, fire would not occur, and yet the light of the fire crystal has not transferred there.

2' *A seed*

When a healthy viable seed of barley or some other plant that has been kept inside a box is planted in a properly prepared field and encounters the conditions of water and manure, a green seedling will gradually appear. Moreover, without dependence on the field, water, manure, and so forth, the seedling would not appear. Because it arises on the basis of those conditions, no cessation occurs. Because those conditions have not transferred to the seedling, no actual arising occurs.

3' *A sour taste*

In regard to "a sour taste," when one sees another person eat something very sour like a pomegranate or a sea buckthorn, one may also start salivating. Because one salivates on the basis of that condition, no cessation occurs. Because the sour taste in the mouth of the other person has not transferred into one's own mouth, no actual arising occurs.

4' *An echo*

When one shouts with a loud voice in a mansion or at the base of a great cliff, one's shout distinctly echoes [between the walls or] among the rocks, exactly like that first shout. Because the echo occurs dependent on one's voice, no cessation occurs. Because one's voice has not transferred into the rocks or the mansion, no actual arising occurs.

(2) *Establishing that the illusory [mind] is inexpressible*

Dependently arisen in that way, the illusory [mind] arises as various appearances, but because it is free from arising, cessation, and duration from the very moment of appearance, it cannot be said to be "this" or "that." Precisely that is established by means of eight common and uncommon examples.

(a) *The four common examples*

These are four in number, as mentioned in the following lines:

> Inexpressible,
> the second topic of the third point,
> should be presented.
> This includes the laughter of an infant
> and the dream of a mute,
> tickling a sensitive spot,
> and sexual pleasure,...[718]

1' *The laughter of an infant*

When a small child who cannot yet speak is laughing, he does so because he experiences something that provokes his laugh, but he cannot specify the exact reason for it. [341] Similarly, when a yogin is practicing the path, he understands that all phenomena appear as just dependently arisen connections and knows that what is thus not established as true is not established. The individually reflexive primordial awareness experiences this by way of recognizing itself as the object of experiential activity, but one is incapable of saying, "It is this." Furthermore, this is not a case of having something that can be expressed and not knowing how to express it. Here one does not know how to express it because it cannot be expressed. It has been taught:

> May what even the omniscient ones lack words for be victorious![719]

Thus the fundamental nature cannot be expressed, but merely as an indication it is termed *inexpressible, transcendent,* and so forth.

Therefore, reach the decisive conclusion that all the phenomena included in apparent existence, samsara and nirvana, are not even slightly established outside of one's mind, and that the mind is also united lucidity and emptiness, beyond all theoretical knowledge and all possibility of expression. Rest at ease in that state without clinging.

2' *The dream of a mute*

It is also like "the dream of a mute." When a mute has a clear dream, he experiences it but does not know how to tell it to others.

3' *Tickling a sensitive spot*

It is like "tickling a sensitive spot." When another person touches a spot where exceptional droplets of the essential constituents are present, an unbearable tickling sensation occurs. Through the catalyst of being touched in such places as the armpit by oneself or another person, a tickling sensation is experienced, but one does not know how to express exactly how it tickles by saying, "It is like this."

4' *Sexual pleasure*

It is like "sexual pleasure." The pleasure of the meeting and uniting of the male and female sexual organs is experienced, but cannot be expressed by saying, "The pleasure is like this."

Because those examples are known in common with worldly people, they are called "the common examples." All the views established up to this point are called "the poisonous view of the time of the cause" and "the view not apart from the waves of the ocean of reality." In brief, because they are not experienced except conceptually, they are not the flawless view. Thus my master taught.

(b) *The four uncommon examples*

Because these are known only in the unexcelled Vajrayana, they are called "the uncommon examples." The four are mentioned in the following lines:

> ...the primordial awareness of the third,
> secret union, the waves of enjoyment,
> and the mandalacakra.[720] [342]

1' *The primordial awareness of the third*

It is like "the primordial awareness of the third," which is the bliss arisen during the third initiation dependent on the catalyst of another, a mudrā consort. In this context, followers of secret mantra in general refer to the actual mudrā consort as the *action mudrā,* but in our tradition a consort is named *action mudrā* because she performs the action of generating the primordial awareness of great bliss. If these are distinguished, both an actual mudrā consort and one of primordial awareness are accepted, because the great venerable lord Drakpa Gyaltsen says:

> The action mudrā is both the actual
> and that of primordial awareness.[721]

In any case, on the basis of union with the appropriate one of those two mudrā consorts of the third initiation, a descending joy is experienced, but one does not know how to express it by saying, "This is the essence of that bliss."

2' *Secret union*

It is like "secret union," which is called "seeking lost meditation by means of the catalyst." This is one of the two ways of seeking meditation that has never arisen, or that has arisen but been lost. Without reference to the catalyst of another person, a mudrā consort, the bliss arisen from stimulating the secret channel with one's hand is experienced, but one does not know how to express it.

3' *The waves of enjoyment*

It is like "the waves of enjoyment," which is a means for seeking lost meditation. As waves appear when the ocean is moved by the wind, so also the circulation of the vital winds of subject and object through both the channels of the rasanā and the lalanā moves the thoughts. The waves are the pulses of the channels of the rasanā and the lalanā located on the right and left of the throat.[722]

This is how to squeeze them: by pressing slightly on the right and left of the throat with the thumbs and middle fingers placed together, the pulse of the three channels will be identified. If the channel through which the drops circulate is pressed, some bliss will arise, but it is harmful to life. If the channel through which the blood circulates is pressed, a red haze will appear. So one should press the middle channel through which the vital winds circulate. Furthermore, if done as though squeezing the neck, throat pains and so forth will occur, so support the head from the back. If pressed intensely, [awareness] will fade away and there will be no primordial awareness to identify, so just press with gradually increasing intensity. When one practices in such a way, a primordial awareness will arise in which all thoughts of subject and object have ceased, but one does not know how to express its essence. [343]

4' *The mandalacakra*

It is like "the mandalacakra." The primordial awareness of the third was in the context of the ripening initiation, whereas this is the sustaining of its stream during the time of the path. When entering into union with an actual or a mudrā consort of primordial awareness, bliss arises, and at the point of the appeals of the goddesses of the retinue and during the melting of the causal Vajra Holder,[723] the bliss of union arises and is experienced, but one does not know how to express it.

Seal all the phenomena of samsara and nirvana with those examples and meditate.

In that way, radiant unceasing lucidity arises as a variety, but its essence is emptiness. Although empty, it still arises as a variety. Establishing the essence to be inexpressible is the extensive explication of their unity.

That is the extensive explication by means of thirty-two examples.

At first, meditate on all of these, each just in passing. Then concentrate and meditate on the basis of whichever examples are most appealing. Thus my master taught.

Furthermore, it is taught:

> ...there are thirty-two
> or thirty-seven examples,...[724]

The meaning: in addition to the thirty-two examples just explained, for the further production of certainty and for enhancement, the four primary examples are collected and presented, making thirty-six examples. Of those four, the foremost one is selected, making thirty-seven.

Of the first of these—the four examples establishing that appearances are the mind—practice the example of a dream, as previously explained. This one example is able to illustrate all four points. The experience of various pleasures and pains dependent on the arising of various objects related to attachment and hatred in a dream establishes that appearances are the mind. What arises in that way in a dream occurs from the combination of numerous conditions, such as the habitual propensities of the day and the condition of having gone to sleep, but the dream will not occur if any one of them is missing, so it is illusory. A dream will not occur unless one has gone to sleep, but sleep has not transferred into the dream, so it is dependently arisen. Because its essence cannot be expressed by saying, "It is this," it is inexpressible. Reach a decisive certainty in this way, and rest without clinging.

Similarly, reach a decisive conclusion and practice with all four points complete in each of these examples as well: the moon in water as the example establishing that mental appearance is illusory, a seedling as the example establishing that [the illusory mind] is dependently arisen, and the waves as the example establishing that [the illusory mind] is inexpressible. [344]

For the one foremost example, of either the secret union or the waves, the usual practice has been to use the latter. So squeeze the waves as explained, and when external appearances have become less clear, rest the mind in the inexpressible without distraction. Serenely rest in a state in which all subject and object has ceased. When that has passed, seal all the phenomena of samsara and nirvana with that sort of experience, and meditate. Again, squeeze the waves. Practice in that way again and again. Thus my master taught.

In that way, because the experience dependent on the four uncommon examples is not just intellectual knowledge, but is experienced, it is the illustrative and symbolic primordial awareness. It is taught:

> The differences of realization
> are presented by means
> of the example of the moon.[725]

Thus, when a person wanting to look at the moon is taught about something made of crystal gem, round in shape, radiating cool white light, with the good qualities of causing the moon lily to blossom, and so forth, that arises as the person's intellectual knowledge in the form of a concept, and he thinks, "The moon is like this." Similarly, because all the views confirmed by means of the four common examples establishing that the mind is inexpressible are also merely concepts or intellectual knowledge, they are called "the poisonous view of the time of the cause" and "the view entailing adherence to an individual philosophical tenet."

Similarly, when the moon's reflection is clearly seen shining in the water, a certainty arises that is not just the previous intellectual understanding. So also, the experience of primordial awareness that has come from cultivating the meditative concentrations of the two stages is the illustrative and symbolic primordial awareness. Hence, just as one is liberated from all those doubts by actually seeing the moon in the sky, if one sustains the stream of that illustrative and symbolic primordial awareness, when the first spiritual level has been actualized the real primordial awareness that is illustrated will be actualized.

Also, this is the meaning of "The differences of realization are presented by means of the example of the moon": seeing the moon of the first day [after new moon] is seeing the moon, but it is not completely seeing the moon. Similarly, on the first spiritual level one sees a little of the primordial awareness of a buddha. Then the moon gradually increases, and on the evening of the full moon one sees the moon completely. Similarly, one gradually progresses through the spiritual levels and, at the point when one has actualized the thirteenth spiritual level of a vajra holder, one sees the entire primordial awareness of a buddha. Thus my master taught. [345]

Furthermore, there is both classifying mere understanding to be the view and classifying the primordial awareness of experience to be the view. The first is this *poisonous view of the time of the cause.* This consists of three topics: the poison of designation, the poison of conceptualization, and the poison of attachment to the deity as perfection.

The first, [the poison of designation, includes] everything from ordinary people's designation of the places, bodies, and experiences of samsara as truly established external objects, to the śrāvaka's designation of them as external objects. That sort of poison is removed by this view of the time of the cause, which has arisen from the extensive presentation establishing that appearances are the mind, and so forth, together with the examples. The second is the poison of conceptualization: except for just the difference of being good thoughts instead of bad thoughts, the view of the time of the cause does not itself transcend the nature of thought. The poison of that is removed by the creation stage. The third is the poison of attachment to the deity as perfection. All the attachment to that deity as sublime is removed by the completion stage. Thus my master taught.

3) *An extremely extensive explication by means of the three continua*

All the phenomena included in samsara and nirvana have been presented as lucidity, emptiness, and their unity. If all phenomena are entirely summarized, nothing is not included within the categories of the ground, the path, and the result, or in the three continua. And each of these is established as the indivisibility of samsara and nirvana.

a) *The presentation of the ground or causal continuum as the indivisibility of samsara and nirvana*

This consists of seven topics, as mentioned in the following lines:

> First, the extensive explication
> consists of the nature of the universal ground,
> the support, how it is supported,
> the causal and the root continuum,
> how they are connected, and,
> through mindfulness of the three appearances,
> how samsara and nirvana are complete
> within the body and the mind.[726]

(1) *The nature or essence of the universal ground*

It is taught:

> The mind, the universal ground, serves as the cause of all samsara and nirvana. It is experiencing and aware, not specifically classifiable, and not fitting into a type or category. It is method,

> pure awareness lucid and unceasing, its essence emptiness, serving as the support in which the habitual propensities of karma are accumulated.[727]

The meaning: in general, the universal ground is both unaffected by conditions and affected. [346]

Concerning the first, it is taught:

> Precisely this is known as samsara.
> Precisely this is nirvana itself.[728]

Thus, if the methods are not applied to one's mind—to precisely this genuine uncontrived cognition—it produces the appearances of samsara; but if the methods are applied, it produces the appearances of nirvana. Therefore it is the cause of all samsara and nirvana. Furthermore, it is not like a productive cause; it arises as one appearance or another by virtue of whether or not it has recognized its own essence.

One might ask, "In that case, is this universal ground composite or noncomposite?"

It is taught, "It is composite," so it is experiencing.

Everything composite is either inanimate, cognitive, or a nonassociated conditioning factor. Of these, this universal ground is cognitive, so it is aware.

It is not at all virtuous or sinful, so it is not specifically classifiable.

It does not fit into the types of either samsara or nirvana. If it were in the class of samsara, its radiant unceasing appearances would not be able to arise as nirvana, and if it fit into the class of nirvana, its radiant and unceasing appearances would not be able to arise as samsara.

In regard to not fitting into a category, the mind that is thus lucid yet empty pervades all the phenomena of samsara and nirvana. If they were not pervaded by lucidity, they would be inanimate external objects, and if they were not pervaded by emptiness, they would be truly established.

Of the relative and the absolute, this is relative, and so it is method.

Because it is not a future mind, it is pure awareness. Because it is not past, it is unceasing. Because it is present, it is lucid.

Because its essence is emptiness, it is not established as anything, and therefore can arise as anything. It is taught:

> Anything is possible
> for the person who
> accepts emptiness.[729]

In brief, precisely this momentary pure awareness of the present, with the nature of united lucidity and emptiness, is the essence or nature of the universal ground. Thus my master taught.

(2) *The support*

"In that case," one might wonder, "dependent upon what support does such a mind exist?"

Although the support is not established as an external object, by virtue of the various habitual propensities existing within that universal ground itself encountering the conditions for their awakening, they arise as the radiant unceasing appearances of the four supporting mandalas. The coarse channels of the body are the supporting container of the sense organs. The subtle channels include all the channels from the three primary ones to the channels equal to the number of body hairs. The channel syllables are the channels in crooked shapes (with the shapes of syllables), from the coarse, which are *puja* and so forth, down to the subtle, which is the inexpressible short *a.* [347] The coarse essential constituent nectars are the five nectars. The subtle pervade all the openings of the hair follicles, and have various colors and the nature of light, like dew on a blade of grass, or the throat feathers of a cuckoo or a pigeon. In regard to the quintessential vital wind of primordial awareness, the coarse involves moving and staying still, speech and expression, and so forth, and the subtle is the pause within. The universal ground exists supported upon these, which appear [as the four mandalas].

(3) *How it is supported*

The body and the mind exist as a single undifferentiated substance, like musk and the scent of musk or a flower and the scent of a flower.

"In that case," one might ask, "would the inanimate and the cognitive not become a single substance?"

They do not. Even the four supporting mandalas are only the confusing appearances of the mind itself, and are not externally established. In brief, this tradition does not accept any external objects other than just mental appearance. Therefore, the slight inability of such masters as Bartön Dorjé Gyaltsen[730] to accept the body and the mind as a single undifferentiated substance is because they slightly misunderstood this key point. Thus my master taught.

(4) *The reason it is defined as the causal continuum*

According to the distinction of whether the methods are applied or not applied, precisely that sort of universal ground serves as the cause of all samsara and nirvana. From a sentient being in hell, to the unity of Vajradhara, that lucid yet empty mind has three different temporary modes of appearance, as presented by the example of copper,[731] but it is a continuum, without the slightest good or bad change in essence, existing without interruption. *Continuum* means "continuous." As it is taught:

> Samsara is maintained
> to be a continuum.[732]

(5) *Classification as the root continuum*

Precisely that is also known as "the root continuum." Dependent on the healthy root of a tree, all the branches, leaves, flowers, and fruits appear. Similarly, as when an umbrella held aloft in the sky casts a shadow on the ground, when the mind, the universal ground, does not recognize its own essence, it serves as the root for the arising of the various confusing appearances of samsara, even though they do not exist. But when the methods are applied, it serves as the root for the appearance of all the good qualities of the path and the result. [348] "Continuum" is the same as mentioned previously, as it is taught:

> Since samsara and nirvana are complete in the causal
> continuum of the universal ground, it is the root
> continuum.[733]

(6) *How the support and the supported are connected*

All the phenomena of samsara and nirvana exist within the mind, the universal ground, in the form of habitual propensities. Dependent on coming in contact with the conditions, precisely those arise in the form of the channel syllables in the body. Dependent on the going and coming of the vital winds and mind in the channel syllables, all the confusing appearances of samsara arise. The three realms arise as the object and the various appearances as the experience. Thus my master taught.

(7) *The calculation of how samsara and nirvana are complete within the body and the mind*

Thus, precisely that which exists in the mind in the form of habitual propensities arises as the channel syllables in the vajra body. All of samsara and nirvana are complete in the body, from which, due to the force of the vital winds and mind gathered there [in the channel syllables], all the appearances of samsara and nirvana arise, although nonexistent.

In the context of impure appearance, of the seed syllables of the six realms that exist in the bhaga,[734] the dependently arisen connections of the vital winds and mind coming and going in the black syllable *tri* of the hells may cause an intense fiery hatred to arise at the point of death due to any suitable stimulus, like meeting a deadly enemy or remembering him. On the basis of that, the vital winds and mind gather in the seed syllable of the hells. That takes control of all the vital winds and mind, and, immediately upon rising from the clear light of death, an intermediate existence like a log of wood burning with fire also appears in the intermediate state. From there, one will definitely be reborn in the hell realms. It is taught:

> What is close and
> what is familiar.[735]

Thus it is taught that the karma of what is close at the transition point and of what is continuously familiar is strongest.

Similarly, by virtue of the vital winds and mind being gathered in the seed syllables of the six realms, conception takes place in a particular realm.

In the context of experiential appearance, dependent on the vital winds and mind gathered in the seed of the hells, the experiences of the purifications of the birthplaces,[736] such as the experiences of the cooking and burning of the hells, arise while one is still living in the human realm. It is taught:

> If dissolved in the mansion of the great mother Prajñāpāramitā and so forth, the dharmakāya reality body is experienced and there is freedom from subject and object.[737]

Similarly, when the vital winds and mind have gathered in the channel syllables of nirvana, pure appearance arises. [349] Thus, with the transformation of appearances as the mode of purification, meditate on pure appearance purifying all the impure appearances of the channel syllables of samsara and so forth. By applying the seal of pure appearance as the result of purification, and taking that as the path, [impure appearance] will become the enlightened bodies and primordial awareness of pure appearance.

In summation, all the phenomena of samsara are complete in the form of the characteristic of the mind, the radiant unceasing lucidity that arises as the various places, bodies, and experiences of samsara. All the phenomena of the path are complete in the form of the qualities of the mind, because, due to the force of the practice, these arise as the variety of the fifteen experiences—the five sets of three—and so forth.[738] The phenomena of the result are complete in the form of the potency of the mind, because it has the ability to actualize the result.

In brief, first perform the three preliminaries as explained previously. Without the main practice of mindfulness of the example and so forth, reach a decisive conclusion, thinking: "In this way, of all these phenomena included in samsara and nirvana, not even a sesame seed is established outside my own mind, this momentary pure awareness. The essence of mind is united lucidity and emptiness, beyond all possibility of expression."

When certainty has arisen, rest in wonder at the natural state, without clinging to even the thought that it is inexpressible. To be without clinging is crucial. Practice the final three topics as before.[739]

In brief, those in the tradition of the Explication for the Assembly do not perform more than a reading transmission for the extensive explication of the Three Continua, but this tradition of the Explication for Disciples makes them the key points of guidance. One will come to understand the reason by looking at the works of the great venerable lord Drakpa Gyaltsen. Thus my master taught.

b) *The presentation of the method continuum as the indivisibility of samsara and nirvana*

It is taught:

> The method continuum consists
> of ripening initiation, the path, and experience.[740]

Accordingly, this consists of three topics:

(1) The ripening initiation
(2) The path of both creation and completion
(3) The primordial awareness of experience arisen from that

If all the phenomena of the method continuum are combined, they are included in these three. This is also known as "the explanatory continuum."[741] In the context of the descriptive words, a scripture that clarifies what a root tantra leaves unclear is referred to as an *explanatory tantra.* [350] Similarly, because the incidental stains existing as the various habitual propensities of samsara and nirvana in the universal ground are purified here, and its own essence is clarified, this is the real explanation of the root that is to be described. Thus my master taught.

(1) *The indivisibility of samsara and nirvana in the ripening initiation*

This consists of three topics, as mentioned in the following lines:

> For the first topic, learn directly from
> the glorious master
> that each of the mandalas, initiations,
> initiation substances, and so forth,
> are also the three seats,
> samsara and nirvana indivisible.[742]

(a) *The indivisibility of samsara and nirvana in the mandalas where the initiations are bestowed*

Furthermore, the three seats must be complete in the mandalas where the initiations are bestowed, the vajra master who bestows them, and the vajra disciples to whom they are bestowed. As for the meaning of "the three seats," the Sanskrit equivalent of *seat* is *pīṭha,* which applies to a type, a place, or a seat. It would be easy to understand if translated as something like "type," but because the venerable lord Drokmi was extremely reticent about the mantra teachings, he translated it as "seat," which is the most difficult to understand. The meaning is: "If all the buddhas are gathered together, they are included in three types."

By means of essence these are the buddhas, bodhisattvas, and wrathful beings. If classified as the three seats, these also include female buddhas, female bodhisattvas, and female wrathful beings, making six seats. In the context of the ground of purification, these would be five seats, because no separate ground of purification exists for the female wrathful beings. However, in general these are three: the seat of the male and female buddhas, the seat of the male and female bodhisattvas, and the seat of the male and female wrathful beings.

Furthermore, in the context of actual completeness, purity, and enlightened actions, completeness must be by means of any of these three types of completeness. Here, the three seats are actually complete in the mandala in the sky, which is the agent of bestowal. Two traditions exist: meditating and not meditating on the celestial mansion in the sky in front. Of these two traditions, that of meditating on it is foremost at the time of the cause.

Therefore, in the center of a celestial mansion with all the complete characteristics, envision a two-tiered square heavenly dais of blue beryl, which is like large and small stacked seats. In the center of it is either a nine-sectioned grid or a lotus with eight petals, in the middle of which resides Akṣobhya indivisible from the root master, displaying the mudrā gesture of the great subjugation of Māra. In front of him, on a jeweled throne covered with numerous silks of divine material, are the initiation substances—the vase, crown, and so forth—created from the manifestations of primordial awareness. [351] The four such as Vairocana are in the four directions. To the southeast of [Akṣobhya] is Locanā, to the southwest is Māmakī, to the northwest is Gaurī, and to the northeast is Tārā, in their peaceful forms. This is the seat of the male and female buddhas.

In the eight primary and intermediate directions of the first heavenly dais are the eight bodhisattvas such as Kṣitigarbha, displaying the eight auspicious substances.[743] In the four corners of the second heavenly dais, with two each in the southeast and the northeast and one each in the southwest and the northwest, are the six goddesses such as Rūpavajrā, holding their individual offering substances. This is the seat of the male and female bodhisattvas.

When a celestial mansion is present, the ten wrathful beings with the consorts of their own light are at the eight points beside the gates and both above and below. When no mansion is present, they are in the ten primary and intermediate directions outside of the outer heavenly dais. This is the seat of the male and female wrathful beings.

Moreover, visualize that those in the eastern direction are looking at oneself and the others are facing the main figure, or that all are facing the main figure, whichever is preferred. Thus my master taught.

In the front mandala, the three seats are also complete by means of purity and enlightened actions. The main father and mother, Gaurī, and so forth are the seat of the male buddhas. If applied down to the ground of purification, the five aggregates are the ground of purification for the five spiritual families at the time of the ground. From the perspective of the incidental stains of attachment to them as ordinary, they are what is to be purified. Precisely these are purified by Gaurī and so forth, because when applied up to the result of purification, they are the essence of the five types of primordial awareness that are mirrorlike and so forth. The four of Pukkasī and so forth are the seat of the female buddhas, because they purify the four base elements that are the ground of purification and because they are the essence of the four immeasurables that are the result of purification.

The eight goddesses are also the seat of the male bodhisattvas, because they purify the eight inner sensory bases[744] such as the eyes, which are the ground of purification, and because they have the same meaning as Mohavajrā at the eyes, and so forth. They are also the seat of the female bodhisattvas, because they purify the six outer sensory bases that are the ground of purification.

The seat of the male and female wrathful beings is complete by means of enlightened actions, because just as summoning and stationing[745] is performed by the four gatekeepers such as Urgarāja in the father tantras, so here the actions of summoning and stationing are performed with the mantras *gaurī akarṣaya jaḥ* and so forth.

Those are also the indivisibility of samsara and nirvana. The various forms are samsara. The essence completely unestablished is nirvana. The indivisibility of those two is inexpressible. [352]

Similarly, by means of enlightened actions the three seats are also complete in all the vajra master's aggregates, constituents, and sensory bases. By means of purity the three seats are also complete in all the vajra disciple's aggregates, constituents, and sensory bases. Thus my master taught.

(b) *The indivisibility of samsara and nirvana in the ritual of bestowing the initiations*

The completeness of the three seats in the vase initiation is as follows: with the prayer of "Blessed ones, tathāgatas," and so forth, the peaceful initiation deities residing in the sky transform into the wrathful and passionate enlightened bodies of the conquerors of the five spiritual families, the enlightened bodies of herukas with eight faces and sixteen arms, embraced by their individual consorts. When they bestow the initiation with a vase that is white like the moon and filled with the nectar of primordial awareness, holding it slightly tilted, all the incidental stains of the disciple's five aggregates are purified into space. The five aggregates of the time of the cause that are transformed into the herukas of the five spiritual families are samsara. Meditating on the herukas of the five spiritual families of the time of the purifying path—by way of the transformation of appearances as the mode of purification—and applying the seal of pure appearance by meditating with the thought, "These are the real herukas of the five spiritual families of the time of the result, residing on the thirteenth spiritual level of a vajra holder, the result of purification," is nirvana. This is the indivisibility of samsara and nirvana.

Similarly, just the distinct proclamation of the vajra song of *kollaire* and so forth by the five consorts transforms the impure four base elements—together with space—into the five consorts, who are the essence of the four immeasurables, with extremely pure great bliss as the fifth. By the recitation of the auspicious lines of "Excellent qualities"[746] and so forth by the eight bodhisattvas or their transformations into the eight goddesses Gaurī and so forth, the inner sensory bases such as the eyes are transformed into the eight goddesses. By the filling of the entire expanse of the sky with the outer, inner, and secret offerings, and by the offering of these to oneself by Rūpavajrā and so forth or their transformations into Rūpa Gaurī and so forth, the outer sensory bases such as form are transformed into the six vajra goddesses. By the male and female wrathful beings' frightening away impeding spirits with fierce terrifying shouts, while roaring like thunder the sound of mantras such as *hūṃ* and *phaṭ*, the eight great joints and the top of the head and soles of the feet—making ten—are transformed into the ten wrathful beings. [353]

In brief, the complete three seats of the time of the ground are samsara. Meditating on precisely those as the deities of the complete three seats of the time of the path (by way of the transformation of appearances), and as the complete three seats residing on the thirteenth spiritual level of a vajra holder as the result of purification, is nirvana. Because it is precisely those complete three seats of the time of the ground that are transformed at the time of the path and the time of the result, this is the indivisibility of samsara and nirvana.

Similarly, the three seats are complete and samsara and nirvana are indivisible during the five initiations of primordial awareness and that of the vajra master.

(c) *The indivisibility of samsara and nirvana in the initiation substances*

The three seats are complete in the initiation substance during the vase initiation. For example, the water of the vase that is the initiation substance during the water initiation of Akṣobhya is just one's mind alone appearing as water; it is not established externally as water. Therefore, because all the phenomena of samsara and nirvana are complete within the momentary mind, the existence of the water as the complete three seats is samsara, and the generation of that as Akṣobhya, the summoning and dissolving of the Akṣobhya of the time of the result, and making them identical, is nirvana. Thus samsara and nirvana are indivisible. Similarly, the three seats are complete in all the substances of the crown and so forth. Thus my master taught.

During the secret initiation, because the clear essence of the aggregates, constituents, outer and inner sensory bases, and the great joints is included in just a speck of the vajra master's essential constituent, the three seats are complete. They are thus also complete in the enlightenment mind existing as the basis of the disciple.[747] In that way, the disciple's enlightenment mind is samsara. The master's enlightenment mind is nirvana. Those two becoming identical is the indivisibility of samsara and nirvana.

During the initiation of primordial awareness dependent on an embodiment of wisdom, the three seats are complete in the aggregates, constituents, and sensory bases of the individual actual mudrā consort and the one of primordial awareness. All the apparent aspects of union endowed with the three perceptions and so forth are samsara. Their totally unestablished nature is nirvana. Because those two are indivisible, this is the indivisibility of samsara and nirvana.

During the initiation of the primordial awareness of the fourth initiation, radiant unceasing lucidity is samsara. Its essence, emptiness free from all conceptual elaborations, is nirvana. Because the fundamental nature of those two is beyond all expression, it is the indivisibility of samsara and nirvana. Thus my master taught. [354]

(2) *The indivisibility of samsara and nirvana in the path*

This consists of two topics:

(a) The indivisibility of samsara and nirvana in the creation stage
(b) The indivisibility of samsara and nirvana in the completion stage

(a) *The indivisibility of samsara and nirvana in the creation stage*

This involves seven topics, as mentioned in the following lines:

> The creation stage consists of the preliminaries,
> the supports, and the ritual of creation,
> the colors, the hand implements,
> the postures, and the branches,
> each of which will, with kind consideration,
> be carefully explained to have the nature
> of indivisible samsara and nirvana.[748]

1' *The indivisibility of samsara and nirvana in the preliminaries*

The ground of purification and the purifying agent, or the indivisibility of samsara and nirvana, or the triad of ground, path, and result, and so forth, are just different names for the same thing. This may be applied to both the common and the uncommon preliminaries. The actual presentation in the text of the great venerable lord Drakpa Gyaltsen commences from the uncommon.[749]

Moreover, in the context of the ground of purification, those in the tradition of the Explication for the Assembly accept that three and a half birthplaces are purified during one practice of the method for direct realization.[750] Regarding the ground of purification, the Gendenpa claim: "The stains of previous lifetimes cannot be purified, just as last year's firewood cannot be burned by this year's fire. The present stains cannot be purified, because they have already been established by karma and afflictions and are not affected by the actions of the antidote, just as charcoal may be scrubbed clean, but will not turn white. Therefore, the three of birth, death, and the intermediate state of the supporting body of a human being who will be reborn in the future are purified."[751]

However, such a position entails accepting that all these impure appearances are truly established external objects. If this were true, where would the deities and celestial mansion be visualized—outside or inside of these present appearances? At the point of buddhahood, at which place would this tainted body be put?

Therefore, as explained before, according to our tradition four and a half birthplaces are purified.[752] In this context, the uncommon preliminaries are the accumulation of the two assemblies.

a' *The accumulation of the assembly of merit*

This consists of two topics:

1'' Accumulation of karma in reference to pure objects
2'' Accumulation of karma in reference to impure objects

1'' *Accumulation of karma in reference to pure objects*

As the support for one's accumulation of karma prior to this lifetime, one took a supporting body in one of the six realms. [355] Karma was accumulated with that body—from actions that were motivated by the three poisons, such as striking, stabbing, slandering, and insulting those who are pure objects, which accumulated karma for rebirth in the three lower realms, to the tainted virtue that becomes the cause for rebirth as a god of the higher realms and for attainment of the enlightenment of the śrāvakas and the pratyekabuddhas. All that virtuous and sinful karma is the ground of purification.

The mode of purification, called "the mode of transforming appearances," is the meditative transformation of impure appearance into pure appearance. Because the supporting body of the one who accumulates karma is just one's own mental appearance, precisely that impure appearance present in the form of habitual propensities in one's own mind is clearly imagined as the pure appearance of Heruka with eight faces and sixteen arms. The objects in reference to which karma is accumulated are also present in the form of habitual propensities in the mind. These are all visualized in the form of the nine deities of Heruka, crowned with the master Akṣobhya. All accumulated karma is clearly imagined and meditated upon [during the Time of the Path], from the homage up to the taking of the vows.

In brief, the particular ground of purification is samsara. The transformation of that into the form of the purifying path and the meditative application of the seal of pure appearance as the result of purification is called "the indivisibility of samsara and nirvana" or "the indivisibility of the triad of ground, path, and result."

2'' *Accumulation of karma in reference to impure objects*[753]

Similarly, meditate on all one's accumulated karma in reference to sentient beings that are impure objects, the accumulating agent, and the objects of the accumulation, as the pure four immeasurables. Apply the seals of the four consorts, who are the result, and meditate.

b' *The accumulation of the assembly of primordial awareness*[754]

Then, when all one's life, karma, and merit are exhausted like an extinguished butter lamp, one darkly and dully dissolves into the clear light of death, but does not recognize one's own essence. Precisely this is coemergent lack of awareness. Such appearances of death are present within the mind in the form of habitual propensities. By means of the purifying mantra beginning with *śūnyatā,* these are meditated upon as the clear light of emptiness.

Furthermore, the heart of the path is that the purification of the impure (corresponding to the mask of samsara) enables one to obtain the pure (corresponding to the mask of nirvana). If these practices are applied to the pure, they are the equivalent of the accumulation of the assemblies during three countless eons. Thus my master taught.

2' *The indivisibility of samsara and nirvana in the supports*

It is taught:

> Wind depends on space,
> and the sphere of water
> depends on that.[755]

Thus the gradual creation of Mount Meru, the outer environment, and so forth from the atoms of wind, water, earth, and fire is the ground of purification. [356] All such impure appearances are used as the substances that are transformed into the forms of the individual base elements of the Time of the Path—the wind mandala and so forth. Apply the seal of thinking that these are the actual four consorts of the time of the result, and meditate. This is the indivisibility of samsara and nirvana in the supports.

3' *The indivisibility of samsara and nirvana in the ritual of creation*

When such a sentient being arises from the death state into the intermediate existence, by the force of karma, conception will again take place in one of the six realms.

In the context of a human being endowed with the six constituents, the father's white constituent is the ground of purification. As the purifying agent, it is visualized in the form of a moon mandala that comes from the melting of the vowels such as *a,* which are the essence of the thirty-two major marks. Apply the seal of mirrorlike primordial awareness that comes from that as the result of purification, and meditate.

Similarly, the mother's red constituent is the ground of purification. The purifying sun comes from the consonant-syllables such as *ka* that are the nature of the eighty minor marks. The result of purification is the primordial awareness of equality.

The consciousness of the intermediate state is the ground of purification. The purifying agents are the hand implements together with the seed syllables. The result of purification is the primordial awareness of discrimination.

The single combination of semen, uterine blood, and the consciousness of the intermediate existence is the ground of purification. The purifying agent is the single combination of the sun, moon, and hand implements. The result of purification is the all-accomplishing primordial awareness.

After that, birth (following the completion of the body in the womb) is the ground of purification. The purifying agent is the totally complete body of enlightenment. The result of purification is the primordial awareness of the basic space of phenomena.

That is the indivisibility of the ground of purification and the purifying agent, or of the triad of ground, path, and result.

4' *The indivisibility of samsara and nirvana in the colors*

When the habitual propensity of ignorance has become solid, it appears as the color white. This is because, just as ignorance is the ground of all the afflictions, so also the color white is the ground of all the colors. All the appearances of such a color white are the ground of purification, which is transformed into the white color of the enlightened body of the causal Vajradhara, the right face of the resultant Vajra Holder, and so forth, in brief, into all the white colors of the Time of the Path, and sealed as the mirrorlike primordial awareness of the time of the result. This is the indivisibility of samsara and nirvana in reference to the color white.

A black radiance occurs when a hateful thought has become coarse, and when hatred has arisen the face turns black and appearances become dark and dull.

The radiance of desire is red, and when desire has arisen appearances become reddish. [357]

Similarly, the five colors of the time of the ground are transformed into the five colors of the Time of the Path, the seal of the five types of primordial awareness of the time of the result is applied, and one meditates.

5' *The indivisibility of samsara and nirvana in the hand implements*

The appearance of ignorance is the cakra. Just as ignorance is the great force that produces all the afflictions, but does not actually arise in a coarse form like desire and hatred, so also the cakra spins around, but remains invisible because the tips of its spokes are extremely sharp. Similarly, all the possible appearances of a cakra during the time of the ground are transformed into the form of a cakra as the hand implement of a deity during the Time of the Path, sealed as the primordial awareness of the time of the result, and meditated upon.

The appearance of hatred is the vajra. Just as hatred cuts through and destroys everything else, so also the vajra is indestructible, and it destroys everything else. It is the same for the axe, the curved knife, and so forth.

Just as greed arises for valuable objects such as jewels, the jewel is the hand implement derived from the concept of greed.

The lotus is created from the appearance of desire, and the crossed vajra, the sword, and so forth, from the appearance of jealousy.

In brief, all the hand implements are for the most part also included among the hand implements of the five spiritual families. The best of hand implements have the forms of creatures. Because all the aggregates, constituents, and sensory bases are complete in one creature such as an elephant, the complete three seats of the triad of ground, path, and result are present in each one. Therefore, those deities holding hand implements in the forms of creatures are the most profound. Thus my master taught.

6' *The indivisibility of samsara and nirvana in the postures*

Extension of the right arms and legs indicates that wisdom, or emptiness, pervades all phenomena. Contraction symbolizes one's realization of such emptiness. Extension of the left limbs indicates that great compassion pervades all phenomena. Contraction symbolizes one's possession of [great compassion] in the mindstream. Crossing [the limbs indicates] unity. And so forth.

In brief, the various forms are samsara or the ground of purification. Its nature is nirvana or the purifying agent. These two are indivisible.

7' *The indivisibility of samsara and nirvana in the branches*

These are the yogas for times when one is not in the meditative equipoise of the creation stage. For example, during the yoga of food, the ordinary food is samsara. [358] Reflecting on it as the essence of purity, the five types of primordial awareness, and the five nectars, and enjoying it while oneself is clearly the chosen deity, is nirvana.

The ordinary substance of the sacrificial cake is samsara. Blessing it as pure nectar, and offering it, is nirvana.

Similarly, during all activities, radiant unceasing form—appearance in a particular form—is samsara. The essence of just that, beyond all possibility of expression, is nirvana. The indivisibility of those two is the indivisibility of samsara and nirvana or the indivisibility of the triad of ground, path, and result.

In brief, this is the advantage of having established that all appearances are the mind. If appearances are held to be external objects, one is unable to accept things in this way. Thus my master taught.

(b) *The indivisibility of samsara and nirvana in the completion stage*

It is taught:

> For the completion stage,
> the body, speech, and mind in samsara,
> and the fully complete result that is
> the primordial awareness of a buddha,
> should be mutually sealed with cause and result,
> and the realization introduced
> as the symbolic primordial awareness.[756]

Thus the complete body [includes everything] from the coarse supporting container of the sense organs to the subtle three channels. The complete speech [includes everything] from coarse talk, laughter, and so forth to the subtle inexpressible short *a* of the navel. As for the complete mind, *mind (yid)* signifies both the mind *(sems)* and the drops *(thig le)*. The latter includes everything from the coarse five nectars to the subtle [drops] that are equal to the number of body hairs, and which are present like dew on the tip of a blade of grass. The former includes everything from the coarse thoughts of subject and object to the subtle, which are all the internal facets of each thought.

When those are taken as the path, during the secret initiation all the forms of the ordinary channels are the ground of purification, samsara.

Meditating that both [the coarse and subtle channels] dissolve into clear light and, from that state, take the form of the channels and of the syllables (the crooked channels) created from the manifestation of primordial awareness in the enlightened body of Hevajra—like a reflection in a mirror—is nirvana. The inhalation, pause, and exhalation of the ordinary vital wind is samsara. The transformation of precisely that into the vajra repetition and so forth is nirvana.

The yogin and the mudrā consort endowed with the three perceptions and so forth during the third initiation is samsara. Residing in the inexpressible as its essence is nirvana.

Although this tradition primarily accepts the vajra waves as the path of the fourth initiation, here the radiant unceasing lucidity of the mind is samsara. The essence, emptiness, is nirvana. [359] Their inseparability is the indivisibility of samsara and nirvana.

The *Sarvaguhya Tantra* teaches:

> Apply the seal of the result to the cause
> and also apply the seal of the cause to the result.[757]

Thus, by taking as the path precisely that united lucidity and emptiness of the mind at the time of the cause, all the incidental stains within it are purified into space. [The mind] nakedly seeing its own essence is the result.

In brief, *seal* means not to transcend. Precisely that cause becomes the result; no other result exists apart from the cause. This is application of the seal of the result to the cause. Because the result does not transcend its own cause, the seal of the cause is applied to the result.

The realization is a symbolic primordial awareness. Taken as the path by means of such exceptional methods, when the vital winds of life and exertion enter the central channel, like a mount and its rider,[758] thoughts of subject and object totally cease. The vital winds that enter the central channel melt the clear essence of the drops, and the primordial awareness of great bliss arises in the mindstream. It is taught:

> The primordial awareness
> of an omniscient one is like that.[759]

Because it illustrates the primordial awareness of the time of the result, it is called *symbolic primordial awareness,* like showing the moon in water to someone who wants to look at the moon.

Similarly, it is taught:

> Be mindful of the six topics common
> to the creation and completion stages,
> and if one wishes to increase the level
> of realization higher and higher,
> also correctly apply the sacred commitments,
> signs, and so forth, and examine this
> with an immaculate mind.[760]

This consists of six topics: the essence of both stages, the divisions, the definitions, the definite number, the reason for liberation, and the sequence. Each initiation has the five sacred commitments of meditative equipoise, subsequent conduct, food, protection, and no separation. For each of these, the various forms are samsara. The essence is nirvana. Similarly, the signs and so forth of the four initiations are the indivisibility of samsara and nirvana, and should be recognized as such.

In brief, all the phenomena included in the ground, path, and result are the indivisibility of samsara and nirvana. This is impossible to explain from each perspective, so one should mentally examine it in detail without fabrication or exaggeration, and practice. Thus my master taught. [360]

(3) *The indivisibility of samsara and nirvana in the primordial awareness of experience arisen from that*

It is taught:

> Dependent on the experiences of samsara,
> wrong view is rejected.
> Through the experiences of the path,
> one vehicle is established.
> Through the experiences of the result,
> sublime delight arises.
> All phenomena are established
> by means of the four authentic qualities.[761]

First, in general, it is taught:

> Everything below the *peak* of existence appears in the experiences of meditative concentration. The unexplainable is illustrated.[762]

Thus, if it does not exist in samsara and nirvana, one can ignore it. All the things that do exist arise as experiences. The habitual propensities of samsara and nirvana exist in the mind, and by virtue of that all the samsara channels and nirvana channels exist in the body. By the dependently arisen connections of the vital winds and mind gathered in those channels, all the appearances of samsara and nirvana arise, although nonexistent. Therefore, if the types of experiences are condensed, they can be gathered into three: [the experiences of samsara, the experiences of the path, and the experiences of the result.]

(a) *The experiences of samsara*

For example, when a stream has been dammed up and not allowed to go anywhere, it will overflow, spill out, and so forth. Similarly, when the vital winds and mind are allowed to run wild, extensive confusing appearances proliferate, but when the vital winds and mind are bound by means of exceptional methods and are unable to go everywhere they want to go, they gather in the suitable channel syllables. Based on that, their appearances arise, even though nonexistent.

When the vital winds and mind have gathered in the seed of the hells, the black syllable *tri* that exists in the lower abdominal triangle among the "syllables of the bhaga," inconceivable sufferings such as the cooking and burning of the hells are experienced, as happened to lord Sachen's disciple Neten Sösher. But by serenely resting in just that state without clinging, that experience of the purification of birthplace will be broken, at which point that black syllable *tri,* the seed of the hells, will have been destroyed and become nonexistent. Thereafter, such a person will never be in danger of being born in the hells. In that way, from the perspective of appearance, these experiences in the form of the hot and cold sufferings of the hells are samsara. Because they are in essence nondual primordial awareness arisen from cultivation of the meditative concentrations of the two stages, they are nirvana.

Similarly, it is taught:

> If the vital winds and mind gather together in the syllables of the six realms that first formed at the navel, there are the dances of the

> six realms, the mantras, being guided there, dreams, and similar experiences, which appear as the entire three worlds.[763] [361]

Thus, whenever the vital winds and mind have gathered in a seed syllable of the six realms, *dances,* which are physical postures, occur. The *mantras* are the speech of various languages. Concerning "being guided there," when a person whose vital winds and mind have gathered in the channel of the hells is guided into any building, the appearance of being guided into a pit of fire or a cavity of ice arises. Wherever one whose vital winds and mind have gathered into the channel of the gods is guided, the experience of being guided into a celestial mansion of jewels occurs. Therefore, due to the key point of appearances being only one's own mind and not established as external objects, these arise corresponding to the individual mental appearance. That is also the meaning of these words:

> We maintain that because a single thing
> appears differently to the mind,
> it is not established as an entity.[764]

And also:

> Who made the ground of glowing iron?[765]

In brief, various sufferings of the six realms may be experienced, but they are not experienced by the force of evil karma; they are nondual primordial awareness arisen from cultivation of the meditative concentration of the two stages. And by means of that, one is liberated from birth in any of the six realms for which the purification of birthplace has occurred.

During postmeditation, think: "Alas! If I am unable to bear and withstand such suffering that is just an experience of the hells without having died and without having changed bodies, what would I do if I were born there? I will never perform unwholesome actions!"

Unerring certainty in the causes and results of actions will arise, the effect of which will be the removal of all wrong views about the nonexistence of cause and result, past and future lives being untrue, and so forth.

(b) *The experiences of the path*

By virtue of the habitual propensities present in the mind from having been a non-Buddhist, those types of channels are present in the body. When the vital winds and mind have gathered in those, one thinks that the individual philosophical tenets of the non-Buddhists advocating Brahmā, Śiva, Fate, and so forth as the primal cause are each true, and certainty arises. When the vital winds and mind have gathered in the channels of the śrāvakas, pratyekabuddhas, Cittamātrins, and Madhyamikas, adherence to particular views and philosophical tenets as true will arise. Although these are different from adherence and attachment to each as true due to the force of karma or due to having been accepted by a spiritual friend, they arise in a form similar to that. [362] Based on this, certainty will arise and one will think, "Numerous stages of the path and different vehicles exist, but they exist merely in the perception of individual beings. In essence they do not transcend unity." Thus my master taught.

(c) *The experiences of the result*

It is taught:

> If dissolved in the mansion of the great mother Prajñāpāramitā and so forth, the dharmakāya reality body is experienced and there is freedom from subject and object.[766]

Thus, dependent on the vital winds and mind gathered in the channel syllables of nirvana, one thinks that the dharmakāya reality body is experienced and thinks that one is free from all thoughts of subject and object. When the vital winds and mind have gathered in the *bhrūṃ, āṃ, jrīṃ,* and *khaṃ* of the heart,[767] one thinks one is actually the sambhogakāya enjoyment bodies of the five spiritual families, and beholds their faces. If the vital winds and mind have gathered in the *laṃ, māṃ, pāṃ,* and *tāṃ,*[768] one thinks one is actually the five consorts. And so forth.

On the basis of that, during postmeditation one will think: "If even my attainment of the qualities of buddhahood in the form of these experiences is so wonderful, if I attained actual buddhahood itself the qualities of it would be immeasurable. Therefore, I must very quickly—without delay—attain buddhahood!"

With intense effort on the path, like a trader who pays no attention to the difficulties and exhaustion on the path if he has seen the profit to come in the trade, one will utterly abandon all sham turmoil and will practice.

It is taught:

> All phenomena are established
> by means of the four authentic qualities.[769]

Similarly, the authentic quality of experience, which is the fifteen experiences—the five sets of three—and so forth, will completely arise in one's mindstream.

At that point one will reach a decisive conclusion, thinking: "That master of mine is the essence of all the buddhas of the three times; he presents without error the fundamental nature of all phenomena; and he is the combined essence of all the buddhas." This is the authentic quality of the master.

One thinks: "Because what occurred just as the master taught is also explained in this way by the great venerable Lord of Yogins in the small treatise of the *Vajra Lines,* that teacher is also certainly beyond all dispute." This is the authentic quality of the treatise.

When one sees that precisely this is also taught in various forms in all the sutras and tantras, and in the teachings of the Sugata such as the *Two-Part Root Tantra,* one thinks, "The Conqueror is infallible." This is the authentic quality of scripture as the perfect word. [363] Thus my master taught.

c) *The resultant indivisibility of samsara and nirvana*

It is taught:

> If the natural cause is reflected upon,
> it is spontaneity,
> and the mass of limitless qualities
> are transformable.
> Thus spontaneity and transformation
> are not contradictory.
> This is the resultant indivisibility
> of samsara and nirvana.[770]

This means the result to be attained by practicing these paths is also present as the indivisibility of samsara and nirvana. Precisely those three resultant bodies of enlightenment—the lucidity of the mind spontaneously present as the nirmāṇakāya emanated body, emptiness as the dharmakāya reality body, and their unity as the sambhogakāya enjoyment body—are called "the Hevajra of the time of the ground." Precisely that is transformed into the Hevajra of the time of the path and, through practice, the fifteen experiences—the five sets of three—and so forth increase as good qualities. When all the incidental stains within the mind have been purified into space, all the good qualities—the qualities of the dharmakāya reality body, which are the ten powers, the four fearless traits, and the four clearly distinct applications of mindfulness—are actualized by way of transformation.[771] Therefore, the Hevajra of the spontaneous ground is samsara. The Hevajra of the time of the path and of the result is nirvana. Like the same copper appearing in separate forms, these arise in different forms, but their essence is nothing but the mind—the lucidity, emptiness, and unity of the time of the ground—and so they are indivisible.

In brief, the sambhogakāya enjoyment body is endowed with the five certainties,[772] and that same mental continuum free from all conceptual elaborations is the dharmakāya reality body. Although it does not stray from that, to the superior disciples it emanates in the form of the circle of the mandala of the sublime nirmāṇakāya emanated bodies such as Hevajra, Cakrasaṃvara, and Guhyasamāja. To the middling disciples it emanates as the middling nirmāṇakāya emanated body, the buddha who displays the twelve deeds. To the inferior disciples it emanates as any form of the environment and its inhabitants that will be appropriate to train them. At that time, the nirmāṇakāya emanated body is designated as samsara and the sambhogakāya enjoyment body as nirvana. In summation, it is taught:

> The buddha called the *sixth* is one,
> but performs numerous dances.[773]

Thus, the buddha of the sixth spiritual family is the buddha of the time of the ground. [364] That single [buddha] appears in the numerous forms of the ground, path, and result. As for how it appears, it is taught:

> It appears like dancers
> and like a fine drawing.[774]

Whatever postures a dancer assumes, such as peaceful, wrathful, lying on the back, face down, right arms or legs extended, and left arms or legs extended, the essence does not become any better than the dancer. Similarly, the appearances of samsara and nirvana arise in various forms, but the essence of the mind itself is never established as better or worse. Thus my master taught.

In summation, introduction is by means of the three aspects of coemergence. If the introduction is ineffective, or in order to stabilize and enhance the introduction, the extensive explication with the examples by means of the three key points of practice is presented. How the ground, path, and result are each the indivisibility of samsara and nirvana is presented as the extensive explication of the Three Continua. If all of that is completely condensed, it is contained in just this united lucidity and emptiness of the mind. Just being introduced to that and recognizing it once is not sufficient. If it is not sustained by attentive mindfulness without forgetting it, one will return to being no different from an ordinary person. From now on, whatever appearances of the time of the ground arise (the environment and its inhabitants, enemies or friends), rest at ease in the real essence without examining their forms. This is the indivisibility of samsara and nirvana, a united lucidity and emptiness in which the appearances of the objects are unceasing, but no grasping arises. Whatever thoughts (movements of the mind) arise within, do not examine their forms. If one rests looking nakedly at the essence, that mere appearance, the lucid aspect, is samsara. Its essence, naked emptiness, is nirvana. Whatever appearances of the path (the yogas of creation and completion) are meditated upon, the one taking refuge during the preliminaries is united lucidity and emptiness. Because the mere appearance of all the sources of refuge and the taking of refuge is lucidity, and not clinging to them is emptiness, the indivisibility of samsara and nirvana is present in taking refuge. Similarly, understand everything—from the awakening of the enlightenment mind to the daily activities—to be the indivisibility of samsara and nirvana, and practice.

In brief, it is taught beginning with the words:

> Precisely this is known as samsara.[775]

The meaning is that precisely this lucidity of the mind is known as *samsara.* Its essence, precisely this emptiness, is *nirvana.* Therefore, samsara—the lucidity of the mind—is not discovered by searching, because precisely this is emptiness. [365] After abandoning this, another emptiness—nirvana—will not be discovered outside. Therefore, one should understand whatever appearances arise to be united lucidity and emptiness, and remain undistracted.

Precisely that is the heart of secret mantra. *Secret* is added to mean that it is secret to the unfortunate. *Mantra* means protection of the mind from conceptual marks. Any radiance of lucidity that arises is a mark. Distinguishing it to be good, bad, and so forth is conceptual. Because mantra is able to protect one from this, it is the heart.

Although a wish-fulfilling jewel has been obtained in hand, if it is not cleansed with the three preparations[776] and prayers are not offered, the attainments will not occur. Similarly, a profound path like this has been obtained, but if it is not practiced the attainments will not occur. If the jewel is placed on the point of a victory banner and worshipped and prayed to, the fulfillment of all wishes occurs. Similarly, once these profound oral instructions have been obtained, if they are practiced with attentive mindfulness, without forgetting them, the sublime and common attainments will occur. Therefore, maintain them at all times, without forgetting.

At first, combine these oral instructions with the circumstance of [something like] the pain of a thorn. The stinging heat is lucidity. The essence of that heat, not discovered by searching, is emptiness. Rest upon that. Then combine the oral instructions with all circumstances. The more firewood of what is to be discarded, the stronger the fire of the antidote. Similarly, by combining them with all impediments and obstacles, and practicing, all the good qualities of experience, realization, and so forth will increase. Thus my master taught.

> The sun of the teachings
> of the wild father and master
> is a path illuminating
> all the phenomena of samsara and nirvana.
> When a hundred thousand great lights
> of confidence shone here,
> the dense darkness of dualistic
> appearances was banished.

Difficult to discover through countless eons,
the vajra words should not be forgotten,
but held in the heart.
Although my heart is empty
and I have recorded secret talk
in rows of words on paper,
please continue to long protect me
with your compassion!

Enough of that unnecessary confused turmoil!
Now I'll live as I please in an isolated
mountain gorge with no people,
sustaining the inexpressible fundamental nature.
One must not waste this! Think about it!

8. Summarizing Notes on the Outer Creation Stage

From the Expansion of the Great Secret Doctrine

Summarizing Notes of Guidance for the Precious Teaching of the "Path with the Result"

The Infallible Version of Khau Drakzongpa

Jamyang Khyentsé Wangchuk (1524–68)

I PROSTRATE AND TAKE REFUGE at the feet of my spiritual father and master, the overlord of a hundred spiritual families, great Heruka himself. Please bless me that appearances arise as the sphere of the mandala.

2. *Explanation of the path in connection with the four initiations concerning the method continuum of the body*[777]

In regard to this, one might ask, "That meditation on the view of the indivisibility of samsara and nirvana in the causal continuum of the universal ground, which primarily targeted the key points of the mind that is the ground of purification, established that the fundamental nature of all phenomena is inexpressible. Is that sufficient?"

It is not. That is called "the view of the time of the cause," "the view equal to that of the Vehicle of the Perfections," and "the view entailing adherence to an individual philosophical tenet." In brief, while it is just possible that the fundamental nature of all phenomena may be experienced dependent on the uncommon examples, the others merely create an intellectual understanding. That much can also be established by means of the reasoning of the Madhyamaka and so forth, for as the Dharma lord Sakya Paṇḍita says:

> If a view greater than
> the view of the Perfections
> were to exist,
> that view would contain
> conceptual elaboration.[778]

A path such as that is much greater than [the path] of an ordinary person. However, other than the identification of lucidity and just resting upon precisely that, no transformation of that lucidity into the deity and the primordial awareness of great bliss and so forth by means of exceptional methods occurs, and so it is slightly less profound. However, it is necessary because—on the basis of that previous presentation—all the paths that are described following will be united with wisdom, or emptiness. [368] And dependent on that, the path will be free from errors.

The heart of the path is this path of the four initiations. In the yoga tantras and the lower tantras, even just the names of the four supporting mandalas, which are the extremely profound ground of purification, are not taught. Because of that, the purifying path, which is the two stages, is not taught. Because that path is absent, it is not possible to quickly obtain the four bodies of enlightenment, which are the result. The *Sampuṭa* says:

> Because the real nature
> of the body is not understood,
> all those practices
> of the eighty-four thousand
> articles of Dharma
> are said to be without result.[779]

No matter how energetic one is in all the practices of Dharma other than the unexcelled Vajrayana, from the vehicle of the śrāvakas through the yoga tantras, it is impossible to achieve the citadel of unity in this lifetime because one does not come to understand the real nature of the body that is the ground of purification, and then target its key points. Thus, "without result" indicates an inferior result and is used as a term of denigration.

Therefore, as the ground of purification, targeting the key points of the body is much more profound than targeting the key points of the mind. For example, if one wants the head to ache and meditates on that for a long time, the head will begin to ache due to the key point of appearances being one's mind. In regard to the body, pain will occur as soon as the head is actually hit with something hard such as a stone.

Moreover, in secret mantra in general, sets consisting of two are prominent: the pair of body and mind as the ground of purification, the pair of creation and completion as the purifying agent, and the pair of the bodies of enlightenment as the result of purification. But it was the custom of the venerable Lord of Yogins to explain by means of sets consisting of four: the four supporting mandalas as the ground of purification, the four classes of tantra, initiations, and paths, and the four bodies of enlightenment as the result. When it is taught, "For the method continuum of the body,"[780] "body" means the four supporting mandalas. As for the path of the four initiations, it is taught:

> Presentation by means of the four fives of the creation stage as the path and so forth.[781]

The four paths are the creation stage, the self-blessing, the mandalacakra, and the vajra waves. By adding the view, the culmination of attainment, and so forth, each of the four initiations includes five topics, for a total of twenty. Or else, by giving the paths the names of the initiations, the four are the path of the vase initiation and so forth. Hence, there are no more than twenty, according to the tradition of the Explication for the Assembly.

However, according to the tradition of the Explication for Disciples, by taking the three essences (which are the view of the creation stage) as the path on the mundane path, the indivisibility of samsara and nirvana as the culmination of attainment is realized on the transcendent path, and one is liberated. [369] If one is unable to reach the culmination of attainment in this lifetime because of weak faculties and lack of diligence, the practice when passing away is necessary. If that also does not turn out exactly right, the practice of the intermediate state is necessary. To evaluate whether or not one will be able to bring the experiences of the intermediate state under control, the dream yoga is necessary. For recognition of dream at night, the illusory body is necessary during the day. Therefore, these practices are presented in sequence. Thus my master taught. In that way, each initiation includes six topics.[782]

a. *The vase initiation*

To begin with, six topics are connected with the vase initiation.

1) *The path: the creation stage*

This consists of two topics:

a) The outer creation stage
b) The inner creation stage[783]

a) *The outer creation stage*

This also consists of two topics:

(1) The practices of the creation stage
(2) The mental focusing

(1) *The practices of the creation stage*

The great venerable lord Drakpa Gyaltsen says in the *Guidance Manual for Jochak:*

> Then, before entering into the practice, receive the initiation of the time of the path from the master and mend the sacred commitments.[784]

Thus, if one is doing the practice in the extensive way, one again requests from the master the initiation in the outer mandala, either colored powder or painted cloth. The term *time of the path* is used because—from first obtaining the initiation of the time of the cause, until the initiation in conjunction with the result—the entire path upon which that person depends is only initiation. This is not the initiation of the body mandala. Thus my master taught.

Furthermore, while an initiation used to be bestowed at this point (as may also be known from the stories of Drokmi Lotsāwa's time), nowadays this practice is not followed.

Similarly, if one has time for the extensive way, it is taught that the basic recitation retreat should also be done during this interval. If this is accomplished it is good, but it is not absolutely indispensable. However, it definitely must be accomplished before one engages in the activities of a vajra master. Thus my master taught.

In brief, the *extensive* practice of the creation stage is to complete the recitation retreat, down to the burnt offering with a tenth of the mantras. The *middling* is requesting the initiation or taking the suitable self-entry and performing the practices of accumulation and purification. The *condensed* is the practices of accumulation and purification alone. Of these three ways, the last one is indispensable and must be completed. Therefore, as explained previously, offer the mandala of seven heaps and so forth in front of the created mandala of either one heap or five, together with the verses beginning, "This pristine, pure realm," composed by the Dharma lord Sakya Paṇḍita.[785] Also perform the hundred syllables as explained before. [370]

(2) *The practices of mental focusing*

This consists of three topics:

(a) Engaging
(b) Resting
(c) Arising

(a) *Engaging*

This is the practice of engaging something special as the object of mental focusing. Seated on a comfortable cushion, correctly maintain the key physical points with the body in the sevenfold posture of Vairocana: the hands held in the mudrā gesture of meditative equipoise except during the specific times of performing mudrā gestures and counting the rosary, the eyes gazing just at the tip of the nose, and so forth. In regard to the methods for direct realization that are to be practiced, both the methods of four branches and of six branches are the practices of a beginner, so the process of direct enlightenment dependent on the vowels such as *a* and the consonant-syllables such as *ka* is definitely required.[786] If other practitioners prefer the elaborate method, it is sufficient to meditate on the six branches. It is absolutely no different for one to meditate on whichever appeals to the mind, such as [two triangular moons] joined together, [sun and moon] not joined together, an emanation of drops, and an emanation of seed syllables. However, [the sun and moon] slightly separated is considered profound because an actual correspondence exists between that and the ground of purification of birth from a womb.

In any case, be motivated by intense aspiration and think: "I must very quickly and without delay reach the citadel of unity for the benefit of all sentient beings."

Begin by taking refuge, and meditate—until the sealing of the lord of the spiritual family, if according to the four branches; and until the eulogy (the branch of Ratnasambahava) if according to the six branches.

The precise way to meditate

The great venerable lord [Sachen] says:

> Intense, lucid, and short,
> are the crucial key points
> for the creation stage.[787]

Intense means that the recited words should be steadily recited without mumbled or interrupted speech, "just audible to one in front," at a volume barely audible nearby.

Lucid means that [the recitation] should not be just words; each word should connect with each visualization. When reciting "I and," clearly focus on oneself. When reciting "the living beings who have been my mother throughout the three realms, all sentient beings equal to the sky," immediately envision all sentient beings as mental objects. When reciting "in the master" and "in the buddhas," feel deep devotion for the main deity of the mandala, thinking "May you be aware of me!" When reciting "in the Dharma," feel devotion toward the volumes of Dharma stacked up like a mountain behind the form of the deity. When reciting "in the Sangha," feel devotion for the goddesses of the retinue. [371] In a similar way, precisely connect each ground of purification and each purifying agent exactly as they occur in the commentaries. Even if one does not know that much, make the particular forms clearly appear as mental objects. In brief, never be without visualization.

Short means that by making both words and meaning lucid and short, not tortuous and long like the spiritual practice of Shangpo Sötré, a pure state without other thoughts will occur. If not already lucid, nothing will become lucid by remaining dull for a long period, and numerous other thoughts will have already arisen in the meantime. And when one rests in a lucid state for a long period, it may have already become affected by other thoughts in the meantime, like water underneath ice. Do not let that happen.

Furthermore, the *Root Tantra* says:

> Like the steady flow
> of a stream of water
> and the steady flicker
> of the tip of a lamp flame.[788]

This presents similies for both the words and the meaning. The streams of water that flow over the edge of a mountain cliff fall without pause, one after the other. In a similar way, recite steadily, without gaps between the words. The tips of a lamp flame also flicker one after the other. Similarly, meditate without any intervals in visualization.

In brief, without allowing the mind to slip into bad habits, never allow the words and the visualization to separate, and without allowing the body to slip into bad habits, never abandon the key physical points until the session is finished, no matter what happens. If one practices with courage and effort, experience will certainly occur immediately. Therefore, these are the crucial points of meditation for the creation stage. The *lucid, intense,* and *short* mentioned here have also been further elaborated with "lucid is lucid words," and so forth, but our tradition is as explained here. Thus my master taught.

(b) *Resting*

This is the actual mental focusing, which consists of two topics:

1' Focusing the mind on the pride
2' Focusing the mind on the forms

1' *Focusing the mind on the pride*

The ground of purification is the "coemergent clinging to an 'I,'" which sentient beings have, and which becomes the root of samsara. That clinging is a lack of awareness, or ignorance. Based on clinging to a self, other beings are established. Thoughts of attachment and hatred arise from that; this is the affliction of affliction. This accumulates karma, which is the affliction of karma. By virtue of that, one is born in samsara, which is the affliction of birth. [372]

Briefly, in order to purify that which causes all the confusing appearances of samsara to arise, after completing the practice up through the branch of the eulogy, serenely set aside the mandala and so forth for a while and meditate with firm pride, thinking: "I am not an ordinary being. I am actually glorious Hevajra, arisen from the accumulation of the two assemblies as the cause, born from the fivefold process of direct enlightenment with the nature of the five types of primordial awareness, the one who delights the goddesses of the retinue and rested in a droplet globe with the nature of the dharmakāya reality body, but then arose due to the urging of the songs of the four goddesses. I am appearance and emptiness indivisible, space and primordial awareness indivisible, the Buddha's dharmakāya reality body and rūpakāya form bodies indivisible, residing on the thirteenth spiritual level of a vajra holder at the time of the result, with all faults exhausted and all good qualities perfected."

When that has been clearly imagined, rest at ease without clinging in just that state, the essence of which is totally unestablished emptiness, transcending all theoretical knowledge and beyond all possibility of expression.

Again, whatever thought may arise, be proud as before, without following after it, thinking, "I am actually glorious Hevajra." Rest upon precisely that, without clinging.

Briefly, this ordinary body arises as just a confusing appearance, in which the very essence of the united lucidity and emptiness of the mind is not recognized. No body of samsara exists as the ground of purification established outside of this momentary mind. When precisely that momentary pure awareness arises in the form of the Hevajra of the time of the path, those grounds of purification transform into the essence of the purifying path. Because the result of purification, or what is to be obtained, is also not established outside of one's mind, precisely this is actually Hevajra residing on the thirteenth spiritual level of a vajra holder. Thinking that, apply the seal of pure appearance and take that as the path. At that point, the ground, path, and result have become indivisible in the perception of the yogin. Precisely that is also the indivisibility of samsara and nirvana. Thus my master taught.

In brief, the creation stage of lucid appearance and firm pride that has not been pervaded by the indivisibility of samsara and nirvana is able to accomplish the common attainments without impediment, but it is somewhat unable to yield the sublime attainment. The labeling of its result by adherents of the *Bodhisattva Commentaries* is also done with this point in mind.[789] [373] Because the way it was explained previously unites the creation and completion stages, that is the main method for achieving buddhahood. But with just one, after those two have been separated, it is not possible to obtain the sublime. Thus my master taught.

Therefore, the *Vajrapañjara* says:

> With the proud yoga
> of being a buddha,
> one will quickly
> achieve buddhahood.[790]

This is the firm pride of thinking that one is actually Buddha Hevajra. And it is also taught:

> The yoga of the union
> of method and wisdom
> was taught by the Tathāgata.[791]

Thus a yogin of unity who understands the essence of that pride to be emptiness will quickly and without delay achieve the citadel of buddhahood. Thus my master taught.

In that way, from a state of firm pride and the knowledge that its essence is inexpressible, practice until the pride vividly arises without depending on attention, and until the thought, "I am actually Hevajra" arises even in a dream.

(c) *Arising*[792]

When one wishes to arise from that session, meditate on the fierce fire dependent on four cakras or, since precisely that meditative equipoise in a lucid yet empty state is itself the completion stage, it is also fine not to meditate on it separately. Be mindful of the purity,[793] and perform the recitations, up to the gathering-in of the mandala. Dedicate the sacrificial cake or, if that is not done, just recite the vajra song and the auspicious prayers to bless the session, and enter into the activities between sessions.

Divide it into four sessions in that way and practice.

2' *Focusing the mind on the forms*

This consists of two topics:

a' Focusing the mind on the general forms
b' Focusing the mind on the individual forms

a' *Focusing the mind on the general forms*

Engaging and arising are as before.

Resting

Think: "I am actually Hevajra."

One might wonder, "What kind of form does Hevajra have?"

He has a body with eight faces, sixteen arms, and four legs, and is in union with mother Vajra Nairātmyā. The eight goddesses of the retinue are present. Outside of them is the celestial mansion. Outside of that is the Dharma tetrahedron. Outside of that are the eight charnel grounds. But it is also taught:

> What are to be purified
> reside inside or outside
> the purifying agent.[794]

Thus the charnel grounds may be visualized either outside the common protection cakra or inside it and outside the uncommon one.

Outside of that tetrahedron is the golden cakra with ten spokes. Outside of that is the vajra fence and pavilion, together with the blazing fire of primordial awareness. Rest without clinging in just that state, in which everything is brilliantly vivid, like a dream, like an illusion, like a moon reflected in water, with one thing not obscured by another, radiantly lucid with the nature of light. [374] Again, imagine clearly and meditate.

Furthermore, according to the accounts of the words of the masters, this creation stage is similar to starting a fire in a great forest. When one has merely eliminated doubts by means of learning and reflection on the meaning of what is to be meditated upon, one may think, "This is it,"and have a brilliant intellectual understanding of it, but it has not actually arisen in the mindstream. For example, much explanation may be given about how to start a fire, so that one thinks, "If a fire were started in this forest in this way, everything would catch fire," but since a fire has not actually been started, not even one branch has burned. Similarly, when guidance is given, and one's mind is first focused on the general forms, it is also possible for meditative concentration to arise for fortunate ones who possess the karma. For others, the appearance of just the general forms is like taking something such as a firebrand and wandering through the entire forest, at which point it is possible that some single thing may catch fire. The arising of experience when focusing one's mind on the individual forms is like concentrating the fire and starting it at a crucial point such as a dry tree, after which it will gradually spread everywhere and all appearances will blaze with fire. Thus my master taught.

b' *Focusing the mind on the individual forms*[795]

Of the four transmission lines of Hevajra possessed by the venerable lords of Sakya, the tradition of Kṛṣṇa is held in somewhat less esteem because no more than just the initiation and reading transmission remain. Because the complete ripening initiations and liberating guidance are possessed for the other three, they are considered more valuable.[796] At this point in the tradition of the esoteric instructions, some procedures also correspond to those traditions. Based on the division into four branches actually presented in the *Root Tantra,* Padmavajra composed a method for accomplishment in four branches, and dependent on the teaching of six branches in the *Vajrapañjara,* Durjayacandra divided it into six. Correspondingly, here also both the four- and six-branch methods for accomplishment agree with those.

Similarly, the great venerable lord Drakpa Gyaltsen used just the central eye for the mental focusing of the creation stage and lord Lama Dampa did not use more than seven visualizations. [375] But in agreement with Saroruha,[797] Ngorchen Dorjé Chang used thirty-two visualizations. Thus my master taught.

Furthermore, usually the followers of the father tantras mostly begin the mental focusing from the jewel of the cranial dome and the followers of the mother tantras mostly begin from the lotus and sun seats. However, in the treatises of nondual Hevajra, beginning the mental focusing from the central eye is accepted as especially profound. Because no exceptional key points as grounds of purification correspond to those other points, it is difficult for meditative concentration to arise immediately. And even when it does arise, it is difficult for faultless [meditative concentration] to arise. Because an exceptional key point as the ground of purification is present here, faultless meditative concentration will quickly arise. For example, in terms of drawing milk from a cow, the milk will come as soon as an udder is pulled, but no milk will come no matter how much other parts of the body such as the horns and the tail are pulled. Similarly, with regard to targeting the key points of the body in the unexcelled Vajrayana, meditative concentration will quickly arise dependent on an exceptional key point, but it will not arise when just any point of the body is targeted. Here, the central channel has three upper ends. The first extends into the aperture of Brahmā at the top of the head, on the basis of which the esoteric instructions of transference are taken as the path. The second extends into the point between the eyebrows. The third extends into the base of the uvula, on the basis of which the instruction for cutting the stream[798] is is taken as the path. The results of purification from targeting the key points of those exceptional grounds of purification are the creation of the cranial dome of the head, the tuft of hair between the eyebrows, the central eye on wrathful deities, and so forth. Thus my master taught.

The precise way to practice

After focusing the mind on the general forms, meditate on the central eye between one's eyebrows, which looks like the left eye standing upright. Because Hevajra is a wrathful being of the angry seer category, the upper and lower corners of the eye become narrow, and the orange eyebrow and eyelash are glowing like fire. The eyeball is black in the center, pale around that, and is bloodshot. When the eye is clearly imagined, blend that and one's mind together indivisibly and rest serenely. It is taught:

> If lucid, cut the stream while lucid. If not lucid, cut the stream while not lucid. Extract the poison of meditation.[799]

The poison of meditation is the thoughts that circulate underneath, which are referred to as "thieving thoughts that are the māras of meditation." [376] According to our tradition, these become extensive yet are unnoticed, in the manner of two thoughts simultaneously entering the mind and circulating underneath what is at the surface of the visualization, like water underneath ice.

What extracts this [poison]? Meditate for a short period, and then rest the mind on an object slightly below and in front of one, such as a pillar or a vase. If the central eye has been clearly imagined, that is good, but even if it has not, rest for a while.

If another thought starts to arise, do not be swept away by it; strongly rest the reflexive awareness upon that object in front.

Again, just before being swept away by another thought, focus the mind on the central eye.

Again, shift the focus out.

In brief, by means of such short and pure states, focus the mind alternately on both the central eye and the object in front, without allowing any other thoughts to arise.

If one is resting at ease in a nonconceptual state blended with calm abiding as before, one need not shift the focus. Rest evenly for as long as it remains.

When one practices in that way, three purities will actualize as the signs of perfection. The central eye seeming to actually appear during meditation is the purity of the individual deity. That it does not appear when one is not meditating is the purity of suchness. The arising of any of the three meditative concentrations[800] of calm abiding is the purity of reflexive awareness.

Furthermore, the mental focusing on the blue flower described before was just focusing the mind. This is very different, because not only does it cause the meditative concentration of calm abiding to arise, but it is also the uncommon cause that establishes a buddha's rūpakāya form bodies. And this calm abiding arises as a calm abiding that completely calms all conceptual marks. As it is taught:

> Extracting the poison of the view by meditating on a thought
> that purifies the mind, which is the path of eliminating entry.[801]

When one practices in this way, calm abiding, the path of eliminating entry, arises as one of the three essences. "Entry" means the uninterrupted entry of one thought after another. The way of "eliminating" that is the complete calming of conceptual marks by means of focusing the mind on something such as the central eye—[the arising of thoughts are arrested] like reining in a horse, or a fly stuck in glue, or damming up a running stream—and then resting serenely in a nonconceptual state. Because that cleanses the stains present within the mind, it "purifies the mind." Because meditating on its essence as the enlightened body of the deity and so forth are good thoughts, it is "a thought." Meditating on that eliminates the poison of the view, which is thoughts like "All phenomena are inexpressible." These are conceptual in nature and are thus the poison of the view. [377]

Furthermore, the central eye brilliantly lucid as though actually present during meditation is the essence of the apparent aspect. During meditation on the central eye, if it is not lucid, and the mind is also focused on pristine emptiness like space, without any other circulation of thoughts, it is the essence of the empty aspect.

Without either of those two occurring, the five signs of clear light may arise, such as twisting and shimmering bunches of bluish thin smoke, or rusty mist, or mirages, the glittering red forms of fireflies, and the flickering and fleeting red forms of lamp flames. And the five signs of the signs and so forth may arise.[802] In a similar way, one thinks that everything below the *peak* of existence appears in the experiences of meditative concentration. The unexplainable is illustrated.[803] Thus appearances of everything possible in samsara and nirvana may arise. Focusing the mind in that state and resting once without thoughts, where the arising of one thought after another is arrested like reining in a racing horse or like a fly stuck in glue, is known as "the essence of unity."

Those manifestations are explained in the *Kālacakra* and so forth to be emptiness sublimely endowed with all aspects. Similarly, it is also appropriate to label them with that term here. As for what this tradition accepts as *sublimely endowed with all aspects,* it accepts that all the phenomena of samsara and nirvana are complete within a single momentary instant of one's mind.

In brief, although both the essence of the apparent aspect and that of the empty aspect are flawed experiences, and that of their unity is a flawless experience, if any of these arise, for a while one is cut out from the herd of those referred to by the phrase "for a sentient being with afflictions" and is placed in the category of those referred to by the line "For a yogin with meditative concentration, experiential appearance occurs."[804] The approximate actual presentations of the explications of the treatise of the *Vajra Lines* seem to say that only flawless experiences arise during the transcendent path. However, until the thirteenth spiritual level of a vajra holder is reached, they arise in combination, with only greater or lesser proportion. Thus my master taught.

If a single experience of the essence has not arisen in the mindstream, no matter how well one acts one will not accomplish genuine benefit for oneself and others, because one has not risen above the state of an ordinary "sentient being." Therefore, meditate with great courage and do whatever it takes for meditative concentration to arise in the mindstream. [378] These paths, transmitted from Vajradhara without interruption, were explained by the Lord of Yogins exactly according to the teaching of Vajra Nairātmyā. Then they were explained by each following master exactly according to the teachings of each previous one, until they reached one's root master. This is a Dharma of the unbroken transmission of the meaning and the words of experience, from which wafts the fresh breath of the ḍākinīs. If one is able to meditate, one will arrive at the beginning of experience within three or four days. So be energetic and meditate!

At the least, meditate until each visualization becomes lucid and convincing. By means of that, the transmission of the meaning will be unbroken. Then, after one goes to an isolated place and meditates on the stream of that previous experience, experience and realization will arise. Thus my master taught.

Arising and so forth are as before.

Meditating in that way, if meditative concentration has arisen just by means of clearly imagining the central eye to that degree, that is sufficient. If it has not arisen, enhancement consists of both clear imagination by means of speech and clear imagination by means of drawing.

First, in regard to clear imagination by means of one's own speech, after the engaging and meditating with divine pride, up to the clear imagination of the central eye, say aloud, "The central eye is black in the center, pale around that, and is bloodshot," and clearly imagine it. Again, rest the attention upon an object in front.

Again, say and clearly imagine that, or else have someone (like a trustworthy friend) sit nearby and say it aloud while one clearly imagines it and meditates. Do whichever of the two is clearest.

Second, focusing the mind on a central eye drawn in front is slightly less profound, so draw it on something like cloth or paper and attach it between one's eyebrows. Make it appear inside a clean mirror in front of one, and focus the mind on it. Before another thought arises, meditate on it between the eyebrows.

In summation, alternate those two [practices] and meditate until any one of the three experiences has arisen.[805]

Furthermore, if an experience of calm abiding has arisen on the basis of the central eye, the other [experiences] will occur in a supplementary way. If no more than a rough approximation occurs here, no more than a rough approximation of the others will also occur, so targeting the key point here is crucial. Thus my master taught.

Similarly, by changing the visualizations for focusing the mind on the individual forms during each of the four sessions, the thirty-two visualizations are completed in eight days. The root of this practice is the precious venerable lord Drakpa Gyaltsen's text on the "nine profound means" of the creation stage according to Saroruha,[806] so it is crucial that it correspond to that. Thus my master taught. [379]

That is the first session of the first day, focusing on the central eye.

For the second session, in addition to the central eye, practice focusing the mind on the two right and left eyes, black in the center, pale around that, and bloodshot, the two corners of the eyes narrowing, and the orange eyebrows and eyelashes glowing with light like fire.

For the third session, focus on the two and a half wrinkles of wrath between the eyebrows. Furthermore, the two on the right and left are somewhat coarse and that in the middle is somewhat thinner. They are azure like the color of beryl, and have the nature of light.

For the fourth session, practice focusing the mind on just the high bridge of the nose, with the openings of the nostrils bright red.

The yoga of arising is as before.

In that way, both engaging and arising are done as before, and the visualizations while resting are changed for the individual sessions.

For the first session of the second day, in addition to the previous visualizations, focus the mind on the fine interior of the lips in the form of the lips of a lotus petal. The outsides of the lips are like the color of clear beryl. Their edges are red like crabapples or coral. Because Hevajra is a wrathful being of the angry seer category, his mouth is not gaping wide open, but [is shaped as if he were] saying [something like], "hey hey." He has forty white and evenly arranged teeth, as well as two pairs of fangs, one upper and one lower; these are about half a tooth longer than all the other teeth, protrude slightly, and have curved points like the shape of a crescent moon. This is the meaning of *ardhentu daṃkṣṭiṇe—endowed with crescent-moon fangs.*[807] The whole interior of the mouth is pure red, with the nature of light. The tongue is thin and supple, with its tip curled slightly upward and flickering about.

For the second session, both ears have cartilage and so forth exactly like one's own now, but with very long earlobes nearly reaching both shoulders.

For the third session, practice focusing the mind on the complete mandala of the face, with just the right plumpness, not with cheeks that have become too emaciated and hollow, and also not like the corpulent angry wrathful beings such as the yamas or the yakṣas. Three wrinkles of suitable length are also present in the flesh of the throat. [The face] has the nature of light. If its blueness is observed, it is blue, and if its clearness is observed, it is clear, like the autumn sky free from the three flaws of the sun, the moon, and atmospheric obscurations.

For the fourth session, focus the mind on the right white face, white like a conch shell, the moon, or a jasmine flower, clear like a crystal jewel, and glowing with light. [380] Its central eye, two other eyes, and two and a half wrinkles of wrath between the eyebrows are also present. The bridge of the nose is high, and the face has a smiling expression. The ear is directly against the ear of the main face. The complete face is like a hundred thousand moons shining at once. The throat has the three designs. Thinking this, practice focusing the mind on each point as before. Meditate that this face has a slightly calmer expression than the main face. The color of the throat corresponds to the color of the body. The throat slightly bulges directly at each individual face. Thus my master taught.

For the first session of the third day, in addition to the previous visualizations, focus the mind on the left red face, red like ruby or polished coral, clear and glowing with light. Focus the mind [on the parts of the face] in sequence, from its central eye to its ears, and on the complete face having a passionate expression, together with the throat.

For the second session, focus the mind on the remaining right faces. Phakpa Rinpoché[808] and others have referred to these as the *back faces,* and since they are located to the back of the right face and so forth, it is appropriate to label them in that way, but they are not located at the actual back of the head like the back face of Saṃvara. It is taught:

> The remaining faces are like bees.[809]

This refers to the remaining right and left faces. One face is beside the right white face, with the ear of this one directly against its ear. And one face is beside that one. Both are also very black, like bees. Their central eyes, two other eyes, three slightly coarse wrinkles of wrath, slightly bulging noses, and earlobes are all present. They have expressions slightly more wrathful than the main face. The throat just bulges at each and has the three designs.

For the third session, focus the mind as before on the two remaining left faces.

Between the last two such faces, at the back of the main face, orange hair floats up, four of the Blessed One's own finger-widths wide, signifying the absence of a back face. Thus my master taught.

For the fourth session, focus the mind on the upper face. Dīpaṃkara explains its color in this way:

> The upper face
> is the color of turquoise,
> and has bared fangs.[810]

All other Indian treatises describe it as smoky. [381] Some followers of the Ngor tradition say that those two are not contradictory, and that it is similar to azure, like the steam of boiling tea. Smoke is a mixture of fire and wind. Therefore, what is being spoken of is a dull rusty color that is a mixture of both the red color of fire and the green color of wind. Meditate in that way.

Furthermore, practice focusing the mind on the upper smoky face upon the head of the main face. The ends of its central eye and other two eyes are broad and the centers are bulging and round. The nose is slightly crinkled and the bulb of the nose is very flared. The mouth gapes widely. The four fangs are fully bared, each protruding beyond all the other teeth. Think that warm blood is inside the mouth. The earlobes are complete. This face is much more wrathful than the main face, and it has a slight cranial dome on the top of the head. The throat is four finger-widths long.

For the first session of the fourth day, in addition to the previous visualizations, focus the mind on the form of the orange hair rising up above all the faces. Furthermore, the hair at the front of the head of the main face is standing up to the right and the left, rising without obscuring the upper face, and floating up beside its right and left cheeks. Similarly, the rising tips of the hair of all the faces float together with the hair of the main face like blazing fire. On the fontanel of the main face, a crossed vajra measuring about four of the Blessed One's finger-widths stands upright, blue in the center, white to the east, yellow to the south, red to the west, and green to the north.

For the second session, focus on the bone cakra on the top of the head, open at the center and fastened at the rear, which surrounds the throat of the upper face. The eight spokes are at eight points directly above the seven faces and the back of the main face. These each have four bone garlands, totaling thirty-two. Furthermore, these bone ornaments are worn as a sort of reminder of spiritual practice at the time of the precipitous pathway of great dullness during the final gathering of the essential constituents, and thus symbolize the thirty-two channel branches in the cakra of great bliss at the top of the head. Thus my master taught.

For the third session, focus on the beryl headbands, which are wrapped with gold at the tops and bottoms and are attached to each of the bone garlands of the cakra at each of the faces. [382] On the surfaces of these, which are inlaid with many precious stones, are pieces of human skull—five for each face—measuring five of the Blessed One's finger-widths, upon which are drawn the forms of dry human heads. It is taught:

> He should attach to the crown
> skulls measuring five finger-widths.[811]

It should be done in this way for the wrathful beings of the angry seer category. Thus my master taught.

Nets stretch from the corner of the mouth of each one of these dry skulls to the corner of the mouth of the next, and half-nets hang from the center of each mouth. White and sparkling like strands of stars, they reach about halfway down the forehead of each face. Ornamental knobs made of gold are on top of each skull, in the centers of which are the hand implements of the five spiritual families. The edges [of the knobs] are encircled by a scrollwork of light rays.

For the fourth session, practice focusing the mind on the ear ornaments in each ear, the rings of bone each wrapped with three and one half bone garlands. At the throat is a necklace with three bone panels, in the center of which is an offering goddess. The edges are encircled by a scrollwork of light rays. The panels are linked together with four bone garlands between each. At the edge is a net of bone garlands with sixteen squares, at the tips of which are bone tassels. This symbolizes the channel cakra of the throat.

These bone ornaments are white, clear, and glittering, with the nature of light, and unbearable to gaze upon with the eyes.

The entire body is transparent from the outside and transparent from the inside, with the nature of light. It is taught:

> Your body has no empty cavity,
> and no flesh, bone, and blood.[812]

Thus it is clear and immaculate. The form of the upper body is broad and the form of the waist and lower body is graceful.

For the first session of the fifth day, in addition to the previous visualizations, focus the mind on the eight right arms.

The statements in the *Kālacakra* about six shoulders and so forth are the particular teachings of that tradition itself. This tradition of the Path with the Result speaks of eight shoulder blades to the right and to the left. Eight upper arms or limbs branch from their ball-and-socket joints. Eight forearms branch from those. Eight hands branch from those. In brief, everything from the shoulder blade to the hand is termed the *arm*. Therefore, the opinions of some that these branch from the forearms, and so forth, are incorrect. The opinion of the Gendenpa that the arms protrude from the rib cage like the legs of a butterfly is silly.

Therefore, focus on the shoulder blade, which has the nature of light, created from the manifestations of primordial awareness. The upper arm and the forearm branch from that. [383] The upper arm, which is of suitable thickness and proportion for a youth of sixteen years, has an upper-arm ornament attached by bone garlands of three bone panels, with bone prongs at the edges. A bracelet is at the joint of the wrist. The palm of the hand of such a beautiful arm is not bright red as though smeared with warm blood, but slightly red, like blue that is tinted by a red glow. This is *wisdom,* with the nature of emptiness. Upon it is held a skull-cup white like the moon, with the forehead facing oneself. This is *method,* with the nature of great bliss. Inside of the skull cup is a white elephant with all the complete characteristics, symbolizing their unity. Moreover, it is taught:

> The elephant and so forth
> should be understood in sequence
> as the diseases of the lungs,

> the breath, and likewise insanity,
> internal hemorrhage, leprosy, smallpox,
> the liver, and the spleen.[813]

Thus these eight creatures symbolize eight diseases and, in a similar way, all the sufferings of sentient beings. To symbolize that these sufferings are dissolved into the space of wisdom and emptiness, the creatures are held facing inward.

The second arm grows from the shoulder blade behind that first shoulder blade, with an upper arm, forearm, and hand, within which is a blue horse.

In the third, behind that, is an orange donkey with a white blaze on its forehead.

In the fourth, behind that, is a red or yellow bull, like these known today.

In the fifth, behind that, is an ashen camel.

In the sixth, behind that, is a red human being.

In the seventh, behind that, is a blue griffin, the hybrid of a garuda and a lion. Its shape, from the mane to the tail, is just like a lion, but it has the beak and horns of a garuda, and wings of flesh above each of its four limbs. It is also called "the lion with eight legs," and is able to fly. Thus my master taught.

In the eighth, behind that, is a cat with a white blaze on its forehead.

Visualize all those creatures in their living forms with complete individual characteristics, and not like corpses.

Focus the mind on the eight arms, the ornaments, and the skull-cups with the creatures. Of the several opinions about counting the front arms themselves as the main arms or counting the two rear ones as the main arms, this tradition accepts the first. Thus my master taught. [384]

For the second session, focus the mind on the eight left arms. In the skull-cup of the first hand, with the forehead of the skull-cup facing oneself, is a yellow earth goddess. The next seven figures are male, from the second skull-cup, which holds a water deity, up through the eighth, which holds Vasudhara. If their hand implements and so forth are observed in detail, they can be envisioned according to the treatise of Divākaracandra.[814] But if one does not incline toward the elaborate, envision each with one face and two arms, adorned with silk and jewels, legs half-crossed, the right hand upon the [right] knee in the gesture of granting the sublime attainment, the left at the heart in the gesture of providing protection, and facing outward. It is taught:

> With earth first and Vasudhara last,
> he bestows the eight qualities of power and wealth.[815]

Concerning the eight qualities of power and wealth, it is taught:

> The eight qualities are the power
> and wealth of enlightened body,
> the power and wealth
> of enlightened speech,
> and likewise the power and wealth
> of enlightened mind,
> the power and wealth of
> miraculous ability, omnipresence,
> whatever is desired,
> and enlightened activities.[816]

Thus the eight deities symbolize giving these eight qualities of power and wealth to living beings. The unbroken oral transmission from the Lord of Yogins accepts just this many faces and arms, so this is mainly observed in the tradition of the esoteric instructions. Thus my master taught.

Practice focusing the mind in sequence on each of those eight arms, the ornaments, and the skull-cups with the deities.

For the third session, on the back, and on the front at the center of the chest, focus on the two bone cakras with eight spokes symbolizing the dharmacakra of the heart. These are connected by eight garlands of bone—two garlands of bone to the right and the left above and two to the right and the left below. It is taught:

> He should wear the ashes
> and the sacred thread of hair
> worn for sacrifices.[817]

This is known as the "ashes," or "sacred thread of hair worn for sacrifices," or "the crossed sacred threads."

What was called the *apron* in the archaic terminology is essentially a waist ornament with five bone panels, three in the front and one at each of the two hips. In their centers are the hand implements of the five spiritual families, encircled by a scrollwork of light rays. These panels are connected by garlands of bone, and have bone garlands with sixty-four squares, which symbolize the nirmāṇacakra at the navel. Long central garlands of bone hang from those, reaching to about the anklebones of the legs. Short garlands on both the right and the left reach to about the middle of the calves. At the tips [of the garlands] are bone spears, at the tips of which are tinkling gold bells.

Hevajra has one hipbone socket on the right and one on the left of the body. [385] Two thighs grow from each of these, each with lower legs and feet. He stands with the two right legs in dancing posture and the big toes of the feet pressing heavily upon the heart of Rudra,[818] with the heels raised and the other toes barely touching the seat. In brief, the form is such that the weight of the body is borne by the big toe of the front foot. The ankle joints are adorned with anklets of three bone panels connected by bone garlands, at the edges of which are prongs.

As for the half-vajra position of the two left legs, they are placed just as the left leg is when assuming the vajra position, and have anklets like the extended right ones.

Several different positions of the legs do occur, but since only the seat of the four stacked up māras is explained in the venerable brothers'[819] methods for accomplishment according to the tradition of the esoteric instructions, this posture is correct for this tradition. Thus my master taught.

Fifty damp human heads, not decayed or old, but fresh and glossy as though just severed, are strung on a human intestine or a cord of hair and hang from the neck down to the thighs. In regard to how they are strung, on the wrathful beings of the angry yakṣa and the yama categories, they dangle as though strung on a cord through the lower jaw, but on those of the angry seer category, one meditates that a knot has been made of the hair of each human head, by which it is fastened to the cord. Thus my master taught.

For the fourth session, mother Vajra Nairātmyā, whose body is blue in color, is in Hevajra's embrace. Father Hevajra is the essence of great bliss, so he is sky blue. Mother Nairātmyā symbolizes wisdom, immutable emptiness, so she is blue like the evening sky with a black luster. The mandala of her face, with the central eye, two other eyes, nose, mouth, and ears is complete, and she is kissing the father. Her hair is orange and she has a bone cakra on the top of her head, a tiara of dry skulls, a necklace, and earrings. With the right hand she strongly brandishes above the father's left shoulder a copper curved knife created from the manifestations of primordial awareness and marked with a five-pronged vajra. She holds a skull-cup filled with the blood of all the māras in her left hand and embraces the father's neck. Her upper body is voluptuous, with very full protruding breasts. Her waist is narrow and her lower body is broad. Since the crossed sacred threads symbolize wisdom, or emptiness, the mother does not need them. [386] She has the apron and a long necklace of fifty dry skulls. The left leg is extended together with the father's, and the big toe presses upon the heart of Rudra. The right is wrapped above the father's left hip. Practice focusing the mind on each of these until a lucid appearance arises.

Similarly, the seats below are Brahmā, who is the Brahmā of the form realm, Indra, who is Śakra, Upendra, who is a god of desire with control of others' emanations,[820] and Rudra, who is Powerful Rudra, Maheśvara. Their shapes, hand implements, and so forth, are explained in detail by Divākaracandra.[821]

However, the great venerable lord Drakpa Gyaltsen says:

> Frightened, they have fallen, dropped their implements, and with palms joined together, gaze up with their faces.[822]

Thus, when Rudra and his retinue were subdued in the past, they fell in terror, dropped their implements, and joined their palms together. Visualize them in that form here.

A sun mandala is under them. Under that is a lotus with pistil and stamens. From the bodies of both father and mother a five-colored bonfire of primordial awareness is crackling and blazing. Practice focusing the mind on all of this.

For the first session of the sixth day, in addition to those previous visualizations, focus the mind on the goddess Gaurī, called "The White Lady," on the front petal to the east. Regarding her, in the past, Rudra Īśvara took for himself eight wives who came from the races of the gods, human beings, and demons. When the Blessed One subdued and blessed them in nondual primordial awareness, the names of the subdued were given to the subduers. When the names of Rudra's eight wives were given to the eight consorts who were followers of the Blessed One, this one who came from the race of the gods was called "The White Lady." The color of her body is black like a bee. Her face is complete with the central eye, the two other eyes, the nose, the mouth, and the ears. She has a cakra in her hair, a tiara of dry skulls, and earrings and a necklace. With bracelets on her wrists and upper arms, she brandishes in the right hand a vajra curved knife that cuts through the six faults of pride and so forth,[823] and the tip of her menacing index finger is level with the point between her eyebrows. As a sign of extracting sentient beings that live like fish in the ocean of samsara, her left hand holds the form of a living rohita fish. [387] The color of the fish is red, symbolizing that to extract sentient beings in such a way is also to hold sentient beings with affectionate compassion. She has the apron. Her left leg is extended with the big toe pressing on the heart of the Brahmā of the desire realm, who has fallen on his back, and who has one face and two arms, is yellow in color, and whose head is turned to the left. A moon seat is under him. She stands in the middle of the blazing fires of primordial awareness.

For the second session, to the south is the first of the six consorts who came from the human race. She is red Caurī, who came from the robber caste. She rattles a ḍāmaru skull-drum with the right hand and holds a pig with the left. This symbolizes that sentient beings, like pigs oppressed by the sleep of ignorance, are awakened by the sound of her ḍāmaru. Thus my master taught. The Indra who is her seat is Śakra of the eastern direction, who is one of the direction guardians. Thus my master taught.

For the third session, to the west is Vetālī, like the color of smelted gold, who came from the race of the zombies, or demons. She holds a turtle in her right hand and a skull-cup filled with nectar in the left, symbolizing the transformation of the desire of passionate turtle-like sentient beings into nectar. She stands upon Upendra Viṣṇu as her seat.

For the fourth session, to the north is "The Voracious Lady," Ghasmarī, green like emerald, who came from the human race and the caste known as "gamblers." She holds the middle of a snake with her right hand and a skull-cup in the left, symbolizing the transformation of hatred into nectar. Rudra, who is her seat, is Maheśvara.

For the first session of the seventh day, to the northeast is "The Haughty Lady." Although the royal caste is exalted, they have little arrogance. The commoner caste has no attitude of supremacy. But the merchant caste has great arrogance or pride, so Pukkasī, who came from that caste, is called

"The Haughty Lady." She is a color like the clear autumn sky. She has a lion in her right hand and an axe in the left. A half-vajra is at the end of the handle, which is eighteen inches long. The blade of the axe is like a round mirror split in half, and it is also marked by a half-vajra on the back. Using the great pride of the lion as an example, this means cutting the pride of sentient beings. As a seat, she stands upon Yama of the southern direction, who is one of the direction guardians. [388]

For the second session, to the southeast is "The Wilderness Lady," Śavarī, white like the moon, who came from the caste of those who live in the mountain cliffs and hunt sentient beings. She holds in her right hand the stem of a lotus with four petals, upon which stands the upright figure of a fully ordained monk. With the left she holds a monk's staff. The meaning is the destruction of the view of a self. As a seat, she stands upon Yakṣa, who is one of the direction guardians.

For the third session, to the southwest is Caṇḍālī, blue like the color of clear beryl, who came from the caste of the outcastes. In her right hand she holds a wheel with four spokes, symbolizing the turning of the Dharma wheel of the four truths. In the left she holds a plow, symbolizing that, with the Dharma wheel, she plows the mindstreams of sentient beings, which are like fallow ground. As a seat, she stands upon Rākṣasa.

For the fourth session, to the northwest is low-caste Ḍombinī, who came from the caste of washerwomen. Her color has been maintained to be like Vajrakarma of the yoga tantras, glittering multicolored, green, and so forth. Since the last of these is the intention of the *Vajrapañjara,* she must be green in the mandala of that tantra. But here, corresponding to the inner elements, she is blue from both feet up through her thighs, red from the lower abdomen up through her hips, white at her stomach, yellow at her chest, and her head and both arms are green. She has a vajra in her right hand, the left points menacingly, and she stands upon Vemacitra as her seat.

Practice focusing the mind on each goddess, beginning from the central eye, down to the bonfire, and if done extensively, until tactile and visual signs are obtained.

Then focus on the lotus of the seat. One may use whichever of the following three appeal to one's mind, and meditate in that way. The *Saṃvarodaya* says:

> The four directions are red,
> fire and wind are yellow,

> the powerful is blue,
> and the false is green.[824]

Or the four directions are red and the intermediate are beautifully shaded. Or they are the same as the colors of the goddesses.

For the first session of the eighth day, in addition to the previous visualizations, focus the mind on the celestial mansion.[825] Its foundation is a variegated vajra, upon which is a heavenly dais measuring one minor unit in height, which serves as the floor, with a blue center and the sections in the east and so forth the colors of the directions. Each of the walls flanking the gates are one minor unit from it in each direction. Below that is the square center of the crossed vajra, with prongs in each direction. [389] Some claim that this is the crossed vajra of the protection cakra, but we maintain that that is invisible, obscured by the tiny vajras spread out like barley. This is the seat of the celestial mansion.

[Below and extending] outside of that [square center] is a sun of very clear fire crystal, maintained by some to be green because it rests upon the green stamens of a lotus. But the precious venerable lord Drakpa Gyaltsen maintained that the sun is clear like a mirror, yet of various colors because it is struck by the light of the celestial mansion's ornaments.

[Below and] outside of that is a lotus extending for a distance of two minor units in a ring surrounding it. The number of those petals is thirty-two or a hundred thousand, whichever is preferred. Thus my master taught.

In the center of the variegated vajra is the square celestial mansion with four gates. The layered five walls do not touch each other in each of the spaces where their outsides and insides join. The outer one is white and the inner one is black. All five walls are visible at the ends of the walls flanking the gates. On top of the walls is a precious frieze made of gold and extending one minor unit out from the walls, with numerous clusters of precious stones on its surface. On top of that are eight precious capitals and supports in each cardinal direction and one in each intermediate direction, making thirty-six. On top of those is a golden flat beam surrounding and covering the walls, flush with them on the inside and extending out two minor units on the outside.

Outside of the center lotus are two white pillars marked with cakras to the east, two yellow pillars marked with jewels to the south, two red pillars marked with lotuses to the west, and two green pillars marked with variegated vajras to the north. These are connected by a circular fence of vajras in the lower spaces between them. Including the capitals and bows that are on top of the pillars, they are level with the golden flat beam. A circular vajra beam goes around the top of the pillars. On top of that, the inner tips of the rafters abut the circular vajra beam and the outer tips are level with the golden flat beam. The roof is laid upon these.

At the outer extremity of each rafter there is a "bird wing." From each of these hangs a spoutless flask made of jewels. Nets and half-nets are suspended. On top of the bird wings is a parapet like a fence of inverted pyramids with designs in relief, like the portion below the bowl of a stupa of great enlightenment. Inside of that parapet are jewel vases filled with various grain liquids, in which various parasols, victory banners, and pendants stand raised. These are attractive and connected by garlands of jewels and flowers in the spaces between them.

On top of the circular vajra beam is also a circular wall. On top of that are a frieze, capitals and supports, and a flat beam. [390] On top of that are laid four vajra crossbeams forming four squares in the cardinal directions and four triangles in the intermediate directions. On top of these the inner tips of the rafters are flush with the square of beams in the center. The outer tips of the rafters extend out, with the bird wings, nets, and half-nets [at the ends]. On top of the bird wings is a parapet, and then the parasols, victory banners, and so forth.

On the surface of the square of beams in the center is also a square wall. From the frieze to the parasols is as before.

In the center [of that roof is a structure] pitched like a pagoda, with a vajra at the peak marked with a jewel pinnacle.

To the right and left of the walls flanking each of the four gates are two pillars, making four, which support an archway of four layers, each shorter by one minor unit from the two sides, but with the surfaces perfectly flush. The colors of the individual ledges are beautifully shaded (or, because in the context of their purity it is taught, "The archways are the purity of the meditative states,")[826] from the bottom they have the colors red, blue, green, and yellow. Each such ledge is also adorned with numerous ornaments. At the peak of that archway is a lotus of four petals, upon which is a Dharma wheel of four or eight spokes, made from gold, with a parasol above. A short distance to the right and left of it are golden deer who have very long necks with silk scarves upon them and who gaze at the Dharma wheel.

Numerous offering goddesses are on the red platform of sensory objects outside the walls.

For the second session, it is taught:

> Residing in the bhaga of the Vajra Queen.[827]

Thus, outside of that celestial mansion, so that people with passionate desire will enter, is the bhaga of the mother, a tetrahedron symbolizing the three gates to liberation,[828] white on the outside and red on the inside. With the tapered root pointing down and the large surface facing up, it has three corners and the nature of light. Outside of that is the uncommon protection cakra, a gold cakra with ten spokes spinning clockwise. Inside of the spokes are the ten wrathful beings, like angry rākṣasa demons. Focus the mind on this.

For the third session, outside of [the uncommon protection cakra] on the vajra ground are the eight charnel grounds. In the charnel ground of Caṇḍogra to the eastern direction is the "*śirīṣa* tree," which is a myrobalan plum tree. Its trunk is huge, with exquisite branches, leaves, and fruit. At its base is white Śakra, with the palm of his right hand placed directly at his forehead, offering homage to the main deity. His left hand holds a vajra and skull-cup at his heart. [391] He is mounted on an elephant. His servant, Devopāsaka, is white in color, has the face of an elephant, holds a curved knife and a skull-cup at his heart with both hands, and emerges from the waist up among the leaves of the tree. The sky above that charnel ground is completely covered by the yellow cloud called Sarvakolāhala. The sound of thunder slowly rumbles from within it, and a drizzling rain falls. A lake is at the root of the tree, and yellow Vāsuki is in it, looking inward [toward the celestial mansion] and bowing to the main deity.

Great fires blaze from the trees or from complete skulls. There are stupas. The charnel grounds are filled with corpses dangling from the branches of the trees, corpses lying on the surface of the earth, corpses impaled on the points of stakes, pieces of heads, pieces of limbs, and pieces of skeletons. Cries of "Phem! Phem!" ring out from the hawks, owls, vultures, jackals, and so forth.

The yogins that live in those charnel grounds should be envisioned according to the identification and method for direct realization of the individual adepts composed by the master Vajrāsanapāda.[829] Thus my master taught. This is good, because benefits and blessings will come from making the forms of those adepts part of the path. In reality, since these charnel grounds appeared at the beginning of the kāliyuga, it was not yet time for the appearance of those adepts. Nevertheless, one should visualize a pair of yogins and yoginīs in each of the charnel grounds. Thus my master taught.

Similarly, visualize each of the trees, direction guardians, clouds, nāgas, fires, adepts, and jackals in each charnel ground down through Kīlikīlarava.

For the fourth session, the vajra ground below is made up of vajras spread out like barley and rice, indigo in color and radiating sparks. At its edges is the "vajra fence" constructed of vertical black vajras the size of Mount Meru, with all the spaces between them filled with vajras from the size of Mount Meru to the size of atoms. These are capped by a ring of horizontal black vajras. On top of that are vertical ones. On top of that are horizontal ones. It is built in that way to whatever height one desires. Its shape has been explained both as square and as round, but here it is round. In the tradition of the esoteric instructions the net is not mentioned separately, but since the fence stands vertically and the net stretches horizontally, both are actually complete. [392] A vajra canopy is mentioned by the great venerable lord Drakpa Gyaltsen:

> The vajra ground, the fence, the canopy, and the pavilion.[830]

A canopy is also mentioned in the front creation according to the *Clear Mirror* by Sempa Chenpo.[831] Therefore, it is not wrong if this is done, but the tradition is mostly without it. Inside of the fence is a wall that goes even higher, constructed in the same way as before, and with a pinnacle of a half-vajra at the peak where the tips come together. This is the vajra pavilion. Everything outside the vajra fence is a bonfire of primordial awareness, difficult to endure, crackling and blazing so that ten million armies of māras cannot bear even to look for faults in it. Practice focusing the mind on all of this.

Those complete the thirty-two visualizations for focusing the mind.

To develop expertise and enhance it, one trains by means of three topics: the vast, the profound, and freedom from flaws of contradiction.

First, for the vast, practice the engaging and resting up through the common protection cakra as described before. Then clearly imagine all appearances to be the mandala. If a great mountain is seen before the eyes or arises as a mental object, clearly imagine it to be the supporting mandala of Hevajra with the supported nine deities, and rest upon that. In a similar way, vividly imagine whatever is seen with the eyes or arises as a mental object—from people, horses, oxen, and so forth, down to atoms—to be the supporting mandala and supported deities. In brief, if the mind is at rest, these appear vividly as the mandala of nine deities. If the mind strays, clearly imagine those objects to which it strays to be the mandala of nine deities and rest serenely upon that, not letting ordinary thoughts occur for even an instant.

Similarly, imagine that the supporting mandala that one has envisioned becomes larger and larger, filling the sky, and that the supported deities also become larger, [growing] to an incredible size, and focus the mind on that.

Second, for the profound, focus the mind again on the environment becoming smaller and smaller, with the celestial mansion, charnel grounds, and protection cakra about the size of a mustard seed, inside of which are the nine deities, as though painted with a hair, and with complete faces, arms, and ornaments, clearly distinct down to the whites and pupils of their eyes. Once again, it becomes larger, filling the sky. Again, it becomes smaller, about the size of a mustard seed. Alternate those two, and focus the mind.

Third, for training in freedom from flaws of contradiction, sometimes meditate on the supporting mandala filling the sky but the supported deities about the size of a mustard seed, without the environment having become larger and without the deities having become smaller. [393]

Sometimes focus the mind on the supporting mandala being about the size of a mustard seed but the supported deities filling the expanse of the sky, without the supported deities having become larger or the supporting mandala having become smaller.

Briefly, this is purification of attachment to the creation stage and development of expertise. Because appearances are the mind, their dimensions are not established and can be meditated upon as anything. Even with material things, a large area can appear inside a small mirror without any omission, and no problem of fixed dimensions arises no matter how many people enter some ancient meditation sites such as the Mañjughoṣa Cave of Sakya.[832] Thus my master taught.

Three perfections come from practicing in that way: perfection of the visualization, the meditation, and the result.

First is perfection of the visualization. When meditating in this way, the supporting mandala and supported deities become simultaneously clear and distinct, with one not obscuring the other, clear and distinct down to the whites and pupils of their eyes. If one rests upon that, even resting for as long as one desires, one remains without conceptual distraction, and if the focus is shifted it can be shifted to anything.

Second is perfection of the meditation. At this point, without the slightest dependence on external substances, yogic exercises, and so forth, just by purposely directing the visualizations and using the gazes, one is able to take the lives of enemies, impeding spirits, and so forth, and to instantly summon tigers, lions, and other wild animals. This is achieved through the vital winds of consciousness[833] being in equilibrium. No more than just that will be achieved by the creation stage alone (which is not pervaded by the completion stage). But with creation and completion stages indivisible as in this system, by means of the vital wind of primordial awareness being in equilibrium one is able to again summon and revive the consciousness of the one killed before, and able to send back to their own places those animals that were summoned before. Thus my master taught.

Third is perfection of the result. This forms the uncommon immediate causes for achieving the interim results up through the sixth spiritual level and the ultimate result of a buddha's rūpakāya form bodies.[834] Thus my master taught. [394]

In this way, a beginner who meditates on the paths that have been explained meditates on the method for direct realization generated from the process for direct enlightenment dependent on the vowels such as *a* and the consonant-syllables such as *ka,* and single-pointedly practices focusing the mind. Thereby, one of the three paths, such as that of eliminating entry,[835] will arise in the mindstream, such as the ability to clearly imagine the supporting mandala and nine supported deities instantaneously and so forth. At that time one has become an individual for whom some bliss has arisen, and one meditates on the method for direct realization generated from the process for direct enlightenment minus the vowels such as *a* and the consonant-syllables such as *ka,* and by targeting the key points of focusing the mind as before. In that way, dependent on single-pointed practice of the nine yogas[836] of both the outer and inner creation stage—

the path of the vase initiation—during meditative equipoise and during postmeditation, the view of the three essences will arise in the mindstream.

2) *The view: the three essences*

This consists of four topics:[837]

a) The arising of the view during meditative equipoise
b) The arising of the view during postmeditation
c) How to produce the view if it has not arisen during those two
d) Enhancement if the view has arisen

a) *The arising of the view during meditative equipoise*

In the case of the essence of the apparent aspect, when the mind is focused on the central eye—[with the image] not just vivid like the intellectual understanding of it described before, but apparent as though actually present between the eyebrows, with the central eye black in the center, pale around that, and bloodshot—this is the phenomenon that is the reverse of the appearances of ignorance. Ignorance in this context is not general ignorance; the central eye not arising as a mental object is ignorance. The reverse of that is the appearance of the central eye as though actually present between the eyebrows. The lucid aspect of that is the phenomenon. In regard to "the true nature free from artificial mind," the essence of that mind—the empty aspect of resting serenely after eliminating all thoughts other than the solely lucid central eye—is the true nature. As for "a single essence but with different facets," from the perspective of the lucid central eye, precisely that phenomenon is primordial unestablished emptiness. The radiance of precisely that emptiness arises unceasingly as the central eye. At that point they are a single essence. But if distinguished by different qualities, these are differentiated as "the phenomenon from the perspective of the lucid aspect" and "the true nature from the perspective of the empty aspect." In brief, meditative concentration will arise in that way. This is called "the path of eliminating entry" because, once the entry of one thought after another, like running water, has been eliminated, the mind rests serenely in a nonconceptual state, like reining in a horse or damming a flow of water. [395]

In the case of the essence of the empty aspect, the mind rests serenely in a completely unestablished state like empty sky, without any meditated deity being lucid and without any of these ordinary appearances arising. This occurs by means of the three modes of arising: the phenomenon that is the reverse of the appearances of ignorance, and so forth. Lucidly resting in emptiness after reversing from the ignorance of not knowing to rest in emptiness is the phenomenon. As the essence of that mind, being naked and free from all circulation of other thoughts is its true nature. Those two have a single essence, but are differentiated by different facets. This is called "the path of severing attachment," because it eliminates mental attachment or clinging to the meditative concentration of the apparent aspect, the form of the deity.

In the case of the essence of unity, the unexplainable appearances of samsara and nirvana illustrated by the five signs of clear light, such as smoke, arise without either the meditated deity or unmeditated emptiness occurring. The arising of the various signs of clear light after reversing from the ignorance in which the appearances of clear light do not arise is the phenomenon. As the essence of that mind, the cessation of the stream of all other subtle and coarse thoughts is the true nature. These two have a single essence, but arise in a form distinguished by different attributes. Thus my master taught.

b) *The arising of the view during postmeditation*

When the meditative concentration of the apparent aspect has arisen during meditative equipoise, and one has entered into subsequent conduct after rising from that meditative concentration, no matter what is seen before the eyes—whether a human being or a mountain or anything else—one will remain at ease upon it without circulation of other thoughts occurring. The appearance before the eyes after reversing from the ignorance in which it is not seen before the eyes is the phenomenon. And so forth. The three characteristics arise as before. Thus my master taught.

c) *How to produce the view if it has not arisen during those two*[838]

In that way, the meditative concentrations of the apparent aspect and the empty aspect are both flawed experiences, because they include exaggeration and denigration. However, when either one has arisen for a while in the mindstream, it will be mastered by the yogin and gradually become flawless. And whichever of those the mind rests upon, if the yogin does not leave it hazy, but energizes and intensifies the pure awareness and rests in an unfabricated state, they will become united. Thus my master taught. [396]

d) *Enhancement if the view has arisen*[839]

Then, to examine whether that meditative concentration is stable or unstable, one engages in the secret conduct that makes everyone tremble. If intense circumstances do not destroy the meditative concentration but assist it, one has arrived at the beginning of the middle gathering of the essential constituents and should perform in public what makes everyone tremble. In regard to the meaning of "makes everyone tremble," it is *avadhūtī*, which means abandoning both subject and object. If analyzed according to the Tibetan language, it is called that because it astonishes everyone in the world and makes them tremble.

First go to an area where even one's name is unknown, and without any certainty of food, clothing, and behavior, abandon all fear, shame, and anxiety, and engage in the conduct. By practicing in that way, when one arrives at the final gathering of the essential constituents, one will seem to swoon from the experience of bliss, and seem to not remember anything. To revive from that, the channel of a two-decade lotus lady who is pleasant and so forth should be sought, and one should engage in the conduct together with an authentic mudrā consort. Engaging in the mundane overt conduct that makes everyone tremble, or in the totally victorious conduct, the path of seeing at the first spiritual level is actualized and twelve sets of a hundred qualities are obtained.

3) *The culmination of attainment as the indivisibility of samsara and nirvana*

It is taught:

> The indivisibility of samsara and nirvana, which was presented before by the master at the time of the cause, is realized at about that point.[840]

Thus the indivisibility of samsara and nirvana is actualized. *Samsara* in this context is impure appearance, the entire environment and its inhabitants in the three realms. But everything now arises as the supporting mandala and supported deities, so that not the slightest impure appearance arises. Then realization gradually increases and one obtains up through the sixth spiritual level, which is the interim result of the vase initiation, and ultimately the rūpakāya form bodies are achieved.

In that way, by meditating on the three essences of the view on the mundane path, the indivisibility of samsara and nirvana is realized as the culmination of attainment on the transcendent path. One who reaches the culmination of attainment in this very lifetime is a person of superior faculties, one for whom the elaborations of the other paths[841] are totally unnecessary. Thus my master taught. [397]

4) *The practice when passing away*

If one has been unable to reach the culmination of attainment in this lifetime, and has made that evaluation, one must alter the aim of the path. By means of the yoga of the practice when passing away, a person with medium faculties reaches the culmination of attainment at the point of death or immediately upon arising from the clear light of death, or is able to achieve Khecara or conception in the womb of a religious woman. Because the intermediate state must be experienced if certainty has not arisen in the practice when passing away, one with inferior faculties must practice the oral instructions of the intermediate state. If certainty does not arise even there, the final resort for one with extremely inferior faculties is prayers for buddhahood through the passage of lifetimes. The three yogas when passing away are for the first type of person.

a) *The transformation of appearances as the practice when passing away*

This consists of two topics:

(1) Training
(2) Putting it into practice

(1) *Training*

In addition to the continual practice explained before, when frightening appearances like banging sounds and booms occur, or human beings appear in front of one, or during any similar sudden circumstances, or while eating food, clearly meditate that everything is Hevajra, appearance and emptiness indivisible. Deliberately not thinking about oneself at all, blend one's own mind together with the deity in front and rest serenely in the inexpressible.

Gain familiarity by means of such practices, and train until a vivid mindfulness that all sudden occurances are Hevajra effortlessly arises, like throwing open a door.

(2) *Putting it into practice*

The *Catuḥpīṭha* says:

> Perform transference when the time comes;
> at the wrong time it will kill the deity.
> By killing the deity, one will definitely
> burn in the lower realms.[842]

Therefore, if the consciousness is transferred at the wrong time the infraction of killing the deity will occur, so the time must be known. And for that, the signs of dying must be correctly understood. Generally, death comes from the exhaustion of one or the exhaustion of two of these: life force, karma, and merit. Death from the exhaustion of one or two is easily averted. But if all three are exhausted, it is impossible to avert death, because this is like the exhaustion of all the cotton and oil in a lamp.

In any case, this is examined by means of three topics:

(a) The outer signs of dying
(b) The inner or solar and lunar signs of dying
(c) The secret or manifest signs of dying

(a) *The outer signs of dying*

The outer signs include a change in one's mind, such as short joys becoming long and long becoming short, a weariness with previous dear companions, a deep dislike of staying in one's area and residence, and a deep desire for another area and new companions. [398] A "discarding of meditation" may also occur, which is a deep dislike of performing spiritual practice. Merit becomes exhausted at the point of death, and by virtue of that the experiences and meditative concentration one had before are obscured and a reversal of devotion occurs. Or else, like a lamp flame flaring up just before burning out, without cause experiential appearances may become more lucid than before. Or else one may dream of a plain of *kāravīra,* known in Tibet as chickweed flowers,[843] wear red clothing in a dream, or ride sentient beings that are not generally ridden, such as donkeys, dogs, pigs, cats, and so forth. In brief, these are signs of some movement of the two immobile cakras. Similar signs in dreams that may occur during the preliminary section of the initiation are explained in the *Abridged Knowledge for Deceiving the Lord of Death.*[844]

(b) *The inner signs of dying*

As for examination of the extensive signs of dying, these may be recognized if all the planets, stars, junctures, and so forth of the time of one's birth are understood, as is known to have occurred for Sangtsa.[845] For everyone else, those cannot be examined because they do not occur with any certainty.

Therefore, the "solar and lunar signs" are examined. Before daybreak, from about the eighth period of the night, observe the key physical points and engage in spiritual practice. From the last of the glow until about the time when the sun dawns at the peak of a suitable mountain on the horizon of the valley, examine through which nostril one's breath circulates. If it circulates through the left for the first, second, and third days of the lunar month, circulates through the right for the fourth, fifth, and sixth, circulates through the left for the seventh, eighth, and ninth, and, in a similar way, circulates through the right for the twenty-eighth, twenty-ninth, and thirtieth, no obstacle is present and everything is fine. Whatever frightening things diviners, oracles, and so forth may say, be at ease; there is no need to be afraid.

Similarly, if the breath circulates for more than three days through the left nostril it is a sign of the accomplishment of some calm and extensive activities. If it circulates for more than three days through the right it is a sign that something like the omens of fierce action will appear to an enemy. So there is no problem.

The opposite, such as circulating through the right for the first, second, and third days, and through the left for the fourth, fifth, and sixth, are inauspicious signs. If that happens for six days, it is a sign of conflict and various physical and mental sufferings to come. If it circulates thus for about half a month, great financial disaster will occur. If it circulates thus for about one month, death or misfortune will occur among relatives, retinue, disciples, and so forth. [399] If it circulates thus for about a month and a half, it is a sign of one's own death. Thus my master taught.

(c) *The secret or manifest signs of dying*

When the eyeballs are pressed with the fingers, circles of light will not appear in the palms of the hands. When the ears are covered with the hands, a humming sound will not arise. When sitting and facing to the west as the sun is about to dawn in the morning, a vapor will not rise from one's head. Feces and urine cannot be retained when a sneeze occurs. When the right hand is clenched in a fist and placed between the eyebrows it appears to be totally broken off at the wrist. These are signs of certain death.

As indicated by those signs, perform "the examination of the life-form," either when the moon is about to appear during the full moon or when the sun's rays dawn over the mountains. Remove one's clothing. Holding a vajra and bell, and facing to the west, stand up and focus the eyes single-pointedly at the heart of one's shadow. When one's vision becomes very blurred, look into the sky in front of one. A vague pale image just like one's form will appear in the sky. If it is flawless, that is sufficient. If it is headless, one will die. If the right arm is missing, a male relative will die, and if the left one is missing, a female relative will die. If the right leg is missing, a male servant will die, and if the left one is missing, a female servant will die. If the limbs are complete but one has no torso, it is a sign of moving to another area. If one has a torso, but with nothing except nebulous roundish holes in it, it is a sign of financial loss to come.[846] It is explained that if no image of the form appears, or it is utterly black, or it is like a shrouded corpse, death cannot be averted.

Concerning the precise way to avert death, it is uncertain when each of those signs explained before may occur, but when any continuously occur, they can be alleviated if one performs the meditations and recitations of Amitāyus, White Tārā, Vijayā, and so forth, and constructs images of them and so forth. If that does not alleviate the signs, it is a indication of exhausted merit. Therefore, they can be alleviated by honoring the master, which is the main method for accumulating merit; by supporting the sangha and giving to the poor and the blind; and by practicing the meditations and recitations of deities that increase merit, such as Vaiśravaṇa and

Gaṇapati. [400] Similarly, when karma has been exhausted, death is difficult to avert, but the signs can be removed by resting the mind in emptiness, the fundamental nature; by sincerely meditating on love and compassion; and so forth. Those are the common methods for averting death.

In regard to the special common methods, if one meditates on the vase retention of the vital winds by means of the yoga of four sessions for a period such as seven days, or if one repeats 15,000 vajra repetitions with prāṇāyāma by means of the yoga of four sessions for seven days, in seven days 105,000 repetitions will be completed. That can avert even death that is predicted to occur at a definite time. And if one always repeats without interruption a thousand prāṇāyāma at daybreak, one will be able to increase one's life span and remove all immediate obstacles. Thus my master taught.

Concerning the uncommon method, it is taught:

> By inhaling emptiness
> living beings live.[847]

This is the way to practice the instruction of the Lord of Yogins for milking the sky or consuming the sky for food. In the morning, when the lines on the palms of the hands can just be seen, maintain the key physical points and sit facing the east or the west at a place where the vast sky is visible. Preceded by just a brief taking of refuge and awakening of the enlightenment mind, perform as before the protection of oneself the yogin, from the protection cakra by pronouncing "*hūṃ,*" through the recitation of *oṃ āḥ hūṃ.* Then look into the sky and, together with inhaling the vital wind through the mouth with the tone *ha,* imagine that all the blue sky in the three-thousandfold world systems is gathered inward in a blue surge, it enters through one's mouth, and one's entire body is totally filled with that pristine blue sky. When the inhalation of the vital wind is complete, swallow together with some saliva. Then draw up the lower vital wind and hold the vase retention as long as possible. When that becomes impossible, release it naturally. If a belch occurs when a hundred, twenty-one, and so forth have been done in that way, death has certainly been averted, but one should meditate energetically for a period such as seven days. Thus my master taught.

If one is unable to alleviate those signs no matter what one does, the time has come, and one should be unattached to this life. Feel delight about one's immediate departure from an impure realm to a pure realm. As a bird is unable to fly if a stone is tied to it, so one will be unable to transfer the consciousness if one is attached to things and so forth. Therefore, give away all the valuables one owns to whomever one likes. At least completely abandon them mentally and do not cling to them as one's own. [401] If the master is living, request initiation and revive the sacred commitments and vows. If he is not living, perform the self-entry oneself in a mandala of colored particles or painted cloth, or intently perform the Time of the Path while recognizing the grounds of purification and the purifying agents, thereby mending the sacred commitments and removing guilt and regrets from the mind. If someone like a trustworthy companion who knows this path is present, instruct him, "When I am dying, remind me of spiritual practice!" Offer the request that those who do not know this path remain silent, because much babbling talk will not only be disturbing, but will also not remind one of spiritual practice.

Furthermore, if these elaborate transferences are not performed before the subtle dissolution it will be difficult, because then the mind will have become nonconceptual and the visualizations will not arise.[848]

1' *The dissolutions*

This consists of two topics:

a' Dissolution of the elements
b' Dissolution of the sense faculties

a' *Dissolution of the elements*

When the body forms it forms from the navel, and similarly when it decays it decays from the navel. Moreover, from birth until the age of twenty-five all the vital winds, drops, and channels expand. Then, until the age of forty-five, all are stable without increasing or decreasing. Then two channels dry up every day and the vital winds and drops dependent on them vanish. That is the reason for physical weakness and unclear sense faculties in old age. Thus my master taught.

Similarly, at death, because the equally-abiding vital wind at the navel first deviates from its place, the body cannot digest food. Then, because the life-sustaining vital wind of the heart deviates from its place, feelings of sadness and so forth arise in the mind. Then, because the upward-circulating vital wind of the throat deviates from its place, it becomes difficult to swallow and one thinks that food and so forth are rising and that one will vomit. Then, because the downward-clearing vital wind of the genital area deviates from its place, feces and urine cannot be controlled and are discharged or retained.

In that way, when the pervasive vital wind of space takes control of and steals the equally-circulating vital wind,[849] the vital wind of the navel deviates. Previously the channel knots and so forth did not disintegrate because they were held by the vital winds, on the basis of which the essential constituents remained, but now the channel knots disintegrate because they have been abandoned by the vital winds. The essential constituents disperse to their final places. Because they gradually dissolve through the rasanā and lalanā into the central channel, the essential constituents in the channels of the body decline. The outer signs are that the legs cannot hold up the body, the neck cannot hold up the head, and the hands cannot hold up a bowl of cooked food. The inner signs are thinking that one is sinking below the earth or thinking that one is being pushed down from above. [402] The secret sign is the inside of one's dwelling filling with rusty brown smoke. Without being frightened by these signs or letting the mind be dazed, clearly imagine the particular signs to be the essence of the master, the chosen deity Hevajra, with eight faces and sixteen arms, appearance and emptiness indivisible. Blend one's mind together with [this visualization] and rest without clinging. Energize the pure awareness and do not become at all distracted.

Then, because the pervasive vital wind of space robs the life-sustaining vital wind, the channel cakra of the heart disintegrates. When water dissolves into fire, the outer signs are the drying up of the mouth, nose, and so forth. Because a great thirst arises, one desires only water. The inner signs are the consciousness being sometimes lucid and sometimes not lucid, so that people and so forth are sometimes recognized and sometimes not recognized. The secret sign is things like mirages appearing.

Then the pervasive vital wind robs the upward-circulating vital wind. The channel cakra of the throat disintegrates. Fire dissolves into wind. The outer sign is the warmth of the body gradually collecting into the torso from the top of the head or from the soles of the feet. Because the inner warmth exits, perspiration on the body evaporates. Lice and so forth are expelled. The secret sign is things like fireflies appearing. Thus my master taught.

Then the pervasive vital wind takes control of the downward-clearing vital wind, and the channel cakra of the genital area disintegrates. Wind dissolves into consciousness. The outer signs are panting and rasping. Exhalation becomes longer but inhalation is difficult. The secret sign is things like blazing lamps appearing.

Then that pervasive vital wind abandons the channel cakra at the top of the head and that disintegrates. The circulation of the breath out and in ceases and one dies. Thus my master taught.

Not allowing the mind to be at all confused about each such sign, blend one's mind with the essence of the master in the form of the chosen deity Hevajra and rest in a state in which appearance and emptiness are indivisible. If one dies in just that state, the practice when passing away has been successful.

b' *Dissolution of the sense faculties*

This consists of two topics: the coarse dissolution and the subtle dissolution.

1'' *The coarse dissolution*

In conjunction with those [signs], the visual consciousness dissolves into form. Because the channel knot in the shape of *maṃ,* which apprehends form, has disintegrated, the eyes do not see form. Similarly, because the *daṃ* of the ears has disintegrated, sound is not heard. And so forth. Because the *aṃ* of the forehead has disintegrated, sensation is not felt, and adjustment is required even if the bed and so forth have been made comfortable, that person stays exactly as he has been left, and so forth.

2'' *The subtle dissolution*

Since the channel cakras have disintegrated in that way, the two immobile cakras disintegrate because no vital winds remain to uphold them. [403] When the white constituent obtained from one's father, which has the nature of water, flows downward, all appearances appear utterly pale, which is called *white radiance.* All concepts derived from passionate desire cease. That is called *appearance.* The red constituent obtained from one's mother goes upward, a radiant red appearance occurs, and all concepts derived from hatred cease, which is called *spreading appearance.* Then, because one's mind penetrates between the white and red constituents, all appearances become utterly black, and the seven concepts derived from ignorance cease, which is called *near-attainment appearance.*

In brief, a clear light in which all the eighty natural concepts[850] have dissolved into space nakedly arises, beyond all possibility of expression and transcending all theoretical knowledge, like the space of the clear autumn sky. Moreover, except for slight variations of length due to greater and lesser merit, this definitely arises for each living being, even the insects in the grass. Thus my master taught.

Those who have stable experience in the clear light of the time of the path nakedly recognize the very essence of that clear light of the time of the ground, and are known to reach the culmination of attainment at precisely that moment, or to attain buddhahood in the clear light of death, the vast domain of the dharmakāya reality body.

As signs that the clear light has been recognized, a glow gradually appears on the corpse, the body becomes smaller, and so forth. At that time it is also beneficial for a trustworthy companion to speak into one's ear an introduction to the clear light. No ear faculty actually exists at that time because all the sense faculties have dissolved, but something is audible in the glow of the clear light, because it is explained that the appearances of colors occur at the time of the white radiance, the red radiance, and so forth.

If no experience of the clear light of the time of the path has arisen in this lifetime, the clear light will appear, but without recognizing it one will be dazed, like falling into a swoon. At that point, precisely that lack of recognition becomes ignorance, and both the rising from the clear light of death and the arising of the intermediate existence will occur like the high and low of a tilting balance scale. When the appearances of the intermediate state arise, even though they may be frightening, scary, and so forth, through mindfulness of them as the chosen deity, the particular appearance will arise in the form of the deity, and one will be liberated at precisely that moment. Thus my master taught. [404]

b) *The transference with a globe of light*

For training, support the back with something like a thick pillow, and do not bump the head. As the key physical point, sit with raised knees and embrace the back of the head with the interlaced fingers of the hands. Imagine a white light, about thumb-sized, within one's heart cakra, from which a globe of light separates. This goes to the anus, totally blocking it, and the inside of the body becomes one piece, as if it has been plastered. Similarly, globes of light separate and block in sequence the urethra, the navel, the mouth, both nostrils, both eyes, both ears, the point between the eyebrows, and the crown of the head. If the consciousness were transferred through those points, in sequence, one would be reborn as a hell being, as an animal, as a god of the desire realm, as a hungry spirit, as a yakṣa king if through the right nostril and as an ordinary yakṣa if through the left, as a human king if through the right eye and as an ordinary person if through the left, as a kinnara spirit if through the two ears, as a god of the form realm [if through the point between the eyebrows], and as a god of the formless realm [if through the crown of the head]. In order not to be reborn in those states, imagine that those doors of samsara are blocked and even the vital wind cannot escape.

Then clearly imagine at one's navel a blue wind mandala, like a half-moon, about the size of a split pea. On top of that is a moon, and on it a blue *hūṃ,* the support of mind, vibrating and about to fly. Simultaneously tensing the body, drawing up the lower vital wind, and pressing the intestines against the spine, intensely say a forceful *hūṃ* or *hig.* While imagining that the wind lifts the vibrating moon and *hūṃ* upward, and that they gradually arrive at the throat, say about twenty *hūṃ*s or *hig*s. Again, with *ka hi* it gradually descends to the navel. Train in that way until signs occur.

When putting it into action, the drawing up to the throat is otherwise as before, but at the twenty-first *hūṃ* or *hig,* while imagining that the *hūṃ* moves quickly like a small bird flying through a skylight and that the clear light at the crown of the head shoots straight out and dissolves into the heart of the master, quickly release the hands and let the body fall back. Rest the mind without clinging. If the breath stops in just that state, the practice when passing away has been successful. If that does not happen, it should be done again. Thus my master taught.

c) *The transference with sound*

All the key physical points and so forth are the same as described previously, but the openings can also be blocked by syllables as in the supreme fourth initiation practice when passing away. Thus my master taught. [405]

Imagine the wind mandala, moon, and *hūṃ* at the heart cakra. The training, putting it into practice, and so forth are as before.

Success can be achieved by doing whichever of these three transferences one prefers, but in this instance one should mainly do the transformation of appearances as the practice when passing away. Thus my master taught.

Practicing in this way, the superior individual will reach the culmination of attainment and the medium will go to Khecara or become an upholder of pure awareness. Even the inferior will be reborn into a religious family, and by virtue of the dependently arisen connections will meet a master who teaches this Dharma, and by practicing will gradually reach the culmination of attainment.

5) *The intermediate state*

If one has died suddenly from something like a stroke without time to do the practice when passing away, or it did not turn out exactly right because the training had not been perfected, then both the arising from the dharmakāya reality body during the clear light of death and the arising of a mental body in the intermediate state will occur like the high and low of a tilting balance scale. Taking that as the path consists of three topics:

a) The intermediate state between birth and death
b) The intermediate state of dream
c) The intermediate state between existences

a) *The intermediate state between birth and death*

During all meditative equipoise and postmeditation, think: "Oh, no! I've died! These appearances are the appearances of the intermediate state. And I can make the appearances of the intermediate state into anything."

Clearly imagine all appearances as the form of the deity, appearance and emptiness indivisible, and rest in inexpressible pure awareness. In particular, it is imperative to not forget attention to the intermediate state when eating food and whenever violent emotions such as fear arise, and to remember the master who completely bestowed the vase initiation, the mandala in which it was bestowed, and the secret name he gave. Thus my master taught.

b) *The intermediate state of dream*

As will be explained, in the context of a dream, think: "Whatever appearances arise, they are not truly established. I can make them into anything." Train in transforming them into the deity and primordial awareness.

Those are training for the intermediate state.

c) *The intermediate state between existences*

Many different opinions about this exist, but here the explication of the treatise written by Yar Bumawa exactly according to the teachings of the great venerable lord of Sakya, and *Liberation on the Precipitous Pathway* composed by Gyalwa Yangönpa, are both taken as authoritative.[851] Furthermore, the explanations of *Liberation on the Precipitous Pathway* that do not agree with the text of Bumawa are set aside. Thus my master taught.

One might wonder, "What is the nature or fundamental condition of the intermediate state between existences?"

It is taught, beginning with these words:

> With the corporeal form
> of a previous existence.[852]

As previously explained, however long one remains in the state of the dharmakāya reality body during the clear light of death, one remains in a swoon without recognizing one's very nature. [406] When one arises from that, the triad of appearance, spreading, and attainment appear in sequence. The eighty natural concepts become clearer, arising in order. Agitated by the vital action winds, the pair *a haṃ*[853] split apart, and as the consciousness exits through the opening of a sense faculty it is also propelled out toward birth in the six realms and instantly arrives in the intermediate state between existences.

Most accept "with the corporeal form of a previous existence" to mean the form of the prior lifetime. But in Bumawa's text, "previous" is said to refer to a magical birth like the first gods in existence, the size of a child of about eight years of age with all sense faculties complete, who can go directly and without impediment anywhere other than the Vajrāsana (the site blessed by the Buddha), Mount Meru, the collected quintessence of the elements, the womb of one's mother created from karma, and blessed shrines. By the magical ability created from karma, one quickly comes and goes anywhere that is thought about, and has some tainted clairvoyance. A mental body such as that will be created.

At that time, unaware at first that one has died, appearances arise of valuables one possessed before, of giving directions to relatives, and so forth. When such things are done, and it is seen that one's share of food has been eliminated, no place is made for one, and that relatives give no reply no matter how much one speaks to them, as well as their sobbing and so forth, one thinks, "Oh, no! Now I've died," and inconceivable suffering arises. The consciousness becomes instantly helpless and vulnerable. Without the stable channels in the body, the mobile vital winds have dispersed, and the consciousness goes without distinction here and there like a bird feather carried by the wind. Because one has no white and red constituents, no illumination of day and night occurs, but a light created from karma is present, a dimness approximately like the pale light of dawn, in the midst of which places, companions, dwellings, food, and conduct are uncertain.

Sometimes sufferings of the elements arise. Four frightful sounds occur. Due to the reversal of the vital wind of earth, a sound like the disintegration of the entire earth seems to scramble the brains. Because the vital wind of fire has reversed, roaring sounds and crackling sounds, as if all appearances were burning with fire, occur. Because the vital wind of water has reversed, a sound like all appearances being swept away by water arises. [407] Because the vital wind of wind has reversed, a sound like all the three-thousandfold world systems being swept away by wind occurs.

Three terrifying abysses appear as the embodiment of the three poisons:[854] three white, red, and black pits close together, with deep invisible bottoms. While one stands between them on a ledge as thin as the back of a knife, the suffering of being terrified of falling into the pits and anguishing about what to do will occur. Sufferings such as these will happen, without distinction between experiencing this and not experiencing that.

One may be oppressed by numerous additional sufferings, such as the darkness thickening because one's relatives change their clothing and tear out their hair, and intense hail and a rain of blood because they weep. The contamination of their grief may block the opening of the womb in which one is to take birth, and one may wander in the intermediate state for many years, as taught in the *Tale of the Prince.*[855]

Generally the length of life is not definite in the intermediate state, but it is explained that most sentient beings remain in the intermediate state for forty-nine days. A small death strikes every seven days, so eulogies are made at seven-day intervals. If an initiation is bestowed on all of the forty-nine days, the preliminary section must be repeated after seven days because that supporting mental body for which the preliminary was done before has died again. Thus my master taught.

In the context of forty-nine days as the length of life, during the first half, or twenty-four and a half days, due to habitual propensities the previous body will appear to be present. Thereafter, the body connected with the ripening of karma will arise, which will have the form of the supporting body in which one will be reborn, such as a furry form with horns, a tail, and so forth if one will be born as an animal.

Similarly, the appearances of the five olfactory lights arise. The frequent occurrence of the term *five light forms* is a textual corruption, and incomprehensible. *Olfactory* refers to the consumption of odors by the mental body in the intermediate state, meaning something like what is to be smelled by it. These are explained as being the embodiment of the five sensory objects. Thus my master taught.

In regard to the colors, the black light of the hell beings, the blue of the animals, the red of the hungry spirits, the green of the anti-gods, the variegated of the human beings, and the white light of being born as a god arise brilliantly sparkling like shining rainbows. In some explications of the treatise of the *Vajra Lines,* the explanation of the light of the hell beings as white is a concealment. Thus my master taught.

When the lights arise in that way, at the point of going to the birthplace for which the most karma has been accumulated, if the mind focuses on the black light, the appearance arises of one's body in a utterly black form, like a chunk of wood burned by fire, blackly plunging down headfirst. [408] Then one gradually takes birth in hell. Similarly, if the mind focuses on the yellow light, the birthplace appears as a repulsive receptacle or a grass hut, and one will be a hungry spirit. If the mind focuses on the blue light, and if the appearance arises of entering an earthen cave or a disgusting building, one will be an animal. If a green light and the appearance of entering a forest arise, one will be an anti-god. If a white light and the appearance of entering a jeweled building arise, one will be a god. If the mind focuses on light of various colors and one appears to enter a temple, one will be a human being.

Furthermore, if one sees male and female lions copulating, and a lake adorned with them, it is a sign of birth in Jambudvīpa. If one sees lakes adorned with elephants, horses, or peacocks or birds with human bodies,[856] and they are copulating, these are signs of birth in the other three continents in sequence.[857]

In brief, the second half of the number of days one lives in the intermediate state becomes established as the intermediate existence of where one will be born. This is difficult to alter after the olfactory lights have been focused upon. Therefore, in regard to spiritual practices done for the benefit of one in the intermediate state, whatever is done during the first half of the number of days is the most powerful. If the basic virtues, the improvement of birthplace, and so forth, are done very quickly, it is easier to change the consciousness of the intermediate state, and the benefit is more powerful. Thus my master taught.

In that way, whatever confusing appearances of terror and so forth occur, think: "I have died and I am in the intermediate state. All these appearances are the appearances of the intermediate state. The material body of ripened karma has been discarded and does not exist. Nobody can do anything to this insubstantial mental body, but I can change it into anything."

Thus, thinking that the excellent master is bestowing initiation into the mandala of glorious Hevajra and introducing one to all appearances as the deity, clearly imagine whatever confusing appearances arise—terror, desire, hatred, the olfactory lights, and so forth—to be the essence of the master in the form of the chosen deity Hevajra, and rest in just that state. Like a cloud forming, Heruka will arrive there surrounded by a retinue of an inconceivable number of spiritual heroes and yoginīs of Khecara, call one by the secret name given by the master before, and make prophecies. Feel devotion for him, blend one's mind with his, and rest without clinging. At precisely that moment one (the yogin) will be placed on a jeweled throne, a pavilion of rainbow light will form, and while a rain of flowers falls and sweet music plays, one will be carried away to Khecara. [409] Thus my master taught.

It is possible for a dangerous māra to impersonate the deity and cause obstacles at that time, which is the reason the secret name given now by the master must be kept secret. Similarly, it is impossible for murderous gods and demons, diviners, dream interpreters, and so forth to see the mental body of the intermediate state, but some malicious spirits may impersonate its form, cause belief in the untruth of the causes and results of actions, and so forth. However, they are totally unreliable, as taught in the tale of the Bönpo who performed the funeral rites for Ramtara at Lugong.[858]

If one is unable to gain liberation in the intermediate state because one has trained little in this lifetime, one should select a womb. When the appearances of a bad birthplace and the olfactory lights arise, leave the mind without desire and attachment to them. Concentrate on a pure land like Sukhāvatī, or the womb of a religious mother. If intense aspirations are made, this will form an auspicious connection and one will be able to block bad birthplaces. If one offers supplications to these ḍākas and ḍākinīs and Dharma protectors of primordial awareness, requests their enlightened actions, and utterly trusts them, they will definitely protect one from bad birthplaces, as the yogin of Rakha Drak was protected by Kṣetrapāla when he was about to be born as a worm inside the corpse of a horse.[859] Thus my master taught.

In summation, if one trains during the day for the intermediate state between birth and death, obtains stability in spiritual practice during the dream state at night, and these esoteric instructions of the intermediate state are sustained even if one is pursued by a pack of seven dogs led by their mother, then one will be happy. Otherwise, with nothing but vague explanations, it will not turn out exactly right. If stability has not been obtained in dreams, even if the esoteric instructions of the intermediate state are understood, one will be distracted by terror and so forth and not remember them. Even if they are somewhat remembered, stability will not be obtained. Therefore, effort in the practices of the intermediate state between birth and death and the intermediate state of dream alone is crucial now. Thus my master taught.

Maṅgalaṃ
Good fortune!

9. Summarizing Notes on the Inner Creation Stage

From the Expansion of the Great Secret Doctrine

Summarizing Notes of Guidance for the Precious Teaching of the "Path with the Result"

The Infallible Version of Khau Drakzongpa

Jamyang Khyentsé Wangchuk (1524–68)

I PROSTRATE AND TAKE REFUGE at the immaculate lotus beneath the feet of the essence of all the buddhas of the past, present, and future, the overlord of a hundred spiritual families, great Heruka, holy Losel Gyatso Drakpa Gyaltsen Palsangpo of matchless kindness. Please bless me to quickly obtain the naturally spontaneous four bodies of enlightenment.

b) *The inner creation stage*[860]

This consists of two topics:

(1) The elimination of doubts by means of study and reflection on the meaning that is to meditated upon[861]
(2) The practices of mental focusing, which are the practice of the meaning that has been analyzed

2) *The practices of mental focusing*

This consists of three topics:

a) Engaging
b) Resting
c) Arising[862]

a) *Engaging*

From taking refuge through the blessing of the sensory bases as enlightened body, speech, and mind are as before. However, the main primordial awareness aspect, in whose body the body mandala of the supporting mandala and supported deities is present like an image reflected in a mirror, is invited, and offerings and eulogies are made. By the catalyst of its absorption, one's body naturally existing as the supporting mandala and supported deities is instantly and clearly illuminated, like raising up a lamp in a darkened temple. Clearly imagine this in sequence.

Moreover, the variegated vajra at the top of the head, and so forth, are envisioned at this and that spot, wherever the grounds of purification are. As explained in the great adept Jetāri's *Method for Accomplishment of the Fourth Mudrā* and in the explication of the treatise entitled *For the Benefit of the Sons,*[863] the principal deities of the five mansions are visualized as herukas with one face and two arms, in the half-vajra position with the toes of the left foot pointing at the thigh of the extended right leg, and with hair, ornaments, and so forth just like the outer heruka. [412] If so inclined, one may visualize them with eight faces and sixteen arms, with the eight right hands holding the hand implements of the individual five spiritual families and the left holding bells with handles made from those. Thus my master taught. It is good if one meditates on each of the three seats also complete in each of the initiation deities. If unable to manage that, it is also sufficient to imagine that vajra assistants equal to the number of deities emanate from a single initiation deity and grant initiation. If one can manage the visualization, initiation is taken by the outer heruka, the nine deities, the 157 deities of the body mandala, and the additional ones. Even if condensed, the initiation definitely must be taken by the outer heruka as well as the principal deities of the five mansions.[864] If so inclined, it is permissible to visualize that everything in apparent existence takes initiation clearly as the deity. Thus my master taught.

Furthermore, visualize the root master in the form of Akṣobhya residing in the center of a lotus with eight petals on top of a two-level heavenly dais of beryl in front of one in the sky. In front of him is a jewel throne covered with various silks, upon which are the initiation substances such as the vase and the crown. The buddhas of the four spiritual families are in the four cardinal directions. The four mothers are in the four intermediate directions. The eight bodhisattvas are in the primary and intermediate directions of the first heavenly dais. The six goddesses are in the four intermediate directions and the east and west of the second dais. The ten wrathful beings with the mothers in the form of their own light are outside the heavenly dais in the primary and intermediate directions, above, and below. Here the celestial mansion is mainly not visualized. Thus my master taught.

During the water initiation of Akṣobhya, by means of the *svabhāva* mantra one no longer envisions oneself with the body mandala or the initiation substance that is the water of the victory vase, which vanish into emptiness. From a state of emptiness appears a *paṃ* that becomes a lotus and a *raṃ* that becomes a sun, upon which is a *hūṃ* that becomes a blue variegated vajra marked with a *hūṃ*. Light rays radiate from that, return, and from their total transformation one (together with the body mandala and the initiation substance) becomes Akṣobhya. And so forth just as usual. In brief, up through the five initiations of pure awareness and that of the vajra master, the sequential generation of the deities of the body mandala as the buddhas of the five spiritual families, Vajrasattva, and Vajradhara, and taking the initiations, is the extremely crucial profound key point of the Time of the Path. Thus my master taught. [413]

While it is the custom of the Kṛṣṇa Yamāri tradition and so forth for both Vairocana and Vajrasattva to have a moon seat, since a sun seat is explained in the explications of the treatise of the *Vajra Lines,* it should be done in that way. It was the custom of Phakpa Rinpoché[865] to have Vajradhara blue, but since it is the causal Vajradhara here during both the cause and the path, he should be white.

In that way, take the four initiations as usual up through the crowning with the lords of the spiritual families, after which the initiation deities in front dissolve into oneself. Finish up through this point if done according to the method for accomplishment in four branches, or up through the branch of Ratnasambhava, the eulogy, if according to that of six branches.

b) *Resting*

In lord Sakya Paṇḍita's catalogue of guidance for the *Clarification of the Meaning Through Symbols*[866] the extensive practice is with seven sessions. The medium is with five sessions, which are on the supported deity of the enlightened-mind vajra, the three middle mansions, and the last mansion with the additional [ten wrathful beings]. The condensed is as described previously, except that there are three sessions, with the three middle mansions done as one. That much is taught, but here it will be in the context of the extensive.

1' *Focusing the mind on the pride*

After finishing the mental focusing of the outer creation stage, one focuses the mind on the pride. Think: "My body channels, channel syllables, essential constituent nectars, and quintessential vital wind of primordial awareness—the four mandalas—are not ordinary forms like this. They are really the naturally spontaneous four bodies of enlightenment that constitute the level of a vajra holder on the thirteenth spiritual level at the time of the result."

Be proud, and rest at ease without clinging in just that state.

2' *Focusing the mind on the general forms*

Practice focusing the mind by thinking: "These 157 deities, together with the twenty-two additional deities, which arise as such radiant unceasing emanations, are actually those particular deities residing on the level of a vajra holder on the thirteenth spiritual level at the time of the result."

3' *Focusing the mind on the individual forms*

a' *Focusing the mind on the support*

As though the mind has entered into it, first intently focus on the blue *hūṃ* in the heart cakra of the enlightened-mind vajra, Akṣobhya, which is the nature of light, has the majestic radiance of ten million suns, and seems to have been drawn with a body hair. From that a blue light, which is the essence of one's mind, floats up blue like the smoke of a stick of incense. [414] When it arrives at the top of the head, the variegated vajra present at the top of the head is illuminated, like raising up a lamp in a dark room. Furthermore, focus the mind on the variegated vajra that has come from all the flesh, blood, bone, and lymph of the top of one's head as its material, and which is white to the east, yellow to the south, red to the west, green to the north, and indigo in the center, with the nature of light, clear, immaculate, and brilliantly present.

Again, those light rays flash downward, together with one's mind, and arrive at the soles of the feet. Focus the mind on the ground of vajras, like barley spread out on a plain, that is blue in color, with the nature of light, and has come from all the flesh, blood, lymph, and bone of the soles of the feet as its material.

Similarly, imagine that the light illuminates wherever it arrives, like the shining sun.

Focus the mind on particular portions of the fence of blue vajras that stands vertically and the net that stretches horizontally, which have come from one's long ribs and short ribs as their material.

The body of the outer Blessed One, with the nature of light, is complete with the major and minor marks, the appearance of which is unceasing. But inside, like a reflected image appearing in a mirror, the vajra pavilion and canopy are filled with blue vajras about the size of barley and rice, without intervening spaces, which have come from the skin as their material, from that of the crown of the head down to that of the soles of the feet.

With all the body hairs as its material, and created from the manifestations of primordial awareness, the net of protruding arrows has the complete characteristics of the notches, feathers, and so forth, and arrowheads of half-vajras. The notches point inward and the arrowheads point outward.

Since the extra arms and legs are projections, they have no grounds of purification, and one does not need to visualize them. In regard to the nails of the main arms and legs, practice focusing the mind on the nails of the outer Blessed One, which are the color of copper, with the nature of light, inside of which, like an image appearing in a mirror, blazes the fire of primordial awareness that has come from one's nails as its material.

Since the hair of the head is not actually mentioned here, it may be left aside. If it is visualized, since it is described in the *Saṃvara* as a mountain of fire, visualize it in that way. Thus my master taught.

Again, blue light like the shining sun floats out from the *hūṃ.* [415] Practice focusing the mind on the wind mandalas, which are like bent bows marked on the handgrips with *yaṃ*s and on the tips with banners. These have come from the material of the wind residing at the ankle joints of the feet that acts as the support for the flexing movement of the feet.

Again, when that light arrives in the lower abdomen, focus the mind on the red tetrahedron fire mandala blazing with fire and marked with a *raṃ,* which has come from all the flesh, blood, and lymph of the lower abdomen as its material.

Then focus the mind on the white spherical water mandala, like a crystal vase filled with water and marked with an *a,* which has come from the flesh, blood, and so forth of the stomach as its material.

Then focus the mind on the cubical earth mandala marked with half-vajras at the four corners and with a *laṃ* in the middle, which has come from the flesh and bone of the chest as its material.

Their mode of existence corresponds to the present grounds of purification. Thus my master taught.

Then practice focusing the mind on the twenty-one cubical Mount Merus with layered terraces, created from the manifestations of primordial awareness, which have come from each of one's twenty-one vertebrae as their material, and which are precisely located as though stacked one upon the other. The two temples of the head and the two corresponding lower corners at the back of the skull, in brief, the four prongs of the variegated vajra, are the upper part of Mount Meru, each in the form of a turret or small cubical room.

Again, when that light arrives at the four palms of the hands and soles of the feet, meditate on the six-foot-square body symbolizing the square celestial mansion. Visualize each of the black, green, red, yellow, and white forms of the corners of the walls in sequence from the inside; these have come from the flesh, bone, and so forth of the palms of both hands as their material. Focus the mind on each of the five-colored corners of the vajra ground at the soles of the feet, like an image reflected in a mirror.

Practice focusing the mind on the frames of the gates, which have come from the material of the four channels in which the vital winds of the four elements circulate through the heart. Visualize them with lintels and thresholds and the two gate panels thrown wide open, and marked with a cakra in the east, a jewel in the south, a lotus in the west, and a variegated vajra in the north.

The layered five walls that have come from the flesh, blood, and fluid of the eyes as their material are the equivalents of the walls in the cardinal directions. Thus my master taught.

The precious yellow frieze, whose surface is adorned with numerous precious stones, has come from the cartilage, flesh, blood, and so forth of the nose as its material. [416]

Each of the teeth has come from the bone of one's teeth as their material, and have the nature of nets and half-nets of pearls strung on red threads.

Each of the extremely red long platforms of sensory objects, within the

Blessed One's lips and tongue, which are red like crabapples, have come from one's tongue and lips as their material.

The precious archways of four layers, which are supported by four pillars, have the complete characteristics of the Dharma wheels, parasols, deer, and so forth, and have come from the cartilage and so forth of one's ears as their material.

Focus the mind on both upper arms as the white pillars marked with cakras, the forearms as the yellow pillars marked with jewels, the thigh bones as the red pillars marked with lotuses, and the shin bones as the green pillars marked with variegated vajras.

Imagine that the light returns and dissolves into the *hūṃ* of the heart cakra.

b' *Focusing the mind on the supported deities*

Again, at the heart cakra of Akṣobhya, the enlightened-mind vajra, focus the mind on the blue *hūṃ* that has the nature of light and seems to have been drawn with a body hair. Blue light, which is the essence of one's mind, rises up from that. The light that emerges from the crown of Akṣobhya's head illuminates Vajrasattva, the lord of the spiritual family. Focus the mind on Vajrasattva, father and mother, whose bodies are white in color, residing in the vajra position, and nearly invisible to the eye.

Then focus the mind on the red hair rising up on the head, the bone cakra on the top of the head, the tiara of five dry skulls, and the prongs of bone garlands.

Then focus the mind in sequence wherever the light arrives and, like the shining sun, illuminates the face, ears, earrings, necklace, upper body, two hands holding the vajra and bell and embracing the mother, brahmin thread, apron, bracelets and anklets, and the half-vajra position in which the toes of the left foot are pointed at the thigh of the extended right leg.

Again, illuminated by the light from the *hūṃ* of the heart cakra, focus the mind in sequence starting from the hair on the head.

Again, illuminated by the light, focus the mind in detail on the eight Māmakīs of the channel branches, who are brandishing curved knives in their right hands, holding skull-cups of blood at their hearts with their left hands, standing in the half-vajra position with the toes of the right feet pointing at the thighs of the extended left legs, and wearing the ornaments, costumes, and so forth.

Then the blue light from the *hūṃ* of the heart cakra radiates and fills the entire expanse of space. Just by its striking the entire environment and its inhabitants, everything transforms into the complete three seats of the spiritual family of Akṣobhya alone. After focusing the mind on that, imagine that everything smoothly melts into blue light with the nature of great bliss. [417] Imagine that this returns together with the light that radiated before, and dissolves into one's Akṣobhya, the main deity and the retinue. Focus the mind. If one does not like the elaboration of this radiating and returning, it is also permissible not to do so. Thus my master taught.

Again, the blue light from the *hūṃ* of the heart cakra of the enlightened-mind vajra floats up blue like the smoke of a stick of incense. It dissolves into the *oṃ* of the heart cakra of the enlightened-speech vajra of the throat. Imagine that it has the majestic light of ten million suns. Red light rises straight up from [the *oṃ*]. The light emerges from the crown of Amitābha's head and illuminates the lord of the spiritual family and all appearances transform into the complete three seats of the spiritual family of Amitābha, melt into light, return, and dissolve into the inner deities, as before.

Similarly, blue light radiates from the heart cakra of the enlightened-mind vajra, dissolves into the *haṃ* of the heart cakra of Vairocana, the enlightened-body vajra at the top of the head, white light radiates from [the *haṃ*], and so forth.

Again, the blue light from the heart cakra of the enlightened-mind vajra goes downward, enters through the top of the head of Ratnasambhava, the enlightened qualities, who is at the navel, dissolves into the *aṃ* of his heart cakra, yellow light radiates from that, and so forth.

Again, focus the mind as before on the blue light that radiates from the heart cakra of the enlightened-mind vajra, enters through the crown of the head of Amoghasiddhi, the enlightened activities, who is at the genital area, and dissolves into the *ha* of his heart cakra. Green light rises up from that, the light illuminates the lord of the spiritual family, and all appearances transform into the complete three seats of the spiritual family of Amoghasiddhi, return in the form of light, and dissolve into the inner deities.

Again, the light of the heart cakra of the enlightened-mind vajra arrives at the eyes. Clearly imagine the support of those sense organs, the channel knot existing in the shape of *maṃ*, as white Mohavajrā looking outward, and so forth, with the body color, hand implements, and so forth of the subject deities as usual. Īrṣyāvajrā is inside the forehead right between the eyebrows and Nairātmyā is just above the dharmacakra of the heart. The subject goddesses are the vital wind known as *circulation* (which creates the condition for the eyes to engage form) arising as deities. If one of the four supporting mandalas did not act as their material, they would not be in the body mandala. [418] These object deities should be visualized facing inward, as though facing together and touching, but not adhering, to the subject deities. Thus my master taught.

The ten wrathful beings are with the female embodiments of pure awareness in the form of their own light. Furthermore, the ten wrathful beings are the channel syllables *hūṃ* that are present at: both elbows; the tops of both shoulders (both joints where the shoulder blades and upper arms are joined); both kneecaps; [one] for the tops and ankles of both feet; the top of the head measured four finger-widths up from the forehead, but a full finger-width above where the cakra of great bliss is at the top of the head, which is between two finger-widths up [from the forehead] and two finger-widths down [from the crown of the head]; at the tip of the genital organ; and at the tip of the tongue. Visualize those at the top of the head and at the genital organ looking outward. The others look inward. But when practicing repulsion, visualize that they look outward. Thus my master taught.

Practice focusing the mind on those in sequence, beginning from the lord of the spiritual family. Thus my master taught.

Just that much is the essential extract of the teachings of that kind spiritual father and master.

Maṅgalaṃ
Good fortune!

10. Summarizing Notes Beginning with the Dream Yoga of the Vase Initiation

From the Expansion of the Great Secret Doctrine

Summarizing Notes of Guidance for the Precious Teaching of the "Path with the Result"

The Infallible Version of Khau Drakzongpa

The Fifth Dalai Lama (1617–82)

I PROSTRATE AND TAKE REFUGE in the spiritual father Tsarchen, the Dharma king who is the essence of all the buddhas of the past, present, and future, and in his spiritual sons and the lineage. Please grace me with your great love.

> Fortunate are those
> with the knowledge to drink
> from a treasury of nectar such as this,
> the great secret Explication for Disciples,
> the quintessence of the elixir
> of the Lord of Yogin's system,
> difficult to find even with the merit
> accumulated for countless eons.
>
> With this sublime method
> for accomplishing buddhahood
> in one lifetime,
> all impure, confused living beings,
> who are the grounds of purification,
> will, by means of the agent of the purifying
> path of the four initiations,

actually achieve the four bodies of enlightenment,
which is the result of purification.

If the eight concerns[867] of this life
appearing here are cast aside,
and the hardship of diligently practicing
the sublime path as the essential point
is relied upon,
it is certain that one will go
to the land of great blissful unity.

The guidance manual for the precious oral instructions of the Path with the Result, the version of Khau Drakzongpa, the oral explanations of Tsarchen Dorjé Chang, was recorded as summarizing notes by Jamyang Khyentsé Wangchuk, but left unfinished after the completion of the instructions for the intermediate state of the vase initiation. I will write summarizing notes beginning with the guidance for the dream yoga, carefully supplemented with the oral explanations of the great vajra holder of the Asha clan, Jamgön Sönam Chokden,[868] which are the exceptional teachings of the Explication for Disciples.

6) *Dream yoga*[869]

Dream yoga is the evaluation of the practice of the Vajrayana path. [420] The precise way to practice it consists of two topics:

a) The preliminaries
b) The main practice

a) *The preliminaries*

Acting without extreme physical exertion and fatigue, with modest speech, without greatly indulging in wide-ranging thoughts, and avoiding rich foods that are the causes of deep sleep, and strong tea and so forth that are the causes of insomnia, engage in all activities gently and moderately. Until midday, whatever appearances of the day arise, think: "These are the appearances of a dream. I absolutely must be able to recognize this dream!"

Also say aloud again and again: "This is a dream," and focus with intense aspiration.

If done too intensely after midday, these actions will form the causes for sudden awakening, so both the aspiration and speech should be done moderately.

b) *The main practice*

This consists of four topics:

(1) Recognition
(2) Training
(3) Multiplication
(4) Resting the mind in reality

All of those include the three topics of the preliminaries, the main practice, and the conclusion.[870]

First is the preliminaries. After gathering in the visualization of the evening yoga session, perform a condensed taking of refuge and awakening of the enlightenment mind, such as the following:

> I take refuge until enlightenment
> in the Buddha, Dharma,
> and sublime Assembly.
>
> By the merit of my acts
> of generosity and so forth,
> may I achieve enlightenment
> for the benefit of living beings.

Perform the stages of protection for oneself, the place, and the yogin as before. If so inclined, offer supplications to the master for recognition of the dream, and so forth.

Second is the main practice.

(1) *Recognition*

While lying comfortably on the right side and going to sleep, clearly imagine in the throat a red lotus with four petals, and on the petals—in a clockwise circle from the front—*a nu ta ra,* with *oṃ* in the center. Make the color white or red, whichever arises as a mental image. To begin with, focus the visualization on the front *a*. Think: "This *a* is the syllable of dream. This appearance is also an appearance of dream. The appearances of dream can be made and transformed into anything. Therefore, I absolutely must recognize the dream!"

In a state uninterrupted by other thoughts, join this with sleep. If one immediately goes to sleep and recognizes the dream, it has worked. If one is still sleepless or if thoughts continue, also focus the mind in sequence on each of the syllables, from the right *nu* until the *oṃ*.

If one does not recognize the dream even then, clearly imagine between the eyebrows a black droplet with the nature of light, about the size of a pea, touching but not adhering, and spinning counterclockwise.

In regard to this, in other paths four dream impediments are taught, but here, according to the custom of the Lord of Yogins, the two impediments are sudden awakening and confusing disturbances. [421] The first is also alleviated by the previously described black droplet. If not alleviated by that, it will be alleviated by focusing the mind on a droplet that is black around the edges, bright and pale in the middle, and spinning forcefully counterclockwise. If even that does not alleviate it, one will be freed from that sudden awakening by focusing the mind on a totally black droplet spinning counterclockwise as before, but with black light rays like charcoal powder that drift down thickly and seem to cover one's entire body. However, previous masters have taught that this may bring extreme dullness and so forth, so it should not be done except as a kind of last resort if nothing has been recognized.

Confusing disturbances are alleviated by means of the transcendent behavior. Strip the body naked at an isolated and vast spot with no people. Perform various unpredictable physical activities, such as running and leaping. Do various unpredictable things with the voice, such as yells and so forth, and say many times, "This is a dream."

In the mind, think single-pointedly: "These are the appearances of a dream."

That will alleviate confusing disturbances.

Or else stay at a dangerous place, like the summit of a cliff where the water crashes against the rocks, a precipice, or the peak of a tall castle. Thinking again and again that one's feeling of terror is the appearance of a dream will alleviate confusing disturbances.

(2) *Training*

When one has thus recognized a dream, and the thought "Things like this are the appearances of a dream" has arisen during a dream, it can be made and transformed into anything. Therefore, train by going to the summit of Mount Meru and looking at the four continents, then even going to the surfaces of the sun and the moon and looking at Brahmā's world, and then gradually directing the mind to pure lands such as Abhirati, recognizing a dream, meeting the buddhas and listening to Dharma, and so forth.

(3) *Multiplication*

When one has become adept in that way, also emanate many of one's bodies—two from one, three from two, and so forth—and make offerings to the buddhas, and go to the lower realms and multiply one's bodies to work for the benefit of sentient beings, and so forth.

(4) *Resting the mind in reality*

The *Root Tantra* says:

> These are neither true nor false, [422]
> and similarly, yoginīs,
> know that I maintain everything
> to be like the moon in water.[871]

Thus, those [experiences] are not true, because after waking from sleep not even a trace of them having happened is apparent. They are also not false, because they were experienced during the dream.

In brief, apply the seal of truthlessness to all appearances and blend them in the indivisibility of samsara and nirvana.

Illusory Body

Illusory body is the evaluation of that dream yoga. This consists of three topics: impure illusory body, pure illusory body, and illusory body consisting of both.

The first is all that appears as the various places, bodies, and experiences in the three realms, these things that arise, although nonexistent, by virtue of the mind affected by karma and affliction, and by encountering various conditions.

The second is the forms of the deities of the stable creation stage and the experiences that arise as the path of the Three Appearances and so forth, because the profound path has been practiced.

Concerning the third, all the phenomena included in samsara and nirvana appear as a variety, yet not even the tip of a hair has ever been established as true. For example, take the appearance of a form in a mirror. When the conditions for that appearance have not been assembled, the natural causal conditions are lacking. When they have been assembled, a reflected form appears. But it disappears as soon as those conditions cease, so it is empty of an enduring essence. Moreover, how it vanishes in this way is inexpressible, so it is empty of a result in the end.

Similarly, no cause for the birth of one's body existed before, when one's parents had not met. The body established now due to various conditions will be destroyed without remaining for long, so it is empty of an enduring essence. Where it has vanished in the end when the body is cremated is inexpressible, so it is empty of a result in the end. When this point is actually experienced, clinging to everything such as praise and blame, and pleasure and pain, will be abandoned and they will be transformed into the path of the indivisibility of samsara and nirvana.

In that way, through the unity of those two—illusory body during the day and dream at night—the culmination of attainment will be reached in the intermediate state.

Moreover, practice many times, again and again, with forms of praise and blame and so forth recited to one's image in a mirror.

In that way, after the instructions about the ground (the fundamental nature of the phenomenon of samsara), the stages of progress on the path—from a brief presentation by means of the three aspects of coemergence, through what has just been explained—have been carefully completed. [423]

As for the explanation of the result, the spiritual level of buddhahood, a superior person actualizes up through the sixth spiritual level and reaches the culmination of attainment in that lifetime. A middling person does so at the clear light of death. An inferior person does so through the transformation of appearances in the intermediate state. Even an extremely inferior person takes rebirth in conjunction with prayers and trains in the remaining spiritual paths. These are the result of the stages of the path of the vase initiation.

Furthermore, the pulsations of the channels dissolve and the path of the creation stage is actualized.

> The stages of guidance connected
> with the vase initiation,
> by which the sixth spiritual level is actualized
> and the culmination of attainment reached,
> have been written according to the oral account
> of an infallible transmission.
> Assembled fortunate ones, dance with joy!

The oral explanations of my lord and master on the stages of practice for the vase initiation have been carefully completed.

b. *The secret initiation*[872]

The path of the secret initiation is the second path meditated on in connection with the four initiations concerning the method continuum of the body.

1) *The path*

This consists of three topics:

a) The preparation
b) The main practice
c) The conclusion[873]

a) *The preparation*

This consists of two topics: the inclusive oral instructions and the included oral instructions, or else the preliminaries for guidance and the preliminaries for the session.

(1) *The preliminaries for guidance*

This consists of three topics: requesting initiation, taking it, and accumulation and purification. The last is done as before.

(2) *The preliminaries for the session*

This consists of three topics:

(a) The three trainings
(b) The three meditations
(c) Observing the three key points

(a) *The three trainings*

This consist of three topics. The first is to perform the training of the five branches.[874] The second is to lessen loud and intense speech, laughter, reading aloud, chanting, and so forth. The third is to rest, lucid yet empty, without clinging.

(b) *The three meditations*

This also consists of three topics. The first is to begin with these verses:

> I take refuge until enlightenment
> in the Buddha, Dharma,
> and sublime Assembly.
>
> By the merit of my acts
> of generosity and so forth,
> may I achieve enlightenment
> for the benefit of living beings.

Then cultivate compassion for sentient beings who have not realized reality.

The second topic is to clearly imagine the protection cakra and the deity with the recitation of each *hūṃ*.

The third is to visualize the eight-faced master on the top of one's head, pray for him to bless one's mindstream, and imagine his dissolution into oneself.

(c) *Observing the three key points*

This also consists of three topics: with the body, observe the sevenfold posture of Vairocana; with the voice, blow out the vital wind in a series of nine; and with the mind, rest at ease in disenchantment.

b) *The main practice*

The *Vajra Lines* teach that during the first gathering of the essential constituents one is guided on the path by the warmths and the signs of the vital winds and the fierce fire. In regard to this, generally the statements in the *Kālacakra* about the yogas of the vital winds of life and exertion,[875] in the *Guhyasamāja* about those of the illusory body, and in the *Saṃvara* and here in the *Hevajra* tradition about those of the self-blessing or the fierce fire of *caṇḍālī,* are synonymous. [424] The *Root Tantra* says:

> Bring down with exhalation,
> control with inhalation,
> summon with filling,
> and paralyze with calm.[876]

Therefore, in the relative sense, these four—the triad of exhalation, inhalation, and the pause, together with filling—are taught to be the four actions that destroy opponents. According to the definitive meaning, these are taught to be the yogas of the vital wind during the completion stage. The Lord of Yogins made these into seven esoteric instructions: prāṇāyāma with vajra repetition, three for exhalation, two for meditative equipoise following inhalation, and union for the pause. These are combined with the eighteen fierce fires and the thirty-two physical yogic exercises.

(1) *The yogas of the vital wind*

(a) *Prāṇāyāma*

This must first be practiced in coordination with the vital wind circulating through the left nostril. If it is circulating through the right nostril, use the methods to make it circulate through the left by means of the instruction of squeezing the breast and expelling the vital wind. When the master is giving guidance, it is also the custom for him to do it in that way.

Then—figuring as one the triad of entry in through the left nostril, the pause within, and exiting—first count the vital wind without error, using something like a rosary, with an innumerable maximum and a minimum of about one hundred. After having counted about twenty, the circulation of the vital wind through either nostril makes no difference.

By meditating in that way, an exceptional meditative concentration, paranormal ability, and so forth will arise for a superior person. The experience of eliminating the entry of thoughts will arise. At least, as when a pure vessel has been cleaned and rinsed, the good qualities of the vital winds made workable will be produced during the practice of the vase retention.

Moreover, when one wishes to produce the good qualities of the meditative concentration of the completion stage, one should invigorate the vital wind. First, focus the mind on the right vital wind of exertion. Slightly alter the natural movement of the vital wind itself as it goes out, and lengthen the exhalation. Shorten both the inhalation and the pause. Count this as before. That removes obstacles. When one is accustomed to that, do the second practice. Naturally lengthen the vital wind of life entering in through the left nostril, and the pause. Shorten the exhalation. That is the supreme longevity practice, and a nonconceptual state will also gradually arise.

During vajra repetition, one transforms the tone of the vital winds of the previous triad of exhalation, inhalation, and the pause into the three seed syllables, beginning with *oṃ* for the inhalation. [425]

(b)–(d) *The three branches of exhalation*

First, make a fist with the right hand, press the back of the middle finger with the index finger, and press the right nostril with the middle finger. After a slight inhalation through the left nostril, exhale forcefully and hold it for while. Rest a bit during the inhalation and the pause.

Second, exhale forcefully through both nostrils. Exhale as before. To begin with, it will go for just about eighteen inches. Then it will arrive at the limits of the three-thousandfold world systems.

Third, for exhalation with sound through the mouth, bring the upper and lower teeth together but not quite touching, and, with the sound "seee," exhale the same way as before.

(e)–(f) *Inhalation*

This consists of two topics. First, directly at the swirl of the navel, clearly imagine a droplet about the size of a new mother bird's egg,[877] white outside and red inside, in the middle of which is a red *a* in the form of a vertical line about the size of a barley kernel. Block the right nostril with the fist of the hand as before. Inhale for a long time through the left nostril while imagining that the vital winds dissolve and are absorbed into the *a* in the form of a vertical line. When the inhalation is complete, rotate the head in a clockwise circle in coordination with its mount, the saliva, and hold the vital wind as long as possible.

Second, clearly imagine a blue tetrahedron in place of the egg, and visualize that the tetrahedron fills the three-thousandfold world systems in the end. Everything else is the same as the previous practice.

For enhancement [of the practice] or for removal of impediments from having excessively expelled the vital wind, use the yogic posture of the cooking tripod of the body.[878] Another name for this is "binding with the sixfold cooking tripod." Focus the mind on a blue vital wind, like the smoke of a stick of incense, which descends from the top of the head and forms a blue pool for about eighteen inches out of the anus. Slightly compress the upper vital wind.

For enhancement [of the practice] and for removal of impediments from excessive inhalation, sit with crossed legs and grasp the anklebone of the left leg with the right hand, grasp the right with the left, and focus the mind on a blue vital wind going up from the genital area and coming out from the top of the head for about eighteen inches.

(g) *The vase retention*

Visualize an *a* in the form of a vertical line at the navel. Since little impediment occurs when compressing the upper vital wind first, soundlessly swallow some saliva and compress it about when it arrives at the navel. Also draw up the lower vital wind and hold both in union. For the number, count as one each circling of the hand from the left knee to the right and then snapping the fingers in the middle. [426] The superior is countless, the middling is sixty-four, and the inferior is uncertain.

At the end of each practice session of the seven yogas of the vital winds, rest without clinging.

(2) *The visualizations of fierce fire*

The number twenty-nine is taught in the *Sampuṭa.* The Lord of Yogins condensed that into eighteen. Furthermore, if all four of the channels, drops, vital wind, and fire are present, it is the dense fierce fire. If two are present, it is the full fierce fire. Fire alone is the naked fierce fire. The eighteen practices of our tradition include five not dependent on cakras, three dependent on cakras, and ten that have come from the key points of esoteric instruction.

(a) *The five not dependent on cakras*

These five are: feeding the lamp flame, Brahmā's lightning, the channel yoga, the wheel of the fire drill, and the yoga of the drops. Each of these also includes eight topics: training in the path, sustaining the view, allowing the natural expression of experiences, an indefinite number of sessions, an indefinite amount in a session, examining the object of inclination, evaluating health, and urging with the stimuli of food and conduct.

1' *Feeding the lamp flame*

For the first of the five, visualize oneself as the deity. Sitting with the knees raised, the arms crossed and the hands grasping the upper arms, and with the feet also crossed, use the yogic posture of the cooking tripod of the body composed of six triangles. Visualize inside the anus a blue mandala of vital wind like a moon sliced in half with the flat surface up, in the lower abdomen a tetrahedron of fire, below the navel an upside-down red *kṣa,* and at the navel an upright red *aṃ.*

Slightly draw up the lower vital wind three times, drawing it up steadily at the end. This stirs the vital wind, which ignites the fire, which strikes the *kṣa,* from which fire blazes. Two round red drops about the size of a pea come from the *aṃ* and dissolve into the *kṣa,* which blazes intensely as when melted butter is dripped into fire. That acts as a catalyst. While the essential constituent drips from the *aṃ* and both the fire and it become like tangled hair, compress the upper vital wind and rest.

2' *Brahmā's lightning*

At the anus, imagine the vital wind in the shape of a bow, and an arrow with the arrowhead pointing down. Visualize the central channel about the size of a medium reed arrow, straight up to the crown of the head. Visualize an upside-down white *haṃ* at the top of the head. By the catalyst of using the lower vital wind as before, the handgrip of the bow turns upward and the arrow goes up inside the channel and strikes the *haṃ*. [427] Focus the mind on the essential constituent dripping from it and bliss pervading the entire body. Hold the vital wind as before. This should not be done more than once in each session. Thus my master taught.

3' *The channel yoga*

Dependent on the triad of exhalation, inhalation, and the pause, clearly imagine the triad of the rasanā, the lalanā, and the central channel in sequence. Visualize the upper ends of the rasanā and lalanā sticking right into the point between the eyebrows, the upper end of the central channel into the crown of the head, and the lower ends of all three into the genital area. Do the vajra repetition of *oṃ* when the vital wind enters in through the lalanā, *āḥ* when it pauses at the opening of the central channel, and *hūṃ* when it exits through the rasanā.

4' *The wheel of the fire drill*

Sit with the knees raised and the arms wrapped around the knees. Visualize an *aṃ* at the navel. The lower end of the central channel sticks into the top of it. Just behind the navel the rasanā wraps three times in a clockwise circle around the central channel. Above that the lalanā wraps three times in a circle counterclockwise. By the catalyst of those two pulling it to the right and to the left, the central channel rubs the *aṃ* and red fire sparkles out. That red fire fills the central channel. Then it gradually fills the entire body.

5' *The yoga of the drops*

This contains four subsections: the union of sun and moon at the heart, the lone hero at the navel, the drop of bliss at the genitals, and the drop between the eyebrows that destroys white hair and wrinkles.

a' *The union of sun and moon at the heart*

If one wants meditative concentration to arise, one practices the union of sun and moon at the heart. Inside the heart cakra, which is like an eggshell, clearly imagine a white drop about the size of a half-pea, united with a red drop about the size of a half-pea on top of it, and the mind as a blue *hūṃ* inside. Then the sound "siiing" emerges from inside the drop, which acts as a catalyst. A small hole emerges in the top of the pendant formed by the drops. Focus the mind on it as though looking at it with one's eyes. Inhale the vital wind soundlessly through the mouth and imagine that it dissolves into the pendant. Light rays of five colors about the size of a hair from a horse's tail stretch out from the hole and wrap [around the pendant] three times from back to front and three times from right to left. Then the end [of the light rays] from the left goes to the rear and arrives about half way across the top [of the pendant]. Hold the vital winds in union. When exhaling, the light rays are released and dissolve into the place where they came from.

b' *The lone hero at the navel*

If one wants lucidity, one should practice the lone hero at the navel. Visualize a white drop at the navel, about the size of a small pea, endowed with the three qualities of being sparkling, spinning, and lucid. Inhale the vital wind soundlessly through the mouth and imagine that it dissolves into that drop. Hold the vital winds in union.

c' *The drop of bliss at the genitals*

If one wants to generate bliss, practice the drop of bliss at the genitals. [428] Inside the jewel of the male organ or inside the bhaga for a woman, visualize a red drop about the size of a mustard seed and endowed with the three qualities. Slightly draw up the lower vital wind, imagine that all the vital wind dissolves into that drop, and perform the union of the vital winds.

If one is afraid that the impediment of dripping will occur from excessive bliss, focusing the attention at the point between the eyes will alleviate it.

d' *The drop between the eyebrows that destroys white hair and wrinkles*

Assume the mudrā position of the cooking tripod. Place the tip of the tongue against the soft palate and suck a little. Imagine an upside-down white *haṃ* with the nature of bliss at the top of the head, an upside-down white *suṃ* just at the uvula, and an upright blue *hūṃ* at the heart cakra. Those are connected by white enlightenment mind, like a silk thread. When the vital wind of exertion is inhaled, it goes toward the back of the skull, warming the *haṃ,* from which a drop like molten crystal with the nature of bliss emerges. Passing through the path that is like a silk thread, the drop dissolves into the *suṃ,* making the *suṃ* into the nature of nectar. Imagining that [this nectar] also falls from [the *suṃ*] as before and dissolves into the *hūṃ,* slowly suck at the soft palate with the tip of the tongue. If so inclined, perform the union of the vital winds together with the inhalation through the left nostril. Do not discard the saliva elsewhere. This is also called "the instruction for milking the uvula."

(b) *The three dependent on cakras*

Those dependent on cakras are:

1' The sharp, which is dependent on one
2' The quick, which is dependent on two
3' The stable, which is dependent on four

1' *The sharp, which is dependent on one cakra*

Clearly imagine the channel cakra of the navel. Use the vital wind of the anus and the fire of the lower abdomen as before. Visualize an *aṃ* as the center of the channel cakra and the syllables *a ka ca ṭa* and so forth as the eight inner branches, all red. Draw up the lower vital wind in the same way as before. While visualizing that the vital wind ignites the fire, which ignites the syllables, and the fire blazes up from them for about four finger-widths, hold the vital winds in union.

2' *The quick, which is dependent on two cakras*

The visualization up to the navel is the same as the previous main practice, but the *aṃ* has transformed into an *oṃ*. Visualize a blue *hūṃ* as the center of the eight channel branches of the heart cakra. Clearly imagine a thin central channel between the *hūṃ* and the *oṃ*. Drawing up the lower vital wind and so forth as before, imagine that fire blazes up from the syllables of the navel and enters through the path of the central channel, and that when the tongue of flame touches the *hūṃ*, white drops fall from it, and the fire and the drops are like tangled hair.

3' *The stable, which is dependent on four cakras*

From the mandala of vital wind at the anus, up to the *kṣa* syllable of fire, clearly imagine everything as in the previous practices. [429] Then clearly imagine the red central channel about as thick as the thread of a spider web, and with a hollow interior. The upper end arrives at the aperture of Brahmā and the lower end just below the navel. To the right, the red rasanā is filled with blood, is slightly thinner than the central channel, and has the nature of fire. To the left, the white lalanā is the same thickness as the rasanā, is filled with the white constituent, and has the nature of water. The upper and lower ends of both are equal to those of the central channel.

At the navel, four channels branch off from the rasanā and from the lalanā, making eight. Sixty-four come from those. An *aṃ* is at the center. For the eight branches, in a clockwise circle from the front are *a ka ca ṭa* and so forth. The outer branches are two sets of the vowels such as *a* in a counterclockwise circle and one set of the consonant-syllables such as *ka,* minus the pair *ha* and *kṣa,* in a clockwise circle. These are upright, and all the channel syllables are red.

At the center of the eight channel branches of the heart cakra is a *hūṃ.* The eight branches are *bhrūṃ, āṃ, jrīṃ,* and *khaṃ* in a clockwise circle from the front in the four directions, and *laṃ, māṃ, pāṃ,* and *tāṃ* in a clockwise circle from the southeast. These are upside-down, and all are blue.

At the center of the channel cakra of the throat is an *oṃ.* The sixteen branches, in a counterclockwise circle from the front, are the sixteen vowels such as *a.* These are upright, and all are red.

At the center of the channel branches at the top of the head is a *haṃ.* The thirty-two branches are the sixteen vowels such as *a* in a counterclockwise circle from the front and the consonant-syllables from *ka* to *ta* in a clockwise circle. These are upside-down, and all are white.

While clearly imagining that, open and close the anus about three times, finally drawing up the lower vital wind. This stirs the vital wind, the fire blazes up through the inside of the rasanā and, circling clockwise, incinerates all the filth and scum inside the channel cakra of the navel. It gradually does the same up to the top of the head, and when the fire touches the *haṃ,* white drops fall from the *haṃ,* pass through the inside of the lalanā, and circling counterclockwise completely fill the channel cakra at the top of the head. The syllables become more lucid.

After gradually traveling in the same way down to the navel, when a drop strikes the *kṣa,* fire blazes from it and goes straight inside the central channel from the *aṃ* up to the *haṃ.* Drops fall from the *haṃ,* causing blazing and dripping just at the point between the eyebrows. Similarly, focus the mind on the blazing and dripping at each point just below all three cakras of the throat, the heart, and the navel, and hold the vital winds in union in the vase retention.

After that, alternately hold twelve vase retentions with the count of sixty-four and twelve uncounted. [430] For the counted ones, use precisely that visualization, and for the uncounted ones, rest without clinging.

(c) *The ten that have come from the key points of esoteric instruction*

Of the ten visualizations of the key points of esoteric instruction, three were within the four yogas of the drops before. Seven remain.

Pale red fire

Use the position of "binding with the sixfold cooking tripod." Imagining that all the inside of one's body is instantaneously filled with pale red fire, hold the vital winds in the vase retention.

The necessary alternation of twelve counted and twelve uncounted is specific to both the dense fierce fire and the pale red fire that were just explained. Generally, the amount to be practiced in a session is indefinite. Thus my master taught.

Blazing fire

Imagine a dark red *raṃ* about to blaze with fire at both soles of the feet. By the catalyst of flexing the toes of the feet, fire blazes from the *raṃ,* passes through the inside of the arteries of the calves and the thighs, and blends together with the fire of the lower abdomen. While meditating that red sparks sparkle from it and fill the entire body, hold the vital winds in union.

The battle of the drops

From the transformation of the fire of the lower abdomen, clearly imagine in the lower abdomen a white drop above and a red drop below, about the size of the thumb joint. By the catalyst of holding the vital winds in union, imagine sparks as before from those two battling drops.

The fire cakra

Visualize a thin column of fire straight from the crown of the head down to the genital area. Visualize a dark red cakra with eight spokes at the navel, and parallel pairs of the vowels such as *a* on top of the spokes in a counterclockwise circle. Imagine that by the catalyst of holding the vital winds in union, the cakra spins and red fire blazes flickering from the cakra at the navel.

Greatly blazing

From precisely that previous visualization, the body is filled with fire below the throat.

Intensely blazing

In addition to the previous one, imagine that the entire body is filled, with the form of the body barely undestroyed, like glowing iron.

Totally blazing

Beginning from one's residence, visualize that all apparent existence is blazing with roaring red fire.

At the end of all eighteen, sustain the view.

2) *The view*

When one practices in that way, four views will arise. By virtue of meditating on the path and by the catalyst of the vital winds and mind gathering in the syllables of the bhaga and so forth, the intense three poisons will arise without reference to external stimuli. This is naturally arisen affliction. [431]

When the vital winds and mind gather at the lower ends of the rasanā and lalanā, the razor-sharp vital wind becomes forceful, intense thoughts arise, and the mind will not stay at rest. This is naturally arisen thought.

When the vital winds and mind gather inside the horizontal channels in the vajra body and in the channels like empty cavities at the lower ends of the central channel and the rasanā, a sluggish awareness, dullness, and so forth will occur without reference to external food and behavior. This is naturally arisen blankness.

When the vital winds and mind gather in the *bhrūṃ* of the heart cakra and so forth, thoughts of subject and object cease. A sublime, empty yet lucid meditative concentration arises, and the body is experienced to be as buoyant as the down of a silk-cotton tree. This is lucid, buoyant, naturally arisen meditative concentration.

The first three are experiences arisen from meditating on the path, but are flawed because they include exaggeration and denigration. The last is the illustrative and symbolic primordial awareness.

3) *The culmination of attainment*

When that sort of view is practiced by means of the three conducts,[879] one is blessed by the inner vital winds and mind, which are the ten father and mother ḍākas and ḍākinīs. Due to that, all the spiritual heroes and ḍākinīs of the twenty-four sacred lands are brought under control. Whatever appears arises as a friend. The mind rests within. The five aggregates are subdued. The five root vital winds are arrested. The flames of the fierce fire blaze. Many drops bloom. The culmination of attainment, which is clearly distinct and completely perfect, is perfected. This is the path of the superior person.

4) *The clear-light practice when passing away*

This consists of three topics:

a) Training
b) Meditation
c) Putting it into action

a) *Training*

Visualize the red central channel of a suitable thickness, with an upside-down *haṃ* at the upper end and an upright *aṃ* at the lower end. When the vital wind of exertion is blown out,[880] imagine that it comes from the *aṃ* and dissolves into the *haṃ*. When the vital wind of life is inhaled, imagine that it comes from the *haṃ* and dissolves into the *aṃ*. When one does this again and again, at the point of death the vital winds of the rasanā and the lalanā will gather into the central channel, and, by the catalyst of that, the mother and child clear lights will meet.

b) *Meditation*

Recall again and again the master who presented the naturally arisen primordial awareness of the secret initiation, *caṇḍālī* as the path, and naturally arisen primordial awareness as the view. Clearly imagine the smoke, mirage, and so forth of the stages of dissolution to be the vowels such as *a* and the consonant-syllables such as *ka*, and recognize them as naturally arisen primordial awareness.

c) *Putting it into action*

This consists of two topics. The first is precisely those practices of transference with light and sound during the vase initiation. The second is "application to the continents and birthplaces," which means precisely that instruction on the birthplaces during the vase initiation. [432]

5) *The intermediate state*

The main practice is the same as that of the vase initiation, but one should think again and again that all the appearances of the intermediate state, such as the three terrifying places,[881] are lucid, clear, naturally arisen primordial awareness.

6) *Dream yoga*

The main practice is the same as that of the vase initiation. But remember and aspire again and again, thinking that *a nu ta ra* and so forth are also naturally arisen primordial awareness, and that one will definitely cause that naturally arisen primordial awareness to arise even in the dream.

Illusory body

For illusory body, the main practice is also like during the vase initiation, but meditate again and again, thinking: "These daytime appearances, which are like a dream, are also naturally arisen primordial awareness."

Finally, by means of these practices, the first gathering of the essential constituents is completed, the pulsations of the channel syllables are dissolved, and, through the transformation of the syllables, the citadel of the sambhogakāya enjoyment body is actualized.

> When all the stages of progression
> by means of the path of the secret initiation,
> from the seventh spiritual level
> up to *cloud of Dharma,*
> have been written according to the key points
> of the infallible instructions,
> the Lord of Yogins will show
> his happy smiling face.[882]

Just that is the essential extract of the teachings of my lord and master on the practice of the path of the secret initiation.

c. *The initiation of primordial awareness dependent on an embodiment of wisdom*

This is the third path meditated on in connection with the four initiations concerning the method continuum of the body.

1) *The path*

The *path of the mandalacakra, the path of the messenger,* or *the path of primordial awareness dependent on an embodiment of wisdom* are synonyms. This also consists of three topics:

a) The preparation
b) The main practice
c) The conclusion[883]

a) *The preparation*

This consists of two topics:

(1) The preliminaries for guidance
(2) The preliminaries for the session

(1) *The preliminaries for guidance*

Accumulation, purification, and so forth are as in the previous initiations.

(2) *The preliminaries for the session*

This also consists of the six topics of the three meditations and observing the three key points, as during the secret initiation.

b) *The main practice*

This consists of five topics:

(1) Purity of the female embodiment of awareness
(2) Equal body and speech
(3) Equal blessing
(4) Equal desire
(5) Key points from the esoteric instructions

(1) *Purity of the female embodiment of awareness*

Of the two, an actual mudrā consort or one of primordial awareness, this is in the context of the former.[884] This female embodiment of pure awareness should have an excellent body, be in the prime of life, have received initiation, and be a worthy recipient.

(2) *Equal body and speech*

Oneself clearly Hevajra and the female embodiment of pure awareness clearly Nairātmyā is equal body. Both reciting the root mantra is equal speech.

(3) *Equal blessing*

One blesses the secret space of the female embodiment of pure awareness as in the method for accomplishment. [433] The female embodiment of pure awareness also blesses one's secret organ as in the main practice of the method for accomplishment, imagining a rosary of *oṃs* around the middle of the vajra and the opening blocked by a *phaṭ*.

(4) *Equal desire*

One thinks that the four joys will be achieved dependent on this female embodiment of pure awareness and the female embodiment of pure awareness also thinks that great bliss will be achieved dependent on oneself.

(5) *Key points from the esoteric instructions*

This consists of five topics:

(a) Descent
(b) Retention
(c) Reversal
(d) Distribution
(e) Preservation

(a) *Descent*

By gazing at the physical beauty, listening to the sound of passionate talk, savoring the scent of the body, tasting the flavor of sucking the lips and so forth, and engaging in the sensations of the embrace and so forth, the female embodiment of pure awareness will become intoxicated with passion and great bliss will arise in oneself.

If one is afraid that the seminal drop will drip because of excessive bliss, in the accounts of former venerable lords it is said that protection with the extreme stare and the secret control are crucial. The first is to make fists with the hands and cross them on the chest, contract the stomach against the spine, tense the four forearm muscles and calf muscles, clench the toes of the feet, look upward, and say *"hal hal"* or *"hūṃ hūṃ."* Since this involves much activity but little bliss, it is called "the primordial awareness of joy." Secret control means to not immediately enter into union.

By bringing vajra and lotus together again, imagine that the enlightenment mind gradually descends from the top of the head and comes down to the tip of the jewel. Rest without clinging to the totally unestablished essence of that bliss.

(b) *Retention*

"Drying up the ocean around Mount Meru" means to contract the stomach against the spine. "Bringing the four continents under control" means to clench the fingers and toes. "Putting the retainer of taste in its own place" means to curl the tongue up against the soft palate. "Raising up the sublime organs" means to roll the eyes up and hold them there.[885]

(c) *Reversal*

"Inhaling with a forcefully vocal *hūṃ*" means to curl the tip of the tongue and intensely say *hūṃ*. "Firing the arrow and bow of the *hūṃ* and *phaṭ* of meditative concentration" means to imagine that when the seminal drop is pulled up by the *hūṃ* and pushed by the *phaṭ* it reverses upward.

(d) *Distribution*

"Tying on the belt of the vital wind" means to hold both hands in upturned fists and rotate them with intense force to the right and to the left, behind and in front of the waist. "Hurling the lasso" means to strongly rub both arms, or else use the technique of drawing a bow and arrow with great force. [434] "Rotating the wheel of a plow" means to rotate the stomach to the right and to the left with great force. "The behavior of a child" means to sit with crossed legs and to hold the arms as in the posture of binding with the sixfold cooking tripod, and to fall supine and face down, and to twist the neck to the right and to the left.

(e) *Preservation*

By acting in that way, one will prevent the loss of the seminal drop. But if it does drip because of excessive bliss or due to contamination or an evil spirit, one should be cleansed. The superior method is to request the four initiations, the middling is to make clay molds, and the inferior is to perform the cleansing ritual of Vidāraṇā.

This is an exceptional instruction directly from the master: place a frying pan upon a gentle fire. Pour both tree-gum resin and white mustard seeds inside, and when the fire melts them, add menstrual blood and the brains of a person who died violently. In addition, stir that with human ashes. When that has been made into a pill that will fit into the opening of the vajra, and it has been inserted, all types of dripping will be stopped.

The brief path

The preliminaries are to gain control of the downward-clearing vital wind, the main practice is descent and retention, and the conclusion is spreading and distribution.

For the first, draw up both knees under the elbows. While meditating on the sun and the moon in the right and left palms of the hands, cross them and cover the knees. Then inhale the vital wind [1] in front, alternating long, short, and very short inhalations, and hold the vital winds in union. Do the same [2] to the right, [3] in front, [4] to the left, and [5] in front, making five. Again, from the front, blow out long, short, and very short exhalations. Afterward, alternate with long, short, and very short inhalations, making three. Toss the head back repeatedly at the end.

For the second, omit the five points of gazing at the form and so forth. Otherwise, from the purity of the female embodiment of awareness, to the descent, [the practice] is as described before. But sit in the position with raised knees as just explained. While sucking on both right index and middle fingers, stare widely with the left eye. Also do the opposite of that with the other hand and eye. This will retain the seminal drop.

For the third, "With the *hing* of an elephant," means to set the balls of the feet on the ground, rest the buttocks on the heels, and pull the enlightenment mind to the navel with *hī hing,* and likewise with *hū hūṃ, hā hag,* and *hī hig,* up to the top of the head. The mudrā movements of the "liberated lion" are to block the ears, eyes, nostrils, upper lips, and lower lips with the thumbs, index fingers, middle fingers, ring fingers, and little fingers in order, rotate the head clockwise three times, rotate it counterclockwise three times, and again shake it in unpredictable ways for a long time. [435]

2) *The view*

When one practices in this way, the view of the four joys arises. The outer is in reference to sequence. From gazing at the form up through touching is joy. The union of *bola* and *kakkola*[886] is sublime joy. Rubbing is joy free from joy. Following that, the union of the four—the channels, drops, vital winds, and genital organs—is coemergent joy.

The inner is in reference to locations, both outer and inner. The outer is when some of the body, most, all, and all appearances—all four—become bliss, joy, and so forth in sequence. For the inner, the arrival at the four cakras of the heart, throat, navel, and genital area are joy and so forth in sequence.

Concerning what is rejected: the slight cessation of thoughts of the eight worldly concerns, the cessation of most, the cessation even of attachment to the female embodiment of pure awareness, and the cessation of attachment to the three joys, are also the four joys in sequence as before.

In reference to essence: the slight arising of bliss, the great arising, nonconceptual bliss, and the unity of bliss and emptiness are as before. The last alone is flawless.

3) *The culmination of attainment*

When that view is practiced by means of the three conducts[887] and made into the path, and the entire three realms arise in the perception[888] of that yogin as the play of the unity of bliss and emptiness, this is the culmination of attainment, which is blissful emptiness of lesser extent.

4) *The practice when passing away*

As the practice when passing away, Vajrasattva will approach when one dies. This consists of three topics:

a) Training
b) Familiarity
c) Putting it into action

a) *Training*

Recall again and again the master who presented the blissful yet empty secret, the path of the mandalacakra, and the view of the unity of bliss and emptiness.

b) *Familiarity*

Train by thinking: "When the stages of subtle dissolution during the triad of appearance, spreading, and attainment[889] occur, I absolutely must experience the view of blissful emptiness."

c) *Putting it into action*

Transference with sound and syllables is as during the vase initiation.

5) *The intermediate state*

Train that all the appearances of the stages of dissolution and the intermediate state are in essence the unity of bliss and emptiness, but in the form of drops like beads of pearl.

6) *Dream yoga*

Reach the decisive conclusion that all the appearances of dream and illusory body are the unity of bliss and emptiness, and meditate.

By means of these practices, the middle gathering of the essential constituents is completed, the pulsations of the essential constituent nectars dissolved, the eleventh and twelfth spiritual levels actualized, the nectars transformed, and the dharmakāya reality body actualized as the result. [436]

> With a feast of the taintless sublime bliss
> arisen from the stages of the path
> of primordial awareness dependent
> on an embodiment of wisdom,
> the sublime methods that actualize

those eleventh and twelfth spiritual levels,
unity is welcomed like a guest from afar.

The practices of the initiation of primordial awareness dependent on an embodiment of wisdom have been written according to the oral account.

d. *The fourth initiation*

1) *The path*

During the final gathering of the essential constituents, guidance is by means of the path of flawless, genuine, primordial awareness. This is the path of the fourth initiation, or the vajra waves. It is called *vajra* because it is emptiness, and *waves* because all appearances have been transformed into the path of sublime blissful emptiness through cultivation of that path and are no other than emptiness. For example, no matter how many rows of the ocean's waves or bubbles may emerge, they emerge out of that ocean, and when they dissolve, they dissolve into it. Thus the bubbles of water are expressions of the water and not different from it.

The practice of this consists of three topics:

a) The preliminaries
b) The main practice
c) The conclusion[890]

a) *The preliminaries*

The preliminaries for guidance are as described previously. The preliminaries for the session, which are the three meditations and observing the three key points, are done as before. After that it is best to complete the thirty-two yogic excercises three times: in sequential order, in reverse order, and at random. If these are not completed, do the training of the five branches.[891]

b) *The main practice*

(1) *The waves of the body, which draw up the lower vital wind*

Cover the tops of the knees with both hands. Contract the stomach against the spine. Strongly blow the vital wind out through the nose three times and strongly inhale three times. While holding the vital winds in union, slowly draw in the lower vital wind, and pull it up at the end. Alternately lift and lower the right and the left buttocks, and compress the vital winds. Also do the same once to the right and once to the left. For all three, when the union of the vital winds is released, first release the lower vital wind. When one is accustomed to that, even if the lower vital wind is released the upper vital wind will not be lost, and so this is called "the vase retention with the perforated bottom."

When one practices with no fixed number of sessions and no fixed amount in a session, bliss will arise in the body and realization in the mind. If the seminal drop drips due to that [bliss] as the catalyst, that can be alleviated by strongly twisting the upper body and gazing upward with the eyes.

(2) *The calm and intense waves of vocal inhalation*

For the first, sit in the vajra position with crossed legs, the fists crossed at the heart, and the body slightly hunched. [437] Inhale soundlessly between the teeth, with the tone of the vital wind in the form of "eee." Straighten the body as that is completed, toss the head back twice, fully pull up the lower vital wind, hold the vital winds in union, and rest in the state of the view. If so inclined, one may also do this to the right and to the left.

For the *intense,* the posture is as before, but imagine the tone of the vital wind as the sound of *hūṃ,* and inhale with sound. The other points are as before.

For both, with oneself clearly the deity, imagine that the vital wind as light rays of five colors comes from the tip of the vajra, passes up to the navel, and gradually dissolves into the top of the head.

(3) *The mental waves of meditative concentration*

From the purity of the female embodiment of awareness, to the descent to the tip of the vajra, [the practice] is the same as during the initiation of primordial awareness dependent on an embodiment of wisdom. But here those two enlightenment minds transform into light rays of various colors with the nature of the vital wind and circle clockwise through the path of the rasanā. Circling clockwise three times through the channel cakra of the navel, the potency of the white essential constituent makes it like daybreak, the potency of the red makes it like the dawning sun, and the potency of the vital wind makes it like an inflated intestine. This occurs in the same way from there up to the channel cakra at the top of the head.

Then the light rays go out through the top of the head, transforming the environment into the celestial mansion and bestowing initiation on the inhabiting sentient beings and transforming them into deities. These sentient beings are also made into the form of light rays and descend together with light rays of five colors. Circling downward counterclockwise through the lalanā, the channel cakras from the top of the head down to the genital area are made as before.

Again, imagine that when the light rays pass through the path of the central channel and go up to the top of the head, one's body is gradually transformed into rainbow light from the bottom. Rest without clinging.

If an action mudrā is actually present, in the context of the purity of the mindstreams of both—the mindstream of oneself and the mindstream of another—precisely that visualization is also done for the embodiment of pure awareness, but the radiation out from the top of her head is not necessary.

Drawing such light of five colors through the rasanā brings the rasanā under control, accomplishes control over the vital wind of exertion, and actualizes the signless gate to liberation. Drawing it through the lalanā does as before for the lalanā, the vital wind of life, and the wishless gate to liberation. Drawing it through the central channel does as before for the central channel, the pause of the vital wind, and the emptiness gate to liberation.

2) *The view*

The view that arises from those practices is the utter purity of all phenomena, the four ascending joys. [438]

Advantages that benefit the body

> Being in conformity with the cause
> vanquishes white hair.
> The ripened grants supreme strength.
> The personally created
> increases supreme strength.
> The immaculate brings immortality.[892]

Thus, when the white and red essential constituents arrive at the navel, it becomes smooth like the surface of a mirror, and cannot even be grasped by the nails. Young flesh grows without white hairs and wrinkles. When they arrive at the heart, one's strength increases so that not even the strength of Nārāyaṇa[893] or a supreme bull elephant can compete. When they stabilize at the throat, the tongue can cover the face. When they stabilize at the top of the head, one will be able to live for a thousand years.

Advantages that benefit the mind

Also, when the constituents stabilize at the previous four places in sequence, one's pure awareness will arise as blissful emptiness, all appearances will arise as blissful emptiness, all experienced tastes will arise as blissful emptiness, and all the phenomena of samsara and nirvana will arise only as united bliss and emptiness.

The good qualities of both body and mind

Again, in sequence, if seen by others one will not be disagreeable but be attractive, some paranormal abilities will arise, one will be able to enjoy all tastes, and one will be able to display various magical abilities.

3) *The culmination of attainment*

By practicing the three conducts[894] as before and maintaining the conduct according to the scriptures in regard to a lotus lady mudrā consort and so forth prophesied by the deity and the master, one will actualize the culmination of attainment, which is blissful emptiness of greater extent. Dependent on finally receiving the resultant initiations, one will actualize the thirteenth spiritual level of a vajra holder.

4) *The practice when passing away, which is transference from the path of mahāmudrā*

This consists of three topics:

a) Training
b) Familiarity
c) Application

a) *Training*

Recall again and again the master—the master who presented the view of the utter purity of all phenomena, the path, and the view of the four ascending joys.

b) *Familiarity*

Recall again and again the view of sublime blissful emptiness.

c) *Application*

This consists of both transference with syllables and transference with sound.

(1) *Transference with syllables*

Block the nine orifices as before. Envision the three channels and the four cakras with the syllables as in the dense fierce fire. Inside the rasanā and lalanā are the white upside-down consonant-syllables such as *ka,* minus *ha* and *kṣa,* and the red upright vowels such as *a.* Furthermore, for those such as *ka kha a ga gha ā,* clearly imagine each of them in a vertical column from the top like this: *ka kha* upside down, *a* upright, *ga gha* upside down, *ā* upright.[895] When the vital wind of exertion exits, imagine that the upper vital winds dissolve into the cakras at the top of the head and at the throat. When the vital wind of life enters, imagine that it dissolves into the cakras of the heart and the navel. [439]

(2) *Transference with sound*

The main practice is precisely that, but *hi ka* and *ka hi* are used instead of the vital winds of life and exertion.

At the moment when one's outer breathing stops, on the basis of a reminder by a companion, the previous experience acts as a catalyst and the result is obtained. This is transference from mahāmudrā.

5)–6) *The intermediate state and dream yoga*

For the triad of the intermediate state, dream yoga, and illusory body, during particular situations the olfactory experiences and so forth are transformed into the primordial awareness of united bliss and emptiness.

The final outlines, the spiritual paths, and how the results are gained are according to the treatise.

> The stages of the path
> of the fourth initiation,
> by which Vajradhara, the actualized
> and united four bodies of enlightenment,
> is to be achieved,
> have been written exactly according
> to the oral explanations
> of the excellent realized expert,
> Śrī Dharmapāla in saffron disguise.[896]

All the stages of the practice of the fourth initiation have been explained without omission.

> This Dharma of the ground, path, and result,
> the Teaching of the Lord of Yogins
> that elegantly explains all the practices
> of the complete doctrine of the Sage,
> is the short path for achieving buddhahood
> in one lifetime.
>
> Drokmi, the venerable Sakyapa
> Lord of Great Kindness,[897]
> and the lineage made this system
> as bright as the sun and moon
> in the Land of Snows,
> but nowadays the complete teaching
> is like a star in the daytime.

May it be our good fortune
that the practice of the essence,
known as the Explication for Disciples,
the infallible tradition of Khau Drakzong,
and not just the vague explication
of the husk of words
in the Explication for the Assembly,
spread in all directions and at all times!

The Sahor monk Ngawang Losang Gyatso has compiled these stages of practice according to the uncommon Explication for Disciples bestowed on Dakchen Dorjé Chang by Müchen Sempa Chenpo, together with the profound key points even more uncommon than the uncommon, transmitted by his father Jamyang Chöjé.[898] Those wanting more extensive elaborations of quotations and so forth can learn them from the *Clarification of the Hidden Meaning* and the compositions of lord Ludrup Gyatso.[899]

Maṅgalaṃ
Good fortune!

11. Heart of the Practice

A Synopsis of the Key Points of the Guidance Manuals of the Path with the Result

Mangthö Ludrup Gyatso (1523–96)

WITH DEVOTED BODY, speech, and mind, I prostrate at the lotus beneath the feet of my venerable lords and masters.

The heart of the practice, a synopsis of the key points of the esoteric instructions of the Teaching of the Path with the Result, is as follows.

Whatever oral instructions are practiced to achieve the sublime, the mind must turn toward the Dharma. For that purpose, meditation on the faults of samsara is crucial. Therefore, by reflecting on the general and specific sufferings of samsara, draw forth a certainty about the sufferings of samsara that is not mere words. If an uncontrived wish arises to abandon the three poisons, which are the afflictions that cause those sufferings, and to abandon evil actions motivated by them, the mind has turned to the Dharma. So please apply the sufferings of samsara directly to one's own situation, develop an attitude of renunciation from the bottom of one's heart, and create an effective certainty in the mindstream.

> In this samsara that tortures the mind
> with the burning suffering of suffering,
> suffering of change,
> and suffering of conditioned existence,
> no opportunity for happiness exists.
> You must reach the city of liberation—
> my dear disciple!

Then one must meditate on the difficulty of gaining the freedoms and endowments. When one has become mindful of the faults of samsara, the mind has turned toward the Dharma, and the mere wish to practice the Dharma has arisen, one may think that it is enough to practice this Dharma at one's leisure. But it is not. One must intensely begin, starting right now. One must draw forth a certainty that this human body with the freedoms and endowments is as difficult to find as a tiny star in the daytime, that once it is found it is quickly destroyed, and that it is as momentary as the dew on a blade of grass.

> The conditioned existence of this life,
> which is like a streak of lightning in the sky,
> can be destroyed now.
> This self-deception of patiently clinging
> to it as permanent is a great defect.
> Be energetic in the Dharma now—
> my dear disciple! [442]

Even if one has such enthusiastic diligence in the practice of Dharma, if the key points are not understood, that Dharma will not work as a path. So one must then have confidence in the causes and results of actions, primarily abandon nonvirtuous actions, and practice any virtue, even the slightest. Without even roughly understanding rejection and acceptance in regard to the causes and results of actions, with a lofty and high view, hypocritical conduct, and foolish behavior, one will be unable to withstand anything, like a ruined building with a rotten foundation.

> Ignoring virtuous and nonvirtuous
> actions and results,
> and then being fanatical about the view,
> having dignified behavior, and so forth,
> may seem so, so profound,
> but like a throne or bridge of grass,
> they will not work as a path—
> my dear disciple!

Then, to remove confusion about the path, the genuine relative enlightenment mind must arise in the mindstream. Without a pristine view in which all phenomena are as ephemeral as a dream or an illusion, one is in danger of taking the wrong path and falling into the abyss of samsara. If this precious enlightenment mind motivated by love and compassion has not arisen in the mindstream, one is in danger of taking a lesser path and falling to the spiritual levels of the śrāvakas and pratyekabuddhas. Therefore, the perfect enlightenment mind known to have emptiness and compassion as its essence—pervaded by the view, the wisdom that realizes emptiness, and the conduct, compassion—must have arisen in the mindstream.

> If one's mindstream has not been tamed
> by the genuine enlightenment mind,
> the sublime path of combined
> emptiness and compassion,
> one is in danger of falling into the abyss
> of confusion that is not the path.
> Think of altruism that benefits others—
> my dear disciple!

Then, for confusion to arise as primordial awareness, one must meditate on awakening the absolute enlightenment mind. If the exceptional wisdom that realizes the fundamental nature of phenomena has arisen in the mindstream, all appearances of the eight worldly concerns and so forth will dissolve like bubbles into water, and then again appear as friends on the path.

> If one has reached the decisive conclusion
> that all the phenomena of apparent existence
> may arise, but are untrue and confusing,
> like the character of an illusion,
> then, by the play of primordial awareness,
> the eight worldly concerns will appear
> as friends on the path—my dear disciple!

Then the mindstream is ripened by profound initiation. For conceptual elaborations to be eliminated by means of the view, one must meditate on the view of the indivisibility of samsara and nirvana. [443] In this regard, resting serenely, without mentally clinging to this naked clear light of one's mind free from the husk of the dualistic appearances of subject and object, is recognition of the natural state of lucidity. Confirming that this lucidity is also not a permanent, stable, eternal thing established forever, but empty of truth like an illusion that is dependent on causes and conditions, is recognition of the natural state of emptiness. Without altering the mind that is understood to be empty while lucid and lucid yet empty, a united lucidity and emptiness, this momentary pure awareness, rest the mind evenly as long as that state remains. This is resolution in unity. Reaching a decisive conclusion about the mind on the basis of these three aspects of coemergence is crucial.

> Clear light free from the filth
> of subject and object is the true nature,
> mind not established as true
> and affected by incidental stains.
> Recognize the natural state
> of united lucidity and emptiness,
> momentary pure awareness—
> my faithful, dear disciple!

Then, to enhance that view, one must be mindful of the three key points of practice. First, to destroy this solid and tenacious attachment to apparent outer objects such as external mountains and fences, apparent phenomena are established to be the mind by means of the eight examples of dream and so forth, and the pure awareness is fully concentrated and rests upon the lucidity of the mind.

This mind of dualistic appearance, the perceiver of apparent external objects, is also established to be untrue by means of the eight examples of an illusion and so forth. Relax and rest the mind in emptiness, empty of both subject and object.

By means of the eight examples confirming that it is dependently arisen and the eight examples confirming that it is inexpressible, this mind empty of both subject and object is also established to be empty of truth and to be inexpressible and transcendent. One rests evenly in unity, the view of the indivisibility of samsara and nirvana. This is the heart of the practice.

> These external objects
> are like last night's dream,
> and the apprehending mind
> the same as lightning now.

Rest vividly in this stainless mind,
as inexpressible as the thoughts of a mute—
my dear disciple!

Then, of the four paths in connection with the four initiations concerning the method continuum of the body, by means of the outer and inner creation stage, which is the path of the vase initiation, one must first sever the obsession with ordinary attachment to appearances. [444] To purify the stains of the five aggregates, the five afflictions, and so forth, which are the ground of purification, special deities are specifically praised, such as Vairocana for the purification of the aggregate of form. However, in this tradition one single purifying deity is able to purify all ordinary attachment to appearances, which are the ground of purification or what are to be purified. Since this is the heart of the path, clearly imagine oneself as Hevajra, father and mother, with the body mandala. Upholding the firm pride of the deity purifies all ordinary attachment. Practicing by means of vividly transforming whatever appearances arise into the form of the deity, one is able to purify all ordinary appearances.

One appears as Hevajra,
father and mother,
and the environment and its inhabitants
as the play of the deity and celestial mansion.
Purify the vulgar stains of ordinary
attachment to appearances
and uphold the pride of the creation stage—
my dear disciple!

When one meditates on the creation stage in this way, the view of the three essences will arise. If one rests lucidly in the state of the creation stage, it is known as "the meditative concentration of the apparent aspect." If the mind rests without anything appearing, like the empty sky, it is known as "the meditative concentration of the empty aspect." If any of the ten signs of clear light appear, such as smoke and mirage, it is known as "the meditative concentration of unity." At that point the view of the vase initiation, mahāmudrā, has arisen in the mindstream. The appearances of the eight worldly concerns have also thinned out. Even when the eight concerns do arise a bit, if they are apprehended with mindfulness of precisely that view of mahāmudrā, the eight concerns will be destroyed on the spot and a growing contentment will arise.

To examine whether that view is stable or flimsy, go at night to places where fear arises and in the day to spots where the eight concerns arise. When fears and the eight concerns do arise, relax and rest in the unity of the view of the indivisibility of samsara and nirvana and the mahāmudrā of the vase initiation. By training again and again in that way, at some point the view will improve and the bliss of refined body and mind will be obtained. The path will gradually be completed by means of the three gatherings of the essential constituents, and the first culmination of attainment—the culmination of attainment as the indivisibility of samsara and nirvana—will be reached without difficulty. Thus my master taught.

> When meditating on the creation stage,
> the ten signs of clear light appear,
> and all appearances are untrue,
> ephemeral, free, and shimmering
> like the smoke of clear light.
> Rest in mahāmudrā—my dear disciple!
>
> To further enhance this view,
> in isolated places or in busy spots
> of the eight concerns,
> practice the three conducts[900]
> without losing mindfulness
> of the mahāmudrā view—
> my dear disciple! [445]

Then, if the culmination of attainment has not been reached in this lifetime, in order to actualize the clear light of death, the three vase-initiation practices when passing away are crucial. Furthermore, after the definite signs of dying have appeared, this vase initiation practice when passing away is necessary during the arising of the coarse stages of the dissolution of the four elements. Thereafter, during the triad of the white radiance, the red radiance, and the black radiance, it is time for the higher initiation practices when passing away, so one must distinguish these situations.

In that way, when the definite signs of dying appear, receive the initiation from the master or the self-entry from oneself, and mend the sacred commitments. Give away all possessions to virtuous recipients, and totally eliminate all remaining activities of this life. Completely transform all the blurry appearances that arise at the point of death into the appearance of Hevajra, and rest the mind comfortably in that state. That is known as "the transformation of appearances as the practice when passing away."

Another is "the transference with a globe of light as the practice when passing away." This body has nine orifices. When practicing that transference, if this consciousness exits through the anus, one will go to the hells, if through the urethra, one will go to the animal realm, if through the navel, one will be reborn as a god of the desire realm, if through the mouth, as a hungry spirit, if through the two nostrils, as a yakṣa, if through the two ears, as a kinnara spirit, if through the two eyes, as a human being, if through the point between the eyebrows, as a god of the form realm, and if through the crown of the head, as a god of the formless realm. So those orifices must be blocked.

Clearly imagining oneself as Hevajra, visualize the central channel straight up the middle of the body, and a drop—a globe of light about the size of a dung pellet—inside the central channel directly at the heart cakra. Clearly imagine that nine globes of light separate from that and block the nine orifices. At the location of the navel is a mandala of the vital wind about the size of the thumb, with the vital wind moving upward. On top of it is a moon mandala, upon which is the essence of one's consciousness, in the form of a blue *hūṃ.* Above the top of the head is the master in the form of Hevajra, surrounded by an assembly of the lineage masters, spiritual heroes, and yoginīs.

The key physical point is to sit with the knees raised and both arms wrapped around the knees. [446] The key vocal point is to intensely pronounce *hūṃ* twenty-one times. The key mental point is to indivisibly blend together one's consciousness and the *hūṃ* at the navel. Concentrate single-pointedly on those three. By long pronunciations of *hūṃ* with the voice, the vital wind of the navel draws up the consciousness in the shape of the *hūṃ,* and at the twentieth pronunciation it arrives at the throat. These three should be done simultaneously: a very intense pronunciation of the twenty-first *hūṃ,* the ejection of the consciousness as the syllable *hūṃ* through the top of the head like a shooting star fired into the heart of the master, and the relaxation of the body and the two arms. Imagine that one's consciousness and the mind of the master as the chosen deity, nondual in the rainbow body of Hevajra, depart for pure Khecara.

When training in this now, train in solitude during the day and at the point of going to sleep at night. Draw the *hūṃ* up to the throat with twenty pronunciations. Drop it to the navel with *ka hi.*

When putting it into action, it is crucial to shoot the consciousness through the crown of the head with the twenty-first *hūṃ.*

> Mend one's essential
> sacred commitments and vows,
> give away to others all that you cherish,
> pray to the sublime master of refuge,
> and sever mental attachments—
> my dear disciple!
>
> By practicing mindfulness
> of the creation stage as the path
> in regard to the forms of clear light
> during the dissolution
> of the four elements of the body,
> transform mental appearance
> into the mandala of the deity Hevajra—
> my dear disciple!
>
> With the nine orifices of the body blocked by light,
> and the mind in the form of a *hūṃ* at the navel,
> fire it with the sound *hūṃ* through the inside
> of the central channel and out the aperture of Brahmā—
> my dear disciple!

If the practice when passing away is not successful, it is imperative to remember the practice of the intermediate state. In that intermediate period when the appearances of this life have receded and the next rebirth has not been taken, the seven circumstances of the four frightful sounds and the three terrifying abysses will appear.[901] At that point the five olfactory experiences like forms of light will clearly occur. At that time, these three remembrances should automatically arise: remembrance of one's master, remembrance of the secret name, and remembrance of the chosen deity Hevajra. Whatever olfactory appearances arise, clearly transform them into the deity Hevajra and relax in that state for as long as the mind remains without clinging!

When one practices in that way, it is certain that one will be led to a pure land by spiritual heroes and yoginīs with parasols, victory banners, streamers, and the sounds of music. [447]

> When suddenly carried friendless
> into the intermediate state,
> the practice of transforming
> the five olfactory lights into the chosen deity
> by means of the three remembrances
> will lead one to the land of Khecara—
> my dear disciple!

Thus, as the preliminaries for stable practice when passing away, and for those of the intermediate state, it is very important to master the instructions of illusory body and dream yoga from this present moment. In a secluded place during the day, inspire one's mindstream with disillusionment and renunciation, and develop expertise in meditative equipoise by resting the mind evenly in a meditative concentration in which all the phenomena of the triad of appearances, sound, and awareness arise, but are without self-nature, like an illusion.

At the point of going to sleep at night, clearly imagine a red lotus with four petals in one's throat. Clearly visualize an *oṃ* in the center and, in a clockwise circle from the front, the four syllables *a nu ta ra* on the four petals. Blending one's mind with the *oṃ* and joining that with sleep, or then blending one's mind with each of the four *a nu ta ra* in sequence and joining that with sleep, recognize the dream. The three remembrances will automatically arise, and various types of clear light will appear, such as a lucid clear light, a blissful clear light, and a nonconceptual clear light. Through developing expertise and so forth by observing pure and impure apparent objects [in dreams], and by multiplication and transformation, a great delight in spiritual practice at night will certainly arise.

> In the mansion of a secluded location
> in the mountain ranges,
> be never apart from disenchantment
> and renunciation.
> With phenomena as ephemeral
> as in an illusion,

train in the illusory body during the day—
my dear disciple!

With the practice of *a nu ta ra*
during the night,
the three Dharma remembrances
will easily appear.

Train the mind in multiplication
and transformation,
gain control, and cultivate meditative
concentration while asleep—
my dear disciple!

Thus the path of the vase initiation, the creation stage with associated practices, is presented as the primary practice of meditative equipoise. In addition to that, if the recitation, sacrificial-cake offering, and so forth are also practiced completely, nowadays one will certainly become a middling yogin.

Then, if one practices the path of the secret initiation, the yoga of the fierce fire of *caṇḍālī*, one should purify the body, purify the voice, and purify the mindstream with the guruyoga and so forth. The main practice is the seven yogas of the vital wind, and primarily the practice of the union of the vital winds in the vase retention, which is crucial. Following that the eighteen visualizations of the fierce fire and so forth are extremely profound, but nowadays this *caṇḍālī* yoga dependent on four cakras is practiced as the continual practice. [448]

Thus this practice of the three higher initiations can be understood from the presentation of the practical guidance of an excellent lord and master. The meaning cannot be presented through mere writing, so I have not written about it.

Therefore, the essence of the freedoms and endowments of fortunate disciples is made meaningful by purifying the mindstream with the Three Appearances, by removing the chaff of conceptual elaborations with the view of the indivisibility of samsara and nirvana, by how to meditate on the four different paths for the four initiations, by the four different views of mahāmudrā from meditation on those, by the four different introductions to those and ways to sustain them, by how to practice the four conducts in order to enhance those, by how the four different culminations of attainment are reached through that type of conduct, by the four different practices when passing away if those have not been reached, by the four different practices in the intermediate state if those have not been successful, and by the instructions of illusory body and dream yoga as the evaluation of those paths. This is the Dharma of our amazing and wonderful practice of the Path with the Result in the tradition of the Explication for Disciples.

> Thus this elixir of the heart
> of the Path with the Result,
> the system of the profound lucid path
> of the Explication for Disciples,
> a heart that is not within everyone's range,
> was received by the kindness of the master.

In that way, to benefit knowledgeable people on the occasion of spreading some of the nectar of the Teaching of the Explication for Disciples at the great Dharma institute of Nyenyö Chagöshong in an iron-female-snake year [1581], and especially because of repeated urging from afar by the fully ordained monk, the vajra holder Samten Lhundrup, this practice of the key points of the Path with the Result is sent by Nāgārjuna[902] from the Pavilion of Long Life at glorious Nyenyö. May good fortune increase!

> If this skylike mind becomes accustomed
> to skylike phenomena as skylike,
> it will also reach skylike enlightenment.
>
> If this illusion-like mind becomes accustomed
> to illusion-like phenomena as illusion-like,
> it will also reach illusion-like enlightenment.

Good fortune!

APPENDIXES

1. Table of Tibetan Transliteration

Ah U	'A 'u
Ah U Ma	'A 'u ma
Ajo Gyalé	A jo Rgyal le
Anyen Shel	A gnyen shel
Apho Phaktön	A pho Phag ston
Apo Gyalpo	A po Rgyal po
Apo Shuché	A po Zhu byas
Aseng	A seng
Asha	'A zhwa
Baldrok	'Bal grog
Balphuk	Sbal phug
Balti Lotsāwa	Sbal ti Lo tsā ba
Bari Lotsāwa	Ba ri Lo tsā ba
Barthang	Bar thang
Bökharwa	Bod mkhar ba
Bönpo	Bon po
Bumrampa Sherap Gyaltsen	'Bum rams pa Shes rab rgyal mtshan
Butön Rinpoché	Bu ston Rin po che
Butön Wangchuk Dar	Bu ston Dbang phyug dar
Chagen	Cha gan

Chagen Wangchuk Gyaltsen	Cha gan Dbang phyug rgyal mtshan
Chakthang	Lcags thang
Chakyi Jinpachen	Lcags kyi byin pa can
Chamchik	Lcam gcig
Chamdo	Chab mdo
Ché	Lce
Chegompa	Lce sgom pa
Chekha	’Chad kha
Chemo Namkha Yeshé	Mched mo Nam mkha’ ye shes
Chetsün Sherap Sengé	Lce btsun Shes rab seng ge
Chidrum	Phyi ’brum
Chögyal Phakpa	Chos rgyal ’Phags pa
Chogyé Trichen Rinpoché	Bco brgyad khri chen Rin po che
Chok	Cog
Chökhor Shongma	Chos ’khor shongs ma
Chökyi Gyalpo	Chos kyi rgyal po
Chölingpa Losang Karmo	Chos gling pa Blo bzang dkar mo
Chölung	Chos lung
Chom Ral	Bcom ral
Chushül	Chu shul
Chuwori	Chu bo ri
Da	Zla
Dagyal	Zla rgyal
Dakchen Dorjé Chang	Bdag chen Rdo rje ’chang
Dakchen Jamyang Chenpo	Bdag chen ’Jam dbyangs chen po
Dakchen Künga Wangchuk	Bdag chen Kun dga’ dbang phyug

Dakchen Lodrö Gyaltsen	Bdag chen Blo gros rgyal mtshan
Dakchen Ngakgi Wangpo	Bdag chen Ngag gi dbang po
Dakchen Rinpoché	Bdag chen Rin po che
Dakpo Lhajé	Dwags po Lha rje
Dampa	Dam pa
Dampa Gyagar	Dam pa rgya gar
Dar	'Dar
Darma Udum	Dar ma 'u dum
Dawa Gyaltsen	Zla ba rgyal mtshan
Dawai Özer	Zla ba'i 'od zer
Dentik Shel	Dan tik shel
Depa Shākya Gyal	Des pa Shākya rgyal
Depa Tönchung	Des pa Ston chung
Dergé	Sde dge
Deshek Phakmodrupa	Bde gshegs Phag mo gru pa
Ding	Ding
Dingmawa	Sding ma ba
Dingri	Ding ri
Do	Mdo
Dojok	Rdo 'jog
Dokham	Mdo khams
Dokmé	Mdog smad
Dokorwa	Do skor ba
Dokuk	Mdog dbugs
Domé	Mdo smad
Dong	Ldong

Dong Nyenchen	Gdong brnyan can
Dönri Drakchen	Don ri Grags chen
Doringpa	Rdo ring pa
Dorjé	Rdo rje
Dorjé Chang	Rdo rje 'chang
Dorjé Gönpo	Rdo rje mgon po
Dorjé Gyaltsen	Rdo rje rgyal mtshan
Dorjé Lekpa	Rdo rje legs pa
Dorjé Phurpa	Rdo rje phur pa
Drachung	Bra chung
Dradül Jepa	Dgra 'dul rje pa
Drakpa Gyaltsen	Grags pa rgyal mtsan
Drakphukpa	Brag phug pa
Drakphukpa Könchok Gyaltsen	Brag phug pa Dkon mchog rgyal mtshan
Drakphukpa Köngyal	Brag phug pa Dkon rgyal
Draktsé	Brag rtse
Draktsé Sonak	Brag rtse So nag
Dralhabar	Dgra lha 'bar
Drangti Darma Nyingpo	Brang ti Dar ma snying po
Drangti Gyalnyen Kharphuk	Brang ti Rgyal gnyen mkhar phug
Drangyul Olkawa	Drang yul 'Ol ka ba
Draphu	Gra phu
Drathangpa Sherap Dawa	Gra thang pa Shes rab zla ba
Dratön	Spra ston
Dreyul	'Bras yul

Drilchen	Dril chen
Drilchen Tangawa	Dril chen Rta rnga ba
Dringtsam	’Bring mtshams
Drokmi Lotsāwa	’Brog mi Lo tsā ba
Drokmi Shākya Yeshé	’Brog mi Shākya ye shes
Drom	’Brom
Drom Tsandawarti	’Brom Tsaṇḍa warti
Drompa Gyang	Grom pa Rgyang
Drompa Lhatsé	Grom pa Lha rtse
Dromphuk	Grom phug
Drongchung	Grong chung
Drönla Cham	’Gron la lcam
Dru	’Bru
Dzeṃgi	Dzeṃ gi
Dzeden Öchak	Mdzes ldan ’od chags
Dzimpa Gyaltsen Pal	’Dzim pa Rgyal mtshan dpal
Dzongpa	Rdzong pa
Ga	Sga
Gangtröpa	Gangs khrod pa
Gara	Ga ra
Gatheng	Sga theng
Gatön Dorjé Drak	Sga ston Rdo rje grags
Gelong Künlo	Dge slong Kun blo
Gendenpa	Dge ldan pa
Gendun Gyatso	Dge ’dun rgya mtsho
Genmodrok	Rgan mo grog

Gephu	Dge phu
Geshé	Dge bshes
Gewa Rapsal	Dge ba rab gsal
Gö Lotsāwa	'Gos Lo tsā ba
Gompa Kyibar	Sgom pa Skyi 'bar
Gompa Ötrak	Sgom pa 'Od grags
Gonga	Sgo lnga
Gongkar	Gong dkar
Gongpa Rapsal	Dgongs pa rab gsal
Gönpawa	Dgon pa ba
Gorum	Sgo rum
Gorumpa	Sgo rum pa
Gugé	Gu ge
Gungthang	Gung thang
Guru Rinchen Chödar	Gu ru rin chen chos dar
Gya Shākya Shönu	Rgya Shākya gzhon nu
Gyagom	Rgya sgom
Gyalchungpa	Rgyal chung pa
Gyalmo Men	Rgyal mo sman
Gyaltsa Talphukpa	Rgyal tsha tal phug pa
Gyaltsap Dampa	Rgyal tshab dam pa
Gyaltsen	Rgyal mtshan
Gyalwa Yangönpa	Rgyal ba Yang dgon pa
Gyalwai Sherap	Rgyal ba'i shes rab
Gyatrul Rinpoché	Rgya sprul Rin po che
Gyerbu	Sgyer bu

Gyerda	Gyer mda'
Gyergom Sewo	Gyer sgom Se bo
Gyerphu	Gyer phu
Gyerphu Dzilung	Gyer phu Rdzi lung
Gyichu	Sgyi chu
Gyichuwa	Sgyi chu ba
Gyijang Ukarwa	Gyi ljang Dbu dkar ba
Gyijo Lotsāwa	Gyi jo Lo tsā ba
Gyönjo Yeshé Pal	Gyon jo Ye shes dpal
Jakshong	'Jag gshongs
Jamgön Ameshap	'Jam mgon A mes zhabs
Jamgön Ngawang Künga Lodrö	'Jam mgon Ngag dbang kun dga' blo gros
Jamgön Ngawang Lekdrup	'Jam mgon Ngag dbang legs grub
Jamgön Sönam Chokden	'Jam mgon Bsod nams mchog ldan
Jamlingpa	Byams gling pa
Jampa Künga Tenpai Gyaltsen	Byams pa kun dga' bstan pa'i rgyal mtshan
Jampa Künga Tenzin	Byams pa kun dga' bstan 'dzin
Jampa Namkha Chimé	Byams pa nam mkha' 'chi med
Jampaiyang Ngawang Lekdrup	'Jam pa'i dbyangs ngag dbang legs grub
Jampaiyang Ngawang Sönam Gyaltsen	'Jam pa'i dbangs ngag dbang bsod nams rgyal mtshan
Jampal Sangpo	'Jam dpal bzang po
Jamyang Chenpo	'Jam dbyangs chen po
Jamyang Dönyö Gyaltsen	'Jam dbyangs don yod rgyal mtshan

Jamyang Khyentsé Wangchuk	'Jam dbyangs mkhyen brtse'i dbang phyug
Jamyang Könchok Sangpo	'Jam dbyangs dkon mchog bzang po
Jamyang Loter Wangpo	'Jam dbyangs blo gter dbang po
Jamyang Rinchen Dorjé	'Jam dbyangs rin chen rdo rje
Jamyang Sangpo	'Jam dbyangs bzang po
Jamyang Sherap Gyatso	'Jam dbyangs shes rab rgya mtsho
Jamyang Sönam Paljor	'Jam dbyangs bsod nams dpal 'byor
Jamyang Tsangnak Phukpa	'Jam dbyangs Gtsang nag phug pa
Jang	Byang
Jangchup Ö	Byang chub 'od
Jangchup Pal	Byang chub dpal
Jangpa Charpa	Byang pa char pa
Jatön Sengé Sangpo	Bya ston Seng ge bzang po
Jaur Drak	Bya 'ur grags
Jegyurwa Sönam Sengé	Byas 'gyur ba Bsod nams seng ge
Jenga Könchok Gyatso	Spyan snga Dkon mchog rgya mtsho
Jetsé	Rje btsad
Jetsün Drakpa Gyaltsen	Rje btsun Grags pa rgyal mtshan
Jeu	Rje'u
Jikmé Palden	'Jigs med dpal ldan
Jingyön	Mjing yon
Jinpa Tashi	Sbyin pa bkra shis
Jiwa Hapsha	Byi ba hab sha
Jonang	Jo nang
Jonangpa	Jo nang pa

José Öchok	Jo sras 'Od mchog
Jowo	Jo bo
Jowo Kadampa	Jo bo Bka' gdams pa
Jowo Lhachik	Jo bo Lha gcig
Jungné Dorjé	'Byung gnas rdo rje
Ka	Ska
Kadam	Bka' gdams
Kadampa	Bka' gdams pa
Kangyur	Bka' 'gyur
Kangyurwa	Bka' 'gyur ba
Karpo Drakpa Rinchen Sengé	Dkar po brag pa Rin chen seng ge
Kartön Chakyi Dorjé	Dkar ston Lcags kyi rdo rje
Kechakpa Khyungpo Hūṃkara	Sked chag pa Khyung po hūṃ ka ra
Kham	Khams
Khamchen Genlhepa	Khams chen Rgan lhas pa
Khangtön	Khang ston
Kharak Thöphu	Kha rag Thod phu
Kharchung	Mkhar chung
Kharchungwa	Mkhar chung ba
Khargolung	Mkhar sgo lung
Khau Drakzongpa	Kha'u brag rdzong pa
Khaupa	Kha'u pa
Khedrup	Mkhas grub
Khenchen	Mkhan chen
Khenpo Appey	Mkhan po A pad
Khön	'Khon

Khoré	Kho re
Khulung	Khu lung
Khumbuwa	Khum bu ba
Khün	'Khun
Khuna Sherap Gyaltsen	Khu na Shes rab rgyal mtshan
Khyapdak Kangyurwa	Khyab bdag Bka' 'gyur ba
Khyapdak Nesarwa	Khyab bdag Gnas gsar ba
Khyapdak Shalupa	Khyab bdag Zhwa lu pa
Khyenrap Chöjé	Mkhyen rab chos rje
Khyenrap Jampa	Mkhyen rab byams pa
Khyenrap Rinpoché	Mkhyen rab Rin po che
Khyentsé Wangchuk	Mkhyen brtse'i dbang phyug
Khyin Lotsāwa	'Khyin Lo tsā ba
Khyung Rinchen Drak	Khyung Rin chen grags
Khyungkar	Khyung dkar
Khyungpo Kechakpa	Khyung po Sked chag pa
Kochak	Ko chag
Kodrakpa	Ko brag pa
Könchok Gyalpo	Dkon mchog rgyal po
Könchok Gyaltsen	Dkon mchog rgyal mtshan
Könchok Palwa	Dkon mchog dpal ba
Könchok Sangpo	Dkon mchog bzang po
Köné	Dkon ne
Künga Bar	Kun dga' 'bar
Künga Drolchok	Kun dga' grol mchog
Künga Gyaltsen	Kun dga' rgyal mtshan

Künga Jamyang	Kun dga' 'jam dbyangs
Künga Lhundrup	Kun dga' lhun grub
Künga Lodrö	Kun dga' blo gros
Künga Nyingpo	Kun dga' snying po
Künga Palden	Kun dga' dpal ldan
Künga Sangpo	Kun dga' bzang po
Künlo	Kun blo
Künpang Chenpo	Kun spangs chen po
Künpang Doringpa	Kun spangs Rdo ring pa
Künpang Drakgyal	Kun spangs Grags rgyal
Künpangpa	Kun spangs pa
Künsang Chökyi Nyima Loden Sherap Künga Gyaltsen Palsangpo	Kun bzang chos kyi nyi ma blo ldan shes rab kun dga' rgyal mtshan dpal bzang po
Kuwa	Ku ba
Kya	Skya
Kyawo Khadang	Skya bo kha gdangs
Kyetsal	Skyed tshal
Kyi Dé	Skyid lde
Kyidé Nyima Gön	Skyid lde Nyi ma mgon
Kyirong	Skyid grong
Kyoda Lama	Skyo mda Bla ma
Kyura Akyap	Kyu ra A skyabs
Lachen Künga Gyaltsen	Bla chen Kun dga' rgyal mtshan
Lachen Küngyalwa	Bla chen Kun rgyal ba
Lama Dampa	Bla ma dam pa
Lamdré	Lam 'bras

Langdarma	Glang dar ma
Langri Thang	Glang ri thang
Langtso Marpo	Glang mtsho dmar po
Lapsum Gyaltsen	Bslab gsum rgyal mtshan
Lapsumpa	Bslab gsum pa
Laru Serkhangpa	La ru Gser khang pa
Laruwa Sönam Sengé	La ra ba Bsod nams seng ge
Latö	La stod
Latö Köngyal	La stod Dkon rgyal
Latö Wangyal	La stod Dbang rgyal
Lawa	Gla ba
Lekpai Sherap	Legs pa'i shes rab
Leng Shākya Tsöndrü	Leng Shākya brtson 'grus
Lha Lama Yeshé Ö	Lha bla ma Ye shes 'od
Lha Thothori Nyanshal	Lha Tho tho ri snyan shal
Lhachik Dzeden Öchak	Lha gcig Mdzes ldan 'od chags
Lhalung Palgyi Dorjé	Lha lung Dpal gyi rdo rje
Lhasa	Lha sa
Lhatsé	Lha rtse
Lhatsün Kali	Lha btsun Ka li
Lhodrak	Lho brag
Lhopa	Lho pa
Lhopa Rinchen Pal	Lho pa Rin chen dpal
Lijin	Li byin
Lingbar	Gling bar
Lingtsang	Gling tshang

Lithesé	Li the se
Lobshé	Slob bshad
Lochen	Lo chen
Lochen Jangtsé	Lo chen Byang rtse
Lodrö Chöphak	Blo gros chos 'phags
Lodrö Gyaltsen Palsangpo	Blo gros rgyal mtshan dpal bzang po
Lodrö Karpo	Blo gros dkar po
Lok	Klog
Lokya Chödrak	Klog skya Chos grags
Losang Karmo	Blo bzang dkar mo
Losel Gyatso	Blo gsal rgya mtsho
Loter Wangpo	Blo gter dbang po
Lotön Dorjé Wangchuk	Lo ston Rdo rje dbang phyug
Lotsāwa Kyabchok	Lo tsā ba Skyabs mchog
Ludrup Gyatso	Klu sgrub rgya mtsho
Ma Lotsāwa Chöbar	Rma Lo tsā ba Chos 'bar
Machik Dzeden Öchak	Ma gcig Mdzes ldan 'od chags
Machik Gyalmo	Ma gcig Rgyal mo
Machik Khargolungma	Ma gcig Mkhar sgo lung ma
Machik Nyitri	Ma gcig Nyi khri
Machik Rima	Ma gcig Ri ma
Machik Shama	Ma gcig Zhwa ma
Machik Shangmo	Ma gcig Zhang mo
Machik Tsetsa	Ma gcig Btsad tsha
Maja Tsokchen	Ma bya tshogs can
Maksorma	Dmag zor ma

Mal Lotsāwa	Mal Lo tsā ba
Mamo Bötong	Ma mo rbod gtong
Mang	Mang
Mangchung	Mang chung
Mangchungma	Mang chung ma
Mangkhar	Mang mkhar
Mangkhar Chudé	Mang mkhar chu sde
Mangkhar Drilchen	Mang mkhar dril chen
Mangkhar Trangok	Mang mkhar 'Phrang 'og
Mangpö Jé	Mang po rje
Mangsang	Mang sang
Mangthö Ludrup Gyatso	Mang thos klu sgrub rgya mtsho
Mangyul	Mang yul
Mar	Dmar
Mar Chökyi Gyalpo	Dmar Chos kyi rgyal po
Mara Serpo	Sma ra ser po
Marpa	Mar pa
Martön Chökyi Gyalpo	Dmar ston Chos kyi rgyal po
Menkhangpa	Sman khang pa
Menyag	Me nyag
Metön	Mes ston
Mön Vajra Rāja	Mon Badzra rā dza
Möndrok	Mon grog
Mönmo Gökyi	Mon mo Sgos skyid
Mor	Rmor
Morchen Dorjé Chang	Rmor chen Rdo rje 'chang

Mü	Mus
Müchen Könchok Gyaltsen	Mus chen Dkon mchog rgyal mtshan
Müchen Sempa Chenpo	Mus chen Sems dpa' chen po
Mugulung	Mu gu lung
Mukhyüchen	Mu khyud can
Müsepa	Mus srad pa
Nālendra	Nā lendra
Nakgom Sönam Gyaltsen	Nag sgom Bsod nams rgyal mtshan
Nakgompa Sögyal	Nag sgom pa Bsod rgyal
Nakgyal	Nags rgyal
Nakpo Rozin	Nag po ro 'dzin
Nakrong Lotsāwa	Nags rong Lo tsā ba
Nam Khaupa	Nam kha'u pa
Namgyal Tsé	Rnam rgyal rtse
Namkha Chimé	Nam mkha' 'chi med
Namkha Döndrup Wangpo	Nam mkha' don grub dbang po
Namkha Dorjé	Nam mkha' rdo rje
Namkha Drimé	Nam mkha' dri med
Namkha Özer	Nam mkha' 'od zer
Namkha Yeshé	Nam mkha' ye shes
Namthang Karpo	Gnam thang dkar po
Namthel Karpo	Gnam thel dkar po
Namtso Chukmo	Gnam mtsho phyug mo
Natsok Draden	Sna tshogs sgra ldan
Nawajewa Nyishupa	Rna ba bye ba nyi shu pa
Nenying	Gnas rnying

Nesar Dorjé Chang	Gnas gsar Rdo rje 'chang
Nesarwa	Gnas gsar ba
Ngakchang Sönam Chöphel	Sngags 'chang Bsod nams chos 'phel
Ngamring	Ngam ring
Ngari	Mnga' ris
Ngaripa Salwai Nyingpo	Mnga' ris pa Gsal ba'i snying po
Ngawang Chödrak	Ngag dbang chos grags
Ngawang Chökyong Sangpo	Ngag dbang chos skyong bzang po
Ngawang Khyentsé	Ngag dbang mkhyen brtse
Ngawang Lhundrup	Ngag dbang lhun grub
Ngawang Losang Gyatso	Ngag dbang blo bzang rgya mtsho
Ngawang Rapten	Ngag dbang rab brtan
Ngönpar Shepa Thop	Mngon par shes pa thob
Ngönshé Thopai Gyalpo	Mngon shes thob pa'i rgyal po
Ngor	Ngor
Ngor Ewaṃ Chöden	Ngor E waṃ chos ldan
Ngorchen Dorjé Chang	Ngor chen Rdo rje 'chang
Ngorchen Künga Sangpo	Ngor chen Kun dga' bzang po
Ngülgyi Khorlochen	Dngul gyi 'khor lo can
Ngurmik	Ngur smrig
Nubpa	Gnubs
Nup	Nub
Nya Ön	Nya dbon
Nyak	Gnyags
Nyak Shirawa	Gnyags Gzhi ra ba
Nyak Wangchuk Gyaltsen	Gnyags Dbang phyug rgyal mtshan

Nyan Lotsāwa	Gnyan Lo tsā ba
Nyang Dorjé Gyaltsen	Nyang Rdo rje rgyal mtshan
Nyatri Tsenpo	Gnya' khri btsan po
Nyemo	Snye mo
Nyen Phuljungwa	Gnyan Phul byung ba
Nyen Thanglha	Gnyan Thang lha
Nyenchenpa	Nyan chen pa
Nyenyö Chagöshong	Mnyan yod Bya rgod gshong
Nyilung	Nyi lung
Nyima Charwa	Nyi ma 'char ba
Nyima Ling	Nyi ma gling
Nyingma	Rnying ma
Nyö Jungpo	Gnyos 'Byung po
Nyö Lotsāwa	Gnyos Lo tsā ba
Ö Dé	'Od lde
Öchok	'Od mchog
Ogyal Thang	'O brgyal thang
Ön Rinpoché	Dbon Rin po che
Ongjo	Ong jo
Ösung	'Od srung
Özer Dorjé	'Od zer rdo rje
Özer Gyaltsen	'Od zer rgyal mtshan
Paṇchen Mati	Paṇ chen Ma ti
Paṇchen Shākchok	Paṇ chen Shāk mchog
Padro	Spa gro
Pal	Dpal

Pal Dé	Dpal lde
Palden Lodrö Gyaltsen	Dpal ldan blo gros rgyal mtshan
Palden Sengé	Dpal ldan seng ge
Palden Tsultrim	Dpal ldan tshul khrims
Palgyi Dorjé	Dpal gyi rdo rje
Palpuk	Dpal spug
Palsangpo	Dpal bzang po
Patsap Lotsāwa	Pa tshab Lo tsā ba
Phadruk	Pha drug
Phakmodrupa	Phag mo gru pa
Phakpa Chönang	'Phags pa chos snang
Phakpa Rinpoché	'Phags pa Rin po che
Phakrika	Phag ri kha
Phamthingpa	Pham thing pa
Phenkhang	Phan khang
Phenyul	'Phan yul
Phoma Takri	Pho ma stag ri
Phulchung	Phul chung
Potala	Po ta la
Purang Lotsāwa	Pu hrangs Lo tsā ba
Ra Nyipa Gyalwa Rinchen	Rwa gnyis pa Rgyal ba rin chen
Ralpachen	Ral pa can
Ram Dingmawa	Ram Sding ma ba
Rasa Trulnang	Ra sa 'Phrul snang
Rawa Mé	Ra ba smad
Re	Dbrad

Ré Könchok	Dbrad Dkon mchog
Remo Köné	Dbrad mo Dkon ne
Rikzin Pema Trinlé	Rig 'dzin Padma 'phrin las
Rinchen Dorjé	Rin chen rdo rje
Rinchen Gyaltsen	Rin chen rgyal mtshan
Rinchen Losang Khyenrap	Rin chen blo bzang mkhyen rab
Rinchen Özer	Rin chen 'od zer
Rinchen Sangpo	Rin chen bzang po
Risur	Ri zur
Ritröpa Lodrö Tenpa	Ri khrod pa Blo gros brtan pa
Rok	Rog
Rokpo	Rog po
Rong	Rong
Rongmu	Rong rmu
Rutok	Ru thogs
Sachen Künga Nyingpo	Sa chen Kun dga' snying po
Sahor	Za hor
Sakya	Sa skya
Sakya Paṇḍita	Sa skya Paṇḍi ta
Sakya Trizin	Sa skya Khri 'dzin
Salo Künga Sönam	Sa lo Kun dga' bsod nams
Samling	Bsam gling
Sampa Wadong	Sram pa Wa gdong
Samten Lhundrup	Bsam gtan lhun grub
Samyé	Bsam yas
Sang	Bzang

Sangri	Bzang ri
Sangri Phukpa	Bzang ri phug pa
Sangtsa	Zangs tsha
Sangtsa Sönam Gyaltsen	Zangs tsha Bsod nams rgyal mtshan
Sangyé Palsang	Sangs rgyas dpal bzang
Sangyü	Bzang rgyud
Sarupa	Sa ru pa
Sawang Lachen	Sa dbang Bla chen
Sé	Se
Sé Kharchungwa	Se Mkhar chung ba
Sé Mönlam Sherap	Se Smon lam shes rab
Sé Yeshé Tsöndrü	Se Ye shes brtson 'grus
Semodo	Se mo do
Sempa Chenpo	Sems dpa' chen po
Senalek	Sad na legs
Sengé Gyaltsen	Seng ge rgyal mtshan
Sengé Nampar Tsenpa	Seng ge rnam par rtsen pa
Serdokchen	Gser mdog can
Sergyi Khorlochen	Gser gyi 'khor lo can
Serkya	Ser skya
Setön Dorjung	Se ston Rdor 'byung
Setön Künrik	Se ston Kun rig
Setön Ripa	Se ston Ri pa
Shākya Yeshé	Shākya ye shes
Shakra Lhatsé	Bzhag ra Lha rtse
Shalu	Zhwa lu

Shalu Gyengong	Zhwa lu Rgyan gong
Shalu Khenchen	Zhwa lu mkhan chen
Shalupa Könchok Tsultrim	Zhwa lu pa Dkon mchog tshul khrims
Shama	Zhwa ma
Shama Könchok	Zhwa ma Dkon mchog
Shang	Zhang
Shang Gönpawa	Zhang Dgon pa ba
Shang Könchok Palwa	Zhang Dkon mchog dpal ba
Shang Kyabpa	Zhang Skyabs pa
Shangshung	Zhang zhung
Shangshung Guruwa	Zhang zhung Gu ru ba
Shangtön	Zhang ston
Shangtön Chöbar	Zhang ston Chos 'bar
Shangtön Gönpawa	Zhang ston Dgon pa ba
Shangtön Sijibar	Zhang ston Gzi brjid 'bar
Shap	Shab
Shapmo Chamchik	Shab mo Lcam gcig
Sharchen Yeshé Gyaltsen	Shar chen Ye shes rgyal mtshan
Sharpa Dorjé Özer	Shar pa Rdo rje 'od zer
Sheldrak	Shel brag
Shen	Gshen
Shengom Rokpo	Gshen sgom Rog po
Shentön	Gshen ston
Sherap Bum	Shes rab 'bum
Sherap Dorjé	Shes rab rdo rje
Sherap Özer	Shes rab 'od zer

Shönu Lodrö	Gzhon nu blo gros
Shönu Sherap	Gzhon nu shes rab
Shu	Zhu
Shuché Ngödrup	Zhu byas Dngos grub
Shun Drakrum	Shun drag rum
Shutön Rokpo	Zhu ston Rog po
Sijibarwa	Gzi brjid 'bar
Siropa	Si ro pa
Sönam Chokden	Bsod nams mchog ldan
Sönam Chöphel	Bsod nams chos 'phel
Sönam Dorjé	Bsod nams rdo rje
Sönam Gyaltsen	Bsod nams rgyal mtshan
Sönam Tsemo	Bsod rnams rtse mo
Songé	Song nge
Songtsen Gampo	Srong btsan sgam po
Sothang	Zo thang
Sur Shākjung	Zur Shāk 'byung
Surchen	Zur chen
Surchung	Zur chung
Surpoché	Zur po che
Tai Situ Jangyal	Ta'i si tu Byang rgyal
Tak	Stag
Tak Lotsāwa	Stag Lo tsā ba
Tak Yeshé Shönu	Stag Ye shes gzhon nu
Takdé Sengé Lung	Stag sde Seng ge lung
Takpoché	Rtag po che

Taktsé	Stag rtse
Tanak	Rta nag
Tanak Thupten	Rta nag thub bstan
Tashi Chödé	Bkra shis chos sde
Tashi Lhunpo	Bkra shis lhun po
Tashi Pal	Bkra shis dpal
Tashi Sengé	Bkra shis seng ge
Tashi Tsekpa Pal	Bkra shis brtegs pa dpal
Tengyur	Bstan 'gyur
Tenzin Sangpo	Bstan 'dzin bzang po
Thatsawa Sengé Gyaltsen	Mtha' rtsa ba Seng ge rgyal mtshan
Thekchen Chöjé	Theg chen chos rje
Thoklha Bönpo	Thog lha bon po
Thönmi Saṃbhota	Thon mi saṃ bho ṭa
Thöphu	Thod phu
Thupten Jigmé Chökyi Wangchuk	Thub bstan 'jigs med chos kyi dbang phyug
Thupten Jinpa	Thub bstan sbyin pa
Tömo Dorjetso	Stod mo Rdo rje mtsho
Tönchung Daryé	Ston chung Dar ye
Tong	Stong
Tongra	Stong ra
Tönpa Dorjé Ö	Ston pa Rdo rje 'od
Tötso	Stod tsho
Trangok	'Phrang 'og
Tri Ralpachen	Khri Ral pa can

Tringyi Shukchen	Sprin gyi shugs can
Trisong Deutsen	Khri srong lde'u btsan
Trogyal Yeshé	Khro rgyal ye shes
Tsal Gungthang	Tshal Gung thang
Tsalung Dongtön	Tsha lung Ldong ston
Tsami	Rtswa mi
Tsang	Gtsang
Tsangkha	Gtsang kha
Tsangrong	Gtsang rong
Tsar	Tshar
Tsarchen	Tshar chen
Tsarchen Losel Gyatso	Tshar chen Blo gsal rgya mtsho
Tsarkha	Tshar kha
Tsarpa	Tshar pa
Tsechen	Rtse chen
Tsedong	Brtse gdong
Tsipriwa Kashipa	Rtsibs ri ba Bka' bzhi pa
Tsodo Nesar	Gtso mdo gnas gsar
Tsokgom	Tshogs sgom
Tsokgom Rinpoché	Tshogs sgom Rin po che
Tsokshé	Tshogs bshad
Tsongkha Tsongön	Gtsong kha mtsho sngon
Tsongpön Pal	Tshong dpon Dpal
Tsuktor Gyalpo	Gtsug tor rgyal po
Tsultrim Drak	Tshul khrims grags
Tsultrim Gyaltsen	Tshul khrims rgyal mtshan

Tsultrim Tashi	Tshul khrims bkra shis
Tsünchung	Btsun chung
Ushang Do	'U shang rdo
Wangchuk Gyalpo	Dbang phyug rgyal po
Wangchuk Gyaltsen	Dbang phyug rgyal mtshan
Wangchuk Rapten	Dbang phyug rab brtan
Wangchukma	Dbang phyug ma
Wangrap	Dbang rab
Yakdepa Namkha Sönam	G.yag sde pa Nam mkha' bsod nams
Yalung	G.ya' lung
Yangdak	Yang dag
Yapjé Dorjé Chang	Yab rje Rdo rje 'chang
Yapjé Künga Lodrö	Yab rje Kun dga' blo gros
Yapjé Sönam Rinchen	Yab rje Bsod nams rin chen
Yardrok Khoplewa	Yar 'brog Khob le ba
Yarlha Shampo	Yar lha sham po
Yarlung	Yar lung
Yarlung Choktrul	Yar lung Mchog sprul
Yarlungpa	Yar lung pa
Yerpa	Yer pa
Yeru	G.yas ru
Yeshé Ö	Ye shes 'od
Yeshé Pal	Ye shes dpal
Yo	G.yo
Yönten Drak	Yon tan grags
Yönten Pal	Yon tan dpal

Yopso	Yob so
Yukharmo	G.yu mkhar mo
Yumten	Yum brtan
Yungdrung Drup	G.yung drung grub

2. Topical Outline of the Texts by Sachen Künga Nyingpo, Jamyang Khyentsé Wangchuk, Künga Palden and Loter Wangpo, and the Fifth Dalai Lama

Explication of the Treatise for Nyak, *by Sachen Künga Nyingpo*

Expansion of the Great Secret Doctrine, Summarizing Notes on the History of the Oral Instructions, by Jamyang Khyentsé Wangchuk

Blazing of a Hundred Brilliant Blessings: A Supplement to the *Expansion of the Great Secret Doctrine,* Summarizing Notes on the History of the Oral Instructions, by Künga Palden and Loter Wangpo

Summarizing Notes on How to Explain and Practice the Dharma, by Jamyang Khyentsé Wangchuk

Summarizing Notes on the Path Presented as the Three Appearances, by Jamyang Khyentsé Wangchuk

Profound Summarizing Notes on the Path Presented as the Three Continua, by Jamyang Khyentsé Wangchuk

Summarizing Notes on the Outer Creation Stage, by Jamyang Khyentsé Wangchuk

Summarizing Notes on the Inner Creation Stage, by Jamyang Khyentsé Wangchuk

Summarizing Notes Beginning with the Dream Yoga of the Vase Initiation, by the Fifth Dalai Lama

Notes

1 The phrase *taking the result as the path ('bras bu lam du byed pa)* is taken from Jetsün Drakpa Gyaltsen's annotations in his father Sachen Künga Nyingpo's *Explication of the Treatise for Nyak,* 11b (p. 11 in the critical edition of the Tibetan text).

2 See Stearns (2001) concerning the early transmission of the *Vajra Lines* and the identification of Sachen's eleven commentaries, and Stearns (2003) for a brief overview of the Sakya tradition and the contents of the *Vajra Lines.* The later tradition singled out three commentaries, describing Sachen's *Explication of the Treatise of the Path with the Result for the Benefit of the Sons (Gzhung bshad sras don ma)* as the vast presentation, his *Explication of the Treatise for Nyak (Gzhung bshad gnyags ma)* as the profound, and the *Treasury of Esoteric Instructions (Man ngag gter mdzod)* by Lama Dampa Sönam Gyaltsen (Bla ma dam pa Bsod nams rgyal mtshan, 1312–75) as a commentary on the meaning of those two works. See Samten Lodrö, *Divine Feast for Those of Good Fortune,* 39b (p. 314).

3 For the historical development of—and controversies about—the Explication for Disciples, see Stearns (2001), 39–45.

4 See Samten Lodrö, *Divine Feast for Those of Good Fortune,* 37b–41b (pp. 310–16). The original Dergé edition of the entire collection was in seventeen volumes; it has gradually been supplemented over the past century and has reached a total of thirty-one volumes in the most recent Indian reprint.

5 See Stearns (2001), 43.

6 See Chagen Wangchuk Gyaltsen, *Story of the Lord of Yogins* and *Detailed Story of the Tibetan Masters of the Path with the Result.* Chagen's biography of Virūpa was written in 1304.

7 Also see Stearns (2001), 44–45.

8 Sakya Paṇḍita, *Epistle Sent to the Buddhas and Bodhisattvas of the Ten Directions,* 58a. Also see Sakya Pandita Kunga Gyaltshen (2002), 244–45.

9 The common term *zhabs pad* can mean either "lotus feet" or "lotus beneath the feet." According to Lama Dampa Sönam Gyaltsen (Bla ma dam pa Bsod nams rgyal mtshan, 1312–75) and Mangthö Ludrup Gyatso (Mang thos klu sgrub rgya mtsho, 1523–96), the latter meaning is preferable here. Deities and great masters are often depicted and visualized standing on, or seated upon, a lotus flower. According to the Sakya tradition, the *Vajra Lines* were spoken by Virūpa and not written down, even though the text itself says "I will write" *(bri bar bya).* Mangthö Ludrup Gyatso explains this troublesome point by saying that Virūpa wrote the *Varja Lines* "with the pen of discernment on the tablet of the mind" *(yid kyi glegs bu la rnam dpyod pir gyis).* He also points out that the phrase *bri bar bya* can mean "I will explain" as well as "I will write." See Mangthö Ludrup Gyatso, *Summarizing*

Notes on the Explications of the Treatise, 11b–12a, and Lama Dampa Sönam Gyaltsen, *Treasury of Esoteric Instructions,* 65b.

10 In translating this sentence I am following the spelling *zin pas* (instead of *zin pa'i*) and the explanation in Sachen Künga Nyingpo, *Explication of the Treatise of the Path with the Result for the Benefit of the Sons,* 134a, 143b.

11 The partial quotation is from the *Magical Net (Sgyu 'phrul drwa ba),* which is another name for the *Litany of the Names of Mañjuśrī ('Jam dpal mtshan brjod).* Toh 360, Kangyur, rgyud 'bum *ka,* 3a3.

12 This translation follows the reading *bskyod* as in the Tengyur and all the commentaries, not *spyod* as in the *Yellow Volume* and the new critical edition.

13 According to all commentaries, the meaning here is actually "dharmakāya reality body" *(chos sku),* not "sambhogakāya enjoyment body" *(longs sku).* See Martön Chökyi Gyalpo, *Account of the Words of My Mañjuśrī Master,* 142b–143a, who mentions that Sakya Paṇḍita told him that Drokmi Lotsāwa ('Brog mi Lo tsā ba Shākya ye shes, 993–1077?) altered the *Vajra Lines* (to *sambhogakāya enjoyment body*) to make it difficult to understand without a master's instructions. All the commentaries explain the concealed meaning of *sambhogakāya enjoyment body* in this context. The translation thus follows the commentaries and the editions of the *Vajra Lines* published with Sachen's *Explication of the Treatise of the Path with the Result for the Benefit of the Sons,* 5b, instead of *dharmakāya reality body (chos sku)* found in the *Vajra Lines* published in the *Yellow Volume* and the new critical edition. See also note 99 and the explanation of this line in the *Explication of the Treatise for Nyak.*

14 In the *Explication of the Treatise for Nyak,* translated in this volume, this line reads "a female on the thirteenth spiritual level" *(sa bcu gsum ma),* as does the edition of the *Vajra Lines* published with Sachen's *Explication of the Treatise of the Path with the Result for the Benefit of the Sons,* 5b. The translation follows this reading, and not "female on the tenth spiritual level" *(sa bcu ma),* which is found in the edition of the *Vajra Lines* published in the *Yellow Volume* and in the new critical edition.

15 According to the various commentaries, the meaning here is actually "svābhāvikakāya essence body" *(ngo bo kyi nyid sku)* and not "sambhogakāya enjoyment body" *(longs sku).* Both Sachen Künga Nyingpo (*Explication of the Treatise of the Path with the Result for the Benefit of the Sons,* 217a) and Martön Chökyi Gyalpo (*Account of the Words of My Mañjuśrī Master,* 144a) say that the *Vajra Lines* were altered here in order to require reliance on a teacher. Therefore, the commentaries explain the concealed meaning of *sambhogakāya enjoyment body (longs sku)* in this context. The translation follows this reading, found in the edition of the *Vajra Lines* published with Sachen's *Explication of the Treatise of the Path with the Result for the Benefit of the Sons,* 5b, instead of *svābhāvikakāya essence body (ngo bo nyid kyi sku)* found in the *Vajra Lines* published in the *Yellow Volume* and the new critical edition. See also note 103 and the explanation of this line in the *Explication of the Treatise for Nyak.*

16 The warmths *(drod)* are various key experiences that arise along the path. These are precursors or foretastes of the actual signs *(rtags)* that arise later. The warmths are like smoke and the signs are like fire. Smoke appears first, indicating the imminent arising of fire. The warmths arise on the mundane path and the signs occur on the transcendent path.

17 The system of the Path with the Result mentions five bodies of enlightenment *(sku lnga):* the nirmāṇakāya emanated body *(sprul sku),* the sambhogakāya enjoyment body *(longs sku),* the dharmakāya reality body *(chos sku),* the svābhāvikakāya essence body *(ngo bo nyid kyi sku),* and the utterly pure svābhāvikakāya essence body *(ngo bo nyid kyi sku shin tu rnam par dag pa).*

18 Vajra Nairātmyā.

19 The terms *root continuum (rtsa rgyud)* and *explanatory continuum (bshad rgyud)* as applied here to the universal ground and the body have an additional resonance in Tibetan because of the dual meaning of the word *rgyud,* which can refer to either the continuum or mindstream of a living being or to a tantra. In the context of its meaning as "tantra" or "tantric scripture," a root tantra such as the *Hevajra Tantra* is clarified by other scriptures referred to as *explanatory tantras,* such as the *Vajrapañjara Tantra* and the *Sampuṭa Tantra.* This additional nuance is sometimes specified in other commentaries.

20 The common term *seat (gdan)* is used in this context for *type (rigs)* or *place (gnas).* Drokmi Lotsāwa is said to have purposely chosen the most obscure meaning of the Indian word *pīṭha* when translating the term into Tibetan.

21 According to the annotations composed by Sachen's son Jetsün Drakpa Gyaltsen (Grags pa rgyal mtshan, 1147–1216), the eleven aspects of the vase initiation are the five initiations of pure awareness, that of the sixth perfect buddha, the vase initiation (or initiation of the vajra master), the ritual permission, the prophecy, the encouragement, and the congratulation. The three types of the secret initiation are that obtained from the father, from the mother, or from the force of liberation. The two types of the initiation of primordial awareness dependent on an embodiment of wisdom are obtained dependent on a support and on experience. The five types of the fourth initiation are the word, meaning, path, result, and with the support of a consort.

22 Meditate on a practice such as this if one is inclined to do so, but do not meditate if not inclined. If one does not meditate when inclined to do so, no enhancement will occur. But if one does meditate when not inclined, impediments will arise.

23 In the new critical edition the three extra syllables from each of these groups written in Drakpa Gyaltsen's small annotations have been printed large as though part of the original text. I have followed the original text and not translated these syllables from the annotations.

24 The terms *fire channel (me ma)* and *sleep channel (gnyid ma)* are names for the rasanā and lalanā below the navel.

25 Alternately, count the length of time the breath is held twelve times and do not count the length twelve times. This practice must be learned from a teacher.

26 According to Jetsün Drakpa Gyaltsen's annotations, the four types of individual and perfect pure awareness are of words, meaning, etymology, and confidence.

27 This is one of the thirty-two major marks of a buddha.

28 According to Jetsün Drakpa Gyaltsen's annotation in the Tibetan text, the four branches are the creation of the sacred-commitment aspect of the deity, the entry of the primordial-awareness aspect, the blessing of the sensory bases and enlightened body, speech, and mind, and the bestowal of initiation.

29 *Hevajra Tantra.* Toh 418, Kangyur, rgyud 'bum *nga,* 15a1.

30 The term *space and secret (mkha' gsang)* is a euphemism for the female and male genitals.

31 The term *extreme stare (bgrad pa'i mtha')* refers to a technique for semen retention. *Secret control (gsang thub pa)* means to not actually enter into union with the consort. These practices must be learned from a teacher.

32 The Sanskrit term *bola* is a code word for the male genitals and *kakkola* is a code word for the female genitals.

33 The six actions *('gyur ba rnam pa drug)* are listed in the third paragraph following this one.

34 For explanation of the terms and practices mentioned in this paragraph, see the tenth text in this volume, under the heading (5) *Key points from the esoteric instructions.*

35 The six protections *(bsrung ba rnam pa drug)* are explained in the section on the fourteen protections in common for the two types of yogins.

36 The source for this quote is uncertain because the identification in the critical edition of the Tibetan text is incorrect.

37 This practice assumes familiarity with the visualization for the vase-initiation transference practice. A syllable *hūṃ,* which is the support of the consciousness, is visualized on a mandala of wind and a moon.

38 In this context, the term *exertion (rtsol ba)* is used for exhalation and the term *life (srog)* is used for inhalation.

39 See note 19.

40 The eight enhancements *(bogs 'byin brgyad)* are: (1–2) alternation between tensing and relaxing the body and mind, (3–4) alternation between shortening and lengthening meditation sessions, (5) alternation of food, (6) relaxed conduct, (7) the key mental point of transferring meditative concentration to various objects, and (8) resorting to the nectar of various objects. See Jetsün Drakpa Gyaltsen, *Clarification of the Instructions on the Inconceivable Composed by the Teacher Kuddāla,* 190a–b. I am grateful to Chogyé Trichen Rinpoché for his explanation of these techniques.

41 These special concoctions are explained in some of the more extensive commentaries. One must learn from a teacher how to prepare them.

42 These are explained by the Fifth Dalai Lama in the section on the secret initiation.

43 These yogas are explained by the Fifth Dalai Lama in the section on the secret initiation.

44 In this specific context, *exertion (rtsol ba)* refers to the vital winds that circulate through the right nostril and *life (srog)* refers to those that circulate through the left.

45 The practices of the calm and intense vocal inhalations are explained by the Fifth Dalai Lama in the section on the fourth initiation.

46 The second and third topics are presented in the section of the mundane path entitled "The Brief Presentation of the Causes for the Arising of Meditative Concentration."

47 The Sanskrit term *sihlaka (sihla)* is frankincense, a code word for the female essential constituent received from one's mother, and *karpūraka (ga bur)* is camphor, a code word for the male essential constituent received from one's father. Both are present in both men and women. The *musk* mentioned in the next sentence is a code word for urine.

48 This line is actually located much later in the *Vajra Lines,* toward the end of the section on the mundane path.

49 According to Khenpo Appey Rinpoché, there are two levels of meaning here. The first is that *elimination (tshar gcad)* refers to the elimination of evil beings, and *acceptance (rjes 'dzin)* refers to the acceptance of disciples. In the tantras, the same terms refer, respectively, to killing, making fruit fall from a tree with a mere glance, and so forth, and to the ability to restore to life, make the fruit rise back into a tree, and so forth.

50 The six actions are listed in the section on retention by means of the key points of esoteric instruction. The calm and intense vocal inhalations are practices of the fourth initiation, and are explained in that context in the work of the Fifth Dalai Lama.

51 The three hot herbs are galingale, long pepper, and black pepper.

52 The eight worldly concerns are profit and loss, pleasure and pain, fame and defamation, and praise and blame.

53 In this context, *vital wind of exertion (rtsol ba)* refers to exhalation, and *vital wind of life (srog)* refers to inhalation.

54 In this context, the *path of exertion (rtsol ba)* refers to the right nostril, and the *path of life (srog)* refers to the left nostril.

55 The quote is missing the word *ten (bcu)* that is found in the *Vajra Lines* itself.

56 The term *morbid depression (snying rlung),* which literally means "wind in the heart," is a Tibetan medical term for a type of respiratory illness that causes severe depression to arise in the mind.

57 See note 47.

58 According to Jetsün Drakpa Gyaltsen's annotation, the four malleable qualities *(mnyen lcug)* are malleability of the vital winds, the channels, the syllables, and the nectars.

59 Physical experiences, mental experiences, and dream experiences.

60 The translation follows the reading *gsum ka (all three)* in the *Gdams ngag mdzod* edition of the Tibetan text cited in the notes to the critical edition, instead of the *gnyis (two)* in the Dehra Dun edition.

61 See note 47.

62 That is, the experiences arise in the mind, the dances occur for the body, and the mantras arise as speech.

63 These forty-two experiences (seven for each of the six realms) are what have just been explained in the text. Purification of the places *(gnas)* or birthplaces *(skye gnas)* refers to the removal or purification of the causes for future rebirth in the six realms. When the vital winds and mind gather in specific channel locations in the subtle vajra body of the practitioner, experiences of being born in different realms may arise. These experiences are said to actually purify or remove the causes for future rebirth in those realms.

64 According to Jetsün Drakpa Gyaltsen's annotation, the ten fathers and mothers are the five nectars and the five vital winds.

65 The commentaries do not explain the meaning of the term *one with a bell (dril can).* Perhaps it is a reference to the bell-like shape of the lower end of the central channel and the one that extends from the left ear to the *wisdom āḥ.*

66 See also Sachen Küinga Nyingpo, *Explication of the Treatise of the Path with the Result for the Benefit of the Sons,* 174b, who gives the name of this place as Narigiri (Na ri gi ri) and describes it as a border region of India where only fruit was eaten. Even the word *cattle* was unknown there.

67 The *external-shape a (phyi dbyibs kyi a)* is the lower end of the central channel.

68 Jetsün Drakpa Gyaltsen's annotation says *meditation hut (bsam gtan gyi khang bu)* is a metaphor for one's mindstream *(rang rgyud).*

69 This is the fourth type of subsequent mindfulness *(rjes dran),* which is subsequent mindfulness of Dharma.

70 The exact quotation has not been located, but another of similar meaning is found in *Hevajra Tantra.* Toh 418, Kangyur, rgyud 'bum *nga,* 26a3.

71 The lower ends of the rasanā and lalanā enter into the central channel. The letter *cha* in some early Indian scripts and in Tibetan is similar in shape to the outline of a body seated in the vajra position.

72 The two paths of accumulation and application.

73 The "in that way" in this quote is not actually found in the *Vajra Lines.*

74 The annotation of Jetsün Drakpa Gyaltsen glosses *shape* as "the body mandala" *(lus kyi dkyil 'khor).*

75 In Buddhist cosmology, Jambudvīpa ('Dzam bu gling) is the southern of the four great continents surrounding Mount Meru. Jambudvīpa is the world of human beings.

76 The Sanskrit term *liṅga* is retained in the Tibetan text. As described here, the term refers to the penis. According to Martön Chökyi Gyalpo (Dmar ston Chos kyi rgyal po), *Account of the Words of My Mañjuśrī Master,* 129a, Sakya Paṇḍita (who was a Sanskrit expert) noted that since *liṅga* also means "sign," the three outer, inner, and secret signs are firm or infallible.

77 The distance of exhalation and inhalation are both reduced by one finger-width.

78 According to Jetsün Drakpa Gyaltsen's annotation, the 1,800 vital winds comprise one cycle of the vital wind *('pho ba gcig gi rlung).*

79 Each initiation is further classified into four, such as the vase initiation of the vase initiation, the vase initiation of the secret initiation, the vase initiation of the initiation of primordial awareness dependent on an embodiment of wisdom, and the vase initiation of the fourth initiation. The same applies for the next three initiations.

80 The beginning of this quote from the *Vajra Lines,* "From the second spiritual level of the path of meditation," has been omitted in the commentary.

81 The word *result* is not found in the *Vajra Lines* itself.

82 The four basic gazes are those of falling, attracting, overpowering, and paralyzing, and the eight branch gazes are those that vanquish an enemy, an army, and so forth.

83 The twelve branches of scripture are the sutras, aphorisms, prophecies, verses, meaningful expressions, legends, extensive teachings, tales of past lives, miraculous events, narratives, fables, and oral instructions. Cf. Dorje and Kapstein (1991), 162, 169.

84 According to Jetsün Drakpa Gyaltsen's annotations, these four are the perfect awareness of the words of the doctrine, meaning, etymology, and confidence.

85 *Magical Net (Sgyu 'phrul drwa ba)* is another name for the *Litany of the Names of Mañjuśrī ('Jam dpal mtshan brjod).* Toh 360, Kangyur, rgyud 'bum *ka,* 3a3.

86 Since *dharmakāya reality body (chos sku)* is specifically mentioned in the passage from the *Vajra Lines,* the explanations in the commentaries by both Lama Dampa (Bla ma dam pa Bsod nams rgyal mtshan, 1312–75) and Martön Chökyi Gyalpo (Dmar ston Chos kyi rgyal po, ca. 1198–ca. 1259) of the initiations received from the sambhogakāya enjoyment body *(longs sku)* and the dharmakāya reality body *(chos sku)* seem preferable, but Sachen's *Explication of the Treatise of the Path with the Result for the Benefit of the Sons* also has *nirmāṇakāya emanated body (sprul sku)* and *sambhogakāya enjoyment body (longs sku).*

87 Jetsün Drakpa Gyaltsen's annotation says, "because the vital wind is stable."

88 These twenty-four are the three bodies of enlightenment, the five types of primordial awareness, the five mudrā consorts, and the eleven herukas.

89 Here the four aspects of the real nature are the previous initiation of the real nature of the deity, and the real nature of the mudrā, mandala, and mantra.

90 The five paranormal abilities are to see from where sentient beings transmigrate, to see where they are reborn, to see distant forms, to hear distant sounds, and to know the thoughts of others.

91 Martön Chökyi Gyalpo, *Account of the Words of My Mañjuśrī Master,* 137b, makes this clear: "If the clear essences of the mudrā consort have been drawn there" *(der phyag rgya'i dangs ma 'drongs na).*

92 Both of these lines are out of order and separated by others in the *Vajra Lines.* Sachen Künga Nyingpo, *Explication of the Treatise of the Path with the Result for the Benefit of the Sons,* 211b, and Martön Chökyi Gyalpo, *Account of the Words of My Mañjuśrī Master,* 138b, both place them here.

93 According to Khenpo Appey Rinpoché, the misprint *pa* should be corrected to *ma (mother).*

94 Here the Sanskrit term *bhaga* is used for the vulva, although in other contexts it is also used to designate the body cavity of the abdomen and lower chest in both males and females.

95 Lama Dampa Sönam Gyaltsen, *Treasury of Esoteric Instructions,* 209b, relates the term *harima* to the Sanskrit *hāri,* which means *robbing ('phrog pa).* All of the vital winds of life and exertion in both channels are robbed by the central channel, and the signs that those winds have entered into the central channel are the arising of the eight qualities of power and wealth, which are seeing the central channel and so forth.

96 Source of quote not located. The translation of the common term *dbang phyug* as "power and wealth" in this specific context follows the explanation in Sachen Künga Nyingpo, *Explication of the Treatise of the Path with the Result for the Benefit of the Sons,* 214b, where it is explained that one gains the *power (dbang)* to have anything that is desired manifest instantly and that one is *wealthy (phyug po)* because these qualities never cease.

97 Source of quote not located.

98 These are some of the thirty-two major marks of a buddha.

99 See Martön Chökyi Gyalpo, *Account of the Words of My Mañjuśrī Master,* 142b–143a, for important comments about this problem. He mentions that Sakya Paṇḍita said that Drokmi Lotsāwa altered the *Vajra Lines* to make it difficult to

understand without a master's instructions. Also see Sachen Künga Nyingpo, *Explication of the Treatise of the Path with the Result for the Benefit of the Sons,* 215a–b.

100 The translation follows the reading *new (gsar)* in the *Vajra Lines* and other commentaries, not *clear (gsal)* in the Dehra Dun edition and the new critical edition.

101 See note 99.

102 These three mandalas are the channels, vital winds, and enlightenment mind.

103 Both Sachen Künga Nyingpo, *Explication of the Treatise of the Path with the Result for the Benefit of the Sons,* 217a, and Martön Chökyi Gyalpo, *Account of the Words of My Mañjuśrī Master,* 144a, say that the *Vajra Lines* were mixed up here in order to require reliance on a teacher, and that this line should be understood as applying to the svābhāvikakāya essence body *(ngo bo kyi nyid sku),* not the sambhogakāya enjoyment body *(longs sku).* Martön Chökyi Gyalpo, *Account of the Words of My Mañjuśrī Master,* 143a, quotes his teacher Sakya Paṇḍita as saying that the great master Drokmi Lotsāwa (Bla chen 'Brog mi) purposely altered the treatise to prevent understanding without access to a master.

104 *Aham iti* in Sanskrit means "I." According to Khenpo Appey Rinpoché, its meaning here is just the opposite: "selflessness" *(bdag med).*

105 *Magical Net (Sgyu 'phrul drwa ba)* is another name for the *Litany of the Names of Mañjuśrī ('Jam dpal mtshan brjod).* Toh 360, Kangyur, rgyud 'bum *ka,* 4a6.

106 Toh 360, Kangyur, rgyud 'bum *ka,* 6a2.

107 A set of verses written at the end of the text by Jetsün Drakpa Gyaltsen when he composed annotations to this commentary have not been translated.

108 Most of this extensive title is missing in the critical edition, which has as its title only *A Comprehensive Explanation of the Precious Teaching of the Path with the Result.* The translation follows the full title in the Dehra Dun reproduction of the original Dergé edition. The term *Khau Drakzongpa* (Kha'u brag rdzong pa) is a name used to designate the Tsarpa (Tshar pa) tradition of the Explication for Disciples (Slob bshad). This term is used because the ancient hermitage of Khau Drakzong near Sakya was the residence of Künpang Doringpa (Kun spangs Rdo ring pa, 1449–1524), who was the main disciple of Dakchen Dorjé Chang (Bdag chen rdo rje 'chang Blo gros rgyal mtshan, 1444–95) and the chief teacher of Tsarchen (Tshar chen Blo gsal rgya mtsho, 1502–66).

109 The author's main teacher, Tsarchen Losel Gyatso (Tshar chen Blo gsal rgya mtsho, 1502–66).

110 The second and third topics are explained later in Jamyang Khyentsé Wangchuk's *How to Explain and Practice the Dharma.*

111 The two assemblies of merit and primordial awareness.

112 Various lists of the twelve major deeds of the Buddha are given. According to one list, the twelve are: remaining in Tuṣita heaven, descent and entry into the womb, taking birth, proficiency in the arts, enjoyment of consorts, renouncing the world, practicing asceticism, reaching the point of enlightenment, vanquishing Māra's host, attaining perfect enlightenment, turning the doctrinal wheel, and passing into the final nirvana. See Dorje and Kapstein (1991), 169. All buddhas are said to attain perfect enlightenment at the Vajrāsana or Vajra Seat of Bodhgayā in the Magadha district of India.

113 The four classes of tantra are unexcelled yoga tantra, yoga tantra, performance tantra, and action tantra.

114 Vasubandhu, *Verses on the Treasury of Abhidharma.* Toh 4089, Tengyur, mngon pa *ku,* 24a3.

115 Sutra not identified.

116 The three trainings *(bslab pa gsum)* are moral disipline *(tshul 'khrims),* meditative concentration *(ting nge 'dzin),* and wisdom *(shes rab).*

117 The six ornaments *(rgyan drug)* are Nāgārjuna, Asaṅga, Dignāga, Āryadeva, Vasubandhu, and Dharmakīrti. The supreme pair *(mchog gnyis)* are Guṇaprabha and Śākyaprabha.

118 The *Volume (Glegs bam)* is the *Yellow Volume (Pod ser),* contained in volume 11, *da,* of the *Sa-skya Lam-'bras Literature Series.* For the first history of the tradition in India, see Jetsün Drakpa Gyaltsen, *Story of the Indian Masters of the Lineage.* For the work of Ngorchen Dorjé Chang Künga Sangpo (Ngor chen rdo rje 'chang Kun dga' bzang po, 1382–1456), which describes the Indian tradition first and then the Tibetan, see Ngorchen Künga Sangpo and Gungruwa Sherap Sangpo, *History of the Esoteric Instructions of the Path with the Result.*

119 According to Lama Dampa Sönam Gyaltsen (Bla ma dam pa Bsod nams rgyal mtshan, 1312–75), the six crucial points *(gnad du che ba drug)* are linked to the teachings of six Indian masters. (1) Padmavajra emphasized the crucial point of meditation on the creation stage. (2) Nāgārjuna emphasized the crucial point of meditation on the vital winds. (3) Kuddāla emphasized the crucial point of meditation on mahāmudrā. (4) Vajraghaṇṭā emphasized the crucial point of the blessing of the master. (5) Indrabhūti emphasized the crucial point of the blissful path of resorting to a mudrā consort. (6) Virūpa emphasized the crucial point of the five dependently arisen connections. See Lama Dampa Sönam Gyaltsen, *Illuminating the Marvelous,* 59b–60b.

120 Lord Lama (Rje bla ma) is Lama Dampa Sönam Gyaltsen (1312–75). See Lama Dampa Sönam Gyaltsen, *Illuminating the Marvelous,* 52a–b.

121 Lord Dorjé Chang (Rje Rdo rje 'chang) is Ngorchen Künga Sangpo (1382–1456). See Ngorchen Künga Sangpo and Gungruwa Sherap Sangpo, *History of the Esoteric Instructions of the Path with the Result,* 220a–221a.

122 Vajrāsanapāda, *Supplication to the Eighty-four Great Adepts.* Toh 3758, Tengyur, rgyud *tshu,* 110b3.

123 The teachings of the Indian yoginī Sukhasiddhī were passed down in Tibet in the Shangpa Kagyü (Shangs pa Bka' brgyud) lineage. Her teacher, Eastern Virūpa (Shar phyogs Birwa pa), who formulated the practices of Varāhī with the Severed Head (Phag mo dbu bcad ma), should not be confused with the Virūpa who formulated the Path with the Result.

124 The *Tantra Trilogy of Hevajra (Kye rdo rje'i rgyud gsum)* is composed of the root tantra of the two-part *Hevajra Tantra* (Toh 417/18, Kangyur, rgyud 'bum *nga*), the uncommon explanatory tantra of the *Vajrapañjara Tantra* (Toh 419, Kangyur, rgyud 'bum *nga*), and the common explanatory tantra of the *Sampuṭa Tantra* (Toh 381, Kangyur, rgyud 'bum, *ga*). For translations of the *Hevajra Tantra,* see Snellgrove (1959) and Farrow and Menon (1992).

125 Vajrāsanapāda, *Supplication to the Eighty-four Great Adepts.* Toh 3758, Tengyur, rgyud *tshu,* 110a7.

126 *Commentary on the Enlightenment Mind (Bodhicittavivaraṇa, Byang chub sems kyi 'grel pa),* Toh 1800/01, Tengyur, rgyud *ngi,* by Nāgārjuna. *Guhyasamāja Tantra (Rgyud gsang ba 'dus pa),* Toh 442, Kangyur, rgyud 'bum *ca. Direct Enlightenment of Vairocana (Vairocanābhisaṃbodhi, Rnam snang mngon byang),* Toh 494, Kangyur, rgyud 'bum *tha.* Also see Jetsün Drakpa Gyaltsen's *Instructions Received in Front of a Stupa: Composed by the Teacher Nāgārjuna.*

127 Vajrāsanapāda, *Supplication to the Eighty-four Great Adepts.* Toh 3758, Tengyur, rgyud *tshu,* 110b3.

128 See note 124 for the *Tantra Trilogy of Hevajra. Realizing Coemergence (Lhan cig skyes grub),* by Virūpa's disciple Ḍombi Heruka, is the *Śrīsahajasiddhi (Dpal lhan cig skyes pa grub pa),* Toh 2223, Tengyur, rgyud *wi,* 68b–70b. For a translation and study of the *Śrīsahajasiddhi,* see Shendge (1967). Drakpa Gyaltsen's explanation of the practice is found in the *Sa-skya Lam-'bras Literature Series,* vol. 11, *da,* 194a–198a.

129 Vajrāsanapāda, *Supplication to the Eighty-four Great Adepts.* Toh 3758, Tengyur, rgyud *tshu,* 110b6.

130 Indrabhūti's text known as the *Stages of Qualities in the Initiation (Dbang yon tan rim pa)* has not been identified. *Jñānatilaka (Ye shes thig le),* Toh 422, Kangyur, rgyud 'bum *nga.* Drakpa Gyaltsen's explanation of the practice is found in the *Sa-skya Lam-'bras Literature Series,* vol. 11, *da,* 231a–240a.

131 Vajrāsanapāda, *Supplication to the Eighty-four Great Adepts.* Toh 3758, Tengyur, rgyud *tshu,* 110b2.

132 *Saroruha's Method for Accomplishment (Sgrub thabs mtsho skyes)* is the *Śrīhevajrasādhana (Dpal dgyes pa rdo rje'i sgrub thabs),* Toh 1218, Tengyur, rgyud *nya. Like the Tip of a Lamp Flame (Mar me'i rtse mo)* is found in the *Sa-skya Lam-'bras Literature Series,* vol. 11, *da,* 221a–223a. Drakpa Gyaltsen's explanation of the practice of the Nine Profound Means *(Zab pa'i tshul dgu)* is contained in the same volume, 210a–221a.

133 Vajrāsanapāda, *Supplication to the Eighty-four Great Adepts.* Toh 3758, Tengyur, rgyud *tshu,* 110b7.

134 The *Complete Path by Means of the Five Aspects of the Inconceivable (Bsam gyis mi khyab pa lngas lam rdzogs pa)* of Kuddāla (Tog rtse pa) is usually just known by its short title, *Inconceivable (Bsam mi khyab),* Toh 2228, Tengyur, rgyud *wi.* A group of texts by Drakpa Gyaltsen explaining the practice of the *Inconceivable* is found in the *Sa-skya Lam-'bras Literature Series,* vol. 11, *da,* 181b–194a.

135 The Sanskrit name Kṛṣṇa and its various Prakrit forms such as Kāṇha and Kahna were all translated into Tibetan as "Nag po pa." Since it is the Prakrit forms that are specifically given for the name of Virūpa's disciple in numerous Tibetan sources, such as Jetsün Drakpa Gyaltsen, *Jeweled Tree for Direct Realization of the Tantras,* 3a, a Prakrit form has been used for his name in the translation. Kāṇha of Deliberate Behavior (Brtul zhugs Nag po pa) is one of the nicknames of Virūpa's disciple Kāṇha, who was also known as Eastern Kāṇha (Shar phyogs Nag po pa). Kṛṣṇasamayavajra (Nag po dam tshig rdo rje), whose real name was Śrībhadra, is the source of one of the four Hevajra transmissions in the Sakya tradition.

136 Vajrāsanapāda, *Supplication to the Eighty-four Great Adepts.* Toh 3758, Tengyur, rgyud *tshu,* 111a4. A biography of this Kṛṣṇacārin (Nag po spyod pa) written by

Jonang Tāranātha (Jo nang Tā ra nā tha, 1575–1635) is now available in an English translation. See Templeman (1989).

137 Kṛṣṇacārin's *Four Stages (Rim pa bzhi pa),* also known as *Olapati (O la pa ti),* Toh 1451, Tengyur, rgyud *wa.* Drakpa Gyaltsen's explanation of the practice is found in the *Sa-skya Lam-'bras Literature Series,* vol. 11, *da,* 223a–229a.

138 Vajrāsanapāda, *Supplication to the Eighty-four Great Adepts.* Toh 3758, Tengyur, rgyud *tshu,* 110b6.

139 The name of this master, Kṛṣṇa Utsiṭa the Immortal (Nag po u tsi ṭa 'chi ba med pa), is a composite of Indian and Tibetan words. According to Jonang Tāranātha, *utsiṣṭapa* means "one clinging to neither purity nor filth." See Templeman (1989), 69. Kṛṣṇa's "treatise," *A Verse on Drawing the Vital Winds into the Central Channel (Rlung dbu mar 'jug pa'i tshigs bcad),* is a single verse usually known as "Straightening the Crooked" *(Yon po bsrang ba).* This verse is found on folio 229b of Drakpa Gyaltsen's explanation of the practice in the *Sa-skya Lam-'bras Literature Series,* vol. 11, *da,* 229a–231a.

140 Medicinal pills, eye salve, and subterranean ability are three of the eight common accomplishments.

141 Vajrāsanapāda, *Supplication to the Eighty-four Great Adepts.* Toh 3758, Tengyur, rgyud *tshu,* 112b7.

142 *Illuminating the Fourth (Bzhi pa snang ba)* has not been located. *Seven Branches (Saptāṅga, Yan lag bdun ldan),* Toh 1888, Tengyur, rgyud *pi. Precious Reality (Tattvaratna, De kho na nyid rin po che),* Toh 1889, Tengyur, rgyud *pi.* Drakpa Gyaltsen's explanation of the practice of the Unwritten Mahāmudrā *(Phyag rgya chen po yi ge med pa)* is contained in the *Sa-skya Lam-'bras Literature Series,* vol. 11 *da,* 203b–210a.

143 Toh 543, Kangyur, rgyud 'bum *na,* 308b6.

144 Nāgārjuna, the originator of Madhyamaka philosophy, is generally believed to have been born sometime between the end of the first century C.E. and the third century C.E.

145 *Mañjuśrī Root Tantra.* Toh 543, Kangyur, rgyud 'bum *na,* 308b1.

146 Asaṅga (ca. 350–400 C.E.) was one of the most important of the Yogācāra philosophers. The influential Yogācāra-Madhyamaka master Śāntarakṣita (d. ca. 788) was active in Tibet during the latter half of the eighth century, and served as the first abbot of Samyé (Bsam yas) Monastery.

147 The four oral transmissions *(snyan brgyud bzhi)* are crucial for the practice of the Path with the Result, and were just explained in the previous paragraphs. These four are the unceasing stream of initiation, the undeclined transmission of blessings, the undisrupted sequence of the oral instructions, and the mind satisfied with devotion. They are mentioned in the *Vajra Lines* and explained in the *Explication of the Treatise for Nyak* and in the following texts by Jamyang Khyentsé Wangchuk.

148 Hevajra is surrounded by eight goddesses in his mandala and Nairātmyā is surrounded by fourteen goddesses in her mandala.

149 An annotation in the Tibetan text says: "Although *ha de byon* appears written in some texts, it was not understood that *ha de* is an [Indian] term for a marketplace. Thus my master taught." The purpose of this annotation is to point out that *har re (abruptly)* in Khyentsé's work is the correct reading, and not *ha de (marketplace)*

as found in some other texts. *Ha de* is probably a Tibetan corruption of a Prakrit form of the Sanskrit word *haṭṭa.*

150 The incomplete verses in the Tibetan text have been translated in full from Lama Dampa Sönam Gyaltsen, *Illuminating the Marvelous,* 53b–54a.

151 The incomplete verses in the Tibetan text have been translated in full from Lama Dampa Sönam Gyaltsen, *Illuminating the Marvelous,* 54b.

152 Lama Dampa Sönam Gyaltsen, *Illuminating the Marvelous,* 55a, provides the one-line song: "A single terrifying hero terrifies the Ganges!"

153 Mahākaruṇika (Thugs rje chen po) is one of the names of Avalokiteśvara, the bodhisattva of compassion.

154 Rāḍha is a district of Bengal just south of Puṇḍravardhana. See Tatz (1987), 702.

155 This famous image of Avalokiteśvara or Mahākaruṇika in the form known as Khasarpaṇa figures in the lives of numerous Indian and Tibetan masters, and was later visited by Drokmi Lotsāwa ('Brog mi Lo tsā ba Shākya ye shes, 993–1077?). According to Tatz (1987), 701, the famous statue was probably located in the Puṇḍravardhana forest of the Vārendra district of northern Bengal. In note 31, Tatz lists sources in which it is mentioned and possible locations for it.

156 Somanātha is the name of a form of Śiva or Maheśvara. Throughout this translation, the spelling *so ba nā tha* in the Tibetan text is understood to be a corruption of the Sanskrit name Somanātha. Some other Tibetan authors do correctly transliterate the Indian word as *so ma nā tha,* and at least one translates the transliterated *so ba nā tha* into Tibetan as "zla ba mgon po" (moon lord*),* a precise translation of the Indian name Somanātha. See Roerich (1959), 24.

157 The term *deliberate behavior (brtul zhugs spyod pa)* in this context refers to the various unconventional types of behavior recommended in the tantric scriptures for specific purposes, such as testing the realization of the yogin or bringing others onto the Buddhist path. Many of Virūpa's earlier acts fit this description.

158 The *Five Cycles of Scripture (Lung skor lnga)* were a mysterious group of texts, said to have been extracts from the *Hevajra Tantra* in 500,000 lines, that was preserved in Oḍḍiyāna (Oḍḍiyāna). Also see Stearns (2001), 12.

159 See note 155 concerning the Khasarpaṇa image. The Mahābodhi image of Śākyamuni Buddha was in Bodhgayā. Somanātha here refers to the stone image into which Virūpa dissolved.

160 In the Hindu pantheon, Kumāra Kārttikeya is the son of Śiva.

161 Dharmakīrti was a great Indian master of epistemology who lived in the seventh century. This Dharma king Aśoka is certainly *not* to be identified with the famous Indian emperor Aśoka (reign ca. 268–33 B.C.E.), but with a much later unidentified ruler. For example, although not to be identified with the king mentioned here, in the thirteenth century a certain Aśokavalla or Aśokacalla was king of the Khasa country, and his dominion extended over Kumayun, a part of Garhwal, and the western part of Nepal. It is also known from a dated inscription at Bodhgayā that this king was a devotee of Hevajra. See Mitra (1989), 187.

162 This strange tale seems to have been taken from an earlier biography of Virūpa written by Bartön Dorjé Gyaltsen (Bar ston Rdo rje rgyal mtshan), a fourteenth-century master of the Path with the Result. The story does not appear in any of the other known biographies of Virūpa. See Bartön Dorjé Gyaltsen, *Amazing and Marvelous Biography of Virūpa, the Lord of Yogins,* 27a–b. The perverted teachings

of the Blue Robed Paṇḍita (Paṇḍi ta Sham sngon can) seem to have been specifically connected to deviant tantric practices known to have been proscribed by the Kaśmīri king Śaṃkaravarman (reigned ca. 883–902). See Ruegg (1984), 377.

163 Toh 543, Kangyur, rgyud 'bum *na,* 325b3.

164 The phrase *conduct of the renunciation of duality (gnyis spangs kyi spyod pa)* refers to the advanced practice of renouncing all distinctions of duality, such as filth and cleanliness, good and bad, and so on.

165 Lord Gayadhara (Rje Ga ya dha ra, d. 1103). For a detailed examination of the identity of this important master, see Stearns (2001), 47–55.

166 *Kriyāsamuccaya (Bya ba kun las btus pa)* of Ācārya Darpaṇa ('Gro ba'i me long). Toh 3305, Tengyur, rgyud *bu.* See also Stearns (2001), 172.

167 The spelling *grub brgya (one hundred adepts)* found throughout Jamyang Khyentsé Wangchuk's work is either being used as a round number for eighty-four or is a printing mistake. The term has been translated everywhere in this book as "eighty-four adepts," according to the actual title of the text. Vīraprabhāsvara's work is *Heart of the Realization of the Eighty-four Adepts, (Caturaśītisiddhasambodhihṛdaya, Grub thob brgyad cu rtsa bzhi'i rtogs pa'i snying po),* Toh 2292, Tengyur, rgyud *shi.* The commentary, by Abhyadattaśrī, is *Expression of the Realization of the Eighty-four Adepts in Dohā Song, With a Commentary (Dohāvṛttisahitacaturaśītisiddhāvadāna, Grub thob brgyad cu rtsa bzhi'i rtogs brjod do ha 'grel pa dang bcas pa),* P5092, *lu.*

168 The five basic precepts *(bslab gzhi lnga)* of a lay practitioner are to refrain from killing, stealing, lying, improper sexual activity, and intoxicants.

169 Potala is the residence of Avalokiteśvara, after which the famous palace of the Dalai Lamas in Tibet was later named.

170 *Viśeṣatsavaṭīkā (Khyad par du 'phags pa'i bstod pa'i rgya cher bshad pa),* by Prajñāvarman (Shes rab go cha). Toh 1110, Tengyur, bstod tshogs *ka.*

171 The *Cintāmāṇidhāraṇī* of Uṣṇīsavimala *(tsinta ma ṇi'i gzungs zhes pa gtsug tor dri med)* and the *Seal of the Mudrā (Mu dra'i phyag rgya)* are unidentified. The *One Hundred Rites of Renunciation and Fulfillment (Spang skong phyag brgya pa),* Toh 267, Kangyur, mdo sde *ya.*

172 King Songtsen Gampo (Srong btsan sgam po, 569?–649?). For information about this king, his Nepalese and Chinese queens, the stories of the two famous images, and the early dynastic history of Tibet in general, see Sørensen (1994). Rasa Trulnang (Ra sa 'phrul snang) is the original name of the Jokhang Temple in Lhasa.

173 For a detailed account of the Tibetan king Trisong Deutsen (Khri srong lde btsan, 730?–785?), his patronage of Buddhism, invitation of the Indian masters Bodhisattva Śāntarakṣita and Guru Padmasambhava, construction of Samyé monastery, and the identification of the "seven men on trial" *(sad mi mi bdun),* see Sørensen (1994), 358–403. The Yogācāra-Madhyamaka master Śāntarakṣita (d. ca. 788) was active in Tibet during the latter half of the eighth century, and served as the first abbot of Samyé Monastery.

174 For information on the Tibetan king Tri Ralpachen (Khri Ral pa can, 806?–841?) and the events during his reign, see Sørensen (1994), 410–27. The three early translators were Kawa Paltsek (Ska ba Dpal brtsegs), Chokro Lü Gyaltsen (Cog ro Klu'i rgyal mtshan), and Shang Yeshedé (Zhang Ye shes sde).

175 For a detailed account of the Tibetan king usually known as Langdarma (Glang dar ma, 803?–842?), see Sørensen (1994), 427–35.

176 The Tibetan text contains the following annotation: "Most texts have 'to Lhasa.'"

177 The translation of this last phrase is uncertain: *spyi tshod la sgos tsha 'debs don mi 'dug.* Cf. Sørensen (1994), 435.

178 The full names of these three were Tsang Rapsal (Gtsang Rab gsal), Yo Gewai Jungné (G.yo Dge ba'i 'byung gnas), and Mar Shākyamuni (Dmar Shākya mu ni).

179 The Tibetan text reads *Karma sha tam,* which is presumably the *Karmaśataka (Mdo sde las brgya pa).* Toh 340, Kangyur, mdo sde *ha.*

180 In accordance with the monastic code of the vinaya, at least five monks must be present when a man takes ordination.

181 Chom Ral (Bcom ral) is the abbreviated name of Chomden Rikpai Raldri (Bcom ldan Rig pa'i ral gri, 1227–1305), a great scholar of the Kadampa (Bka' gdams pa) tradition.

182 Source of quote not located. The identification in the critical edition of the Tibetan text is incorrect.

183 The Great Translator Rinchen Sangpo (Lo chen Rin chen bzang po, 958–1055).

184 Jowo Lhachik (Jo bo Lha gcig) is an epithet of the famous Indian master Atiśa (982–1055).

185 See Roerich (1976), 83–85, for an account of the activities of the Indian paṇḍita Dharmapāla and the Tibetan monk Shangshung Gyalwai Sherap (Zhang zhung Rgyal ba'i shes rab).

186 Patsap Lotsāwa (Pa tshab Nyi ma grags, b. 1055).

187 The story of Gö Lotsāwa ('Gos Lo tsā ba Khug pa lhas btsas) and his relationship with Drokmi Lotsāwa and Gayadhara is told in section 3, *The specific history of the Precious Teaching.*

188 The Path of Padmavajra is the Nine Profound Means (Zab mo'i tshul dgu).

189 See Stearns (2001), 47–55, concerning the controversial Indian master Prajñāgupta (Shes rab gsang ba). The Tibetan text contains the following annotation: "This one and the Red Mendicant in the lineage of Maksorma are one. Thus my master taught." This note has been copied in the wrong place in the critical edition of the Tibetan text. The Path of Indrabhūti is the same as the Complete Path by Means of the Mudrā Consort (Phyag rgyas lam rdzogs pa).

190 The Tibetan text contains the following annotation: "He was the junior Amoghavajra, who traveled to Tibet. Thus my master taught." The Unwritten is the Unwritten Mahāmudrā (Phyag chen yi ge med pa).

191 See Stearns (2001), 189–90, for the story of Purang Lochung Shönu Sherap (Pu hrangs Lo chung Gzhon nu shes rab).

192 See Sørensen (1994), 465–80, for more information about the three princes of Lhatsé (Lha rtse) and their descendants.

193 This prophecy from the Avalokiteśvara Khasarpaṇa image in India is actually given later in the text, during the description of Drokmi Lotsāwa's earlier years in India and Nepal.

194 Aśvaghoṣa, *Fifty Verses on the Master (Gurupañcāśikā, Bla ma lnga bcu pa).* Toh 3721, Tengyur, rgyud *tshu.* This is a famous text describing the correct way to relate to a spiritual master in the practice of Buddhism. It has been translated as *Fifty*

Verses of Guru Devotion, Dharamsala: Translation Bureau of the Library of Tibetan Works and Archives, 1976.

195 See Stearns (2001), 47–55, concerning the controversies about the confusing accounts of the Indian masters Gayadhara and Prajñāgupta, both of whom were known by some of these same pseudonyms.

196 The teachings of the Indian master Maitrīpa (1007–85) became especially important for the Kagyü tradition in Tibet. See also Tatz (1987).

197 Sé Mönlam Sherap was a disciple of Gö Lotsāwa. For more details of this story see Stearns (2001), 93–97.

198 The Ārya tradition of Guhyasamāja is the transmission passed down from the Indian master Ārya Nāgārjuna.

199 Sur Shākjung (Zur Shāk 'byung) is the important Nyingma master Surpoché Shākya Jungné (Zur po che Shākya 'byung gnas, 1002–62), whose studies with Drokmi Lotsāwa are related later in the text. See also note 217.

200 As explained in the following paragraphs, Gayadhara had earlier promised not to teach the Path with the Result to anyone else after teaching it to Drokmi Lotsāwa.

201 See also Stearns (2001), 53–54, 192.

202 Vajrāsanapāda, *Supplication to the Eighty-four Great Adepts.* Toh 3758, Tengyur, rgyud *tshu,* 112a4. Curiously, this verse says "from the royal caste," whereas Gayadhara is otherwise described as being from a caste of scribes to royalty.

203 For Gyijo Dawai Özer (Gyi jo Zla ba'i 'od zer), see Stearns (2001), 219, etc.

204 For Nyö Lotsāwa Yönten Drak (Gnyos Lo tsā ba Yon tan grags, b. 961?), see Stearns (2001), 220, etc.

205 Sé and Rok are Drokmi Lotsāwa's disciples Gyergom Sewo (Gyer sgom Se bo) and Shengom Rokpo (Gshen sgom Rog po). See also Stearns (2001), 233–34.

206 Also see Sørensen (1994), 465–80, for more information about the three princes of Lhatsé (Lha rtse) and their descendents. Lotön Dorjé Wangchuk (Lo ston Rdo rje dbang phyug) was one of the seven men of Central Tibet (Dbus) and Tsang (Gtsang) who took monastic vows in Kham (Khams) and then returned to Central Tibet and Tsang to revive the transmission of the Vinaya there. He built the temple of Gyengong (Rgyan gong) after his return to Tsang. See Sørensen (1994), 448–49, n. 1634. Tsongé Sherap Sengé (Tshong ge Shes rab seng ge) was one of Lotön's companions in seeking ordination in Kham. See Sørensen, 449, n. 1633. He is referred to here as Chetsün Sherap Sengé (Lce btsun Shes rab seng ge), signifying that he was a member of the Ché (Lce) clan of Shalu (Zhwa lu), where the temple of Gyengong was located.

207 The Tibetan text contains the following annotation here: "It was about at an equal level with Khyungkar in the lower valley of Dar, where the place called Chödé is now, where there are some mantra practitioners. Thus my master taught." Drokmi Lotsāwa was born in 993. This note has been copied in the wrong place in the critical edition of the Tibetan text.

208 For the Newar master Śāntabhadra, who is known by many names, see Stearns (2001), 206–7.

209 Also see Stearns (2001), 207–9, for information about these six famous masters and what Drokmi received from each.

210 This is the same famous image visited centuries before by Virūpa, as described in his story.

211 A Buddhist monk's staff has rings on it that jingle when shaken to beg for alms.

212 See Stearns (2001), 217, concerning the identification of Śrīparvata in India.

213 See Chimpa and Chattopadhyaya (1990), 294, concerning King Canaka of the Pāla dynasty. However, Canaka's name is not found in the accepted lists of the Pāla dynasty rulers.

214 The Mahābodhi is a famous image of the Buddha at Bodhgayā, where Buddha Śākyamuni reached complete enlightenment at the spot known as the Vajrāsana, "Vajra Seat," under the Bodhi tree.

215 See Stearns (2001), 220, for information about the controversial group of *Rali* tantras.

216 A load *(khal)* is a unit of measure equivalent to about 25 to 30 pounds or 12 to 14 kilos. See Jackson (1996), 216, n. 478.

217 Surpoché Shākya Jungné (Zur po che Shākya 'byung gnas, 1002–62) was one of the great masters of the Nyingma (Rnying ma) tradition and is particularly important for the transmission of the Mind Series of the Great Perfection (Sems sde Rdzogs chen). The story of his life is translated in Dudjom (1991), 617–35. For details on Surpoché's relationship with Gayadhara and Drokmi Lotsāwa, see Stearns (2001), 214–16, etc.

218 Yangdak Heruka (Yang dag Heruka) is one of the eight great Mahāyoga deities of the Nyingma tradition.

219 For stories about the Nyingma master Surchung Sherap Drakpa (Zur chung Shes rab grags pa), see Roerich (1976), 114–15, 118–24.

220 *Saroruha's Method for Accomplishment* and the *Inconceivable* are connected to two of the Nine Cycles of the Path. The Mental Series (Sems phyogs or Sems sde) is one of the three classes of the Atiyoga teachings of the Great Perfection (Rdzogs chen). See Dudjom (1991), 538–53, for information on its lineage, and 319–26 for the nature of its teachings.

221 Pañjaranātha (Gur gyi mgon po) is the form of Mahākāla that is the special protector of the Path with the Result teachings.

222 The Indian master Nāropa gave a similar prophecy to his Tibetan disciple Marpa Lotsāwa (Mar pa Lo tsā ba Chos kyi blo gros, 1000?–1081?). For a translation of the episode in Marpa's life, see Heruka (1982), 92–93.

223 *Ratnajvāla (Rin chen 'bar ba).* Toh 1251, Tengyur, rgyud *nya.* This is a method for the accomplishment of Hevajra according to the tradition of Ḍombi Heruka.

224 The translator Nyan Lo Darma Trak (Gnyan Lo Dar ma grags) brought the teachings of the Dharma protector Caturmukha (Mgon po Zhal bzhi pa) to Tibet. In some histories this episode with Indra is told with Ra Lotsāwa (Rwa Lo tsā ba Rdo rje grags pa) instead of Nyan Lotsāwa. See Stearns (2001), 213.

225 For more information about Gyijang Ukarwa (Gyi ljang Dbu dkar ba), his teacher Nakpo Rozin (Nag po ro 'dzin), and his importance for the transmission of Mahākāla teachings to Tibet, see Stearns (2001), 223–24. The Red Mendicant (Atsārya Dmar po), whose actual name was Prajñāgupta, was one of the most controversial Indian masters of this period. For a discussion of Prajñāgupta's identity and the frequent confusion about this teacher and Gayadhara, see Stearns (2001), 52–53. The protector *(mgon po)* is Mahākāla.

226 Khön Könchok Gyalpo ('Khon Dkon mchog rgyal po, 1034–1102) founded the monastery of Sakya in 1073 and was the father of Sachen Künga Nyingpo. The

twenty-eight Wangchukma are the female protectors in the mandala of Vajrakīla. See Smith (2001), 300, for Dezhung Rinpoché's comments about them.

227 The *Compendium of Lessons* (*Śikṣāsamuccaya, Bslab pa kun las btus pa,* Toh 3939/40) is a collection of early Mahayana teaching compiled by the Indian master Śāntideva. For a complete translation, see Śāntideva (1981).

228 The phrase "concerning conduct" translates the Tibetan term *spyod phyogs,* which is used to designate texts concerned with proper conduct, apparently including sutras such as the *Avataṃsaka.*

229 Bodhisattva Vajragarbha (Rdo rje snying po) wrote one of the most important Sanskrit commentaries on the *Hevajra Tantra.* His work is the *Hevajrapiṇḍārthaṭīkā (Kye'i rdo rje bsdus pa'i don gyi rgya cher 'grel pa),* Toh 1180, Tengyur, rgyud *ka.* This commentary is one of the *Bodhisattva Trilogy (Sems 'grel skor gsum).*

230 More often known as Namkha Yeshé (Nam mkha' ye shes), this woman was also a disciple of Drokmi Lotsāwa. Her story is told later in the text, where she is listed as the fourth of Drokmi's main female disciples.

231 Mamo Bötong (Ma mo rbod gtong) is one of the three mundane deities from among the eight great Mahāyoga deities of the Nyingma tradition.

232 Khecara (Mkha' spyod) is a paradise especially associated with ḍākinīs such as Vajrayoginī.

233 Some other histories, such as Ngorchen Künga Sangpo and Gungruwa Sherap Sangpo, *History of the Esoteric Instructions of the Path with the Result,* 230a, say that Drom taught the Unwritten Mahāmudrā (Phyag chen yi ge med pa), not the *Inconceivable (Bsam mi khyab).*

234 For information about these three men, see Stearns (2001), 233–34.

235 For the statement by Martön (Dmar ston) in the *Incisive Vajra (Zhib mo rdo rje),* see Stearns (2001), 114–15.

236 Sé Kharchungwa (Se Mkhar chung ba) is the epithet of Setön Künrik (Se ston Kun rig, 1025–1122). The translation follows the Dehra Dun edition reading of *mdog smad* for Sé's birthplace, not the *mdo smad* in the critical edition of the Tibetan text. Sé was born in Tsang, not eastern Tibet.

237 As mentioned previously, Drokmi Lotsāwa followed a custom of giving three initiations, of which the second was "the initiation to mend the sacred commitments."

238 As Drokmi previously told Könchok Gyalpo, he had promised one of his teachers not to explain the scriptures to those who fully received the instructions and not to explain the oral instructions to those who fully received the scriptures.

239 That is, the *Tantra Trilogy of Hevajra,* comprised of the *Hevajra Tantra, Vajrapañjara Tantra,* and *Sampuṭa Tantra.*

240 A measure *(bre)* is one twentieth of a load *(khal),* roughly equivalent to 1.35 pounds or 650 grams. See Jackson (1996), 216, n. 477.

241 A load *(khal)* is a unit of measure equivalent to about 25 to 30 pounds or 12 to 14 kilos.

242 Dzeden Öchak was Drokmi's consort.

243 Three modes of gathering the essential constituents *(khams 'dus lugs gsum)* are mentioned in the *Vajra Lines* and the commentaries. Sachen Künga Nyingpo, in the *Explication of the Treatise for Nyak,* says: "The three modes of gathering the essential constituents are: the natural gathering of the essential constituents for one with residual karma, the gathering of the essential constituents through blessings

for one with devotion, and the gathering of the essential constituents through exertion for one with diligence." However, Jamyang Khyentsé Wangchuk here lists four corresponding to the examples of the four women.

244 Kuddāla, *Inconceivable.* Toh 2228, Tengyur, rgyud *wi,* 101a1. The Tibetan translation of these lines in the Dergé Tengyur is by Gö Lotsāwa, and differs slightly from that made by Drokmi Lotsāwa, which is the version quoted in the text. This verse is used in the context of what is known as *resorting to the nectar of various objects (yul sna tshogs kyi bdud rtsi bsten pa),* which is an important theme in the Path with the Result.

245 Machik Shama (Ma gcig Zha ma, 1062–1149) and her brother Khumbuwa Chögyal (Khum bu ba Chos rgyal, 1069–1144), whose story is related later in the text.

246 Nakgyal (Nags rgyal) is the name of both a place near Jonang and the local goddess of that area.

247 Sakya Paṇḍita Künga Gyaltsen (Sa skya paṇḍi ta Kun dga' rgyal mtshan, 1182–1251), one of the greatest masters of the Path with the Result.

248 The story of Drokmi's disciple Drom Depa Tönchung was related previously.

249 These are all practices connected with the special form of Vajrayoginī or Vajravarāhī known as Khecarī (Mkha' spyod ma). Short texts for all the practices mentioned here were later written by Drakpa Gyaltsen and are found in volume 3 of the *Complete Works of the Great Masters of the Sa skya Sect of Tibetan Buddhism.*

250 The Shangtön brothers (Zhang ston sku mched) were named Sijibar (Gzi brjid 'bar) and Chöbar (Chos 'bar, 1053–1135). The elder brother, Shangtön Chöbar, became the main lineage holder of the tradition, later teaching the Path with the Result to Sachen Künga Nyingpo.

251 According to Khenpo Appey Rinpoché, *finishing (rtsi gras)* refers to making the texts straight, trimming the pages evenly, varnishing them, and so forth.

252 The Chinese queen Ongjo (Rgya bza' Ong jo) was a Chinese princess who became the queen of King Songtsen Gampo (Srong btsan sgam po, 569?–649?). The king sent Thönmi Saṃbhoṭa (Thon mi Saṃ bho ṭa) to India to study the written language, and Thönmi is credited with devising the Tibetan script upon his return to Tibet. Ma Lotsāwa Chöbar (Rma Lo tsā ba Chos 'bar, 1044–89) was a Tibetan translator who studied in India with the Kaśmīri master Jayānanda, the Tibetan master Tsami Sangyé Drakpa (Rtswa mi Sangs rgyas grags pa), who was abbot of Nālandā and a great translator, and the famous Indian master Abhayākaragupta. See also Roerich (1976), 219–20, where this is all described in more detail.

253 See Roerich (1976), 222–24, for extensive details about all seven signs of obstacles.

254 Dampa Gyagar (Dam pa rgya gar) is another name for Phadampa Sangyé (Pha dam pa Sangs rgyas, d. 1105), the founder of the tradition of Pacification (Zhi byed) in Tibet. For Phadampa and his system of meditation, which combined the teachings of the tantras and the Perfection of Wisdom teachings (Prajñāpāramitā), see Roerich (1976), 867–981, and Edou (1996), 31–38.

255 See Roerich (1976), 224–25, for further details of this story.

256 Lhajé Nubpa (Lha rje Rnubs pa) is perhaps to be identified with Lhajé Hūṃchung (Lha rje Hūṃ chung), also known as Lhajé Nubchung (Lha rje Gnubs chung), who is in the Rong lineage of transmitted precepts in the Nyingma tradition. He was possibly the teacher with whom Milarepa (Mi la ras pa, 1028?–1111?)

studied the Great Perfection (Rdzogs chen) as a young man. See Dudjom (1991), 615, and Martin (1982), 54–58.

257 *Certainty About Reality in the Glorious Guhyagarbha.* Toh 832, Kangyur, rnying rgyud *kha,* 112a3. The quote seems to be a combination of several lines in the original.

258 The phrase *threefold purity ('khor gsum yongs dag)* refers to performing an act with full awareness of the nonsubstantiality of the person doing the action, the action itself, and the object of the action.

259 Machik and her brother would have to sleep lying against the bellies of yaks on the path to keep warm at night.

260 *Saroruha's Method for Accomplishment (Sgrub thabs mtsho skyes)* is the *Śrīhevajra-sādhana (Dpal dgyes pa rdo rje'i sgrub thabs),* Toh 1218, Tengyur, rgyud *nya.* The four states or categories *(gnas pa bzhi)* are repeatedly mentioned in the explanations of *Saroruha's Method for Accomplishment* when referring to four phases in the creation stage linked to the four bodies of enlightenment, four types of individuals, and so forth.

261 The Tibetan master and translator Tsami Sangyé Drakpa (Rtswa mi Sangs rgyas grags pa) was the abbot of the great monastic university of Nālandā.

262 Lord Gönpawa (Dgon pa ba) is Shangtön Chöbar (Zhang ston Chos 'bar, 1053–1135). His comment about Machik's excessive fondness for songs of experience is baffling. But according to Khenpo Appey Rinpoché, it simply means that she liked songs too much.

263 Sachen Künga Nyingpo (Sa chen Kun dga' snying po, 1092–1158).

264 Jetsün Drakpa Gyaltsen, *Eulogy of the Master's Life,* 166a1.

265 Jamyang Dönyö Gyaltsen ('Jam dbyangs don yod rgyal mtshan, 1310–44) was the elder brother of lord Lama Dampa (Rje Bla ma dam pa Bsod nams rgyal mtshan, 1312–75).

266 Sachen's father had studied with Drokmi Lotsāwa and other translators.

267 The translator Bari Lotsāwa Rinchen Drakpa (Ba ri Lo tsā ba Rin chen grags pa, 1040–1111).

268 Acala (Mi g.yo ba) is the specific protector associated with Mañjuśrī/Mañjughoṣa.

269 The teachings Sachen received when he was twelve years old have come to be known as *Parting from the Four Attachments (Zhen pa bzhi bral).* These four phrases summarize the entire Mahayana path and have continued to be the basis for the extensive teachings on Mind Training (Blo sbyong) in the Sakya tradition up to the present day. See Chogyé Trichen Rinpoché (2003) and Sakya Trizin and Ngawang Samten (1982).

270 "A type of black smallpox" *('brum bu me dbal nag po).* Tibetan medical tradition recognizes three white and three black forms of smallpox.

271 This figure is said to have actually been the Māra King with a Rosary of Skulls (Bdud rgyal thod phreng can), who is one of the specific protectors of the deity Vajrakīla.

272 The *Precision of Epistemology (Pramāṇaviniścaya, Tshad ma rnam nges)* is one of the Indian master Dharmakīrti's Seven Sets on Epistemology.

273 The *One Hundred Methods for Accomplishment (Sgrub thabs brgya rtsa),* also known as the *One Hundred Methods of Bari (Ba ri brgya rtsa),* is a collection of methods for accomplishment received by Bari Lotsāwa from the Indian master

Vajrāsanapāda. The collection is contained in volume 12 of the *Sgrub thabs kun btus,* Dehra Dun: G. T. K. Lodoy, N. Gyaltsen, and N. Lungtok, 1970.

274 Khön Dralhabar ('Khon Dgra lha 'bar) is also known as Sherap Bar (Shes rab 'bar) and Gyichuwa (Sgyi chu ba).

275 The people in Sachen's dream were his future disciples, some of whom are identified and discussed below. Mount Malaya is the name of a legendary mountain on the southern tip of the Indian subcontinent. See Stearns (2001), 250.

276 Kṛṣṇa is Kṛṣṇasamayavajra (Nag po dam tshig rdo rje), who was the source of one of the four Hevajra transmissions in the Sakya tradition. Phamthingpa (Pham thing pa) is the epithet of four Newar brothers who lived in the Kathmandu Valley in Nepal, with whom Mal Lotsāwa (Mal Lo tsā ba Blo gros grags pa) studied. See Stearns (2001), 206–7, about difficulties in identifying the different Phamthingpa brothers.

277 Master Ngaripa was Drokmi's disciple Salwai Nyingpo (Gsal ba'i snying po), from whom Gyichuwa had received the *Tantra Trilogy of Hevajra* and many other transmissions.

278 Master Nam Khaupa (Gnam kha'u pa), whose personal name was Darma Gyaltsen (Dar ma rgyal mtshan), was one of Sachen's previous teachers. For some stories about him, see Stearns (2001), 137, etc.

279 The venerable brothers *(rje btsun sku mched)* are Sachen's sons Sönam Tsemo (Bsod nams rtse mo, 1142–82) and Drakpa Gyaltsen (Grags pa rgyal mtshan, 1147–1216), who would never have been born if Sachen had become a monk.

280 According to Jetsün Drakpa Gyaltsen, *Biography of the Glorious Great Sakyapa Künga Nyingpo,* 13a, the *Eight Branches (Yan lag brgyad pa)* is the teaching on the eight fundamental branches of medical diagnosis in the Tibetan tradition.

281 The teachings of Nāro Khecarī (Nā ro Mkha' spyod ma) are part of the Cakrasaṃvara uncommon explication for disciples. The special teachings of Rakta Yamāri (Gshin rje'i gshed dmar) are from Virūpa. The lineage of Pañjaranātha (Gur gyi mgon po) transmitted through the great translator Lochen Rinchen Sangpo (Lo chen Rin chen bzang po, 958–1055) is the most important of the Mahākāla transmissions for the Sakya tradition. Also see Vitali (2001).

282 The followers of the new translations *(gsar ma ba)* were followers of the Dharma teachings newly translated into Tibetan beginning in the eleventh century.

283 Chagen Wangchuk Gyaltsen, *Detailed Story of the Tibetan Masters of the Path with the Result,* 77&78b (both numbers are written on the same Tibetan page), says the Shangtön brothers learned the Great Perfection teachings of the *Cycle of the Brahmin (Bram ze'i skor)* and the *Great Perfection of Tsamunti (Rdzogs chen tsa mun ti)* from their grandfather and were experts in these practices. The *Cycle of the Brahmin* is a group of Nyingma tantras of the Atiyoga class that were introduced into Tibet by Padmasambhava and Vimalamitra. It is listed as nos. 112–28 in Kaneko (1982), 127–49. The *Great Perfection of Tsamunti (Rdzogs chen tsa munti)* has not been identified.

284 The lords of the three spiritual families *(rigs gsum mgon po)* are the bodhisattvas Avalokiteśvara, Mañjuśrī, and Vajrapāṇi.

285 The Mañjughoṣa Cave ('Jam dbyangs phug pa) is the cave where Sachen had received the teachings of *Parting from the Four Attachments* from Mañjughoṣa when he was twelve years old. When Sachen was blessed by Shang Gönbawa

(Zhang Dgon pa ba) he wrote a eulogy to his master in which he said that he had been cured of the illness by Shangtön's compassion. See Sachen Künga Nyingpo, *Eulogy to Shangtön.*

286 As pointed out to me during a visit to Sakya, Baldrok ('Bal grog) and Möndrok (Mon grog) are the names of two ridges located a considerable distance to either side of the white patch on the mountain.

287 Koṭalipa (Ko ṭa li pa) is a form of the name Kuddāla (Tog rtse pa). The spelling Kuddāla is found in the extant Sanskrit texts. Vīṇāpa (the corrupt spelling *bi na sa* is in the text) was an early predecessor of Kuddāla in the lineage of the *Inconceivable (Bsam mi khyab).*

288 Mangthö Ludrup Gyatso, *Bright Sun of Pure Altruism,* 130, dates this meeting with Virūpa to the year 1138 *(sa rta),* when Sachen was forty-six years old. The experience of receiving these prolonged teachings from Virūpa caused a stunning eulogy to arise in Sachen's mind. See Sachen Künga Nyingpo, *Eulogy to Glorious Virūpa.* The identification of the seventy-two tantric teachings has created much confusion. The Great Abbot of Mustang, Sönam Lhundrup (Glo bo mkhan chen Bsod nams lhun grub, 1456–1531), finally wrote a short text to clarify the issue. He enumerates fifty anuttarayoga, four yoga, three caryā, and fifteen kriyā tantras. See Sönam Lhundrup, *Bright Lamp.* Explanations of the other teachings from Virūpa are found in the *Red Volume (Pod dmar)* contained in volume 13, *pa,* of the *Sa skya Lam 'bras Literature Series.*

289 See Sachen Künga Nyingpo, *Versified Summary of Everything.* According to Mangthö Ludrup Gyatso, *Bright Sun of Pure Altruism,* 130, Sachen first taught the Path with the Result to Aseng in 1041 *(lcags mo bya).*

290 The main spiritual son is Sachen's son and disciple Drakpa Gyaltsen, who is believed to have attained final enlightenment in the pure realm of Serdokchen (Gser mdog can), as mentioned later in the text.

291 Dakchen Rinpoché (Bdag chen Rin po che) is Dakchen Lodrö Gyaltsen (Bdag chen Blo gros rgyal mtshan, 1444–95). See Stearns (2001), 16–25, for a discussion of Sachen's eleven commentaries and the disciples who requested them.

292 Shuché Ngödrup (Zhu byas Dngos grub) was one of Sachen's main disciples and the requestor of one of the eleven commentaries.

293 Yarlungpa (Yar lung pa) could be either Yarlungpa Jangchup Gyaltsen (Yar lung pa Byang chub rgyal mtshan) or Yarlungpa Drakpa Gyaltsen (Yar lung pa Grags pa rgyal mtshan), both of whom were active in the second half of the thirteenth century.

294 See Sachen Künga Nyingpo, *Versified Summary of Everything.*

295 See note 63 concerning the purification of the places *(gnas)* or birthplaces *(skye gnas).*

296 The practices of the vocal inhalations *(ngag 'dren)* are explained by the Fifth Dalai Lama in the text translated later in the volume.

297 The profound path *(lam zab)* is the term given to the meditations of guruyoga in the Path with the Result.

298 Jetsün Drakpa Gyaltsen, *Dreams of the Venerable Lord,* 199b4. The quote given here is considerably different from the passage in the extant text itself.

299 The venerable brothers are Jetsün Drakpa Gyaltsen and Lopön Sönam Tsemo. The Gorum Temple (Sgo rum) was the oldest temple in Sakya.

300 The syllables *hrīḥ kṣṭi* are from the mantra of Yamāri.

301 According to Chogyé Trichen Rinpoché, a blending ritual *(bsre ba'i cho ga)* blends together the primordial-awareness aspect *(ye shes pa)* and the sacred-commitment aspect *(dam tshig pa)* of a deity.

302 Nyak Wangchuk Gyaltsen (Gnyags Dbang phyug rgyal mtshan), for whom the *Explication of the Treatise for Nyak* was taught.

303 See Jetsün Drakpa Gyaltsen, *Instruction by the Venerable Lord to Gatön Dorjé Drak.*

304 Purification of birth in the hells *(dmyal ba'i gnas sbyong).* See note 63.

305 Purification of birth as an animal *(dud 'gro'i gnas sbyong).* See note 63.

306 Durjayacandra (Mi thub zla ba) was the teacher of Vīravajra, who was the teacher of Drokmi Lotsāwa.

307 Potala is the residence of the bodhisattva Avalokiteśvara.

308 Jetsün Drakpa Gyaltsen, *Eulogy of the Master's Life,* 166b3.

309 Jetsün Drakpa Gyaltsen, *Dreams of the Venerable Lord,* 198b–199a.

310 With the exception of *Application to Precisely This Scripture (Lung 'di nyid dang sbyar ba),* which is found in volume 11, *da,* of the *Sa-skya Lam-'bras Literature Series,* these texts are found among Sönam Tsemo's writings in the *Complete Works of the Great Masters of the Sa skya Sect of Tibetan Buddhism. Precisely this scripture* in the title of the text refers to the *Hevajra Tantra.*

311 The great paṇḍita of Kaśmīr is Śākyaśrībhadra (1140s–1225?).

312 The celestial demon Rāhu was believed to devour the sun and cause eclipses.

313 That is, Sakya Paṇḍita Künga Gyaltsen.

314 The interpreter was previously identified as Namthel Karpo. Nyen Thanglha would seem to be another name for this deity.

315 In about 1244 Sakya Paṇḍita was summoned to the court of the Mongol prince Ködan Khan. In 1258, Qubilai Khan (1215–94), who would later become the first Emperor of the Yüan Dynasty in China, requested from Sakya Paṇḍita's nephew, Chögyal Phakpa (Chos rgyal 'Phags pa, 1235–80), the complete Hevajra initiation, in gratitude for which Qubilai is said to have offered Phakpa the three regions of Tibet.

316 These lines are all found in Sakya Paṇḍita Künga Gyaltsen, *Clarification of the Meaning Through Symbols.*

317 Nyen Phuljungwa Tsuktor Gyalpo (Gnyan Phul byung ba Gtsug tor rgyal po) was an important disciple of Sachen Künga Nyingpo. He edited the many miscellaneous explanations of difficult points in the Path with the Result that Sachen had written down for his sons into the most extensive of Sachen's eleven commentaries on the *Vajra Lines.* See Sachen Künga Nyingpo, *Explication of the Treatise of the Path with the Result for the Benefit of the Sons.*

318 Source not located.

319 Vajradhara and Nairātmyā are considered to be indivisible and thus are counted as one.

320 Jetsün Drakpa Gyaltsen, *Summarizing Outline,* 161b3.

321 The ten directions are the eight primary and intermediate directions, above, and below. According to the Kālacakra tradition, Mount Meru is surrounded by seven mountains.

322 The two texts by Drakpa Gyaltsen are found in the *Yellow Volume (Pod ser),* which is contained in volume 11, *da,* of the *Sa-skya Lam-'bras Literature Series.*

323 See Sakya Paṇḍita Künga Gyaltsen, *Explication of the Five Dependently Arisen Connections* and *Explication of the Seal of the Four Mandalas.*

324 This is a confusing reference. The questions of the Kadam master Dokorwa (Do skor ba) and Sakya Paṇḍita's replies to them are contained in Sakya Paṇḍita's *Collected Works, na,* 217a–220a. No comments by Phakpa Rinpoché are found there.

325 The great Kagyü (Bka' brgyud) master Gyalwa Yangönpa Gyaltsen Pal (Rgyal ba Yang dgon pa Rgyal mtshan dpal, 1213–58) received the Path with the Result of the Sakya tradition from Sakya Paṇḍita and that of the Shama tradition from Gyalwa Kodrakpa (Rgyal ba Ko brag pa, 1170–1249).

326 See Stearns (2001) for a translation and study of the *Incisive Vajra (Zhib mo rdo rje)* by Martön Chökyi Gyalpo (Dmar ston Chos kyi rgyal po, ca. 1198–ca. 1259) and information about his life and works. Also see Stearns (2001), 198, for information on Gangtön Sherap (Sgang ston Shes rab) and Karpo Drakpa Rinchen Sengé (Dkar po brag pa Rin chen seng ge).

327 The adept Yönten Pal (Grub thob Yon tan dpal, 1237–1323).

328 Tsokgom Rinchen Pal (Tshogs sgom Rin chen dpal, 1210–1307).

329 Sangtsa Sönam Gyaltsen (Zangs tsha Bsod nams rgyal mtshan, 1184–1239) was the younger brother of Sakya Paṇḍita and the father of Chögyal Phakpa.

330 A hybrid yak-cow *(mdzo)* is a hybrid between a yak and cattle. It progresses slowly and deliberately, often stopping to graze.

331 Shang Könchok Pal (Zhang Dkon mchog dpal, 1240–1307).

332 Drakphukpa Sönam Pal (Brag phug pa Bsod nams dpal, 1277–1346).

333 The great adept Nyenchenpa (Grub chen Nyan chen pa) is Nyenchen Sönam Tenpa (Nyan chen Bsod nams brtan pa, 1222–1317).

334 Lama Dampa Sönam Gyaltsen (Bla ma dam pa Bsod nams rgyal mtshan, 1312–75).

335 Ritröpa Lodrö Tenpa (Ri khrod pa Blo gros brtan pa, 1316–58).

336 The Path with the Result master Yeshé Pal (Lam 'bras pa Ye shes dpal, 1281–1365).

337 Losang Karmo (Blo bzang dkar mo) taught the Path with the Result to Bodong Paṇchen Cholé Namgyal (Bo dong paṇ chen Phyogs las rnam rgyal, 1376–1451).

338 Palden Tsultrim (Dpal ldan tshul khrims, 1333–99).

339 The great adept Buddhashrī (Grub chen Buddha shrī, 1339–1419).

340 Sharchen Yeshé Gyaltsen (Shar chen Ye shes rgyal mtshan, d. 1406).

341 Sempa Chenpo (Sems dpa' chen po) is an epithet of Müchen Könchok Gyaltsen (Mus chen Dkon mchog rgyal mtshan, 1388–1469).

342 Dakchen Dorjé Chang (Bdag chen rdo rje 'chang) is an epithet of Dakchen Lodrö Gyaltsen (Bdag chen Blo gros rgyal mtshan, 1444–95).

343 La is Laruwa Sönam Sengé (La ru ba Bsod nams seng ge), who was invited to China by the Emperor Siddhipala (1303–23) and passed away there at the age of eighty-seven. Nyen is Nyenchen Sönam Tenpa (Nyan chen Bsod nams brtan pa, 1222–1317), an important disciple of Tsokgom Künga Pal. Shang is Shang Könchok Pal (Zhang Dkon mchog dpal, 1240–1307), the most important of Phakpa Rinpoché's disciples.

344 Gangtröpa Drakpa Pal (Gangs khrod pa Grags pa dpal, b. 1292), also known as the omniscient Pangkhangpa (Kun mKhyen Spang khang pa), was the third abbot of Ngamring monastery.

345 Mati Paṇchen (Ma ti Paṇ chen 'Jam dbyangs blo gros rgyal mtshan, 1294–1376). Individual withdrawal *(so sor sdud pa)* is the first branch of the six-branch yoga of the Kālacakra. The omniscient Jonangpa is Dolpopa Sherap Gyaltsen (Dol po pa Shes rab rgyal mtshan, 1292–1361).

346 The Time of the Path (Lam dus) is a common name for the daily Hevajra method for accomplishment *(sādhana, sgrub thabs)*. Thekchen Chöjé (Theg chen chos rje Kun dga' bkra shis, 1349–1425).

347 The venerable father (Rje btsun Yab) is Jamyang Namkha Gyaltsen ('Jam dbyangs Nam mkha' rgyal mtshan, 1398–1472).

348 Lachen Künga Gyaltsen (Bla chen Kun dga' rgyal mtshan, 1344–1418) of the Khön ('Khon) family. He was the nephew of Lama Dampa and the father of Dakchen Jamyang Namkha Gyaltsen (Bdag chen 'Jam dbyangs Nam mkha' rgyal mtshan, 1398–1472), who was the father of Dakchen Lodrö Gyaltsen (Bdag chen Blo gros rgyal mtshan, 1444–95).

349 The great adept Künlo (Grub chen Kun dga' blo gros, 1365–1443). Nya Ön (Nya dbon Kun dga' dpal, 1285–1379) was also one of the main disciples of the Jonang master Dolpopa Sherap Gyaltsen. Yakdepa (G.yag sde pa Nam mkha' bsod nams, 1299–1378).

350 Jamyang Könchok Sangpo ('Jam dbyangs dkon mchog bzang po, 1398–1475).

351 Künpang Chenpo (Kun spangs chen po Kun bzang chos kyi nyi ma, 1449–1524), most often referred to by the epithet Künpang Doringpa (Kun spangs Rdo ring pa), was the most important disciple of Dakchen Dorjé Chang (Bdag chen rdo rje 'chang Blo gros rgyal mtshan, 1444–95), and became the main teacher of Tsarchen Losel Gyatso (Tshar chen Blo gsal rgya mtsho, 1502–66).

352 The author's main teacher, Tsarchen Losel Gyatso.

353 Dakchen Dorjé Chang Lodrö Gyaltsen.

354 *Hevajra Tantra.* Toh 418, Kangyur, rgyud 'bum *nga,* 27a7. Assuming that the reader would have this quote from the tantra memorized, the text only gives the first and last lines. The entire passage has been provided in the translation.

355 *Hevajra Tantra.* Toh 418, Kangyur, rgyud 'bum *nga,* 27b1.

356 This criticism is particularly directed at the Dzongpa (Rdzong pa) tradition of the Path with the Result.

357 *Hevajra Tantra.* Toh 417, Kangyur, rgyud 'bum *nga,* 12b5.

358 Virūpa, *Vajra Lines.* Toh 2284, Tengyur, rgyud *zhi,* 139b1.

359 Sachen Künga Nyingpo, *Versified Summary of Everything,* 95a.

360 See Jetsün Drakpa Gyaltsen, *Clear Reply to a Request.*

361 Ngorchen Künga Sangpo (Ngor chen Kun dga' bzang po, 1382–1456).

362 Toh 113, Kangyur, mdo sde *ja,* 181b2. The line in the sutra is different from that in the quote.

363 Toh 101, Kangyur, mdo sde *nga,* 94a2.

364 The *Sutra of the White Lotus of the Excellent Doctrine.* Toh 113, Kangyur, mdo sde *ja,* 181b3. Khedrup Delek PalSang (Mkhas grub Dge legs dpal bzang, 1385–1438) was one of the greatest disciples and Dharma heirs of Tsongkhapa Losang Drakpa (Tsong kha pa Blo bzang grags pa, 1357–1438).

365 The *Sutra of the White Lotus of the Excellent Doctrine.* Toh 113, Kangyur, mdo sde *ja,* 181b3.

366 Müchen Könchok Gyaltsen (Mus chen Dkon mchog rgyal mtshan, 1388–1469).

367 Khyenrap Chöjé (Mkhyen rab Chos rje Rin chen mchog grub, 1436–97).

368 Phakmodrupa (Phag mo gru pa Rdo rje rgyal po, 1110–70). For information about Phakmodrupa and his works concerning the Path with the Result, see Stearns (2001), 26–32.

369 Dakpo Lhajé (Dwags po Lha rje) is an epithet of the great Kagyü master Gampopa Sönam Rinchen (Sgam po pa Bsod nams rin chen, 1079–1153).

370 Sakya Paṇḍita Künga Gyaltsen, *Distinguishing the Three Vows,* 41b1. Only the first line of these verses from Sakya Paṇḍita's famous work is given in the text. The full set of verses has been included in the translation. Also see Sakya Pandita Kunga Gyaltshen (2002), 162.

371 For a study of Chegompa (Lce sgom pa), see Sørensen (1999). Gyaltsa Talphukpa (Rgyal tsha tal phug pa Rin chen mgon, 1118–95) founded the Trophu Kagyü (Khro phu Bka' brgyud) tradition.

372 For a study of the life and spiritual songs of Kodrakpa (Ko brag pa Bsod nams rgyal mtshan, 1170–1249), see Stearns (2000). For a study of the life and Tibetan legacy of Paṇḍita Vibhūticandra, see Stearns (1996).

373 Lord of Yogins is an epithet of Virūpa.

374 Chagen's personal name was Wangchuk Gyaltsen (Dbang phyug rgyal mtshan). Other sources agree that Chagen received the Shama tradition of the Path with the Result from Lady Machik Nyitri (Ma gcig Nyi khri), but usually say that he received the Sakya tradition from the omniscient Phurangpa Sangyé Drak (Kun mkhyen Phu hrangs pa Sangs rgyas grags), who was a disciple of Sakya Paṇḍita. For example, see Ngorchen Künga Sangpo and Gungruwa Sherap Sangpo, *History of the Esoteric Instructions of the Path with the Result,* 235a. Chagen was also a disciple of Chögyal Phakpa (Chos rgyal 'Phags pa Blo gros rgyal mtshan, 1235–80).

375 Künpang Drakgyal is also known by the epithet Peerless Master (Bla ma Mnyam med pa). Tai Situ Jangyal (Ta Si Byang rgyal) is Tai Situ Jangchup Gyaltsen (Ta'i Si tu Byang chub rgyal mtshan, 1302–1364), who became the supreme political ruler of Tibet. For information on both these figures, see van der Kuijp (1994).

376 Jonang Künpang Chenpo (Jo nang Kun spangs chen po) is an epithet of Thukjé Tsöndru (Thugs rje brtson 'grus, 1243–1313), also known as Küntu Sangpo (Kun tu bzang po) and Mikyö Dorjé (Mi bskyod rdo rje). He founded the monastery of Jonang.

377 Sé Kharchungwa (Se Mkhar chung ba) is an epithet of Setön Künrik (Se ston Kun rig, 1025–1122), the most important disciple of Drokmi Lotsāwa, whose story was told previously.

378 Individual withdrawal *(sor sdud)* is the first branch of the six-branch yoga of the Kālacakra completion-stage practices. Also see Ngorchen Künga Sangpo and Gungruwa Sherap Sangpo, *History of the Esoteric Instructions of the Path with the Result,* 235b–236b, for quotes from the work of Latö Wangyal (La stod Dbang rgyal) in which he emphasizes *seven necessary points* and *seven unnecessary points.* The Chinese *hoshang* Mahāyāna (*hva shang* Mā ha yā na) debated the Indian master Kamalaśīla at Samyé Monastery in Tibet toward the end of the eighth century. The Chinese master advocated the instantaneous approach to realization, while the Indian teacher taught the gradual approach. According to Tibetan sources, Kamalaśīla was victorious.

379 See notes 344 and 345.

380 Lochen Jangtsé is Lochen Jangchup Tsemo (Lo chen Byang chub rtse mo, 1302–80).

381 Woven into these verses is the name Jampa (love) Künga (to delight all) Tenpai (of the doctrine) Gyaltsen (victory banner). Jampa Künga Tenpai Gyaltsen (Byams pa Kun dga' bstan pa'i rgyal mtshan, 1829–70) was the fifty-fourth abbot of Ngor Monastery and the teacher of the coauthor of this text, Jamyang Loter Wangpo ('Jam dbyangs blo gter dbang po, 1847–1914). See also Jackson (1989), 83.

382 This is the most famous image of Mahākāla Pañjaranātha at Sakya, which had been given to Sachen by his teacher Mal Lotsāwa (Mal Lo tsā ba Blo gros grags pa). For details, see Vitali (2001).

383 Jamyang Chenpo Namkha Gyaltsen ('Jam dbyangs chen po Nam mkha' rgyal mtshan, 1398–1472).

384 Jamyang Könchok Sangpo ('Jam dbyangs dkon mchog bzang po, 1398–1475) was the disciple of the great adept Künga Lodrö (Grub chen Kun dga' blo gros, 1365–1443).

385 Dakchen Künga Wangchuk (Bdag chen Kun dga' dbang phyug, 1418–62), of the Khön family at Sakya.

386 The important Sakya monastery of Nālendra (Nā lendra) was founded by Rongtön Sheja Künrik (Rong ston Shes bya kun rig, 1367–1449) in 1437.

387 With the exception of the text for bestowing the path initiation, these works are found in volume 18, *tsha,* of the *Sa-skya Lam-'bras Literature Series.*

388 Doringpa (Rdo ring pa) is the epithet of Künsang Chökyi Nyima (Kun bzang chos kyi nyi ma, 1449–1524).

389 The goddess Kurukullā (Rig byed ma) is one of the Thirteen Golden Dharmas (Gser chos bcu gsum) of the Sakya tradition listed in the following note.

390 The Thirteen Golden Dharmas (Gser chos bcu gsum) of the Sakya tradition are Nāro Khecarī (Nā ro Mkha' spyod ma), Indra Khecarī (Indra Mkha' spyod ma), and Maitrī Khecarī (Maitrī Mkha' spyod ma), who are known as the Khecarī Trilogy (Mkha' spyod skor gsum); Kurukullā (Ku ru ku lle), Gaṇapati (Tshogs bdag), and Ṭakkirāja ('Dod rgyal), who are known as the Greater Red Trilogy (Dmar chen skor gsum); Kurukullā with a Golden Heartdrop (Ku ru ku lle gser gyi snying thig can), Red Norgyunma (Nor rgyun ma dmar mo), and the goddess Tinuma (Lha mo Ti nu ma), who are known as the Lesser Red Trilogy (Dmar chung skor gsum); and Chimé Dorjé Lhamo ('Chi med rdo rje lha mo), Red Jambhala (Dzam dmar), Siṃhamukha (Seng gdong ma), and Black Mañjuśrī ('Jam dpal nag po). Multicolored Garuda (Khyung khra) is sometimes included in the list instead of one of the other deities. The large and small Dharma protectors are Pañjaranātha and Caturmukha.

391 The *aṣṭā* is the root mantra *(rtsa sngags)* of Hevajra.

392 Gorumpa (Sgo rum pa) is the epithet of Gorum Künga Lekpa (Sgo rum Kun dga' legs pa, 1477–1544).

393 Marpa of Lhodrak (Mar pa Lho brag pa) is the famous Kagyü master Marpa Lotsāwa Chökyi Lodrö (Mar pa Lo tsā ba Chos kyi blo gros, 1000?–1081?).

394 The Sakya throne-holder Salo Jamyang Künga Sönam (Sa lo 'Jam dbyangs kun dga' bsod nams, 1485–1533), and Könchok Tsultrim (Kun mchog tshul khrims, 1445–1517), the abbot of Shalu Monastery.

395 "Fire-dragon" (*me 'brug,* 1556) has been corrected in the translation to "wood-dragon" (*shing 'brug,* 1544).

396 Gendün Gyatso (Dge 'dun rgya mtsho, 1475–1542) was the second Dalai Lama.

397 The great Gelukpa monastery of Tashi Lhunpo (Bkra shis lhun po) was founded in 1447 by the first Dalai Lama, Gendün Drup (Dge 'dun grub, 1391–1474).

398 In this context, the Dharma cycle of Khecarī refers to the practices of Vajrayoginī in the Sakya tradition. The main practice is Nāro Khecarī (Nā ro Mkha' spyod ma), but the practices of Indra Khecarī (Indra Mkha' spyod ma) and Maitrī Khecarī (Mai trī Mkha' spyod ma) are also used. These are three of the Thirteen Golden Dharmas of Sakya.

399 Tsarchen's *Sunbeams (Nyi ma'i 'od zer)* is the definitive commentary on the creation stage of Hevajra according to the tradition of the Explication for Disciples. It is found in volume 10, *tha,* of the *Sa-skya Lam-'bras Literature Series.* The *Rosary of Jewels (Nor bu'i phreng ba),* Tsarchen's explanation of the Hevajra initiation, supplementing the earlier work of Lopön Sönam Tsemo (Slob dpon Bsod nams rtse mo, 1142–82) entitled *Stream of Initiation (Dbang chu),* is found in volume 18, *tsha,* of the *Sa-skya Lam-'bras Literature Series.*

400 These are short names for the long mantras of Hevajra, Khecarī, Vajrabhairava, and Mahākāla.

401 Dakchen Ngakgi Wangpo (Bdag chen Ngag gi dbang po) is probably the Sakya master of the Khön family, Dakchen Ngakgi Wangchuk (Bdag chen Ngag gi dbang phyug, d. 1544).

402 Palpuk (Dpal spug) was the hermitage of Butön Rinchen Drup (Bu ston Rin chen grub, 1290–1364) at Shalu Monastery.

403 The following annotation appears in the Tibetan text: "Although earth-rabbit (1579) appears in the autobiography of Drupa, earth-dragon (1568) appears in the writings of Wangrap, Yapjé, and the Fifth Dalai Lama, who are in agreement." Drupa ('Bru pa) is Ngakchang Sönam Chöphel (Sngags 'chang Bsod nams chos 'phel, 1527–1603), Wangrap (Dbang rab) is Wangchuk Rapten (Dbang phyug rab brtan, 1558–1636), Yapjé (Yab rje) is the Sakya throne-holder Yapjé Künga Lodrö (Yab rje Kun dga' blo gros, 1729–83), and the Fifth Dalai Lama is Ngawang Losang Gyatso (Ngag dbang blo bzang rgya mtsho, 1617–82).

404 Künga Drolchok (Kun dga' grol mchog, 1507–66) was a great nonsectarian master who specialized in the teachings of the Jonang, Sakya, and Shangpa Kagyü traditions. At that time, he was the head of the Jonang tradition.

405 These are two of the experiences of clear light.

406 Ludrup Gyatso's works are found in volume 15, *ba,* of the *Sa-skya Lam-'bras Literature Series.*

407 Paṇchen Ngawang Chödrak (Paṇ chen Ngag dbang chos grags, 1572–1641).

408 The following annotation appears in the Tibetan text: "Yapjé Dorjé Chang said that Ludrup Gyatso passed away when he was seventy-one, in a water-snake year (1593), but since it is clear from the autobiography that he was still living up to the fifth month of a wood-horse year (1594), when he was seventy-two, a definitive year for his passing has not been determined." It is now known that Mangthö Ludrup Gyatso died in 1596. Yapjé Dorjé Chang is the Sakya throne-holder Yapjé Künga Lodrö (Yab rje Kun dga' blo gros, 1729–83).

409 Bökharwa (Bod mkhar ba) is the epithet of Maitri Döndrup Gyaltsen (Mai tri Don grub rgyal mtshan, 1527–87).

410 By visualizing the Sangha members on the crown of his head Bökharwa honored them as superior to himself.

411 According to Chogyé Trichen Rinpoché, Dong Nyenchen (Gdong brnyan can) is an epithet of the Dharma protector Caturmukha.

412 *Head of state (sde srid)* is a very high political title, but it is uncertain which specific ruler is indicated here. One would guess the Desi of Tsang (Gtsang Sde srid).

413 Buffalo-faced Mighty Enemy of Time (Dus dgra'i dbang po ma he'i zhal) is an epithet of the deity Vajrabhairava.

414 The following annotation appears in the Tibetan text: "In the supplement to the autobiography it is explained as an earth-rabbit year (1639), but this appears to be a textual error in which the years do not match. This statement by Yapjé Dorjé Chang that it was a water-rabbit year (1603) is flawless."

415 The term Khaupa (Kha'u pa) is a short form of Khau Drakzongpa (Kha'u brag rdzong pa), a name used to designate the Tsarpa (Tshar pa) tradition of the Explication for Disciples (Slob bshad). This term is used because the ancient hermitage of Khau Drakzong near Sakya was the residence of Künpang Doringpa (Kun spangs Rdo ring pa, 1449–1524), who was the main disciple of Dakchen Dorjé Chang and the chief teacher of Tsarchen.

416 Dingmawa Lapsum Gyaltsen (Sding ma ba Bslab gsum rgyal mtshan, 1526–77).

417 There are several different explanations of the seven branches of union *(kha sbyor yan lag bdun)*. According to one list, the seven are nonsubstantiality, union with awareness in the form of the consort, supreme bliss, the sambhogakāya enjoyment body, no cessation of the experience, total compassion, and no interruption of the experience. Cf. Dorje and Kapstein (1991), 153–54.

418 The great Ngakchang of Dru ('Bru'i sngags 'chang) is Ngakchang Sönam Chöphel (Sngags 'chang Bsod nams chos 'phel, 1527–1603).

419 Paṇchen Ngawang Chödrak's texts on the Path with the Result are found in volume 25, *ra,* of the *Sa-skya Lam-'bras Literature Series.* His commentary on the *Hevajra Tantra* is found in volume 10, *tha.*

420 The *aṣṭā* is the root mantra of Hevajra.

421 Paṇchen Ngawang Chödrak did later teach the Path with the Result to the Sakya throne-holder Jamgön Ameshap Ngawang Künga Sönam ('Jam mgon A mes zhabs Ngag dbang kun dga' bsod nams, 1597–1659).

422 Lapsumpa (Bslab gsum pa) is Dingmawa Lapsum Gyaltsen (Sding ma ba Bslab gsum rgyal mtshan, 1526–77).

423 The Three Venerable Lords in White (Rje btsun dkar po rnam gsum) are Sachen Künga Nyingpo and his sons Sönam Tsemo and Drakpa Gyaltsen. They wore white robes because they were laymen.

424 Kangyurwa (Bka' 'gyur ba) is the epithet of the master Sönam Chokden (Bsod nams mchog ldan, 1603–59).

425 Shalu Khenchen (Zha lu mkhan chen), Great Abbot of Shalu, is an epithet of Rinchen Sönam Chokdrup (Rin chen bsod nams mchog grub, 1602–81). The incorrect reading of water-horse (*chu rta,* 1582) has been corrected to water-tiger (*chu stag,* 1602) in the translation, in accordance with the date in Shalu Khenchen's long biography.

426 The Gongkar (Gong dkar) tradition is a branch of the Dzongpa (Rdzong pa) lineage transmitted through Dzongpa Künga Namgyal (Rdzong pa Kun dga' rnam rgyal, 1432–96), who founded the monastery of Gongkar Dorjeden (Gong dkar rdo rje gdan) in 1469.

427 The *devapicu* is the heart mantra *(snying po'i bsngags)* of Hevajra.

428 The date has been corrected in the translation from "iron-bird" *(lcags bya)* to "iron-mouse" *(lcags byi)*.

429 The Fifth Dalai Lama's name was Ngawang Losang Gyatso (Ngag dbang blo bzang rgya mtsho, 1617–82).

430 The Dalai Lama's work is translated in the present volume.

431 See note 399.

432 Surchen (Zur chen) is Sur Chöying Rangdrol (Zur Chos dbyings rang grol, 1610–57).

433 The trilogy of red deities (Dmar po skor gsum) is an important group of three deities practiced in the Sakya tradition. The three are Kurukullā (Ku ru ku lle, Rig byed ma), Gaṇapati (Tshogs bdag), and Ṭakkirāja ('Dod rgyal). These deities are three of the Thirteen Golden Dharmas of Sakya. The eastern emperor is the Emperor of China.

434 Tenzin Sangpo was a master of Nālendra who was also from the noble Che lineage of Shalu.

435 The texts of the *Blue Volume (Pod sngon)*, the special Nālendra teachings of the Path with the Result, are found in volume 31, *e waṃ*, of the *Sa-skya Lam-'bras Literature Series*.

436 Rongtön Sheja Künrik (1367–1449), Thekchen Chöjé Künga Tashi (1349–1425), Ngorchen Künga Sangpo (1382–1456), Müchen Könchok Gyaltsen (1388–1469), and Khyenrap Chöjé Rinchen Chokdrup (1436–97).

437 See note 63 for the meaning of *purifying the places (gnas sbyong)*.

438 Lord Ön Rinpoché (Rje Dbon Rin po che) is Lord Ön Ngawang Tenzin Lhundrup (Rje dbon Ngag dbang bstan 'dzin lhun grub).

439 Khyapdak Shalupa (Khyab bdag Zha lu pa) is an epithet of Shalu Khenchen (Zha lu mkhan chen), the Great Abbot of Shalu, Rinchen Sönam Chokdrup (Rin chen bsod nams mchog grub, 1602–81).

440 Morchen Dorjé Chang (Rmor chen Rdo rje 'chang) is the epithet of Morchen Künga Lhundrup (Rmor chen Kun dga' lhun grub, 1654–1728). Rongtön Sheja Künrik (1367–1449). See note 435 for the *Blue Volume*.

441 Shuché Ngödrup (Zhu byas Dngos grub) was one of Sachen's main disciples and the requestor of one of the eleven commentaries on the *Vajra Lines*. Sangtsa Sönam Gyaltsen (Zangs tsha Bsod nams rgyal mtshan, 1184–1239) was the younger brother of Sakya Paṇḍita and the father of Chögyal Phakpa.

442 *Vajra Rosary (Vajrāvalī, Rdo rje pheng ba)*, Toh 3140, Tengyur, rgyud *phu*. This is a collection of tantric initiations and practices compiled by the Indian master Abhayākaragupta. The mandalas for purification are the Sarvavid (Kun rig) mandalas.

443 The Sakya throne-holder Jamgön Ameshap ('Jam mgon A mes zhabs Ngag dbang kun dga' bsod nams, 1597–1659).

444 The ritual permission of the ten wrathful deities *(khro bo bcu)* is a special initiation of Pañjaranātha Mahākāla. The guidance of the six transmissions of the *Perfection*

of Wisdom (Sher phyin bka' babs drug gi khrid) is an instruction text written by Rongtön Sheja Künrik (1367–1449). The phrase *upper actions (stod las)* refers to the two-day great initiation of Vajrakīla. The initiation of the *lower actions (smad las)* is sometimes given on a third day. See note 273 for the *One Hundred Methods for Accomplishment (Sgrub thabs brgya rtsa).*

445 The Dakchen (Bdag chen) at Sakya was the throne-holder Jamyang Sönam Wangchuk ('Jam dbyangs bsod nams dbang phyug, 1638–85), and his son was the throne-holder Ngawang Künga Tashi (Ngag dbang kun dga' bkra shis, 1656–1711).

446 Khyapdak Nesarwa (Khyab bdag Gnas gsar ba) is the epithet of Künga Lekpai Jungné (Kun dga' legs pa'i 'byung gnas, 1704–60).

447 Damchen Dorjé Lekpa (Dam can Rdo rje legs pa) is one of the main Dharma protectors of the Nyingma tradition.

448 Nāro Khecarī is the special form of Vajrayoginī transmitted from the great Indian master Nāropa. The three white deities *(dkar po lha gsum)* are White Amitāyus (Tshe dpag med dkar po), White Tārā in the form known as the Wish-fulfilling Wheel (Sgrol dkar Yid bzhin 'khor lo), and White Sarasvatī (Dbyangs can ma dkar mo). The Rock Fortress (Brag rdzong ma) is a special teaching of Pañjaranātha. See note 390 for the Thirteen Golden Dharmas. The large and small protectors are Pañjaranātha and Caturmukha.

449 Yapjé Dorjé Chang is the Sakya throne-holder Yapjé Künga Lodrö (Yab rje Kun dga' blo gros, 1729–83).

450 The Khön ('Khon) family line of Sakya is known by three special names: divine family line *(lha rigs),* Khön hereditary line *('khon gdung),* and Sakyapa *(sa skya pa).*

451 According to Chogyé Trichen Rinpoché, the protector of Nyen (Gnyan mgon) is Caturmukha. The teachings of Caturmukha were brought to Tibet by Nyen Lotsāwa Darma Trak (Gnyan Lo tsā ba Dar ma grags).

452 The Lord of Yogins, Virūpa, was able to control the sun, and Künga Lodrö was practicing the Virūpa Protection (Bir srung) according to the teachings of the Path with the Result. It is traditionally believed that solar eclipses are caused when the sun is devoured by the celestial demon Rāhu.

453 According to Jackson (1989), 82, Jampa Namkha Chimé (Byams pa nam mkha' 'chi med) was born in 1765.

454 There were four palaces *(bla brang)* at the monastery of Ngor Ewaṃ Chöden, with the names Khangsar (Khang gsar), Phendé (Phan bde) or Phenkhang (Phan khang), Thartsé (Thar rtse), and Luding (Klu sdings).

455 One of the requirements to become Ngor abbot was to pass four minor examinations *(rgyugs chung bzhi)* on four small tantric texts *(rgyud chung bzhi)* of the tradition: the *Hevajra Tantra,* Ngorchen Könchok Lhundrup's (Ngor chen Dkon mchog lhun grub, 1497–1557) *Ornament to Beautify the Jeweled Tree* (*Ljon shing mdzes rgyan,* which is an explanation of Jetsün Drakpa Gyaltsen's *Jeweled Tree for Direct Realization*) and his *Ornament to Beautify the Three Means* (*Tshul gsum mdzes rgyan,* which is an explanation of Lopön Sönam Tsemo's *Classification of the Tantras in General*), and Sakya Paṇḍita's *Distinguishing the Three Vows.* See Jackson (1989), 50. The seven treatises necessary for all *(kun tu dgos pa'i gzhung bdun)* are: (1) Sachen's *Fragments of the Tantras (Rgyud sde'i dum bu),* (2) Sönam Tsemo's *Classification of the Tantras in General,* (3) Drakpa Gyaltsen's *Jeweled Tree for Direct Realization,* (4) Drakpa Gyaltsen's *Summarizing Outline (Stong thun),* (5) Drakpa

Gyaltsen's *Eulogy to the Father Hevajra in Daṇḍaka Metre (Yab kyi bstod pa daṇḍa ka),* (6) Drakpa Gyaltsen's *Immaculate Ornament: Eulogy to the Mother Nairātmyā (Yum gyi bstod pa dri ma med pa'i rgyan),* and (7) Sakya Paṇḍita's *Commentary on the Eulogy to Nairātmyā (Bdag med bstod pa'i rnam 'grel).* These seven works are enumerated by their short titles in a verse by Drakpa Gyaltsen quoted by Tsangjampa Dorjé Gyaltsen (Gtsang byams pa Rdo rje rgyal mtshan, 1424–98). See Tsangjampa Dorjé Gyaltsen, *River of Explication,* 3a.

456 Ngawang Chökyong Sangpo (Ngag dbang chos skyong bzang po, b. 1723) was the fortieth abbot of Ngor Monastery. See Jackson (1989), 82.

457 Jamgön Ngawang Künga Lodrö ('Jam mgon Ngag dbang kun dga' blo gros) is the Sakya throne-holder Yapjé Künga Lodrö (Yab rje Kun dga' blo gros, 1729–83).

458 Padmakāra is one of the names of Guru Padmasambhava.

459 The throne of Ngorchen Dorjé Chang Künga Sangpo at Ngor Monastery.

460 Sawang Lachen (Sa dbang Bla chen) was the king of Dergé (Sde dge), often known as Dergé Yapchen (Sde dge Yab chen), who later took ordination and became a respected scholar. Also see Smith (2001), 24–25. Sawang Lachen is the Dharma king mentioned in the next paragraph.

461 According to Jackson (1989), 82, Jampa Namkha Chimé died in 1820.

462 See note 455 concerning the seven treatises necessary for all.

463 See note 460.

464 The Omniscient Khyentsé Wangpo was the famed nonsectarian master Jamyang Khyentsé Wangpo ('Jam dbyangs mKhyen brtse'i dbang po, 1820–92). Sawang Lachen (Sa dbang Bla chen) was the king of Dergé. Künga Palden (Kun dga' dpal ldan) was the author of the earlier portions of the present text.

465 See note 455 concerning the seven treatises necessary for all.

466 That is, lay, novice, and complete ordination.

467 The Jowo Kadampa (Jo bo Bka' gdams pa) is the Kadampa tradition established by Dromtön Gyalwai Jungné ('Brom ston Rgyal ba'i 'byung gnas, 1005–64) based upon the teachings of the Indian master Jowo Atiśa (Jo bo A ti sha, 982–1055).

468 The vow of individual liberation, the bodhisattva vow, and the Vajrayana vows and sacred commitments.

469 The eighteen famous treatises *(grags chen bco brgyad)* are sometimes divided into six groups, as follows. Six Treatises on the Perfections: (1) *Abhisamayālaṃkāra (Mngon rtogs rgyan),* (2) *Mahāyānasūtrālaṃkāra (Mdo sde rgyan),* (3) *Madhyāntavibhāga (Dbus mtha' rnam 'byed),* (4) *Dharmadharmatāvibhāga (Chos dang chos nyid rnam 'byed),* (5) *Ratnagotravibhāṅga (Rgyud bla ma),* (6) *Bodhisattvacaryāvatāra (Byang chub sems dpa'i spyod pa la 'jug pa).* Two Vinaya Scriptures: (7) *Pratimokṣasūtra (So so thar pa'i mdo),* (8) *Vinayamūlasūtra ('Dul ba mdo rtsa).* Three Madhyamaka Treatises: (9) *Mūlamadhyamakakārika (Dbu ma rtsa ba shes rab),* (10) *Catuḥśataka (Dbu ma bzhi brgya pa),* (11) *Madhyamakāvatāra (Dbu ma la 'jug pa).* Two Abhidharma Treatises: (12) *Abhidharmasamuccaya (Mngon pa kun btus),* (13) *Abhidharmakośa (Mngon pa mdzod).* Four Treatises on Epistemology: (14) *Pramāṇasamuccaya (Tshad ma kun btus),* (15) *Pramāṇavārttika (Tshad ma rnam 'grel),* (16) *Pramāṇaviniścaya (Tshad ma rnam nges),* (17) Sakya Paṇḍita's *Treasury of Epistemology (Tshad ma rigs gter).* One Treatise on the Three Vows: (18) Sakya Paṇḍita's *Distinguishing the Three Vows (Sdom gsum rab dbye).* For a slightly different list, see Jackson (1987), vol. 1: 158.

470 The *One Hundred Systems of Guidance (Khrid brgya)* is an important collection of guidance manuals compiled by Jonang Künga Drolchok (Jo nang Kun dga' grol mchog, 1507–66). It has been published in volume 12 of the *Gdams ngag mdzod,* Delhi: N. Lungtok and N. Gyaltsan, 1972. The "eight great systems of guidance in our own tradition" *(rang lugs khrid chen brgyad)* are unidentified. The Stages of the Path *(lam rim)* and Mind Training *(blo sbyong)* are two fundamental Mahayana teachings most commonly taught according to the Kadampa and Gelukpa traditions. The seven mandalas of Ngor *(ngor dkyil bdun)* are three traditions of Hevajra, two of Cakrasaṃvara, and two of Guhyasamāja. The *Ocean of Methods for Accomplishment (Sgrub thabs rgya mtsho)* is a collection passed down through the Indian master Abhayākaragupta.

471 Jampaiyang Ngawang Sönam Gyaltsen ('Jam pa'i dbyangs ngag dbang bsod nams rgyal mtshan, ca. 1830s–90s) was the fifty-fifth abbot of Ngor Monastery. Jamyang Sherap Gyatso ('Jam dbyangs shes rab rgya mtsho, d. 1873?) was the fifty-sixth abbot of Ngor. Palden Lodrö Gyaltsen (Dpal ldan blo gros rgyal mtshan, 1840–1900) was the fifty-seventh abbot of Ngor. Jamyang Rinchen Dorjé ('Jam dbyangs rin chen rdo rje, 1837–1901) was the fifty-eighth abbot of Ngor. See Jackson (1989), 83. The author of this section of the text is Jamyang Loter Wangpo ('Jam dbyangs blo gter dbang po, 1847–1914).

472 Künga Palden's title of *eastern Dharma lord (shar chos rje)* refers to his position at the great monastery of Dergé, where there was an *eastern master (shar bla ma)* and a *western master (nub bla ma).* See Jackson (2003), 595–96 n. 225. The translation follows the spelling *shar chos rje* in the Dergé edition, not the *sham chos rje* in the Dehra Dun and critical editions.

473 The name Losel Gyatso (Blo gsal rgya mtsho), which is the name of Tsarchen, the author's teacher, is woven into the first three lines of verse: intellect *(blo gros),* clear *(gsal),* and ocean *(rgya mtsho).*

474 The term *threefold greatness (che ba gsum)* is used to describe the final result. As explained later in the text: "The result is threefold greatness: the greatness of benefit for oneself, which is being endowed with the four bodies of enlightenment and the five types of primordial awareness, the greatness of benefit for others, which is enabling the blind to regain sight and so forth, and the greatness for both oneself and others, which is buddhahood together with one's circle in a single group."

475 The translation is made with the assumption that the phrase "path with the cause" *(lam rgyu dang bcas pa)* should be placed after the phrase "by implication" *(shugs kyis),* and not before it as in the Tibetan text.

476 Sakya Paṇḍita Künga Gyaltsen, *Clarification of the Meaning Through Symbols,* 105b4.

477 *Hevajra Tantra.* Toh 418, Kangyur, rgyud 'bum *nga,* 22a3. This is a famous quote that most people reading this text would have memorized. Only the first two lines are actually given in the text. The third line has been included in the translation because it is part of the following explanation.

478 Gyaltsap Dampa Künga Wangchuk (Rgyal tshab dam pa Kun dga' dbang phyug, 1424–78) was the nephew of Ngor chen Kun dga' bzang po (1382–1457) and served as the fourth abbot of Ngor monastery. His text entitled *Great Proclamation*

(Khyab mo che) does not seem to have survived. I am grateful to Chogyé Trichen Rinpoché for this identification.

479 The text mistakenly reads *Identification of the esoteric instructions that are explained ('chad byed kyi man ngag ngos gzung ba la)*. This has been replaced in the translation with the correct subject heading given in the original outline: *The description—how the "path with the result" is presented in the treatise (rjod byed gzhung gis bstan tshul gyis lam 'bras bu dang bcas pa)*. The other topic comes later, but with different wording.

480 King Indrabhūti of Oḍḍiyāna is said to have received various teachings of the tantras from Buddha Śākyamuni himself, and to have reached complete enlightenment during the initiation of Guhyasamāja bestowed by the Buddha.

481 Sachen's *Explication of the Treatise for Nyak* explains the four modes of protection *(bsrung tshul rnam pa bzhi)*: "All of [the sacred commitments] perfectly arising in one's mindstream protects them from damage, subsequent mindfulness of their number protects them from damage, the arising of an experience protects them from damage, and exceptional devotion to an excellent master protects them from damage."

482 Sachen Künga Nyingpo, *Versified Summary of Everything*, 95a4.

483 Virūpa, *Vajra Lines*. Toh 2284, Tengyur, rgyud *zhi*, 139b3.

484 Jetsün Drakpa Gyaltsen, *Root Text on the View of the Indivisibility of Samsara and Nirvana*, 97a5.

485 Puṇḍarīka, *Immaculate Light (Vimalaprabhā, Dri med 'od)*. Toh 845, dus 'khor 'grel bshad (in the Kangyur) *shrī*, 32a1.

486 Because they studied with the great adept Virūpa himself, the author of the treatise of the *Vajra Lines*.

487 *Sampuṭa Tantra*. Toh 381, Kangyur, rgyud 'bum *ga*, 104a2. The first line is found in the tantra, although in a somewhat different form, but the last line is not.

488 Toh 381, Kangyur, rgyud 'bum *ga*, 104a1.

489 Sachen Künga Nyingpo, *Versified Summary of Everything*, 95a3. The information in the note to the critical edition of the Tibetan text is incorrect.

490 In the *Explication of the Treatise for Nyak*, Sachen Künga Nyingpo lists the five sets of three *(lnga gsum bco lnga)*, also known as the fifteen experiences *(nyams bco lnga)*: "(1) The three paths—which are the path of eliminating entry, the path of severing attachment, and the path of great enlightenment; (2) the three experiences—which are the physical experiences, mental experiences, and dream experiences; (3) the three dependently arisen connections—which are the dependently arisen connections of the reversal of the vital winds, the visual appearances, and dreams; (4) the three warmths—which are the warmth preceded by thought, the warmth of the gathering of the nine essential constituents, and the warmth of the blazing and gathering of the drops; and (5) the three meditative concentrations—which are the meditative concentration of the characteristic as a variety, the meditative concentration of the nature as emptiness, and the meditative concentration of the essence as their unity."

491 Virūpa, *Vajra Lines*. Toh 2284, Tengyur, rgyud *zhi*, 139b3.

492 The Path with the Result master Yeshé Pal (Lam 'bras pa Ye shes dpal, 1281–1365).

493 Lord Müsepa (Rje Mus srad pa) is Müsepa Dorjé Gyaltsen (Mus srad pa Rdo rje rgyal mtshan, 1424–98), also known as Tsangjampa (Gtsang byams pa), who was

a great master of the Dzongpa (Rdzong pa) tradition of the Path with the Result. These sixty texts make up the *Yellow Volume,* contained in volume 11, *da,* of the *Sa-skya Lam-'bras Literature Series.*

494 Jetsün Drakpa Gyaltsen, *Catalogue of the Volume,* 3b4. The wording of this extant copy of Drakpa Gyaltsen's catalogue is quite different from the quote.

495 Shang Gönpawa commanded Sachen to keep the teachings secret for eighteen years.

496 See Sachen Künga Nyingpo, *Versified Summary of Everything.*

497 All of these texts, and those mentioned in the following paragraphs, with the exception of the seven Dharma teachings for beginners, are found in volume 11, *da,* of the *Sa-skya Lam-'bras Literature Series.*

498 All the phrases in quotation marks in this paragraph are from the *Vajra Lines* of Virūpa.

499 In this context, *path of liberation (grol lam)* refers to the practices of the higher three initiations that may involve an actual consort.

500 These seven texts are not included in the *Yellow Volume,* and are found in the collected works of Sönam Tsemo and Drakpa Gyaltsen.

501 "Precisely this scripture" means the *Hevajra Tantra.*

502 The *Little Red Volume (Pusti dmar chung)* is contained in volume 13, *pa,* of the *Sa-skya Lam-'bras Literature Series.*

503 The *Black Volume (Pod nag)* of the Sakya throne-holder Lama Dampa Sönam Gyaltsen (Bla ma dam pa Bsod nams rgyal mtshan, 1312–75) fills volume 16, *ma,* of the *Sa-skya Lam-'bras Literature Series.*

504 Most of these texts composed by Müchen Könchok Gyaltsen (Mus chen Dkon mchog rgyal mtshan, 1388–1469) and Dakchen Lodrö Gyaltsen (Bdag chen Blo gros rgyal mtshan, 1444–95) are located in volumes 13, *pa,* and 18, *tsha,* of the *Sa-skya Lam-'bras Literature Series.*

505 The relation of the different texts in the *Little Red Volume* to the four authentic qualities is noted in the catalogue to the collection written by Gyaltsap Künga Wangchuk (Rgyal tshab Kun dga' dbang phyug, 1424–78), which is found at the beginning of the volume.

506 These four texts from the *Yellow Volume* are found in volume 11, *da,* of the *Sa-skya Lam-'bras Literature Series.*

507 See Jetsün Drakpa Gyaltsen, *Guidance Manual for Jochak.*

508 *Hevajra Tantra.* Toh 418, Kangyur, rgyud 'bum *nga,* 27a7.

509 *Vajrapañjara Tantra.* Toh 419, Kangyur, rgyud 'bum *nga,* 54b6.

510 *Hevajra Tantra.* Toh 418, Kangyur, rgyud 'bum *nga,* 27b1.

511 Jetsün Drakpa Gyaltsen's *Jeweled Tree for Direct Realization of the Tantras.*

512 The critical edition of the Tibetan text has mistakenly changed *key point (gnad)* to *initiation (dbang).*

513 The four texts from the *Yellow Volume* briefly mentioned in the following four paragraphs are found in volume 11, *da,* of the *Sa-skya Lam-'bras Literature Series.*

514 Vajraghaṇṭā, *Condensed Ritual for the Initiation of Glorious Cakrasaṃvara.* Toh 1431, Tengyur, rgyud *wa,* 219b6.

515 Vajraghaṇṭā, *Condensed Ritual for the Initiation of Glorious Cakrasaṃvara.* Toh 1431, Tengyur, rgyud *wa,* 219b6.

516 Sakya Paṇḍita, *Distinguishing the Three Vows,* 20a2. Also see Sakya Pandita Kunga Gyaltshen (2002), 101 and 297.

517 *Hevajra Tantra.* Toh 417, Kangyur, rgyud 'bum *nga,* 11b4. The wording in the tantra itself is much different.

518 See Sakya Paṇḍita Künga Gyaltsen, *Clarifying the Meaning of the Essence,* 13b–14a: "The eight that are like the faces are the rituals of accepting disciples, the propitiation, the earth ritual, the preliminary section, the drawing and the arranging of decorations, the attainment and offerings, the entry and bestowal of initiation, and the conclusion ritual."

519 The adept Yönten Pal (Grub thob Yon tan dpal, 1237–1323) and Tsokgom Rinchen Pal (Tshogs sgom Rin chen dpal, 1210–1307).

520 See note 490 for the fifteen experiences.

521 Lord Gönpawa is Shangtön Chöbar (Zhang ston Chos 'bar, 1053–1135), who prophesied to Sachen that he should practice for eighteen years before he even mentioned the existence of the Path with the Result to anyone else.

522 According to Chogyé Trichen Rinpoché, this is a traditional saying of the Sakya tradition, and probably the words of Sachen Künga Nyingpo.

523 Dharmapāla was the ordination name of Virūpa, who is believed to have later taken rebirth as Tsarchen.

524 The author's teacher, Tsarchen Losel Gyatso (1502–66).

525 The following annotation appears at this point in the Tibetan text: "If the initiation of the vajra master is not bestowed in detail during the causal initiation, the parasol and so forth are not used. If it is bestowed in detail, it is done like this during the prayers. Thus my master taught. The ritual feast is held after the completion of the key points of guidance."

526 The *Ocean of Good Qualities (Yon tan rgya mtsho ma)* is a eulogy to Drakpa Gyaltsen written by his nephew, Sakya Paṇḍita. See Sakya Paṇḍita Künga Gyaltsen, *Eulogy to the Venerable Lord Drakpa Gyaltsen.* The following annotation appears at this point in the Tibetan text: "After the mantra path begins, instead of reciting the *Heart Sutra,* the protection cakra is visualized, the *bhāyanāsa* mantra is recited, and the disciples offer the outer, inner, and secret mandalas according to the verses composed by Sakya Paṇḍita. During this period the master performs the condensed Dharma sacrificial-cake dedication of Hevajra." See Sakya Paṇḍita Künga Gyaltsen, *Three Outer, Inner, and Secret Mandalas.*

527 The term *seat (gdan)* is used in this context to mean "type" *(rigs)* or "place" *(gnas).* The three seats are the seat of the buddhas and bodhisattvas, the seat of the female embodiments of pure awareness and the goddesses, and the seat of the wrathful males and wrathful females. Sometimes the three are listed as THE buddhas, the bodhisattvas, and the wrathful beings.

528 The Sanskrit word *śabda* means "sound," which is the last of the eight requisite offerings. The following annotation appears at this point in the Tibetan text: "The disciples, chanting and performing the mudrā hand gestures."

529 The following annotation appears here in the Tibetan text: "If the building is spacious this is actually done, and if it is small it is sufficient to imagine it. Thus my master taught."

530 The complete verses are found on folio 107a of volume 13, *pa,* of the *Sa-skya Lam-'bras Literature Series.*

531 Only the beginning and final syllables of many lines are quoted here from a text on performing the thirty-seven-heap mandala offering composed by Chögyal Phakpa (Chos rgyal 'Phags pa Blo gros rgyal mtshan, 1235–80). See Chögyal Phakpa, *Esoteric Instructions for Offering a Mandala and Supplications to the Master.*

532 Toh 1802, Tengyur, rgyud *ngi,* 53b5.

533 Nāgārjuna, *Five Stages.* Toh 1802, Tengyur, rgyud *ngi,* 53b5.

534 Aśvaghoṣa, *Fifty Verses on the Master.* Toh 3721, Tengyur, rgyud *tshu,* 10b4.

535 This quote was not located in Nāgabodhi's *Jewel Rosary (Nor bu'i phreng ba),* Toh 1840, but a similar verse is found in Aśvaghoṣa's *Fifty Verses on the Master,* Toh 3721, Tengyur, rgyud *tshu,* 10b5.

536 Toh 442, Kangyur, rgyud 'bum *ca,* 110b7–111a1.

537 Toh 419, Kangyur, rgyud 'bum *nga,* 49b3.

538 Aśvaghoṣa, *Fifty Verses on the Master.* Toh 3721, Tengyur, rgyud *tshu,* 11a7.

539 Source not located.

540 Nāgārjuna, *Jewel Rosary.* Toh 4158, Tengyur, spring yig *ge,* 1b5.

541 *Correctness of the Explanation, (Vyākhyāyukti).* Toh 4061, Tengyur, sems tsam *shi,* 65b4.

542 The gods with control of other's emanations *(gzhan 'phrul dbang byed)* are one of the six classes of gods in the desire realm.

543 The *Gate for Entering the Dharma (Chos la 'jug pa'i sgo)* and the *Classification of the Tantras in General (Rgyud sde spyi'i rnam gzhag)* are contained in volume 2 of *The Complete Works of the Great Masters of the Sa skya Sect of Tibetan Buddhism.*

544 Sachen Künga Nyingpo, *Versified Summary of Everything,* 95a4. The information in the note to the critical edition of the Tibetan text is incorrect.

545 Toh 381, Kangyur, rgyud 'bum *ga,* 104a1. The last line is not found in the tantra.

546 These works are all found in the *Yellow Volume,* in vol. 11, *da,* of the *Sa-skya Lam-'bras Literature Series.*

547 The texts dealing with these subjects are all found in the *Yellow Volume,* in vol. 11, *da,* of the *Sa-skya Lam-'bras Literature Series.*

548 Sachen Künga Nyingpo, *Versified Summary of Everything,* 95a4. The information in the note to the critical edition of the Tibetan text is incorrect.

549 Lama Dampa Sönam Gyaltsen, *Complete Clarification of the Hidden Meaning.* Quote not located.

550 Jetsün Drakpa Gyaltsen, *Guidance Manual for Jochak,* 150a5.

551 This is an alternate title for Jetsün Drakpa Gyaltsen, *Clear Reply to a Request.*

552 Virūpa, *Vajra Lines.* Toh 2284, Tengyur, rgyud *zhi,* 139b1.

553 *Hevajra Tantra.* Toh 418, Kangyur, rgyud 'bum *nga,* 27b1.

554 See Lama Dampa Sönam Gyaltsen, *Complete Clarification of the Hidden Meaning.*

555 Dakchen Dorjé Chang (Bdag chen rdo rje 'chang) is an epithet of the Sakya throne-holder Dakchen Lodrö Gyaltsen (Bdag chen Blo gros rgyal mtshan, 1444–95). His father was the Sakya throne-holder Jamyang Namkha Gyaltsen ('Jam dbyangs Nam mkha' rgyal mtshan, 1398–1472), who had received the transmission from his own father Lachen Künga Gyaltsen (Bla chen Kun dga' rgyal mtshan, 1344–1418) and from Thekchen Chöje (Theg chen chos rje Kun dga' bkra shis, 1349–1425), who was also of the Khön ('Khon) family line. Jamyang Könchok Sangpo ('Jam dbyangs dkon mchog bzang po, 1398–1475). The great adept Künga Lodrö (Grub chen Kun dga' blo gros, 1365–1443). Nya Ön (Nya dbon Kun

dga' dpal, 1285–1379) was one of the main disciples of both Lama Dampa (Bla ma Dam pa) and the Jonang master Dolpopa Sherap Gyaltsen (Dol po pa Shes rab rgyal mtshan, 1291–1361). Yakdepa Namkha Sönam (G.yag sde pa Nam mkha' bsod nams, 1299–1378). Sempa Chenpo (Sems dpa' chen po) is an epithet of Müchen Könchok Gyaltsen (Mus chen Dkon mchog rgyal mtshan, 1388–1469).

556 See note 550.

557 Nine uncommon preliminary practices are utilized for all the yogas of the path. Briefly, these are three purifications of body, speech, and mind; three key points of body, speech, and mind; and three preliminary meditations.

558 The threefold formula for taking refuge according to the Mahayana entails taking refuge in the Buddha, Dharma, and Sangha. In the Vajrayana the fourfold refuge formula, which includes the spiritual masters or gurus, is used. The following annotation appears at this point in the Tibetan text: "The Three Appearances are explained in common with the Vehicle of the Perfections and Secret Mantra. Since they are not according to the Vehicle of the Perfections alone, it is suitable for the sources of refuge and so forth to be used in common."

559 The venerable lord Künpangpa (Rje btsun Kun spangs pa) is Künpang Doringpa (Kun spangs Rdo ring pa, 1449–1524), Tsarchen's main teacher. Anyone performing this practice now would extend the visualization of the lineage up to the present day.

560 The following annotation appears at this point in the Tibetan text: "The supporting mandala with the supported deities."

561 The phrase *heart of enlightenment (byang chub snying po)* has two meanings: the Vajrāsana at Bodhgayā in India, where every buddha is said to reach enlightenment, and the actual enlightenment of a buddha.

562 The brief instructions known as *Parting from the Four Attachments (Zhen pa bzhi bral)* were received by Sachen Künga Nyingpo directly from the bodhisattva Mañjughoṣa and have continued to be the basis for the extensive teachings on Mind Training *(blo sbyong)* in the Sakya tradition up to the present day. The lines of prayer given here are not actually part of the original teaching, but are commonly used during its practice.

563 The following annotation appears at this point in the Tibetan text: "of various colors, like the sun dawning."

564 Śāntideva, *Engaging in the Conduct of a Bodhisattva.* Toh 3871, Tengyur, dbu ma *la,* 14a3. The *Sutra of Three Heaps (Āryatriskandhakanāma mahāyanasūtra, 'Phags pa phung po gsum pa zhes bya ba theg pa chen po'i mdo).* Toh 284.

565 The following annotation appears at this point in the Tibetan text: "It is also permissible to enter into the individual key points after the refuge prayers, without doing the practice of awakening the enlightenment mind."

566 Virūpa, *Vajra Lines.* Toh 2284, Tengyur, rgyud *zhi,* 139a7.

567 Jetsün Drakpa Gyaltsen, *Instructions on Parting from the Four Attachments,* 298b2.

568 Jetsün Drakpa Gyaltsen, *Clear Reply to a Request,* 8b.

569 Śāntideva, *Engaging in the Conduct of a Bodhisattva.* Toh 3871, Tengyur, dbu ma *la,* 10b1.

570 The three poisons are desire, hatred, and ignorance.

571 The term *olfactory light (bsnam bya'i 'od)* refers to experiences in the intermediate state between lifetimes. It is explained later in this book by Jamyang Khyentsé

Wangchuk in his text on the outer creation stage: "The appearances of the five olfactory lights arise. *Olfactory* refers to the consumption of odors by the mental body in the intermediate state, meaning something like what is to be smelled by it. These are explained as being the embodiment of the five sensory objects."

572 Vasubandhu, *Verses on the Treasury of Abhidharma.* Toh 4089, Tengyur, mngon pa *ku,* 10a3.

573 A *measure (bre)* is about 1.35 pounds, and is one twentieth of a *load (khal),* which is about twenty-five to thirty pounds. See Jackson (1996), 216 nn. 477–78.

574 Vasubandhu, *Explication of the Treasury of Abhidharma.* Toh 4090, Tengyur, mngon pa *khu,* 154b3. The information in the note to the critical edition of the Tibetan text is incorrect.

575 In the translation, the spelling *mdo med* has been understood as a mistake for *don med.*

576 The Indian master Vasubandhu's *Verses on the Treasury of Abhidharma,* Toh 4089, Tengyur, mngon pa *ku,* and his brother Asaṅga's *Bhūmivastu (Sa'i dngos gzhi)* or *Yogacaryābhūmi (Rnal 'byor spyod pa'i sa),* Toh 4035, Tengyur, sems tsam *tshi.*

577 The gods of the four races of the great kings *(rgyal chen ris bzhi pa'i lha)* are one of the six types of gods in the desire realm.

578 *Sutra of One Hundred Parables on Deeds (Karmaśataka, Las brgya pa),* Toh 340. The descriptions were not located in this sutra, but similar ones are found in Nāgārjuna's *Letter to a Friend,* Toh 4182, Tengyur, spring yig *nge,* 99b4–100a1.

579 The five inexpiable acts *(mtshams med lnga)* are matricide, patricide, killing an arhat, creating a schism in the Sangha, and maliciously causing blood to flow from a buddha's body.

580 Source not located.

581 Vasubandhu, *Verses on the Treasury of Abhidharma.* Toh 4089, Tengyur, mngon pa *ku,* 9a4.

582 The following annotation appears at this point in the Tibetan text: "This is also known as 'the forest of sword leaves.'"

583 The *Compendium of Lessons* (*Śikṣāsamuccaya, Bslab pa kun las btus pa,* Toh 3939/40) is a compendium of early Mahayana teaching collected by the Indian master Śāntideva. For a complete translation, see Śāntideva (1981).

584 See Śāntideva (1981), 58–60, for the hells described in the narrative of Saṅgharakṣita.

585 The Indian master Smṛtijñāna visited Tibet in the late tenth and early eleventh centuries and translated a number of texts into Tibetan. He worked menial jobs until he learned the Tibetan language and was recognized as an Indian paṇḍita.

586 The Tibetan text seems to place Rājagṛha (Rgyal po'i khab) in the region of Vaiśālī (Yangs pa can), which does not agree with actual Indian geography.

587 Nāgārjuna, *Letter to a Friend.* Toh 4182, Tengyur, spring yig *nge,* 45a2.

588 Nāgārjuna, *Letter to a Friend.* Toh 4182, Tengyur, spring yig *nge,* 45a3.

589 Nāgārjuna, *Letter to a Friend.* Toh 4182, Tengyur, spring yig *nge,* 45a4.

590 The lists of the eight tribes of gods and demons vary. For an extremely detailed listing of these groups according to the Nyingma tradition, see Dorje and Kapstein (1991), 158–59.

591 *Lalitavistara Sutra.* Toh 95, Kangyur, mdo sde *kha,* 88a2.

592 The four summations *(sdom bzhi)* of the doctrine: all composite things are impermanent *('dus byas thams cad mi rtag pa)*, all that is tainted is suffering *(zag bcas thams cad sdug bsngal ba)*, all phenomena lack self-nature *(chos thams cad bdag med pa)*, nirvana is peace *(mya ngan las 'das pa zhi ba)*.

593 Nāgārjuna, *Letter to a Friend.* Toh 4182, Tengyur, spring yig *nge*, 45a6.

594 Source of quote not located. The information in the note to the critical edition of the Tibetan text does not apply to this quote.

595 Source of quote not located. The information in the note to the critical edition of the Tibetan text does not apply to this quote.

596 Source of quote not located. The information in the note to the critical edition of the Tibetan text does not apply to this quote.

597 Śāntideva, *Engaging in the Conduct of a Bodhisattva.* Toh 3871, Tengyur, dbu ma *la*, 8b6.

598 *Sutra of a Bouquet of Flowers (Āryakusumasañcayanāma mahāyānasūtra, 'Phags pa mdo sde me tog gi tshogs shes bya ba theg pa chen po'i mdo).* Toh 266, Kangyur, mdo sde *'a*.

599 Nāgārjuna, *Jewel Rosary.* Toh 4158, spring yig *ge*, 1b5. The wording is somewhat different.

600 Source of quote not located.

601 Nāgārjuna, *Jewel Rosary.* Toh 4158, spring yig *ge*, 1b5.

602 According to Dezhung Rinpoché, the four powers *(stobs bzhi)* are the power of the support (in other words, the visualized deity, such as Vajrasattva), the power of repudiating the sin, the power of activating the antidote, and the power of restoration.

603 Prajñāvarman, *Commentary on the Udanavarga.* Toh 4100, Tengyur, mngon pa *tu*, 72b5.

604 Virūpa, *Vajra Lines.* Toh 2284, Tengyur, rgyud *zhi*, 139a7.

605 Maitreya, *Sūtrālaṃkāra.* Toh 4020, Tengyur, sems tsam *phi*, 26b7.

606 Candrakīrti, *Entering the Madhyamaka.* Toh 3861, Tengyur, dbu ma *'a*, 214b3.

607 It is a Tibetan custom to place a soft piece of *palate butter (rkan mar)* on the palate of a newborn child for it to have something to suck.

608 Candrakīrti, *Entering the Madhyamaka.* Toh 3861, Tengyur, dbu ma *'a*, 214b2.

609 Dakchen Dorjé Chang (Bdag chen rdo rje 'chang) is an epithet of Dakchen Lodrö Gyaltsen (Bdag chen Blo gros rgyal mtshan, 1444–95).

610 Jetsün Drakpa Gyaltsen, *Guidance Manual for Jochak*, 153a3. Important differences in wording are found when this quote and the passage in the extant text are compared.

611 This sentence has been added after the time of the author, Jamyang Khyentsé Wangchuk ('Jam dbyangs mkhyen brtse'i dbang phyug, 1524–68), referred to here as Jamgön Khyentsé ('Jam mgon Mkhyen brtse). According to Chogyé Trichen Rinpoché, the term *hol kong (special section)* indicates important special instructions written out separately *(zur du bris)*. Rinpoché also specified that this entire text is the work of Khyentsé Wangchuk. Dorjé Chang Wangrap (Rdo rje 'chang Dbang rab) is Wangchuk Rapten (Dbang phyug rab brtan, 1558–1636), a disciple of both Tsarchen and Khyentsé.

612 The lord in Kyirong (Skyid grong Jo bo) is an ancient holy image of Avalokiteśvara in the town of Kyirong (Skyid grong) near the Tibetan border with Nepal.

613 Bhūripa, *Extensive Confession of Glorious Cakrasaṃvara.* Toh 1533, Tengyur, rgyud *za,* 95a4.

614 According to Chogyé Trichen Rinpoché, the *Fine Path of the Bodhisattvas (Rgyal sras lam bzang)* is an alternate title for one of Sakya Paṇḍita's most important works, *Elucidating the Intention of the Sage (Thub pa'i dgongs gsal).* This alternate title is taken from a line in the opening verses of the work. See Sakya Paṇḍita Künga Gyaltsen, *Elucidating the Intention of the Sage,* 2b. The information in the note to the critical edition of the Tibetan text is incorrect.

615 *Samādhirāja Sutra.* Toh 127, Kangyur, mdo sde *da.*

616 Sakya Paṇḍita Künga Gyaltsen, *Elucidating the Intention of the Sage,* 57b6. The wording is different in the actual text.

617 Yaśomitra, *Commentary on the Treasury of Abhidharma.* Toh 4092, Tengyur, mngon pa *gu,* 5a3.

618 Gendenpa is another name for the Gelukpa tradition.

619 Jetsün Drakpa Gyaltsen, *Instructions on Parting from the Four Attachments,* 297b2. This is the last of the four lines of *Parting from the Four Attachments (Zhen pa bzhi bral),* spoken by the bodhisattva Mañjughoṣa to Sachen Künga Nyingpo. The line quoted here reads *ensues (zhugs)* instead of *occurs (byung),* which is in the original.

620 *Sutra of Definitive Commentary on the Intention (Saṃdhinirmocana).* Toh 106, Kangyur, mdo sde *ca,* 11b4 and 21a5.

621 See note 490 for the fifteen experiences.

622 Virūpa, *Vajra Lines.* Toh 2284, Tengyur, rgyud *zhi,* 139b7.

623 The root text is the *Saṃvaraviṃśaka (Sdom pa nyi shu pa),* a twenty-verse work on the bodhisattva vows composed by the Indian master Candragomin. Drakpa Gyaltsen's commentary is the *Byang chub sems dpa'i sdom pa gsal bar ston pa shlo ka nyi shu pa'i rnam par bshad pa,* found in volume 4, *ta,* 249a–277a, of the *Complete Works of the Great Masters of the Sa skya Sect of Tibetan Buddhism.*

624 These famous verses by the Indian master Atiśa (982–1055) are referred to in the Tibetan text by a condensed name. They have been provided in full in the translation.

625 The four immeasurables *(tshad med bzhi)* are immeasurable love, compassion, joy, and equanimity.

626 See Sakya Paṇḍita Künga Gyaltsen, *Three Outer, Inner, and Secret Mandalas.*

627 Aśvaghoṣa, *Fifty Verses on the Master.* Toh 3721, Tengyur, rgyud *tshu.*

628 Venerable lord Kangyurwa (Rje btsun Bka' 'gyur ba) is an epithet of Sönam Chokden (Bsod nams mchog ldan, 1603–59). According to Chogyé Trichen Rinpoché, this final addendum describing how the supportive reading transmissions and explanations are given was written by the Fifth Dalai Lama Ngawang Losang Gyatso (Ngag dbang blo bzang rgya mtsho, 1617–82). The phrase "reading transmission of the sacred commitments" *(sa ma ya'i lung)* refers to the transmission of a commentary on the sacred commitments.

629 Tsarchen Losel Gyatso (Tshar chen Blo gsal rgya mtsho, 1502–66).

630 This third section was apparently never written by Jamyang Khyentsé Wangchuk, who passed away before completing the set of texts translated in this book. His work was later supplemented by the text of the Fifth Dalai Lama translated in this volume, in which brief explanations of the result ensuing from the practice are found.

631 See Jetsün Drakpa Gyaltsen, *Guidance Manual for Jochak,* 154a. The extant text by Drakpa Gyaltsen contains significantly different wording.

632 In addition to the southern continent of Jambudvīpa, which is the world of human beings, the other three continents around Mount Meru are Pūrvavideha in the east, Aparagodanīya in the west, and Uttarakuru in the north.

633 The three seed syllables are probably *oṃ, āḥ,* and *hūṃ,* which are the seed syllables of enlightened body, speech, and mind. Acccording to Chogyé Trichen Rinpoché, the term *nyid dwangs kyi sum dwangs* is synonymous with the term *dwangs ma'i dwangs ma,* and is translated here as "clear quintessence of the clear essences."

634 The four supporting mandalas *(rten dkyil 'khor bzhi)* are the body channels *(lus rtsa),* the channel syllables *(rtsa yi ge),* the essential constituent nectars *(khams bdud rtsi),* and the quintessential vital wind of primordial awareness *(snying po ye shes kyi rlung).*

635 Source of quote not located. The information in the note to the critical edition of the Tibetan text is incorrect. Goram Sönam Sengé (Go rams Bsod nams seng ge, 1429–89) says this quote is from the Indian master Garbharipa's *Entry into the Tantras (Rgyud la 'jug pa),* which is not found in the Tengyur. According to Chogyé Trichen Rinpoché, "cause" *(rgyu)* refers to the human body endowed with the six constituents as just explained.

636 *Hevajra Tantra.* Toh 418, Kangyur, rgyud 'bum *nga,* 29a6.

637 *Hevajra Tantra.* Toh 418, Kangyur, rgyud 'bum *nga,* 29a6.

638 A third topic with this heading is not found in the text, but these topics are basically explained in the third and final section concerning the resultant indivisibility of samsara and nirvana.

639 The sacred commitment of protection *(bsrung ba'i dam tshig)* is one of the five sacred commitments of the vase initiation. Also see the following note.

640 As explained by Sachen Künga Nyingpo in his *Explication of the Treatise for Nyak,* each of the four initiations has the five sacred commitments of meditative equipoise, subsequent conduct, food, protection, and no separation. The "remaining nineteen" are the remaining four of the vase initiation and the fifteen of the other three initiations.

641 See Jetsün Drakpa Gyaltsen, *Rejection of Confusion About the Root Infractions,* which is the fundamental text concerning the vows and sacred commitments in the Sakya tradition. Dakchen Dorjé Chang (Bdag chen rdo rje 'chang) is an epithet of the Sakya throne-holder Dakchen Lodrö Gyaltsen (Bdag chen Blo gros rgyal mtshan, 1444–95), not Ngorchen Künga Sangpo as mistakenly stated in the note to the critical edition of the Tibetan text. Lodrö Gyaltsen's *Clarification of the Intention of the* Refutation of Confusion: *A Commentary on the Sacred Commitments (Dam tshig gi rnam bshad 'grel pa 'khrul spong gi dgongs pa rab tu gsal ba),* is found in volume 20, *wa,* of the *Sa-skya Lam-'bras Literature Series.*

642 Paṇchen Shākchok is Serdok Paṇchen Shākya Chokden (Gser mdog Paṇ chen Shākya mchog ldan, 1428–1507). His work, *Total Clarification of the Sacred Commitments: A Definitive Reply to Criticisms of the* Rejection of Confusion *('Khrul spong gi brgal lan rnam par nges pa'i dam tshig rab tu gsal ba),* is found in *The Complete Works (Gsung 'bum) of Gser-mdog Paṇ-chen Shākya mchog-ldan,* vol. 23, Thimphu: Kunzang Tobgey, 1975. The most important of the Gendenpa refutations was written by Tsongkapa Losang Drakpa (Tsong kha pa Blo bzang grags pa,

1357–1419). See his *Sheaves of Attainment: An Explication of Moral Discipline in Secret Mantra (Gsang sngags kyi tshul khrims kyi rnam bshad dngos grub kyi snye ma),* in *The Collected Works (Gsung 'bum) of the Incomparable Lord Tsong-kha-pa Blo-bzang grags-pa,* vol. 1, Mongolian Lama Gurudeva: New Delhi, 1978. Jamlingpa is Jamling Paṇchen Sönam Namgyal (Byams gling Paṇ chen Bsod nams rnam rgyal, 1400–1475). His work is not available.

643 This second topic is the subject of the following text by Jamyang Khyentsé Wangchuk, entitled *Summarizing Notes on the Outer Creation Stage.*

644 The section on this third topic was apparently never written by Jamyang Khyentsé Wangchuk, who passed away before completing the set of texts translated in this book. His work was later supplemented by the text of the Fifth Dalai Lama translated in this volume, in which brief explanations of the result ensuing from the practice are found.

645 *Hevajra Tantra.* Toh 417, Kangyur, rgyud 'bum *nga,* 12b5. *Precisely that* in the first line refers to *primordial awareness.*

646 The venerable lord Künpangpa (Rje btsun Kun spangs pa) is Künpang Doringpa (Kun spangs Rdo ring pa, 1449–1524), Tsarchen's main teacher. Anyone performing this practice now would extend the visualization of the lineage up to the present day.

647 The following annotation is found at this point in the Tibetan text: "and after offering with the verses 'This pristine, pure realm,' and so forth composed by the Dharma lord Sakya Paṇḍita." See Sakya Paṇḍita Künga Gyaltsen, *Three Outer, Inner, and Secret Mandalas.*

648 The thirty-seven-heap mandala offering composed by Chögyal Phakpa (Chos rgyal 'Phags pa Blo gros rgyal mtshan, 1235–80) is referred to here by the opening words of a famous set of verses. See Chögyal Phakpa, *Esoteric Instructions for Offering a Mandala and Supplications to the Master.*

649 *Hevajra Tantra.* Toh 417, Kangyur, rgyud 'bum *nga,* 10a2.

650 Saraha, *Treasury of Dohā in a Song.* Toh 2224, Tengyur, rgyud *wi,* 74a3.

651 Tilopa, *Treasury of Dohā.* Toh 2281, Tengyur, rgyud *zhi,* 136b2. The quote is somewhat different from the Tengyur text.

652 *Hevajra Tantra.* Toh 417, Kangyur, rgyud 'bum *nga,* 10a3.

653 *Condensed Verses on the Perfection of Wisdom.* Toh 13, Kangyur, sher phyin *ka,* 12a2.

654 Toh 442, Kangyur, rgyud 'bum *ca,* 110b7–111a1.

655 Source not located.

656 Although the text says this quote is from the *Guhyasamāja Tantra,* it is found in Nāgārjuna, *Five Stages.* Toh 1802, Tengyur, rgyud *ngi,* 53b4.

657 *Five Stages.* Toh 1802, Tengyur, rgyud *ngi,* 48a3.

658 *Yoginīsañcārya.* Toh 375, Kangyur, rgyud 'bum *ga,* 34a1.

659 *Saṃvarodaya Tantra.* Toh 373, Kangyur, rgyud 'bum *kha,* 302b2.

660 Toh 381, Kangyur, rgyud 'bum *ga,* 80b4.

661 Toh 419, Kangyur, rgyud 'bum *nga,* 65a6.

662 Sakya Paṇḍita, *Uncommon Supplication to the Excellent Master,* 201a3.

663 Toh 13, Kangyur, sher phyin *ka,* 9a7.

664 Toh 13, Kangyur, sher phyin *ka,* 9a7.

665 Toh 13, Kangyur, sher phyin *ka,* 13a7.

666 No sutra by this name was located in the Kangyur.

667 Virūpa, *Vajra Lines*. Toh 2284, Tengyur, rgyud *zhi*, 142b6.

668 Vajraghaṇṭā, *Five Stages of Glorious Cakrasaṃvara*. Toh 1433, Tengyur, rgyud *wa*, 224b6.

669 Saraha, *Treasury of Dohā in a Song*. Toh 2224, Tengyur, rgyud *wi*, 71b3.

670 *Yoginīsañcārya*. Toh 375, Kangyur, rgyud 'bum *ga*, 34a1. Only the first line of this well-known quote is actually given in the Tibetan text. It is quoted in full here.

671 *Saṃvarodaya Tantra*. Toh 373, Kangyur, rgyud *kha*, 302b2. Only the first line of this is given in the Tibetan text. It is quoted in full here.

672 Source not located. Only the first line of this well-known quote is actually given in the Tibetan text.

673 Source not located. Only the first line of this well-known quote is actually given in the Tibetan text.

674 The renunciation of duality *(gnyis spangs)* refers to the advanced practice of renouncing all distinctions of duality, such as filth and cleanliness, good and bad, and so on.

675 This verse is missing in the new critical edition of the Tibetan text and in the text reproduced in Dehra Dun, but is present in the original Dergé edition.

676 Additional verses can be inserted after these lines to bring this supplication up to date.

677 At this point it is only necessary to repeat the following words: "I pray to the precious master, the essence of all the buddhas of the three times. Please bless my mindstream."

678 The *Ever Excellent (Kun bzang ma)* is a supplication to the lineage of the Path with the Result composed by Tsarchen Losel Gyatso (Tshar chen Blo gsal rgya mtsho, 1502–66). It is referred to here by its opening words, *ever excellent (kun bzang)*. See Tsarchen Losel Gyatso, *Supplication to the Masters of Three Combined Lineages of the Precious Teaching*.

679 The Tibetan text seems to be corrupt here. The phrase *dbu skra nas yas mar 'od du zhu ste* has not been included in the translation.

680 Only the first line of this well-known prayer is actually printed in the Tibetan text. It has been translated in full as written by Dezhung Rinpoché.

681 Only the first two lines of this well-known prayer are actually printed in the Tibetan text. The complete verse has been translated as written by Chogyé Trichen Rinpoché. Young Sudhana (Gzhon nu Nor bzang) was a legendary devoted disciple who is the hero of the *Gaṇḍavyūha Sūtra*.

682 Reading *snang ba'i ngo bo (essence of appearances)* as a scribal mistake for *snang ba'i dngos po (apparent things)*.

683 See Jetsün Drakpa Gyaltsen, *Commentary on the View of the Indivisibility of Samsara and Nirvana* and *Catalogue of the Volume*, and Sakya Paṇḍita Künga Gyaltsen, *Catalogue of the Guiding Instructions of the Path with the Result* and *Clarification of the Meaning Through Symbols*.

684 Jetsün Drakpa Gyaltsen, *Root Text on the View of the Indivisibility of Samsara and Nirvana*, 96a6.

685 Jetsün Drakpa Gyaltsen, *Root Text on the View of the Indivisibility of Samsara and Nirvana*, 96b1.

686 Jetsün Drakpa Gyaltsen, *Root Text on the View of the Indivisibility of Samsara and Nirvana*, 96b1.

687 The translation of this sentence is uncertain. The Dergé and Indian editions are very different.

688 Sakya Paṇḍita Künga Gyaltsen, *Elucidating the Intention of the Sage,* 57b6.

689 Jamyang Khyentsé Wangchuk makes this comment to defend the mahāmudrā teachings of the Kagyü traditions—of which he was also a master and lineage holder—against accusations from persons who might misunderstand the intent of Sakya Paṇḍita's statement.

690 Sakya Paṇḍita Künga Gyaltsen, *Distinguishing the Three Vows,* 25b4. Also see Sakya Pandita Kunga Gyaltshen (2002), 117 and 303.

691 Sakya Paṇḍita Künga Gyaltsen, *Reply to the Questions of the Yogin Truma,* 250a6.

692 Jetsün Drakpa Gyaltsen, *Root Text on the View of the Indivisibility of Samsara and Nirvana,* 96b2.

693 The *nāda* is the tiny zig-zag line rising up from the circular nasal sign above the seed syllable *hūṃ* in the heart.

694 See note 490 for the fifteen experiences.

695 The five signs are like smoke, mirage, fireflies, burning lamp flames, and a cloudless sky. The five signs of the signs *(rtags kyi rtags lnga)* are like darkness, rainbows, lightning, moonbeams, and sunbeams.

696 Jetsün Drakpa Gyaltsen, *Root Text on the View of the Indivisibility of Samsara and Nirvana,* 96b3.

697 Jamyang Khyentsé Wangchuk explained this example in the section on the identification of the Dharma to be explained: "When a piece of copper is used for a dog dish, it is an inferior thing and an object of disgust, but when the very same copper is used for an ornament, whether an anklet or a bracelet, or something like the plate of a king, there is no feeling of disgust and, in addition, it becomes a beautiful and amazing thing. When that same copper has been made into something like a buddha image, and consecrated, it is used as an object for prostrations and offerings, on the basis of which it becomes an object for the accumulation of the assembly of merit. Although it appears in this way in temporarily sublime or inferior forms, the essence of the copper itself has not improved in the least."

698 Mañjughoṣa's statement is the last line of the basic verses of *Parting from the Four Attachments.* See Jetsün Drakpa Gyaltsen, *Instructions on Parting from the Four Attachments,* 297b2.

699 Jetsün Drakpa Gyaltsen, *Clear Reply to a Request,* 9a. The identification of the text in the note to the critical edition of the Tibetan text is incorrect.

700 Jetsün Drakpa Gyaltsen, *Root Text on the View of the Indivisibility of Samsara and Nirvana,* 96b4.

701 Jetsün Drakpa Gyaltsen, *Root Text on the View of the Indivisibility of Samsara and Nirvana,* 96b4.

702 The translation follows the reading in the original Dergé edition, which lists three topics, instead of the altered reading in the Dehra Dun and critical editions that replace *dang gsum* with *dge ba'i rtsa ba bsngo ba dang bzhi.*

703 In a confusing way, this third general topic is prematurely inserted here after only the first example of the main practice. Thus the third general topic is presented before the second general topic has been completed. These conclusion practices are also to be performed after each of the following examples, even though only presented here once.

704 According to the glossary in Parfionovitch et al. (1992), *thar nu* is *Euphorbia wallichiana / Euphorbia kansuensis (Chinese spurge).*

705 According to Chogyé Trichen Rinpoché, *kashokanta (ka sho kanta)* is a poisonous plant. Its Tibetan name is *thang phrom.* According to the glossary in Parfionovitch et al. (1992), *thang phrom (dkar po)* is *Datura metel / Datura stramonium (datura),* but *thang phrom nag po* is *Scopolia lurida (scopolia).*

706 According to Chogyé Trichen Rinpoché, *jinchen thulu (byin chen thu lu)* is a striped insect found in fields.

707 According to Chogyé Trichen Rinpoché, *bocha gapa (sbo cha ga pa)* is a black berry *(shing tog nag po)* used for rosary beads in Vaiśravaṇa practice.

708 According to Chogyé Trichen Rinpoché, *ug chos* is a red flower. According to the glossary in Parfionovitch et al. (1992), *ug chos dmar po* is *Incarvillea younghusbandii / Incarvillea delavayi (red incarvillea).* According to Chogyé Trichen Rinpoché, *btsun pa* is a reddish color.

709 Jetsün Drakpa Gyaltsen, *Root Text on the View of the Indivisibility of Samsara and Nirvana,* 96b4.

710 According to Chogyé Trichen Rinpoché, in this context *sense consciousness (dbang shes)* is an abbreviation for *consciousness of the visual sense organ (mig gi dbang po'i rnam shes).*

711 See Jetsün Drakpa Gyaltsen, *Commentary on the View of the Indivisibility of Samsara and Nirvana,* and Lama Dampa Sönam Gyaltsen, *Complete Clarification of the Hidden Meaning.*

712 Jetsün Drakpa Gyaltsen, *Root Text on the View of the Indivisibility of Samsara and Nirvana,* 96b5.

713 According to ancient cosmology, a volcanic iron mountain range that resembles the face of a horse *(rta gdong)* encircles our world system. The "fire of the horse's face" *(rta gdong gi me)* is believed to erupt from the mouths of the volcanos and to cause the excess water of the oceans to evaporate, thereby maintaining their proper level. See Jamgön Kongtrul (2005), 446.

714 Jetsün Drakpa Gyaltsen, *Root Text on the View of the Indivisibility of Samsara and Nirvana,* 96b5.

715 Toh 381, Kangyur, rgyud 'bum *ga,* 86a3.

716 Jetsün Drakpa Gyaltsen, *Root Text on the View of the Indivisibility of Samsara and Nirvana,* 96b5.

717 Jetsün Drakpa Gyaltsen, *Root Text on the View of the Indivisibility of Samsara and Nirvana,* 96b5.

718 Jetsün Drakpa Gyaltsen, *Root Text on the View of the Indivisibility of Samsara and Nirvana,* 96b6.

719 Yoginī Cinṭa, *Realization of Reality.* Toh 2222, Tengyur, rgyud *wi,* 63a7.

720 Jetsün Drakpa Gyaltsen, *Root Text on the View of the Indivisibility of Samsara and Nirvana,* 96b6.

721 Jetsün Drakpa Gyaltsen, *Clear Reply to a Request,* 9b6. The information in the note to the critical edition of the Tibetan text is incorrect.

722 The terms rasanā *(ro ma),* lalanā *(rkyang ma),* and central channel *(dbu ma)* mentioned in this practice do not seem to have the usual meaning of right, left, and central channels in the subtle body. Here the terms seem to refer to three channels or veins located on each side of the throat.

723 The appeals of the goddesses and the melting of the causal Vajra Holder occur during the practice of the Hevajra Time of the Path.

724 Jetsün Drakpa Gyaltsen, *Root Text on the View of the Indivisibility of Samsara and Nirvana,* 96b4.

725 Jetsün Drakpa Gyaltsen, *Clear Reply to a Request,* 9b6.

726 Jetsün Drakpa Gyaltsen, *Root Text on the View of the Indivisibility of Samsara and Nirvana,* 97a1.

727 Jetsün Drakpa Gyaltsen, *Summary of Writings About the Universal Ground,* 65a. The wording of this quotation is quite different from the passage in the extant text.

728 *Hevajra Tantra.* Toh 418, Kangyur, rgyud 'bum *nga,* 20b4.

729 Nāgārjuna, *Root Verses on the Madhyamaka.* Toh 3824, Tengyur, dbu ma *tsa,* 15a4.

730 Bartön Dorjé Gyaltsen (Bar ston Rdo rje rgyal mtshan) was a fourteenth-century master of the Path with the Result whose works seem to have been passed down primarily in the Dzongpa (Rdzong pa) lineage of the Sakya tradition.

731 See note 697 for Jamyang Khyentsé Wangchuk's explanation of the example of copper.

732 *Vajra Peak Tantra.* Toh 480, Kangyur, rgyud 'bum *nya,* 148b5.

733 Virūpa, *Vajra Lines.* Toh 2284, Tengyur, rgyud *zhi,* 139b1.

734 Here the Sanskrit term *bhaga* is used to designate the body cavity of the abdomen and lower chest in both males and females. In other contexts the same term is also used for the vulva.

735 Vasubandhu, *Explication of the Treasury of Abhidharma.* Toh 4090, Tengyur, mngon pa *khu,* 94b5.

736 See note 63.

737 Virūpa, *Vajra Lines.* Toh 2284, Tengyur, rgyud *zhi,* 140b3.

738 See note 490 for the fifteen experiences.

739 These three are: (1) dedicating the basic virtue, (2) meditating on compassion for infinite sentient beings, and (3) combining all activities with resting evenly, and practicing without parting from that.

740 Jetsün Drakpa Gyaltsen, *Root Text on the View of the Indivisibility of Samsara and Nirvana,* 97a1.

741 See note 19.

742 Jetsün Drakpa Gyaltsen, *Root Text on the View of the Indivisibility of Samsara and Nirvana,* 97a2.

743 The eight auspicious substances are a mirror, yogurt, cotton grass *(rtswa dur ba),* Bengal quince *(shing tog bil ba),* a conch shell with a clockwise spiral, bezoar *(ghi wang),* vermilion, and white mustard seed.

744 Six sensory bases are usually enumerated. The extra two here are Maitreya, who is the veins and tendons *(rtsa rgyus),* and Samantabhadra, who is the joints *(tshig mtshams).*

745 Summoning and stationing deities at their places in the mandala.

746 The vajra song beginning with *kollaire,* which is taken from the *Hevajra Tantra,* is recited near the end of the daily practice of the method for accomplishment of Hevajra, and is followed with a series of verses in Tibetan beginning with the words "Excellent qualities" *(phun sum tshogs pa).*

747 In this specific context, the terms *essential constituent (khams)* and *enlightenment mind (byang sems)* are euphemisms for the reproductive fluids that are present in both men and women.

748 Jetsün Drakpa Gyaltsen, *Root Text on the View of the Indivisibility of Samsara and Nirvana,* 97a2.

749 See Jetsün Drakpa Gyaltsen, *Commentary on the View of the Indivisibility of Samsara and Nirvana.*

750 In this context, the term *method for direct realization (mngon rtogs)* is a synonym for *method for accomplishment (sgrub thabs),* meaning specifically the Hevajra Time of the Path. According to Chogyé Trichen Rinpoché, the three and a half birthplaces (or modes of birth) are birth from a womb, birth from an egg, birth from heat and moisture, and half of the process of miraculous birth.

751 This seems to be a generalized statement of the Gendenpa or Gelukpa position.

752 The four and a half birthplaces (or modes of birth) *(skye gnas phyed dang lnga)* are unidentified. According to Khenpo Appey Rinpoché, this is perhaps a mistaken spelling, since no explanation of more than four is found in any text.

753 The number *two (gnyis pa)* for this heading is found only in the original Dergé edition.

754 According to Chogyé Trichen Rinpoché, the phrase *yul ma dag pa las,* found in both the Dehra Dun edition and the critical edition of the Tibetan text, should been replaced by *ye shes kyi,* which is found in the original Dergé edition.

755 *Condensed Verses on the Perfection of Wisdom.* Toh 13, Kangyur, sher phyin *ka,* 11b4.

756 Jetsün Drakpa Gyaltsen, *Root Text on the View of the Indivisibility of Samsara and Nirvana,* 97a3.

757 The text reads *Sarvaguhya Tantra (Thams cad gsang ba'i rgyud),* but the verse (with the two lines reversed) was located in the *Later Tantra (Rgyud phyi ma)* of the *Guhyasamāja.* Toh 443, Kangyur, rgyud 'bum *ca,* 151b6.

758 The vital winds are like a mount and the conceptual mind is like its rider.

759 *Hevajra Tantra.* Toh 417, Kangyur, rgyud 'bum *nga,* 10b3.

760 Jetsün Drakpa Gyaltsen, *Root Text on the View of the Indivisibility of Samsara and Nirvana,* 97a4.

761 Jetsün Drakpa Gyaltsen, *Root Text on the View of the Indivisibility of Samsara and Nirvana,* 97a5.

762 Virūpa, *Vajra Lines.* Toh 2284, Tengyur, rgyud *zhi,* 140b4.

763 Virūpa, *Vajra Lines.* Toh 2284, Tengyur, rgyud *zhi,* 140b2.

764 Asaṅga, *Summary of the Mahayana.* Toh 4048, Tengyur, sems tsam *ri,* 16a2.

765 Śāntideva. *Engaging in the Conduct of a Bodhisattva.* Toh 3871, Tengyur, dbu ma *la,* 10b1.

766 Virūpa, *Vajra Lines.* Toh 2284, Tengyur, rgyud *zhi,* 140b3.

767 The fifth syllable, *hūṃ,* is missing in the Tibetan text. Perhaps the *hūṃ* is assumed because it is the seed syllable of Hevajra.

768 The first syllable, *aṃ,* is missing in the Tibetan text. Perhaps the *aṃ* is assumed because it is the seed syllable of Nairātmyā.

769 Jetsün Drakpa Gyaltsen, *Root Text on the View of the Indivisibility of Samsara and Nirvana,* 97a5.

770 Jetsün Drakpa Gyaltsen, *Root Text on the View of the Indivisibility of Samsara and Nirvana,* 97a5.

771 The ten powers *(stobs bcu)* of a buddha are the powers of knowing what are and are not appropriate circumstances; knowing the ripening of actions; knowing various inclinations; knowing various constituents; knowing who has supreme faculties and inferior faculties; knowing the paths going everywhere; knowing meditation, liberation, meditative concentration, absorption, and so forth; knowing previous lifetimes; knowing the transference of consciousness at death and birth; and knowing the cessation of taints. The four fearless traits *(mi 'jigs pa bzhi)* are being fearless in perfect realization, fearless in perfect renunciation, fearless in showing the phenomena of obstacles, and fearless in teaching the path of certain renunciation. As mentioned in the *Vajra Lines* and the *Explication of the Treatise for Nyak,* the four applications of mindfulness *(dran pa nyer bar bzhag pa'i bzhi)* are application of mindfulness of the body, of the deity, of mantra, and of Dharma.

772 The five certainties of teacher, doctrine, retinue, place, and time.

773 In his *Lamp Summarizing Conduct* (Toh 1803, Tengyur, rgyud *ngi,* 66a5), Āryadeva says this quote is from the *Tantra Equaling the Sky (Nam mkha' dang mnyam pa'i rgyud),* but it has not been located in that scripture.

774 This quote is also mentioned in Āryadeva, *Lamp Summarizing Conduct,* Toh 1803, Tengyur, rgyud *ngi,* 66a5.

775 *Hevajra Tantra.* Toh 418, Kangyur, rgyud 'bum *nga,* 20b4. The next line says, "Precisely this is nirvana itself."

776 The three preparations are to remove whatever covers the jewel, to wash it, and to polish it.

777 The numbering of the outline in this text continues from that in the previous text, in which the second general heading was *The stages of guiding the person,* and, within that, the first topic was *Meditation on the view of the indivisibility of samsara and nirvana in the causal continuum of the universal ground.*

778 Sakya Paṇḍita, *Distinguishing the Three Vows,* 229b6. Also see Sakya Pandita Kunga Gyaltshen (2002), 129 and 308.

779 This quote was not located in the *Sampuṭa Tantra,* but a very similar passage is found in the tantra known as *Requested by Four Goddesses (Caturdeviparipṛcchā, Lha mo bzhis yongs su zhus pa).* Toh 446, Kangyur, rgyud 'bum *ca,* 279a5.

780 Virūpa, *Vajra Lines.* Toh 2284, Tengyur, rgyud *zhi,* 139b1.

781 Virūpa, *Vajra Lines.* Toh 2284, Tengyur, rgyud *zhi,* 139b1.

782 The six topics are the path, view, culmination of attainment, practice when passing away, intermediate-state practice, and dream yoga. Illusory body is considered to be a subcategory of dream yoga.

783 This topic is explained in the following text by Jamyang Khyentsé Wangchuk, which begins with the inner creation stage as the second topic.

784 Jetsün Drakpa Gyaltsen, *Guidance Manual for Jochak,* 156a1.

785 See Sakya Paṇḍita Künga Gyaltsen, *Three Outer, Inner, and Secret Mandalas.*

786 The term *direct enlightenment (mngon byang)* refers here to the creation process of the deity during the daily Hevajra practice of the Time of the Path. In the more detailed versions, this involves the visualization of all the Sanskrit vowels and consonant-syllables and their transformation into moon or sun disks. As mentioned in the following lines, other practices use only the visualization of drops and seed syllables.

787 According to Dezhung Rinpoché, these are the words of Sachen Künga Nyingpo.

788 *Hevajra Tantra.* Toh 417, Kangyur, rgyud 'bum *nga,* 10a5.

789 The *Bodhisattva Commentaries (Sems 'grel)* are a set of Indian treatises often known as the *Bodhisattva Trilogy (Sems 'grel skor gsum):* (1) the *Vimalaprabhā* (Toh 1347), an immense commentary on the *Kālacakra Tantra* by Kalkī Puṇḍarīka, (2) the *Hevajrapiṇḍārthaṭīkā* (Toh 1180), a commentary on the *Hevajra Tantra* by Bodhisattva Vajragarbha, and (3) the *Lakṣābhidhānāduddhṛta laghutantra piṇḍārthavivaraṇa* (Toh 1402), a commentary on the *Cakrasaṃvara Tantra* by Bodhisattva Vajrapāṇi. Followers of these texts often criticize the practice of the creation stage as an insufficient means for attaining complete enlightenment, and emphasize the practice of the completion stage.

790 Toh 419, Kangyur, rgyud 'bum *nga,* 31b1.

791 The *Later Tantra.* Toh 443, Kangyur, rgyud 'bum *ca,* 150a1.

792 In a confusing way, this third topic is prematurely inserted here before the completion of the second topic. This explanation of arising also applies to the following sections in this text, as well as the discussion of the inner creation stage, where it is listed in the outline, but not explained.

793 The expression *mindful of the purity (dag pa dran pa)* refers to a series of verses in the Hevajra Time of the Path that express the pure significance of Hevajra's various qualities.

794 According to Chogyé Trichen Rinpoché, this is an oral saying within the tradition of the Path with the Result *(lam 'bras kyi lung tshig).*

795 The Tibetan text numbers this as the third instead of the second topic, which seems to be a scribal mistake.

796 The other three transmissions of Hevajra are those of Virūpa's Path with the Result, of Ḍombi Heruka, and of Padmavajra (also known as Saroruha).

797 For Saroruha's method, see Jetsün Drakpa Gyaltsen, *Creation Stage Adorned with Nine Profound Means,* 215b–216a.

798 According to Chogyé Trichen Rinpoché, the *instruction for cutting the stream (rgyun gcod kyi gdams pa)* is another name for the *instruction for milking the uvula (lce chung ba bzho ba'i gdams pa),* a practice of the secret initiation explained by the Fifth Dalai Lama under the heading of *The drop between the eyebrows that destroys white hair and wrinkles.*

799 Jetsün Drakpa Gyaltsen, *Creation Stage Adorned with Nine Profound Means,* 214a.

800 The three meditative concentrations are the meditative concentration of the characteristic as a variety, the meditative concentration of the nature as emptiness, and the meditative concentration of the essence as their unity. These are three of the fifteen experiences.

801 Virūpa, *Vajra Lines.* Toh 2284, Tengyur, rgyud *zhi,* 139b4.

802 The five signs are like smoke, mirage, fireflies, burning lamp flames, and a cloudless sky. The five signs of the signs are like darkness, rainbows, lightning, moonbeams, and sunbeams.

803 Although not marked as quotes, these two sentences are from Virūpa's *Vajra Lines.* Toh 2284, Tengyur, rgyud *zhi,* 140b4.

804 Virūpa, *Vajra Lines.* Toh 2284, Tengyur, rgyud *zhi,* 139a7.

805 The term *three experiences (nyams gsum)* usually refers to physical, mental, and dream experiences, but here it probably refers to the three essences *(ngo bo nyid gsum)* that are the view of the creation stage practice of the vase initiation: the

essence of the apparent aspect *(snang phyogs)*, the empty aspect *(stong phyogs)*, and their unity *(zung 'jug)*. These were just discussed in the text.

806 See Jetsün Drakpa Gyaltsen, *Creation Stage Adorned with Nine Profound Means,* 215b–216a, etc.

807 The Sanskrit words *ardhentu daṃkṣṭiṇe* are from the root mantra of Hevajra.

808 Phakpa Rinpoché ('Phags pa Rin po che) is Chögyal Phakpa (Chos rgyal 'Phags pa, 1235–80).

809 *Hevajra Tantra.* Toh 418, Kangyur, rgyud 'bum *nga,* 23b7.

810 Dīpaṃkara, *Jeweled Lamp: A Method for the Accomplishment of Glorious Hevajra.* Toh 1268, Tengyur, rgyud *ta,* 31a4. Dīpaṃkara (Mar me mdzad) is the Indian master Atiśa (982–1055).

811 *Hevajra Tantra.* Toh 417, Kangyur, rgyud 'bum *nga,* 7a6.

812 Nāgārjuna, *Five Stages.* Toh 1802, Tengyur, rgyud *ngi,* 52a2.

813 *Vajrapañjara Tantra.* Toh 419, Kangyur, rgyud 'bum *nga,* 42b4. The information in the note to the critical edition of the Tibetan text is incorrect.

814 The text referred to here is probably Divākaracandra (Nyin mo'i 'byung gnas zla ba), *Śrīherukabhūtanāmamaṇḍalavidhi* (*Dpal he ru ka 'byung ba shes bya ba'i dkyil 'khor gyi cho ga*). Toh 1261, Tengyur, rgyud *nya.*

815 According to Jamgön Ameshap ('Jam mgon A mes zhabs Ngag dbang kun dga' bsod nams, 1597–1659) this quote is from the *Hevajra Tantra,* but it was not located there.

816 Candrakīrti, *Illuminating Lamp.* Toh 1785, Tengyur, rgyud *ha,* 183b1.

817 *Hevajra Tantra.* Toh 417, Kangyur, rgyud 'bum *nga,* 7a7.

818 Rudra is another name for the god Śiva or Maheśvara.

819 The venerable brothers are Sönam Tsemo (Bsod nams rtse mo, 1142–82) and Drakpa Gyaltsen (Grags pa rgyal mtshan, 1147–1216).

820 The gods with control of others' emanations *(gzhan 'phrul dbang byed)* are one of the six classes of gods in the desire realm.

821 See note 814.

822 Jetsün Drakpa Gyaltsen, *Eulogy in Daṇḍaka Metre to Glorious Hevajra,* 236b2.

823 The six faults *(skyon drug)* are probably the same as the six afflictions *(nyon mongs drug):* desire, hatred, ignorance, pride, doubt, and wrong view.

824 Toh 373, Kangyur, rgyud 'bum *kha,* 286a2. *Powerful* means "the northeast" and *false* means "the southwest." The quote is quite different from the lines in the tantra itself.

825 I am grateful to Hubert Decleer for his help in deciphering some parts of the following section on the celestial mansion.

826 The four meditative states *(bsam gtan bzhi)* are (1) the meditative state with both thoughts and discernment, (2) the meditative state with no thoughts but with discernment alone, (3) the meditative state of mental action devoid of thoughts and discernment, and (4) the meditative state of mental action united with delight. Cf. Dorje and Kapstein (1991), 134.

827 *Hevajra Tantra.* Toh 417, Kangyur, rgyud 'bum *nga,* 1a2.

828 The three gates to liberation *(rnam thar sgo gsum)* are the emptiness, wishless, and signless gates to liberation.

829 The identification of this work is uncertain. Perhaps the reference is to Vajrāsanapāda's *Supplication to the Eighty-four Great Adepts.* Toh 3758, Tengyur, rgyud *tshu.*

830 Jetsün Drakpa Gyaltsen, *Eulogy in Daṇḍaka Metre to Glorious Hevajra,* 237a3.

831 Sempa Chenpo (Sems dpa' chen po) is an epithet of Müchen Könchok Gyaltsen (Mus chen Dkon mchog rgyal mtshan, 1388–1469). The *Clear Mirror (Gsal ba'i me long)* is Müchen's text for the bestowal of the Hevajra initiation, contained in volume 13, *pa,* of the *Sa-skya Lam-'bras Literature Series.*

832 The Mañjughoṣa Cave of Sakya is the meditation cave of Sachen Künga Nyingpo, where he received from the bodhisattva Mañjughoṣa the instructions of *Parting from the Four Attachments,* and later received from Virūpa many teachings of the Path with the Result.

833 According to Chogyé Trichen Rinpoché, *vital winds of consciousness (rnam shes kyi rlung)* is another term for *vital action winds (las kyi rlung).*

834 The rūpakāya form bodies are the nirmāṇakāya emanated body and the sambhogakāya enjoyment body.

835 The three paths are three of the fifteen experiences. They are the path of eliminating entry *('jug pa sel ba'i lam),* the path of severing attachment *(chags pa gcod pa'i lam),* and the path of great enlightenment *(byang chub chen po'i lam).*

836 The Hevajra practice is usually said to consist of ten yogas, two of which are the yogas of the creation and completion stages during meditative equipoise, and eight of which are during postmeditation. Perhaps, in the specific context of the practice of the creation stage of the vase initiation here, the completion stage is not being counted. The eight yogas practiced other than during meditative equipoise are the yogas of sleep, arising, recitation, bathing, eating food, offering sacrificial cakes, conduct, and passion.

837 The Tibetan text seems to be corrupt here. The phrase *in the case of the essence of the apparent aspect (snang phyogs la mtshon na)* has been omitted from the translation.

838 The Tibetan text seems to be corrupt here. According to the earlier outline, the third topic should be *How to produce it if it has not arisen during those two (de gnyis la ma skyes na bskyed pa'i thabs),* but the text actually has *Enhancement (bogs 'byin pa),* which is the fourth topic. This has been replaced in the translation with the original heading.

839 This heading has been inserted here according to the original outline, with the heading *Enhancement (bogs 'byin pa)* moved from the earlier mistaken location. This should be the fourth topic.

840 Virūpa, *Vajra Lines.* Toh 2284, Tengyur, rgyud *zhi,* 141b1.

841 According to Chogyé Trichen Rinpoché, *other paths (gzhan gyi lam)* means the practices of the transference of consciousness and so forth.

842 Toh 428, Kangyur, rgyud 'bum *nga,* 226b3.

843 According to the glossary in Parfionovitch, et al. (1992), *re lcag pa* is *Stellera chamaejasme (chickweed).* According to Chogyé Trichen Rinpoché, it is a type of red flower.

844 The *Abridged Knowledge for Deceiving the Lord of Death ('Chi bdag bslu ba bsdus pa'i rtogs pa)* has not been identified.

845 Sangtsa Sönam Gyaltsen (Zangs tsha Bsod nams rgyal mtshan, 1184–1239) was the younger brother of Sakya Paṇḍita and the father of Chögyal Phakpa. He was a great astrological expert famed for having predicted the exact time of his own death.

846 The translation of this sentence is uncertain.

847 According to Chogyé Trichen Rinpoché, this is an oral saying from the tradition of the Path with the Result.

848 The elaborate transference practices are explained just following.

849 *Equally-circulating (mnyam rgyu)* is another name for the *equally-abiding (mnyam gnas)* vital wind mentioned in the previous paragraph.

850 The eighty natural concepts are listed in Jamgön Kongtrul (2003), 507–9.

851 The great venerable lord of Sakya is Sachen Künga Nyingpo. The text on the intermediate state by Yar Bumawa (G.yar sbu ma ba) has not survived. *Liberation on the Precipitous Pathway ('Phrang sgrol)* is a text on the intermediate state written by the Kagyü master Gyalwa Yangönpa Gyaltsen Pal (Rgyal ba Yang dgon pa Rgyal mtshan dpal, 1213–58), who received the Path with the Result of the Sakya tradition from Sakya Paṇḍita and the Shama tradition from Gyalwa Kodrakpa (Rgyal ba Ko brag pa, 1170–1249). A series of texts in Yangönpa's collected writings concerning *Liberation on the Precipitous Pathway of the Intermediate State (Bar do 'phrang sgrol)* are found in *Collected Works (Gsung 'bum) of Yang-dgon-pa Rgyal-mtshan-dpal,* Thimphu: Kunzang Topgey, 1976, vols. 2 and 3.

852 Vasubandhu, *Verses on the Treasury of Abhidharma.* Toh 4089, Tengyur, mngon pa *ku,* 7a7. The line in the quote and that in Vasubandhu's text are somewhat different.

853 *A* and *haṃ* are two channel syllables in the vajra body. *Aham* in Sanskrit means "I."

854 The three poisons are desire, hatred, and ignorance.

855 The *Tale of the Prince (Rgyal po'i bu'i gtam rgyud)* has not been identified.

856 The bird with a human body *(bya shang shang)* is a creature with the lower body of a bird, the upper body of a human, and wings.

857 The southern continent of Jambudvīpa is the world of human beings. The other three continents are Pūrvavideha in the east, Aparagodanīya in the west, and Uttarakuru in the north.

858 In the translation, the spelling *kṣa gong* in the Dehra Dun edition and the critical edition of the Tibetan text has been replaced by *klu gong,* which is found in the original Dergé edition. According to Chogyé Trichen Rinpoché, Ramtara (Ram rta ra) was a minister of the Tibetan king Trisong Detsen (Khri srong lde btsan). It is said that when Ramtara died, a Bönpo priest performed rituals, and a malicious spirit impersonated Ramtara's mental body and appeared to the king. Guru Padmasambhava also did rituals, and told the king that the form that had appeared to him was not his minister, but a demon attempting to cause obstacles. I am grateful to Guru Rinchen Chödar for this information.

859 According to Chogyé Trichen Rinpoché, Rakha Drak (Ra kha brags) was a retreat center of Sera (Se ra) Monastery near Lhasa. When a certain yogin who lived there died, his rebirth as a worm inside the corpse of a horse was prevented by his guardian deity, Kṣetrapāla, who is a special protector of Tārā.

860 The outline here continues from Jamyang Khyentsé Wangchuk's previous text on the outer creation stage, where the inner creation stage was listed but not explained.

861 This topic is not explained in the present text.

862 *Arising* is not explained again here in the context of the inner creation stage. It was explained previously by Jamyang Khyentsé Wangchuk in the text on the outer creation text, and that explanation should be applied here as well.

863 Mahāsiddha Jetāri's *Method for Accomplishment of the Fourth Mudrā (Phyag rgya bzhi pa'i sgrub thabs)* has not been identified. *For the Benefit of the Sons (Sras don ma)* is the most important of Sachen Künga Nyingpo's eleven commentaries on the *Vajra Lines* of Virūpa. See Sachen Künga Nyingpo, *Explication of the Treatise of the Path with the Result for the Benefit of the Sons.*

864 The following annotation appears at this point in the Tibetan text: "In the explication of the treatise of the *Vajra Lines* by Chilgom, who received the Path with the Result eighteen times from the great venerable lord Drakpa Gyaltsen, it is explained that initiation is taken by the goddesses of the retinue."

865 Phakpa Rinpoché ('Phags pa Rin po che) is Chögyal Phakpa (Chos rgyal 'Phags pa, 1235–80).

866 See Sakya Paṇḍita Künga Gyaltsen, *Clarification of the Meaning Through Symbols,* although the following description does not seem to match what is actually found in that text.

867 The eight worldly concerns are profit and loss, pleasure and pain, fame and defamation, and praise and blame.

868 Jamgön Sönam Chokden ('Jam mgon Bsod nams mchog ldan, 1603–59), often known by the epithet Kangyurwa (Bka' 'gyur ba).

869 This is the sixth topic continuing from the outline in Jamyang Khyentsé Wangchuk's earlier text on the outer creation stage, where the fifth topic was the intermediate-state practices of the vase initiation.

870 The preliminaries are only explained in this section, but should be understood to apply to all the sections following. The conclusion is not explained here, and is the same as that explained in the previous texts by Jamyang Khyentsé Wangchuk.

871 *Hevajra Tantra.* Toh 418, Kangyur, rgyud 'bum *nga,* 18a3.

872 The outline continues here from the previous text on the outer creation stage, where the vase initiation was the first topic.

873 The conclusion is not explained here, and is the same as that explained in the previous texts by Jamyang Khyentsé Wangchuk.

874 The training of the five branches *(yan lag lnga),* which are like warm-up exercises, is explained in other texts such as Lama Dampa Sönam Gyaltsen, *Complete Clarification of the Hidden Meaning,* 229b.

875 The term *exertion (rtsol)* is used both for the vital winds that circulate in the right channel of the rasanā and for the exhalation of breath. The term *life (srog)* is used both for the vital winds that circulate in the left channel of the lalanā and for the inhalation of breath. The Sanskrit term *prāṇāyāma* is translated into Tibetan as "*srog rtsol.*"

876 *Hevajra Tantra.* Toh 417, Kangyur, rgyud 'bum *nga,* 13a6.

877 According to Tibetan tradition, a bird's first eggs are small, but then get larger as the mother gets older.

878 This position is explained six paragraphs following under the heading *Feeding the lamp flame.*

879 The three conducts *(spyod pa gsum)* are probably the main categories of unconventional behavior referred to as *deliberate conduct (brtul zhugs spyod pa),* which are called *avadhūti, totally good (kun tu bzang po),* and *completely victorious (phyogs las rnam rgyal).* In this context, the Sanskrit term *avadhūti* means "sinful behavior" *(sdig pa spyod pa),* "nondual behavior" *(gnyis spangs),* or "behavior that makes everyone tremble" *(kun 'dar).* It purifies sins, destroys dualistic mind, and uproots the tendency to cling to things as true. The second conduct is called *totally good* because the essence of the behavior is always good, no matter whether it appears externally to be good or bad. The third is known as *completely victorious* because one has actually achieved victory over the afflictions, the four māras have been tamed, one has the power to benefit sentient beings, and the obscuration of knowledge has been destroyed. In the Path with the Result, the term *three conducts (spyod pa gsum)* could also refer to the bases for the miraculous *(rdzu 'phrul gyi rkang pa),* the applications of mindfulness *(dran pa nye bar gzhag pa),* and the perfect renunciations *(yang dag par spong ba),* which are the antidotes for the three precipitous pathways *('phrang gsum)* of appearances rising up as the enemy *(snang ba dgrar langs),* emptiness rising up as the enemy *(stong pa dgrar langs),* and great dullness *(bying ba chen po).*

880 In the Tibetan text, the phrase "and inhaled" *(te nang du rngubs)* would seem to be a mistake here and has not been translated.

881 As explained earlier by Jamyang Khyentsé Wangchuk in the text on the outer creation stage, these three places *(gnas)* are otherwise referred to as the three terrifying abysses *(g.yang sa):* "Three terrifying abysses appear as the embodiment of the three poisons: three white, red, and black pits close together, with deep invisible bottoms. While one stands between them on a ledge as thin as the back of a knife, the suffering of being terrified of falling into the pits and anguishing about what to do will occur." The three poisons are desire, hatred, and ignorance.

882 The following annotation appears at this point in the Tibetan text: "Annotation: in the tradition of the venerable lords of Sakya itself, there are six spiritual levels for the vase initiation, four spiritual levels for the secret initiation, two spiritual levels for the initiation of primordial awareness dependent on an embodiment of wisdom, and the twelfth and a half—the *path of study*—and half of the thirteenth—the *path of no more study*—for the fourth initiation."

883 The conclusion is not explained here, and is the same as that explained in the previous texts by Jamyang Khyentsé Wangchuk.

884 According to Chogyé Trichen Rinpoché, the reading of *latter (phyi ma)* found in the Dehra Dun and critical editions should be corrected to *former (snga ma).*

885 These practices mentioned in quotation marks here and in the next paragraph are known as the *six actions ('gyur ba rnam pa drug),* and were explained in Sachen Künga Nyingpo's *Explication of the Treatise for Nyak.*

886 The Sanskrit term *bola* is a code word for the male genitals and *kakkola* is a code word for the female genitals.

887 For the three conducts, see note 879.

888 The reading of *ngo bor (in essence)* has been understood as a scribal mistake for *ngor (in the perception).*

889 The three experiences of appearance *(snang ba)*, spreading *(mched pa)*, and near-attainment *(nyer thob)* were explained by Jamyang Khyentsé Wangchuk in the text on the outer creation stage.

890 The conclusion is not explained here, and is the same as that explained in the previous texts by Jamyang Khyentsé Wangchuk.

891 The thirty-two yogic exercises *('phrin las so gnyis)* and the training of the five branches *(yan lag lnga)* are explained in separate texts.

892 Source of quote not located. The identification in the critical edition of the Tibetan text is incorrect.

893 Nārāyaṇa is the name of a mighty elephant and also an epithet of the god Viṣṇu.

894 For the three conducts, see note 879.

895 In the original Tibetan text these syllables are stacked in a vertical column. The translation follows the original Dergé edition and the Dehra Dun reproduction, and not the new critical edition of the Tibetan text where the syllables have been incorrectly copied.

896 Śrī Dharmapāla was Virūpa's name while he was still a monk. In this verse the Fifth Dalai Lama is eulogizing his own master, Jamgön Sönam Chokden ('Jam mgon Bsod nams mchog ldan, 1603–59), as being Virūpa himself in the saffron robes of a monk.

897 Drokmi is Drokmi Lotsāwa. Sakyapa Lord of Great Kindness is an epithet of Sachen Künga Nyingpo.

898 Ngawang Losang Gyatso is the Fifth Dalai Lama. Dakchen Dorjé Chang (Bdag chen rdo rje 'chang) is the epithet of Dakchen Lodrö Gyaltsen (Bdag chen Blo gros rgyal mtshan, 1444–95). Müchen Sempa Chenpo (Mus chen Sems dpa' chen po) is an epithet of Müchen Könchok Gyaltsen (Mus chen Dkon mchog rgyal mtshan, 1388–1469). Jamyang Chöjé ('Jam dbyangs Chos rje) is an epithet of Jamyang Namkha Gyaltsen ('Jam dbyangs Nam mkha' rgyal mtshan, 1398–1472), who was the father of Dakchen Dorjé Chang.

899 The *Clarification of the Hidden Meaning (Sbas don gsal ba)* is the text by Lama Dampa (Bla ma dam pa Bsod nams rgyal mtshan, 1312–75) on the Three Appearances and the Three Continua. See Lama Dampa Sönam Gyaltsen, *Complete Clarification of the Hidden Meaning.* Lord Ludrup Gyatso is Mangthö Ludrup Gyatso (Mang thos klu sgrub rgya mtsho, 1523–96), who wrote a complete set of texts on the Explication for Disciples according to the words of his teacher Tsarchen Losel Gyatso (Tshar chen Blo gsal rgya mtsho, 1502–66).

900 See note 879.

901 The four frightful sounds *('jigs pa'i sgra bzhi)* and three terrifying abysses *(ya nga ba'i g.yang sa gsum)* were explained by Jamyang Khyentsé Wangchuk in the text on the outer creation stage: "Four frightful sounds occur. Due to the reversal of the vital wind of earth, a sound like the disintegration of the entire earth seems to scramble the brains. Because the vital wind of fire has reversed, roaring sounds and crackling sounds, as if all appearances were burning with fire, occur. Because the vital wind of water has reversed, a sound like all appearances being swept away by water arises. Because the vital wind of wind has reversed, a sound like all the three-thousandfold world systems being swept away by wind occurs." See note 881 for the three abysses.

902 Nāgārjuna (Nā gardzu na) is the Sanskritized form of Ludrup (Klu sgrub), the name of the author Mangthö Ludrup Gyatso (Maṇg thos klu sgrub rgya mtsho, 1523–96).

Glossary

accumulate the assemblies *(tshogs gsog).* The two assemblies of merit *(bsod nams)* and primordial awareness *(ye shes)* must be accumulated to reach full enlightenment.

allow the natural expression *(byung rgyal du btang/skyang).* A phrase indicating how to deal with the various experiences that arise during meditation. According to Chogyé Trichen Rinpoché, the essential point is to allow all experiences to arise naturally, without attachment to the pleasant ones and without viewing the disturbing ones as faults.

bhaga *(bha ga).* A Sanskrit word not translated into Tibetan. The term is used to designate a certain physical region of the body, mostly the abdomen below the navel, but sometimes also extending up to the heart cakra. Many of the key channel syllables are located in this region according to the Hevajra tradition. The same term is also used for the vulva.

bodies of enlightenment *(sku).* The system of the Path with the Result speaks of five bodies of enlightenment: the nirmāṇakāya emanated body *(sprul sku),* the sambhogakāya enjoyment body *(longs sku),* the dharmakāya reality body *(chos sku),* the svābhāvikakāya essence body *(ngo bo nyid kyi sku),* and the utterly pure svābhāvikakāya essence body *(ngo bo nyid kyi sku shin tu rnam par dag pa).*

caṇḍālī *(gtum mo).* Literally, "fierce woman." A Sanskrit term used for the fire visualized inside the body during completion stage practices.

clear essences *(dwangs ma).* The clear or pure essences of the nine or ten father and mother ḍākas and ḍākinīs, which are the nine or ten essential constituents of the vital winds and mind in a human body.

conqueror *(rgyal ba).* A buddha. May also be used as an epithet for a great Buddhist master. The Conqueror is Śākyamuni Buddha.

continuum *(rgyud).* The Tibetan word *rgyud* was used to translate two Sanskrit words—*tantra* and *saṃtāna*—that are not synonyms in Sanskrit. The word *tantra* is primarily used for certain scriptures, systems of practice, and so forth. The word *saṃtāna* is used to mean "continuum," in the sense of the stream of being, mindstream, or continuum that constitutes a living being. In Tibetan, the word *rgyud* was used for both meanings. In this book *continuum* means the continuity, or continuum, of a living being. Furthermore, the terms *root continuum (rtsa rgyud)* and *explanatory continuum (bshad rgyud)* have an additional resonance in Tibetan because of the dual meaning of the Tibetan word *rgyud.* In the context of its meaning as "tantra" or "tantric scripture," a root tantra such as the *Hevajra Tantra* is clarified by other scriptures referred to as *explanatory tantras,* such as the *Vajrapañjara* and the *Sampuṭa.*

culmination of attainment *(grub mtha').* A culmination or limit of attainment is associated with each of the four initiations. These culminations of realization or attainment result from the specific practices of the respective initiations. These results arise at certain points along the path, and are not the ultimate and final results. The same Tibetan term also means "philosophical tenet," which is not applicable in this context.

ḍākas and ḍākinīs *(mkha' 'gro).* The neuter Tibetan term *mkha' 'gro* is purposely used throughout the Tibetan texts. This term is the Tibetan translation of the masculine Sanskrit term *ḍāka,* but is also used as an abbreviation for the feminine Tibetan term *mkha' 'gro ma,* which is the Tibetan translation of the Sanskrit term *ḍākinī.* Thus an inherent ambiguity is often present in the use of the Tibetan term without the feminine ending *ma.* In the translated texts the term *mkha' 'gro* is used to embrace both the masculine and feminine meanings. In many instances the intended gender is clear from context. But when the meaning is ambiguous, the single term *mkha' 'gro* has been translated as "ḍākas and ḍākinīs." This decision is based on conversations with His Holiness Sakya Trizin, Khenpo Appey Rinpoché, and Dezhung Rinpoché.

dissolution of the four pulsations *('gros bzhi thim).* The four pulsations are the pulsations of: the channels; the syllables (which are channels in the crooked forms of syllables); the drops, enlightenment minds, or nectars (terms used synonymously at various times); and the vital winds. The advance and retreat *('jug ldog)* of these four in and out of the samsara channels of the rasanā and lalanā and the central channel of nirvana is referred to as *pulsation ('gros).* When the four pulsations have gone into the central channel and no longer retreat, this is referred to as the *dissolution of the four pulsations ('gros bzhi thim).*

drop/seminal drop *(thig le).* The translation "seminal drop" has been used for the physical reproductive fluids. The term "drop" has been used in other contexts involving the visualization of drops not related to the reproductive fluids.

enlightenment mind *(byang sems).* This term is often used in the tantric sense in the translated texts. It can refer to semen, to the reproductive fluids in both males and females, and to the clear essences of the essential constituents. Context dictates meaning. Often several layers of meaning exist simultaneously.

female embodiment of pure awareness *(rig ma).* One of the common terms used for the female consort, whether visualized or actual. Another similar term is *female embodiment of wisdom (shes rab ma).*

five dependently arisen connections *(rten 'brel lnga).* The Path with the Result emphasizes five dependently arisen connections: the outer dependently arisen connections, the inner dependently arisen connections, the secret dependently arisen connections, the dependently arisen connections of reality, and the ultimate dependently arisen connections. Sakya Paṇḍita said that the way to make this key Buddhist tenet of dependent arising into the path of meditation was only explained in full detail in the teachings of the Path with the Result. It is perhaps *the* fundamental theme of this tradition.

four fourfold initiations *(dbang bzhi bzhi).* Each of the four initiations is further classified into four, such as the vase initiation of the vase initiation, the vase initiation of the secret initiation, the vase initiation of the initiation of primordial awareness dependent on an embodiment of wisdom, and the vase initiation of the fourth initiation.

four malleable qualities *(mnyen lcug bzhi).* The ability to totally control the vital winds, the channels, the syllables, and the nectars, which have become completely malleable.

four supporting mandalas *(rten dkyil 'khor bzhi).* The four mandalas are the channels of the body, the channel syllables, the essential constituent nectars (enlightenment mind, drops), and the vital wind of primordial awareness. These are the supports that transform into the four bodies of enlightenment. The universal ground consciousness, or mind, is supported by these four and transforms into the fifth body of enlightenment.

gathering of the essential constituents *(khams 'dus pa).* The first, the middle, and the final gatherings represent the gradual clearing and purification of the nine or ten essential constituents within the body. The four or five vital winds and the five enlightenment minds gather into different channel locations within the body due to the practice of yoga. As these nine or ten essential constituents—the ḍākinīs and ḍākas or buddhas—gather into those specific locations, the ordinary body is transformed into a rainbow body.

heruka. Sanskrit term used in the Buddhist tantric tradition for a male semi-wrathful deity.

initiation of primordial awareness dependent on an embodiment of wisdom *(shes rab ye shes kyi dbang).* The term *wisdom (shes rab)* refers to the female, whether visualized or actual, who is the *embodiment of wisdom (shes rab ma).* Through the practices of the third initiation, which are dependent on her, the coemergent *primordial awareness (ye shes)* arises. Chogyé

Trichen Rinpoché glossed the name of the third initiation with the phrase "coemergent primordial awareness dependent on a female embodiment of wisdom" *(**shes rab** ma la brten nas lhan cig skyes pa'i **ye shes**).* His Holiness Sakya Trizin agreed with this definition and Sachen Künga Nyingpo also clearly defines the term in the *Explication of the Treatise for Nyak.*

lalanā *(ro ma).* One of the three main channels. The lalanā is located to the left of the central channel.

nine or ten essential constituents *(khams bcu/dgu).* Five of the essential constituents are the five vital winds of earth, water, fire, wind, and space, which are also referred to as the five ḍākinīs. The essential physical constituents of feces, urine, blood, reproductive fluid, and flesh are also referred to as the five nectars, or as the ḍākas or the enlightened bodies of the tathāgatas. Sometimes the vital wind of space is considered to be all-pervasive, and so the reference is to just nine essential constituents.

omniscient one *(thams cad mkhyen pa).* A buddha. May also be used as an epithet for a great Buddhist master. The Omniscient One is Śākyamuni Buddha.

paṇḍita. Sanskrit title for a learned master or scholar.

rasanā *(rkyang ma).* One of the three main channels. The rasanā is located to the right of the central channel.

reading transmission *(lung).* The reading aloud of a text by a teacher who has previously heard the reading of the text from his or her teacher. In this way, the reading transmission is traced back in an unbroken line to the author of the work.

sugata *(bde bar gshegs pa).* A buddha. Literally, "one gone to bliss."

three seats *(gdan gsum).* The word *seat* is used to designate a group of deities. The three seats are usually listed as the seat of the buddhas and bodhisattvas, the seat of the female embodiments of pure awareness and the goddesses, and the seat of the male and female wrathful beings. Sometimes the three are listed as the buddhas, the bodhisattvas, and the wrathful beings.

top of the head *(spyi bo),* **crown of the head** *(spyi gtsug),* **aperture of Brahmā** *(tshangs pa'i bu ga),* **cranial dome** *(uṣṇiṣa, gtsug tor).* These terms are often very specific. The top of the head is eight finger-widths above the eyebrows. The crown of the head is twelve finger-widths above the eyebrows, and the aperture of Brahmā refers to the juncture of the bones of the skull at that point. The cranial dome is a knob or dome that protrudes from the crown of the head at the point of enlightenment.

total release *(la dor).* This obscure term refers to the total release of knots in the channels, of pains and so forth in the channels, and of attachment to various experiences. It refers to definitive techniques for the elimination of these hindrances so that they are permanently removed.

universal ground *(kun gzhi)* The mental ground of an individual that is the basis for all the experiences included in samsara and nirvana.

vajra position *(rdo rje'i skyil krung).* The sitting position most often used for meditation, with the side of the left foot placed upon the right thigh and the side of the right foot placed upon the left thigh.

vast domain *(zhing khams).* Four vast domains are associated with the four buddha bodies. In this context alone, the English translation "vast domain" has been used to clearly distinguish between this specific meaning and the more common general meaning of "paradise" or "pure realm."

vital wind of exertion *(rtsol).* A term used both for the vital winds that circulate through the right channel of the rasanā and for the exhalation of breath. The path of the vital wind of exertion is thus the right nostril.

vital wind of life *(srog).* A term used both for the vital winds that circulate through the left channel of the lalanā and for the inhalation of breath. The path of the vital wind of life is thus the left nostril.

vital winds and mind *(rlung sems).* Synonymous with the ten essential constituents and with the ten inner father and mother ḍākas and ḍākinīs. Five of the essential constituents are the five vital winds of earth, water, fire, wind, and space, which are also referred to as the five ḍākinīs. In the phrase *vital winds and mind,* the word *mind (sems)* is an abbreviation for the five enlightenment minds *(byang sems),* which are the clear essences of the physical constituents of feces, urine, blood, reproductive fluid, and flesh. These five are also referred to as the five father ḍākas or as the enlightened bodies of the tathāgatas. To complicate matters, the enlightenment mind, or *mind* in this phrase, is the support of the *mind* in the usual sense of the word. Thus a double level of meaning is always present. States of mind are dependent on the inner movements and locations of the vital winds and enlightenment minds within the channel network of the subtle body.

vowels such as *a* and consonant-syllables such *as ka* *(ā li kā li).* The fifty vowels and consonant-syllables of the Sanskrit language. The crooked channel syllables in the subtle body are in the shapes of these syllables.

warmths and signs *(drod rtags).* The warmths are various key experiences that arise along the path. These are precursors or foretastes of the actual signs that arise later. The warmths are like smoke and the signs are like fire. Smoke appears first, indicating the imminent arising of fire. The warmths arise on the mundane path and the signs arise on the transcendent path.

Bibliography

Works Cited by the Authors

Kangyur (Canonical Scriptures)

Catuḥpīṭha Tantra. Śrīcatuḥpīṭhamahāyoginītantrarājanāma. Rnal 'byor ma'i rgyud kyi rgyal po chen po dpal gdan bzhi pa zhes bya ba. Toh 428, rgyud 'bum *nga,* 81a–231b. P67, *nga.*

Certainty About Reality in the Glorious Guhyagarbha. Śrīguhyagarbhatattva-viniścaya. Dpal gsang ba'i snying po de kho na nyid rnam par nges pa. Toh 832, rnying rgyud *kha,* 110b–132a.

Condensed Verses on the Perfection of Wisdom. Āryaprajñāpāramitāsañcayagātha. 'Phags pa shes rab kyi pha rol tu phyin pa sdud pa tshigs su bcad pa. Toh 13, sher phyin *ka,* 1b–19b. P735, *tsi.*

Guhyasamāja Tantra. Sarvatathāgatakāyavākcittarahasyaguhyasamājanāmamahā-kalparāja. De bzhin gshegs pa thams cad kyi sku gsung thugs kyi gsang chen gsang ba 'dus pa zhes bya ba brtag pa'i rgyal po chen po. Toh 442, rgyud 'bum *ca,* 90a–148a. P81, *ca.*

Hevajra Tantra. Hevajratantrarājanāma. Kye rdo rje zhes bya ba rgyud kyi rgyal po / Kye'i rdo rje mkha' 'gro ma dra ba'i sdom pa'i rgyud kyi rgyal po. Also known as the *Two Parts. Brtags pa gnyis pa.* Toh 417/18, rgyud 'bum *nga,* 1b–30a. P10, *ka.*

Lalitavistara Sutra. Āryalalitavistaranāmamahāyānasūtra. 'Phags pa rgya cher rol pa zhes bya ba theg pa chen po'i mdo. Toh 95, mdo sde *kha,* 1b–216b. P763, *ku.*

Later Tantra. Rgyud phyi ma. The last chapter of the *Guhyasamāja Tantra.* Toh 443, rgyud 'bum *ca,* 148a–157b. P81, *ca.*

Magical Net. Sgyu 'phrul drwa ba. Another name for the *Litany of the Names of Mañjuśrī. Mañjuśrījñānasattvasyaparamārthanāmasaṃgīti. 'Jam dpal ye shes sems dpa'i don dam pa'i mtshan yang dag par brjod pa.* Toh 360, rgyud 'bum *ka,* 1b–13b. P2, *ka.*

Mañjuśrī Root Tantra. Āryamañjuśrīmūlatantra. 'Phags pa 'jam dpal gyi rtsa ba'i rgyud. Toh 543, rgyud 'bum *na,* 105a–351a. P162, *na.*

Noble Sutra on Upholding Basic Virtue. Āryakuśalamūlasaṃparigrahanāma mahāyānasūtra. 'Phags pa dge ba'i rtsa ba yongs su 'dzin pa zhes bya ba theg pa chen po'i mdo. Toh 101, mdo sde *nga,* 1b–227b. P769, *gu.*

Sampuṭa Tantra. Sampuṭanāmamahātantra. Yang dag par sbyor ba zhes bya ba'i rgyud chen po. Toh 381, rgyud 'bum *ga,* 73b–158b. P26, *ga.*

Saṃvarodaya Tantra. Śrīmahāsamvarodayatantrarājanāma. Dpal bde mchog 'byung ba zhes bya ba'i rgyud kyi rgyal po chen po. Toh 373, rgyud 'bum *kha,* 265a–311a. P20, *ga.*

Sarvaguhya Tantra. Thams cad gsang ba'i rgyud. Apparently another name for the *Later Tantra. Rgyud phyi ma.* Toh 443, rgyud 'bum *ca,* 148a–157b. P81, *ca.*

Sutra of Definitive Commentary on the Intention. Āryasaṃdhinirmocananāma mahāyānasūtra. 'Phags pa dgongs pa nges par 'grel pa zhes bya ba theg pa chen po'i mdo. Toh 106, mdo sde *ca,* 1b–55b. P664, *ngu.*

Sutra of the White Lotus of the Excellent Doctrine. Saddharmapuṇḍarīkanāma mahāyānasūtra. Dam pa'i chos pad ma dkar po zhes bya ba theg pa chen po'i mdo. Toh 113, mdo sde *ja,* 1b–180b. P781, *chu.*

Vajra Peak Tantra. Vajraśekharamahāguhyayogatantra. Gsang ba rnal 'byor chen po'i rgyud rdo rje rtse mo. Toh 480, rgyud 'bum *nya,* 142b–274a. P113, *nya.*

Vajrapañjara Tantra. Āryaḍākinīvajrapañjaramahātantrarājakalpanāma. 'Phags pa mkha' 'gro ma rdo rje gur zhes bya ba'i rgyud kyi rgyal po chen po'i brtag pa. Toh 419, rgyud 'bum *nga,* 30a–65b. P11, *ka.*

Yoginīsañcārya. Rnal 'byor ma'i kun tu spyod pa. Toh 375, rgyud 'bum *ga,* 34a–44b. P23, *ga.*

Tengyur (Canonical Treatises)

Āryadeva. *Lamp Summarizing Conduct. Caryāmelāpakapradīpa. Spyod pa bsdus pa'i sgron ma.* Toh 1803, rgyud *ngi,* 57a–106b. P2668, *gi.*

Asaṅga. *Summary of the Mahayana. Mahāyānasaṃgraha. Theg pa chen po bsdus pa.* Toh 4048, sems tsam *ri,* 1b–43a. P5549, *li.*

Aśvaghoṣa. *Fifty Verses on the Master. Gurupañcāśikā. Bla ma lnga bcu pa.* Toh 3721, rgyud *tshu,* 10a–12a. P4544, *nu.*

Bhūripa. *Extensive Confession of Glorious Cakrasaṃvara. Dpal 'khor lo bde mchog gi rgyun bshags rgyas pa.* Toh 1533, rgyud *za,* 93b–95b. P2244, *phi.*

Candrakīrti. *Entering the Madhyamaka. Madhyamakāvatāranāma. Dbu ma la 'jug pa shes bya ba.* Toh 3861, dbu ma *'a,* 201b–219a. P5262, *'a.*

———. *Illuminating Lamp. Pradipodyotananāmaṭikā. Sgron ma gsal bar byed pa shes bya ba'i rgya cher bshad pa.* Toh 1785, rgyud *ha,* 1b–201a.

Dīpaṃkara. *Jeweled Lamp: A Method for the Accomplishment of Glorious Hevajra. Śrīhevajraratnapradīpasādhananāma. Dpal dgyes pa rdo rje'i sgrub thabs rin po che'i sgron ma.* Toh 1268, rgyud *ta,* 28b–34b. P2424, *za.*

Kuddāla. *Inconceivable. Bsam mi khyab.* Short title for *Esoteric Instructions on the Stages of the Inconceivable. Acintyakramopadeśanāma. Bsam gyis mi khyab pa'i rim pa'i man ngag ces bya ba.* Toh 2228, rgyud *wi,* 99b–104b. P3072, *mi.*

Maitreya. *Sūtrālaṃkāra.* Short title for *Mahāyānasūtrālaṃkāranāmakārikā. Theg pa chen po mdo sde'i rgyan zhes bya ba'i tshig le'ur byas pa.* Toh 4020, sems tsam *phi,* 1b–39a. P5521, *phi.*

Nāgabodhi. *Jewel Rosary. Nor bu'i phreng ba.* Short title for *Jewel Rosary: An Explication of the* Five Stages. *Rim pa lnga pa'i bshad pa nor bui'i phreng ba zhes bya ba.* Toh 1840, rgyud *chi,* 14a–157a. P2697, *ngi.*

Nāgārjuna. *Five Stages. Pañcakrama. Rim pa lnga pa.* Toh 1802, rgyud *ngi,* 45a–57a. P2667, *gi.*

———. *Jewel Rosary. Rājaparikathāratnamālā. Rgyal po la gtam bya ba rin po che'i phreng ba.* Toh 4158, spring yig *ge,* 107a–128a. P5658, *nge.*

———. *Letter to a Friend. Suhṛllekha. Bshes pa'i spring yig.* Toh 4182, spring yig *nge,* 40b–46b. P5622, *nge.*

———. *Root Verses on the Madhyamaka. Prajñānāmamūlamadhyamakakārikā. Dbu ma rtsa ba'i tshig le'ur byas pa shes rab ces bya ba.* Toh 3824, dbu ma *tsa,* 1b–19a. P5224, *tsa.*

Prajñākaramati. *Commentary on Difficult Points in* Engaging in the Conduct of a Bodhisattva. *Bodhicaryāvatārapañjikā. Byang chub kyi spyod pa la 'jug pa'i dka' 'grel.* Toh 3872, dbu ma *la,* 41b–288a. P5273, *la.*

Prajñāvarman. *Commentary on the* Udanavarga. *Udanavargavivaraṇa. Che du brjod pa'i tshoms kyi rnam par 'grel pa.* Toh 4100, mngon pa *tu,* 45b–223a. P5601, *du.*

Puṇḍarīka, Kalkī. *Immaculate Light. Dri med 'od.* Short title for *Vimala-*

prabhānāma mūlatantrānusāriṇīdvādaśasāhasrikālagukālacakratantrarājaṭīkā. Bsdus pa'i rgyud kyi rgyal po dus kyi 'khor lo'i 'grel bshad / rtsa ba'i rgyud kyi rjes su 'jug pa stong phrag bcu gnyis pa dri ma med pa'i 'od. Toh 845, dus 'khor 'grel bshad (in the Kangyur) *shrī,* 1b–469a. P2064, Tengyur, *ka.*

Śāntideva. *Engaging in the Conduct of a Bodhisattva. Bodhisattvacaryāvatāra. Byang chub sems dpa'i spyod pa la 'jug pa.* Toh 3871, dbu ma *la,* 1b–40a. P5272, *la.*

Saraha. *Treasury of Dohā in a Song. Dohākoṣagīti. Do hā mdzod kyi glu.* Toh 2224, rgyud *wi,* 70b–77a. P3068, *mi.*

Tilopa. *Treasury of Dohā. Dohākoṣa. Do hā mdzod.* Toh 2281, rgyud *zhi,* 136a–137b. P3128, *tsi.*

Vajraghaṇṭā. *Condensed Ritual for the Initiation of Glorious Cakrasaṃvara. Śrīcakrasaṃvaraṣekaprakriyopadeśanāma. Dpal 'khor lo sdom pa'i dbang gi bya ba mdor bsdus pa zhes bya ba.* Toh 1431, rgyud *wa,* 219b–222b. P2148, *na.*

———. *Five Stages of Glorious Cakrasaṃvara. Śrīcakrasaṃvarapañcakrama. Dpal 'khor lo sdom pa'i rim pa lnga pa.* Toh 1433, rgyud *wa,* 224b–227a. P2150, *na.*

Vajrāsanapāda. *Supplication to the Eighty-four Great Adepts. Grub thob brgyad cu rtsa bzhi'i gsol 'debs.* Toh 3758, rgyud *tshu,* 110a–113b. P4578, *nu.*

Vasubandhu. *Correctness of the Explanation. Vyākhyāyukti. Rnam par bshad pa'i rigs pa.* Toh 4061, sems tsam *shi,* 29a–134b. P5562, *si.*

———. *Explication of the* Treasury of Abhidharma. *Abhidharmakoṣabhāṣya. Chos mngon pa'i mdzod kyi bshad pa.* Toh 4090, mngon pa *khu,* 26b–258a. P5591, *gu.*

———. *Verses on the Treasury of Abhidharma. Abhidharmakoṣakārikā. Chos mngon pa'i mdzod kyi tshig le'ur byas pa.* Toh 4089, mngon pa *ku,* 1b–25a. P5591, *gu.*

Virūpa. *Vajra Lines. Rdo rje'i tshig rkang.* Short title for *Vajra Lines: Root Text of the Path with the Result. Lam 'bras bu dang bcas pa'i rtsa ba rdo rje'i tshig rkang.* Toh 2284, rgyud *zhi,* 139a–143b. P3131, *tsi.*

Yaśomitra. *Commentary on the* Treasury of Abhidharma. *Abhidharmakoṣaṭīkā. Chos mngon pa mdzod kyi 'grel bshad.* Toh 4092, mngon pa *gu,* 1b–330a. P5593, *cu.*

Yoginī Cinta. *Realization of Reality That Subsequently Clarifies Entities. Vyakta-*

bhāvānugatatattvasiddhi. Dngos po gsal ba'i rjes su 'gro ba'i de kho na nyid grub pa. Toh 2222, rgyud *wi,* 63a–68b. P3066, *mi.*

Tibetan Works

Chögyal Phakpa Lodrö Gyaltsen (Chos rgyal 'Phags pa Blo gros rgyal mtshan). *Esoteric Instructions for Offering a Mandala and Supplications to the Master. Bla ma la maṇḍal dbul zhing gsol ba gdab pa'i man ngag.* In *The Complete Works of the Great Masters of the Sa skya Sect of Tibetan Buddhism. Sa skya pa'i bka' 'bum,* vol. 6, *Collected Works pa,* 195a–196a. Tokyo: The Toyo Bunko, 1968.

Jetsün Drakpa Gyaltsen (Rje btsun Grags pa rgyal mtshan). *Catalogue of the Volume.* Short title for *Catalogue of the Volume that Clarifies the Meaning of the Precious Teaching of the Path with the Result. Gsung ngag rin po che lam 'bras bu dang bcas pa'i don gsal bar byed pa glegs bam gyi dkar chags.* In *Sa-skya Lam-'bras Literature Series,* vol. 11 *da,* 1a–4b. Dehra Dun: Sakya Centre, 1983.

———. *Clear Reply to a Request. Zhus lan gsal ba.* Alternate name for the *Versified Guidance Manual for Guiding Disciples Precisely According to the Treatise of the Path with the Result. Lam 'bras gzhung ji lta ba bzhin tu dkri ba'i khrid yig tshigs bcad ma.* In *Sa-skya Lam-'bras Literature Series,* vol. 13 *pa,* 8a–10a. Dehra Dun: Sakya Centre, 1983.

———. *Commentary on the View of the Indivisibility of Samsara and Nirvana. 'Khor 'das dbyer med kyi lta ba'i 'grel pa.* In *Sa-skya Lam-'bras Literature Series,* vol. 11 *da,* 97b–122a. Dehra Dun: Sakya Centre, 1983.

———. *Creation Stage Adorned with Nine Profound Means Formulated by the Teacher Padmavajra. Slob dpon padma badzras mdzad pa'i bskyed rim zab pa'i tshul dgus brgyan pa.* In *Sa-skya Lam-'bras Literature Series,* vol. 11 *da,* 210a–221a. Dehra Dun: Sakya Centre, 1983.

———. *Dreams of the Venerable Lord. Rje btsun pa'i mnal lam.* In *The Complete Works of the Great Masters of the Sa skya Sect of Tibetan Buddhism. Sa skya pa'i bka' 'bum,* vol. 4, *Collected Works nya,* 197b–201a. Tokyo: The Toyo Bunko, 1968.

———. *Eulogy of the Master's Life. Bla ma'i rnam thar bstod pa khyod nyi ma.* In *The Complete Works of the Great Masters of the Sa skya Sect of Tibetan Buddhism. Sa skya pa'i bka' 'bum,* vol. 3, *Collected Works cha,* 165b–167a. Tokyo: The Toyo Bunko, 1968.

———. *Guidance Manual for Jochak. Khrid yig Jo lcags ma.* Alternate title for *Fundamental Treatise for Guiding Disciples Precisely According to the Treatise.*

Gzhung ji lta ba bzhin du dkri ba'i gzhung shing. In *Sa-skya Lam-'bras Literature Series,* vol. 11 *da,* 150b–157b. Dehra Dun: Sakya Centre, 1983.

———. *Instructions on Parting from the Four Attachments. Zhen pa bzhi bral gyi gdams pa.* In *The Complete Works of the Great Masters of the Sa skya Sect of Tibetan Buddhism. Sa skya pa'i bka' 'bum,* vol. 4, *Collected Works ta,* 297a–299b. Tokyo: The Toyo Bunko, 1968.

———. *Praise in Daṇḍaka Metre to Glorious Hevajra. Dpal kyi rdo rje'i bstod pa daṇḍa ka.* In *The Complete Works of the Great Masters of the Sa skya Sect of Tibetan Buddhism. Sa skya pa'i bka' 'bum,* vol. 3, *Collected Works ja,* 236a–238b. Tokyo: The Toyo Bunko, 1968.

———. *Rejection of Confusion About the Root Infractions. Rtsa ltung 'khrul spong.* Short title for *Rejection of Confusion: A Clarifying Commentary on the Fourteen Root Infractions. Rtsa ba'i ltung ba bcu bzhi pa'i 'grel pa gsal byed 'khrul spong.* In *The Complete Works of the Great Masters of the Sa skya Sect of Tibetan Buddhism. Sa skya pa'i bka' 'bum,* vol. 3, *Collected Works ja,* 123a–184a. Tokyo: The Toyo Bunko, 1968.

———. *Root Text on the View of the Indivisibility of Samsara and Nirvana. 'Khor 'das dbyer med kyi lta ba'i rtsa ba.* In *Sa-skya Lam-'bras Literature Series,* vol. 11 *da,* 96a–97b. Dehra Dun: Sakya Centre, 1983.

———. *Summarizing Outline of the* Classification of the Tantras in General *and the* Direct Realization of the Tantras. *Rgyud sde spyi'i rnam gzhag dang rgyud kyi mngon par rtogs pa'i stong thun sa bcad.* In the *Complete Works of the Great Masters of the Sa skya Sect of Tibetan Buddhism,* vol. 3, *Collected Works cha,* 140a–162a. Tokyo: The Toyo Bunko, 1968.

———. *Summary of Writings About the Universal Ground. Kun gzhi'i yi ge'i don bsdus pa.* In *Sa-skya Lam-'bras Literature Series,* vol. 11 *da,* 64b–66a. Dehra Dun: Sakya Centre, 1983.

Sachen Künga Nyingpo (Sa chen Kun dga' snying po). *Versified Summary of Everything. Thams cad kyi don bsdus pa'i tshigs su bcad pa.* In *Sa-skya Lam-'bras Literature Series,* vol. 11 *da,* 94b–96a. Dehra Dun: Sakya Centre, 1983.

Sakya Paṇḍita Künga Gyaltsen (Sa skya Paṇḍi ta Kun dga' rgyal mtshan). *Catalogue of the Guiding Instructions of the Path with the Result. Lam 'bras bu dang bcas pa'i khrid kyi dkar chag.* In *The Complete Works of the Great Masters of the Sa skya Sect of Tibetan Buddhism. Sa skya pa'i bka' 'bum,* vol. 5, *Collected Works na,* 142b–147a. Tokyo: The Toyo Bunko, 1968.

———. *Clarification of the Meaning Through Symbols. Brda don gsal ba.* In *Sa-skya*

Lam-'bras Literature Series, vol. 13 *pa,* 103a–106b. Dehra Dun: Sakya Centre, 1983.

———. *Distinguishing the Three Vows. Sdom pa gsum gyi rab tu dbye ba.* In *The Complete Works of the Great Masters of the Sa skya Sect of Tibetan Buddhism. Sa skya pa'i bka' 'bum,* vol. 5, *Collected Works na,* 1a–48b. Tokyo: The Toyo Bunko, 1968.

———. *Elucidating the Intention of the Sage. Thub pa'i dgongs pa rab tu gsal ba.* In *The Complete Works of the Great Masters of the Sa skya Sect of Tibetan Buddhism. Sa skya pa'i bka' 'bum,* vol. 5, *Collected Works tha,* 1a–99a. Tokyo: The Toyo Bunko, 1968.

———. *Explication of the Five Dependently Arisen Connections. Rten 'brel lnga'i bshad pa.* In *Sa-skya Lam-'bras Literature Series,* vol. 13 *pa,* 110a–114a. Dehra Dun: Sakya Centre, 1983.

———. *Explication of the Seal of the Four Mandalas. 'Khor bzhi'i rgya'i bshad pa.* In *Sa-skya Lam-'bras Literature Series,* vol. 13 *pa,* 115b–117a. Dehra Dun: Sakya Centre, 1983.

———. *Fine Path of the Bodhisattvas. Rgyal sras lam bzang.* Alternate title for *Elucidating the Intention of the Sage.*

———. *Reply to the Questions of the Yogin Truma. Rnal 'byor pa phru ma'i dris lan.* In *The Complete Works of the Great Masters of the Sa skya Sect of Tibetan Buddhism. Sa skya pa'i bka' 'bum,* vol. 5, *Collected Works na,* 249b–250b. Tokyo: The Toyo Bunko, 1968.

———. *Three Outer, Inner, and Secret Mandalas. Phyi nang gsang gsum gyi maṇḍal.* In *Sa-skya Lam-'bras Literature Series,* vol. 13 *pa,* 25a–26b. Dehra Dun: Sakya Centre, 1983.

———. *Uncommon Supplication to the Excellent Master. Bla ma dam pa la thun mong ma yin pa'i sgo nas gsol ba 'debs pa.* In *The Complete Works of the Great Masters of the Sa skya Sect of Tibetan Buddhism. Sa skya pa'i bka' 'bum,* vol. 5, *Collected Works na,* 201a–202a. Tokyo: The Toyo Bunko, 1968.

Works Consulted by the Translator

Tibetan Works

Bartön Dorjé Gyaltsen (Bar ston Rdo rje rgyal mtshan). *Amazing and Marvelous Biography of Virūpa, the Lord of Yogins. Rnal 'byor dbang phyug bir wa pa'i rnam thar ngo mtshar rmad byung*. In *Lam 'bras bla brgyud kyi rnam thar*, 2a–28a. Rajpur: Sakya Centre, 1985.

Chagen Wangchuk Gyaltsen (Cha rgan Dbang phyug rgyal mtshan). *Detailed Story of the Tibetan Masters of the Path with the Result, with Additional Information on the Origins of Tibet and the Doctrine. Lam 'bras kyi bla ma bod kyi lo rgyus rgyas pa bod dang bstan pa'i byung 'dems ma*. Beijing: Library of the Cultural Palace of Nationalities. Unpublished *dbu med* ms., 92 fols.

———. *Story of the Lord of Yogins Composed by Chagen. Cha rgan gyi mdzad pa'i rnal 'byor dbang phyug gi lo rgyus*. Beijing: Library of the Cultural Palace of Nationalities. Unpublished *dbu med* ms., 12 fols.

Jamyang Khyentsé Wangchuk ('Jam dbyangs mkhyen brtse'i dbang phyug). *Expansion of the Great Secret Doctrine: Summarizing Notes on the History of the Oral Instructions. From the Comprehensive Explanation of the Precious Teaching of the "Path with the Result." The Infallible Version of Khau Drakzongpa. The Practice of the Old Monk Khyentsé. Gsung ngag rin po che lam 'bras bu dang bcas pa'i khog phub kyi rnam bshad las / gdams ngag byung tshul gyi zin bris gsang chen bstan pa rgyas byed ces bya ba kha'u brag rdzong pa'i bzhed pa ma nor ba ban rgan mkhyen brtse'i nyams len*. In *Sa-skya Lam-'bras Literature Series*, vol. 14 *pha*, 1b–78a (pp. 2–155). Dehra Dun: Sakya Centre, 1983.

———. *Profound Summarizing Notes on the Path Presented as the Three Continua. From the* Expansion of the Great Secret Doctrine, *Summarizing Notes of Guidance for the Precious Teaching of the "Path with the Result." The Special Dharma of Khau Drakzongpa. The Practice of the Old Monk Khyentsé. Gsung ngag rin po che lam 'bras bu dang bcas pa'i khrid kyi zin bris gsang chen bstan pa rgyas byed ces bya ba las / rgyud gsum du bstan pa'i lam gyi zin bris zab mo kha'u brag rdzong pa'i khyad chos ban rgan mkhyen brtse'i nyams len*. In *Sa-skya Lam-'bras Literature Series*, vol. 14 *pha*, 1a–45a (pp. 345–433). Dehra Dun: Sakya Centre, 1983.

———. *Summarizing Notes on How to Explain and Practice the Dharma. From the Comprehensive Explanation of the Precious Teaching of the "Path with the Result." The Infallible Version of Khau Drakzongpa. The Practice of the Old Monk Khyentsé. Gsung ngag rin po che lam 'bras bu dang bcas pa'i khog phub kyi rnam bshad las / byung ba'i chos la bshad sgrub bya tshul gyi zin bris kha'u brag rdzong pa'i bzhed pa ma nor ba ban rgan mkhyen brtse'i nyams len*. In *Sa-skya Lam-'bras Literature Series*, vol. 14 *pha*, 98a–113a (pp. 195–225). Dehra Dun: Sakya Centre, 1983.

———. *Summarizing Notes on the Inner Creation Stage. From the* Expansion of the Great Secret Doctrine, *Summarizing Notes of Guidance for the Precious Teaching of the "Path with the Result." The Infallible Version of Khau Drakzongpa. Gsung ngag rin po che lam 'bras bu dang bcas pa'i khrid kyi zin bris gsang chen bstan pa rgyas byed ces bya ba las / nang bskyed rim gyi zin bris kha'u brag rdzong pa'i bzhed pa ma nor ba.* In *Sa-skya Lam-'bras Literature Series,* vol. 14 *pha,* 1a–7a (pp. 505–17). Dehra Dun: Sakya Centre, 1983.

———. *Summarizing Notes on the Outer Creation Stage. From the* Expansion of the Great Secret Doctrine, *Summarizing Notes of Guidance for the Precious Teaching of the "Path with the Result." The Infallible Version of Khau Drakzongpa. Gsung ngag rin po che lam 'bras bu dang bcas pa'i khrid kyi zin bris gsang chen bstan pa rgyas byed ces bya ba las / phyi bskyed rim gyi zin bris kha'u brag rdzong pa'i bzhed pa ma nor ba.* In *Sa-skya Lam-'bras Literature Series,* vol. 14 *pha,* 1a–35a (pp. 435–503). Dehra Dun: Sakya Centre, 1983.

———. *Summarizing Notes on the Path Presented as the Three Appearances. From the* Expansion of the Great Secret Doctrine, *Summarizing Notes of Guidance for the Precious Teaching of the "Path with the Result." The Infallible Version of Khau Drakzongpa. Gsung ngag rin po che lam 'bras bu dang bcas pa'i khrid kyi zin bris gsang chen bstan pa rgyas byed ces bya ba las / snang ba gsum du bstan pa'i lam gyi zin bris kha'u brag rdzong pa'i bzhed pa ma nor ba.* In *Sa-skya Lam-'bras Literature Series,* vol. 14 *pha,* 1a–46a (pp. 253–343). Dehra Dun: Sakya Centre, 1983.

Jetsün Drakpa Gyaltsen (Rje btsun Grags pa rgyal mtshan). *Biography of the Glorious Great Sakyapa Künga Nyingpo. Dpal sa skya pa chen po kun dga' snying po'i rnam thar.* In *Sa-skya Lam-'bras Literature Series,* vol. 1 *ka,* 9b–16b. Dehra Dun: Sakya Centre, 1983.

———. *Clarification of the Instructions on the Inconceivable Composed by the Teacher Kuddāla. Slob dpon tog rtse pa pas mdzad pa'i bsam mi khyab kyi gdams pa gsal bar byed pa.* In *Sa-skya Lam-'bras Literature Series,* vol. 11 *da,* 183a–192b. Dehra Dun: Sakya Centre, 1983.

———. *Instruction by the Venerable Lord to Gatön Dorjé Drak. Rje btsun gyis dga' ston rdo rje grags la gdams pa.* In *Sa-skya Lam-'bras Literature Series,* vol. 13 *pa,* 21a–25a. Dehra Dun: Sakya Centre, 1983.

———. *Instructions Received in Front of a Stupa: Composed by the Teacher Nāgārjuna. Slob dpon klu sgrub kyis mdzad pa'i mchod rten drung thob.* In *Sa-skya Lam-'bras Literature Series,* vol. 11 *da,* 200b–203a. Dehra Dun: Sakya Centre, 1983.

———. *Jeweled Tree for Direct Realization of the Tantras. Rgyud kyi mngon par rtogs pa rin po che'i ljon shing.* In *Sa-skya Lam-'bras Literature Series,* vol. 22 *za,* 1a–139a. Dehra Dun: Sakya Centre, 1983.

———. *Story of the Indian Masters of the Lineage. Bla ma brgyud pa rgya gar ba'i lo rgyus.* In *Sa-skya Lam-'bras Literature Series,* vol. 11 *da,* 291a–297a. Dehra Dun: Sakya Centre, 1983.

———. *Story of the Tibetan Masters of the Lineage. Bla ma brgyud pa bod kyi lo rgyus.* In *Sa-skya Lam-'bras Literature Series,* vol. 11 *da,* 297b–300a. Dehra Dun: Sakya Centre, 1983.

Kuddāla (Tog rtse pa). *Glorious Kuddāla's Oral Instructions on the Inconceivable. Dpal tog rtse pa'i bsam mi khyab kyi gdams ngag.* In *Sa-skya Lam-'bras Literature Series,* vol. 11 *da,* 174a–181b. Dehra Dun: Sakya Centre, 1983.

Künga Palden and Jamyang Loter Wangpo (Kun dga' dpal ldan and 'Jam dbyangs blo gter dbang po). *Blazing of a Hundred Brilliant Blessings: A Supplement to the* Expansion of the Great Secret Doctrine, *Summarizing Notes on the History of the Oral Instructions. From the Comprehensive Explanation of the Precious Teaching of the "Path with the Result." Gsung ngag rin po che lam 'bras bu dang bcas pa'i khog phub rnam bshad las gdams ngag gi byung tshul zin ris gsang chen bstan pa rgyas byed kyi zhal skong byin rlabs gzi brgya 'bar ba.* In *Sa-skya Lam-'bras Literature Series,* vol. 14 *pha,* 78a–98a (pp. 155–95). Dehra Dun: Sakya Centre, 1983.

Lama Dampa Sönam Gyaltsen (Bla ma dam pa Bsod nams rgyal mtshan). *Illuminating the Marvelous: Biographies of the Lineal Masters. Bla ma brgyud pa'i rnam par thar pa ngo mtshar snang ba.* In *Sa-skya Lam-'bras Literature Series,* vol. 16 *ma,* 1b–61a. Dehra Dun: Sakya Centre, 1983.

———. *Complete Clarification of the Hidden Meaning: Guidance Manual for Guiding Disciples Precisely According to the Treatise of the Path with the Result. Lam 'bras bu dang bcas pa'i gzhung ji lta ba bzhin dkri ba'i khrid yig sbas don kun gsal.* In *Sa-skya Lam-'bras Literature Series,* vol. 16 *ma,* 226a–272a. Dehra Dun: Sakya Centre, 1983.

———. *Treasury of Esoteric Instructions: An Explication of the Oral Instructions of the Path with the Result. Lam 'bras bu dang bcas pa'i gdams ngag gi rnam par bshad pa man ngag gter mdzod.* In *Sa-skya Lam-'bras Literature Series,* vol. 16 *ma,* 62a–216b. Dehra Dun: Sakya Centre, 1983.

Mangthö Ludrup Gyatso (Mang thos klu sgrub rgya mtsho). *Bright Sun of Pure Altruism: A Chronicle of the Doctrine. Bstan rtsis gsal ba'i nyin byed lhag bsam rab dkar.* Lhasa: Bod ljongs mi dmangs dpe skrun khang, 1987.

———. *Heart of the Practice: A Synopsis of the Key Points of the Guidance Manuals of the Path with the Result. Lam 'bras khrid dpe gnad dril ba'i nyams len snying po.* In *Sa-skya Lam-'bras Literature Series,* vol. 18 *tsha,* 113b–119a. Dehra Dun: Sakya Centre, 1983.

———. *Summarizing Notes on the Explications of the Treatise: The Words of Ludrup Gyatso. Gzhung bshad zin bris klu sgrub rgya mtsho'i gsung.* In *Mang thos klu sgrub rgya mtsho'i gsung skor,* vol. *ca,* 1a–42b (pp. 345–428). Kathmandu: Sa skya rgyal yongs gsung rab slob gnyer khang, 1999.

Martön Chökyi Gyalpo (Dmar ston Chos kyi rgyal po). *Account of the Words of My Mañjuśrī Master: A Commentary on the Treatise of the* Vajra Lines. *A Teaching of Mar Chögyal. Gzhung rdo rje'i tshig rkang gi 'grel pa 'jam dbyangs bla ma'i gsung sgros ma zhes dmar chos rgyal gyi gsung.* In *Sa-skya Lam-'bras Literature Series,* vol. 30 *a,* 1a–148a. Dehra Dun: Sakya Centre, 1983.

Ngawang Losang Gyatso, the Fifth Dalai Lama (Ngag dbang blo bzang rgya mtsho). *Summarizing Notes Beginning with the Dream Yoga of the Vase Initiation. From the* Expansion of the Great Secret Doctrine, *Summarizing Notes of Guidance for the Precious Teaching of the "Path with the Result." The Infallible Version of Khau Drakzongpa. Gsung ngag rin po che lam 'bras bu dang bcas pa'i khrid kyi zin bris gsang chen bstan pa rgyas byed ces bya ba las / bum dbang gi rmi lam man gyi zin bris kha'u brag rdzong pa'i bzhed pa ma nor ba.* In *Sa-skya Lam-'bras Literature Series,* vol. 14 *pha,* 1a–18a (pp. 519–53). Dehra Dun: Sakya Centre, 1983.

Ngorchen Künga Sangpo and Gungruwa Sherap Sangpo (Ngor chen Kun dga' bzang po and Gung ru ba Shes rab bzang po). *History of the Esoteric Instructions of the Path with the Result: Sunlight on the Expansion of the Doctrine of the Precious Teaching. Lam 'bras bu dang bcas pa'i man ngag gi byung tshul gsung ngag rin po che bstan pa rgyas pa'i nyi 'od.* In *The Complete Works of the Great Masters of the Sa skya Sect of Tibetan Buddhism. Sa skya pa'i bka' 'bum,* vol. 9, *Collected Works ka,* 218a–251b. Tokyo: The Toyo Bunko, 1968.

Sachen Künga Nyingpo (Sa chen Kun dga' snying po). *Eulogy to Glorious Virūpa. Dpal ldan bi rū pa la bstod pa.* In *The Complete Works of the Great Masters of the Sa skya Sect of Tibetan Buddhism. Sa skya pa'i bka' 'bum,* vol. 1, *Collected Works ka,* 1b–3b Tokyo: The Toyo Bunko, 1968.

———. *Eulogy to Shangtön. Zhang ston la bstod pa.* In *The Complete Works of the Great Masters of the Sa skya Sect of Tibetan Buddhism. Sa skya pa'i bka' 'bum,* vol. 1, *Collected Works ka,* 3b–4a. Tokyo: The Toyo Bunko, 1968.

———. *Explication of the Treatise for Nyak. Gzhung bshad gnyags ma.* In *Sa-skya Lam-'bras Literature Series,* vol. 11 *da,* 11a–64b. Dehra Dun: Sakya Centre, 1983.

———. *Explication of the Treatise of the Path with the Result for the Benefit of the Sons. Lam 'bras gzhung bshad sras don ma.* In *Sa-skya Lam-'bras Literature Series,* vol. 12 *na,* 1a–222b. Dehra Dun: Sakya Centre, 1983.

Sakya Paṇḍita Künga Gyaltsen (Sa skya Paṇḍi ta Kun dga' rgyal mtshan). *Clarifying the Meaning of the Essence: An Explication of the Root Mantra. Rtsa sngags kyi rnams bshad snying po don gsal.* In *Sa-skya Lam-'bras Literature Series,* vol. 13 *pa,* 13a–18b. Dehra Dun: Sakya Centre, 1983.

———. *Epistle Sent to the Buddhas and Bodhisattvas of the Ten Directions. Phyogs bcu'i sangs rgyas dang byang chub sems dpa' rnams la zhu ba'i 'phrin yig.* In *The Complete Works of the Great Masters of the Sa skya Sect of Tibetan Buddhism. Sa skya pa'i bka' 'bum,* vol. 5, *Collected Works na,* 55a–69a. Tokyo: The Toyo Bunko, 1968.

———. *Eulogy to the Venerable Lord Drakpa Gyaltsen. Rje btsun grags pa rgyal mtshan gyi bstod pa.* In *The Complete Works of the Great Masters of the Sa skya Sect of Tibetan Buddhism. Sa skya pa'i bka' 'bum,* vol. 5, *Collected Works na,* 50a–51b. Tokyo: The Toyo Bunko, 1968.

———. *Profound-Path Guruyoga. Lam zab bla ma'i rnal 'byor.* In *Sa-skya Lam-'bras Literature Series,* vol. 13 *pa,* 139b–148a. Dehra Dun: Sakya Centre, 1983.

Samten Lodrö, the Great Abbot (Mkhan chen Bsam gtan blo gros). *Divine Feast for Those of Good Fortune: A Partial Biography of the Lord of Secrets, the Vajra-holder Jamyang Loter Wangpo, which is a Fine Tree of Virtuous Gems that Grants the Sublime Attainment and Causes the Natural Liberation of Body, Speech, and Mind. Gsang bdag rdo rje 'dzin pa 'jam dbyangs blo gter dbang po'i rnam par thar pa cha tsam brjod pa mchog sbyin sgo gsum rang grol dge legs nor bu'i ljon bzang skal bzang lha yi dga' ston.* In *Sa-skya Lam-'bras Literature Series,* vol. 8 *nya,* 1a–50a (pp. 237–335). Dehra Dun: Sakya Centre, 1983.

Sönam Lhundrup, the Great Abbot of Mustang (Glo bo Mkhan chen Bsod nams lhun grub). *Bright Lamp: A Catalogue of the Seventy-two Tantras. Rgyud sde bdun cu rtsa gnyis kyi dkar chag gsal ba'i sgron me. Dbu med* ms., 1 fol. Kathmandu: Nepal-German Manuscript Preservation Project, Reel no. L-102/28, running no. L-1256.

Tsangjampa Dorjé Gyaltsen (Gtsang byams pa Rdo rje rgyal mtshan). *River of Explication to Wash Away the Stains of Slander. Rnam bshad chu rgyun log smra'i dri ma 'khrud byed.* In *Sngon byon pa'i sa skya pa'i mkhas pa rnams kyi sngags skor,* vol. *kha,* 1a–133b (pp. 371–636). Kathmandu: Sa skya rgyal yongs gsung rab slob gnyer khang, 2003.

Tsarchen Losel Gyatso (Tshar chen Blo gsal rgya mtsho). *Supplication to the Masters of Three Combined Lineages of the Precious Teaching, Together with a Prayer Concerning the Stages of the Path. Gsung ngag rin po che brgyud pa gsum 'dus kyi bla ma la gsol ba 'debs pa lam rim smon lam dang bcas pa.* In *Sa-skya Lam-'bras Literature Series,* vol. 14 *pha,* 5a–11b (pp. 235–48). Dehra Dun: Sakya Centre, 1983.

Virūpa. *Vajra Lines. Rdo rje'i tshig rkang.* Short title for *Oral Instructions, together with Esoteric Instructions, of the Path with the Result. Lam 'bras bu dang bcas pa'i gdams ngag dang man ngag tu bcas pa.* In *Sa-skya Lam-'bras Literature Series,* vol. 11 *da,* 5b–10a, and vol. 12 *na,* 1b–6a. Dehra Dun: Sakya Centre, 1983.

Other Works

Chimpa, Lama, and Alaka Chattopadhyaya, trans. (1990). *Tāranātha's History of Buddhism in India.* Delhi: Motilal Banarsidass.

Chogyé Trichen Rinpoché (2003). *Parting from the Four Attachments: Jetsun Drakpa Gyaltsen's Song of Experience on Mind Training and the View.* Ithaca: Snow Lion Publications.

Dorje, Gyurme and Matthew Kapstein (1991). *The Nyingma School of Tibetan Buddhism: Its Fundamentals and History.* Vol. 2. Boston: Wisdom Publications.

Dudjom Rinpoché, Jikdrel Yeshé Dorje (1991). *The Nyingma School of Tibetan Buddhism: Its Fundamentals and History.* Vol. 1. Translated by Gyurme Dorje and Matthew Kapstein. Boston: Wisdom Publications.

Edou, Jérôme (1996). *Machig Labdrön and the Foundations of Chöd.* Ithaca: Snow Lion Publications.

Farrow, G. W., and I. Menon (1992). *The Concealed Essence of the Hevajra Tantra.* Delhi: Motilal Banarsidass.

Heruka, Tsang Nyön (1982). *The Life of Marpa the Translator.* Translated by the Nālandā Translation Committee. Boulder: Prajñā Press.

Jackson, David P. (1987). *The Entrance Gate for the Wise (Section III).* 2 vols. Vienna: Arbeitskreis für Tibetische und Buddhistische Studien Universität Wien.

——— (1989). "Sources on the Chronology and Succession of the Abbots of Ngor E-waṃ-chos-ldan." *Berliner Indologische Studien.* Band 4/5: 49–93.

——— (1996). *A History of Tibetan Painting.* Vienna: Österreichische Akademie der Wissenschaften.

——— (2003). *A Saint in Seattle: The Life of the Tibetan Mystic Dezhung Rinpoche.* Boston: Wisdom Publications.

Jamgön Kongtrul Lodrö Taye (2003). *The Treasury of Knowledge: Book Five: Buddhist Ethics.* Translated by the Kalu Rinpoché Translation Group. Ithaca: Snow Lion Publications.

——— (2005). *The Treasury of Knowledge: Book Six, Part Four: Systems of Buddhist Tantra.* Translated by the Kalu Rinpoché Translation Group. (This volume translated by Elio Guarisco and Ingrid McLeod.) Ithaca: Snow Lion Publications.

Kaneko, Eiichi (1982). *Ko-Tantora Zenshū Kaidai Mokuroku.* (Catalogue to the Gting skyes Edition of the *Rnying ma rgyud 'bum*). Tokyo: Kokusho Kankūkai.

Kuijp, Leonard W. J. van der (1994). "Fourteenth Century Tibetan Cultural History I: Ta'i-si-tu Byang-chub rgyal-mtshan as a Man of Religion." *Indo-Iranian Journal* 37: 139–49.

Martin, Dan (1982). "The Early Education of Milarepa." *The Journal of the Tibetan Society,* 2: 53–76.

Mitra, Debala (1989). "Some Images of Heruka-Hevajra." In *Studies in Art and Archaeology of Bihar and Bengal,* 179–88. Delhi: Sri Satguru Publishers.

Parfionovitch, Yuri, Fernand Meyer, and Gyurme Dorje, eds. (1992). *Tibetan Medical Paintings: Illustrations to the Blue Beryl Treatise of Sangye Gyamtso (1653-1705).* New York: Harry N. Abrams.

Roerich, George N., trans. (1959). *Biography of Dharmasvamin.* Patna: K. Jayaswal Research Institute.

———, trans. (1976). *The Blue Annals.* Delhi: Motilal Banarsidass.

Ruegg, David Seyfort (1984). "Problems in the Transmission of Vajrayana Buddhism in the Western Himalaya about the Year 1000." *Acta Indologica* VI: 369–81.

Sakya Pandita Kunga Gyaltshen (2002). *A Clear Differentiation of the Three Codes.* Translated by Jared Douglas Rhoton. Albany: State University of New York Press.

Sakya Trizin, H.H., and Ngawang Samten Chophel, trans. (1982). *A Collection of Instructions on Parting from the Four Attachments.* Singapore: The Singapore Buddha Sasana Society.

Śāntideva (1981). *Śikṣā Samuccaya: A Compendium of Buddhist Doctrine.* Translated from the Sanskrit by Cecil Bendall and W. H. D. Rouse. Reprint of 1922 London edition. Delhi: Motilal Banarsidass.

Shendge, Malati J. (1967). "*Śrīsahajasiddhi.*" *Indo-Iranian Journal* 10, no. 2/3: 126–49.

Smith, E. Gene (2001). *Among Tibetan Texts: History & Literature of the Himalayan Plateau.* Boston: Wisdom Publications.

Snellgrove, David (1959). *The Hevajra Tantra.* 2 vols. London: Oxford University Press.

Sørensen, Per K. (1994). *Tibetan Buddhist Historiography: The Mirror Illuminating the Royal Geneaologies: An Annotated Translation of the XIVth Century Tibetan Chronicle rGyal-rabs gsal-ba'i me-long.* Wiesbaden: Harrassowitz Verlag.

——— (1999). "The Prolific Ascetic lCe-sgom Śes-rab rdo-rje *alias* lCe-sgom zhig-po: Allusive, but Elusive." *Journal of the Nepal Research Centre* XI: 175–200.

Stearns, Cyrus (1996). "The Life and Tibetan Legacy of the Indian *Mahāpaṇḍita* Vibhūticandra." *Journal of the International Association of Buddhist Studies,* 19, no. 1: 127–71.

——— (1999). *The Buddha from Dolpo: A Study of the Life and Thought of the Tibetan Master Dolpopa Sherab Gyaltsen.* Albany: State University of New York Press.

——— (2000). *Hermit of Go Cliffs: Timeless Instructions from a Tibetan Mystic.* Boston: Wisdom Publications.

——— (2001). *Luminous Lives: The Story of the Early Masters of the Lam 'bras Tradition in Tibet.* Boston: Wisdom Publications.

——— (2003). "The Sakya School." In *Portraits of the Masters: Bronze Sculptures of the Tibetan Buddhist Lineages,* ed. Donald Dinwiddie, 204–19. Chicago & London: Serindia Publications Inc and Oliver Hoare Ltd.

Tatz, Mark (1987). "The Life of the Siddha Philosopher Maitrīgupta." *The Journal of the American Oriental Society,* 107, no. 4: 695–711.

Templeman, David (1989). *Tāranātha's Life of Kṛṣṇācārya/Kāṇha.* Dharamsala: Library of Tibetan Works and Archives.

Ui, Hakuju, Munetada Suzuki, Yensho Kanakura, and Tokan Tada, eds. (1934). *A Complete Catalogue of the Tibetan Buddhist Canons (Bkaḥ-ḥgyur and Bstan-ḥgyur).* Sendai: Tohoku Imperial University.

Vitali, Roberto (2001). "Sa skya and the mNga' ris skor gsum legacy: the case of Rin chen bzang po's flying mask." *Lungta 14: Aspects of Tibetan History* (spring 2001): 5–44.

Index

About the Contributors

Cyrus Stearns first began to study Buddhism with Dezhung Rinpoché (1906–87) in 1973. Since that time he has studied with and translated for many Tibetan teachers, especially Dezhung Rinpoché and Chogyé Trichen Rinpoché. Cyrus has a Ph.D. in Buddhist Studies from the University of Washington and lived for about eight years in Nepal, India, and Southeast Asia. Among his other publications are *The Buddha from Dolpo, Hermit of Go Cliffs,* and *Luminous Lives.* Cyrus has three daughters and lives on Whidbey Island, Washington.

Geshe Thupten Jinpa was trained as a monk at the Shartse College of Ganden Monastic University, South India, where he received the Geshe Lharam degree. Jinpa also holds a B.A. honors in philosophy and a Ph.D. in religious studies, both from Cambridge University, England.

Jinpa has been the principal English-language translator for His Holiness the Dalai Lama for nearly two decades and has translated and edited numerous books by the Dalai Lama. His own works include *Songs of Spiritual Experience* (coauthored) and *Self, Reality and Reason in Tibetan Philosophy.* He is currently the president of the Institute of Tibetan Classics and lives in Montreal with his wife and two daughters.

The Institute of Tibetan Classics

The Institute of Tibetan Classics is a nonprofit, charitable educational organization based in Montreal, Canada. It is dedicated to two primary objectives: (1) to preserve and promote the study and deep appreciation of Tibet's rich intellectual, spiritual, and artistic heritage, especially among the Tibetan-speaking communities worldwide; and (2) to make the classical Tibetan knowledge and literature a truly global heritage, its spiritual and intellectual resources open to all.

To learn more about the Institute of Tibetan Classics and its various projects, please visit www.tibetanclassics.org or write to this address:

Institute of Tibetan Classics
304 Aberdare Road
Montreal (Quebec) H3P 3K3
Canada

Following is a list of the thirty-two proposed volumes in *The Library of Tibetan Classics.* Some volumes are translations of single texts, while others are compilations of multiple texts, and each volume will be roughly the same length. Except for those volumes already published, the renderings of titles below are only tentative and are liable to change. The Institute of Tibetan Classics has contracted numerous established translators in its efforts, and progress is proceeding on multiple volumes simultaneously, with several near completion as of this writing.

1. *Mind Training: The Great Collection,* compiled by Shönu Gyalchok and Könchok Gyaltsen (fifteenth century). NOW AVAILABLE
2. *The Book of Kadam: The Core Texts,* attributed to Atiśa and Dromtönpa (eleventh century)
3. *The Great Chariot: A Treatise on the Great Perfection,* Longchen Rapjampa (1308–63)
4. *Taking the Result As the Path: Core Teachings of the Sakya Lamdré Tradition,* Jamyang Khyentsé Wangchuk (1524–68) et al. NOW AVAILABLE
5. *Mahāmudrā and Related Instructions: Core Teachings of the Kagyü School*
6. *Stages of the Path and the Ear-Whispered Instructions: Core Teachings of the Geluk School*
7. *Ocean of Definitive Meaning: A Teaching for the Mountain Hermit,* Dölpopa Sherap Gyaltsen (1292–1361)
8. *Miscellaneous Tibetan Buddhist Lineages: The Core Teachings,* Jamgön Kongtrül (1813–90)
9. *Sutra, Tantra, and the Mind Cycle: Core Teachings of the Bön School*
10. *The Stages of the Doctrine: Selected Key Texts*
11. *The Bodhisattva's Altruistic Ideal: Selected Key Texts*
12. *The Ethics of the Three Codes*
13. *Sādhanas: Vajrayana Buddhist Meditation Manuals*
14. *Ornament of Stainless Light: An Exposition of the Kālacakra Tantra,* Khedrup Norsang Gyatso (1423–1513). NOW AVAILABLE
15. *Lamp Thoroughly Illuminating the Five Stages of Completion,* Tsongkhapa (1357–1419)
16. *Studies in the Perfection of Wisdom*

17. *Treatises on Buddha Nature*
18. *Differentiations of the Profound View: Interpretations of Emptiness in Tibet*
19. *Elucidation of the Intent: A Thorough Exposition of "Entering the Middle Way,"* Tsongkhapa (1357–1419)
20. *Tibetan Buddhist Epistemology I: The Sakya School*
21. *Tibetan Buddhist Epistemology II: The Geluk School*
22. *Tibetan Buddhist Psychology and Phenomenology: Selected Texts*
23. *Ornament of Higher Knowledge: A Exposition of Vasubandhu's "Treasury of Higher Knowledge,"* Chim Jampalyang (thirteenth century)
24. *A Beautiful Adornment of Mount Meru: Presentation of Classical Indian Philosophies,* Changkya Rölpai Dorjé (1717–86)
25. *The Crystal Mirror of Philosophical Systems: A Tibetan Study of Asian Religions Thought,* Thuken Losang Chökyi Nyima (1737–1802)
26. *Gateway for Being Learned and Realized: Selected Texts*
27. *The Well-Uttered Insights: Advice on Everyday Wisdom, Civility, and Basic Human Values*
28. *A Mirror of Beryl: A Historical Introduction to Tibetan Medical Science,* Desi Sangyé Gyatso (1653–1705)
29. *Selected Texts on Tibetan Astronomy and Astrology*
30. *Art and Literature: An Anthology*
31. *Tales from the Tibetan Operas*
32. *Selected Historical Works*

To stay informed about *The Library of Tibetan Classics,* please write:

Wisdom Publications
Attn: Library of Tibetan Classics Information
199 Elm Street
Somerville, MA 02144 USA

or send a request by email to info@wisdompubs.org.

A complete catalog containing descriptions of each volume can be found online at www.wisdompubs.org.

Wisdom Publications

Wisdom Publications is dedicated to making available authentic Buddhist works for the benefit of all. We publish translations of the sutras and tantras, commentaries and teachings of past and contemporary Buddhist masters, and original works by the world's leading Buddhist scholars. We publish our titles with the appreciation of Buddhism as a living philosophy and with the special commitment to preserve and transmit important works from all the major Buddhist traditions.

Wisdom Publications
199 Elm Street
Somerville, Massachusetts 02144 USA
Telephone: (617) 776-7416
www.wisdompubs.org

Wisdom is a nonprofit, charitable 501(c)(3) organization affiliated with the Foundation for the Preservation of the Mahayana Tradition (FPMT).

Mind Training
The Great Collection
Translated and edited by Thupten Jinpa
768 pages, cloth, ISBN 0-86171-440-7,
$49.95

"The practice of mind training *(lojong)* is based on the essential Mahayana teachings of impermanence, compassion, and the exchange of self and other that the eleventh-century master Atisha brought to Tibet from India. The lojong teachings are a source of inspiration and guidance shared by masters of all Tibetan traditions. This makes Thupten Jinpa's translation of *Mind Training: The Great Collection* a natural choice for publication as part of the *Library of Tibetan Classics* series. For the first time, this early collection of the instructions of the great Kadampa masters has been translated in its entirety. The clarity and raw power of these thousand-year-old teachings are astonishingly fresh, whether studied as a complete anthology or opened at random for inspiring verses on the heart of Buddhist practice."—*Buddhadharma: The Practitioner's Quarterly*

"Thupten Jinpa has done us all a great service by editing and translating this marvelous volume. In an era when Buddhist meditation is largely equated with simply calming the mind and developing mindfulness, this compendium of methods for training the mind gives a glimpse of the tremendous richness and depth of the Buddhist tradition for enhancing mental health and balance and realizing the full potential of consciousness in terms of wisdom and compassion. With the current rise of positive psychology, in which researchers are seeking a fresh vision of genuine happiness and well-being, this volume can break new ground in bridging the ancient wisdom of Buddhism with cutting-edge psychology. Such collaborative inquiry between spirituality and science is especially timely in today's troubled and divisive world."—B. Alan Wallace, author of *The Attention Revolution*, and translator of *Natural Liberation*

A Note About Dust Jackets

In response to readers' requests, Wisdom has elected to change the dust jackets on the *Library of Tibetan Classics* series from the vellum covers initially produced to conventional paper jackets. If you have purchased either of the first two volumes in the series, *Ornament of Stainless Light* or *Mind Training,* and would like to receive a replacement jacket free of charge, please email us at info@wisdompubs.org with your mailing address. You can also send your request to Wisdom Publications, 199 Elm St., Somerville MA, 02144.